Blackstone's Statutes on

LANDLORD AND TENANT

Edited by

Stuart Bridge

Fellow of Queens' College
Lecturer in Law in the University of Cambridge
Barrister of the Middle Temple

BLACKSTONE PRESS LIMITED

First published in Great Britain 1991 by Blackstone Press Limited,
9-15 Aldine Street, London W12 8AW. Telephone 081 740 1173

ISBN: 1 85431 118 2

British Library Cataloguing in Publication Data
A CIP catalogue record for this book is available from the British Library

Typeset by Style Photosetting Ltd, Mayfield, East Sussex
Printed by Loader Jackson Printers, Arlesey, Bedfordshire

CONTENTS

EDITOR'S PREFACE

This is a collection of statutes for the use of students. Statutory provisions are printed in their amended form, those repealed are simply omitted, and repeals 'with savings' are generally ignored as being of little interest to the likely reader. Two sets of repealed provisions are included (in italics), as they cast an important interpretative light on others which remain extant.

The prime difficulty for an editor of a work of this kind is selection, which in the area of landlord and tenant law soon becomes elimination. I am grateful for those of my colleagues who have made suggestions for inclusion and exclusion. It will be impossible to please everyone; I may have pleased no one. I hope to have covered the major statutes which will be of interest to those who are studying a basic landlord and tenant course. Future editions are contemplated, and both author and publisher will be ready to react favourably to comment of a constructive kind.

Checking the proofs has been a singularly unedifying process, even for a landlord and tenant fan. Jane (my wife), Van Morrison and Bruce Springsteen have all helped at critical times when the mind was no longer willing, and the progress of Leeds United has been a huge encouragement, as I am sure it has to many, over the course of a long academic season. Gordon Strachan was my first choice as dedicatee, but with his recent (richly deserved) accolade of Footballer of the Year he does not perhaps need another at the moment. I have enjoyed the affection, loyalty, and companionship of Cleo for many years now. In the hope that our relationship will long continue, it is to her that I dedicate this book.

Stuart Bridge

To Cleo

COMMON LAW PROCEDURE ACT 1852
(15 & 16 Vict. c. 76)

[30 June 1852]

210. Proceedings in Ejectment by Landlord for Nonpayment of Rent.

In all Cases between Landlord and Tenant, as often as it shall happen that One Half Year's Rent shall be in arrear, and the Landlord or Lessor, to whom the same is due, hath Right by Law to re-enter for the Nonpayment thereof, such Landlord or Lessor shall and may, without any formal Demand or Re-entry, serve a Writ in Ejectment for the Recovery of the demised Premises, which Service shall stand in the Place and Stead of a Demand and Re-entry; and in case if Judgment against the Defendant for Nonappearance, if it shall be made appear to the Court where the said Action is depending, by Affidavit, or be proved upon the Trial in case the Defendant appears, that Half a Year's Rent was due before the said Writ was served, and that no sufficient Distress was to be found on the demised Premises, countervailing the Arrears then due, and that the Lessor had Power to re-enter, then and in every such Case the Lessor shall recover Judgment and Execution, in the same Manner as if the Rent in arrear had been legally demanded, and a Re-entry made; and in case the Lessee or his Assignee, or other Person claiming or deriving under the said Lease, shall permit and suffer Judgment to be had and recovered on such Trial in Ejectment, and Execution to be executed thereon, without paying the Rent and Arrears, together with full Costs, and without proceeding for Relief in Equity within Six Months after such Execution executed, then and in such Case the said Lessee, his Assignee, and all other Persons claiming and deriving under the said Lease, shall be barred and foreclosed from all Relief or Remedy in Law or Equity, other than by bringing Error for Reversal of such Judgment, in case the same shall be erroneous, and the said Landlord or Lessor shall from thenceforth hold the said demised Premises discharged from such Lease; provided that nothing herein contained shall extend to bar the Right of any Mortgagee of such Lease, or any Part thereof, who shall not be in possession, so as such Mortgagee shall and do, within Six Months after such Judgment obtained and Execution executed, pay all Rent in arrear, and all Costs and Damages sustained by such Lessor or Person entitled to the Remainder or Reversion as aforesaid, and perform all the Covenants and Agreements which, on the Part and Behalf of the First Lessee are and ought to be performed.

211. Lessee proceeding in Equity not to have Injunction or Relief without Payment of Rent and Costs.

In case the said Lessee, his Assignee, or other Person claiming any Right, Title, or Interest, in Law or Equity, of, in, or to the said Lease, shall, within the Time aforesaid, proceed for Relief in any Court of Equity, such Person shall not have or continue any Injunction against the Proceedings at Law on such Ejectment, unless he does or shall, within Forty Days next after a full and perfect Answer shall be made by the Claimant in such Ejectment, bring into Court, and lodge with the proper Officer such Sum and Sums of Money as the Lessor or Landlord shall in his Answer swear to be due and in arrear over and above all just Allowances, and also the Costs taxed in the said Suit, there to remain till the Hearing of the Cause, or to be paid out to the Lessor or Landlord on good Security, subject to the Decree of the Court; and in case such Proceedings for Relief in Equity shall be taken within the Time aforesaid, and after Execution is executed, the Lessor or Landlord shall be accountable only for so much and no more as he shall really and bonâ fide, without Fraud, Deceit, or wilful Neglect, make of the demised Premises from the Time of his entering into the actual Possession thereof; and if what shall be so made by the Lessor or Landlord happen to be less than the Rent reserved on the said Lease, then the said Lessee or his Assignee, before he shall be restored to his Possession, shall pay such Lessor or Landlord, what the Money so by him made fell short of the reserved Rent for the Time such Lessor or Landlord held the said Lands.

212. Tenant paying all Rent with Costs, Proceedings to cease.
If the Tenant or his Assignee do or shall, at any Time before the Trial in such Ejectment, pay or tender to the Lessor or Landlord, his Executors or Administrators, or his or their Attorney in that Cause, or pay into the Court where the same Cause is depending, all the Rent and Arrears, together with the Costs, then and in such Case, all further Proceedings on the said Ejectment shall cease and be discontinued; and if such Lessee, his Executors, Administrators, or Assigns, shall, upon such Proceedings as aforesaid, be relieved in Equity, he and they shall have, hold, and enjoy the demised Lands, according to the Lease thereof made, without any new Lease.

APPORTIONMENT ACT 1870
(33 & 34 Vict. c. 35)

An Act for the better Apportionment of Rents and other periodical Payments
[1 August 1870]

2. Rents, &c. to accrue from day to day and be apportionable in respect of time.
All rents, annuities, dividends, and other periodical payments in the nature of income (whether reserved or made payable under an instrument in writing or otherwise) shall, like interest on money lent, be considered as accruing from day to day, and shall be apportionable in respect of time accordingly.

3. Apportioned part of rent &c. to be payable when the next entire portion shall have become due.
The apportioned part of any such rent, annuity, dividend, or other payment shall be payable or recoverable in the case of a continuing rent, annuity, or other such payment when the entire portion of which such apportioned part shall form part shall become due and payable, and not before, and in the case of a rent, annuity, or other such payment determined by re-entry, death, or otherwise when the next entire portion of the same would have been payable if the same had not so determined, and not before.

4. Persons shall have the same remedies for recovering apportioned parts as for entire portions.
All persons and their respective heirs, executors, administrators, and assigns, and also the executors, administrators, and assigns respectively of persons whose interests determine with their own deaths, shall have such or the same remedies at law and in equity for recovering such apportioned parts as aforesaid when payable (allowing proportionate parts of all just allowances) as they respectively would have had for recovering such entire portions as aforesaid if entitled thereto respectively; provided that persons liable to pay rents reserved out of or charged on lands or other hereditaments of any tenure, and the same lands or other hereditaments, shall not be resorted to for any such apportioned part forming part of an entire or continuing rent

as aforesaid specifically, but the entire or continuing rent, including such apportioned part, shall be recovered and received by the heir or other person who, if the rent had not been apportionable under this Act or otherwise, would have been entitled to such entire or continuing rent, and such apportioned part shall be recoverable from such heir or other person by the executors or other parties entitled under this Act to the same by action at law or suit in equity.

5. Interpretation of terms.

In the construction of this Act—

The word "rents" includes rent service, rentcharge, and rent seck, and also tithes and all periodical payments or renderings in lieu of or in the nature of rent or tithe.

The word "annuities" includes salaries and pensions.

The word "dividends" includes (besides dividends strictly so called) all payments made by the name of dividend, bonus, or otherwise out of the revenue of trading or other public companies, divisible between all or any of the members of such respective companies, whether such payments shall be usually made or declared at any fixed times or otherwise; and all such divisible revenue shall, for the purposes of this Act, be deemed to have accrued by equal daily increment during and within the period for or in respect of which the payment of the same revenue shall be declared or expressed to be made, but the said word "dividend" does not include payments in the nature of a return or reimbursement of capital.

6. Act not to apply to policies of assurance.

Nothing in this Act contained shall render apportionable any annual sums made payable in policies of assurance of any description.

7. Nor where stipulation made to the contrary.

The provisions of this Act shall not extend to any case in which it is or shall be expressly stipulated that no apportionment shall take place.

LAW OF PROPERTY ACT 1922
(1922, c. 16)

[29 June 1922]

PART VII

PROVISIONS RESPECTING LEASEHOLDS

Conversion of Perpetually Renewable Leaseholds into Long Terms

145. Conversion of perpetually renewable leaseholds.

For the purpose of converting perpetually renewable leases and underleases (not being an interest in perpetually renewable copyhold land enfranchised by Part V. of this Act, but including a perpetually renewable underlease derived out of an interest in perpetually renewable copyhold land) into long terms, for preventing the creation of perpetually renewable leasehold interests and for providing for the interests of the persons affected, the provisions contained in the Fifteenth Schedule to this Act shall have effect.

190. Special definitions applicable to Part VII.

In Part VII. of this Act—

(i) "Lessor" means the person for the time being entitled in reversion expectant on the interest demised, or, where the reversion is encumbered, the person having power to accept a surrender of the lease, or underlease;

(ii) "Lessee" and "underlessee" include the persons respectively deriving title under them;

(iii)   "A perpetually renewable lease or underlease" means a lease or underlease the holder of which is entitled to enforce (whether or not subject to the fulfilment of any condition) the perpetual renewal thereof, and includes a lease or underlease for a life or lives or for a term of years, whether determinable with life or lives or not, which is perpetually renewable as aforesaid, but does not include copyhold land held for a life or lives or for years, whether or not determinable with life, where the tenant had before the commencement of this Act a right of perpetual renewal subject or not to the fulfilment of any condition;

(iv)   "Underlease," unless the context otherwise requires, includes a subterm created out of a derivative leasehold interest.

Section 145.   FIFTEENTH SCHEDULE

PROVISIONS RELATING TO PERPETUALLY RENEWABLE LEASES AND UNDERLEASES

1.   Conversion of perpetually renewable leases into long terms.

(1)   Land comprised in a perpetually renewable lease which was subsisting at the commencement of this Act shall, by virtue of this Act, vest in the person who at such commencement was entitled to such lease, for a term of two thousand years, to be calculated from the date at which the existing term or interest commenced, at the rent and subject to the lessees' covenants and conditions (if any) which under the lease would have been payable or enforceable during the subsistence of such term or interest.

(2)   The rent, covenants and conditions (if any) shall (subject to the express provisions of this Act to the contrary) be payable and enforceable during the subsistence of the term created by this Act; and that term shall take effect in substitution for the term or interest created by the lease, and be subject to the like power of re-entry (if any) and other provisions which affected the term or interest created by the lease, but without any right of renewal.

2.   Conversion of perpetually renewable underleases into long terms.

(1)   Land comprised in any underlease, which at the commencement of this Act was perpetually renewable and was derived out of a head term affected by this Act, shall, by virtue of this Act, vest in the person who at such commencement was entitled to the subterm or interest for a term of two thousand years less one day, to be calculated from the date at which the head term created by this Act commenced, at the rent and subject to the underlessee's covenants and conditions (if any) which under the underlease would have been payable or enforceable during the subsistence of such subterm or interest.

(2)   The rent, covenants and conditions (if any) shall (subject to the express provisions of this Act to the contrary) be payable and enforceable during the subsistence of the subterm created by this Act; and that subterm shall take effect in substitution for the subterm or interest created by the underlease, and be subject to the like power of re-entry (if any) and other provisions which affected the subterm or interest created by the underlease, but without any right of renewal.

(3)   The foregoing provisions of this section shall also apply to any perpetually renewable subterm or interest which, at the commencement of this Act, was derived out of any other subterm or interest, but so that in every case the subterm created by this Act shall be one day less in duration than the derivative term created by this Act, out of which it takes effect.

SETTLED LAND ACT 1925
(1925, c. 18)

PART II
POWERS OF A TENANT FOR LIFE

Leasing Powers

41. Power to lease for ordinary or building or mining or forestry purposes.
A tenant for life may lease the settled land, or any part thereof, or any easement, right, or privilege of any kind over or in relation to the land, for any purpose whatever, whether involving waste or not, for any term not exceeding—

(i)   In case of a building lease, nine hundred and ninety-nine years;

(ii)   In case of a mining lease, one hundred years;

(iii)   In case of a forestry lease, nine hundred and ninety-nine years;

(iv)   In case of any other lease, fifty years.

42. Regulations respecting leases generally.

(1)   Save as hereinafter provided, every lease—

(i)   shall be by deed, and be made to take effect in possession not later than twelve months after its date, or in reversion after an existing lease having not more than seven years to run at the date of the new lease;

(ii)   shall reserve the best rent that can reasonably be obtained, regard being had to any fine taken, and to any money laid out or to be laid out for the benefit of the settled land, and generally to the circumstances of the case;

(iii)   shall contain a covenant by the lessee for payment of the rent, and a condition of re-entry on the rent not being paid within a time therein specified not exceeding thirty days.

(2)   A counterpart of every lease shall be executed by the lessee and delivered to the tenant for life or statutory owner, of which execution and delivery the execution of the lease by the tenant for life or statutory owner shall be sufficient evidence.

(3)   A statement, contained in a lease or in an indorsement thereon, signed by the tenant for life or statutory owner, respecting any matter of fact or of calculation under this Act in relation to the lease, shall, in favour of the lessee and of those claiming under him, be sufficient evidence of the matter stated.

(4)   A fine received on the grant of a lease under any power conferred by this Act shall be deemed to be capital money arising under this Act.

(5)   A lease at the best rent that can be reasonably obtained without fine, and whereby the lessee is not exempted from punishment for waste, may be made—

(i)   Where the term does not exceed twenty-one years—

(a)   without any notice of an intention to make the lease having been given under this Act; and

(b)   notwithstanding that there are no trustees of the settlement; and

(ii)   Where the term does not extend beyond three years from the date of the writing, by any writing under hand only containing an agreement instead of a covenant by the lessee for payment of rent.

43. Leasing powers for special objects.
The leasing power of a tenant for life extends to the making of—

(i)   a lease for giving effect (in such manner and so far as the law permits) to a covenant of renewal, performance whereof could be enforced against the owner for the time being of the settled land; and

(ii)   a lease for confirming, as far as may be, a previous lease being void or voidable, but so that every lease, as and when confirmed, shall be such a lease as might at the date of the original lease have been lawfully granted under this Act or otherwise, as the case may require.

Provisions as to building, mining and forestry leases

44. Regulations respecting building leases.

(1)   Every building lease shall be made partly in consideration of the lessee, or some person by whose direction the lease is granted, or some other person having erected or agreeing to erect buildings, new or additional, or having improved or repaired or agreeing to improve or repair buildings, or having executed or agreeing to execute on the land leased, an improvement authorised by this Act for or in connexion with building purposes.

(2)   A peppercorn rent or a nominal or other rent less than the rent ultimately payable, may be made payable for the first five years or any less part of the term.

(3)   Where the land is contracted to be leased in lots the entire amount of rent to be ultimately payable may be apportioned among the lots in any manner:

Provided that—

(i)   the annual rent reserved by any lease shall not be less than 50p; and

(ii)   the total amount of the rents reserved on all leases for the time being granted shall not be less than the total amount of the rents which in order that the leases may be in conformity with this Act, ought to be reserved in respect of the whole land for the time being leased; and

(iii)   the rent reserved by any lease shall not exceed one-fifth part of the full annual value of the land comprised in that lease with the buildings thereon when completed.

45. Regulations respecting mining leases.

(1)   In a mining lease—

(i)   the rent may be made to be ascertainable by or to vary according to the acreage worked or by or according to the quantities of any mineral or substance gotten, made merchantable, converted, carried away, or disposed of, in or from the settled land, or any other land, or by or according to any facilities given in that behalf; and

(ii)   the rent may also be made to vary according to the price of the minerals or substances gotten, or any of them, and such price may be the saleable value, or the price or value appearing in any trade or market or other price list or return from time to time, or may be the marketable value as ascertained in any manner prescribed by the lease (including a reference to arbitration), or may be an average of any such prices or values taken during a specified period; and

(iii)   a fixed or minimum rent may be made payable, with or without power for the lessee, in case the rent, according to acreage or quantity or otherwise, in any specified period does not produce an amount equal to the fixed or minimum rent, to make up the deficiency in any subsequent specified period, free of rent other than the fixed or minimum rent.

(2)   A lease may be made partly in consideration of the lessee having executed, or agreeing to execute, on the land leased an improvement authorised by this Act, for or in connexion with mining purposes.

46. Variation of building or mining lease according to circumstances of district.

(1)   Where it is shown to the court with respect to the district in which any settled land is situate, either—

(i)   that it is the custom for land therein to be leased for building or mining purposes for a longer term or on other conditions than the term or conditions specified in that behalf in this Act; or

(ii)   that it is difficult to make leases for building or mining purposes of land therein, except for a longer term or on other conditions than the term and conditions specified in that behalf in this Act;

the court may, if it thinks fit, authorise generally the tenant for life or statutory owner to make from time to time leases of or affecting the settled land in that district, or parts thereof for any term or on any conditions as in the order of the court expressed, or may, if it thinks fit, authorise the tenant for life or statutory owner to make any such lease in any particular case.

(2) Thereupon the tenant for life or statutory owner, and, subject to any direction in the order of the court to the contrary, each of his successors in title being a tenant for life or statutory owner, may make in any case, or in the particular case, a lease of the settled land, or part thereof, in conformity with the order.

47. Capitalisation of part of mining rent.

Under a mining lease, whether the mines or minerals leased are already opened or in work or not, unless a contrary intention is expressed in the settlement, there shall be from time to time set aside, as capital money arising under this Act, part of the rent as follows, namely – where the tenant for life or statutory owner is impeachable for waste in respect of minerals, three fourths parts of the rent, and otherwise one fourth part thereof, and in every such case the residue of the rent shall go as rents and profits.

48. Regulations respecting forestry leases.

(1) In the case of a forestry lease—

(i) a peppercorn rent or a nominal or other rent less than the rent ultimately payable, may be made payable for the first ten years or any less part of the term;

(ii) the rent may be made to be ascertainable by or to vary according to the value of the timber on the land comprised in the lease, or the produce thereof, which may during any year be cut, converted, carried away, or otherwise disposed of;

(iii) a fixed or minimum rent may be made payable, with or without power for the lessee, in case the rent according to value in any specified period does not produce an amount equal to the fixed or minimum rent, to make up the deficiency in any subsequent specified period, free of rent other than the fixed or minimum rent; and

(iv) any other provisions may be made for the sharing of the proceeds or profits of the user of the land between the reversioner and the Forestry Commissioners.

(2) In this section the expression "timber" includes all forest products.

PART VI
GENERAL PROVISIONS AS TO TRUSTEES

101. Notice to trustees.

(1) Save as otherwise expressly provided by this Act, a tenant for life or statutory owner, when intending to make a sale, exchange, lease, mortgage, or charge or to grant an option—

(a) shall give notice of his intention in that behalf to each of the trustees of the settlement, by posting registered letters, containing the notice, addressed to the trustees severally, each at his usual or last known place of abode in the United Kingdom; and

(b) shall give a like notice to the solicitor for the trustees, if any such solicitor is known to the tenant for life or statutory owner, by posting a registered letter, containing the notice, addressed to the solicitor at his place of business in the United Kingdom; every letter under this section being posted not less than one month before the making or granting by the tenant for life or statutory owner of the sale, exchange, lease, mortgage, charge, or option, or of a contract for the same:

Provided that a notice under this section shall not be valid unless at the date thereof the trustee is a trust corporation, or the number of trustees is not less than two.

(2) The notice required by this section of intention to make a sale, exchange, or lease, or to grant an option may be notice of a general intention in that behalf.

(3) The tenant for life or statutory owner is, upon request by a trustee of the settlement, to furnish to him such particulars and information as may reasonably be required by him from time to time with reference to sales, exchanges, or leases effected, or in progress, or immediately intended.

(4)   Any trustee, by writing under his hand, may waive notice either in any particular case, or generally, and may accept less than one month's notice.

(5)   A person dealing in good faith with the tenant for life is not concerned to inquire respecting the giving of any such notice as is required by this section.

PART VII
RESTRICTIONS, SAVINGS AND PROTECTION OF PURCHASERS

110.   Protection of purchasers, &c.

(1)   On a sale, exchange, lease, mortgage, charge, or other disposition, a purchaser dealing in good faith with a tenant for life or statutory owner shall, as against all parties entitled under the settlement, be conclusively taken to have given the best price, consideration, or rent, as the case may require, that could reasonably be obtained by the tenant for life or statutory owner, and to have complied with all the requisitions of this Act.

(2)   A purchaser of a legal estate in settled land shall not, except as hereby expressly provided, be bound or entitled to call for the production of the trust instrument or any information concerning that instrument or any ad valorem stamp duty thereon, and whether or not he has notice of its contents he shall, save as hereinafter provided, be bound and entitled if the last or only principal vesting instrument contains the statements and particulars required by this Act to assume that—

(a)   the person in whom the land is by the said instrument vested or declared to be vested is the tenant for life or statutory owner and has all the powers of a tenant for life under this Act, including such additional or larger powers, if any, as are therein mentioned;

(b)   the persons by the said instrument stated to be the trustees of the settlement, or their successors appearing to be duly appointed, are the properly constituted trustees of the settlement;

(c)   the statements and particulars required by this Act and contained (expressly or by reference) in the said instrument were correct at the date thereof;

(d)   the statements contained in any deed executed in accordance with this Act declaring who are the trustees of the settlement for the purposes of this Act are correct;

(e)   the statements contained in any deed of discharge, executed in accordance with this Act, are correct:

Provided that, as regards the first vesting instrument executed for the purpose of giving effect to—

(a)   a settlement subsisting at the commencement of this Act; or

(b)   an instrument which by virtue of this Act is deemed to be a settlement; or

(c)   a settlement which by virtue of this Act is deemed to have been made by any person after the commencement of this Act; or

(d)   an instrument inter vivos intended to create a settlement of a legal estate in land which is executed after the commencement of this Act and does not comply with the requirements of this Act with respect to the method of effecting such a settlement; a purchaser shall be concerned to see—

(i)   that the land disposed of to him is comprised in such settlement or instrument;

(ii)   that the person in whom the settled land is by such vesting instrument vested, or declared to be vested, is the person in whom it ought to be vested as tenant for life or statutory owner;

(iii)   that the persons thereby stated to be the trustees of the settlement are the properly constituted trustees of the settlement.

(3)   A purchaser of a legal estate in settled land from a personal representative shall be entitled to act on the following assumptions:—

(i) If the capital money, if any, payable in respect of the transaction is paid to the personal representative, that such representative is acting under his statutory or other powers and requires the money for purposes of administration;

(ii) If such capital money is, by the direction of the personal representative, paid to persons who are stated to be the trustees of a settlement, that such persons are the duly constituted trustees of the settlement for the purposes of this Act, and that the personal representative is acting under his statutory powers during a minority;

(iii) In any other case, that the personal representative is acting under his statutory or other powers.

(4) Where no capital money arises under a transaction, a disposition by a tenant for life or statutory owner shall, in favour of a purchaser of a legal estate, have effect under this Act notwithstanding that at the date of the transaction there are no trustees of the settlement.

(5) If a conveyance of or an assent relating to land formerly subject to a vesting instrument does not state who are the trustees of the settlement for the purposes of this Act, a purchaser of a legal estate shall be bound and entitled to act on the assumption that the person in whom the land was thereby vested was entitled to the land free from all limitations, powers, and charges taking effect under that settlement, absolutely and beneficially, or, if so expressed in the conveyance or assent, as personal representative, or trustee for sale or otherwise, and that every statement of fact in such conveyance or assent is correct.

PART IX
SUPPLEMENTARY PROVISIONS

117. Definitions.

(1) In this Act, unless the context otherwise requires, the following expressions have the meanings hereby assigned to them respectively, that is to say:—

(i) "Building purposes" include the erecting and the improving of, and the adding to, and the repairing of buildings; and a "building lease" is a lease for any building purposes or purposes connected therewith;

(ii) "Capital money arising under this Act" means capital money arising under the powers and provisions of this Act or the Acts replaced by this Act, and receivable for the trusts and purposes of the settlement and includes securities representing capital money;

(iii) "Death duty" means estate duty . . . and every other duty leviable or payable on death;

(iv) "Determinable fee" means a fee determinable whether by limitation or condition;

(v) "Disposition" and "conveyance" include a mortgage, charge by way of legal mortgage, lease, assent, vesting declaration, vesting instrument, disclaimer, release and every other assurance of property or of an interest therein by any instrument, except a will, and "dispose of" and "convey" have corresponding meanings;

(vi) "Dower" includes "freebench";

(vii) "Hereditaments" mean real property which on an intestacy might before the commencement of this Act have devolved on an heir;

(viii) "Instrument" does not include a statute unless the statute creates a settlement;

(ix) "Land" includes land of any tenure, and mines and minerals whether or not held apart from the surface, buildings or parts of buildings (whether the division is horizontal, vertical or made in any other way) and other corporeal hereditaments; also a manor, an advowson, and a rent and other incorporeal hereditaments, and an easement, right, privilege, or benefit in, over, or derived from land, and any estate or interest in land not being an undivided share in land;

(x) "Lease" includes an agreement for a lease, and "forestry lease" means a lease to the Forestry Commissioners for any purpose for which they are authorised to acquire land by the Forestry Act 1919;

(xi) "Legal mortgage" means a mortgage by demise or sub-demise or a charge by way of legal mortgage, and "legal mortgagee" has a corresponding meaning; "legal estate" means an estate interest or charge in or over land (subsisting or created at law) which is by statute authorised to subsist or to be created at law; and "equitable interests" mean all other interests and charges in or over land or in the proceeds of sale thereof; an equitable interest "capable of subsisting at law" means such an equitable interest as could validly subsist at law, if clothed with the legal estate; and "estate owner" means the owner of a legal estate;

(xii) "Limitation" includes a trust, and "trust" includes an implied or constructive trust;

(xiv) "Manor" includes lordship, and reputed manor or lordship; and "manorial incident" has the same meaning as in the Law of Property Act 1922;

(xv) "Mines and minerals" mean mines and minerals whether already opened or in work or not, and include all minerals and substances in, on, or under the land, obtainable by underground or by surface working; and "mining purposes" include the sinking and searching for, winning, working, getting, making merchantable, smelting or otherwise converting or working for the purposes of any manufacture, carrying away, and disposing of mines and minerals, in or under the settled land, or any other land, and the erection of buildings, and the execution of engineering and other works suitable for those purposes; and a "mining lease" is a lease for any mining purposes or purposes connected therewith, and includes a grant or licence for any mining purposes;

(xvi) "Minister" means the Minister of Agriculture, Fisheries and Food;

(xvii) "Notice" includes constructive notice;

(xviii) "Personal representative" means the executor, original or by representation, or administrator, for the time being of a deceased person, and where there are special personal representatives for the purposes of settled land means those personal representatives;

(xix) "Possession" includes receipt of rents and profits, or the right to receive the same, if any; and "income" includes rents and profits;

(xx) "Property" includes any thing in action, and any interest in real or personal property;

(xxi) "Purchaser" means a purchaser in good faith for value, and includes a lessee, mortgagee or other person who in good faith acquires an interest in settled land for value; and in reference to a legal estate includes a chargee by way of legal mortgage;

(xxii) "Rent" includes yearly or other rent, and toll, duty, royalty, or other reservation, by the acre, or the ton, or otherwise; and, in relation to rent, "payment" includes delivery; and "fine" includes premium or fore-gift, and any payment, consideration, or benefit in the nature of a fine, premium, or fore-gift;

(xxiii) "Securities" include stocks, funds, and shares;

(xxiv) "Settled land" includes land which is deemed to be settled land; "settlement" includes an instrument or instruments which under this Act or the Acts which it replaces is or are deemed to be or which together constitute a settlement, and a settlement which is deemed to have been made by any person or to be subsisting for the purposes of this Act; "a settlement subsisting at the commencement of this Act" includes a settlement created by virtue of this Act immediately on the commencement thereof; and "trustees of the settlement" mean the trustees thereof for the purposes of this Act howsoever appointed or constituted;

(xxv) "Small dwellings" mean dwelling-houses of a rateable value not exceeding one hundred pounds per annum;

(xxvi) "Statutory owner" means the trustees of the settlement or other persons who, during a minority, or at any other time when there is no tenant for life, have the powers of a tenant for life under this Act, but does not include the trustees of the settlement, where by virtue of an order of the court or otherwise the trustees have power to convey the settled land in the name of the tenant for life;

(xxvii) "Steward" includes deputy steward, or other proper officer, of a manor;

(xxviii) "Tenant for life" includes a person (not being a statutory owner) who has the powers of a tenant for life under this Act, and also (where the context requires) one of two or more persons who together constitute the tenant for life, or have the powers of a tenant for life; and "tenant in tail" includes a person entitled to an entailed interest in any property; and "entailed interest" has the same meaning as in the Law of Property Act 1925;

(xxix) A "term of years absolute" means a term of years, taking effect either in possession or in reversion, with or without impeachment for waste, whether at a rent or not and whether subject or not to another legal estate, and whether certain or liable to determination by notice, re-entry, operation of law, or by a provision for cesser on redemption, or in any other event (other than the dropping of a life, or the determination of a determinable life interest), but does not include any term of years determinable with life or lives or with the cesser of a determinable life interest, nor, if created after the commencement of this Act, a term of years which is not expressed to take effect in possession within twenty-one years after the creation thereof where required by statute to take effect within that period; and in this definition the expression "term of years" includes a term for less than a year, or for a year or years and a fraction of a year or from year to year;

(xxx) "Trust corporation" means the Public Trustee or a corporation either appointed by the court in any particular case to be a trustee or entitled by rules made under subsection (3) of section four of the Public Trustee Act 1906, to act as custodian trustee, and "trust for sale" "trustees for sale" and "power to postpone a sale" have the same meanings as in the Law of Property Act 1925;

(xxxi) In relation to settled land "vesting deed" or "vesting order" means the instrument whereby settled land is conveyed to or vested or declared to be vested in a tenant for life or statutory owner; "vesting assent" means the instrument whereby a personal representative, after the death of a tenant for life or statutory owner, or the survivor of two or more tenants for life or statutory owners, vests settled land in a person entitled as tenant for life or statutory owner; "vesting instrument" means a vesting deed, a vesting assent or, where the land affected remains settled land, a vesting order; "principal vesting instrument" includes any vesting instrument other than a subsidiary vesting deed; and "trust instrument" means the instrument whereby the trusts of the settled land are declared, and includes any two or more such instruments and a settlement or instrument which is deemed to be a trust instrument;

(xxxii) "United Kingdom" means Great Britain and Northern Ireland;

(xxxiii) "Will" includes codicil.

(1A) Any reference in this Act to money, securities or proceeds of sale being paid or transferred into court shall be construed as referring to the money, securities or proceeds being paid or transferred into the Supreme Court or any other court that has jurisdiction, and any reference in this Act to the court, in a context referring to the investment or application of money, securities or proceeds of sale paid or transferred into court, shall be construed, in the case of money, securities or proceeds paid or transferred into the Supreme Court, as referring to the High Court, and, in the case of money, securities or proceeds paid or transferred into another court, as referring to that other court.

(2) Where an equitable interest in or power over property arises by statute or operation of law, references to the "creation" of an interest or power include any interest or power so arising.

(3)   References to registration under the Land Charges Act 1925, apply to any registration made under any statute which is by the Land Charges Act 1925, to have effect as if the registration had been made under that Act.

LAW OF PROPERTY ACT 1925
(1925, c. 20)

An Act to consolidate the enactments relating to Conveyancing and the Law of Property in England and Wales.   [9 April 1925]

PART I
GENERAL PRINCIPLES AS TO LEGAL ESTATES, EQUITABLE INTERESTS AND POWERS

1.   Legal estates and equitable interests.

(1)   The only estates in land which are capable of subsisting or of being conveyed or created at law are—

(a)   An estate in fee simple absolute in possession;

(b)   A term of years absolute.

(2)   The only interests or charges in or over land which are capable of subsisting or of being conveyed or created at law are—

(a)   An easement, right, or privilege in or over land for an interest equivalent to an estate in fee simple absolute in possession or a term of years absolute;

(b)   A rentcharge in possession issuing out of or charged on land being either perpetual or for a term of years absolute;

(c)   A charge by way of legal mortgage;

(d)   and any other similar charge on land which is not created by an instrument;

(e)   Rights of entry exercisable over or in respect of a legal term of years absolute, or annexed, for any purpose, to a legal rentcharge.

(3)   All other estates, interests, and charges in or over land take effect as equitable interests.

(4)   The estates, interests, and charges which under this section are authorised to subsist or to be conveyed or created at law are (when subsisting or conveyed or created at law) in this Act referred to as "legal estates," and have the same incidents as legal estates subsisting at the commencement of this Act; and the owner of a legal estate is referred to as "an estate owner" and his legal estate is referred to as his estate.

(5)   A legal estate may subsist concurrently with or subject to any other legal estate in the same land in like manner as it could have done before the commencement of this Act.

(6)   A legal estate is not capable of subsisting or of being created in an undivided share in land or of being held by an infant.

(7)   Every power of appointment over, or power to convey or charge land or any interest therein, whether created by a statute or other instrument or implied by law, and whether created before or after the commencement of this Act (not being a power vested in a legal mortgagee or an estate owner in right of his estate and exercisable by him or by another person in his name and on his behalf), operates only in equity.

(8)   Estates, interests, and charges in or over land which are not legal estates are in this Act referred to as "equitable interests" and powers which by this Act are to operate in equity only are in this Act referred to as "equitable powers."

(9)   The provisions in any statute or other instrument requiring land to be conveyed to uses shall take effect as directions that the land shall (subject to creating or reserving thereout any legal estate authorised by this Act which may be required) be conveyed to a person of full age upon the requisite trusts.

(10)   The repeal of the Statute of Uses (as amended) does not affect the operation thereof in regard to dealings taking effect before the commencement of this Act.

5. Satisfied terms, whether created out of freehold or leasehold land to cease.

(1)   Where the purposes of a term of years created or limited at any time out of freehold land, become satisfied either before or after the commencement of this Act (whether or not that term either by express declaration or by construction of law becomes attendant upon the freehold reversion) it shall merge in the reversion expectant thereon and shall cease accordingly.

(2)   Where the purposes of a term of years created or limited, at any time, out of leasehold land, become satisfied after the commencement of this Act, that term shall merge in the reversion expectant thereon and shall cease accordingly.

(3)   Where the purposes are satisfied only as respects part of the land comprised in a term, this section shall have effect as if a separate term had been created in regard to that part of the land.

6. Saving of lessors' and lessees' covenants.

(1)   Nothing in this Part of this Act affects prejudicially the right to enforce any lessor's or lessee's covenants, agreements or conditions (including a valid option to purchase or right of pre-emption over the reversion), contained in any such instrument as is in this section mentioned, the benefit or burden of which runs with the reversion or the term.

(2)   This section applies where the covenant, agreement or condition is contained in any instrument—

(a)   creating a term of years absolute, or

(b)   varying the rights of the lessor or lessee under the instrument creating the term.

8. Saving of certain legal powers to lease.

(1)   All leases or tenancies at a rent for a term of years absolute authorised to be granted by a mortgagor or mortgagee or by the Settled Land Act, 1925, or any other statute (whether or not extended by any instrument) may be granted in the name and on behalf of the estate owner by the person empowered to grant the same, whether being an estate owner or not, with the same effect and priority as if this Part of this Act had not been passed; but this section does not (except as respects the usual qualified covenant for quiet enjoyment) authorise any person granting a lease in the name of an estate owner to impose any personal liability on him.

(2)   Where a rentcharge is held for a legal estate, the owner thereof may under the statutory power or under any corresponding power, create a legal term of years absolute for securing or compelling payment of the same; but in other cases terms created under any such power shall, unless and until the estate owner of the land charged gives legal effect to the transaction, take effect only as equitable interests.

PART II
CONTRACTS, CONVEYANCES AND OTHER INSTRUMENTS

44. Statutory commencements of title.

(1)   After the commencement of this Act fifteen years shall be substituted for forty years as the period of commencement of title which a purchaser of land may require; nevertheless earlier title than fifteen years may be required in cases similar to those in which earlier title than forty years might immediately before the commencement of this Act be required.

(2)   Under a contract to grant or assign a term of years, whether derived or to be derived out of freehold or leasehold land, the intended lessee or assign shall not be entitled to call for the title to the freehold.

(3)   Under a contract to sell and assign a term of years derived out of a leasehold interest in land, the intended assign shall not have the right to call for the title to the leasehold reversion.

(4) On a contract to grant a lease for a term of years to be derived out of a leasehold interest, with a leasehold reversion, the intended lessee shall not have the right to call for the title to that reversion.

(5) Where by reason of any of the three last preceding subsections, an intending lessee or assign is not entitled to call for the title to the freehold or to a leasehold reversion, as the case may be, he shall not, where the contract is made after the commencement of this Act, be deemed to be affected with notice of any matter or thing of which, if he had contracted that such title should be furnished, he might have had notice.

(6) Where land of copyhold or customary tenure has been converted into freehold by enfranchisement, then, under a contract to sell and convey the freehold, the purchaser shall not have the right to call for the title to make the enfranchisement.

(7) Where the manorial incidents formerly affecting any land have been extinguished, then, under a contract to sell and convey the freehold, the purchaser shall not have the right to call for the title of the person entering into any compensation agreement or giving a receipt for the compensation money to enter into such agreement or to give such receipt, and shall not be deemed to be affected with notice of any matter or thing of which, if he had contracted that such title should be furnished, he might have had notice.

(8) A purchaser shall not be deemed to be or ever to have been affected with notice of any matter or thing of which, if he had investigated the title or made enquiries in regard to matters prior to the period of commencement of title fixed by this Act, or by any other statute, or by any rule of law, he might have had notice, unless he actually makes such investigation or enquiries.

(9) Where a lease whether made before or after the commencement of this Act, is made under a power contained in a settlement, will, Act of Parliament, or other instrument, any preliminary contract for or relating to the lease shall not, for the purpose of the deduction of title to an intended assign, form part of the title, or evidence of the title, to the lease.

(10) This section, save where otherwise expressly provided, applies to contracts for sale whether made before or after the commencement of this Act, and applies to contracts for exchange in like manner as to contracts for sale, save that it applies only to contracts for exchange made after such commencement.

(11) This section applies only if and so far as a contrary intention is not expressed in the contract.

45. Other statutory conditions of sale.

(1) A purchaser of any property shall not—

(a) require the production, or any abstract or copy, of any deed, will, or other document, dated or made before the time prescribed by law, or stipulated, for the commencement of the title, even though the same creates a power subsequently exercised by an instrument abstracted in the abstract furnished to the purchaser; or

(b) require any information, or make any requisition, objection, or inquiry, with respect to any such deed, will, or document, or the title prior to that time, notwithstanding that any such deed, will, or other document, or that prior title, is recited, agreed to be produced, or noticed;

and he shall assume, unless the contrary appears, that the recitals, contained in the abstracted instruments, of any deed, will, or other document, forming part of that prior title, are correct, and give all the material contents of the deed, will, or other document so recited, and that every document so recited was duly executed by all necessary parties, and perfected, if and as required, by fine, recovery, acknowledgement, inrolment, or otherwise:

Provided that this subsection shall not deprive a purchaser of the right to require the production, or an abstract or copy of—

(i) any power of attorney under which any abstracted document is executed; or

(ii) any document creating or disposing of an interest, power or obligation which is not shown to have ceased or expired, and subject to which any part of the property is disposed of by an abstracted document; or

(iii) any document creating any limitation or trust by reference to which any part of the property is disposed of by an abstracted document.

(2) Where land sold is held by lease (other than an under-lease), the purchaser shall assume, unless the contrary appears, that the lease was duly granted; and, on production of the receipt for the last payment due for rent under the lease before the date of actual completion of the purchase, he shall assume, unless the contrary appears, that all the covenants and provisions of the lease have been duly performed and observed up to the date of actual completion of the purchase.

(3) Where land sold is held by under-lease, the purchaser shall assume, unless the contrary appears, that the under-lease and every superior lease were duly granted; and, on production of the receipt for the last payment due for rent under the under-lease before the date of actual completion of the purchase, he shall assume, unless the contrary appears, that all the covenants and provisions of the under-lease have been duly performed and observed up to the date of actual completion of the purchase, and further that all rent due under every superior lease, and all the covenants and provisions of every superior lease, have been paid and duly performed and observed up to that date.

(4) On a sale of any property, the following expenses shall be borne by the purchaser where he requires them to be incurred for the purpose of verifying the abstract or any other purpose, that is to say—

(a) the expenses of the production and inspection of all Acts of Parliament, inclosure awards, records, proceedings of courts, court rolls, deeds, wills, probates, letters of administration, and other documents, not in the possession of the vendor or his mortgagee or trustee, and the expenses of all journeys incidental to such production or inspection; and

(b) the expenses of searching for, procuring, making, verifying, and producing all certificates, declarations, evidences, and information not in the possession of the vendor or his mortgagee or trustee, and all attested, stamped, office, or other copies or abstracts of, or extracts from, any Acts of Parliament or other documents aforesaid, not in the possession of the vendor or his mortgagee or trustee;

and where the vendor or his mortgagee or trustee retains possession of any document, the expenses of making any copy thereof, attested or unattested, which a purchaser requires to be delivered to him, shall be borne by that purchaser.

(5) On a sale of any property in lots, a purchaser of two or more lots, held wholly or partly under the same title, shall not have a right to more than one abstract of the common title, except at his own expense.

(6) Recitals, statements, and descriptions of facts, matters, and parties contained in deeds, instruments, Acts of Parliament, or statutory declarations, twenty years old at the date of the contract, shall, unless and except so far as they may be proved to be inaccurate, be taken to be sufficient evidence of the truth of such facts, matters, and descriptions.

(7) The inability of a vendor to furnish a purchaser with an acknowledgment of his right to production and delivery of copies of documents of title or with a legal covenant to produce and furnish copies of documents of title shall not be an objection to title in case the purchaser will, on the completion of the contract, have an equitable right to the production of such documents.

(8) Such acknowledgments of the right of production or covenants for production and such undertakings or covenants for safe custody of documents as the purchaser can and does require shall be furnished or made at his expense, and the vendor shall bear the expense of perusal and execution on behalf of and by himself, and on behalf of and

by necessary parties other than the purchaser.

(9)   A vendor shall be entitled to retain documents of title where—

(a)   he retains any part of the land to which the documents relate; or

(b)   the document consists of a trust instrument or other instrument creating a trust which is still subsisting, or an instrument relating to the appointment or discharge of a trustee of a subsisting trust.

(10)   This section applies to contracts for sale made before or after the commencement of this Act, and applies to contracts for exchange in like manner as to contracts for sale, except that it applies only to contracts for exchange made after such commencement:

Provided that this section shall apply subject to any stipulation or contrary intention expressed in the contract.

(11)   Nothing in this section shall be construed as binding a purchaser to complete his purchase in any case where, on a contract made independently of this section, and containing stipulations similar to the provisions of this section, or any of them, specific performance of the contract would not be enforced against him by the court.

48.   Stipulations preventing a purchaser, lessee, or underlessee from employing his own solicitor to be void.

(1)   Any stipulation made on the sale of any interest in land after the commencement of this Act to the effect that the conveyance to, or the registration of the title of, the purchaser shall be prepared or carried out at the expense of the purchaser by a solicitor appointed by or acting for the vendor, and any stipulation which might restrict a purchaser in the selection of a solicitor to act on his behalf in relation to any interest in land agreed to be purchased, shall be void; and, if a sale is effected by demise or subdemise, then, for the purposes of this subsection, the instrument required for giving effect to the transaction shall be deemed to be a conveyance:

Provided that nothing in this subsection shall effect any right reserved to a vendor to furnish a form of conveyance to a purchaser from which the draft can be prepared, or to charge a reasonable fee therefor, or, where a perpetual rentcharge is to be reserved as the only consideration in money or money's worth, the right of a vendor to stipulate that the draft conveyance is to be prepared by his solicitor at the expense of the purchaser.

(2)   Any covenant or stipulation contained in, or entered into with reference to any lease or underlease made before or after the commencement of this Act—

(a)   whereby the right of preparing, at the expense of a purchaser, any conveyance of the estate or interest of the lessee or underlessee in the demised premises or in any part thereof, or of otherwise carrying out, at the expense of the purchaser, any dealing with such estate or interest, is expressed to be reserved to or vested in the lessor or underlessor or his solicitor; or

(b)   which in any way restricts the right of the purchaser to have such conveyance carried out on his behalf by a solicitor appointed by him;

shall be void:

Provided that, where any covenant or stipulation is rendered void by this subsection, there shall be implied in lieu thereof a covenant or stipulation that the lessee or underlessee shall register with the lessor or his solicitor within six months from the date thereof, or as soon after the expiration of that period as may be practicable, all conveyances and devolutions (including probates or letters of administration) affecting the lease or underlease and pay a fee of one guinea in respect of each registration, and the power of entry (if any) on breach of any covenant contained in the lease or underlease shall apply and extend to the breach of any covenant so to be implied.

(3)   Save where a sale is effected by demise or sub-demise, this section does not affect the law relating to the preparation of a lease or underlease or the draft thereof.

(4) In this section "lease" and "underlease" include any agreement therefor or other tenancy, and "lessee" and "underlessee" and "lessor" and "underlessor" have corresponding meanings.

Conveyances and other Instruments

52. Conveyances to be by deed.

(1) All conveyances of land or of any interest therein are void for the purpose of conveying or creating a legal estate unless made by deed.

(2) This section does not apply to—

(a) assents by a personal representative;

(b) disclaimers made in accordance with sections 178 to 180 or sections 315 to 319 of the Insolvency Act 1986, or not required to be evidenced in writing;

(c) surrenders by operation of law, including surrenders which may, by law, be effected without writing;

(d) leases or tenancies or other assurances not required by law to be made in writing;

(e) receipts other than those falling within section 115 below;

(f) vesting orders of the court or other competent authority;

(g) conveyances taking effect by operation of law.

53. Instruments required to be in writing.

(1) Subject to the provisions hereinafter contained with respect to the creation of interests in land by parol—

(a) no interest in land can be created or disposed of except by writing signed by the person creating or conveying the same, or by his agent thereunto lawfully authorised in writing, or by will, or by operation of law;

(b) a declaration of trust respecting any land or any interest therein must be manifested and proved by some writing signed by some person who is able to declare such trust or by his will;

(c) a disposition of an equitable interest or trust subsisting at the time of the disposition, must be in writing signed by the person disposing of the same, or by his agent thereunto lawfully authorised in writing or by will.

(2) This section does not affect the creation or operation of resulting, implied or constructive trusts.

54. Creation of interests in land by parol.

(1) All interests in land created by parol and not put in writing and signed by the persons so creating the same, or by their agents thereunto lawfully authorised in writing, have, notwithstanding any consideration having been given for the same, the force and effect of interests at will only.

(2) Nothing in the foregoing provisions of this Part of this Act shall affect the creation by parol of leases taking effect in possession for a term not exceeding three years (whether or not the lessee is given power to extend the term) at the best rent which can be reasonably obtained without taking a fine.

55. Savings in regard to last two sections.

Nothing in the last two foregoing sections shall—

(a) invalidate dispositions by will; or

(b) affect any interest validly created before the commencement of this Act; or

(c) affect the right to acquire an interest in land by virtue of taking possession; or

(d) affect the operation of the law relating to part performance.

56. Persons taking who are not parties and as to indentures.

(1) A person may take an immediate or other interest in land or other property, or the benefit of any condition, right of entry, covenant or agreement over or respecting

land or other property, although he may not be named as a party to the conveyance or other instrument.

(2)   A deed between parties, to effect its objects, has the effect of an indenture though not indented or expressed to be an indenture.

61.   Construction of expressions used in deeds and other instruments.

In all deeds, contracts, wills, orders and other instruments executed, made or coming into operation after the commencement of this Act, unless the context otherwise requires—

(a)   "Month" means calendar month;

(b)   "Person" includes a corporation;

(c)   The singular includes the plural and vice versâ;

(d)   The masculine includes the feminine and vice versâ.

62.   General words implied in conveyances.

(1)   A conveyance of land shall be deemed to include and shall by virtue of this Act operate to convey, with the land, all buildings, erections, fixtures, commons, hedges, ditches, fences, ways, waters, watercourses, liberties, privileges, easements, rights, and advantages whatsoever, appertaining or reputed to appertain to the land, or any part thereof, or, at the time of conveyance, demised, occupied, or enjoyed with, or reputed or known as part or parcel of or appurtenant to the land or any part thereof.

(2)   A conveyance of land, having houses or other buildings thereon, shall be deemed to include and shall by virtue of this Act operate to convey, with the land, houses, or other buildings, all outhouses, erections, fixtures, cellars, areas, courts, courtyards, cisterns, sewers, gutters, drains, ways, passages, lights, watercourses, liberties, privileges, easements, rights, and advantages whatsoever, appertaining or reputed to appertain to the land, houses, or other buildings conveyed, or any of them, or any part thereof, or, at the time of conveyance, demised, occupied, or enjoyed with, or reputed or known as part or parcel of or appurtenant to, the land, houses, or other buildings conveyed, or any of them, or any part thereof.

(3)   A conveyance of a manor shall be deemed to include and shall by virtue of this Act operate to convey, with the manor, all pastures, feedings, wastes, warrens, commons, mines, minerals, quarries, furzes, trees, woods, underwoods, coppices, and the ground and soil thereof, fishings, fisheries, fowlings, courts leet, courts baron, and other courts, view of frankpledge and all that to view of frankpledge doth belong, mills, mulctures, customs, tolls, duties, reliefs, heriots, fines, sums of money, amerciaments, waifs, estrays, chief-rents, quitrents, rentscharge, rents seck, rents of assize, fee farm rents, services, royalties, jurisdictions, franchises, liberties, privileges, easements, profits, advantages, rights, emoluments, and hereditaments whatsoever, to the manor appertaining or reputed to appertain, or, at the time of conveyance, demised, occupied, or enjoyed with the same, or reputed or known as part, parcel, or member thereof.

For the purposes of this subsection the right to compensation for manorial incidents on the extinguishment thereof shall be deemed to be a right appertaining to the manor.

(4)   This section applies only if and as far as a contrary intention is not expressed in the conveyance, and has effect subject to the terms of the conveyance and to the provisions therein contained.

(5)   This section shall not be construed as giving to any person a better title to any property, right, or thing in this section mentioned than the title which the conveyance gives to him to the land or manor expressed to be conveyed, or as conveying to him any property, right, or thing in this section mentioned, further or otherwise than as the same could have been conveyed to him by the conveying parties.

(6)   This section applies to conveyances made after the thirty-first day of December, eighteen hundred and eighty-one.

63. All estate clause implied.

(1) Every conveyance is effectual to pass all the estate, right, title, interest, claim, and demand which the conveying parties respectively have, in, to, or on the property conveyed, or expressed or intended so to be, or which they respectively have power to convey in, to, or on the same.

(2) This section applies only if and as far as a contrary intention is not expressed in the conveyance, and has effect subject to the terms of the conveyance and to the provisions therein contained.

(3) This section applies to conveyances made after the thirty-first day of December, eighteen hundred and eighty-one.

Covenants

76. Covenants for title.

(1) In a conveyance there shall, in the several cases in this section mentioned, be deemed to be included and there shall in those several cases, by virtue of this Act, be implied, a covenant to the effect in this section stated, by the person or by each person who conveys, as far as regards the subject-matter or share of subject matter expressed to be conveyed by him, with the person, if one, to whom the conveyance is made, or with the persons jointly, if more than one, to whom the conveyance is made as joint tenants, or with each of the persons, if more than one, to whom the conveyance is (when the law permits) made as tenants in common, that is to say:

(A) In a conveyance for valuable consideration, other than a mortgage, a covenant by a person who conveys and is expressed to convey as beneficial owner in the terms set out in Part I. of the Second Schedule to this Act;

(B) In a conveyance of leasehold property for valuable consideration, other than a mortgage, a further covenant by a person who conveys and is expressed to convey as beneficial owner in the terms set out in Part II. of the Second Schedule to this Act;

(C) In a conveyance by way of mortgage (including a charge) a covenant by a person who conveys or charges and is expressed to convey or charge as beneficial owner in the terms set out in Part III. of the Second Schedule to this Act;

(D) In a conveyance by way of mortgage (including a charge) of freehold property subject to a rent or of leasehold property, a further covenant by a person who conveys or charges and is expressed to convey or charge as beneficial owner in the terms set out in Part IV. of the Second Schedule to this Act;

(E) In a conveyance by way of settlement, a covenant by a person who conveys and is expressed to convey as settlor in the terms set out in Part V. of the Second Schedule to this Act;

(F) In any conveyance, a covenant by every person who conveys and is expressed to convey as trustee or mortgagee, or as personal representative of a deceased person, or under an order of the court, in the terms set out in Part VI. of the Second Schedule to this Act, which covenant shall be deemed to extend to every such person's own acts only, and may be implied in an assent by a personal representative in like manner as in a conveyance by deed.

(2) Where in a conveyance it is expressed that by direction of a person expressed to direct as beneficial owner another person conveys, then, for the purposes of this section, the person giving the direction, whether he conveys and is expressed to convey as beneficial owner or not, shall be deemed to convey and to be expressed to convey as beneficial owner the subject-matter so conveyed by his direction; and a covenant on his part shall be implied accordingly.

(3) Where a wife conveys and is expressed to convey as beneficial owner, and the husband also conveys and is expressed to convey as beneficial owner, then, for the purposes of this section, the wife shall be deemed to convey and to be expressed to convey by direction of the husband, as beneficial owner; and, in addition to the covenant

implied on the part of the wife, there shall also be implied, first, a covenant on the part of the husband as the person giving that direction, and secondly, a covenant on the part of the husband in the same terms as the covenant implied on the part of the wife.

(4) Where in a conveyance a person conveying is not expressed to convey as beneficial owner, or as settlor, or as trustee, or as mortgagee, or as personal representative of a deceased person, or under an order of the court, or by direction of a person as beneficial owner, no covenant on the part of the person conveying shall be, by virtue of this section, implied in the conveyance.

(5) In this section a conveyance does not include a demise by way of lease at a rent, but does include a charge and "convey" has a corresponding meaning.

(6) The benefit of a covenant implied as aforesaid shall be annexed and incident to, and shall go with, the estate or interest of the implied covenantee, and shall be capable of being enforced by every person in whom that estate or interest is, for the whole or any part thereof, from time to time vested.

(7) A covenant implied as aforesaid may be varied or extended by a deed or an assent, and, as so varied or extended, shall, as far as may be, operate in the like manner, and with all the like incidents, effects, and consequences, as if such variations or extensions were directed in this section to be implied.

(8) This section applies to conveyances made after the thirty-first day of December, eighteen hundred and eighty-one, but only to assents by a personal representative made after the commencement of this Act

77. Implied covenants in conveyances subject to rents.

(1) In addition to the covenants implied under the last preceding section, there shall in the several cases in this section mentioned, be deemed to be included and implied, a covenant to the effect in this section stated, by and with such persons as are hereinafter mentioned, that is to say:—

(A) In a conveyance for valuable consideration, other than a mortgage, of the entirety of the land affected by a rentcharge, a covenant by the grantee or joint and several covenants by the grantees, if more than one, with the conveying parties and with each of them, if more than one, in the terms set out in Part VII. of the Second Schedule to this Act. Where a rentcharge has been apportioned in respect of any land, with the consent of the owner of the rentcharge, the covenants in this paragraph shall be implied in the conveyance of that land in like manner as if the apportioned rentcharge were the rentcharge referred to, and the document creating the rentcharge related solely to that land:

(B) In a conveyance for valuable consideration, other than a mortgage, of part of land affected by a rentcharge, subject to a part of that rentcharge which has been or is by that conveyance apportioned (but in either case without the consent of the owner of the rentcharge) in respect of the land conveyed:—

(i) A covenant by the grantee of the land or joint and several covenants by the grantees, if more than one, with the conveying parties and with each of them, if more than one, in the terms set out in paragraph (i) of Part VIII. of the Second Schedule to this Act;

(ii) A covenant by a person who conveys or is expressed to convey as beneficial owner, or joint and several covenants by the persons who so convey or are expressed to so convey, if at the date of the conveyance any part of the land affected by such rentcharge is retained, with the grantees of the land and with each of them (if more than one) in the terms set out in paragraph (ii) of Part VIII. of the Second Schedule to this Act:

(C) In a conveyance for valuable consideration, other than a mortgage, of the entirety of the land comprised in a lease, for the residue of the term or interest created by the lease, a covenant by the assignee or joint and several covenants by the assignees (if more than one) with the conveying parties and with each of them (if more than one) in the terms set out in Part IX. of the Second Schedule to this Act. Where a rent has been apportioned in respect of any land, with the consent of the lessor, the covenants in this paragraph shall be implied in the conveyance of that land in like manner as if the apportioned rent were the original rent reserved, and the lease related solely to that land:

(D)   In a conveyance for valuable consideration, other than a mortgage, of part of the land comprised in a lease, for the residue of the term or interest created by the lease, subject to a part of the rent which has been or is by the conveyance apportioned (but in either case without the consent of the lessor) in respect of the land conveyed:—

(i)   A covenant by the assignee of the land, or joint and several covenants by the assignees, if more than one, with the conveying parties and with each of them, if more than one, in the terms set out in paragraph (i) of Part X. of the Second Schedule to this Act;

(ii)   A covenant by a person who conveys or is expressed to convey as beneficial owner, or joint and several covenants by the persons who so convey or are expressed to so convey, if at the date of the conveyance any part of the land comprised in the lease is retained, with the assignees of the land and with each of them (if more than one) in the terms set out in paragraph (ii) of Part X. of the Second Schedule to this Act.

(2)   Where in a conveyance for valuable consideration, other than a mortgage, part of land affected by a rentcharge, or part of land comprised in a lease is, without the consent of the owner of the rentcharge or of the lessor, as the case may be, expressed to be conveyed—

(i)   subject to or charged with the entire rent—

then paragraph (B) (i) or (D) (i) of the last subsection, as the case may require, shall have effect as if the entire rent were the apportioned rent; or

(ii)   discharged or exonerated from the entire rent—

then paragraph (B) (ii) or (D) (ii) of the last subsection, as the case may require, shall have effect as if the entire rent were the balance of the rent, and the words "other than the covenant to pay the entire rent" had been omitted.

(3)   In this section "conveyance" does not include a demise by way of lease at a rent.

(4)   Any covenant which would be implied under this section by reason of a person conveying or being expressed to convey as beneficial owner may, by express reference to this section, be implied, with or without variation, in a conveyance, whether or not for valuable consideration, by a person who conveys or is expressed to convey as settlor, or as trustee, or as mortgagee, or as personal representative of a deceased person, or under an order of the court.

(5)   The benefit of a covenant implied as aforesaid shall be annexed and incident to, and shall go with, the estate or interest of the implied covenantee, and shall be capable of being enforced by every person in whom that estate or interest is, for the whole or any part thereof, from time to time vested.

(6)   A covenant implied as aforesaid may be varied or extended by deed, and, as so varied or extended, shall, as far as may be, operate in the like manner, and with all the like incidents, effects and consequences, as if such variations or extensions were directed in this section to be implied.

(7)   In particular any covenant implied under this section may be extended by providing that—

(a)   the land conveyed; or

(b)   the part of the land affected by the rentcharge which remains vested in the covenantor; or

(c)   the part of the land demised which remains vested in the covenantor;

shall, as the case may require, stand charged with the payment of all money which may become payable under the implied covenant.

(8)   This section applies only to conveyances made after the commencement of this Act.

78. Benefit of covenants relating to land.

(1) A covenant relating to any land of the covenantee shall be deemed to be made with the covenantee and his successors in title and the persons deriving title under him or them, and shall have effect as if such successors and other persons were expressed.

For the purposes of this subsection in connexion with covenants restrictive of the user of land "successors in title" shall be deemed to include the owners and occupiers for the time being of the land of the covenantee intended to be benefited.

(2) This section applies to covenants made after the commencement of this Act, but the repeal of section fifty-eight of the Conveyancing Act 1881 does not affect the operation of covenants to which that section applied.

79. Burden of covenants relating to land.

(1) A covenant relating to any land of a covenantor or capable of being bound by him, shall, unless a contrary intention is expressed, be deemed to be made by the covenantor on behalf of himself his successors in title and the persons deriving title under him or them, and, subject as aforesaid, shall have effect as if such successors and other persons were expressed.

This subsection extends to a covenant to do some act relating to the land, notwithstanding that the subject-matter may not be in existence when the covenant is made.

(2) For the purposes of this section in connexion with covenants restrictive of the user of land "successors in title" shall be deemed to include the owners and occupiers for the time being of such land.

(3) This section applies only to covenants made after the commencement of this Act.

84. Power to discharge or modify restrictive covenants affecting land.

(1) The Lands Tribunal shall (without prejudice to any concurrent jurisdiction of the court) have power from time to time, on the application of any person interested in any freehold land affected by any restriction arising under covenant or otherwise as to the user thereof or the building thereon, by order wholly or partially to discharge or modify any such restriction on being satisfied—

(a) that by reason of changes in the character of the property or the neighbourhood or other circumstances of the case which the Lands Tribunal may deem material, the restriction ought to be deemed obsolete; or

(aa) that (in a case falling within subsection (1A) below) the continued existence thereof would impede some reasonable user of the land for public or private purposes or, as the case may be, would unless modified so impede such user; or

(b) that the persons of full age and capacity for the time being or from time to time entitled to the benefit of the restriction, whether in respect of estates in fee simple or any lesser estates or interests in the property to which the benefit of the restriction is annexed, have agreed, either expressly or by implication, by their acts or omissions, to the same being discharged or modified; or

(c) that the proposed discharge or modification will not injure the persons entitled to the benefit of the restriction;

and an order discharging or modifying a restriction under this subsection may direct the applicant to pay to any person entitled to the benefit of the restriction such sum by way of consideration as the Tribunal may think it just to award under one, but not both, of the following heads, that is to say, either—

(i) a sum to make up for any loss or disadvantage suffered by that person in consequence of the discharge or modification; or

(ii) a sum to make up for any effect which the restriction had, at the time when it was imposed, in reducing the consideration then received for the land affected by it.

(1A) Subsection (1)(aa) above authorises the discharge or modification of a restriction by reference to its impeding some reasonable user of land in any case in which the Lands Tribunal is satisfied that the restriction, in impeding that user, either—

(a) does not secure to persons entitled to the benefit of it any practical benefits of substantial value or advantage to them; or

(b) is contrary to the public interest;

and that money will be an adequate compensation for the loss or disadvantage (if any) which any such person will suffer from the discharge or modification.

(1B) In determining whether a case is one falling within subsection (1A) above, and in determining whether (in any such case or otherwise) a restriction ought to be discharged or modified, the Lands Tribunal shall take into account the development plan and any declared or ascertainable pattern for the grant or refusal of planning permissions in the relevant areas, as well as the period at which and context in which the restriction was created or imposed and any other material circumstances.

(1C) It is hereby declared that the power conferred by this section to modify a restriction includes power to add such further provisions restricting the user of or the building on the land affected as appear to the Lands Tribunal to be reasonable in view of the relaxation of the existing provisions, and as may be accepted by the applicant; and the Lands Tribunal may accordingly refuse to modify a restriction without some such addition.

(2) The court shall have power on the application of any person interested—

(a) to declare whether or not in any particular case any freehold land is, or would in any given event be, affected by a restriction imposed by any instrument; or

(b) to declare what, upon the true construction of any instrument purporting to impose a restriction, is the nature and extent of the restriction thereby imposed and whether the same is, or would in any given event be, enforceable and if so by whom.

Neither subsections (7) and (11) of this section nor, unless the contrary is expressed, any later enactment providing for this section not to apply to any restrictions shall affect the operation of this subsection or the operation for purposes of this subsection of any other provisions of this section.

(3) The Lands Tribunal shall, before making any order under this section, direct such enquiries, if any, to be made of any government department or local authority, and such notices, if any, whether by way of advertisement or otherwise, to be given to such of the persons who appear to be entitled to the benefit of the restriction intended to be discharged, modified, or dealt with as, having regard to any enquiries, notices or other proceedings previously made, given or taken, the Lands Tribunal may think fit.

(3A) On an application to the Lands Tribunal under this section the Lands Tribunal shall give any necessary directions as to the persons who are or are not to be admitted (as appearing to be entitled to the benefit of the restriction) to oppose the application, and no appeal shall lie against any such direction; but rules under the Lands Tribunal Act 1949 shall make provision whereby, in cases in which there arises on such an application (whether or not in connection with the admission of persons to oppose) any such question as is referred to in subsection (2)(a) or (b) of this section, the proceedings on the application can and, if the rules so provide, shall be suspended to enable the decision of the court to be obtained on that question by an application under that subsection, or by means of a case stated by the Lands Tribunal, or otherwise, as may be provided by those rules or by rules of court.

(5) Any order made under this section shall be binding on all persons, whether ascertained or of full age or capacity or not, then entitled or thereafter capable of becoming entitled to the benefit of any restriction, which is thereby discharged, modified or dealt with, and whether such persons are parties to the proceedings or have been served with notice or not.

(6) An order may be made under this section notwithstanding that any instrument which is alleged to impose the restriction intended to be discharged, modified, or dealt

with, may not have been produced to the court or the Lands Tribunal, and the court or the Lands Tribunal may act on such evidence of that instrument as it may think sufficient.

(7) This section applies to restrictions whether subsisting at the commencement of this Act or imposed thereafter, but this section does not apply where the restriction was imposed on the occasion of a disposition made gratuitously or for a nominal consideration for public purposes.

(8) This section applies whether the land affected by the restrictions is registered or not, but, in the case of registered land, the Land Registrar shall give effect on the register to any order under this section in accordance with the Land Registration Act 1925.

(9) Where any proceedings by action or otherwise are taken to enforce a restrictive covenant, any person against whom the proceedings are taken, may in such proceedings apply to the court for an order giving leave to apply to the Lands Tribunal under this section, and staying the proceedings in the meantime.

(11) This section does not apply to restrictions imposed by the Commissioners of Works under any statutory power for the protection of any Royal Park or Garden or to restrictions of a like character imposed upon the occasion of any enfranchisement effected before the commencement of this Act in any manor vested in His Majesty in right of the Crown or the Duchy of Lancaster, nor (subject to subsection (11A) below) to restrictions created or imposed—

    (a) for naval, military or air force purposes,

    (b) for civil aviation purposes under the powers of the Air Navigation Act 1920, of section 19 or 23 of the Civil Aviation Act 1949 or of section 30 or 41 of the Civil Aviation Act 1982.

(11A) Subsection (11) of this section—

    (a) shall exclude the application of this section to a restriction falling within subsection (11)(a), and not created or imposed in connection with the use of any land as an aerodrome, only so long as the restriction is enforceable by or on behalf of the Crown; and

    (b) shall exclude the application of this section to a restriction falling within subsection (11)(b), or created or imposed in connection with the use of any land as an aerodrome, only so long as the restriction is enforceable by or on behalf of the Crown or any public or international authority.

(12) Where a term of more than forty years is created in land (whether before or after the commencement of this Act) this section shall, after the expiration of twenty-five years of the term, apply to restrictions affecting such leasehold land in like manner as it would have applied had the land been freehold:

Provided that this subsection shall not apply to mining leases.

PART V

LEASES AND TENANCIES

139. Effect of extinguishment of reversion.

(1) Where a reversion expectant on a lease of land is surrendered or merged, the estate or interest which as against the lessee for the time being confers the next vested right to the land, shall be deemed the reversion for the purpose of preserving the same incidents and obligations as would have affected the original reversion had there been no surrender or merger thereof.

(2) This section applies to surrenders or mergers effected after the first day of October, eighteen hundred and forty-five.

140. Apportionment of conditions on severance.

(1) Notwithstanding the severance by conveyance, surrender, or otherwise of the reversionary estate in any land comprised in a lease, and notwithstanding the avoidance

or cesser in any other manner of the term granted by a lease as to part only of the land comprised therein, every condition or right of re-entry, and every other condition contained in the lease, shall be apportioned, and shall remain annexed to the severed parts of the reversionary estate as severed, and shall be in force with respect to the term whereon each severed part is reversionary, or the term in the part of the land as to which the term has not been surrendered, or has not been avoided or has not otherwise ceased, in like manner as if the land comprised in each severed part, or the land as to which the term remains subsisting, as the case may be, had alone originally been comprised in the lease.

(2) In this section "right of re-entry" includes a right to determine the lease by notice to quit or otherwise; but where the notice is served by a person entitled to a severed part of the reversion so that it extends to part only of the land demised, the lessee may within one month determine the lease in regard to the rest of the land by giving to the owner of the reversionary estate therein a counter notice expiring at the same time as the original notice.

(3) This section applies to leases made before or after the commencement of this Act and whether the severance of the reversionary estate or the partial avoidance or cesser of the term was effected before or after such commencement:

Provided that, where the lease was made before the first day of January eighteen hundred and eighty-two nothing in this section shall affect the operation of a severance of the reversionary estate or partial avoidance or cesser of the term which was effected before the commencement of this Act.

141. Rent and benefit of lessee's covenants to run with the reversion.

(1) Rent reserved by a lease, and the benefit of every covenant or provision therein contained, having reference to the subject-matter thereof, and on the lessee's part to be observed or performed, and every condition of re-entry and other condition therein contained, shall be annexed and incident to and shall go with the reversionary estate in the land, or in any part thereof, immediately expectant on the term granted by the lease, notwithstanding severance of that reversionary estate, and without prejudice to any liability affecting a covenantor or his estate.

(2) Any such rent, covenant or provision shall be capable of being recovered, received, enforced, and taken advantage of, by the person from time to time entitled, subject to the term, to the income of the whole or any part, as the case may require, of the land leased.

(3) Where that person becomes entitled by conveyance or otherwise, such rent, covenant or provision may be recovered, received, enforced or taken advantage of by him notwithstanding that he becomes so entitled after the condition of re-entry or forfeiture has become enforceable, but this subsection does not render enforceable any condition of re-entry or other condition waived or released before such person becomes entitled as aforesaid.

(4) This section applies to leases made before or after the commencement of this Act, but does not affect the operation of—

(a) any severance of the reversionary estate; or

(b) any acquisition by conveyance or otherwise of the right to receive or enforce any rent covenant or provision;

effected before the commencement of this Act.

142. Obligation of lessor's covenants to run with reversion.

(1) The obligation under a condition or of a covenant entered into by a lessor with reference to the subject-matter of the lease shall, if and as far as the lessor has power to bind the reversionary estate immediately expectant on the term granted by the lease, be annexed and incident to and shall go with that reversionary estate, or the several parts thereof, notwithstanding severance of that reversionary estate, and may be taken

advantage of and enforced by the person in whom the term is from time to time vested by conveyance, devolution in law, or otherwise; and, if and as far as the lessor has power to bind the person from time to time entitled to that reversionary estate, the obligation aforesaid may be taken advantage of and enforced against any person so entitled.

(2)   This section applies to leases made before or after the commencement of this Act, whether the severance of the reversionary estate was effected before or after such commencement:

Provided that, where the lease was made before the first day of January eighteen hundred and eighty-two, nothing in this section shall affect the operation of any severance of the reversionary estate effected before such commencement.

This section takes effect without prejudice to any liability affecting a covenantor or his estate.

143.   Effect of licences granted to lessees.

(1)   Where a licence is granted to a lessee to do any act, the licence, unless otherwise expressed, extends only—

    (a)   to the permission actually given; or

    (b)   to the specific breach of any provision or covenant referred to; or

    (c)   to any other matter thereby specifically authorised to be done;

and the licence does not prevent any proceeding for any subsequent breach unless otherwise specified in the licence.

(2)   Notwithstanding any such licence—

    (a)   All rights under covenants and powers of re-entry contained in the lease remain in full force and are available as against any subsequent breach of covenant, condition or other matter not specifically authorised or waived, in the same manner as if no licence had been granted; and

    (b)   The condition or right of entry remains in force in all respects as if the licence had not been granted, save in respect of the particular matter authorised to be done.

(3)   Where in any lease there is a power or condition of re-entry on the lessee assigning, subletting or doing any other specified act without a licence, and a licence is granted—

    (a)   to any one of two or more lessees to do any act, or to deal with his equitable share or interest; or

    (b)   to any lessee, or to any one of two or more lessees to assign or underlet part only of the property, or to do any act in respect of part only of the property;

the licence does not operate to extinguish the right of entry in case of any breach of covenant or condition by the co-lessees of the other shares or interests in the property, or by the lessee or lessees of the rest of the property (as the case may be) in respect of such shares or interests or remaining property, but the right of entry remains in force in respect of the shares, interests or property not the subject of the licence.

This subsection does not authorise the grant after the commencement of this Act of a licence to create an undivided share in a legal estate.

(4)   This section applies to licences granted after the thirteenth day of August, eighteen hundred and fifty-nine.

144.   No fine to be exacted for licence to assign.

In all leases containing a covenant, condition, or agreement against assigning, underletting, or parting with the possession, or disposing of the land or property leased without licence or consent, such covenant, condition, or agreement shall, unless the lease contains an express provision to the contrary, be deemed to be subject to a proviso to the effect that no fine or sum of money in the nature of a fine shall be payable for or in respect of such licence or consent; but this proviso does not preclude the right to require the payment of a reasonable sum in respect of any legal or other expense incurred in relation to such licence or consent.

145. Lessee to give notice of ejectment to lessor.

Every lessee to whom there is delivered any writ for the recovery of premises demised to or held by him, or to whose knowledge any such writ comes, shall forthwith give notice thereof to his lessor or his bailiff or receiver, and, if he fails so to do, he shall be liable to forfeit to the person of whom he holds the premises an amount equal to the value of three years' improved or rack rent of the premises, to be recovered by action in any court having jurisdiction in respect of claims for such an amount.

146. Restrictions on and relief against forfeiture of leases and underleases.

(1) A right of re-entry or forfeiture under any proviso or stipulation in a lease for a breach of any covenant or condition in the lease shall not be enforceable, by action or otherwise, unless and until the lessor serves on the lessee a notice—

(a) specifying the particular breach complained of; and

(b) if the breach is capable of remedy, requiring the lessee to remedy the breach; and

(c) in any case, requiring the lessee to make compensation in money for the breach;

and the lessee fails, within a reasonable time thereafter, to remedy the breach, if it is capable of remedy, and to make reasonable compensation in money, to the satisfaction of the lessor, for the breach.

(2) Where a lessor is proceeding, by action or otherwise, to enforce such a right of re-entry or forfeiture, the lessee may, in the lessor's action, if any, or in any action brought by himself, apply to the court for relief; and the court may grant or refuse relief, as the court, having regard to the proceedings and conduct of the parties under the foregoing provisions of this section, and to all the other circumstances, thinks fit; and in case of relief may grant it on such terms, if any, as to costs, expenses, damages, compensation, penalty, or otherwise, including the granting of an injunction to restrain any like breach in the future, as the court, in the circumstances of each case, thinks fit.

(3) A lessor shall be entitled to recover as a debt due to him from a lessee, and in addition to damages (if any), all reasonable costs and expenses properly incurred by the lessor in the employment of a solicitor and surveyor or valuer, or otherwise, in reference to any breach giving rise to a right of re-entry or forfeiture which, at the request of the lessee, is waived by the lessor, or from which the lessee is relieved, under the provisions of this Act.

(4) Where a lessor is proceeding by action or otherwise to enforce a right of re-entry or forfeiture under any covenant, proviso, or stipulation in a lease, or for non-payment of rent, the court may, on application by any person claiming as under-lessee any estate or interest in the property comprised in the lease or any part thereof, either in the lessor's action (if any) or in any action brought by such person for that purpose, make an order vesting, for the whole term of the lease or any less term, the property comprised in the lease or any part thereof in any person entitled as under-lessee to any estate or interest in such property upon such conditions as to execution of any deed or other document, payment of rent, costs, expenses, damages, compensation, giving security, or otherwise, as the court in the circumstances of each case may think fit, but in no case shall any such under-lessee be entitled to require a lease to be granted to him for any longer term than he had under his original sub-lease.

(5) For the purposes of this section—

(a) "Lease" includes an original or derivative under-lease; also an agreement for a lease where the lessee has become entitled to have his lease granted; also a grant at a fee farm rent, or securing a rent by condition;

(b) "Lessee" includes an original or derivative under-lessee, and the persons deriving title under a lessee; also a grantee under any such grant as aforesaid and the persons deriving title under him;

(c) "Lessor" includes an original or derivative under-lessor, and the persons deriving title under a lessor; also a person making such grant as aforesaid and the persons deriving title under him;

(d) "Under-lease" includes an agreement for an underlease where the under-lessee has become entitled to have his underlease granted;

(e) "Under-lessee" includes any person deriving title under an under-lessee.

(6) This section applies although the proviso or stipulation under which the right of re-entry or forfeiture accrues is inserted in the lease in pursuance of the directions of any Act of Parliament.

(7) For the purposes of this section a lease limited to continue as long only as the lessee abstains from committing a breach of covenant shall be and take effect as a lease to continue for any longer term for which it could subsist, but determinable by a proviso for re-entry on such a breach.

(8) This section does not extend—

(i) To a covenant or condition against assigning, underletting, parting with the possession, or disposing of the land leased where the breach occurred before the commencement of this Act; or

(ii) In the case of a mining lease, to a covenant or condition for allowing the lessor to have access to or inspect books, accounts, records, weighing machines or other things, or to enter or inspect the mine or the workings thereof.

(9) This section does not apply to a condition for forfeiture on the bankruptcy of the lessee or on taking in execution of the lessee's interest if contained in a lease of—

(a) Agricultural or pastoral land;

(b) Mines or minerals;

(c) A house used or intended to be used as a public-house or beershop;

(d) A house let as a dwelling-house, with the use of any furniture, books, works of art, or other chattels not being in the nature of fixtures;

(e) Any property with respect to which the personal qualifications of the tenant are of importance for the preservation of the value or character of the property, or on the ground of neighbourhood to the lessor, or to any person holding under him.

(10) Where a condition of forfeiture on the bankruptcy of the lessee or on taking in execution of the lessee's interest is contained in any lease, other than a lease of any of the classes mentioned in the last sub-section, then—

(a) if the lessee's interest is sold within one year from the bankruptcy or taking in execution, this section applies to the forfeiture condition aforesaid;

(b) if the lessee's interest is not sold before the expiration of that year, this section only applies to the forfeiture condition aforesaid during the first year from the date of the bankruptcy or taking in execution.

(11) This section does not, save as otherwise mentioned, affect the law relating to re-entry or forfeiture or relief in case of non-payment of rent.

(12) This section has effect notwithstanding any stipulation to the contrary.

(13) The county court has jurisdiction under this section—

(a) in any case where the lessor is proceeding by action in court to enforce the right of entry or forfeiture; and

(b) where the lessor is proceeding to enforce the said right otherwise than by action, in a case where the net annual value for rating of the property comprised in the lease does not exceed the county court limit.

147. Relief against notice to effect decorative repairs.

(1) After a notice is served on a lessee relating to the internal decorative repairs to a house or other building, he may apply to the court for relief, and if, having regard to all the circumstances of the case (including in particular the length of the lessee's term or interest remaining unexpired), the court is satisfied that the notice is unreasonable,

it may, by order, wholly or partially relieve the lessee from liability for such repairs.

(2)   This section does not apply:—

(i)   where the liability arises under an express covenant or agreement to put the property in a decorative state of repair and the covenant or agreement has never been performed;

(ii)   to any matter necessary or proper—

(a)   for putting or keeping the property in a sanitary condition, or

(b)   for the maintenance or preservation of the structure;

(iii)   to any statutory liability to keep a house in all respects reasonably fit for human habitation;

(iv)   to any covenant or stipulation to yield up the house or other building in a specified state of repair at the end of the term.

(3)   In this section "lease" includes an underlease and an agreement for a lease, and "lessee" has a corresponding meaning and includes any person liable to effect the repairs.

(4)   This section applies whether the notice is served before or after the commencement of this Act, and has effect notwithstanding any stipulation to the contrary.

(5)   The county court has jurisdiction under this section where the net annual value for rating of the house or other building does not exceed the county court limit.

148.   Waiver of a covenant in a lease.

(1)   Where any actual waiver by a lessor or the persons deriving title under him of the benefit of any covenant or condition in any lease is proved to have taken place in any particular instance, such waiver shall not be deemed to extend to any instance, or to any breach of covenant or condition save that to which such waiver specially relates, nor operate as a general waiver of the benefit of any such covenant or condition.

(2)   This section applies unless a contrary intention appears and extends to waivers effected after the twenty-third day of July, eighteen hundred and sixty.

149.   Abolition of interesse termini, and as to reversionary leases and leases for lives.

(1)   The doctrine of interesse termini is hereby abolished.

(2)   As from the commencement of this Act all terms of years absolute shall, whether the interest is created before or after such commencement, be capable of taking effect at law or in equity, according to the estate interest or powers of the grantor, from the date fixed for commencement of the term, without actual entry.

(3)   A term, at a rent or granted in consideration of a fine, limited after the commencement of this Act to take effect more than twenty-one years from the date of the instrument purporting to create it, shall be void, and any contract made after such commencement to create such a term shall likewise be void; but this subsection does not apply to any term taking effect in equity under a settlement, or created out of an equitable interest under a settlement, or under an equitable power for mortgage, indemnity or other like purposes.

(4)   Nothing in subsections (1) and (2) of this section prejudicially affects the right of any person to recover any rent or to enforce or take advantage of any covenants or conditions, or, as respects terms or interests created before the commencement of this Act, operates to vary any statutory or other obligations imposed in respect of such terms or interests.

(5)   Nothing in this Act affects the rule of law that a legal term, whether or not being a mortgage term, may be created to take effect in reversion expectant on a longer term, which rule is hereby confirmed.

(6)   Any lease or underlease, at a rent, or in consideration of a fine, for life or lives or for any term of years determinable with life or lives, or on the marriage of the lessee, or any contract therefor, made before or after the commencement of this Act, or created

by virtue of Part V. of the Law of Property Act 1922, shall take effect as a lease, underlease or contract therefor, for a term of ninety years determinable after the death or marriage (as the case may be) of the original lessee, or of the survivor of the original lessees, by at least one month's notice in writing given to determine the same on one of the quarter days applicable to the tenancy, either by the lessor or the persons deriving title under him, to the person entitled to the leasehold interest, or if no such person is in existence by affixing the same to the premises, or by the lessee or other persons in whom the leasehold interest is vested to the lessor or the persons deriving title under him:

Provided that—

(a)   this subsection shall not apply to any term taking effect in equity under a settlement or created out of an equitable interest under a settlement for mortgage, indemnity, or other like purposes;

(b)   the person in whom the leasehold interest is vested by virtue of Part V. of the Law of Property Act, 1922, shall, for the purposes of this subsection, be deemed an original lessee;

(c)   if the lease, underlease, or contract therefor is made determinable on the dropping of the lives of persons other than or besides the lessees, then the notice shall be capable of being served after the death of any person or of the survivor of any persons (whether or not including the lessees) on the cesser of whose life or lives the lease, underlease, or contract is made determinable, instead of after the death of the original lessee or of the survivor of the original lessees;

(d)   if there are no quarter days specially applicable to the tenancy, notice may be given to determine the tenancy on one of the usual quarter days.

150.   Surrender of a lease, without prejudice to underleases with a view to the grant of a new lease.

(1)   A lease may be surrendered with a view to the acceptance of a new lease in place thereof, without a surrender of any under-lease derived thereout.

(2)   A new lease may be granted and accepted, in place of any lease so surrendered, without any such surrender of an under-lease as aforesaid, and the new lease operates as if all under-leases derived out of the surrendered lease had been surrendered before the surrender of that lease was effected.

(3)   The lessee under the new lease and any person deriving title under him is entitled to the same rights and remedies in respect of the rent reserved by and the covenants, agreements and conditions contained in any under-lease as if the original lease had not been surrendered but was or remained vested in him.

(4)   Each under-lessee and any person deriving title under him is entitled to hold and enjoy the land comprised in his under-lease (subject to the payment of any rent reserved by and to the observance of the covenants agreements and conditions contained in the under-lease) as if the lease out of which the under-lease was derived had not been surrendered.

(5)   The lessor granting the new lease and any person deriving title under him is entitled to the same remedies, by distress or entry in and upon the land comprised in any such under-lease for rent reserved by or for breach of any covenant, agreement or condition contained in the new lease (so far only as the rents reserved by or the covenants, agreements or conditions contained in the new lease do not exceed or impose greater burdens than those reserved by or contained in the original lease out of which the under-lease is derived) as he would have had—

(a)   If the original lease had remained on foot; or

(b)   If a new under-lease derived out of the new lease had been granted to the under-lessee or a person deriving title under him;

as the case may require.

(6) This section does not affect the powers of the court to give relief against forfeiture.

151. Provision as to attornments by tenants.

(1) Where land is subject to a lease—

(a) the conveyance of a reversion in the land expectant on the determination of the lease; or

(b) the creation or conveyance of a rentcharge to issue or issuing out of the land; shall be valid without any attornment of the lessee:

Nothing in this subsection—

(i) affects the validity of any payment of rent by the lessee to the person making the conveyance or grant before notice of the conveyance or grant is given to him by the person entitled thereunder; or

(ii) renders the lessee liable for any breach of covenant to pay rent, on account of his failure to pay rent to the person entitled under the conveyance or grant before such notice is given to the lessee.

(2) An attornment by the lessee in respect of any land to a person claiming to be entitled to the interest in the land of the lessor, if made without the consent of the lessor, shall be void.

This subsection does not apply to an attornment—

(a) made pursuant to a judgment of a court of competent jurisdiction: or

(b) to a mortgagee, by a lessee holding under a lease from the mortgagor where the right of redemption is barred; or

(c) to any other person rightfully deriving title under the lessor.

152. Leases invalidated by reason of non-compliance with terms of powers under which they are granted.

(1) Where in the intended exercise of any power of leasing, whether conferred by an Act of Parliament or any other instrument, a lease (in this section referred to as an invalid lease) is granted, which by reason of any failure to comply with the terms of the power is invalid, then—

(a) as against the person entitled after the determination of the interest of the grantor to the reversion; or

(b) as against any other person who, subject to any lease properly granted under the power, would have been entitled to the land comprised in the lease;

the lease, if it was made in good faith, and the lessee has entered thereunder, shall take effect in equity as a contract for the grant, at the request of the lessee, of a valid lease under the power, of like effect as the invalid lease, subject to such variations as may be necessary in order to comply with the terms of the power:

Provided that a lessee under an invalid lease shall not, by virtue of any such implied contract, be entitled to obtain a variation of the lease if the other persons who would have been bound by the contract are willing and able to confirm the lease without variation.

(2) Where a lease granted in the intended exercise of such a power is invalid by reason of the grantor not having power to grant the lease at the date thereof, but the grantor's interest in the land comprised therein continues after the time when he might, in the exercise of the power, have properly granted a lease in the like terms, the lease shall take effect as a valid lease in like manner as if it had been granted at that time.

(3) Where during the continuance of the possession taken under an invalid lease the person for the time being entitled, subject to such possession, to the land comprised therein or to the rents and profits thereof, is able to confirm the lease without variation, the lessee, or other person who would have been bound by the lease had it been valid, shall, at the request of the person so able to confirm the lease, be bound to accept a

confirmation thereof, and thereupon the lease shall have effect and be deemed to have had effect as a valid lease from the grant thereof.

Confirmation under this subsection may be by a memorandum in writing signed by or on behalf of the persons respectively confirming and accepting the confirmation of the lease.

(4)   Where a receipt or a memorandum in writing confirming an invalid lease is, upon or before the acceptance of rent thereunder, signed by or on behalf of the person accepting the rent, that acceptance shall, as against that person, be deemed to be a confirmation of the lease.

(5)   The foregoing provisions of this section do not affect prejudicially—

(a)   any right of action or other right or remedy to which, but for those provisions or any enactment replaced by those provisions, the lessee named in an invalid lease would or might have been entitled under any covenant on the part of the grantor for title or quiet enjoyment contained therein or implied thereby; or

(b)   any right of re-entry or other right or remedy to which, but for those provisions or any enactment replaced thereby, the grantor or other person for the time being entitled to the reversion expectant on the termination of the lease, would or might have been entitled by reason of any breach of the covenants, conditions or provisions contained in the lease and binding on the lessee.

(6)   Where a valid power of leasing is vested in or may be exercised by a person who grants a lease which, by reason of the determination of the interest of the grantor or otherwise, cannot have effect and continuance according to the terms thereof independently of the power, the lease shall for the purposes of this section be deemed to have been granted in the intended exercise of the power although the power is not referred to in the lease.

(7)   This section does not apply to a lease of land held on charitable, ecclesiastical or public trusts.

(8)   This section takes effect without prejudice to the provision in this Act for the grant of leases in the name and on behalf of the estate owner of the land affected.

153.   Enlargement of residue of long terms into fee simple estates.

(1)   Where a residue unexpired of not less than two hundred years of a term, which, as originally created, was for not less than three hundred years, is subsisting in land, whether being the whole land originally comprised in the term, or part only thereof,—

(a)   without any trust or right of redemption affecting the term in favour of the freeholder, or other person entitled in reversion expectant on the term; and

(b)   without any rent, or with merely a peppercorn rent or other rent having no money value, incident to the reversion, or having had a rent, not being merely a peppercorn rent or other rent having no money value, originally so incident, which subsequently has been released or has become barred by lapse of time, or has in any other way ceased to be payable;

the term may be enlarged into a fee simple in the manner, and subject to the restrictions in this section provided.

(2)   This section applies to and includes every such term as aforesaid whenever created, whether or not having the freehold as the immediate reversion thereon; but does not apply to—

(i)   Any term liable to be determined by re-entry for condition broken; or

(ii)   Any term created by subdemise out of a superior term, itself incapable of being enlarged into fee simple.

(3)   This section extends to mortgage terms, where the right of redemption is barred.

(4)   A rent not exceeding the yearly sum of one pound which has not been collected or paid for a continuous period of twenty years or upwards shall, for the purposes of this section, be deemed to have ceased to be payable:

Provided that, of the said period, at least five years must have elapsed after the commencement of this Act.

(5) Where a rent incident to a reversion expectant on a term to which this section applies is deemed to have ceased to be payable for the purposes aforesaid, no claim for such rent or for any arrears thereof shall be capable of being enforced.

(6) Each of the following persons, namely—

(i) Any person beneficially entitled in right of the term, whether subject to any incumbrance or not, to possession of any land comprised in the term, and, in the case of a married woman without the concurrence of her husband, whether or not she is entitled for her separate use or as her separate property;

(ii) Any person being in receipt of income as trustee, in right of the term, or having the term vested in him in trust for sale, whether subject to any incumbrance or not;

(iii) Any person in whom, as personal representative of any deceased person, the term is vested, whether subject to any incumbrance or not;

shall, so far as regards the land to which he is entitled, or in which he is interested in right of the term, in any such character as aforesaid, have power by deed to declare to the effect that, from and after the execution of the deed, the term shall be enlarged into a fee simple.

(7) Thereupon, by virtue of the deed and of this Act, the term shall become and be enlarged accordingly, and the person in whom the term was previously vested shall acquire and have in the land a fee simple instead of the term.

(8) The estate in fee simple so acquired by enlargement shall be subject to all the same trusts, powers, executory limitations over, rights, and equities, and to all the same covenants and provisions relating to user and enjoyment, and to all the same obligations of every kind, as the term would have been subject to if it had not been so enlarged.

(9) But where—

(a) any land so held for the residue of a term has been settled in trust by reference to other land, being freehold land, so as to go along with that other land, or, in the case of settlements coming into operation before the commencement of this Act, so as to go along with that other land as far as the law permits; and

(b) at the time of enlargement, the ultimate beneficial interest in the term, whether subject to any subsisting particular estate or not, has not become absolutely and indefeasibly vested in any person, free from charges or powers of charging created by a settlement;

the estate in fee simple acquired as aforesaid shall, without prejudice to any conveyance for value previously made by a person having a contingent or defeasible interest in the term, be liable to be, and shall be, conveyed by means of a subsidiary vesting instrument and settled in like manner as the other land, being freehold land, aforesaid, and until so conveyed and settled shall devolve beneficially as if it had been so conveyed and settled.

(10) The estate in fee simple so acquired shall, whether the term was originally created without impeachment of waste or not, include the fee simple in all mines and minerals which at the time of enlargement have not been severed in right or in fact, or have not been severed or reserved by an inclosure Act or award.

154. Application of Part V. to existing leases.

This Part of this Act, except where otherwise expressly provided, applies to leases created before or after the commencement of this Act, and "lease" includes an under-lease or other tenancy.

PART XI
MISCELLANEOUS

Notices

196.   Regulations respecting notices.

(1)   Any notice required or authorised to be served or given by this Act shall be in writing.

(2)   Any notice required or authorised by this Act to be served on a lessee or mortgagor shall be sufficient, although only addressed to the lessee or mortgagor by that designation, without his name, or generally to the persons interested, without any name, and notwithstanding that any person to be affected by the notice is absent, under disability, unborn, or unascertained.

(3)   Any notice required or authorised by this Act to be served shall be sufficiently served if it is left at the last-known place of abode or business in the United Kingdom of the lessee, lessor, mortgagee, mortgagor, or other person to be served, or, in case of a notice required or authorised to be served on a lessee or mortgagor, is affixed or left for him on the land or any house or building comprised in the lease or mortgage, or, in case of a mining lease, is left for the lessee at the office or counting-house of the mine.

(4)   Any notice required or authorised by this Act to be served shall also be sufficiently served, if it is sent by post in a registered letter addressed to the lessee, lessor, mortgagee, mortgagor, or other person to be served, by name, at the aforesaid place of abode or business, office, or counting-house, and if that letter is not returned through the post-office undelivered; and that service shall be deemed to be made at the time at which the registered letter would in the ordinary course be delivered.

(5)   The provisions of this section shall extend to notices required to be served by any instrument affecting property executed or coming into operation after the commencement of this Act unless a contrary intention appears.

(6)   This section does not apply to notices served in proceedings in the court.

198.   Registration under the Land Charges Act 1925, to be notice.

(1)   The registration of any instrument or matter in any register kept under the Land Charges Act 1972 or any local land charges register shall be deemed to constitute actual notice of such instrument or matter, and of the fact of such registration, to all persons and for all purposes connected with the land affected, as from the date of registration or other prescribed date and so long as the registration continues in force.

(2)   This section operates without prejudice to the provisions of this Act respecting the making of further advances by a mortgagee, and applies only to instruments and matters required or authorised to be registered in any such register.

199.   Restrictions on constructive notice.

(1)   A purchaser shall not be prejudicially affected by notice of—

(i)   any instrument or matter capable of registration under the provisions of the Land Charges Act 1925, or any enactment which it replaces, which is void or not enforceable as against him under that Act or enactment, by reason of the non-registration thereof;

(ii)   any other instrument or matter or any fact or thing unless—

(a)   it is within his own knowledge, or would have come to his knowledge if such inquiries and inspections had been made as ought reasonably to have been made by him; or

(b)   in the same transaction with respect to which a question of notice to the purchaser arises, it has come to the knowledge of his counsel, as such, or of his solicitor or other agent, as such, or would have come to the knowledge of his solicitor or other agent, as such, if such inquiries and inspections had been made as ought reasonably to have been made by the solicitor or other agent.

(2)   Paragraph (ii) of the last subsection shall not exempt a purchaser from any liability under, or any obligation to perform or observe, any covenant, condition, provision, or restriction contained in any instrument under which his title is derived, mediately or immediately; and such liability or obligation may be enforced in the same manner and to the same extent as if that paragraph had not been enacted.

(3)   A purchaser shall not by reason of anything in this section be affected by notice in any case where he would not have been so affected if this section had not been enacted.

(4)   This section applies to purchases made either before or after the commencement of this Act.

PART XII
CONSTRUCTION, JURISDICTION, AND GENERAL PROVISIONS

205.   General definitions.

(1)   In this Act unless the context otherwise requires, the following expressions have the meanings hereby assigned to them respectively, that is to say:—

(i)   "Bankruptcy" includes liquidation by arrangement; also in relation to a corporation means the winding up thereof;

(ii)   "Conveyance" includes a mortgage, charge, lease, assent, vesting declaration, vesting instrument, disclaimer, release and every other assurance of property or of an interest therein by any instrument, except a will; "convey" has a corresponding meaning; and "disposition" includes a conveyance and also a devise, bequest, or an appointment of property contained in a will; and "dispose of" has a corresponding meaning;

(iii)   "Building purposes" include the erecting and improving of, and the adding to, and the repairing of buildings; and a "building lease" is a lease for building purposes or purposes connected therewith;

(iiiA)   "the county court limit", in relation to any enactment contained in this Act, means the amount for the time being specified by an Order in Council under section 145 of the County Courts Act 1984 as the county court limit for the purposes of that enactment (or, where no such Order in Council has been made, the corresponding limit specified by Order in Council under section 192 of the County Courts Act 1959);

(iv)   "Death duty" means estate duty, and every other duty leviable or payable on a death;

(v)   "Estate owner" means the owner of a legal estate, but an infant is not capable of being an estate owner;

(vi)   "Gazette" means the London Gazette;

(vii)   "Incumbrance" includes a legal or equitable mortgage and a trust for securing money, and a lien, and a charge of a portion, annuity, or other capital or annual sum; and "incumbrancer" has a meaning corresponding with that of incumbrance, and includes every person entitled to the benefit of an incumbrance, or to require payment or discharge thereof;

(viii)   "Instrument" does not include a statute, unless the statute creates a settlement;

(ix)   "Land" includes land of any tenure, and mines and minerals, whether or not held apart from the surface, buildings or parts of buildings (whether the division is horizontal, vertical or made in any other way) and other corporeal hereditaments; also a manor, an advowson, and a rent and other incorporeal hereditaments, and an easement, right, privilege, or benefit in, over, or derived from land; but not an undivided share in land; and "mines and minerals" include any strata or seam of minerals or substances in or under any land, and powers of working and getting the same but not an undivided share thereof; and "manor" includes a lordship, and reputed manor or lordship; and "hereditament" means any real property which on an intestacy occurring before the commencement of this Act might have devolved upon an heir;

(x) "Legal estates" mean the estates, interests and charges, in or over land (subsisting or created at law) which are by this Act authorised to subsist or to be created as legal estates; "equitable interests" mean all the other interests and charges in or over land or in the proceeds of sale thereof; an equitable interest "capable of subsisting as a legal estate" means such as could validly subsist or be created as a legal estate under this Act;

(xi) "Legal powers" include the powers vested in a chargee by way of legal mortgage or in an estate owner under which a legal estate can be transferred or created; and "equitable powers" mean all the powers in or over land under which equitable interests or powers only can be transferred or created;

(xii) "Limitation Acts" mean the Real Property Limitation Acts, 1833, 1837 and 1874, and "limitation" includes a trust;

(xiii) "Mental disorder" has the meaning assigned to it by section 1 of the Mental Health Act 1983, and "receiver", in relation to a person suffering from a mental disorder, means a receiver appointed for that person under Part VIII of the Mental Health Act 1959 or Part VII of the said Act of 1983;

(xiv) a "mining lease" means a lease for mining purposes, that is, the searching for, winning, working, getting, making merchantable, carrying away, or disposing of mines and minerals, or purposes connected therewith, and includes a grant or licence for mining purposes;

(xv) "Minister" means the Minister of Agriculture, Fisheries and Food;

(xvi) "Mortgage" includes any charge or lien on any property for securing money or money's worth; "legal mortgage" means a mortgage by demise or subdemise or a charge by way of legal mortgage and "legal mortgagee" has a corresponding meaning; "mortgage money" means money or money's worth secured by a mortgage; "mortgagor" includes any person from time to time deriving title under the original mortgagor or entitled to redeem a mortgage according to his estate interest or right in the mortgaged property; "mortgagee" includes a chargee by way of legal mortgage and any person from time to time deriving title under the original mortgagee; and "mortgagee in possession" is, for the purposes of this Act, a mortgagee who, in right of the mortgage, has entered into and is in possession of the mortgaged property; and "right of redemption" includes an option to repurchase only if the option in effect creates a right of redemption;

(xvii) "Notice" includes constructive notice;

(xviii) "Personal representative" means the executor, original or by representation, or administrator for the time being of a deceased person, and as regards any liability for the payment of death duties includes any person who takes possession of or intermeddles with the property of a deceased person without the authority of the personal representatives or the court;

(xix) "Possession" includes receipt of rents and profits or the right to receive the same, if any; and "income" includes rents and profits;

(xx) "Property" includes any thing in action, and any interest in real or personal property;

(xxi) "Purchaser" means a purchaser in good faith for valuable consideration and includes a lessee, mortgagee or other person who for valuable consideration acquires an interest in property except that in Part I. of this Act and elsewhere where so expressly provided "purchaser" only means a person who acquires an interest in or charge on property for money or money's worth; and in reference to a legal estate includes a chargee by way of legal mortgage; and where the context so requires "purchaser" includes an intending purchaser; "purchase" has a meaning corresponding with that of "purchaser"; and "valuable consideration" includes marriage but does not include a nominal consideration in money;

(xxii) "Registered land" has the same meaning as in the Land Registration Act 1925, and "Land Registrar" means the Chief Land Registrar under that Act;

(xxiii) "Rent" includes a rent service or a rentcharge, or other rent, toll, duty, royalty, or annual or periodical payment in money or money's worth, reserved or issuing out of or charged upon land, but does not include mortgage interest; "rentcharge" includes a fee farm rent; "fine" includes a premium or foregift and any payment, consideration, or benefit in the nature of a fine, premium or foregift; "lessor" includes an underlessor and a person deriving title under a lessor or underlessor; and "lessee" includes an underlessee and a person deriving title under a lessee or under-lessee, and "lease" includes an underlease or other tenancy;

(xxiv) "Sale" includes an extinguishment of manorial incidents, but in other respects means a sale properly so called;

(xxv) "Securities" include stocks, funds and shares;

(xxvi) "Tenant for life," "statutory owner," "settled land," "settlement," "vesting deed," "subsidiary vesting deed," "vesting order," "vesting instrument," "trust instrument," "capital money," and "trustees of the settlement" have the same meanings as in the Settled Land Act 1925;

(xxvii) "Term of years absolute" means a term of years (taking effect either in possession or in reversion whether or not at a rent) with or without impeachment for waste, subject or not to another legal estate, and either certain or liable to determination by notice, re-entry, operation of law, or by a provision for cesser on redemption, or in any other event (other than the dropping of a life, or the determination of a determinable life interest); but does not include any term of years determinable with life or lives or with the cesser of a determinable life interest, nor, if created after the commencement of this Act, a term of years which is not expressed to take effect in possession within twenty-one years after the creation thereof where required by this Act to take effect within that period; and in this definition the expression "term of years" includes a term for less than a year, or for a year or years and a fraction of a year or from year to year;

(xxviii) "Trust Corporation" means the Public Trustee or a corporation either appointed by the court in any particular case to be a trustee or entitled by rules made under subsection (3) of section four of the Public Trustee Act, 1906, to act as custodian trustee;

(xxix) "Trust for sale," in relation to land, means an immediate binding trust for sale, whether or not exercisable at the request or with the consent of any person, and with or without a power at discretion to postpone the sale; "trustees for sale" mean the persons (including a personal representative) holding land on trust for sale; and "power to postpone a sale" means power to postpone in the exercise of a discretion;

(xxx) "United Kingdom" means Great Britain and Northern Ireland;

(xxxi) "Will" includes codicil.

(1A) Any reference in this Act to money being paid into court shall be construed as referring to the money being paid into the Supreme Court or any other court that has jurisdiction, and any reference in this Act to the court, in a context referring to the investment or application of money paid into court, shall be construed, in the case of money paid into the Supreme Court, as referring to the High Court, and in the case of money paid into another court, as referring to that other court.

(2) Where an equitable interest in or power over property arises by statute or operation of law, references to the creation of an interest or power include references to any interest or power so arising.

(3) References to registration under the Land Charges Act, 1925, apply to any registration made under any other statute which is by the Land Charges Act, 1925, to have effect as if the registration had been made under that Act.

Sections 76 and 77.   SECOND SCHEDULE.

IMPLIED COVENANTS

PART I

COVENANT IMPLIED IN A CONVEYANCE FOR VALUABLE CONSIDERATION, OTHER THAN A MORTGAGE, BY A PERSON WHO CONVEYS AND IS EXPRESSED TO CONVEY AS BENEFICIAL OWNER.

That, notwithstanding anything by the person who so conveys or any one through whom he derives title otherwise than by purchase for value, made, done, executed, or omitted, or knowingly suffered, the person who so conveys, has, with the concurrence of every other person, if any, conveying by his direction, full power to convey the subject-matter expressed to be conveyed, subject as, if so expressed, and in the manner in which, it is expressed to be conveyed, and that, notwithstanding anything as aforesaid, that subject-matter shall remain to and be quietly entered upon, received, and held, occupied, enjoyed, and taken, by the person to whom the conveyance is expressed to be made, and any person deriving title under him, and the benefit thereof shall be received and taken accordingly, without any lawful interruption or disturbance by the person who so conveys or any person conveying by his direction, or rightfully claiming or to claim by, through, under, or in trust for the person who so conveys, or any person conveying by his direction, or by, through, or under any one (not being a person claiming in respect of an estate or interest subject whereto the conveyance is expressly made), through whom the person who so conveys derives title, otherwise than by purchase for value:

And that, freed and discharged from, or otherwise by the person who so conveys sufficiently indemnified against, all such estates, incumbrances, claims, and demands, other than those subject to which the conveyance is expressly made, as, either before or after the date of the conveyance, have been or shall be made, occasioned, or suffered by that person or by any person conveying by his direction, or by any person rightfully claiming by, through, under, or in trust for the person who so conveys, or by, through, or under any person conveying by his direction, by, through, or under any one through whom the person who so conveys derives title, otherwise than by purchase for value:

And further, that the person who so conveys, and any person conveying by his direction, and every other person having or rightfully claiming any estate or interest in the subject-matter of conveyance, other than an estate or interest subject whereto the conveyance is expressly made, by, through, under, or in trust for the person who so conveys, or by, through, or under any person conveying by his direction, or by, through, or under any one through whom the person who so conveys derives title, otherwise than by purchase for value, will, from time to time and at all times after the date of the conveyance, on the request and at the cost of any person to whom the conveyance is expressed to be made, or of any person deriving title under him, execute and do all such lawful assurances and things for further or more perfectly assuring the subject-matter of the conveyance to the person to whom the conveyance is made, and to those deriving title under him, subject as, if so expressed, and in the manner in which the conveyance is expressed to be made, as by him or them or any of them shall be reasonably required.

In the above covenant a purchase for value shall not be deemed to include a conveyance in consideration of marriage.

PART II

FURTHER COVENANT IMPLIED IN A CONVEYANCE OF LEASEHOLD PROPERTY FOR VALUABLE CONSIDERATION, OTHER THAN A MORTGAGE, BY A PERSON WHO CONVEYS AND IS EXPRESSED TO CONVEY AS BENEFICIAL OWNER.

That, notwithstanding anything by the person who so conveys, or any one through whom he derives title, otherwise than by purchase for value, made, done, executed, or omitted, or knowingly suffered, the lease or grant creating the term or estate for which the land is conveyed is, at the time of conveyance, a good, valid, and effectual lease or grant of the property conveyed, and is in full force, unforfeited, unsurrendered, and has in nowise become void or voidable, and that, notwithstanding anything as aforesaid, all the rents reserved by, and all the covenants, conditions, and agreements contained in, the lease or grant, and on the part of the lessee or grantee and the persons deriving title under him to be paid, observed, and performed, have been paid, observed, and performed up to the time of conveyance.

In the above covenant a purchase for value shall not be deemed to include a conveyance in consideration of marriage.

PART III
COVENANT IMPLIED IN A CONVEYANCE BY WAY OF MORTGAGE BY A PERSON WHO CONVEYS AND IS EXPRESSED TO CONVEY AS BENEFICIAL OWNER.

That the person who so conveys, has, with the concurrence of every other person, if any, conveying by his direction, full power to convey the subject-matter expressed to be conveyed by him, subject as, if so expressed, and in the manner in which it is expressed to be conveyed:

And also that, if default is made in payment of the money intended to be secured by the conveyance, or any interest thereon, or any part of that money or interest, contrary to any provision in the conveyance, it shall be lawful for the person to whom the conveyance is expressed to be made, and the persons deriving title under him, to enter into and upon, or receive, and thenceforth quietly hold, occupy, and enjoy or take and have, the subject-matter expressed to be conveyed, or any part thereof, without any lawful interruption or disturbance by the person who so conveys, or any person conveying by his direction, or any other person (not being a person claiming in respect of an estate or interest subject whereto the conveyance is expressly made):

And that, freed and discharged from, or otherwise by the person who so conveys sufficiently indemnified against, all estates, incumbrances, claims, and demands whatever, other than those subject whereto the conveyance is expressly made:

And further, that the person who so conveys and every person conveying by his direction, and every person deriving title under any of them, and every other person having or rightfully claiming any estate or interest in the subject-matter of conveyance, or any part thereof, other than an estate or interest subject whereto the conveyance is expressly made, will from time to time and at all times, on the request of any person to whom the conveyance is expressed to be made, or of any person deriving title under him, but, as long as any right of redemption exists under the conveyance, at the cost of the person so conveying, or of those deriving title under him, and afterwards at the cost of the person making the request, execute and do all such lawful assurances and things for further or more perfectly assuring the subject-matter of conveyance and every part thereof to the person to whom the conveyance is made, and to those deriving title under him, subject as, if so expressed, and in the manner in which the conveyance is expressed to be made, as by him or them or any of them shall be reasonably required.

The above covenant in the case of a charge shall have effect as if for references to "conveys," "conveyed" and "conveyance" there were substituted respectively references to "charges," "charged" and "charge."

PART IV
COVENANT IMPLIED IN A CONVEYANCE BY WAY OF MORTGAGE OF FREEHOLD PROPERTY SUBJECT TO A RENT OR OF LEASEHOLD PROPERTY BY A PERSON WHO CONVEYS AND IS EXPRESSED TO CONVEY AS BENEFICIAL OWNER.

That the lease or grant creating the term or estate for which the land is held is, at the time of conveyance, a good, valid, and effectual lease or grant of the land conveyed and is in full force, unforfeited, and unsurrendered and has in nowise become void or voidable, and that all the rents reserved by, and all the covenants, conditions, and agreements contained in, the lease or grant, and on the part of the lessee or grantee and the persons deriving title under him to be paid, observed, and performed, have been paid, observed, and performed up to the time of conveyance:

And also that the person so conveying, or the persons deriving title under him, will at all times, as long as any money remains owing on the security of the conveyance, pay, observe, and perform, or cause to be paid, observed, and performed all the rents reserved by, and all the covenants, conditions, and agreements contained in, the lease or grant, and on the part of the lessee or grantee and the persons deriving title under him to be paid, observed, and performed, and will keep the person to whom the conveyance is made, and those deriving title under him, indemnified against all actions, proceedings, costs, charges, damages, claims and demands, if any, to be incurred or sustained by him or them by reason of the non-payment of such rent or the non-observance or non-performance of such covenants, conditions, and agreements, or any of them.

The above covenant in the case of a charge shall have effect as if for references to "conveys," "conveyed" and "conveyance" there were substituted respectively references to "charges," "charged" and "charge."

PART V
COVENANT IMPLIED IN A CONVEYANCE BY WAY OF SETTLEMENT, BY A PERSON WHO CONVEYS AND IS EXPRESSED TO CONVEY AS SETTLOR.

That the person so conveying, and every person deriving title under him by deed or act or operation of law in his lifetime subsequent to that conveyance, or by testamentary disposition or devolution in law, on his death, will, from time to time, and at all times, after the date of that conveyance, at the request and cost of any person deriving title thereunder, execute and do all such lawful assurances and things for further or more perfectly assuring the subject-matter of the conveyance to the persons to whom the conveyance is made and those deriving title under them, as by them or any of them shall be reasonably required, subject as, if so expressed, and in the manner in which the conveyance is expressed to be made.

PART VI
COVENANT IMPLIED IN ANY CONVEYANCE, BY EVERY PERSON WHO CONVEYS AND IS EXPRESSED TO CONVEY AS TRUSTEE OR MORTGAGEE, OR AS PERSONAL REPRESENTATIVE OF A DECEASED PERSON, OR UNDER AN ORDER OF THE COURT

That the person so conveying has not executed or done, or knowingly suffered, or been party or privy to, any deed or thing, whereby or by means whereof the subject-matter of the conveyance, or any part thereof, is or may be impeached, charged, affected, or incumbered in title, estate, or otherwise, or whereby or by means whereof the person who so conveys is in anywise hindered from conveying the subject-matter of the conveyance, or any part thereof, in the manner in which it is expressed to be conveyed.

The foregoing covenant may be implied in an assent in like manner as in a conveyance by deed.

PART VII
COVENANT IMPLIED IN A CONVEYANCE FOR VALUABLE CONSIDERATION, OTHER THAN A MORTGAGE, OF THE ENTIRETY OF LAND AFFECTED BY A RENTCHARGE.

That the grantees or the persons deriving title under them will at all times, from the date of the conveyance or other date therein stated, duly pay the said rentcharge and observe and perform all the covenants, agreements and conditions contained in the deed or other document creating the rentcharge, and thenceforth on the part of the owner of the land to be observed and performed:

And also will at all times, from the date aforesaid, save harmless and keep indemnified the conveying parties and their respective estates and effects, from and against all proceedings, costs, claims and expenses on account of any omission to pay the said rentcharge or any part thereof, or any breach of any of the said covenants agreements and conditions.

PART VIII
COVENANTS IMPLIED IN A CONVEYANCE FOR VALUABLE CONSIDERATION, OTHER THAN A MORTGAGE, OF PART OF LAND AFFECTED BY A RENTCHARGE, SUBJECT TO A PART (NOT LEGALLY APPORTIONED) OF THAT RENTCHARGE.

(i)   That the grantees, or the persons deriving title under them, will at all times, from the date of the conveyance or other date therein stated, pay the apportioned rent and observe and perform all the covenants (other than the covenant to pay the entire rent) and conditions contained in the deed or other document creating the rentcharge, so far as the same relate to the land conveyed:

And also will at all times, from the date aforesaid, save harmless and keep indemnified the conveying parties and their respective estates and effects, from and against all proceedings, costs, claims and expenses on account of any omission to pay the said apportioned rent, or any breach of any of the said covenants and conditions, so far as the same relate as aforesaid.

(ii)   That the conveying parties, or the persons deriving title under them, will at all times, from the date of the conveyance or other date therein stated, pay the balance of the rentcharge (after deducting the apportioned rent aforesaid, and any other rents similarly apportioned in respect of land not retained), and observe and perform all the covenants, other than the covenant to pay the entire rent, and conditions contained in the deed or other document creating the rentcharge, so far as the same relate to the land not included in the conveyance and remaining vested in the covenantors:

And also will at all times, from the date aforesaid, save harmless and keep indemnified the grantees and their estates and effects, from and against all proceedings, costs, claims and expenses on account of any omission to pay the aforesaid balance of the rentcharge, or any breach of any of the said covenants and conditions so far as they relate as aforesaid.

PART IX
COVENANT IN A CONVEYANCE FOR VALUABLE CONSIDERATION, OTHER THAN A MORTGAGE, OF THE ENTIRETY OF THE LAND COMPRISED IN A LEASE FOR THE RESIDUE OF THE TERM OR INTEREST CREATED BY THE LEASE.

That the assignees, or the persons deriving title under them, will at all times, from the date of the conveyance or other date therein stated, duly pay all rent becoming due under the lease creating the term or interest for which the land is conveyed, and observe and perform all the covenants, agreements and conditions therein contained and thenceforth on the part of the lessees to be observed and performed:

And also will at all times, from the date aforesaid, save harmless and keep indemnified the conveying parties and their estates and effects, from and against all proceedings, costs, claims and expenses on account of any omission to pay the said rent or any breach of any of the said covenants, agreements and conditions.

PART X
COVENANTS IMPLIED IN A CONVEYANCE FOR VALUABLE CONSIDERATION, OTHER THAN A MORTGAGE, OF PART OF THE LAND COMPRISED IN A LEASE, FOR THE RESIDUE OF THE TERM OR INTEREST CREATED BY THE LEASE, SUBJECT TO A PART (NOT LEGALLY APPORTIONED) OF THAT RENT.

(i) That the assignees, or the persons deriving title under them, will at all times, from the date of the conveyance or other date therein stated, pay the apportioned rent and observe and perform all the covenants, other than the covenant to pay the entire rent, agreements and conditions contained in the lease creating the term or interest for which the land is conveyed, and thenceforth on the part of the lessees to be observed and performed, so far as the same relate to the land conveyed:

And also will at all times from the date aforesaid save harmless and keep indemnified, the conveying parties and their respective estates and effects, from and against all proceedings, costs, claims and expenses on account of any omission to pay the said apportioned rent or any breach of any of the said covenants, agreements and conditions so far as the same relate as aforesaid.

(ii) That the conveying parties, or the persons deriving title under them, will at all times, from the date of the conveyance, or other date therein stated, pay the balance of the rent (after deducting the apportioned rent aforesaid and any other rents similarly apportioned in respect of land not retained) and observe and perform all the covenants, other than the covenant to pay the entire rent, agreements and conditions contained in the lease and on the part of the lessees to be observed and performed so far as the same relate to the land demised (other than the land comprised in the conveyance) and remaining vested in the covenantors:

And also will at all times, from the date aforesaid, save harmless and keep indemnified, the assignees and their estates and effects, from and against all proceedings, costs, claims and expenses on account of any omission to pay the aforesaid balance of the rent or any breach of any of the said covenants, agreements and conditions so far as they relate as aforesaid.

LAND REGISTRATION ACT 1925
(15 Geo. 5, c. 21)

An Act to consolidate the Land Transfer Acts and the statute law relating to registered land.
[9 April 1925]

PART I
PRELIMINARY

1. Registers to be continued.

(1) The Chief Land Registrar shall continue to keep a register of title to freehold land and leasehold land.

(2) The register need not be kept in documentary form.

2. What estates may be registered.

(1) After the commencement of this Act, estates capable of subsisting as legal estates shall be the only interests in land in respect of which a proprietor can be registered and all other interests in registered land (except overriding interests and interests entered on the register at or before such commencement) shall take effect in equity as minor interests, but all interests (except undivided shares in land) entered on the register at such commencement which are not legal estates shall be capable of being dealt with under this Act:

Provided that, on the occasion of the first dealing with any such interest, the register shall be rectified in such manner as may be provided by rules made to secure that the entries therein shall be similar to those which would have been made if the title to the land had been registered after the commencement of this Act.

(2) Subject as aforesaid, and save as otherwise expressly provided by this Act, this Act applies to land registered under any enactment replaced by this Act in like manner as it applies to land registered under this Act.

3. Interpretation.

In this Act unless the context otherwise requires, the following expressions have the meanings hereby assigned to them respectively, that is to say:-

(i) "Charge by way of legal mortgage" means a mortgage created by charge under which, by virtue of the Law of Property Act 1925, the mortgagee is to be treated as an estate owner in like manner as if a mortgage term by demise or subdemise were vested in him, and "legal mortgage" has the same meaning as in that Act;

(ii) "the court" means the High Court or, where county courts have jurisdiction by virtue of rules made under section 138(1) of this Act, the county court;

(iv) "Estate owner" means the owner of a legal estate, but an infant is not capable of being an estate owner;

(v) "Gazette" means the London Gazette;

(vi) "Income" includes rents and profits;

(vii) "Instrument" does not include a statute, unless the statute creates a settlement;

(viii) "Land" includes land of any tenure (including land, subject or not to manorial incidents, enfranchised under Part V. of the Law of Property Act 1922), and mines and minerals, whether or not held with the surface, buildings or parts of buildings (whether the division is horizontal, vertical or made in any other way) and other corporeal hereditaments; also a manor, and a rent and other incorporeal hereditaments, and an easement, right, privilege, or benefit in, over, or derived from land; but not an undivided share in land; and "hereditaments" mean real property which on an intestacy might, before the commencement of this Act, have devolved on an heir;

(ix) "Land charge" means a land charge of any class described in section 2 of the Land Charges Act 1972 or a local land charge;

(x) "Lease" includes an under-lease and any tenancy or agreement for a lease, under-lease or tenancy;

(xi) "Legal estates" mean the estates interests and charges in or over land subsisting or created at law which are by the Law of Property Act 1925, authorised to subsist or to be created at law; and "Equitable interests" mean all the other interests and charges in or over land or in the proceeds of sale thereof; an equitable interest "capable of subsisting at law" means such as could validly subsist at law if clothed with the legal estate;

(xii) "Limitation Acts" mean the Real Property Limitation Acts, 1833, 1837 and 1874, and any Acts amending those Acts;

(xiii) "Manorial incidents" have the same meaning as in Part V. of the Law of Property Act 1922;

(xiv) "Mines and minerals" include any strata or seam of minerals or substances in or under any land, and powers of working and getting the same, but not an undivided share thereof;

(xv) "Minor interests" mean the interests not capable of being disposed of or created by registered dispositions and capable of being overridden (whether or not a purchaser has notice thereof) by the proprietors unless protected as provided by this Act, and all rights and interests which are not registered or protected on the register and are not overriding interests, and include—

(a) in the case of land held on trust for sale, all interests and powers which are under the Law of Property Act 1925, capable of being overridden by the trustees for sale, whether or not such interests and powers are so protected; and

(b)   in the case of settled land, all interests and powers which are under the Settled Land Act, 1925, and the Law of Property Act 1925, or either of them, capable of being overridden by the tenant for life or statutory owner, whether or not such interests and powers are so protected as aforesaid;

(xvi)   "Overriding interests." mean all the incumbrances, interests, rights, and powers not entered on the register but subject to which registered dispositions are by this Act to take effect, and in regard to land registered at the commencement of this Act include the matters which are by any enactment repealed by this Act declared not to be incumbrances;

(xvii)   "Personal representative" means the executor, original or by representation, or administrator for the time being of a deceased person, and as regards any liability for the payment of death duties includes any person who takes possession of or intermeddles with the property of a deceased person without the authority of the personal representatives or the court; and where there are special personal representatives for the purposes of any settled land, it means, in relation to that land, those representatives;

(xviii)   "Possession" includes receipt of rents and profits or the right to receive the same, if any;

(xix)   "Prescribed" means prescribed by general rules made in pursuance of this Act;

(xx)   "Proprietor" means the registered proprietor for the time being of an estate in land or of a charge;

(xxi)   "Purchaser" means a purchaser in good faith for valuable consideration and includes a lessee, mortgagee, or other person who for valuable consideration acquires any interest in land or in any charge on land;

(xxii)   "Registered dispositions" mean dispositions which take effect under the powers conferred on the proprietor by way of transfer, charge, lease or otherwise and to which (when required to be registered) special effect or priority is given by this Act on registration;

(xxiii)   "Registered estate," in reference to land, means the legal estate, or other registered interest, if any, as respects which a person is for the time being registered as proprietor, but does not include a registered charge and a "registered charge" includes a mortgage or incumbrance registered as a charge under this Act;

(xxiv)   "Registered land" means land or any estate or interest in land the title to which is registered under this Act or any enactment replaced by this Act, and includes any easement, right, privilege, or benefit which is appurtenant or appendant thereto, and any mines and minerals within or under the same and held therewith;

(xxv)   "Rent" includes a rent service or a rent charge, or other rent, toll, duty, royalty, or annual or periodical payment, in money or money's worth, issuing out of or charged upon land, but does not include mortgage interest;

(xxvi)   "Settled land" "settlement" "tenant for life" "statutory owner" "trustees of the settlement" "capital money" "trust corporation" "trust instrument" "vesting deed" "vesting order" "vesting assent" and "vesting instrument" have the same meanings as in the Settled Land Act, 1925;

(xxvii)   A "term of years absolute" means a term of years, whether at a rent or not, taking effect either in possession or in reversion, with or without impeachment for waste, subject or not to another legal estate and either certain or liable to determination by notice, re-entry, operation of law, or by a provision for cesser on redemption, or in any other event (other than the dropping of a life, or the determination of a determinable life interest), but does not include any term of years determinable with life or lives or with the cesser of a determinable life interest, nor, if created after the commencement of this Act, a term of years which is not expressed to take effect in possession within twenty-one years after the creation thereof where required by the Law of Property Act, 1925, to take effect within that period; and in this definition the expression "term of years" includes a term for less than a year, or for a year or years and a fraction of a year or from year to year;

(xxviii) "Trust for sale," in relation to land, means an immediate binding trust for sale, whether or not exercisable at the request or with the consent of any person, and with or without a power at discretion to postpone the sale;

(xxix) "Trustees for sale" mean the persons (including a personal representative) holding land on trust for sale;

(xxx) "United Kingdom" means Great Britain and Northern Ireland;

(xxxi) "Valuable consideration" includes marriage, but does not include a nominal consideration in money;

(xxxii) "Will" includes codicil.

PART II
REGISTRATION OF LAND

Leasehold Land

8. Application for registration of leasehold land.

(1) Where the title to be registered is a title to a leasehold interest in land—

(a) any estate owner (including a tenant for life, statutory owner, personal representative, or trustee for sale, but not including a mortgagee where there is a subsisting right of redemption), holding under a lease for a term of years absolute of which more than twenty-one are unexpired, whether subject or not to incumbrances, or

(b) any other person (not being a mortgagee as aforesaid and not being a person who has merely contracted to buy the leasehold interest) who is entitled to require a legal leasehold estate held under such a lease as aforesaid (whether subject or not to incumbrances) to be vested in him,

may apply to the registrar to be registered in respect of such estate, or in the case of a person not being in a fiduciary position to have registered in his stead any nominee, as proprietor with an absolute title, with a good leasehold title or with a possessory title:

Provided that—

(i) Where an absolute title is required, the applicant or his nominee shall not be registered as proprietor until and unless the title both to the leasehold and to the freehold, and to any intermediate leasehold that may exist, is approved by the registrar;

(ii) Where a good leasehold title is required, the applicant or his nominee shall not be registered as proprietor until and unless the title to the leasehold interest is approved by the registrar;

(iii) Where a possessory title is required, the applicant or his nominee may be registered as proprietor on giving such evidence of title and serving such notices, if any, as may for the time being be prescribed;

(iv) If on an application for registration with a possessory title the registrar is satisfied as to the title to the leasehold interest, he may register it as good leasehold, whether the applicant consents to such registration or not, but in that case no higher fee shall be charged than would have been charged for registration with possessory title.

(1A) An application for registration in respect of leasehold land held under a lease in relation to the grant or assignment of which section 123(1) of this Act applies (whether by virtue of this Act or any later enactment) may be made within the period allowed by section 123(1), or any authorised extension of that period, notwithstanding that the lease was granted for a term of not more than twenty-one years or that the unexpired term of the lease is not more than twenty-one years.

(2) Leasehold land held under a lease containing a prohibition or restriction on dealings therewith inter vivas shall not be registered under this Act unless and until

provision is made in the prescribed manner for preventing any dealing therewith in contravention of the prohibition or restriction by an entry on the register to that effect, or otherwise.

(3) Where on an application to register a mortgage term, wherein no right of redemption is subsisting, it appears that the applicant is entitled in equity to the superior term, if any, out of which it was created, the registrar shall register him as proprietor of the superior term without any entry to the effect that the legal interest in that term is outstanding, and on such registration the superior term shall vest in the proprietor and the mortgage term shall merge therein:

Provided that this subsection shall not apply where the mortgage term does not comprise the whole of the land included in the superior term, unless in that case the rent, if any, payable in respect of the superior term has been apportioned, or the rent is of no money value or no rent is reserved, and unless the covenants, if any, entered into for the benefit of the reversion have been apportioned (either expressly or by implication) as respects the land comprised in the mortgage term.

9.   Effect of first registration with absolute title.

Where the registered land is a leasehold interest, the registration under this Act of any person as first proprietor thereof with an absolute title shall be deemed to vest in such person the possession of the leasehold interest described, with all implied or expressed rights, privileges, and appurtenances attached to such interest, subject to the following obligations, rights, and interests, that is to say,—

(a)   Subject to all implied and express covenants, obligations, and liabilities incident to the registered land; and

(b)   Subject to the incumbrances and other entries (if any) appearing on the register; and

(c)   Unless the contrary is expressed on the register, subject to such overriding interests, if any, as affect the registered land; and

(d)   Where such first proprietor is not entitled for his own benefit to the registered land subject, as between himself and the persons entitled to minor interests, to any minor interests of such persons of which he has notice;

but free from all other estates and interests whatsoever, including estates and interests of His Majesty.

10.   Effect of first registration with good leasehold title.

Where the registered land is a leasehold interest, the registration of a person as first proprietor thereof with a good leasehold title shall not affect or prejudice the enforcement of any estate, right or interest affecting or in derogation of the title of the lessor to grant the lease, but, save as aforesaid, shall have the same effect as registration with an absolute title.

11.   Effect of first registration with possessory title.

Where the registered land is a leasehold interest, the registration of a person as first proprietor thereof with a possessory title shall not affect or prejudice the enforcement of any estate, right, or interest (whether in respect of the lessor's title or otherwise) adverse to or in derogation of the title of such first registered proprietor, and subsisting or capable of arising at the time of the registration of such proprietor; but, save as aforesaid, shall have the same effect as registration with an absolute title.

12.   Qualified title.

(1)   Where on examination it appears to the registrar that the title, either of the lessor to the reversion or of the lessee to the leasehold interest, can be established only for a limited period, or subject to certain reservations, the registrar may, upon the request in writing of the person applying to be registered, by an entry made in the register, except from the effect of registration any estate, right or interest—

(a)   arising before a specified date, or

(b)   arising under a specified instrument, or otherwise particularly described in the register,

and a title registered subject to any such exception shall be called a qualified title.

(2)   Where the registered land is a leasehold interest, the registration of a person as first proprietor thereof with a qualified title shall not affect or prejudice the enforcement of any estate, right, or interest appearing by the register to be excepted, but, save as aforesaid, shall have the same effect as registration with a good leasehold title or an absolute title, as the case may be.

PART III
REGISTERED DEALINGS WITH REGISTERED LAND
Dispositions of Leasehold Land

21.   Powers of disposition of registered leaseholds.

(1)   Where the registered land is a leasehold interest the proprietor may, in the prescribed manner, transfer the registered estate in the land or any part thereof, and, subject to any entry in the register to the contrary may in the prescribed manner—

(a)   transfer all or any of the leasehold mines and minerals apart from the surface; or the surface without all or any of the leasehold mines and minerals;

(b)   grant (to the extent of the registered estate) any annuity or rentcharge in possession, easement, right or privilege in, over, or derived from the registered land or any part thereof, in any form which sufficiently refers, in the prescribed manner, to the registered lease, and to the dominant tenement, whether being registered land or not;

(c)   transfer the registered land or any part thereof subject to a reservation to any person of any such annuity, rentcharge, easement, right, or privilege;

(d)   grant (subject or not to the reservation of an easement, right or privilege) an underlease of the registered land, or any part thereof, or of all or any mines and minerals apart from the surface, or of the surface without all or any of the mines and minerals, or of an easement, right or privilege, in or over the registered land or any part thereof, for any term of years absolute of less duration than the registered estate and for any purpose (but where by way of mortgage, subject to the provisions of this Act and of the Law of Property Act, 1925, relating thereto), and in any form which sufficiently refers in the prescribed manner to the registered land, and in the case of an easement, right, or privilege, to the dominant tenement, whether being registered land or not.

(2)   A disposition of registered leasehold land may be made subject to a rent legally apportioned in the prescribed manner, or to a rent not so apportioned.

(3)   An underlease for a term, not exceeding twenty-one years, to take effect in possession or within one year from the date thereof, may be granted and shall take effect under this section, notwithstanding that a caution, notice of deposit of a certificate, restriction, or inhibition (other than a bankruptcy inhibition) may be subsisting, but subject to the interests intended to be protected by any such caution, notice, restriction, or inhibition.

(4)   The foregoing powers of disposition shall (subject to the express provisions of this Act and of the Law of Property Act, 1925, relating to mortgages) apply to dispositions by the registered proprietor by way of charge or mortgage, but no estate, other than a legal estate, shall be capable of being disposed of or created under this section.

(5)   In this Act "transfer" or "disposition" when referring to registered leasehold land includes any disposition authorised as aforesaid, and "transferee" has a corresponding meaning.

22.   Registration of dispositions of leaseholds.

(1)   A transfer of the registered estate in the land or part thereof shall be completed by the registrar entering on the register the transferee as proprietor of the estate

transferred, but until such entry is made the transferor shall be deemed to remain the proprietor of the registered estate; and where part only of the land is transferred, notice thereof shall also be noted on the register.

(2) All interests transferred or created by dispositions by the registered proprietor other than the transfer of his registered estate in the land or in part thereof shall (subject to the provisions relating to mortgages) be completed by registration in the same manner and with the same effect as provided by this Act with respect to transfers of the registered estate, and notice thereof shall also be noted on the register in accordance with this Act:

Provided that nothing in this subsection—

(a) shall authorise the registration of an underlease originally granted for a term not exceeding twenty-one years, or require the entry of a notice of such an underlease; or

(b) shall authorise the registration of a mortgage term where there is a subsisting right of redemption, or

(c) shall render necessary the registration of any easement, right, or privilege except as appurtenant to registered land, or the entry of notice thereof except as against the registered title of the servient land.

Every such disposition shall, when registered, take effect as a registered disposition, and an underlease made by the registered proprietor which is not required to be registered or noted on the register shall nevertheless take effect as if it were a registered disposition immediately on being granted.

(3) The general words implied in conveyances under the Law of Property Act, 1925, shall apply, so far as applicable thereto, to transfers of a registered leasehold estate.

23. Effect of registration of dispositions of leaseholds.

(1) In the case of a leasehold estate registered with an absolute title, a disposition (including a subdemise thereof) for valuable consideration shall, when registered, be deemed to vest in the transferee or underlessee the estate transferred or created to the extent of the registered estate, or for the term created by the subdemise, as the case may require, with all implied or expressed rights, privileges, and appurtenances attached to the estate transferred or created, including (subject to any entry to the contrary on the register) the appropriate rights and interests which would under the Law of Property Act, 1925, have been transferred if the land had not been registered, but subject as follows:—

(a) To all implied and express covenants, obligations, and liabilities incident to the estate transferred or created; and

(b) To the incumbrances and other entries (if any) appearing on the register and any charge for capital transfer tax subject to which the disposition takes effect under section 73 of this Act; and

(c) Unless the contrary is expressed on the register, to the overriding interests, if any, affecting the estate transferred or created,

but free from all other estates and interests whatsoever, including estates and interests of His Majesty; and the transfer or subdemise shall operate in like manner as if the registered transferor or sublessor were (subject to any entry to the contrary on the register) absolutely entitled to the registered lease for his own benefit.

(2) In the case of a leasehold estate registered with a good leasehold title, a disposition (including a subdemise thereof) for valuable consideration shall, when registered, have the same effect as it would have had if the land had been registered with an absolute title, save that it shall not affect or prejudice the enforcement of any right or interest affecting or in derogation of the title of the lessor to grant the lease.

(3) In the case of a leasehold estate registered with a qualified title, a disposition (including a subdemise thereof) for valuable consideration shall, when registered, have the same effect as it would have had if the land had been registered with an absolute

title, save that such disposition shall not affect or prejudice the enforcement of any right or interest (whether in respect of the lessor's title or otherwise) appearing by the register to be excepted.

(4) In the case of a leasehold estate registered with a possessory title, a disposition (including a subdemise thereof) for valuable consideration shall not affect or prejudice the enforcement of any right or interest (whether in respect of the lessor's title or otherwise) adverse to or in derogation of the title of the first registered proprietor, and subsisting or capable of arising at the time of the registration of such proprietor, but save as aforesaid shall, when registered, have the same effect as it would have had if the land had been registered with an absolute title.

(5) Where any such disposition is made without valuable consideration it shall, so far as the transferee or underlessee is concerned, be subject to any minor interests subject to which the transferor or sublessor held the same; but, save as aforesaid, shall, when registered, in all respects, and in particular as respects any registered dealings on the part of the transferee or underlessee, have the same effect as if the disposition had been made for valuable consideration.

24. Implied covenants on transfers of leaseholds.

(1) On the transfer, otherwise than by way of underlease, of any leasehold interest in land under this Act, unless there be an entry on the register negativing such implication, there shall be implied—

(a) on the part of the transferor, a covenant with the transferee that, notwithstanding anything by such transferor done, omitted, or knowingly suffered, the rent, covenants, and conditions reserved and contained by and in the registered lease, and on the part of the lessee to be paid, performed, and observed have been so paid, performed, and observed up to the date of the transfer; and

(b) on the part of the transferee, a covenant with the transferor, that during the residue of the term the transferee and the persons deriving title under him will pay, perform, and observe the rent, covenants, and conditions by and in the registered lease reserved and contained, and on the part of the lessee to be paid, performed, and observed, and will keep the transferor and the persons deriving title under him indemnified against all actions, expenses, and claims on account of the non-payment of the said rent or any part thereof, or the breach of the said covenants or conditions, or any of them.

(2) On a transfer of part of the land held under a lease, the covenant implied on the part of the transferee by this section shall be limited to the payment of the apportioned rent, if any, and the performance and observance of the covenants by the lessee and conditions in the registered lease so far only as they affect the part transferred. Where the transferor remains owner of part of the land comprised in the lease, there shall also be implied on his part, as respects the part retained, a covenant with the transferee similar to that implied on the part of the transferee under this subsection.

Subsidiary Provisions

46. Determination or variation of leases, incumbrances, &c.

The registrar shall, on proof to his satisfaction of—

(a) the determination of any lease, rentcharge, or other estate or interest the title to which is registered under this Act; or

(b) the discharge or determination (whole or partial) or variation of any lease, incumbrance, rentcharge, easement, right or other interest in land which is noted on the register as an incumbrance,

notify in the prescribed manner on the register the determination (whole or partial) or variation of such lease or other interest.

PART IV
NOTICES, CAUTIONS, INHIBITIONS AND RESTRICTIONS
Notices

48. Registration of notice of lease.

(1) Any lessee or other person entitled to or interested in a lease of registered land, where the term granted is not an overriding interest, may apply to the registrar to register notice of such lease in the prescribed manner, and when so registered, every proprietor and the persons deriving title under him shall be deemed to be affected with notice of such lease, as being an incumbrance on the registered land in respect of which the notice is entered:

Provided that a proprietor of a charge or incumbrance registered or protected on the register prior to the registration of such notice shall not be deemed to be so affected by the notice unless such proprietor is, by reason of the lease having been made under a statutory or other power or by reason of his concurrence or otherwise, bound by the terms of the lease.

(2) In order to register notice of a lease, if the proprietor of the registered land affected does not concur in the registration thereof, the applicant shall obtain an order of the court authorising the registration of notice of the lease, and shall deliver the order to the registrar, accompanied with the original lease or a copy thereof, and thereupon the registrar shall make a note in the register identifying the lease or copy so deposited, and the lease or copy so deposited shall be deemed to be the instrument of which notice is given; but if the proprietor concurs in the notice being registered, notice may be entered in such manner as may be agreed upon:

Provided that, where the lease is binding on the proprietor of the land, neither the concurrence of such proprietor nor an order of the court shall be required.

Protection of various Interests

59. Writs, orders, deeds of arrangement, pending actions, &c.

(1) A writ, order, deed of arrangement, pending action, or other interest which in the case of unregistered land may be protected by registration under the Land Charges Act, 1925, shall, where the land affected or the charge securing the debt affected is registered, be protected only by lodging a creditor's notice, a bankruptcy inhibition or a caution against dealings with the land or the charge.

(2) Registration of a land charge (other than a local land charge) shall, where the land affected is registered, be effected only by registering under this Act a notice caution or other prescribed entry:

Provided that before a land charge including a local land charge affecting registered land (being a charge to secure money) is realised, it shall be registered and take effect as a registered charge under this Act in the prescribed manner, without prejudice to the priority conferred by the land charge.

(4) When a land charge protected by notice has been discharged as to all or any part of the land comprised therein, the notices relating thereto and to all devolutions of and dealings therewith shall be vacated as to the registered land affected by the discharge.

(5) The foregoing provisions of this section shall apply only to writs and orders, deeds of arrangement, pending actions and land charges which if the land were unregistered would for purposes of protection be required to be registered or re-registered after the commencement of this Act under the Land Charges Act, 1925; and for the purposes of this section a land charge does not include a puisne mortgage.

(6) Subject to the provisions of this Act relating to fraud and to the title of a trustee in bankruptcy, a purchaser acquiring title under a registered disposition, shall not be concerned with any pending action, writ, order, deed of arrangement, or other document, matter, or claim (not being an overriding interest or a charge for capital

transfer tax subject to which the disposition takes effect under section 73 of this Act) which is not protected by a caution or other entry on the register, whether he has or has not notice thereof, express, implied, or constructive.

(7)   In this section references to registration under the Land Charges Act, 1925, apply to any registration made under any other statute which, in the case of unregistered land, is by the Land Charges Act, 1925, to have effect as if the registration had been made under that Act.

PART VI
GENERAL PROVISIONS AS TO REGISTRATION AND THE EFFECT THEREOF

69.   Effect of registration on the legal estate.

(1)   The proprietor of land (whether he was registered before or after the commencement of this Act) shall be deemed to have vested in him without any conveyance, where the registered land is freehold, the legal estate in fee simple in possession, and where the registered land is leasehold the legal term created by the registered lease, but subject to the overriding interests, if any, including any mortgage term or charge by way of legal mortgage created by or under the Law of Property Act, 1925, or this Act or otherwise which has priority to the registered estate.

(2)   Where any legal estate or term left outstanding at the date of first registration (whether before or after the commencement of this Act), or disposed of or created under section forty-nine of the Land Transfer Act, 1875, before the commencement of this Act, becomes satisfied, or the proprietor of the land becomes entitled to require the same to be vested in or surrendered to him, and the entry, if any, for protecting the same on the register has been cancelled, the same shall thereupon, without any conveyance, vest in the proprietor of the land, as if the same had been conveyed or surrendered to him as the case may be.

(3)   If and when any person is registered as first proprietor of land in a compulsory area after the commencement of this Act, the provisions of the Law of Property Act, 1925, for getting in legal estates shall apply to any legal estate in the land which was expressed to be conveyed or created in favour of a purchaser or lessee before the commencement of this Act but which failed to pass or to be created by reason of the omission of such purchaser or lessee to be registered as proprietor of the land under the Land Transfer Acts, 1875 and 1897, and shall operate to vest that legal estate in the person so registered as proprietor on his registration, but subject to any mortgage term or charge by way of legal mortgage having priority thereto.

(4)   The estate for the time being vested in the proprietor shall only be capable of being disposed of or dealt with by him in manner authorised by this Act.

(5)   Nothing in this section operates to render valid a lease registered with possessory or good leasehold title.

70.   Liability of registered land to overriding interests.

(1)   All registered land shall, unless under the provisions of this Act the contrary is expressed on the register, be deemed to be subject to such of the following overriding interests as may be for the time being subsisting in reference thereto, and such interests shall not be treated as incumbrances within the meaning of this Act, (that is to say):—

(a)   Rights of common, drainage rights, customary rights (until extinguished), public rights, profits à prendre, rights of sheepwalk, rights of way, watercourses, rights of water, and other easements not being equitable easements required to be protected by notice on the register;

(b)   Liability to repair highways by reason of tenure, quit-rents, crown rents, heriots, and other rents and charges (until extinguished) having their origin in tenure;

(c)   Liability to repair the chancel of any church;

    (d)   Liability in respect of embankments, and sea and river walls;

    (e)   payments in lieu of tithe, and charges or annuities payable for the redemption of tithe rentcharges;

    (f)   Subject to the provisions of this Act, rights acquired or in course of being acquired under the Limitation Acts;

    (g)   The rights of every person in actual occupation of the land or in receipt of the rents and profits thereof, save where enquiry is made of such person and the rights are not disclosed;

    (h)   In the case of a possessory, qualified, or good leasehold title, all estates, rights, interests, and powers excepted from the effect of registration;

    (i)   Rights under local land charges unless and until registered or protected on the register in the prescribed manner;

    (j)   Rights of fishing and sporting, seignorial and manorial rights of all descriptions (until extinguished), and franchises;

    (k)   Leases granted for a term not exceeding twenty one years;

    (l)   In respect of land registered before the commencement of this Act, rights to mines and minerals, and rights of entry, search, and user, and other rights and reservations incidental to or required for the purpose of giving full effect to the enjoyment of rights to mines and minerals or of property in mines or minerals, being rights which, where the title was first registered before the first day of January, eighteen hundred and ninety-eight, were created before that date, and where the title was first registered after the thirty-first day of December, eighteen hundred and ninety-seven, were created before the date of first registration:

Provided that, where it is proved to the satisfaction of the registrar that any land registered or about to be registered is exempt from land tax, or tithe rentcharge or payments in lieu of tithe, or from charges or annuities payable for the redemption of tithe rentcharge, the registrar may notify the fact on the register in the prescribed manner.

(2)   Where at the time of first registration any easement, right, privilege, or benefit created by an instrument and appearing on the title adversely affects the land, the registrar shall enter a note thereof on the register.

(3)   Where the existence of any overriding interest mentioned in this section is proved to the satisfaction of the registrar or admitted, he may (subject to any prescribed exceptions) enter notice of the same or of a claim thereto on the register, but no claim to an easement, right, or privilege not created by an instrument shall be noted against the title to the servient land if the proprietor of such land (after the prescribed notice is given to him) shows sufficient cause to the contrary.

77.   Conversion of title.

(1)   Where land is registered with a good leasehold title, or satisfies the conditions for such registration under this section, the registrar may, and on application by the proprietor shall, if he is satisfied as to the title to the freehold and the title to any intermediate leasehold, enter the title as absolute.

(2)   Where land is registered with a possessory title, the registrar may, and on application by the proprietor shall—

    (a)   if he is satisfied as to the title, or

    (b)   if the land has been so registered for at least twelve years and he is satisfied that the proprietor is in possession,

enter the title in the case of freehold land as absolute and in the case of leasehold land as good leasehold.

(3)   Where land is registered with a qualified title, the registrar may, and on application by the proprietor shall, if he is satisfied as to the title, enter it in the case of freehold land as absolute and in the case of leasehold land as good leasehold.

(4) If any claim adverse to the title of the proprietor has been made, an entry shall not be made in the register under this section unless and until the claim has been disposed of.

(5) No fee shall be charged for the making of an entry in the register under this section at the instance of the registrar or on an application by the proprietor made in connection with a transfer for valuable consideration of the land to which the application relates.

(6) Any person, other than the proprietor, who suffers loss by reason of any entry on the register made by virtue of this section shall be entitled to be indemnified under this Act as if a mistake had been made in the register.

PART XI
COMPULSORY REGISTRATION

123. Effect of Act in areas where registration is compulsory.

(1) In any area in which an Order in Council declaring that registration of title to land within that area is to be compulsory on sale is for the time being in force, every conveyance on sale of freehold land and every grant of a term of years absolute of more than twenty-one years from the date of delivery of the grant, and every assignment on sale of leasehold land held for a term of years absolute having more than twenty-one years to run from the date of delivery of the assignment, shall (save as hereinafter provided), on the expiration of two months from the date thereof or of any authorised extension of that period, become void so far as regards the grant or conveyance of the legal estate in the freehold or leasehold land comprised in the conveyance, grant, or assignment, or so much of such land as is situated within the area affected, unless the grantee (that is to say, the person who is entitled to be registered as proprietor of the freehold or leasehold land) or his successor in title or assign has in the meantime applied to be registered as proprietor of such land:

Provided that the registrar, or the court on appeal from the registrar, may, on the application of any persons interested in any particular case in which the registrar or the court is satisfied that the application for first registration cannot be made within the said period, or can only be made within that period by incurring unreasonable expense, or that the application has not been made within the said period by reason of some accident or other sufficient cause, make an order extending the said period; and if such order be made, then, upon the registration of the grantee or his successor or assign, a note of the order shall be endorsed on the conveyance, grant or assignment:

In the case of land in an area where, at the date of the commencement of this Act, registration of title is already compulsory on sale, this subsection shall apply to every such conveyance, grant, or assignment, executed on or after that date.

(2) Rules under this Act may provide for applying the provisions thereof to dealings with the land which may take place between the date of such conveyance, grant, or assignment and the date of application to register as if such dealings had taken place after the date of first registration, and for registration to be effected as of the date of the application to register.

(3) In this section the expressions "conveyance on sale" and "assignment on sale" mean an instrument made on sale by virtue whereof there is conferred or completed a title under which an application for registration as first proprietor of land may be made under this Act, and include a conveyance or assignment by way of exchange where money is paid for equality of exchange, but do not include an enfranchisement or extinguishment of manorial incidents, whether under the Law of Property Act, 1922, or otherwise, or an assignment or surrender of a lease to the owner of the immediate reversion containing a declaration that the term is to merge in such reversion.

LANDLORD AND TENANT ACT 1927
(1927, c. 36)

An Act to provide for the payment of compensation for improvements and goodwill to tenants of premises used for business purposes, or the grant of a new lease in lieu thereof; and to amend the law of landlord and tenant. [22 December 1927]

PART I
COMPENSATION FOR IMPROVEMENTS AND GOODWILL ON THE TERMINATION OF TENANCIES OF BUSINESS PREMISES

1. Tenant's right to compensation for improvements.

(1) Subject to the provisions of this Part of this Act, a tenant of a holding to which this Part of this Act applies shall, if a claim for the purpose is made in the prescribed manner and within the time limited by section forty-seven of the Landlord and Tenant Act 1954 be entitled, at the termination of the tenancy, on quitting his holding, to be paid by his landlord compensation in respect of any improvement (including the erection of any building) on his holding made by him or his predecessors in title, not being a trade or other fixture which the tenant is by law entitled to remove, which at the termination of the tenancy adds to the letting value of the holding:

Provided that the sum to be paid as compensation for any improvement shall not exceed—

(a) the net addition to the value of the holding as a whole which may be determined to be the direct result of the improvement; or

(b) the reasonable cost of carrying out the improvement at the termination of the tenancy, subject to a deduction of an amount equal to the cost (if any) of putting the works constituting the improvement into a reasonable state of repair, except so far as such cost is covered by the liability of the tenant under any covenant or agreement as to the repair of the premises.

(2) In determining the amount of such net addition as aforesaid, regard shall be had to the purposes for which it is intended that the premises shall be used after the termination of the tenancy, and if it is shown that it is intended to demolish or to make structural alterations in the premises or any part thereof or to use the premises for a different purpose, regard shall be had to the effect of such demolition, alteration or change of user on the additional value attributable to the improvement, and to the length of time likely to elapse between the termination of the tenancy and the demolition, alteration or change of user.

(3) In the absence of agreement between the parties, all questions as to the right to compensation under this section, or as to the amount thereof, shall be determined by the tribunal hereinafter mentioned, and if the tribunal determines that, on account of the intention to demolish or alter or to change the user of the premises, no compensation or a reduced amount of compensation shall be paid, the tribunal may authorise a further application for compensation to be made by the tenant if effect is not given to the intention within such time as may be fixed by the tribunal.

2. Limitation on tenant's right to compensation in certain cases.

(1) A tenant shall not be entitled to compensation under this Part of this Act—

(a) in respect of any improvement made before the commencement of this Act; or

(b) in respect of any improvement made in pursuance of a statutory obligation, or of any improvement which the tenant or his predecessors in title were under an obligation to make in pursuance of a contract entered into, whether before or after the passing of this Act, for valuable consideration, including a building lease; or

(c) in respect of any improvement made less than three years before the termination of the tenancy; or

(d) if within two months after the making of the claim under section one, subsection (1), of this Act the landlord serves on the tenant notice that he is willing and able to grant to the tenant, or obtain the grant to him of, a renewal of the tenancy at such rent and for such term as, failing agreement, the tribunal may consider reasonable; and, where such a notice is so served and the tenant does not within one month from the service of the notice send to the landlord an acceptance in writing of the offer, the tenant shall be deemed to have declined the offer.

(2) Where an offer of the renewal of a tenancy by the landlord under this section is accepted by the tenant, the rent fixed by the tribunal shall be the rent which in the opinion of the tribunal a willing lessee other than the tenant would agree to give and a willing lessor would agree to accept for the premises, having regard to the terms of the lease, but irrespective of the value attributable to the improvement in respect of which compensation would have been payable.

(3) The tribunal in determining the compensation for an improvement shall in reduction of the tenant's claim take into consideration any benefits which the tenant or his predecessors in title may have received from the landlord or his predecessors in title in consideration expressly or impliedly of the improvement.

3. Landlord's right to object.

(1) Where a tenant of a holding to which this Part of this Act applies proposes to make an improvement on his holding, he shall serve on his landlord notice of his intention to make such improvement, together with a specification and plan showing the proposed improvement and the part of the existing premises affected thereby, and if the landlord, within three months after the service of the notice, serves on the tenant notice of objection, the tenant may, in the prescribed manner, apply to the tribunal, and the tribunal may, after ascertaining that notice of such intention has been served upon any superior landlords interested and after giving such persons an opportunity of being heard, if satisfied that the improvement—

(a) is of such a nature as to be calculated to add to the letting value of the holding at the termination of the tenancy; and

(b) is reasonable and suitable to the character thereof; and

(c) will not diminish the value of any other property belonging to the same landlord, or to any superior landlord from whom the immediate landlord of the tenant directly or indirectly holds;

and after making such modifications (if any) in the specification or plan as the tribunal thinks fit, or imposing such other conditions as the tribunal may think reasonable, certify in the prescribed manner that the improvement is a proper improvement.

Provided that, if the landlord proves that he has offered to execute the improvement himself in consideration of a reasonable increase of rent, or of such increase of rent as the tribunal may determine, the tribunal shall not give a certificate under this section unless it is subsequently shown to the satisfaction of the tribunal that the landlord has failed to carry out his undertaking.

(2) In considering whether the improvement is reasonable and suitable to the character of the holding, the tribunal shall have regard to any evidence brought before it by the landlord or any superior landlord (but not any other person) that the improvement is calculated to injure the amenity or convenience of the neighbourhood.

(3) The tenant shall, at the request of any superior landlord or at the request of the tribunal, supply such copies of the plans and specifications of the proposed improvement as may be required.

(4) Where no such notice of objection as aforesaid to a proposed improvement has been served within the time allowed by this section, or where the tribunal has certified an improvement to be a proper improvement, it shall be lawful for the tenant as against the immediate and any superior landlord to execute the improvement according to the

plan and specification served on the landlord, or according to such plan and specification as modified by the tribunal or by agreement between the tenant and the landlord or landlords affected, anything in any lease of the premises to the contrary notwithstanding:

Provided that nothing in this subsection shall authorise a tenant to execute an improvement in contravention of any restriction created or imposed—

    (a)   for naval, military or air force purposes;

    (b)   for civil aviation purposes under the powers of the Air Navigation Act, 1920;

    (c)   for securing any rights of the public over the foreshore or bed of the sea.

(5)   A tenant shall not be entitled to claim compensation under this Part of this Act in respect of any improvement unless he has, or his predecessors in title have, served notice of the proposal to make the improvement under this section, and (in case the landlord has served notice of objection thereto) the improvement has been certified by the tribunal to be a proper improvement and the tenant has complied with the conditions, if any, imposed by the tribunal, nor unless the improvement is completed within such time after the service on the landlord of the notice of the proposed improvement as may be agreed between the tenant and the landlord or may be fixed by the tribunal, and where proceedings have been taken before the tribunal, the tribunal may defer making any order as to costs until the expiration of the time so fixed for the completion of the improvement.

(6)   Where a tenant has executed an improvement of which he has served notice in accordance with this section and with respect to which either no notice of objection has been served by the landlord or a certificate that it is a proper improvement has been obtained from the tribunal, the tenant may require the landlord to furnish to him a certificate that the improvement has been duly executed; and if the landlord refuses or fails within one month after the service of the requisition to do so, the tenant may apply to the tribunal who, if satisfied that the improvement has been duly executed, shall give a certificate to that effect.

Where the landlord furnishes such a certificate, the tenant shall be liable to pay any reasonable expenses incurred for the purpose by the landlord, and if any question arises as to the reasonableness of such expenses, it shall be determined by the tribunal.

8.   Rights of mesne landlords.

(1)   Where, in the case of any holding, there are several persons standing in the relation to each other of lessor and lessee, the following provisions shall apply:—

Any mesne landlord who has paid or is liable to pay compensation under this Part of this Act shall, at the end of his term, be entitled to compensation from his immediate landlord in like manner and on the same conditions as if he had himself made the improvement in question, except that it shall be sufficient if the claim for compensation is made at least two months before the expiration of his term:

A mesne landlord shall not be entitled to make a claim under this section unless he has, within the time and in the manner prescribed, served on his immediate superior landlord copies of all documents relating to proposed improvements and claims which have been sent to him in pursuance of this Part of this Act:

Where such copies are so served, the said superior landlord shall have, in addition to the mesne landlord, the powers conferred by or in pursuance of this Part of this Act in like manner as if he were the immediate landlord of the occupying tenant, and shall, in the manner and to the extent prescribed, be at liberty to appear before the tribunal and shall be bound by the proceedings:

(2)   In this section, references to a landlord shall include references to his predecessors in title.

9.   Restriction on contracting out.

This Part of this Act shall apply notwithstanding any contract to the contrary, being a contract made at any time after the eighth day of February, nineteen hundred and twenty-seven:

10. Right of entry.

The landlord of a holding to which this Part of this Act applies, or any person authorised by him may at all reasonable times enter on the holding or any part of it, for the purpose of executing any improvement he has undertaken to execute and of making any inspection of the premises which may reasonably be required for the purposes of this Part of this Act.

11. Right to make deductions.

(1) Out of any money payable to a tenant by way of compensation under this Part of this Act, the landlord shall be entitled to deduct any sum due to him from the tenant under or in respect of the tenancy.

(2) Out of any money due to the landlord from the tenant under or in respect of the tenancy, the tenant shall be entitled to deduct any sum payable to him by the landlord by way of compensation under this Part of this Act.

12. Application of 13 & 14 Geo. 5. c. 9. s. 20.

Section twenty of the Agricultural Holdings Act, 1923 (which relates to charges in respect of money paid for compensation), as set out and modified in the First Schedule to this Act, shall apply to the case of money paid for compensation under this Part of this Act, including any proper costs, charges, or expenses incurred by a landlord in opposing any proposal by a tenant to execute an improvement, or in contesting a claim for compensation, and to money expended by a landlord in executing an improvement the notice of a proposal to execute which has been served on him by a tenant under this Part of this Act.

13. Power to apply and raise capital money.

(1) Capital money arising under the Settled Land Act, 1925 (either as originally enacted or as applied in relation to trusts for sale by section twenty-eight of the Law of Property Act, 1925), or under the University and College Estates Act, 1925, may be applied—

(a) in payment as for an improvement authorised by the Act of any money expended and costs incurred by a landlord under or in pursuance of this Part of this Act in or about the execution of any improvement;

(b) in payment of any sum due to a tenant under this Part of this Act in respect of compensation for an improvement and any costs, charges, and expenses incidental thereto;

(c) in payment of the costs, charges, and expenses of opposing any proposal by a tenant to execute an improvement.

(2) The satisfaction of a claim for such compensation as aforesaid shall be included amongst the purposes for which a tenant for life, statutory owner, trustee for sale, or personal representative may raise money under section seventy-one of the Settled Land Act, 1925.

(3) Where the landlord liable to pay compensation for an improvement is a tenant for life or in a fiduciary position, he may require the sum payable as compensation and any costs, charges, and expenses incidental thereto, to be paid out of any capital money held on the same trusts as the settled land.

In this subsection "capital money" includes any personal estate held on the same trusts as the land, and "settled land" includes land held on trust for sale or vested in a personal representative.

14. Power to sell or grant leases notwithstanding restrictions.

Where the powers of a landlord to sell or grant leases are subject to any statutory or other restrictions, he shall, notwithstanding any such restrictions or any rule of law to the contrary, be entitled to offer to sell or grant any such reversion or lease as would under this Part of this Act relieve him from liability to pay compensation thereunder, and to convey and grant the same, and to execute any lease which he may be ordered to grant under this Part of this Act.

15. Provisions as to reversionary leases.

(1) Where the amount which a landlord is liable to pay as compensation for an improvement under this Part of this Act has been determined by agreement or by an award of the tribunal, and the landlord had before the passing of this Act granted or agreed to grant a reversionary lease commencing on or after the termination of the then existing tenancy, the rent payable under the reversionary lease shall, if the tribunal so directs, be increased by such amount as, failing agreement, may be determined by the tribunal having regard to the addition to the letting value of the holding attributable to the improvement:

Provided that no such increase shall be permissible unless the landlord has served or caused to be served on the reversionary lessee copies of all documents relating to the improvement when proposed which were sent to the landlord in pursuance of this Part of this Act.

(2) The reversionary lessee shall have the same right of objection to the proposed improvement and of appearing and being heard at any proceedings before the tribunal relative to the proposed improvement as if he were a superior landlord, and if the amount of compensation for the improvement is determined by the tribunal, any question as to the increase of rent under the reversionary lease shall, where practicable, be settled in the course of the same proceedings.

16. Landlord's right to reimbursement of increased taxes, rates or insurance premiums.

Where the landlord is liable to pay any rates (including water rate) in respect of any premises comprised in a holding, or has undertaken to pay the premiums on any fire insurance policy on any such premises, and in consequence of any improvement executed by the tenant on the premises under this Act the assessment of the premises or the rate of premium on the policy is increased, the tenant shall be liable to pay to the landlord sums equal to the amount by which—

(a) the rates payable by the landlord are increased by reason of the increase of such assessment;

(b) the fire premium payable by the landlord is increased by reason of the increase in the rate of premium;

and the sums so payable by the tenant shall be deemed to be in the nature of rent and shall be recoverable as such from the tenant.

17. Holdings to which Part I applies.

(1) The holdings to which this Part of this Act applies are any premises held under a lease, other than a mining lease, made whether before or after the commencement of this Act, and used wholly or partly for carrying on thereat any trade or business, and not being agricultural holdings within the meaning of the Agricultural Holdings Act 1986.

(2) This Part of this Act shall not apply to any holding let to a tenant as the holder of any office, appointment or employment, from the landlord, and continuing so long as the tenant holds such office, appointment or employment, but in the case of a tenancy created after the commencement of this Act, only if the contract is in writing and expresses the purpose for which the tenancy is created.

(3) For the purposes of this section, premises shall not be deemed to be premises used for carrying on thereat a trade or business—

(a) by reason of their being used for the purpose of carrying on thereat any profession;

(b) by reason that the tenant thereof carries on the business of subletting the premises as residential flats, whether or not the provision of meals or any other service for the occupants of the flats is undertaken by the tenant:

Provided that, so far as this Part of this Act relates to improvements, premises regularly used for carrying on a profession shall be deemed to be premises used for carrying on a trade or business.

(4) In the case of premises used partly for purposes of a trade or business and partly for other purposes, this Part of this Act shall apply to improvements only if and so far as they are improvements in relation to the trade or business.

PART II
GENERAL AMENDMENTS OF THE LAW OF LANDLORD AND TENANT

18. Provisions as to covenents to repair.

(1) Damages for a breach of a covenant or agreement to keep or put premises in repair during the currency of a lease, or to leave or put premises in repair at the termination of a lease, whether such covenant or agreement is expressed or implied, and whether general or specific, shall in no case exceed the amount (if any) by which the value of the reversion (whether immediate or not) in the premises is diminished owing to the breach of such covenant or agreement as aforesaid; and in particular no damage shall be recovered for a breach of any such covenant or agreement to leave or put premises in repair at the termination of a lease, if it is shown that the premises, in whatever state of repair they might be, would at or shortly after the termination of the tenancy have been or be pulled down, or such structural alterations made therein as would render valueless the repairs covered by the covenant or agreement.

(2) A right of re-entry or forfeiture for a breach of any such covenant or agreement as aforesaid shall not be enforceable, by action or otherwise, unless the lessor proves that the fact that such a notice as is required by section one hundred and forty-six of the Law of Property Act, 1925, had been served on the lessee was known either—

(a) to the lessee; or

(b) to an under-lessee holding under an under-lease which reserved a nominal reversion only to the lessee; or

(c) to the person who last paid the rent due under the lease either on his own behalf or as agent for the lessee or under-lessee;

and that a time reasonably sufficient to enable the repairs to be executed had elapsed since the time when the fact of the service of the notice came to the knowledge of any such person.

Where a notice has been sent by registered post addressed to a person at his last known place of abode in the United Kingdom, then, for the purposes of this subsection, that person shall be deemed, unless the contrary is proved, to have had knowledge of the fact that the notice had been served as from the time at which the letter would have been delivered in the ordinary course of post.

This subsection shall be construed as one with section one hundred and forty-six of the Law of Property Act, 1925.

(3) This section applies whether the lease was created before or after the commencement of this Act.

19. Provisions as to covenants not to assign, &c. without licence or consent.

(1) In all leases whether made before or after the commencement of this Act containing a covenant condition or agreement against assigning, underletting, charging or parting with the possession of demised premises or any part thereof without licence or consent, such covenant condition or agreement shall, notwithstanding any express provision to the contrary, be deemed to be subject—

(a)   to a proviso to the effect that such licence or consent is not to be unreasonably withheld, but this proviso does not preclude the right of the landlord to require payment of a reasonable sum in respect of any legal or other expenses incurred in connection with such licence or consent; and

(b)   (if the lease is for more than forty years, and is made in consideration wholly or partially of the erection, or the substantial improvement, addition or alteration of buildings, and the lessor is not a Government department or local or public authority, or a statutory or public utility company) to a proviso to the effect that in the case of any assignment, under-letting, charging or parting with the possession (whether by the holders of the lease or any under-tenant whether immediate or not) effected more than seven years before the end of the term no consent or licence shall be required, if notice in writing of the transaction is given to the lessor within six months after the transaction is effected.

(2)   In all leases whether made before or after the commencement of this Act containing a covenant condition or agreement against the making of improvements without licence or consent, such covenant condition or agreement shall be deemed, notwithstanding any express provision to the contrary, to be subject to a proviso that such licence or consent is not to be unreasonably withheld; but this proviso does not preclude the right to require as a condition of such licence or consent the payment of a reasonable sum in respect of any damage to or diminution in the value of the premises or any neighbouring premises belonging to the landlord, and of any legal or other expenses properly incurred in connection with such licence or consent nor, in the case of an improvement which does not add to the letting value of the holding, does it preclude the right to require as a condition of such licence or consent, where such a requirement would be reasonable, an undertaking on the part of the tenant to reinstate the premises in the condition in which they were before the improvement was executed.

(3)   In all leases whether made before or after the commencement of this Act containing a covenant condition or agreement against the alteration of the user of the demised premises, without licence or consent, such covenant condition or agreement shall, if the alteration does not involve any structural alteration of the premises, be deemed, notwithstanding any express provision to the contrary, to be subject to a proviso that no fine or sum of money in the nature of a fine, whether by way of increase of rent or otherwise, shall be payable for or in respect of such licence or consent; but this proviso does not preclude the right of the landlord to require payment of a reasonable sum in respect of any damage to or diminution in the value of the premises or any neighbouring premises belonging to him and of any legal or other expenses incurred in connection with such licence or consent.

Where a dispute as to the reasonableness of any such sum has been determined by a court of competent jurisdiction, the landlord shall be bound to grant the licence or consent on payment of the sum so determined to be reasonable.

(4)   This section shall not apply to leases of agricultural holdings within the meaning of the Agricultural Holdings Act 1986, and paragraph (b) of subsection (1), subsection (2) and subsection (3) of this section shall not apply to mining leases.

20.   Apportionment of rents.

(1)   An order of apportionment of a rent reserved by a lease or any such other rent or payment as is mentioned in section ten of the Inclosure Act, 1854, may be made by the Minister of Agriculture and Fisheries under sections ten to fourteen of that Act, on the application of any person interested in the rent or payment, or any part thereof, or in the land in respect of which such rent or payment is payable, without the concurrence of any other person:

Provided that the Minister may in any such case, on the application of any person entitled to the rent or payment or any part thereof, require as a condition of making the order that any apportioned part of the rent or payment which does not exceed the yearly sum of £5 shall be redeemed forthwith in accordance with sections 8 to 10 of the Rentcharges Act 1977 (which, for the purposes of this section, shall have effect with the necessary modifications).

(1A)   An order of apportionment under sections 10 to 14 of the said Act of 1854 may provide for the amount apportioned to any part of the land in respect of which the rent or payment is payable to be nil.

(2)   Where the reason for the application was due to any action taken by a person other than the applicant, the Minister shall, notwithstanding anything in section fourteen of the Inclosure Act, 1854, have power to direct by whom and in what manner the expenses of the application or any part thereof are to be paid.

PART III
GENERAL

21.   Provisions as to tribunal.

The tribunal for the purposes of Part I of this Act shall be the court exercising jurisdiction in accordance with the provisions of section sixty-three of the Landlord and Tenant Act 1954.

23.   Service of notices.

(1)   Any notice, request, demand or other instrument under this Act shall be in writing and may be served on the person on whom it is to be served either personally, or by leaving it for him at his last known place of abode in England or Wales, or by sending it through the post in a registered letter addressed to him there, or, in the case of a local or public authority or a statutory or a public utility company, to the secretary or other proper officer at the principal office of such authority or company, and in the case of a notice to a landlord, the person on whom it is to be served shall include any agent of the landlord duly authorised in that behalf.

(2)   Unless or until a tenant of a holding shall have received notice that the person theretofore entitled to the rents and profits of the holding (hereinafter referred to as "the original landlord") has ceased to be so entitled, and also notice of the name and address of the person who has become entitled to such rents and profits, any claim, notice, request, demand, or other instrument which the tenant shall serve upon or deliver to the original landlord shall be deemed to have been served upon or delivered to the landlord of such holding.

24.   Application to Crown, Duchy, ecclesiastical and charity lands.

(1)   This Act shall apply to land belonging to His Majesty in right of the Crown or the Duchy of Lancaster and to land belonging to the Duchy of Cornwall, and to land belonging to any Government department, and for that purpose the provisions of the Agricultural Holdings Act, 1923, relating to Crown and Duchy lands, as set out and adapted in Part I of the Second Schedule to this Act, shall have effect.

(2)   The provisions of the Agricultural Holdings Act, 1923, with respect to the application of that Act to ecclesiastical and charity lands, as set out and adapted in Part II of the Second Schedule to this Act, shall apply for the purposes of this Act.

(4)   Where any land is vested in the official custodian for charities in trust for any charity, the trustees of the charity and not the custodian shall be deemed to be the landlord for the purposes of this Act.

25.   Interpretation.

(1)   For the purposes of this Act, unless the context otherwise requires—

The expression "tenant" means any person entitled in possession to the holding under any contract of tenancy, whether the interest of such tenant was acquired by original contract, assignment, operation of law or otherwise;

The expression "landlord" means any person who under a lease is, as between himself and the tenant or other lessee, for the time being entitled to the rents and profits of the demised premises payable under the lease;

The expression "predecessor in title" in relation to a tenant or landlord means any person through whom the tenant or landlord has derived title, whether by assignment, by will, by intestacy, or by operation of law;

The expression "lease" means a lease, under-lease or other tenancy, assignment operating as a lease or under-lease, or an agreement for such lease, under-lease tenancy, or assignment;

The expression "mining lease" means a lease for any mining purpose or purposes connected therewith, and "mining purposes" include the sinking and searching for, winning, working, getting, making merchantable, smelting or otherwise converting or working for the purposes of any manufacture, carrying away, and disposing of mines and minerals, in or under land, and the erection of buildings, and the execution of engineering and other works suitable for those purposes;

The expression "term of years absolute" has the same meaning as in the Law of Property Act, 1925;

The expression "statutory company" means any company constituted by or under an Act of Parliament to construct, work or carry on any tramway, hydraulic power, dock, canal or railway undertaking; and the expression "public utility company" means any company within the meaning of the Companies (Consolidation) Act, 1908, or a society registered under the Industrial and Provident Societies Acts, 1893 to 1913, carrying on any such undertaking;

The expression "prescribed" means prescribed by County Court Rules, except that in relation to proceedings before the High Court, it means prescribed by rules of the Supreme Court.

(2)   The designation of landlord and tenant shall continue to apply to the parties until the conclusion of any proceedings taken under or in pursuance of this Act in respect of compensation.

26.   Short title, commencement and extent.

(1)   This Act may be cited as the Landlord and Tenant Act, 1927.

(3)   This Act shall extend to England and Wales only.

SCHEDULES

Section 12.   FIRST SCHEDULE

PROVISIONS AS TO CHARGES

(1)   A landlord, on paying to the tenant the amount due to him under Part I of this Act, in respect of compensation for an improvement under that Part, or on expending after notice given in accordance with that Part such amount as may be necessary to execute an improvement, shall be entitled to obtain from the Minister of Agriculture and Fisheries (hereinafter referred to as the Minister) an order in favour of himself and the persons deriving title under him charging the holding, or any part thereof, with repayment of the amount paid or expended, including any proper costs, charges or expenses incurred by a landlord in opposing any proposal by a tenant to execute an improvement or in contesting a claim for compensation, and of all costs properly incurred by him in obtaining the charge, with such interest, and by such instalments, and with such directions for giving effect to the charge, as the Minister thinks fit.

(2)   Where the landlord obtaining the charge is not an absolute owner of the holding for his own benefit, no instalment or interest shall be made payable after the time when

the improvement in respect whereof compensation is paid will, in the opinion of the Minister, have become exhausted.

(3)   Where the estate or interest of a landlord is determinable or liable to forfeiture by reason of his creating or suffering any charge thereon, that estate or interest shall not be determined or forfeited by reason of his obtaining such a charge, anything in any deed, will or other instrument to the contrary thereof notwithstanding.

(4)   The sum charged shall be a charge on the holding, or the part thereof charged, for the landlord's interest therein and for interests in the reversion immediately expectant on the termination of the lease; but so that, in any case where the landlord's interest is an interest in a leasehold, the charge shall not extend beyond that leasehold interest.

(5)   Any company now or hereafter incorporated by Parliament, and having power to advance money for the improvement of land, may take an assignment of any charge made under this Schedule, upon such terms and conditions as may be agreed upon between the company and the person entitled to the charge, and may assign any charge so acquired by them.

(6)   Where a charge may be made under this Schedule for compensation due under an award, the tribunal making the award shall, at the request and cost of the person entitled to obtain the charge, certify the amount to be charged and the term for which the charge may properly be made, having regard to the time at which each improvement in respect of which compensation is awarded is to be deemed to be exhausted.

(7)   A charge under this Schedule may be registered under section ten of the Land Charges Act, 1925, as a land charge of Class A.

Section 24.   SECOND SCHEDULE

PART I
APPLICATION TO CROWN AND DUCHY LAND

1.—(a)   With respect to any land belonging to His Majesty in right of the Crown, or to a Government department, for the purposes of this Act, the Commissioners of Crown Lands, or other the proper officer or body having charge of the land for the time being, or, in case there is no such officer or body, then such person as His Majesty may appoint in writing under the Royal Sign Manual, shall represent His Majesty, and shall be deemed to be the landlord.

2.—(a)   With respect to land belonging to His Majesty in right of the Duchy of Lancaster, for the purposes of this Act, the Chancellor of the Duchy shall represent His Majesty, and shall be deemed to be the landlord.

(b)   The amount of any compensation under Part I. of this Act payable by the Chancellor of the Duchy shall be raised and paid as an expense incurred in improvement of land belonging to His Majesty in right of the Duchy within section twenty-five of the Act of the Fifty-seventh year of King George the Third, chapter ninety-seven.

3.—(a)   With respect to land belonging to the Duchy of Cornwall, for the purposes of this Act, such person as the Duke of Cornwall, or the possessor for the time being of the Duchy of Cornwall appoints, shall represent the Duke of Cornwall or other the possessor aforesaid, and be deemed to be the landlord, and may do any act or thing under this Act which a landlord is authorised or required to do thereunder.

(b)   Any compensation under Part I. of this Act payable by the Duke of Cornwall, or other the possessor aforesaid, shall be paid, and advances therefor made, in the manner and subject to the provisions of section eight of the Duchy of Cornwall Management Act, 1863, with respect to improvements of land mentioned in that section.

PART II
APPLICATION TO ECCLESIASTICAL AND CHARITY LAND

1.—(a) Where lands are assigned or secured as the endowment of a see, the powers by this Act conferred on a landlord in respect of charging land shall not be exercised by the bishop in respect of those lands, except with the previous approval in writing of the Estates Committee of the Ecclesiastical Commissioners.

(c) The Ecclesiastical Commissioners may, if they think fit, on behalf of an ecclesiastical corporation, out of any money in their hands, pay to the tenant the amount of compensation due to him under Part I. of this Act, and thereupon they may, instead of the corporation obtain from the minister a charge on the holding in respect thereof in favour of themselves.

2. The powers by this Act conferred on a landlord in respect of charging land shall not be exercised by trustees for ecclesiastical or charitable purposes, except with the approval in writing of the Charity Commissioners or the Board of Education, as the case may require.

LEASEHOLD PROPERTY (REPAIRS) ACT 1938
(1 & 2 Geo. 6, c. 34)

An act to amend the law as to the enforcement by landlords of obligations to repair and similar obligations arising under leases.   [23 June 1938]

1. Restriction on enforcement of repairing covenants in long leases of small houses.

(1) Where a lessor serves on a lessee under subsection (1) of section one hundred and forty-six of the Law of Property Act, 1925, a notice that relates to a breach of a covenant or agreement to keep or put in repair during the currency of the lease all or any of the property comprised in the lease and at the date of the service of the notice three years or more of the term of the lease remain unexpired, the lessee may within twenty-eight days from that date serve on the lessor a counter-notice to the effect that he claims the benefit of this Act.

(2) A right to damages for a breach of such a covenant as aforesaid shall not be enforceable by action commenced at any time at which three years or more of the term of the lease remain unexpired unless the lessor has served on the lessee not less than one month before the commencement of the action such a notice as is specified in subsection (1) of section one hundred and forty-six of the Law of Property Act, 1925, and where a notice is served under this subsection, the lessee may, within twenty-eight days from the date of the service thereof, serve on the lessor a counter-notice to the effect that he claims the benefit of this Act.

(3) Where a counter-notice is served by a lessee under this section, then, notwithstanding anything in any enactment or rule of law, no proceedings, by action or otherwise, shall be taken by the lessor for the enforcement of any right of re-entry or forfeiture under any proviso or stipulation in the lease for breach of the covenant or agreement in question, or for damages for breach thereof, otherwise than with the leave of the court.

(4) A notice served under subsection (1) of section one hundred and forty-six of the Law of Property Act, 1925, in the circumstances specified in subsection (1) of this section, and a notice served under subsection (2) of this section shall not be valid unless it contains a statement, in characters not less conspicuous than those used in any other part of the notice, to the effect that the lessee is entitled under this Act to serve on the lessor a counter-notice claiming the benefit of this Act, and a statement in the like characters specifying the time within which, and the manner in which, under this Act a counter-notice may be served and specifying the name and address for service of the lessor.

(5) Leave for the purposes of this section shall not be given unless the lessor proves—

(a) that the immediate remedying of the breach in question is requisite for preventing substantial diminution in the value of his reversion, or that the value thereof has been substantially diminished by the breach;

(b) that the immediate remedying of the breach is required for giving effect in relation to the premises to the purposes of any enactment, or of any byelaw or other provision having effect under an enactment, or for giving effect to any order of a court or requirement of any authority under any enactment or any such byelaw or other provision as aforesaid;

(c) in a case in which the lessee is not in occupation of the whole of the premises as respects which the covenant or agreement is proposed to be enforced, that the immediate remedying of the breach is required in the interests of the occupier of those premises or of part thereof;

(d) that the breach can be immediately remedied at an expense that is relatively small in comparison with the much greater expense that would probably be occasioned by postponement of the necessary work; or

(e) special circumstances which in the opinion of the court, render it just and equitable that leave should be given.

(6) The court may, in granting or in refusing leave for the purposes of this section, impose such terms and conditions on the lessor or on the lessee as it may think fit.

2. Restriction on right to recover expenses of survey, &c.

A lessor on whom a counter-notice is served under the preceding section shall not be entitled to the benefit of subsection (3) of section one hundred and forty-six of the Law of Property Act, 1925, (which relates to costs and expenses incurred by a lessor in reference to breaches of covenant), so far as regards any costs or expenses incurred in reference to the breach in question, unless he makes an application for leave for the purposes of the preceding section, and on such an application the court shall have power to direct whether and to what extent the lessor is to be entitled to the benefit thereof.

3. Saving for obligation to repair on taking possession.

This Act shall not apply to a breach of a covenant or agreement in so far as it imposes on the lessee an obligation to put premises in repair that is to be performed upon the lessee taking possession of the premises or within a reasonable time thereafter.

5. Application to past breaches.

This Act applies to leases created, and to breaches occurring, before or after the commencement of this Act.

6. Court having jurisdiction under this Act.

(1) In this Act the expression "the court" means the county court, except in a case in which any proceedings by action for which leave may be given would have to be taken in a court other than the county court, and means in the said excepted case that other court.

7. Application of certain provisions of 15 & 16 Geo. 5. c. 20.

(1) In this Act the expressions "lessor," "lessee" and "lease" have the meanings assigned to them respectively by sections one hundred and forty-six and one hundred and fifty-four of the Law of Property Act, 1925, except that they do not include any reference to such a grant as is mentioned in the said section one hundred and forty-six, or to the person making, or to the grantee under such a grant, or to persons deriving title under such a person; and "lease" means a lease for a term of seven years or more, not being a lease of an agricultural holding within the meaning of the Agricultural Holdings Act 1986.

(2)   The provisions of section one hundred and ninety-six of the said Act (which relate to the service of notices) shall extend to notices and counter-notices required or authorised by this Act.

8.   Short title and extent.
(1)   This Act may be cited as the Leasehold Property (Repairs) Act, 1938.
(2)   This Act shall not extend to Scotland or to Northern Ireland.

LANDLORD AND TENANT ACT 1954
(1954, c. 56)

An Act to provide security of tenure for occupying tenants under certain leases of residential property at low rents and for occupying sub-tenants of tenants under such leases; to enable tenants occupying property for business, professional or certain other purposes to obtain new tenancies in certain cases; to amend and extend the Landlord and Tenant Act, 1927, the Leasehold Property (Repairs) Act, 1938, and section eighty-four of the Law of Property Act, 1925; to confer jurisdiction on the County Court in certain disputes between landlords and tenants; to make provision for the termination of tenancies of derelict land; and for purposes connected with the matters aforesaid.   [30 July, 1954]

PART I
SECURITY OF TENURE FOR RESIDENTIAL TENANTS

Security of tenure for tenants under ground leases, etc.

1.   Protection of residential tenants on termination of long tenancies at low rents.
On the termination in accordance with the provisions of this Part of this Act of a tenancy to which this section applies the tenant shall be entitled to the protection of the Rent Act subject to and in accordance with those provisions.

2.   Tenancies to which s. 1 applies.
(1)   The foregoing section applies to any long tenancy at a low rent, being a tenancy as respects which for the time being the following condition (hereinafter referred to as "the qualifying condition") is fulfilled, that is to say that the circumstances (as respects the property comprised in the tenancy, the use of that property, and all other relevant matters) are such that on the coming to an end of the tenancy at that time the tenant would, if the tenancy had not been one at a low rent, be entitled by virtue of the Rent Act to retain possession of the whole or part of the property comprised in the tenancy.

(1A)   For the purpose only of determining whether the qualifying condition is fulfilled with respect to a tenancy which is entered into on or after 1st April 1990 (otherwise than, where the property comprised in the tenancy had a rateable value on 31st March 1990, in pursuance of a contract made before 1st April 1990), for section 4(4)(b) and (5) of that Act substitute—

"(b)   on the date the contract for the grant of the tenancy was made (or, if there was no such contract, on the date the tenancy was entered into) R exceeded £25,000 under the formula—

$$R = \frac{P \times I}{1 - (1 + I)^{-T}}$$

where—

P is the premium payable as a condition of the grant of the tenancy (and includes a payment of money's worth) or, where no premium is so payable, zero,

I is 0.06, and

T is the term, expressed in years, granted by the tenancy (disregarding any right to terminate the tenancy before the end of the term or to extend the tenancy)."

(2)   At any time before, but not more than twelve months before, the term date application may be made to the court as respects any long tenancy at a low rent, not being at the time of the application a tenancy as respects which the qualifying condition is fulfilled, for an order declaring that the tenancy is not to be treated for the purposes of this Part of this Act as a tenancy to which the foregoing section applies; and where such an application is made—

(a)   the court, if satisfied that the tenancy is not likely, immediately before the term date, to be a tenancy to which the foregoing section applies, but not otherwise, shall make the order;

(b)   if the court makes the order, then notwithstanding anything in subsection (1) of this section the tenancy shall not thereafter be treated as a tenancy to which the foregoing section applies.

(3)   Anything authorised or required to be done under the following provisions of this Part of this Act in relation to tenancies to which the foregoing section applies shall, if done before the term date in relation to a long tenancy at a low rent, not be treated as invalid by reason only that at the time at which it was done the qualifying condition was not fulfilled as respects the tenancy.

(4)   In this Part of this Act the expression "long tenancy" means a tenancy granted for a term of years certain exceeding twenty-one years, whether or not subsequently extended by act of the parties or by any enactment.

(5)   In this Part of this Act the expression "tenancy at a low rent" means a tenancy the rent payable in respect whereof (or, where that rent is a progressive rent, the maximum rent payable in respect whereof) is less than,—

(a)   where the tenancy was entered into before 1st April 1990 or (where the property comprised in the tenancy had a rateable value on 31st March 1990) is entered into on or after 1st April 1990 in pursuance of a contract made before that date, two-thirds of the rateable value of the property; and for the purposes of this subsection the rateable value of the property is that which would be taken as its rateable value for the purposes of section 5(1) of the Rent Act 1977; and,

(b)   where the tenancy is entered into on or after 1st April 1990 (otherwise than, where the property comprised in the tenancy had a rateable value on 31st March 1990, in pursuance of a contract made before 1st April 1990), is payable at a rate of,—

(i)   £1,000 or less a year if the property is in Greater London, and

(ii)   £250 or less a year if the property is elsewhere.

(6)   In this Part of this Act the expression "term date", in relation to a tenancy granted for a term of years certain, means the date of expiry of the term.

(7)   In determining whether a long tenancy is, or at any time was, a tenancy at a low rent there shall be disregarded such part (if any) of the sums payable by the tenant as is expressed (in whatever terms) to be payable in respect of rates, services, repairs, maintenance, or insurance, unless it could not have been regarded by the parties as a part so payable.

In this section "long tenancy" does not include a tenancy which is, or may become, terminable before the end of the term by notice given to the tenant.

(8)   The Secretary of State may by order replace any amount referred to in subsections (1A) and (5)(b) of this section and the number in the definition of "I" in subsection (1A) by such amount or number as is specified in the order; and such an order shall be made by statutory instrument which shall be subject to annulment in pursuance of a resolution of either House of Parliament.

Continuation and termination of tenancies to which s. 1 applies

3.   Continuation of tenancies to which s. 1 applies.

(1)   A tenancy which is current immediately before the term date and is then a tenancy to which section one of this Act applies shall not come to an end on that date

except by being terminated under the provisions of this Part of this Act, and if not then so terminated shall subject to those provisions continue until so terminated and shall, while continuing by virtue of this section, be deemed (notwithstanding any change in circumstances) to be a tenancy to which section one of this Act applies.

(2)   Where by virtue of the last foregoing subsection a tenancy is continued after the term date, then—

(a)   if the premises qualifying for protection are the whole of the property comprised in the tenancy, the tenancy shall continue at the same rent and in other respects on the same terms as before the term date;

(b)   if the premises qualifying for protection are only part of the property comprised in the tenancy, the tenancy while continuing after the term date shall have effect as a tenancy of those premises to the exclusion of the remainder of the property, and at a rent to be ascertained by apportioning the rent payable before the term date as between those premises and the remainder of the property, and in other respects on the same terms (subject to any necessary modifications) as before the term date.

(3)   In this Part of this Act the expression "the premises qualifying for protection" means the aggregate of the premises of which, if the tenancy in question were not one at a low rent, the tenant would be entitled to retain possession by virtue of the Rent Act after the coming to an end of the tenancy at the term date.

(4)   Any question arising under paragraph (b) of subsection (2) of this section as to the premises comprised in a tenancy continuing as mentioned in that paragraph, as to the rent payable in respect of a tenancy so continuing, or as to any of the terms of such a tenancy, shall be determined by agreement between the landlord and the tenant or, on the application of either of them, by the court.

4.   Termination of tenancy by the landlord.

(1)   The landlord may terminate a tenancy to which section one of this Act applies by notice given to the tenant in the prescribed form specifying the date at which the tenancy is to come to an end (hereinafter referred to as "the date of termination"), being either the term date of the tenancy or a later date:

Provided that this subsection has effect subject to the provisions of this Part of this Act as to the annulment of notices in certain cases and subject to the provisions of Part IV of this Act as to the interim continuation of tenancies pending the disposal of applications to the court.

(2)   A notice under the last foregoing subsection shall not have effect unless it is given not more than twelve nor less than six months before the date of termination specified therein.

(3)   A notice under subsection (1) of this section shall not have effect unless it specifies the premises which the landlord believes to be, or to be likely to be, the premises qualifying for protection and either—

(a)   it contains proposals for a statutory tenancy, as defined by subsection (3) of section seven of this Act, or

(b)   it contains notice that, if the tenant is not willing to give up possession at the date of termination of the tenancy, of all the property then comprised in the tenancy, the landlord proposes to apply to the court, on one or more of the grounds mentioned in section twelve of this Act, for possession of the property comprised in the tenancy, and states the ground or grounds on which he proposes to apply.

(4)   A notice under subsection (1) of this section shall invite the tenant, within two months after the giving of the notice, to notify the landlord in writing whether he is willing to give up possession as mentioned in paragraph (b) of the last foregoing subsection.

(5)   A notice under subsection (1) of this section containing proposals such as are mentioned in paragraph (a) of subsection (3) of this section is hereinafter referred to as

a "landlord's notice proposing a statutory tenancy", and a notice under subsection (1) of this section not containing such proposals is hereinafter referred to as a "landlord's notice to resume possession".

(6) References in this Part of this Act to an election by the tenant to retain possession are references to his notifying the landlord, in accordance with subsection (4) of this section, that he will not be willing to give up possession.

5. Termination of tenancy by the tenant.

(1) A tenancy to which section one of this Act applies may be brought to an end at the term date thereof by not less than one month's notice in writing given by the tenant to the immediate landlord.

(2) A tenancy continuing after the term date thereof by virtue of section three of this Act may be brought to an end at any time by not less than one month's notice in writing given by the tenant to the immediate landlord, whether the notice is given after or before the term date of the tenancy.

(3) The fact that the landlord has given a notice under subsection (1) of the last foregoing section, or that the tenant has elected to retain possession, shall not prevent the tenant from giving a notice terminating the tenancy at a date earlier than the date of termination specified in the landlord's notice.

Statutory tenancies arising under Part I

6. Application of Rent Acts where tenant retains possession.

(1) Where a tenancy is terminated by a landlord's notice proposing a statutory tenancy the Rent Act shall apply, subject as hereinafter provided, as if the tenancy (hereinafter referred to as "the former tenancy")—

(a) had been a tenancy of the dwelling-house, as hereinafter defined, and

(b) had not been a tenancy at a low rent and, except or regards the duration of the tenancy and the amount of the rent, had been a tenancy on the terms agreed or determined in accordance with the next following section and no other terms.

(2) The Rent Act shall not apply as aforesaid, if at the end of the period of two months after the service of the landlord's notice the qualifying condition was not fulfilled as respects the tenancy, unless the tenant has elected to retain possession.

(3) In this Part of this Act the expression "the dwelling-house" means the premises agreed between the landlord and the tenant or determined by the court,—

(a) if the agreement or determination is made on or after the term date of the former tenancy, to be the premises which as respects that tenancy are the premises qualifying for protection.

(b) if the agreement or determination is made before the term date of the former tenancy, to be the premises which are likely to be the premises qualifying for protection.

7. Settlement of terms of statutory tenancy.

(1) The terms on which the tenant and any successor to his statutory tenancy may retain possession of the dwelling-house during that period other than the amount of the rent shall be such as may be agreed between the landlord and the tenant or determined by the court.

(2) A landlord's notice proposing a statutory tenancy and anything done in pursuance thereof shall cease to have effect if by the beginning of the period of two months ending with the date of termination specified in the notice any of the following matters, that is to say,—

(a) what premises are to constitute the dwelling-house;

(b) as regards the rent of the dwelling-house during the period of the statutory tenancy, the intervals at which instalments of that rent are to be payable, and whether they are to be payable in advance or in arrear;

   (c)   whether any, and if so what, initial repairs (as defined in the next following section) are to be carried out on the dwelling-house;

   (d)   whether initial repairs to be so carried out are to be carried out by the landlord or by the tenant, or which of them are to be carried out by the landlord and which by the tenant; and

   (e)   the matters required by the next following section to be agreed or determined in relation to repairs before the beginning of the period of the statutory tenancy,

has not been agreed between the landlord and the tenant and no application has been made by the beginning of the said period of two months for the determination by the court of such of those matters as have not been agreed:

   Provided that this subsection shall not have effect if at the end of the period of two months after the service of the landlord's notice the qualifying condition was not fulfilled as respects the tenancy unless the tenant has elected to retain possession.

   (3)   In paragraph (a) of subsection (3) of section four of this Act, the expression "proposals for a statutory tenancy" means proposals as to the rent of the dwelling-house during the period of the statutory tenancy, proposals as to the matters specified in paragraphs (b) to (e) of the last foregoing subsection, and such other proposals (if any) as to the terms mentioned in subsection (1) of this section as the landlord may include in his notice.

   (4)   Any such proposals—

   (a)   shall be made, and be expressed to be made, on the assumption that the dwelling-house will be the premises specified in the landlord's notice in accordance with subsection (3) of section four of this Act;

   (b)   shall not be treated as failing to satisfy the requirements of the said subsection (3) by reason only of a difference between the premises to which the proposals relate and the premises subsequently agreed or determined to be the dwelling-house,

and in the event of any such difference the landlord shall not be bound by his proposals notwithstanding that they may have been accepted by the tenant.

   (5)   An application for securing a determination by the court in accordance with the foregoing provisions of this section shall be made by the landlord, and—

   (a)   shall be made during the currency of the landlord's notice proposing a statutory tenancy and not earlier than two months after the giving thereof, so however that if the tenant has elected to retain possession it may be made at a time not earlier than one month after the giving of the notice;

   (b)   subject to the provisions of the last foregoing subsection, shall not be made for the determination of any matter as to which agreement has already been reached between the landlord and the tenant.

   (6)   In this Part of this Act the expression "the period of the statutory tenancy" means the period beginning with the coming to an end of the former tenancy and ending with the earliest date by which the tenant, and any successor to his statutory tenancy, have ceased to retain possession of the dwelling-house by virtue of the Rent Act.

8.   Provisions as to repairs during period of statutory tenancy.

   (1)   Where it is agreed between the landlord and the tenant, or determined by the court, that the terms mentioned in subsection (1) of the last foregoing section shall include the carrying out of specified repairs (hereinafter referred to as "initial repairs"), and any of the initial repairs are required in consequence of failure by the tenant to fulfil his obligations under the former tenancy, the landlord shall be entitled to a payment (hereinafter referred to as a "payment for accrued tenant's repairs") of an amount equal to the cost reasonably incurred by the landlord in ascertaining what repairs are required as aforesaid and in carrying out such of the initial repairs as are so required and as respects which it has been agreed or determined as aforesaid that they are to be carried out by the landlord, excluding any part of that cost which is recoverable by the landlord

otherwise than from the tenant or his predecessor in title.

(2) A payment for accrued tenant's repairs may be made either by instalments or otherwise, as may be agreed or determined as aforesaid; and the provisions of the First Schedule to this Act shall have effect as to the time for, and method of, recovery of such payments, the persons from whom they are to be recoverable, and otherwise in relation thereto.

(3) The obligations of the landlord and the tenant as respects the repair of the dwelling-house during the period of the statutory tenancy shall, subject to the foregoing provisions of this section, be such as may be agreed between them or as may be determined by the court.

(4) The matters referred to in paragraph (e) of subsection (2) of the last foregoing section are:

(a) which of the initial repairs (if any) are required in consequence of failure by the tenant to fulfil his obligations under the former tenancy and, where there are any initial repairs so required, the amount to be included in the payment for accrued tenant's repairs in respect of the cost incurred by the landlord in ascertaining what initial repairs are so required;

(b) the estimated cost of the repairs so required, in so far as they are to be carried out by the landlord;

(c) whether any payment for accrued tenant's repairs is to be payable by instalments or otherwise, and if by instalments the amount of each instalment (subject to any necessary reduction of the last), the time at which the first is to be payable and the frequency of the instalments;

(d) whether there are to be any, and if so what, obligations as respects the repair of the dwelling-house during the period of the statutory tenancy, other than the execution of initial repairs.

(5) The provisions of the Second Schedule to this Act shall have effect as respects cases where the landlord or the tenant fails to carry out initial repairs, as to the cost of carrying out such repairs in certain cases and as to the making of a record, where required by the landlord or by the tenant, of the state of repair of the dwelling-house.

9. Principles to be observed in determining terms of statutory tenancy as to repairs and rent.

(1) Where it falls to the court to determine what initial repairs (if any) should be carried out by the landlord, the court shall not, except with the consent of the landlord and the tenant, require the carrying out of initial repairs in excess of what is required to bring the dwelling-house into good repair or the carrying out of any repairs not specified by the landlord in his application as repairs which he is willing to carry out.

(2) In the last foregoing subsection the expression "good repair" means good repair as respects both structure and decoration, having regard to the age, character and locality of the dwelling-house.

(3) Notwithstanding anything in subsection (1) of section seven of this Act, the court shall not have power to determine that any initial repairs shall be carried out by the tenant except with his consent.

(4) Any obligations imposed by the court under this Part of this Act as to keeping the dwelling-house in repair during the period of the statutory tenancy shall not be such as to require the dwelling-house to be kept in a better state of repair than the state which may be expected to subsist after the completion of any initial repairs to be carried out or, in the absence of any agreement or determination requiring the carrying out of initial repairs, in a better state of repair than the state subsisting at the time of the court's determination of what obligations are to be imposed.

10. Provisions as to liabilities under tenant's covenants in former lease.

(1) If on the termination of the former tenancy the tenant retains possession of the

dwelling-house by virtue of section six of this Act, any liability, whether of the tenant or of any predecessor in title of his, arising under the terms of the former tenancy shall be extinguished:

Provided that this subsection shall not affect any liability—

(a)   for failure to pay rent or rates or to insure or keep insured, or

(b)   in respect of the use of any premises for immoral or illegal purposes.

or any liability under the terms of the former tenancy in so far as those terms related to property other than the dwelling-house.

(2)   During the period of the statutory tenancy no order shall be made for the recovery of possession of the dwelling-house from the tenant in any of the circumstances specified in Cases 1 to 3 in Schedule 15 to the Rent Act (which relate to the recovery of possession where an obligation of the tenancy has been broken or where certain specified acts or defaults have been committed) by reason only of any act or default which occurred before the date of termination of the former tenancy.

Provisions as to possession on termination of long tenancy

12.   Grounds for resumption of possession by landlord.

(1)   The grounds on which a landlord may apply to the court for possession of the property comprised in a tenancy to which section one of this Act applies are the following:—

(a)   that for purposes of redevelopment after the termination of the tenancy the landlord proposes to demolish or reconstruct the whole or a substantial part of the relevant premises;

(b)   the grounds specified in the Third Schedule to this Act (which correspond, subject to the necessary modifications, to the Cases 1 to 9 in Schedule 15 to the Rent Act which specify circumstances in which a court may make an order for possession under that Act).

(2)   In this section the expression "the relevant premises" means—

(a)   as respects any time after the term date, the premises of which, if the tenancy were not one at a low rent, the tenant would have been entitled to retain possession by virtue of the Rent Act after the coming to an end of the tenancy at the term date;

(b)   as respects any time before the term date, the premises agreed between the landlord and the tenant or determined by the court to be likely to be the premises of which, if the tenancy were not one at a low rent, the tenant would be entitled to retain possession as aforesaid.

13.   Landlord's application for possession.

(1)   Where a landlord's notice to resume possession has been served and either—

(a)   the tenant elects to retain possession, or

(b)   at the end of the period of two months after the service of the landlord's notice the qualifying condition is fulfilled as respects the tenancy,

the landlord may apply to the court for an order under this section on such of the grounds mentioned in the last foregoing section as may be specified in the notice:

Provided that the application shall not be made later than two months after the tenant elects to retain possession, or, if he has not elected to retain possession, later than four months after the service of the notice.

(2)   Where the ground or one of the grounds for claiming possession specified in the landlord's notice was that mentioned in paragraph (a) of subsection (1) of the last foregoing section, then if on such an application the court is satisfied that the landlord has established that ground as respects premises specified in the application, and is further satisfied,—

(a)   that on the said ground possession of the specified premises will be required by the landlord on the termination of the tenancy; and

(b)   that the landlord has made such preparations (including the obtaining, or, if that is not reasonably practicable in the circumstances, preparations relating to the obtaining, of any requisite permission or consent, whether from any authority whose permission or consent is required under any enactment or from the owner of any interest in any property) for proceeding with the redevelopment as are reasonable in the circumstances,

the court shall order that the tenant shall, on the termination of the tenancy, give up possession of all the property then comprised in the tenancy.

(3)   Where in a case falling within the last foregoing subsection the court is not satisfied as therein mentioned, but would be satisfied if the date of termination of the tenancy had been such date (in this subsection referred to as "the postponed date") as the court may determine, being a date later, but not more than one year later, than the date of termination specified in the landlord's notice, the court shall, if the landlord so requires, make an order specifying the postponed date and otherwise to the following effect, that is to say:—

(a)   that the tenancy shall not come to an end on the date of termination specified in the landlord's notice but shall continue thereafter, as respects the whole of the property comprised therein, at the same rent and in other respects on the same terms as before that date;

(b)   that unless the tenancy comes to an end before the postponed date, the tenant shall on that date give up possession of all the property then comprised in the tenancy.

(4)   Where the ground or one of the grounds for claiming possession specified in the landlord's notice was one mentioned in the Third Schedule to this Act, then if on an application made in accordance with subsection (1) of this section the court is satisfied that the landlord has established that ground and that it is reasonable that the landlord should be granted possession, the court shall order that the tenant shall, on the termination of the tenancy, give up possession of all the property then comprised in the tenancy.

(5)   Nothing in the foregoing provisions of this section shall prejudice any power of the tenant under section five of this Act to terminate the tenancy; and subsection (2) of that section shall apply where the tenancy is continued by an order under subsection (3) of this section as it applies where the tenancy is continued by virtue of section three of this Act.

14.   Provisions where tenant not ordered to give up possession.

(1)   The provisions of this section shall have effect where in a case falling within paragraph (a) or (b) of subsection (1) of the last foregoing section the landlord does not obtain an order under the last foregoing section.

(2)   If at the expiration of the period within which an application under the last foregoing section may be made the landlord has not made such an application, the landlord's notice, and anything done in pursuance thereof, shall thereupon cease to have effect.

(3)   If before the expiration of the said period the landlord has made an application under the last foregoing section, but the result of the application, at the time when it is finally disposed of, is that no order is made, the landlord's notice shall cease to have effect; but if within one month after the application to the court is finally disposed of the landlord gives a landlord's notice proposing a statutory tenancy, the earliest date which may be specified therein as the date of termination shall, notwithstanding anything in subsection (2) of section four of this Act, be the expiration of three months from the giving of the subsequent notice.

(4)   The reference in the last foregoing subsection to the time at which an application is finally disposed of shall be construed as a reference to the earliest time at which the proceedings on the application (including any proceedings on or in consequence of an

appeal) have been determined and any time for appealing or further appealing has expired, except that if the application is withdrawn or any appeal is abandoned the reference shall be construed as a reference to the time of withdrawal or abandonment.

(5) A landlord's notice to resume possession may be withdrawn at any time by notice in writing served on the tenant (without prejudice, however, to the power of the court to make an order as to costs if the notice is withdrawn after the landlord has made an application under the last foregoing section); and if within one month of the withdrawal of a landlord's notice to resume possession the landlord gives a landlord's notice proposing a statutory tenancy, the earliest date which may be specified therein as the date of termination shall, notwithstanding anything in subsection (2) of section four of this Act, be the expiration of three months from the giving of the subsequent notice or six months from the giving of the withdrawn notice, whichever is the later.

(6) Where by virtue of subsection (3) or (5) of this section the landlord gives a landlord's notice proposing a statutory tenancy which specifies as the date of termination a date earlier than six months after the giving of the notice, subsection (2) of section seven of this Act shall apply in relation to the notice with the substitution, for references to the period of two months ending with the date of termination specified in the notice and the beginning of that period, of references to the period of three months beginning with the giving of the notice and the end of that period.

General and supplementary provisions

16. Relief for tenant where landlord proceeding to enforce covenants.

(1) The provisions of the next following subsection shall have effect where, in the case of a tenancy to which section one of this Act applies,—

(a) the immediate landlord has brought proceedings to enforce a right of re-entry or forfeiture or a right to damages in respect of a failure to comply with any terms of the tenancy,

(b) the tenant has made application in the proceedings for relief under this section, and

(c) the court makes an order for the recovery from the tenant of possession of the property comprised in the tenancy or for the payment by the tenant of such damages as aforesaid, and the order is made at a time earlier than seven months before the term date of the tenancy.

(2) The operation of the order shall be suspended for a period of fourteen days from the making thereof, and if before the end of that period the tenant gives notice in writing to the immediate landlord that he desires that the provisions of the two following paragraphs shall have effect, and lodges a copy of the notice in the court,—

(a) the order shall not have effect except if and in so far as it provides for the payment of costs, and

(b) the tenancy shall thereafter have effect, and this Part of this Act shall have effect in relation thereto, as if it had been granted for a term expiring at the expiration of seven months from the making of the order.

(3) In any case falling within paragraphs (a) and (b) of subsection (1) of this section, the court shall not make any such order as is mentioned in paragraph (c) thereof unless the time of the making of the order falls earlier than seven months before the term date of the tenancy:

Provided that (without prejudice to section ten of this Act) this subsection shall not prevent the making of an order for the payment of damages in respect of a failure, as respects any premises, to comply with the terms of a tenancy if, at the time when the order is made, the tenancy has come to an end as respects those premises.

(4) The foregoing provisions of this section shall not have effect in relation to a failure to comply with—

(a) any term of a tenancy as to payment of rent or rates or as to insuring or keeping insured any premises, or

(b) any term restricting the use of any premises for immoral or illegal purposes.

(5) References in this section to proceedings to enforce a right to damages in respect of a failure to comply with any terms of a tenancy shall be construed as including references to proceedings for recovery from the tenant of expenditure incurred by or recovered from the immediate landlord in consequence of such a failure on the part of the tenant.

(6) Nothing in the foregoing provisions of this section shall prejudice any right to apply for relief under any other enactment.

(7) Subsection (3) of section two of this Act shall not have effect in relation to this section.

17. Prohibition of agreements excluding Part I.

The provisions of this Part of this Act shall have effect notwithstanding any agreement to the contrary:

Provided that nothing in this Part of this Act shall be construed as preventing the surrender of a tenancy.

18. Duty of tenants of residential property to give information to landlords or superior landlords.

(1) Where the property comprised in a long tenancy at a low rent is or includes residential premises, then at any time during the last two years of the term of the tenancy, or (if the tenancy is being continued after the term date by subsection (1) of section three of this Act) at any time while the tenancy is being so continued, the immediate landlord or any superior landlord may give to the tenant or any sub-tenant of premises comprised in the long tenancy a notice in the prescribed form requiring him to notify the landlord or superior landlord, as the case may be,—

(a) whether the interest of the person to whom the notice is given has effect subject to any sub-tenancy on which that interest is immediately expectant and, if so,

(b) what premises are comprised in the sub-tenancy, for what term it has effect (or, if it is terminable by notice, by what notice it can be terminated), what is the rent payable thereunder, who is the sub-tenant and (to the best of the knowledge and belief of the person to whom the notice is given) whether the sub-tenant is in occupation of the premises comprised in the sub-tenancy or any part of those premises and, if not, what is the sub-tenant's address,

and it shall be the duty of the person to whom such a notice is given to comply therewith within one month of the giving of the notice.

(2) In this section the expression "residential premises" means premises normally used, or adapted for use, as one or more dwellings, the expression "sub-tenant" in relation to a long tenancy means the owner of a tenancy created (whether immediately or derivatively) out of the long tenancy and includes a person retaining possession of any premises by virtue of the Rent Act after the coming to an end of a sub-tenancy, and the expression "sub-tenancy" includes a right so to retain possession.

19. Application of Part I to tenancies granted in continuation of long tenancies.

(1) Where on the coming to an end of a tenancy at a low rent the person who was tenant thereunder immediately before the coming to an end thereof becomes (whether by grant or by implication of law) tenant of the whole or any part of the property comprised therein under another tenancy at a low rent, then if the first tenancy was a long tenancy or is deemed by virtue of this subsection to have been a long tenancy the second tenancy shall be deemed for the purposes of this Part of this Act to be a long tenancy irrespective of its terms.

(2)   In relation to a tenancy from year to year or other tenancy not granted for a term of years certain, being a tenancy which by virtue of the last foregoing subsection is to be deemed to be a long tenancy, this Part of this Act shall have effect subject to the modifications set out in the Fourth Schedule to this Act.

20.   Assumptions on which court to determine future questions.

Where under this Part of this Act any question falls to be determined by the court by reference to the circumstances at a future date, the court shall have regard to all rights, interests and obligations under or relating to the tenancy as they subsist at the time of the determination and to all relevant circumstances as they then subsist and shall assume, except in so far as the contrary is shown, that those rights, interests, obligations and circumstances will continue to subsist unchanged until the said future date.

21.   Meaning of "the landlord" in Part I and provisions as to mesne landlords, etc.

(1)   Subject to the provisions of this section, in this Part of this Act the expression "the landlord", in relation to a tenancy (in this section referred to as "the relevant tenancy"), means the person (whether or not he is the immediate landlord) who is the owner of that interest in the property comprised in the relevant tenancy which for the time being fulfils the following conditions, that is to say—

(a)   that it is an interest in reversion expectant (whether immediately or not) on the termination of the relevant tenancy, and

(b)   that it is either the fee simple or a tenancy the duration of which is at least five years longer than that of the relevant tenancy.

and is not itself in reversion expectant (whether immediately or not) on an interest which fulfils those conditions.

(2)   References in this Part of this Act to a notice to quit given by the landlord are references to a notice to quit given by the immediate landlord.

(3)   For the purposes of subsection (1) of this section the question whether a tenancy (hereinafter referred to as "the superior tenancy") is to be treated as having a duration at least five years longer than that of the relevant tenancy shall be determined as follows:—

(a)   if the term date of the relevant tenancy has not passed, the superior tenancy shall be so treated unless it is due to expire at a time earlier than five years after the term date or can be brought to an end at such a time by notice to quit given by the landlord;

(b)   if the term date of the relevant tenancy has passed, the superior tenancy shall be so treated unless it is due to expire within five years or can be brought to an end within five years by notice to quit given by the landlord.

(4)   In relation to the premises constituting the dwelling-house where the Rent Act applies by virtue of subsection (1) of section six of this Act, the expression "the landlord", as respects any time falling within the period of the statutory tenancy, means the person who as respects those premises is the landlord of the tenant for the purposes of the Rent Act:

Provided that in relation to the carrying out of initial repairs, and to any payment for accrued tenant's repairs, the said expression, as respects any time falling within that period, means the person whose interest in the dwelling-house fulfils the following conditions, that is to say:—

(a)   that it is not due to expire within five years and is not capable of being brought to an end within five years by notice to quit given by the landlord, and

(b)   that it is not itself in reversion expectant on an interest which is not due to expire or capable of being brought to an end as aforesaid.

(5)   The provisions of the Fifth Schedule to this Act shall have effect for the application of this Part of this Act to cases where the immediate landlord of the tenant is not the owner of the fee simple in respect of the premises in question.

(6) Notwithstanding anything in subsection (1) of this section, if at any time the interest which apart from this subsection would be the interest of the landlord is an interest not bound by this Part of this Act and is not the interest of the immediate landlord, then as respects that time the expression "the landlord" means in this Part of this Act (subject to the provisions of subsection (2) of this section) the person (whether or not he is the immediate landlord) who has the interest in the property comprised in the relevant tenancy immediately derived out of the interest not bound by this Part of this Act.

In this subsection the expression "interest not bound by this Part of this Act" means an interest which belongs to Her Majesty in right of the Crown and is not under the management of the Crown Estate Commissioners or an interest belonging to a Government department or held on behalf of Her Majesty for the purposes of a Government department.

22. Interpretation of Part I.

(1) In this Part of this Act:—

"date of termination" has the meaning assigned to it by subsection (1) of section four of this Act;

"the dwelling-house" has the meaning assigned to it by subsection (3) of section six of this Act;

"election to retain possession" has the meaning assigned to it by subsection (6) of section four of this Act;

"former tenancy" has the meaning assigned to it by subsection (1) of section six of this Act;

"initial repairs" has the meaning assigned to it by subsection (1) of section eight of this Act;

"the landlord" has the meaning assigned to it by the last foregoing section;

"landlord's notice proposing a statutory tenancy" and "landlord's notice to resume possession" have the meanings assigned to them respectively by subsection (5) of section four of this Act;

"long tenancy" has the meaning assigned to it by subsection (4) of section two of this Act;

"order" includes judgment;

"payment for accrued tenant's repairs" has the meaning assigned to it by subsection (1) of section eight of this Act;

"the period of the statutory tenancy" has the meaning assigned to it by subsection (6) of section seven of this Act;

"premises qualifying for protection" has the meaning assigned to it by subsection (3) of section three of this Act;

"qualifying condition" has the meaning assigned to it by subsection (1) of section two of this Act;

"the Rent Act" means the Rent Act 1977 as it applies to regulated tenancies but exclusive of Parts II to V thereof;

"tenancy at a low rent" has the meaning assigned to it by subsection (5) of section two of this Act;

"term date" has the meaning assigned to it by subsection (6) of section two of this Act.

(2) In relation to the premises constituting the dwelling-house the expression "the tenant" in this Part of this Act means the tenant under the former tenancy and, except as respects any payment for accrued tenant's repairs not payable by instalments, includes any successor to his statutory tenancy, and the expression "successor to his statutory tenancy", in relation to that tenant, means a person who after that tenant's death retains possession of the dwelling-house by virtue of the Rent Act.

(3) In determining, for the purposes of any provision of this Part of this Act, whether the property comprised in a tenancy, or any part of that property, was let as a separate dwelling, the nature of the property or part at the time of the creation of the tenancy shall be deemed to have been the same as its nature at the time in relation to which the question arises, and the purpose for which it was let under the tenancy shall be deemed to have been the same as the purpose for which it is or was used at the last-mentioned time.

PART II
SECURITY OF TENURE FOR BUSINESS, PROFESSIONAL AND OTHER TENANTS

Tenancies to which Part II applies

23. Tenancies to which Part II applies.

(1) Subject to the provisions of this Act, this Part of this Act applies to any tenancy where the property comprised in the tenancy is or includes premises which are occupied by the tenant and are so occupied for the purposes of a business carried on by him or for those and other purposes.

(2) In this Part of this Act the expression "business" includes a trade, profession or employment and includes any activity carried on by a body of persons, whether corporate or unincorporate.

(3) In the following provisions of this Part of this Act the expression "the holding", in relation to a tenancy to which this Part of this Act applies, means the property comprised in the tenancy, there being excluded any part thereof which is occupied neither by the tenant nor by a person employed by the tenant and so employed for the purposes of a business by reason of which the tenancy is one to which this Part of this Act applies.

(4) Where the tenant is carrying on a business, in all or any part of the property comprised in a tenancy, in breach of a prohibition (however expressed) of use for business purposes which subsists under the terms of the tenancy and extends to the whole of that property, this Part of this Act shall not apply to the tenancy unless the immediate landlord or his predecessor in title has consented to the breach or the immediate landlord has acquiesced therein.

In this subsection the reference to a prohibition of use for business purposes does not include a prohibition of use for the purposes of a specified business, or of use for purposes of any but a specified business, but save as aforesaid includes a prohibition of use for the purposes of some one or more only of the classes of business specified in the definition of that expression in subsection (2) of this section.

24. Continuation of tenancies to which Part II applies and grant of new tenancies.

(1) A tenancy to which this Part of this Act applies shall not come to an end unless terminated in accordance with the provisions of this Part of this Act; and, subject to the provisions of section 29 of this Act, the tenant under such a tenancy may apply to the court for a new tenancy—

(a) if the landlord has given notice under section 25 of this Act to terminate the tenancy, or

(b) if the tenant has made a request for a new tenancy in accordance with section 26 of this Act.

(2) The last foregoing subsection shall not prevent the coming to an end of a tenancy by notice to quit given by the tenant, by surrender or forfeiture, or by the forfeiture of a superior tenancy, unless—

(a) in the case of a notice to quit, the notice was given before the tenant had been in occupation in right of the tenancy for one month; or

(b) in the case of an instrument of surrender, the instrument was executed before, or was executed in pursuance of an agreement made before, the tenant had been in occupation in right of the tenancy for one month.

(3) Notwithstanding anything in subsection (1) of this section,—

(a) where a tenancy to which this Part of this Act applies ceases to be such a tenancy, it shall not come to an end by reason only of the cesser, but if it was granted for a term of years certain and has been continued by subsection (1) of this section then (without prejudice to the termination thereof in accordance with any terms of the tenancy) it may be terminated by not less than three nor more than six months' notice in writing given by the landlord to the tenant;

(b) where, at a time when a tenancy is not one to which this Part of this Act applies, the landlord gives notice to quit, the operation of the notice shall not be affected by reason that the tenancy becomes one to which this Part of this Act applies after the giving of the notice.

24A. Rent while tenancy continues by virtue of s. 24 of Act of 1954.

(1) The landlord of a tenancy to which this Part of this Act applies may,—

(a) if he has given notice under section 25 of this Act to terminate the tenancy; or

(b) if the tenant has made a request for a new tenancy in accordance with section 26 of this Act;

apply to the court to determine a rent which it would be reasonable for the tenant to pay while the tenancy continues by virtue of section 24 of this Act, and the court may determine a rent accordingly.

(2) A rent determined in proceedings under this section shall be deemed to be the rent payable under the tenancy from the date on which the proceedings were commenced or the date specified in the landlord's notice or the tenant's request, whichever is the later.

(3) In determining a rent under this section the court shall have regard to the rent payable under the terms of the tenancy, but otherwise subsections (1) and (2) of section 34 of this Act shall apply to the determination as they would apply to the determination of a rent under that section if a new tenancy from year to year of the whole of the property comprised in the tenancy were granted to the tenant by order of the court.

25. Termination of tenancy by the landlord.

(1) The landlord may terminate a tenancy to which this Part of this Act applies by a notice given to the tenant in the prescribed form specifying the date at which the tenancy is to come to an end (hereinafter referred to as "the date of termination"):

Provided that this subsection has effect subject to the provisions of Part IV of this Act as to the interim continuation of tenancies pending the disposal of applications to the court.

(2) Subject to the provisions of the next following subsection, a notice under this section shall not have effect unless it is given not more than twelve nor less than six months before the date of termination specified therein.

(3) In the case of a tenancy which apart from this Act could have been brought to an end by notice to quit given by the landlord—

(a) the date of termination specified in a notice under this section shall not be earlier than the earliest date on which apart from this Part of this Act the tenancy could have been brought to an end by notice to quit given by the landlord on the date of the giving of the notice under this section; and

(b) where apart from this Part of this Act more than six months' notice to quit would have been required to bring the tenancy to an end, the last foregoing subsection shall have effect with the substitution for twelve months of a period six months longer than the length of notice to quit which would have been required as aforesaid.

(4)   In the case of any other tenancy, a notice under this section shall not specify a date of termination earlier than the date on which apart from this Part of this Act the tenancy would have come to an end by effluxion of time.

(5)   A notice under this section shall not have effect unless it requires the tenant, within two months after the giving of the notice, to notify the landlord in writing whether or not, at the date of termination, the tenant will be willing to give up possession of the property comprised in the tenancy.

(6)   A notice under this section shall not have effect unless it states whether the landlord would oppose an application to the court under this Part of this Act for the grant of a new tenancy and, if so, also states on which of the grounds mentioned in section thirty of this Act he would do so.

26.   Tenant's request for a new tenancy.

(1)   A tenant's request for a new tenancy may be made where the tenancy under which he holds for the time being (hereinafter referred to as "the current tenancy") is a tenancy granted for a term of years certain exceeding one year, whether or not continued by section twenty-four of this Act, or granted for a term of years certain and thereafter from year to year.

(2)   A tenant's request for a new tenancy shall be for a tenancy beginning with such date, not more than twelve nor less than six months after the making of the request, as may be specified therein:

Provided that the said date shall not be earlier than the date on which apart from this Act the current tenancy would come to an end by effluxion of time or could be brought to an end by notice to quit given by the tenant.

(3)   A tenant's request for a new tenancy shall not have effect unless it is made by notice in the prescribed form given to the landlord and sets out the tenant's proposals as to the property to be comprised in the new tenancy (being either the whole or part of the property comprised in the current tenancy), as to the rent to be payable under the new tenancy and as to the other terms of the new tenancy.

(4)   A tenant's request for a new tenancy shall not be made if the landlord has already given notice under the last foregoing section to terminate the current tenancy, or if the tenant has already given notice to quit or notice under the next following section; and no such notice shall be given by the landlord or the tenant after the making by the tenant of a request for a new tenancy.

(5)   Where the tenant makes a request for a new tenancy in accordance with the foregoing provisions of this section, the current tenancy shall, subject to the provisions of subsection (2) of section thirty-six of this Act and the provisions of Part IV of this Act as to the interim continuation of tenancies, terminate immediately before the date specified in the request for the beginning of the new tenancy.

(6)   Within two months of the making of a tenant's request for a new tenancy the landlord may give notice to the tenant that he will oppose an application to the court for the grant of a new tenancy, and any such notice shall state on which of the grounds mentioned in section thirty of this Act the landlord will oppose the application.

27.   Termination by tenant of tenancy for fixed term.

(1)   Where the tenant under a tenancy to which this Part of this Act applies, being a tenancy granted for a term of years certain, gives to the immediate landlord, not later than three months before the date on which apart from this Act the tenancy would come to an end by effluxion of time, a notice in writing that the tenant does not desire the tenancy to be continued, section twenty-four of this Act shall not have effect in relation to the tenancy, unless the notice is given before the tenant has been in occupation in right of the tenancy for one month.

(2)   A tenancy granted for a term of years certain which is continuing by virtue of section twenty-four of this Act may be brought to an end on any quarter day by not less

than three months' notice in writing given by the tenant to the immediate landlord, whether the notice is given after the date on which apart from this Act the tenancy would have come to an end or before that date, but not before the tenant has been in occupation in right of the tenancy for one month.

28. Renewal of tenancies by agreement.

Where the landlord and tenant agree for the grant to the tenant of a future tenancy of the holding, or of the holding with other land, on terms and from a date specified in the agreement, the current tenancy shall continue until that date but no longer, and shall not be a tenancy to which this Part of this Act applies.

Application to court for new tenancies

29. Order by court for grant of a new tenancy.

(1) Subject to the provisions of this Act, on an application under subsection (1) of section twenty-four of this Act for a new tenancy the court shall make an order for the grant of a tenancy comprising such property, at such rent and on such other terms, as are hereinafter provided.

(2) Where such an application is made in consequence of a notice given by the landlord under section twenty-five of this Act, it shall not be entertained unless the tenant has duly notified the landlord that he will not be willing at the date of termination to give up possession of the property comprised in the tenancy.

(3) No application under subsection (1) of section twenty-four of this Act shall be entertained unless it is made not less than two nor more than four months after the giving of the landlord's notice under section twenty-five of this Act or, as the case may be, after the making of the tenant's request for a new tenancy.

30. Opposition by landlord to application for new tenancy.

(1) The grounds on which a landlord may oppose an application under subsection (1) of section twenty-four of this Act are such of the following grounds as may be stated in the landlord's notice under section twenty-five of this Act or, as the case may be, under subsection (6) of section twenty-six thereof, that is to say:—

(a) where under the current tenancy the tenant has any obligations as respects the repair and maintenance of the holding, that the tenant ought not to be granted a new tenancy in view of the state of repair of the holding, being a state resulting from the tenant's failure to comply with the said obligations;

(b) that the tenant ought not to be granted a new tenancy in view of his persistent delay in paying rent which has become due;

(c) that the tenant ought not to be granted a new tenancy in view of other substantial breaches by him of his obligations under the current tenancy, or for any other reason connected with the tenant's use or management of the holding;

(d) that the landlord has offered and is willing to provide or secure the provision of alternative accommodation for the tenant, that the terms on which the alternative accommodation is available are reasonable having regard to the terms of the current tenancy and to all other relevant circumstances, and that the accommodation and the time at which it will be available are suitable for the tenant's requirements (including the requirement to preserve goodwill) having regard to the nature and class of his business and to the situation and extent of, and facilities afforded by, the holding;

(e) where the current tenancy was created by the subletting of part only of the property comprised in a superior tenancy and the landlord is the owner of an interest in reversion expectant on the termination of that superior tenancy, that the aggregate of the rents reasonably obtainable on separate lettings of the holding and the remainder of that property would be substantially less than the rent reasonably obtainable on a letting of that property as a whole, that on the termination of the current tenancy the landlord requires possession of the holding for the purpose of letting or otherwise disposing of the said property as a whole, and that in view thereof the tenant ought not to be granted a new tenancy;

(f)   that on the termination of the current tenancy the landlord intends to demolish or reconstruct the premises comprised in the holding or a substantial part of those premises or to carry out substantial work of construction on the holding or part thereof and that he could not reasonably do so without obtaining possession of the holding;

(g)   subject as hereinafter provided, that on the termination of the current tenancy the landlord intends to occupy the holding for the purposes, or partly for the purposes, of a business to be carried on by him therein, or as his residence.

(2)   The landlord shall not be entitled to oppose an application on the ground specified in paragraph (g) of the last foregoing subsection if the interest of the landlord, or an interest which has merged in that interest and but for the merger would be the interest of the landlord, was purchased or created after the beginning of the period of five years which ends with the termination of the current tenancy, and at all times since the purchase or creation thereof the holding has been comprised in a tenancy or successive tenancies of the description specified in subsection (1) of section twenty-three of this Act.

(3)   Where the landlord has a controlling interest in a company any business to be carried on by the company shall be treated for the purposes of subsection (1)(g) of this section as a business to be carried on by him.

For the purposes of this subsection, a person has a controlling interest in a company if and only if either—

(a)   he is a member of it and able, without the consent of any other person, to appoint or remove the holders of at least a majority of the directorships; or

(b)   he holds more than one-half of its equity share capital, there being disregarded any shares held by him in a fiduciary capacity or as nominee for another person;

and in this subsection "company" and "share" have the meanings assigned to them by section 455(1) of the Companies Act 1948 and "equity share capital" the meaning assigned to it by section 154(5) of that Act.

31. Dismissal of application for new tenancy where landlord successfully opposes.

(1)   If the landlord opposes an application under subsection (1) of section twenty-four of this Act on grounds on which he is entitled to oppose it in accordance with the last foregoing section and establishes any of those grounds to the satisfaction of the court, the court shall not make an order for the grant of a new tenancy.

(2)   Where in a case not falling within the last foregoing subsection the landlord opposes an application under the said subsection (1) on one or more of the grounds specified in paragraphs (d), (e) and (f) of subsection (1) of the last foregoing section but establishes none of those grounds to the satisfaction of the court, then if the court would have been satisfied of any of those grounds if the date of termination specified in the landlord's notice or, as the case may be, the date specified in the tenant's request for a new tenancy as the date from which the new tenancy is to begin, had been such later date as the court may determine, being a date not more than one year later than the date so specified,—

(a)   the court shall make a declaration to that effect, stating of which of the said grounds the court would have been satisfied as aforesaid and specifying the date determined by the court as aforesaid, but shall not make an order for the grant of a new tenancy;

(b)   if, within fourteen days after the making of the declaration, the tenant so requires the court shall make an order substituting the said date for the date specified in the said landlord's notice or tenant's request, and thereupon that notice or request shall have effect accordingly.

31A. Grant of new tenancy in some cases where section 30(1)(f) applies.

(1)   Where the landlord opposes an application under section 24(1) of this Act on the ground specified in paragraph (f) of section 30(1) of this Act the court shall not hold that the landlord could not reasonably carry out the demolition, reconstruction or work of construction intended without obtaining possession of the holding if—

(a)   the tenant agrees to the inclusion in the terms of the new tenancy of terms giving the landlord access and other facilities for carrying out the work intended and, given that access and those facilities, the landlord could reasonably carry out the work without obtaining possession of the holding and without interfering to a substantial extent or for a substantial time with the use of the holding for the purposes of the business carried on by the tenant; or

(b)   the tenant is willing to accept a tenancy of an economically separable part of the holding and either paragraph (a) of this section is satisfied with respect to that part or possession of the remainder of the holding would be reasonably sufficient to enable the landlord to carry out the intended work.

(2)   For the purposes of subsection (1)(b) of this section a part of a holding shall be deemed to be an economically separable part if, and only if, the aggregate of the rents which, after the completion of the intended work, would be reasonably obtainable on separate lettings of that part and the remainder of the premises affected by or resulting from the work would not be substantially less than the rent which would then be reasonably obtainable on a letting of those premises as a whole.

32. Property to be comprised in new tenancy.

(1)   Subject to the following provisions of this section, an order under section 29 of this Act for the grant of a new tenancy shall be an order for the grant of a new tenancy of the holding; and in the absence of agreement between the landlord and the tenant as to the property which constitutes the holding the court shall in the order designate that property by reference to the circumstances existing at the date of the order.

(1A)   Where the court, by virtue of paragraph (b) of section 31A(1) of this Act, makes an order under section 29 of this Act for the grant of a new tenancy in a case where the tenant is willing to accept a tenancy of part of the holding, the order shall be an order for the grant of a new tenancy of that part only.

(2)   The foregoing provisions of this section shall not apply in a case where the property comprised in the current tenancy includes other property besides the holding and the landlord requires any new tenancy ordered to be granted under section 29 of this Act to be a tenancy of the whole of the property comprised in the current tenancy; but in any such case—

(a)   any order under the said section 29 for the grant of a new tenancy shall be an order for the grant of a new tenancy of the whole of the property comprised in the current tenancy, and

(b)   references in the following provisions of this Part of this Act to the holding shall be construed as references to the whole of that property.

(3)   Where the current tenancy includes rights enjoyed by the tenant in connection with the holding, those rights shall be included in a tenancy ordered to be granted under section 29 of this Act, except as otherwise agreed between the landlord and the tenant or, in default of such agreement, determined by the court.

33. Duration of new tenancy.

Where on an application under this Part of this Act the court makes an order for the grant of a new tenancy, the new tenancy shall be such tenancy as may be agreed between the landlord and the tenant, or, in default of such an agreement, shall be such a tenancy as may be determined by the court to be reasonable in all the circumstances, being, if it is a tenancy for a term of years certain, a tenancy for a term not exceeding fourteen years, and shall begin on the coming to an end of the current tenancy.

34. Rent under new tenancy.

(1) The rent payable under a tenancy granted by order of the court under this Part of this Act shall be such as may be agreed between the landlord and the tenant or as, in default of such agreement, may be determined by the court to be that at which, having regard to the terms of the tenancy (other than those relating to rent), the holding might reasonably be expected to be let in the open market by a willing lessor, there being disregarded—

(a) any effect on rent of the fact that the tenant has or his predecessors in title have been in occupation of the holding,

(b) any goodwill attached to the holding by reason of the carrying on thereat of the business of the tenant (where by him or by a predecessor of his in that business),

(c) any effect on rent of an improvement to which this paragraph applies,

(d) in the case of a holding comprising licensed premises, any addition to its value attributable to the licence, if it appears to the court that having regard to the terms of the current tenancy and any other relevant circumstances the benefit of the licence belongs to the tenant.

(2) Paragraph (c) of the foregoing subsection applies to any improvement carried out by a person who at the time it was carried out was the tenant, but only if it was carried out otherwise than in pursuance of an obligation to his immediate landlord and either it was carried out during the current tenancy or the following conditions are satisfied, that is to say,—

(a) that it was completed not more than twenty-one years before the application for the new tenancy was made; and

(b) that the holding or any part of it affected by the improvement has at all times since the completion of the improvement been comprised in tenancies of the description specified in section 23(1) of this Act; and

(c) that at the termination of each of those tenancies the tenant did not quit.

(3) Where the rent is determined by the court the court may, if it thinks fit, further determine that the terms of the tenancy shall include such provision for varying the rent as may be specified in the determination.

35. Other terms of new tenancy.

The terms of a tenancy granted by order of the court under this Part of this Act (other than terms as to the duration thereof and as to the rent payable thereunder) shall be such as may be agreed between the landlord and the tenant or as, in default of such agreement, may be determined by the court; and in determining those terms the court shall have regard to the terms of the current tenancy and to all relevant circumstances.

36. Carrying out of order for new tenancy.

(1) Where under this Part of this Act the court makes an order for the grant of a new tenancy, then, unless the order is revoked under the next following subsection or the landlord and the tenant agree not to act upon the order, the landlord shall be bound to execute or make in favour of the tenant, and the tenant shall be bound to accept, a lease or agreement for a tenancy of the holding embodying the terms agreed between the landlord and the tenant or determined by the court in accordance with the foregoing provisions of this Part of this Act; and where the landlord executes or makes such a lease or agreement the tenant shall be bound, if so required by the landlord, to execute a counterpart or duplicate thereof.

(2) If the tenant, within fourteen days after the making of an order under this Part of this Act for the grant of a new tenancy, applies to the court for the revocation of the order the court shall revoke the order; and where the order is so revoked, then, if it is so agreed between the landlord and the tenant or determined by the court, the current tenancy shall continue, beyond the date at which it would have come to an end apart from this subsection, for such period as may be so agreed or determined to be necessary

to afford to the landlord a reasonable opportunity for reletting or otherwise disposing of the premises which would have been comprised in the new tenancy; and while the current tenancy continues by virtue of this subsection it shall not be a tenancy to which this Part of this Act applies.

(3)   Where an order is revoked under the last foregoing subsection any provision thereof as to payment of costs shall not cease to have effect by reason only of the revocation; but the court may, if it thinks fit, revoke or vary any such provision or, where no costs have been awarded in the proceedings for the revoked order, award such costs.

(4)   A lease executed or agreement made under this section, in a case where the interest of the lessor is subject to a mortgage, shall be deemed to be one authorised by section ninety-nine of the Law of Property Act, 1925 (which confers certain powers of leasing on mortgagors in possession), and subsection (13) of that section (which allows those powers to be restricted or excluded by agreement) shall not have effect in relation to such a lease or agreement.

37.   Compensation where order for new tenancy precluded on certain grounds.

(1)   Where on the making of an application under section 24 of this Act the court is precluded (whether by subsection (1) or subsection (2) of section 31 of this Act) from making an order for the grant of a new tenancy by reason of any of the grounds specified in paragraphs (e), (f) and (g) of subsection (1) of section 30 of this Act and not of any grounds specified in any other paragraph of that subsection, or where no other ground is specified in the landlord's notice under section 25 of this Act or, as the case may be, under section 26(6) thereof, than those specified in the said paragraphs (e), (f) and (g) and either no application under the said section 24 is made or such an application is withdrawn, then, subject to the provisions of this Act, the tenant shall be entitled on quitting the holding to recover from the landlord by way of compensation an amount determined in accordance with the following provisions of this section.

(2)   The said amount shall be as follows, that is to say,—

(a)   where the conditions specified in the next following subsection are satisfied it shall be the product of the appropriate multiplier and twice the rateable value of the holding,

(b)   in any other case it shall be the product of the appropriate multiplier and the rateable value of the holding.

(3)   The said conditions are—

(a)   that, during the whole of the fourteen years immediately preceding the termination of the current tenancy, premises being or comprised in the holding have been occupied for the purposes of a business carried on by the occupier or for those and other purposes;

(b)   that, if during those fourteen years there was a change in the occupier of the premises, the person who was the occupier immediately after the change was the successor to the business carried on by the person who was the occupier immediately before the change.

(4)   Where the court is precluded from making an order for the grant of a new tenancy under this Part of this Act in the circumstances mentioned in subsection (1) of this section, the court shall on the application of the tenant certify that fact.

(5)   For the purposes of subsection (2) of this section the rateable value of the holding shall be determined as follows:—

(a)   where in the valuation list in force at the date on which the landlord's notice under section 25 or, as the case may be, subsection (6) of section 26 of this Act is given a value is then shown as the annual value (as hereinafter defined) of the holding, the rateable value of the holding shall be taken to be that value;

(b)   where no such value is so shown with respect to the holding but such a value or such values is or are so shown with respect to premises comprised in or comprising the holding or part of it, the rateable value of the holding shall be taken to be such value as is found by a proper apportionment or aggregation of the value or values so shown;

(c) where the rateable value of the holding cannot be ascertained in accordance with the foregoing paragraphs of this subsection, it shall be taken to be the value which, apart from any exemption from assessment to rates, would on a proper assessment be the value to be entered in the said valuation list as the annual value of the holding;

and any dispute arising, whether in proceedings before the court or otherwise, as to the determination for those purposes of the rateable value of the holding shall be referred to the Commissioners of Inland Revenue for decision by a valuation officer.

An appeal shall lie to the Lands Tribunal from any decision of a valuation officer under this subsection, but subject thereto any such decision shall be final.

(6) The Commissioners of Inland Revenue may by statutory instrument make rules prescribing the procedure in connection with references under this section.

(7) In this section—

the reference to the termination of the current tenancy is a reference to the date of termination specified in the landlord's notice under section 25 of this Act or, as the case may be, the date specified in the tenant's request for a new tenancy as the date from which the new tenancy is to begin;

the expression "annual value" means rateable value except that where the rateable value differs from the net annual value the said expression means net annual value;

the expression "valuation officer" means any officer of the Commissioners of Inland Revenue for the time being authorised by a certificate of the Commissioners to act in relation to a valuation list.

(8) In subsection (2) of this section "the appropriate multiplier" means such multiplier as the Secretary of State may by order made by statutory instrument prescribe.

(9) A statutory instrument containing an order under subsection (8) of this section shall be subject to annulment in pursuance of a resolution of either House of Parliament.

38. Restriction on agreements excluding provisions of Part II.

(1) Any agreement relating to a tenancy to which this Part of this Act applies (whether contained in the instrument creating the tenancy or not) shall be void (except as provided by subsection (4) of this section) in so far as it purports to preclude the tenant from making an application or request under this Part of this Act or provides for the termination or the surrender of the tenancy in the event of his making such an application or request or for the imposition of any penalty or disability on the tenant in that event.

(2) Where—

(a) during the whole of the five years immediately preceding the date on which the tenant under a tenancy to which this Part of this Act applies is to quit the holding, premises being or comprised in the holding have been occupied for the purposes of a business carried on by the occupier or for those and other purposes, and

(b) if during those five years there was a change in the occupier of the premises, the person who was the occupier immediately after the change was the successor to the business carried on by the person who was the occupier immediately before the change,

any agreement (whether contained in the instrument creating the tenancy or not and whether made before or after the termination of that tenancy) which purports to exclude or reduce compensation under the last foregoing section shall to that extent be void, so however that this subsection shall not affect any agreement as to the amount of any such compensation which is made after the right to compensation has accrued.

(3) In a case not falling within the last foregoing subsection the right to compensation conferred by the last foregoing section may be excluded or modified by agreement.

(4)   The court may—

(a)   on the joint application of the persons who will be the landlord and the tenant in relation to a tenancy to be granted for a term of years certain which will be a tenancy to which this Part of this Act applies, authorise an agreement excluding in relation to that tenancy the provisions of sections 24 to 28 of this Act; and

(b)   on the joint application of the persons who are the landlord and the tenant in relation to a tenancy to which this Part of this Act applies, authorise an agreement for the surrender of the tenancy on such date or in such circumstances as may be specified in the agreement and on such terms (if any) as may be so specified;

if the agreement is contained in or endorsed on the instrument creating the tenancy or such other instrument as the court may specify; and an agreement contained in or endorsed on an instrument in pursuance of an authorisation given under this subsection shall be valid notwithstanding anything in the preceding provisions of this section.

General and supplementary provisions

39.   Saving for compulsory acquisitions.

(2)   If the amount of the compensation which would have been payable under section thirty-seven of this Act if the tenancy had come to an end in circumstances giving rise to compensation under that section and the date at which the acquiring authority obtained possession had been the termination of the current tenancy exceeds the amount of the compensation payable under section 121 of the Land Clauses Consolidation Act 1845 or section 20 of the Compulsory Purchase Act 1965 in the case of a tenancy to which this Part of this Act applies, that compensation shall be increased by the amount of the excess.

(3)   Nothing in section twenty-four of this Act shall affect the operation of the said section one hundred and twenty-one.

40.   Duty of tenants and landlords of business premises to give information to each other.

(1)   Where any person having an interest in any business premises, being an interest in reversion expectant (whether immediately or not) on a tenancy of those premises, serves on the tenant a notice in the prescribed form requiring him to do so, it shall be the duty of the tenant to notify that person in writing within one month of the service of the notice—

(a)   whether he occupies the premises or any part thereof wholly or partly for the purposes of a business carried on by him, and

(b)   whether his tenancy has effect subject to any sub-tenancy on which his tenancy is immediately expectant and, if so, what premises are comprised in the sub-tenancy, for what term it has effect (or, if it is terminable by notice, by what notice it can be terminated), what is the rent payable thereunder, who is the sub-tenant, and (to the best of his knowledge and belief) whether the sub-tenant is in occupation of the premises or of part of the premises comprised in the sub-tenancy and, if not, what is the sub-tenant's address.

(2)   Where the tenant of any business premises, being a tenant under such a tenancy as is mentioned in subsection (1) of section twenty-six of this Act, serves on any of the persons mentioned in the next following subsection a notice in the prescribed form requiring him to do so, it shall be the duty of that person to notify the tenant in writing within one month after the service of the notice—

(a)   whether he is the owner of the fee simple in respect of those premises or any part thereof or the mortgagee in possession of such an owner and, if not,

(b)   (to the best of his knowledge and belief) the name and address of the person who is his or, as the case may be, his mortgagor's immediate landlord in respect of those premises or of the part in respect of which he or his mortgagor is not the owner in fee simple, for what term his or his mortgagor's tenancy thereof has effect and what is the earliest date (if any) at which that tenancy is terminable by notice to quit given by the landlord.

(3)   The persons referred to in the last foregoing subsection are, in relation to the tenant of any business premises,—

(a)   any person having an interest in the premises, being an interest in reversion expectant (whether immediately or not) on the tenant's, and

(b)   any person being a mortgagee in possession in respect of such an interest in reversion as is mentioned in paragraph (a) of this subsection;

and the information which any such person as is mentioned in paragraph (a) of this subsection is required to give under the last foregoing subsection shall include information whether there is a mortgagee in possession of his interest in the premises and, if so, what is the name and address of the mortgagee.

(4)   The foregoing provisions of this section shall not apply to a notice served by or on the tenant more than two years before the date on which apart from this Act his tenancy would come to an end by effluxion of time or could be brought to an end by notice to quit given by the landlord.

(5)   In this section—

the expression "business premises" means premises used wholly or partly for the purposes of a business;

the expression "mortgagee in possession" includes a receiver appointed by the mortgagee or by the court who is in receipt of the rents and profits, and the expression "his mortgagor" shall be construed accordingly;

the expression "sub-tenant" includes a person retaining possession of any premises by virtue of the Rent Act 1977 after the coming to an end of a sub-tenancy, and the expression "sub-tenancy" includes a right so to retain possession.

41.   Trusts.

(1)   Where a tenancy is held on trust, occupation by all or any of the beneficiaries under the trust, and the carrying on of a business by all or any of the beneficiaries, shall be treated for the purposes of section twenty-three of this Act as equivalent to occupation or the carrying on of a business by the tenant; and in relation to a tenancy to which this Part of this Act applies by virtue of the foregoing provisions of this subsection—

(a)   references (however expressed) in this Part of this Act and in the Ninth Schedule to this Act to the business of, or to carrying on of business, use, occupation or enjoyment by, the tenant shall be construed as including references to the business of, or to carrying on of business, use, occupation or enjoyment by, the beneficiaries or beneficiary;

(b)   the reference in paragraph (d) of subsection (1) of section thirty-four of this Act to the tenant shall be construed as including the beneficiaries or beneficiary; and

(c)   a change in the persons of the trustees shall not be treated as a change in the person of the tenant.

(2)   Where the landlord's interest is held on trust the references in paragraph (g) of subsection (1) of section thirty of this Act to the landlord shall be construed as including references to the beneficiaries under the trust or any of them; but, except in the case of a trust arising under a will or on the intestacy of any person, the reference in subsection (2) of that section to the creation of the interest therein mentioned shall be construed as including the creation of the trust.

41A.   Partnerships.

(1)   The following provisions of this section shall apply where—

(a)   a tenancy is held jointly by two or more persons (in this section referred to as the joint tenants); and

(b)   the property comprised in the tenancy is or includes premises occupied for the purposes of a business; and

(c)   the business (or some other business) was at some time during the existence of the tenancy carried on in partnership by all the persons who were then the joint tenants or by those and other persons and the joint tenants' interest in the premises was then partnership property; and

(d)   the business is carried on (whether alone or in partnership with other persons) by one or some only of the joint tenants and no part of the property comprised in the tenancy is occupied, in right of the tenancy, for the purposes of a business carried on (whether alone or in partnership with other persons) by the other or others.

(2)   In the following provisions of this section those of the joint tenants who for the time being carry on the business are referred to as the business tenants and the others as the other joint tenants.

(3)   Any notice given by the business tenants which, had it been given by all the joint tenants, would have been—

(a)   a tenant's request for a new tenancy made in accordance with section 26 of this Act; or

(b)   a notice under subsection (1) or subsection (2) of section 27 of this Act; shall be treated as such if it states that it is given by virtue of this section and sets out the facts by virtue of which the persons giving it are the business tenants; and references in those sections and in section 24A of this Act to the tenant shall be construed accordingly.

(4)   A notice given by the landlord to the business tenants which, had it been given to all the joint tenants, would have been a notice under section 25 of this Act shall be treated as such a notice, and references in that section to the tenant shall be construed accordingly.

(5)   An application under section 24(1) of this Act for a new tenancy may, instead of being made by all the joint tenants, be made by the business tenants alone; and where it is so made—

(a)   this Part of this Act shall have effect, in relation to it, as if the references therein to the tenant included references to the business tenants alone; and

(b)   the business tenants shall be liable, to the exclusion of the other joint tenants, for the payment of rent and the discharge of any other obligation under the current tenancy for any rental period beginning after the date specified in the landlord's notice under section 25 of this Act or, as the case may be, beginning on or after the date specified in their request for a new tenancy.

(6)   Where the court makes an order under section 29(1) of this Act for the grant of a new tenancy on an application made by the business tenants it may order the grant to be made to them or to them jointly with the persons carrying on the business in partnership with them, and may order the grant to be made subject to the satisfaction, within a time specified by the order, of such conditions as to guarantors, sureties or otherwise as appear to the court equitable, having regard to the omission of the other joint tenants from the persons who will be the tenant under the new tenancy.

(7)   The business tenants shall be entitled to recover any amount payable by way of compensation under section 37 or section 59 of this Act.

42.   Groups of companies.

(1)   For the purposes of this section two bodies corporate shall be taken to be members of a group if and only if one is a subsidiary of the other or both are subsidiaries of a third body corporate.

In this subsection "subsidiary" has the meaning given by section 736 of the Companies Act 1985.

(2)   Where a tenancy is held by a member of a group, occupation by another member of the group, and the carrying on of a business by another member of the group, shall

be treated for the purposes of section 23 of this Act as equivalent to occupation or the carrying on of a business by the member of the group holding the tenancy: and in relation to a tenancy to which this Part of this Act applies by virtue of the foregoing provisions of this subsection—

(a)   references (however expressed) in this Part of this Act and in the Ninth Schedule to this Act to the business of or to use occupation or enjoyment by the tenant shall be construed as including references to the business of or to use occupation or enjoyment by the said other member;

(b)   the reference in paragraph (d) of subsection (1) of section 34 of this Act to the tenant shall be construed as including the said other member; and

(c)   an assignment of the tenancy from one member of the group to another shall not be treated as a change in the person of the tenant.

(3)   Where the landlord's interest is held by a member of a group—

(a)   the reference in paragraph (g) of subsection (1) of section 30 of this Act to intended occupation by the landlord for the purposes of a business to be carried on by him shall be construed as including intended occupation by any member of the group for the purposes of a business to be carried on by that member; and

(b)   the reference in subsection (2) of that section to the purchase or creation of any interest shall be construed as a reference to a purchase from or creation by a person other than a member of the group.

43.   Tenancies excluded from Part II

(1)   This Part of this Act does not apply—

(a)   to a tenancy of an agricultural holding or a tenancy which would be a tenancy of an agricultural holding if subsection (3) of section (2) of the Agricultural Holdings Act 1986 did not have effect or, in a case where approval was given under subsection (1) of that section, if that approval had not been given.

(b)   to a tenancy created by a mining lease;

(d)   to a tenancy of premises licensed for the sale of intoxicating liquor for consumption on the premises, other than—

(i)   premises which are structurally adapted to be used, and are bona fide used, for a business which comprises one or both of the following, namely, the reception of guests and travellers desiring to sleep on the premises and the carrying on of a restaurant, being a business a substantial proportion of which consists of transactions other than the sale of intoxicating liquor;

(ii)   premises adapted to be used, and bona fide used, only for one or more of the following purposes, namely, for judicial or public administrative purposes, or as a theatre or place of public or private entertainment, or as public gardens or picture galleries, or for exhibitions, or for any similar purpose to which the holding of the licence is merely ancillary;

(iii)   premises adapted to be used, and bona fide used, as refreshment rooms at a railway station.

(2)   This Part of this Act does not apply to a tenancy granted by reason that the tenant was the holder of an office, appointment or employment from the grantor thereof and continuing only so long as the tenant holds the office, appointment or employment, or terminable by the grantor on the tenant's ceasing to hold it, or coming to an end at a time fixed by reference to the time at which the tenant ceases to hold it:

Provided that this subsection shall not have effect in relation to a tenancy granted after the commencement of this Act unless the tenancy was granted by an instrument in writing which expressed the purpose for which the tenancy was granted.

(3)   This Part of this Act does not apply to a tenancy granted for a term certain not exceeding six months unless—

(a) the tenancy contains provision for renewing the term or for extending it beyond six months from its beginning; or

(b) the tenant has been in occupation for a period which, together with any period during which any predecessor in the carrying on of the business carried on by the tenant was in occupation, exceeds twelve months.

43A. Jurisdiction of county court to make declaration.

Where the rateable value of the holding is such that the jurisdiction conferred on the court by any other provision of this Part of this Act is, by virtue of section 63 of this Act, exercisable by the county court, the county court shall have jurisdiction (but without prejudice to the jurisdiction of the High Court) to make any declaration as to any matter arising under this Part of this Act, whether or not any other relief is sought in the proceedings.

44. Meaning of "the landlord" in Part II, and provisions as to mesne landlords, etc.

(1) Subject to the next following subsection, in this Part of this Act the expression "the landlord", in relation to a tenancy (in this section referred to as "the relevant tenancy"), means the person (whether or not he is the immediate landlord) who is the owner of that interest in the property comprised in the relevant tenancy which for the time being fulfils the following conditions, that is to say—

(a) that it is an interest in reversion expectant (whether immediately or not) on the termination of the relevant tenancy, and

(b) that it is either the fee simple or a tenancy which will not come to an end within fourteen months by effluxion of time and, if it is such a tenancy, that no notice has been given by virtue of which it will come to an end within fourteen months or any further time by which it may be continued under section 36(2) or section 64 of this Act,

and is not itself in reversion expectant (whether immediately or not) on an interest which fulfils those conditions.

(2) References in this Part of this Act to a notice to quit given by the landlord are references to a notice to quit given by the immediate landlord.

(3) The provisions of the Sixth Schedule to this Act shall have effect for the application of this Part of this Act to cases where the immediate landlord of the tenant is not the owner of the fee simple in respect of the holding.

46. Interpretation of Part II

In this Part of this Act:—

"business" has the meaning assigned to it by subsection (2) of section twenty-three of this Act;

"current tenancy" has the meaning assigned to it by subsection (1) of section twenty-six of this Act;

"date of termination" has the meaning assigned to it by subsection (1) of section twenty-five of this Act;

subject to the provisions of section thirty-two of this Act, "the holding" has the meaning assigned to it by subsection (3) of section twenty-three of this Act;

"mining lease" has the same meaning as in the Landlord and Tenant Act, 1927.

PART III
COMPENSATION FOR IMPROVEMENTS

47. Time for making claims for compensation for improvements.

(1) Where a tenancy is terminated by notice to quit, whether given by the landlord or by the tenant, or by a notice given by any person under Part I or Part II of this Act, the time for making a claim for compensation at the termination of the tenancy shall be a time falling within the period of three months beginning on the date on which the notice is given:

Provided that where the tenancy is terminated by a tenant's request for a new tenancy under section twenty-six of this Act, the said time shall be a time falling within the period of three months beginning on the date on which the landlord gives notice, or (if he has not given such a notice) the latest date on which he could have given notice, under subsection (6) of the said section twenty-six or, as the case may be, paragraph (a) of subsection (4) of section fifty-seven or paragraph (b) of subsection (1) of section fifty-eight of this Act.

(2)   Where a tenancy comes to an end by effluxion of time, the time for making such a claim shall be a time not earlier than six nor later than three months before the coming to an end of the tenancy.

(3)   Where a tenancy is terminated by forfeiture or re-entry, the time for making such a claim shall be a time falling within the period of three months beginning with the effective date of the order of the court for the recovery of possession of the land comprised in the tenancy or, if the tenancy is terminated by re-entry without such an order, the period of three months beginning with the date of the re-entry.

(4)   In the last foregoing subsection the reference to the effective date of an order is a reference to the date on which the order is to take effect according to the terms thereof or the date on which it ceases to be subject to appeal, whichever is the later.

48.   Amendments as to limitations on tenant's right to compensation.

(1)   So much of paragraph (b) of subsection (1) of section two of the Act of 1927 as provides that a tenant shall not be entitled to compensation in respect of any improvement made in pursuance of a statutory obligation shall not apply to any improvement begun after the commencement of this Act, but section three of the Act of 1927 (which enables a landlord to object to a proposed improvement) shall not have effect in relation to an improvement made in pursuance of a statutory obligation except so much thereof as—

(a)   requires the tenant to serve on the landlord notice of his intention to make the improvement together with such a plan and specification as are mentioned in that section and to supply copies of the plan and specification at the request of any superior landlord; and

(b)   enables the tenant to obtain at his expense a certificate from the landlord or the tribunal that the improvement has been duly executed.

(2)   Paragraph (c) of the said subsection (1) (which provides that a tenant shall not be entitled to compensation in respect of any improvement made less than three years before the termination of the tenancy) shall not apply to any improvement begun after the commencement of this Act.

(3)   No notice shall be served after the commencement of this Act under paragraph (d) of the said subsection (1) (which excludes rights to compensation where the landlord serves on the tenant notice offering a renewal of the tenancy on reasonable terms).

50.   Interpretation of Part III.

In this Part of this Act the expression "Act of 1927" means the Landlord and Tenant Act, 1927, the expression "compensation" means compensation under Part I of that Act in respect of an improvement, and other expressions used in this Part of this Act and in the Act of 1927 have the same meanings in this Part of this Act as in that Act.

PART IV
MISCELLANEOUS AND SUPPLEMENTARY

51.   Extension of Leasehold Property (Repairs) Act, 1938.

(1)   The Leasehold Property (Repairs) Act, 1938 (which restricts the enforcement of repairing covenants in long leases of small houses) shall extend to every tenancy (whether of a house or of other property, and without regard to rateable value) where the following conditions are fulfilled, that is to say,—

   (a)   that the tenancy was granted for a term of years certain of not less than seven years;

   (b)   that three years or more of the term remain unexpired at the date of the service of the notice of dilapidations or, as the case may be, at the date of commencement of the action for damages; and

   (c)   that the property comprised in the tenancy is not an agricultural holding.

   (3)   The said Act of 1938 shall apply where there is an interest belonging to Her Majesty in right of the Crown or to a Government department, or held on behalf of Her Majesty for the purposes of a Government department, in like manner as if that interest were an interest not so belonging or held.

   (4)   Subsection (2) of section twenty-three of the Landlord and Tenant Act, 1927 (which authorises a tenant to serve documents on the person to whom he has been paying rent) shall apply in relation to any counter-notice to be served under the said Act of 1938.

   (5)   This section shall apply to tenancies granted, and to breaches occurring, before or after the commencement of this Act, except that it shall not apply where the notice of dilapidations was served, or the action for damages begun, before the commencement of this Act.

   (6)   In this section the expression "notice of dilapidations" means a notice under subsection (1) of section one hundred and forty-six of the Law of Property Act, 1925.

53. Jurisdiction of county court where lessor refuses licence or consent.

   (1)   Where a landlord withholds his licence or consent—

   (a)   to an assignment of the tenancy or a subletting, charging or parting with the possession of the demised property or any part thereof, or

   (b)   to the making of an improvement on the demised property or any part thereof, or

   (c)   to a change in the use of the demised property or any part thereof, or to the making of a specified use of that property,

and the High Court has jurisdiction to make a declaration that the licence or consent was unreasonably withheld, then without prejudice to the jurisdiction of the High Court the county court shall have the like jurisdiction whatever the net annual value for rating of the demised property is to be taken to be for the purposes of the County Courts Act 1984 and notwithstanding that the tenant does not seek any relief other than the declaration.

   (2)   Where on the making of an application to the county court for such a declaration the court is satisfied that the licence or consent was unreasonably withheld, the court shall make a declaration accordingly.

   (3)   The foregoing provisions of this section shall have effect whether the tenancy in question was created before or after the commencement of this Act and whether the refusal of the licence or consent occurred before or after the commencement of this Act.

   (4)   Nothing in this section shall be construed as conferring jurisdiction on the county court to grant any relief other than such a declaration as aforesaid.

54. Determination of tenancies of derelict land.

Where a landlord, having power to serve a notice to quit, on an application to the county court satisfies the court—

   (a)   that he has taken all reasonable steps to communicate with the person last known to him to be the tenant, and has failed to do so,

   (b)   that during the period of six months ending with the date of the application neither the tenant nor any person claiming under him has been in occupation of the property comprised in the tenancy or any part thereof, and

   (c)   that during the said period either no rent was payable by the tenant or the rent payable has not been paid, the court may if it thinks fit by order determine the tenancy as from the date of the order.

55. Compensation for possession obtained by misrepresentation.

(1) Where under Part I of this Act an order is made for possession of the property comprised in a tenancy, or under Part II of this Act the court refuses an order for the grant of a new tenancy, and it is subsequently made to appear to the court that the order was obtained, or the court induced to refuse the grant, by misrepresentation or the concealment of material facts, the court may order the landlord to pay to the tenant such sum as appears sufficient as compensation for damage or loss sustained by the tenant as the result of the order or refusal.

(2) In this section the expression "the landlord" means the person applying for possession or opposing an application for the grant of a new tenancy, and the expression "the tenant" means the person against whom the order for possession was made or to whom the grant of a new tenancy was refused.

56. Application to Crown.

(1) Subject to the provisions of this and the four next following sections, Part II of this Act shall apply where there is an interest belonging to Her Majesty in right of the Crown or the Duchy of Lancaster or belonging to the Duchy of Cornwall, or belonging to a Government department or held on behalf of Her Majesty for the purposes of a Government department, in like manner as if that interest were an interest not so belonging or held.

(2) The provisions of the Eighth Schedule to this Act shall have effect as respects the application of Part II of this Act to cases where the interest of the landlord belongs to Her Majesty in right of the Crown or the Duchy of Lancaster or to the Duchy of Cornwall.

(3) Where a tenancy is held by or on behalf of a Government department and the property comprised therein is or includes premises occupied for any purposes of a Government department, the tenancy shall be one to which Part II of this Act applies; and for the purposes of any provision of the said Part II of the Ninth Schedule to this Act which is applicable only if either or both of the following conditions are satisfied, that is to say—

(a) that any premises have during any period been occupied for the purposes of the tenant's business;

(b) that on any change of occupier of any premises the new occupier succeeded to the business of the former occupier,

the said conditions shall be deemed to be satisfied respectively, in relation to such a tenancy, if during that period or, as the case may be, immediately before and immediately after the change, the premises were occupied for the purposes of a Government department.

(4) The last foregoing subsection shall apply in relation to any premises provided by a Government department without any rent being payable to the department therefor as if the premises were occupied for the purposes of a Government department.

(5) The provisions of Parts III and IV of this Act amending any other enactment which binds the Crown or applies to land belonging to Her Majesty in right of the Crown or the Duchy of Lancaster, or land belonging to the Duchy of Cornwall, or to land belonging to any Government department, shall bind the Crown or apply to such land.

(6) Sections fifty-three and fifty-four of this Act shall apply where the interest of the landlord, or any other interest in the land in question, belongs to Her Majesty in right of the Crown or the Duchy of Lancaster or to the Duchy of Cornwall, or belongs to a Government department or is held on behalf of Her Majesty for the purposes of a Government department, in like manner as if that interest were an interest not so belonging or held.

(7) Part I of this Act shall apply where—

(a) there is an interest belonging to Her Majesty in right of the Crown and that interest is under the management of the Crown Estate Commissioners; or

(b) there is an interest belonging to Her Majesty in right of the Duchy of Lancaster or belonging to the Duchy of Cornwall;

as if it were an interest not so belonging.

57. Modification on grounds of public interest of rights under Part II.

(1) Where the interest of the landlord or any superior landlord in the property comprised in any tenancy belongs to or is held for the purposes of a Government department or is held by a local authority, statutory undertakers or a development corporation, the Minister or Board in charge of any Government department may certify that it is requisite for the purposes of the first-mentioned department, or, as the case may be, of the authority, undertakers or corporation, that the use or occupation of the property or a part thereof shall be changed by a specified date.

(2) A certificate under the last foregoing subsection shall not be given unless the owner of the interest belonging or held as mentioned in the last foregoing subsection has given to the tenant a notice stating—

(a) that the question of the giving of such a certificate is under consideration by the Minister or Board specified in the notice, and

(b) that if within twenty-one days of the giving of the notice the tenant makes to that Minister or Board representations in writing with respect to that question, they will be considered before the question is determined,

and if the tenant makes any such representations within the said twenty-one days the Minister or Board shall consider them before determining whether to give the certificate.

(3) Where a certificate has been given under subsection (1) of this section in relation to any tenancy, then,—

(a) if a notice given under subsection (1) of section twenty-five of this Act specifies as the date of termination a date not earlier than the date specified in the certificate and contains a copy of the certificate subsections (5) and (6) of that section shall not apply to the notice and no application for a new tenancy shall be made by the tenant under section twenty-four of this Act;

(b) if such a notice specifies an earlier date as the date of termination and contains a copy of the certificate, then if the court makes an order under Part II of this Act for the grant of a new tenancy the new tenancy shall be for a term expiring not later than the date specified in the certificate and shall not be a tenancy to which Part II of this Act applies.

(4) Where a tenant makes a request for a new tenancy under section twenty-six of this Act, and the interest of the landlord or any superior landlord in the property comprised in the current tenancy belongs or is held as mentioned in subsection (1) of this section, the following provisions shall have effect:—

(a) if a certificate has been given under the said subsection (1) in relation to the current tenancy, and within two months after the making of the request the landlord gives notice to the tenant that the certificate has been given and the notice contains a copy of the certificate, then,—

(i) if the date specified in the certificate is not later than that specified in the tenant's request for a new tenancy, the tenant shall not make an application under section twenty-four of this Act for the grant of a new tenancy;

(ii) if, in any other case, the court makes an order under Part II of this Act for the grant of a new tenancy the new tenancy shall be for a term expiring not later than the date specified in the certificate and shall not be a tenancy to which Part II of this Act applies;

(b)   if no such certificate has been given but notice under subsection (2) of this section has been given before the making of the request or within two months thereafter, the request shall not have effect, without prejudice however to the making of a new request when the Minister or Board has determined whether to give a certificate.

(5)   Where application is made to the court under Part II of this Act for the grant of a new tenancy and the landlord's interest in the property comprised in the tenancy belongs or is held as mentioned in subsection (1) of this section, the Minister or Board in charge of any Government department may certify that it is necessary in the public interest that if the landlord makes an application in that behalf the court shall determine as a term of the new tenancy that it shall be terminable by six months' notice to quit given by the landlord.

Subsection (2) of this section shall apply in relation to a certificate under this subsection, and if notice under the said subsection (2) has been given to the tenant—

(a)   the court shall not determine the application for the grant of a new tenancy until the Minister or Board has determined whether to give a certificate,

(b)   if a certificate is given, the court shall on the application of the landlord determine as a term of the new tenancy that it shall be terminable as aforesaid, and section twenty-five of this Act shall apply accordingly.

(6)   The foregoing provisions of this section shall apply to an interest held by a Regional Health Authority, Area Health Authority, District Health Authority, Family Practitioner Committee or special health authority as they apply to an interest held by a local authority but with the substitution, for the reference to the purposes of the authority, of a reference to the purposes of the National Health Service Act 1977.

(7)   Where the interest of the landlord or any superior landlord in the property comprised in any tenancy belongs to the National Trust the Minister of Works may certify that it is requisite, for the purpose of securing that the property will as from a specified date be used or occupied in a manner better suited to the nature thereof, that the use or occupation of the property should be changed; and subsections (2) to (4) of this section shall apply in relation to certificates under this subsection, and to cases where the interest of the landlord or any superior landlord belongs to the National Trust, as those subsections apply in relation to certificates under subsection (1) of this section and to cases where the interest of the landlord or any superior landlord belongs or is held as mentioned in that subsection.

(8)   In this and the next following section the expression "Government department" does not include the Commissioners of Crown Lands and the expression "landlord" has the same meaning as in Part II of this Act; and in the last foregoing subsection the expression "National Trust" means the National Trust for Places of Historic Interest or Natural Beauty.

58.   Termination on special grounds of tenancies to which Part II applies.

(1)   Where the landlord's interest in the property comprised in any tenancy belongs to or is held for the purposes of a Government department, and the Minister or Board in charge of any Government department certifies that for reasons of national security it is necessary that the use or occupation of the property should be discontinued or changed, then—

(a)   if the landlord gives a notice under subsection (1) of section twenty-five of this Act containing a copy of the certificate, subsections (5) and (6) of that section shall not apply to the notice and no application for a new tenancy shall be made by the tenant under section twenty-four of this Act;

(b)   if (whether before or after the giving of the certificate) the tenant makes a request for a new tenancy under section twenty-six of this Act, and within two months after the making of the request the landlord gives notice to the tenant that the certificate has been given and the notice contains a copy of the certificate,—

(i)   the tenant shall not make an application under section twenty-four of this Act for the grant of a new tenancy, and

(ii)   if the notice specifies as the date on which the tenancy is to terminate a date earlier than that specified in the tenant's request as the date on which the new tenancy is to begin but neither earlier than six months from the giving of the notice nor earlier than the earliest date at which apart from this Act the tenancy would come to an end or could be brought to an end, the tenancy shall terminate on the date specified in the notice instead of that specified in the request.

(2)   Where the landlord's interest in the property comprised in any tenancy belongs to or is held for the purposes of a Government department, nothing in this Act shall invalidate an agreement to the effect—

(a)   that on the giving of such a certificate as is mentioned in the last foregoing subsection the tenancy may be terminated by notice to quit given by the landlord of such length as may be specified in the agreement, if the notice contains a copy of the certificate; and

(b)   that after the giving of such a notice containing such a copy the tenancy shall not be one to which Part II of this Act applies.

(3)   Where the landlord's interest in the property comprised in any tenancy is held by statutory undertakers, nothing in this Act shall invalidate an agreement to the effect—

(a)   that where the Minister or Board in charge of a Government department certifies that possession of the property comprised in the tenancy or a part thereof is urgently required for carrying out repairs (whether on that property or elsewhere) which are needed for the proper operation of the landlord's undertaking, the tenancy may be terminated by notice to quit given by the landlord of such length as may be specified in the agreement, if the notice contains a copy of the certificate; and

(b)   that after the giving of such a notice containing such a copy, the tenancy shall not be one to which Part II of this Act applies.

(4)   Where the court makes an order under Part II of this Act for the grant of a new tenancy and the Minister or Board in charge of any Government department certifies that the public interest requires the tenancy to be subject to such a term as is mentioned in paragraph (a) or (b) of this subsection, as the case may be, then—

(a)   if the landlord's interest in the property comprised in the tenancy belongs to or is held for the purposes of a Government department, the court shall on the application of the landlord determine as a term of the new tenancy that such an agreement as is mentioned in subsection (2) of this section and specifying such length of notice as is mentioned in the certificate shall be embodied in the new tenancy;

(b)   if the landlord's interest in that property is held by statutory undertakers, the court shall on the application of the landlord determine as a term of the new tenancy that such an agreement as is mentioned in subsection (3) of this section and specifying such length of notice as is mentioned in the certificate shall be embodied in the new tenancy.

59.   Compensation for exercise of powers under ss. 57 and 58.

(1)   Where by virtue of any certificate given for the purposes of either of the two last foregoing sections or subject to subsections (1A) or (1B) below, sections 60A or 60B below, the tenant is precluded from obtaining an order for the grant of a new tenancy, or of a new tenancy for a term expiring later than a specified date, the tenant shall be entitled on quitting the premises to recover from the owner of the interest by virtue of which the certificate was given an amount by way of compensation, and subsections (2), (3) and (5) to (7) of section thirty-seven of this Act shall with the necessary modifications apply for the purposes of ascertaining the amount.

(1A)   No compensation shall be recoverable under subsection (1) above where the certificate was given under section 60A below and either—

(a)   the premises vested in the Welsh Development Agency under section 7 (property of Welsh Industrial Estates Corporation) or 8 (land held under Local Employment Act 1972) of the Welsh Development Agency Act 1975, or

(b)   the tenant was not tenant of the premises when the said Agency acquired the interest by virtue of which the certificate was given.

(1B)   No compensation shall be recoverable under subsection (1) above where the certificate was given under section 60B below and either—

(a)   the premises are premises which—

(i)   were vested in the Welsh Development Agency by section 8 of the Welsh Development Agency Act 1975 or were acquired by the Agency when no tenancy subsisted in the premises; and

(ii)   vested in the Development Board for Rural Wales under section 24 of the Development of Rural Wales Act 1976; or

(b)   the tenant was not the tenant of the premises when the Board acquired the interest by virtue of which the certificate was given.

(2)   Subsections (2) and (3) of section thirty-eight of this Act shall apply to compensation under this section as they apply to compensation under section thirty-seven of this Act.

60.   Special provisions as to premises provided under Distribution of Industry Acts 1945 and 1950, etc.

(1)   Where the property comprised in a tenancy consists of premises of which the Minister of Technology or the English Industrial Estates Corporation is the landlord, being premises situated in a locality which is either—

(a)   a development area or

(b)   an intermediate area

and the Minister of Technology certifies that it is necessary or expedient for achieving the purpose mentioned in section 2(1) of the said Act of 1972 that the use or occupation of the property should be changed, paragraphs (a) and (b) of subsection (1) of section fifty-eight of this Act shall apply as they apply where such a certificate is given as is mentioned in that subsection.

(2)   Where the court makes an order under Part II of this Act for the grant of a new tenancy of any such premises as aforesaid, and the Minister of Technology certifies that it is necessary or expedient as aforesaid that the tenancy should be subject to a term, specified in the certificate, prohibiting or restricting the tenant from assigning the tenancy or sub-letting, charging or parting with possession of the premises or any part thereof or changing the use of premises or any part thereof, the court shall determine that the terms of the tenancy shall include the terms specified in the certificate.

(3)   In this section "development area" and "intermediate area" mean an area for the time being specified as a development area or, as the case may be, as an intermediate area by an order made, or having effect as if made, under section 1 of the Industrial Development Act 1982.

60A.   Welsh Development Agency premises.

(1)   Where the property comprised in a tenancy consists of premises of which the Welsh Development Agency is the landlord, and the Secretary of State certifies that it is necessary or expedient, for the purpose of providing employment appropriate to the needs of the area in which the premises are situated, that the use or occupation of the property should be changed, paragraphs (a) and (b) of section 58(1) above shall apply as they apply where such a certificate is given as is mentioned in that subsection.

(2)   Where the court makes an order under Part II of this Act for the grant of a new tenancy of any such premises as aforesaid, and the Secretary of State certifies that it is necessary or expedient as aforesaid that the tenancy should be subject to a term, specified in the certificate, prohibiting or restricting the tenant from assigning the

tenancy or subletting, charging or parting with possession of the premises or any part of the premises or changing the use of the premises or any part of the premises, the court shall determine that the terms of the tenancy shall include the terms specified in the certificate.

60B. Development Board for Rural Wales premises.

(1) Where the property comprised in the tenancy consists of premises of which the Development Board for Rural Wales is the landlord, and the Secretary of State certifies that it is necessary or expedient, for the purpose of providing employment appropriate to the needs of the area in which the premises are situated, that the use or occupation of the property should be changed, paragraphs (a) and (b) of section 58(1) above shall apply as they apply where such a certificate is given as is mentioned in that subsection.

(2) Where the court makes an order under Part II of this Act for the grant of a new tenancy of any such premises as aforesaid, and the Secretary of State certifies that it is necessary or expedient as aforesaid that the tenancy should be subject to a term, specified in the certificate, prohibiting or restricting the tenant from assigning the tenancy or sub-letting, charging or parting with possession of the premises or any part of the premises or changing the use of the premises or any part of the premises, the court shall determine that the terms of the tenancy shall include the terms specified in the certificate.

63. Jurisdiction of court for purposes of Parts I and II and of Part I of Landlord and Tenant Act, 1927.

(1) Any jurisdiction conferred on the court by any provision of Part I of this Act shall be exercised by the county court.

(2) Any jurisdiction conferred on the court by any provision of Part II of this Act or conferred on the tribunal by Part I of the Landlord and Tenant Act, 1927, shall, subject to the provisions of this section, be exercised,—

(a) where the rateable value of the holding is not over the county court limit, by the county court;

(b) where it is over the county court limit, by the High Court.

(3) Any jurisdiction exercisable under the last foregoing subsection may by agreement in writing between the parties be transferred from the county court to the High Court or from the High Court to a county court specified in the agreement.

(4) The following provisions shall have effect as respects transfer of proceedings from or to the High Court or the county court, that is to say—

(a) where an application is made to the one but by virtue of subsection (2) of this section cannot be entertained except by the other, the application shall not be treated as improperly made but any proceedings thereon shall be transferred to the other court;

(b) any proceedings under the provisions of Part II of this Act or of Part I of the Landlord and Tenant Act, 1927, which are pending before one of those courts may by order of that court made on the application of any person interested be transferred to the other court, if it appears to the court making the order that it is desirable that the proceedings and any proceedings before the other court should both be entertained by the other court.

(5) In any proceedings where in accordance with the foregoing provisions of this section the county court exercises jurisdiction the powers of the judge of summoning one or more assessors under subsection (1) of section eighty-eight of the County Courts Act, 1934, may be exercised notwithstanding that no application is made in that behalf by any party to the proceedings.

(6) Where in any such proceedings an assessor is summoned by a judge under the said subsection (1),—

(a) he may, if so directed by the judge, inspect the land to which the proceedings relate without the judge and report to the judge in writing thereon;

(b)   the judge may on consideration of the report and any observations of the parties thereon give such judgment or make such order in the proceedings as may be just;

(c)   the remuneration of the assessor shall be at such rate as may be determined by the Lord Chancellor with the approval of the Treasury and shall be defrayed out of moneys provided by Parliament.

(7)   In this section the expression "the holding"—

(a)   in relation to proceedings under Part II of this Act, has the meaning assigned to it by subsection (3) of section twenty-three of this Act,

(b)   in relation to proceedings under Part I of the Landlord and Tenant Act, 1927, has the same meaning as in the said Part I.

(8)   Subsections (5) to (7) of section thirty-seven of this Act shall apply for determining the rateable value of the holding for the purposes of this section as they apply for the purposes of subsection (2) of the said section thirty-seven, but with the substitution in paragraph (a) of the said subsection (5) of a reference to the time at which application is made to the court for the reference to the date mentioned in that subsection.

(9)   Nothing in this section shall prejudice the operation of section one hundred and eleven of the County Courts Act, 1934 (which relates to the removal into the High Court of proceedings commenced in a county court).

64.   Interim continuation of tenancies pending determination by court.

(1)   In any case where—

(a)   a notice to terminate a tenancy has been given under Part I or Part II of this Act or a request for a new tenancy has been made under Part II thereof, and

(b)   an application to the court has been made under the said Part I or the said Part II, as the case may be, and

(c)   apart from this section the effect of the notice or request would be to terminate the tenancy before the expiration of the period of three months beginning with the date on which the application is finally disposed of,

the effect of the notice or request shall be to terminate the tenancy at the expiration of the said period of three months and not at any other time.

(2)   The reference in paragraph (c) of subsection (1) of this section to the date on which an application is finally disposed of shall be construed as a reference to the earliest date by which the proceedings on the application (including any proceedings on or in consequence of an appeal) have been determined and any time for appealing or further appealing has expired, except that if the application is withdrawn or any appeal is abandoned the reference shall be construed as a reference to the date of the withdrawal or abandonment.

65.   Provisions as to reversions.

(1)   Where by virtue of any provision of this Act a tenancy (in this subsection referred to as "the inferior tenancy") is continued for a period such as to extend to or beyond the end of the term of a superior tenancy, the superior tenancy shall, for the purposes of this Act and of any other enactment and of any rule of law, be deemed so long as it subsists to be an interest in reversion expectant upon the termination of the inferior tenancy and, if there is no intermediate tenancy, to be the interest in reversion immediately expectant upon the termination thereof.

(2)   In the case of a tenancy continuing by virtue of any provision of this Act after the coming to an end of the interest in reversion immediately expectant upon the termination thereof, subsection (1) of section one hundred and thirty-nine of the Law of Property Act, 1925 (which relates to the effect of the extinguishment of a reversion) shall apply as if references in the said subsection (1) to the surrender or merger of the reversion included references to the coming to an end of the reversion for any reason other than surrender or merger.

(3)   Where by virtue of any provision of this Act a tenancy (in this subsection referred to as "the continuing tenancy") is continued beyond the beginning of a reversionary tenancy which was granted (whether before or after the commencement of this Act) so as to begin on or after the date on which apart from this Act the continuing tenancy would have come to an end, the reversionary tenancy shall have effect as if it had been granted subject to the continuing tenancy.

(4)   Where by virtue of any provision of this Act a tenancy (in this subsection referred to as "the new tenancy") is granted for a period beginning on the same date as a reversionary tenancy or for a period such as to extend beyond the beginning of the term of a reversionary tenancy, whether the reversionary tenancy in question was granted before or after the commencement of this Act, the reversionary tenancy shall have effect as if it had been granted subject to the new tenancy.

66.   Provisions as to notices.

(1)   Any form of notice required by this Act to be prescribed shall be prescribed by regulations made by the Secretary of State by statutory instrument.

(2)   Where the form of a notice to be served on persons of any description is to be prescribed for any of the purposes of this Act, the form to be prescribed shall include such an explanation of the relevant provisions of this Act as appears to the Secretary of State requisite for informing persons of that description of their rights and obligations under those provisions.

(3)   Different forms of notice may be prescribed for the purposes of the operation of any provision of this Act in relation to different cases.

(4)   Section twenty-three of the Landlord and Tenant Act, 1927 (which relates to the service of notices) shall apply for the purposes of this Act.

(5)   Any statutory instrument under this section shall be subject to annulment in pursuance of a resolution of either House of Parliament.

67.   Provisions as to mortgagees in possession.

Anything authorised or required by the provisions of this Act, other than subsection (2) or (3) of section forty, to be done at any time by, to or with the landlord, or a landlord of a specified description, shall, if at that time the interest of the landlord in question is subject to a mortgage and the mortgagee is in possession or a receiver appointed by the mortgagee or by the court is in receipt of the rents and profits, be deemed to be authorised or required to be done by, to or with the mortgagee instead of that landlord.

68.   Repeal of enactments and transitional provisions.

(2)   The transitional provisions set out in the Ninth Schedule to this Act shall have effect.

69.   Interpretation.

(1)   In this Act the following expressions have the meanings hereby assigned to them respectively, that is to say:—

> "agricultural holding" has the same meaning as in the Agricultural Holdings Act 1986;
>
> "development corporation" has the same meaning as in the New Towns Act, 1946;
>
> "Local authority" has the same meaning as in the Town and Country Planning Act, 1947 except that it includes the Broads Authority and a joint authority established by Part IV of the Local Government Act 1985;
>
> "mortgage" includes a charge or lien and "mortgagor" and "mortgagee" shall be construed accordingly;
>
> "notice to quit" means a notice to terminate a tenancy (whether a periodical tenancy or a tenancy for a term of years certain) given in accordance with the provisions (whether express or implied) of that tenancy;

"repairs" includes any work of maintenance, decoration or restoration, and references to repairing, to keeping or yielding up in repair and to state of repair shall be construed accordingly;

"statutory undertakers" has the same meaning as in the Town and Country Planning Act, 1947, except that it includes the British Coal Corporation;

"tenancy" means a tenancy created either immediately or derivatively out of the freehold, whether by a lease or underlease, by an agreement for a lease or underlease or by a tenancy agreement or in pursuance of any enactment (including this Act), but does not include a mortgage term or any interest arising in favour of a mortgagor by his attorning tenant to his mortgagee, and references to the granting of a tenancy and to demised property shall be construed accordingly;

"terms", in relation to a tenancy, includes conditions.

(2)   References in this Act to an agreement between the landlord and the tenant (except in section seventeen and subsections (1) and (2) of section thirty-eight thereof) shall be construed as references to an agreement in writing between them.

(3)   References in this Act to an action for any relief shall be construed as including references to a claim for that relief by way of counterclaim in any proceedings.

70.   Short title and citation, commencement and extent.

(1)   This Act may be cited as the Landlord and Tenant Act, 1954, and the Landlord and Tenant Act, 1927, and this Act may be cited together as the Landlord and Tenant Acts, 1927 and 1954.

(2)   This Act shall come into operation on the first day of October, nineteen hundred and fifty-four.

(3)   This Act shall not extend to Scotland or to Northern Ireland.

SCHEDULES

Section 8.   FIRST SCHEDULE

SUPPLEMENTARY PROVISIONS AS TO PAYMENTS FOR ACCRUED TENANT'S REPAIRS

PART I
PROVISIONS AS TO MAKING OF PAYMENT IN LUMP SUM

1.   Subject to the provisions of this Part of this Schedule, a payment for accrued tenant's repairs which is to be payable otherwise than by instalments shall become payable when the relevant initial repairs have been completed, unless the landlord and the tenant agree that it shall become payable wholly or in part at some other date.

2.   Where it is determined by the court that a payment for accrued tenant's repairs is to be payable otherwise than by instalments, the court may determine that any specified part of the payment shall become payable when any specified part of the relevant initial repairs has been completed.

3.   A payment for accrued tenant's repairs which is payable otherwise than by instalments, or any part of such a payment, shall be recoverable from the tenant.

4.—(1)   Where it has been agreed or determined that a payment for accrued tenant's repairs should be paid otherwise than by instalments, and the period of the statutory tenancy ends before the relevant initial repairs have been begun, or at a time when they have been begun but not completed, the following provisions shall have effect.

(2)   If the relevant initial repairs have not been begun and are no longer required, then notwithstanding anything in section eight of this Act no payment for accrued tenant's repairs shall be recoverable.

(3)   In any other case, the time for recovery of the payment for accrued tenant's repairs shall be the same as if all the relevant initial repairs had been completed

immediately before the end of the period of the statutory tenancy, and the amount of the payment shall be as hereinafter provided:—

(a) if the relevant initial repairs have not been begun, the amount of the payment shall be the estimated cost of the repairs or of so much thereof as is still required;

(b) if the relevant initial repairs have been begun but not completed, the amount of the payment shall be an amount equal to the expenses reasonably incurred by the landlord for the purposes of so much of the relevant initial repairs as has been carried out together (unless the remainder is no longer required) with the estimated cost of the remainder or of so much thereof as is still required:

Provided that there shall be disregarded so much (if any) of the said expenses or estimated cost as is recoverable by the landlord otherwise than from the tenant or his predecessor in title.

(4) Any question arising under this paragraph whether repairs are no longer required, whether any expenses were incurred, or reasonably incurred, by the landlord, or as to the amount of the estimated cost of any repairs shall be determined by agreement between the landlord and the tenant or by the court on the application of either of them.

(5) For the purposes of this paragraph initial repairs shall be deemed to be no longer required after the end of the period of the statutory tenancy if, and only if, it is shown that the dwelling-house, in whatever state of repair it may then be, is at or shortly after the end of that period to be pulled down, or that such structural alterations are to be made in the dwelling-house as would render those repairs valueless if they were completed.

(6) In a case falling within sub-paragraph (1) of this paragraph where a payment for accrued tenant's repairs would, apart from this paragraph, include an amount in respect of cost incurred by the landlord in ascertaining what initial repairs are required in consequence of failure by the tenant to fulfil his obligations under the former tenancy, the following provisions shall have effect—

(a) that amount shall be recoverable notwithstanding anything in sub-paragraph (2) of this paragraph;

(b) in a case falling within sub-paragraph (3) of this paragraph the said amount shall be recoverable in addition to the amount specified in that sub-paragraph;

(c) the time for recovery of the said amount shall, as well in a case falling within sub-paragraph (2) of this paragraph as in one falling within sub-paragraph (3) thereof, be that mentioned in the said sub-paragraph (3).

5. In relation to a case where the court exercises the power conferred by paragraph 2 of this Schedule references in the last foregoing paragraph to the relevant initial repairs shall be construed as references to any such part of those repairs as is referred to in the said paragraph 2, being a part which at the material time has not been begun or, as the case may be, has been begun but not completed, and references to the payment for accrued tenant's repairs shall be construed accordingly.

PART II
PROVISIONS AS TO MAKING OF PAYMENT BY INSTALMENTS

6. Subject to the provisions of this Part of this Schedule, where under Part I of this Act it is agreed or determined that a payment for accrued tenant's repairs is to be payable by instalments, the instalments shall become payable at the times so agreed or determined.

7. Any such instalment becoming payable at a time falling before the end of the period of the statutory tenancy shall be payable by the tenant.

8.—(1) Where the landlord is not the immediate landlord of the dwelling-house, the landlord and the immediate landlord may serve on the tenant a notice in the prescribed form requiring him to pay the instalments of the payment for accrued tenant's repairs to the immediate landlord for transmission to the landlord.

(2)   A notice under the last foregoing sub-paragraph may be revoked by a subsequent notice given to the tenant by the landlord, with or without the concurrence of the immediate landlord.

9.   Any instalment becoming payable at a time when the landlord is the immediate landlord or when a notice under sub-paragraph (1) of the last foregoing paragraph is in force shall be recoverable by the immediate landlord in the like manner and subject to the like provisions as the rent.

10.   If the period of the statutory tenancy comes to an end before all instalments of the payment for accrued tenant's repairs have been paid, the remaining instalments shall become payable immediately after the end of that period, shall be recoverable by the person who immediately before the end thereof was the landlord, and shall be so recoverable from the person who immediately before the end thereof was the tenant.

11.   In the application of the last foregoing paragraph to a case where the period of the statutory tenancy comes to an end before the relevant initial repairs have been begun, or at a time when they have been begun but not completed, the provisions of paragraph 4 of this Schedule shall have effect (with the necessary modifications) for limiting the recovery of any remaining instalments under the last foregoing paragraph.

12.   Where, during the period of the statutory tenancy and before all instalments of the payment for accrued tenant's repairs have become payable, the interest of the landlord comes to an end or ceases to be an interest falling within paragraphs (a) and (b) of the proviso to subsection (4) of section twenty-one of this Act, he shall thereupon be entitled to recover from the person who thereupon becomes the landlord such amount (if any) as is equal to so much of the expenses reasonably incurred by the landlord—

(a)   in ascertaining what initial repairs are required in consequence of failure by the tenant to fulfil his obligations under the former tenancy; and

(b)   for the purposes of the relevant initial repairs;

as is recoverable from the tenant and has not been recovered.

PART III
VARIATION OF AGREEMENT OR DETERMINATION AS TO TIME FOR MAKING PAYMENT

13.   The tenant may apply to the court for the variation, on the grounds and to the extent hereinafter specified, of any agreement or determination for the making of a payment for accrued tenant's repairs.

14.   The grounds on which an agreement or determination may be varied on an application under the last foregoing paragraph are the following:—

(a)   that the expenditure reasonably incurred by the landlord in carrying out the relevant initial repairs substantially exceeded the estimated cost thereof; or

(b)   that the applicant is not the person who was the tenant at the time of the previous agreement or determination and that there are considerations arising out of the personal circumstances of the applicant which ought to be taken into account in determining the manner of making the payment.

15.   The extent to which an agreement or determination may be so varied on an application under paragraph 13 of this Schedule is the following:—

(a)   if the agreement or determination was for the making of the payment otherwise than by instalments, and the payment has not been fully made, by substituting therefor a determination that the payment or balance of the payment should be made by instalments;

(b)   if the agreement or determination was for the making of a payment by instalments, by substituting for the instalments agreed or determined instalments of such smaller amounts, payable at such times, as may be determined by the court.

16.   Where an agreement or determination is varied under this Part of this Schedule, the foregoing provisions of this Schedule shall thereafter apply with the necessary modifications.

PART IV
SUPPLEMENTARY

17.   Any failure by the tenant to make a payment for accrued tenant's repairs, or any part or instalment of such a payment, at the time when it becomes due shall be treated as a breach of the obligations of the tenancy for the purposes of Case 1 in Schedule 15 to the Rent Act (which relates to recovery of possession where the rent has not been paid or any other obligation of the tenancy has not been performed).

18.   Where any sum in respect of a payment for accrued tenant's repairs has been recovered in advance of the carrying out of the relevant initial repairs, then in any case where paragraph 4 or 11 of this Schedule applies such repayment shall be made as may be just.

19.   In this Schedule the expression "immediate landlord" means the person who as respects the dwelling-house is the landlord of the tenant for the purposes of the Rent Act and the expression "relevant initial repairs" means the repairs in respect of which the payment for accrued tenant's repairs is payable.

Section 8.   SECOND SCHEDULE

FURTHER PROVISIONS AS TO REPAIR WHERE TENANT RETAINS POSSESSION

Failure of landlord to carry out initial repairs

1.—(1)   Where—
   (a)   the tenant retains possession of the dwelling-house by virtue of subsection (1) of section six of this Act, and
   (b)   by virtue of an agreement or of a determination of the court, the landlord is required to carry out initial repairs to the dwelling-house,
then if on an application made by the tenant during the period of the statutory tenancy the court is satisfied that the initial repairs have not been carried out within a reasonable time in accordance with the agreement or determination the court may by order direct that, until the discharge of the order as hereinafter provided or the end of the period of the statutory tenancy, whichever first occurs, the rent payable in respect of the dwelling-house shall be reduced to such amount specified in the order as the court may think just having regard to the extent to which the landlord has failed to comply with the agreement or determination.

(2)   Where the court under the last foregoing sub-paragraph orders a reduction of rent, the court may further order that during the same period any instalments of a payment for accrued tenant's repairs shall be suspended.

(3)   An order under this paragraph may include a provision that the reduction of rent shall take effect from a specified date before the making of the order, being such date as the court thinks just having regard to the landlord's delay in carrying out the initial repairs; and where an order contains such a provision then, in addition to the reduction ordered by virtue of sub-paragraph (1) of this paragraph, such number of payments of rent next falling due after the date of the order shall be reduced by such amount as may be specified in the order for the purpose of giving effect to the said provision.

2.   Where an order under paragraph 1 of this Schedule is in force, and on an application by the landlord the court is satisfied that the initial repairs have been carried out in accordance with the agreement or with the determination of the court, as the case may be, the court shall discharge the order, but without prejudice to the operation

thereof as respects any period before the date on which it is discharged or to any reduction ordered by virtue of sub-paragraph (3) of the last foregoing paragraph.

3. If, while an order under paragraph 1 of this Schedule is in force, it is agreed between the landlord and the tenant that the initial repairs in question have been carried out as mentioned in the last foregoing paragraph, the order shall be discharged by virtue of that agreement in the like manner as if it had been discharged by the court.

Failure of tenant to carry out initial repairs

4. Where, by virtue of an agreement or of a determination of the court, the tenant is required to carry out initial repairs to the dwelling-house, failure by the tenant to carry out the repairs within a reasonable time in accordance with the agreement or determination shall be treated as a breach of the obligations of the tenancy for the purposes of Case 1 in Schedule 15 to the Rent Act (which relates to recovery of possession where the rent has not been paid or any other obligation of the tenancy has not been performed).

Expenses and receipts: mortgages, settlements, etc.

5. Any amount paid by a mortgagee in respect of expenses incurred in carrying out initial repairs in accordance with an agreement or determination under Part I of this Act, or in respect of any payment made in pursuance of a liability imposed by paragraph 12 of the First Schedule to this Act, shall be treated as if it were secured by the mortgage, with the like priority and with interest at the same rate as the mortgage money, so however that (without prejudice to the recovery of interest) any such amount shall not be recoverable from the mortgagor personally.

6. The purposes authorised for the application of capital money by section seventy-three of the Settled Land Act, 1925, by that section as applied by section twenty-eight of the Law of Property Act, 1925, in relation to trusts for sale, and by section twenty-six of the Universities and College Estates Act, 1925, and the purposes authorised by section seventy-one of the Settled Land Act, 1925, by that section as applied as aforesaid, and by section thirty of the Universities and College Estates Act, 1925, as purposes for which moneys may be raised by mortgage, shall include the payment of any such expenses as are mentioned in the last foregoing paragraph and the making of any such payment as is mentioned in that paragraph:

Provided that the like provisions shall have effect as to the repayment of capital money applied by virtue of this paragraph as have effect in the case of improvements authorised by Part II of the Third Schedule to the Settled Land Act, 1925 (which specifies improvements the cost of which may be required to be replaced out of income).

Record of state of repair of dwelling-house

7. A landlord's notice proposing a statutory tenancy may contain a requirement that if the tenant retains possession by virtue of subsection (1) of section six of this Act a record shall be made of the state of repair of the dwelling-house.

8. Where the landlord gives such a notice which does not contain such a requirement, then if the tenant elects to retain possession his notification in that behalf may include a requirement that a record shall be made of the state of repair of the dwelling-house.

9. Where the tenant retains possession of the dwelling-house by virtue of subsection (1) of section six of this Act and either the landlord or the tenant has made such a requirement as is mentioned in either of the two last foregoing paragraphs, the record of the state of repair of the dwelling-house shall be made as soon as may be after the completion of any initial repairs to be carried out or, in the absence of any agreement or determination requiring the carrying out of initial repairs, as soon as may be after the beginning of the period of the statutory tenancy.

10. Any record required to be made under the last foregoing paragraph shall be made by a person appointed, in default of agreement between the landlord and the tenant, by the President of the Royal Institution of Chartered Surveyors.

11. The cost of making any such record as aforesaid shall, in default of agreement between the landlord and the tenant, be borne by them in equal shares.

Sections 12, 13.

THIRD SCHEDULE

GROUNDS FOR POSSESSION ON TERMINATION OF TENANCY

1. The grounds referred to in paragraph (b) of subsection (1) of section twelve of this Act are the following, that is to say:—

(a) that suitable alternative accommodation will be available for the tenant at the date of termination of the tenancy;

(b) that the tenant has failed to comply with any term of the tenancy as to payment of rent or rates or as to insuring or keeping insured any premises;

(c) that the tenant or a person residing or lodging with him or being his sub-tenant has been guilty of conduct which is a nuisance or annoyance to adjoining occupiers, or has been convicted of using any premises comprised in the tenancy or allowing such premises to be used for an immoral or illegal purpose and, where the person in question is a lodger or sub-tenant, that the tenant has not taken such steps as he ought reasonably to have taken for the removal of the lodger or sub-tenant;

(e) that premises comprised in the tenancy, and consisting of or including the relevant premises, are reasonably required by the landlord for occupation as a residence for himself or any son or daughter of his over eighteen years of age or his father or mother or the father or mother of his spouse, and (if the landlord is not the immediate landlord) that he will be the immediate landlord at the date of termination:

Provided that the court shall not make an order under section thirteen of this Act on the grounds specified in sub-paragraph (e) of this paragraph—

(a) if the interest of the landlord, or an interest which has merged in that interest and but for the merger would be the interest of the landlord, was purchased or created after the 18th February 1966; or

(b) if the court is satisfied that having regard to all the circumstances of the case, including the question whether other accommodation is available for the landlord or the tenant, greater hardship would be caused by making the order than by refusing to make it.

2. Part IV of Schedule 15 to the Rent Act (which relates to the circumstances in which suitable accommodation is to be deemed to be available for the tenant) shall apply for the purposes of this Schedule as it applies for the purposes of section 98(1)(a) of that Act.

Section 19.

FOURTH SCHEDULE

MODIFICATIONS OF PART I IN RELATION TO PERIODICAL TENANCIES

1. In relation to such a tenancy as is mentioned in subsection (2) of section nineteen of this Act, Part I of this Act shall have effect subject to the following provisions of this Schedule.

2. For subsection (6) of section two there shall be substituted the following:—

"(6) In this Part of this Act the expression "term date", in relation to any such tenancy as is mentioned in subsection (2) of section nineteen of this Act, means the first date after the commencement of this Act on which apart from this Act the tenancy could have been brought to an end by notice to quit given by the landlord."

3.   For subsection (1) of section five there shall be substituted the following:—

"(1)   A tenancy to which section one of this Act applies may be brought to an end at the term date thereof by notice in writing given by the tenant to the immediate landlord.

The length of any such notice shall be not less than one month nor less than the length of the notice by which the tenant could apart from this Act have brought the tenancy to an end at the term date thereof."

4.   Notwithstanding anything in subsection (2) of section three, where by virtue of subsection (1) of that section the tenancy is continued after the term date thereof the provisions of Part I as to the termination of a tenancy by notice shall have effect in substitution for and not in addition to any such provisions included in the terms on which the tenancy had effect before the term date thereof.

5.   Where the tenancy is not terminated under the provisions of Part I of this Act at the term date thereof, then, whether or not it would have continued after that date apart from this Act, it shall be treated for the purposes of this Act as being continued by virtue of subsection (1) of section three thereof.

Section 21.   FIFTH SCHEDULE

PROVISIONS FOR PURPOSES OF PART I WHERE IMMEDIATE LANDLORD IS NOT THE FREEHOLDER

Definitions

1.—(1)   In this Schedule the following expressions have the meanings hereby assigned to them in relation to a tenancy (in this Schedule referred to as "the relevant tenancy"), that is to say:—

"the competent landlord" means the person who in relation to the relevant tenancy is for the time being the landlord (as defined by section twenty-one of this Act) for the purposes of Part I of this Act;

"mesne landlord" means a tenant whose interest is intermediate between the relevant tenancy and the interest of the competent landlord; and

"superior landlord", except in paragraph 9 of this Schedule, means a person (whether the owner of the fee simple or a tenant) whose interest is superior to the interest of the competent landlord.

(2)   References in this Schedule to "other landlords" are references to persons who are either mesne landlords or superior landlords.

Acts of competent landlord binding on other landlords

2.   Any notice given by the competent landlord under subsection (1) of section four of this Act, any agreement made under Part I of this Act between that landlord and the tenant under the relevant tenancy, and any determination of the court under the said Part I in proceedings between that landlord and that tenant, shall bind the interest of every other landlord (if any).

Provisions as to consent of other landlords to acts of competent landlord

3.—(1)   Where in the four next following paragraphs reference is made to other landlords or to mesne landlords, the reference shall be taken not to include a mesne landlord whose interest is due to expire within the period of two months beginning with the relevant date or is terminable within that period by notice to quit given by his landlord.

(2)   In this paragraph the expression "the relevant date" means—

(a)   if the term date of the relevant tenancy has not passed, that date;

(b)   if that date has passed, and no notice has been given under subsection (1) of section four of this Act to terminate the relevant tenancy, the earliest date at which that tenancy could be brought to an end by such a notice;

(c)   if such a notice has been given, the date of termination specified in the notice.

4.—(1)   If a notice is given by the competent landlord under subsection (1) of section four of this Act, or an agreement under Part I of this Act is made with the tenant by that landlord, without the written consent of every other landlord (if any), any other landlord whose written consent has not been given thereto shall, subject to the next following paragraph, be entitled to compensation from the competent landlord for any loss arising in consequence of the giving of the notice or the making of the agreement.

(2)   The amount of any compensaton under this paragraph shall, in default of agreement, be determined by the court on the application of the person claiming it.

5.   The competent landlord may serve on any other landlord a notice in the prescribed form requiring him to consent to the giving or making of any such notice or agreement as aforesaid; and if within one month after the service of a notice under this paragraph—

(a)   the consent has not been given, or

(b)   conditions have been imposed on the giving of the consent which are in the opinion of the court unreasonable in all the circumstances,

the court, on an application by the competent landlord, may if it thinks fit order that the other landlord shall be deemed to have consented, either without qualification or subject to such conditions (including conditions as to the modification of the proposed notice or agreement or as to the payment of compensaton by the competent landlord) as may be specified in the order.

6.—(1)   It may be made a condition either—

(a)   of the giving of consent by a person whose consent is required under paragraph 4 of this Schedule, or

(b)   of the making of an order under the last foregoing paragraph,

that the initial repairs which the competent landlord will agree to carry out, or which, as the case may be, he will specify in accordance with subsection (1) of section nine of this Act as repairs which he is willing to carry out, shall include such repairs as may be specified in the consent or order.

(2)   In so far as any cost reasonably incurred by the competent landlord in carrying out repairs specified in accordance with the last foregoing sub-paragraph is not recovered by way of payment for accrued tenant's repairs and is not recoverable (apart from this sub-paragraph) otherwise than by way of such payment, it shall be recoverable by the competent landlord from the person whose consent was or is deemed to have been given subject to the condition or (if he is dead) from his personal representatives as a debt due from him at the time of his death.

7.—(1)   Where under Part I of this Act the competent landlord is required by an agreement, or by a determination of the court, to carry out initial repairs to any premises, he may serve on any mesne landlord a notice requiring him to pay to the competent landlord a contribution towards the cost reasonably incurred by the competent landlord in carrying out those repairs, if and in so far as that cost is not recovered by way of payment for accrued tenant's repairs and is not recoverable (apart from this sub-paragraph) otherwise than by way of such payment.

(2)   Where a notice has been served under the last foregoing sub-paragraph, then in default of agreement between the competent landlord and the mesne landlord on whom the notice was served the court may order the mesne landlord to pay such a contribution as aforesaid.

(3)   A contribution ordered under this paragraph shall be such as the court determines to be reasonable having regard to the difference between the rent under the relevant tenancy and the rent which, if the tenant retains possession, will be recoverable during the period of the statutory tenancy.

Failure of competent landlord to carry out initial repairs

8.   Where, in consequence of the failure of the competent landlord to carry out initial repairs, the amount of any payment of rent is reduced under paragraph 1 of the Second Schedule to this Act, and the competent landlord is not the immediate landlord of the tenant, the person who is for the time being the immediate landlord shall be entitled to recover from the competent landlord the amount of the reduction.

Relief in proceedings by superior landlord

9.—(1)   Where in the case of a tenancy to which section one of this Act applies—

(a)   the interest of the immediate landlord is itself a tenancy (in this paragraph referred to as "the mesne tenancy"), and

(b)   a superior landlord has brought proceedings to enforce a right of re-entry or forfeiture in respect of a failure to comply with any terms of the mesne tenancy or of a superior tenancy having effect subject to the mesne tenancy, and

(c)   the court makes an order for the recovery by the superior landlord of possession of the property comprised in the tenancy,

the tenant shall not be required to give up possession of that property unless he has been a party to the proceedings or has been given notice of the order; and the provisions of the next following sub-paragraph shall have effect where he has been such a party or has been given such a notice:

Provided that where the tenant has been a party to the proceedings the said provisions shall not apply unless he has at any time before the making of the order made application in the proceedings for relief under this paragraph.

(2)   If the tenant within fourteen days after the making of the order, or where he has not been a party to the proceedings, within fourteen days after the said notice, gives notice in writing to the superior landlord that he desires that the following provisions of this sub-paragraph shall have effect and lodges a copy of the notice in the court—

(a)   the tenant shall not be required to give up possession of the said property but the tenancy mentioned in head (b) of the last foregoing sub-paragraph shall be deemed as between the tenant and the superior landlord to have been surrendered on the date of the order; and

(b)   if the term date of the tenant's tenancy would otherwise fall later, it shall be deemed for the purposes of Part I of this Act to fall at the expiration of seven months from the making of the order.

(3)   Nothing in the foregoing provisions of this paragraph shall prejudice the operation of any order for the recovery of possession from the tenant under the mesne tenancy, or from the tenant under any superior tenancy having effect subject to the mesne tenancy.

(4)   Subsections (4), (6) and (7) of section sixteen of this Act shall with the necessary modifications apply for the purposes of this paragraph.

Relief for mesne landlord against damages for breach of covenant

10.—(1)   The provisions of the next following sub-paragraph shall have effect where, in the case of a tenancy to which section one of this Act applies,—

(a)   the competent landlord is not the immediate landlord, and

(b)   the competent landlord has brought proceedings against a mesne landlord to enforce a right to damages in respect of a failure to comply with any terms of the mesne landlord's tenancy, and

(c)   the mesne landlord has made application in the proceedings for relief under this paragraph, and

(d)   the court makes an order for the payment by the mesne landlord of any such damages as aforesaid.

(2)   The operation of the order shall be suspended for a period of fourteen days from the making thereof, and if before the end of that period the mesne landlord gives notice in writing to the competent landlord that he desires that the provisions of heads (a) and (b) of this sub-paragraph shall have effect, and lodges a copy of the notice in the court—

(a)   the order shall not be enforceable except if and in so far as it provides for the payment of costs, and

(b)   the interest of the mesne landlord (unless it has then come to an end) shall be deemed to be surrendered, and his rights and liabilities thereunder to be extinguished, as from the date of the giving of the notice.

(3)   Subsections (4) to (7) of section sixteen of this Act shall with the necessary modifications apply for the purposes of this paragraph.

Provisions as to liabilities under tenants' covenants in superior leases

11.—(1)   Where subsection (1) of section ten of this Act applies, any terms to which this paragraph applies shall cease to have effect in so far as they relate to the premises constituting the dwelling-house, and any liability of the competent landlord or any mesne landlord or of any predecessor in title of the competent landlord or of any mesne landlord, under any such terms, in so far as it related to those premises and was a liability subsisting at the termination of the relevant tenancy, shall be deemed to have been extinguished on the termination of that tenancy.

(2)   This paragraph applies to any terms of any tenancy owned by the competent landlord or by any other landlord, whether to be performed during that tenancy or on or after the expiration or determination thereof, except any such terms as are mentioned in paragraph (a) or (b) of the proviso to subsection (1) of section ten of this Act:

Provided that where any term to which this paragraph applies relates both to the dwelling-house and to other premises, nothing in this paragraph shall affect its operation in relation to the other premises.

(3)   Notwithstanding anything in sub-paragraph (1) of this paragraph, if the interest of the competent landlord, being a tenancy, or the interest of any mesne landlord, has not come to an end by the end of the period of the statutory tenancy, and the terms on which that interest was held included an obligation to repair or maintain the dwelling-house or the dwelling-house and other premises, then as from the end of the period of the statutory tenancy the instrument creating the interest of the competent landlord or mesne landlord shall be deemed to contain a covenant with the grantor of the interest that the grantee of the interest will at all times maintain the dwelling-house in a state of repair no less good than that in which it was after the completion of any initial repairs to be carried out thereon in accordance with the provisions of Part I of this Act, and will yield up possession of the dwelling-house in such a state on the coming to an end of the interest of the said landlord.

(4)   Where, in a case falling within sub-paragraph (1) of this paragraph, the competent landlord satisfies the court—

(a)   that the obligations under the tenancy which in relation to him is the immediate mesne tenancy differ from the obligations under the relevant tenancy, and

(b)   that if the obligations under the relevant tenancy had been the same as those under the first-mentioned tenancy he would have been entitled to recover any amount by way of payment for accrued tenant's repairs which he is not entitled to recover,

he shall be entitled to recover that amount from the tenant under the first-mentioned tenancy, or, if that tenancy has come to an end, from the person who was the tenant thereunder immediately before it came to an end.

(5)   Where in accordance with the last foregoing sub-paragraph, or with that sub-paragraph as applied by the following provisions of this sub-paragraph, any sum is recoverable from a person, the last foregoing sub-paragraph shall with the necessary modifications apply as between him and the person entitled to the interest (if any) which

in relation to him is the immediate mesne tenancy or, if such an interest formerly subsisted but has come to an end, as between him and the person last entitled to that interest.

(6) In this paragraph the expression "the immediate mesne tenancy", in relation to the competent landlord or to a mesne landlord, means the tenancy on which his interest in those premises is immediately expectant.

Section 44.

SIXTH SCHEDULE

PROVISIONS FOR PURPOSES OF PART II WHERE IMMEDIATE LANDLORD IS NOT THE FREEHOLDER

Definitions

1. In this Schedule the following expressions have the meanings hereby assigned to them in relation to a tenancy (in this Schedule referred to as "the relevant tenancy"), that is to say:—

"the competent landlord" means the person who in relation to the tenancy is for the time being the landlord (as defined by section 44 of this Act) for the purposes of Part II of this Act;

"mesne landlord" means a tenant whose interest is intermediate between the relevant tenancy and the interest of the competent landlord; and

"superior landlord" means a person (whether the owner of the fee simple or a tenant) whose interest is superior to the interest of the competent landlord.

Power of court to order reversionary tenancies

2. Where the period for which in accordance with the provisions of Part II of this Act it is agreed or determined by the court that a new tenancy should be granted thereunder will extend beyond the date on which the interest of the immediate landlord will come to an end, the power of the court under Part II of this Act to order such a grant shall include power to order the grant of a new tenancy until the expiration of that interest and also to order the grant of such a reversionary tenancy or reversionary tenancies as may be required to secure that the combined effects of those grants will be equivalent to the grant of a tenancy for that period; and the provisions of Part II of this Act shall, subject to the necessary modifications, apply in relation to the grant of a tenancy together with one or more reversionary tenancies as they apply in relation to the grant of one new tenancy.

Acts of competent landlord binding on other landlords

3.—(1) Any notice given by the competent landlord under Part II of this Act to terminate the relevant tenancy, and any agreement made between that landlord and the tenant as to the granting, duration, or terms of a future tenancy, being an agreement made for the purposes of the said Part II, shall bind the interest of any mesne landlord notwithstanding that he has not consented to the giving of the notice or was not a party to the agreement.

(2) The competent landlord shall have power for the purposes of Part II of this Act to give effect to any agreement with the tenant for the grant of a new tenancy beginning with the coming to an end of the relevant tenancy, notwithstanding that the competent landlord will not be the immediate landlord at the commencement of the new tenancy, and any instrument made in the exercise of the power conferred by this sub-paragraph shall have effect as if the mesne landlord had been a party thereto.

(3) Nothing in the foregoing provisions of this paragraph shall prejudice the provisions of the next following paragraph.

Provisions as to consent of mesne landlord to acts of competent landlord

4.—(1) If the competent landlord, not being the immediate landlord, gives any such notice or makes any such agreement as is mentioned in sub-paragraph (1) of the last foregoing paragraph without the consent of every mesne landlord, any mesne landlord whose consent has not been given thereto shall be entitled to compensation from the competent landlord for any loss arising in consequence of the giving of the notice or the making of the agreement.

(2) If the competent landlord applies to any mesne landlord for his consent to such a notice or agreement, that consent shall not be unreasonably withheld, but may be given subject to any conditions which may be reasonable (including conditions as to the modification of the proposed notice or agreement or as to the payment of compensation by the competent landlord).

(3) Any question arising under this paragraph whether consent has been unreasonably withheld or whether any conditions imposed on the giving of consent are unreasonable shall be determined by the court.

Consent of superior landlord required for agreements affecting his interest

5. An agreement between the competent landlord and the tenant made for the purposes of Part II of this Act in a case where—

(a) the competent landlord is himself a tenant, and

(b) the agreement would apart from this paragraph operate as respects any period after the coming to an end of the interest of the competent landlord,

shall not have effect unless every superior landlord who will be the immediate landlord of the tenant during any part of that period is a party to the agreement.

Withdrawal by competent landlord of notice given by mesne landlord

6. Where the competent landlord has given a notice under section 25 of this Act to terminate the relevant tenancy and, within two months after the giving of the notice, a superior landlord—

(a) becomes the competent landlord; and

(b) gives to the tenant notice in the prescribed form that he withdraws the notice previously given;

the notice under section 25 of this Act shall cease to have effect, but without prejudice to the giving of a further notice under that section by the competent landlord.

Duty to inform superior landlords

7. If the competent landlord's interest in the property comprised in the relevant tenancy is a tenancy which will come or can be brought to an end within sixteen months (or any further time by which it may be continued under section 36(2) or section 64 of this Act) and he gives to the tenant under the relevant tenancy a notice under section 25 of this Act to terminate the tenancy or is given by him a notice under section 26(3) of this Act:—

(a) the competent landlord shall forthwith send a copy of the notice to his immediate landlord; and

(b) any superior landlord whose interest in the property is a tenancy shall forthwith send to his immediate landlord any copy which has been sent to him in pursuance of the preceding sub-paragraph or this sub-paragraph.

Section 56.   EIGHTH SCHEDULE

APPLICATION OF PART II TO LAND BELONGING TO CROWN AND DUCHIES OF LANCASTER AND CORNWALL

1. Where an interest in any property comprised in a tenancy belongs to Her Majesty in right of the Duchy of Lancaster, then for the purposes of Part II of this Act the Chancellor of the Duchy shall represent Her Majesty and shall be deemed to be the owner of the interest.

2. Where an interest in any property comprised in a tenancy belongs to the Duchy of Cornwall, then for the purposes of Part II of this Act such person as the Duke of Cornwall, or other the possessor for the time being of the Duchy of Cornwall, appoints shall represent the Duke of Cornwall or other the possessor aforesaid, and shall be deemed to be the owner of the interest and may do any act or thing under the said Part II which the owner of that interest is authorised or required to do thereunder.

4. The amount of any compensation payable under section thirty-seven of this Act by the Chancellor of the Duchy of Lancaster shall be raised and paid as an expense incurred in improvement of land belonging to Her Majesty in right of the Duchy within section twenty-five of the Act of the fifty-seventh year of King George the Third, Chapter ninety-seven.

5. Any compensation payable under section thirty-seven of this Act by the person representing the Duke of Cornwall or other the possessor for the time being of the Duchy of Cornwall shall be paid, and advances therefor made, in the manner and subject to the provisions of section eight of the Duchy of Cornwall Management Act, 1863 with respect to improvements of land mentioned in that section.

Sections 41, 42, 56, 68.   NINTH SCHEDULE

TRANSITIONAL PROVISIONS

3. Where immediately before the commencement of this Act a person was protected by section seven of the Leasehold Property (Temporary Provisions) Act, 1951, against the making of an order or giving of a judgment for possession or ejectment, the Rent Acts shall apply in relation to the dwelling-house to which that person's protection extended immediately before the commencement of this Act as if section fifteen of this Act had always had effect.

4. For the purposes of section twenty-six and subsection (2) of section forty of this Act a tenancy which is not such a tenancy as is mentioned in subsection (1) of the said section twenty-six but is a tenancy to which Part II of this Act applies and in respect of which the following conditions are satisfied, that is to say—

    (a) that it took effect before the commencement of this Act at the coming to an end by effluxion of time or notice to quit of a tenancy which is such a tenancy as is mentioned in subsection (1) of the said section twenty-six or is by virtue of this paragraph deemed to be such a tenancy; and

    (b) that if this Act had then been in force the tenancy at the coming to an end of which it took effect would have been one to which Part II of this Act applies; and

    (c) that the tenant is either the tenant under the tenancy at the coming to an end of which it took effect or a successor to his business,

shall be deemed to be such a tenancy as is mentioned in subsection (1) of the said section twenty-six.

5.—(1) A tenant under a tenancy which was current at the commencement of this Act shall not in any case be entitled to compensation under section thirty-seven or fifty-nine of this Act unless at the date on which he is to quit the holding the holding or part thereof has continuously been occupied for the purposes of the carrying on of the tenant's business (whether by him or by any other person) for at least five years.

(2) Where a tenant under a tenancy which was current at the commencement of this Act would but for this sub-paragraph be entitled both to—

(a) compensation under section thirty-seven or section fifty-nine of this Act; and

(b) compensation payable, under the provisions creating the tenancy, on the termination of the tenancy,

he shall be entitled, at his option, to the one or the other, but not to both.

6.—(1) Where the landlord's interest in the property comprised in a tenancy which, immediately before the commencement of this Act, was terminable by less than six months' notice to quit given by the landlord belongs to or is held for the purposes of a Government Department or is held by statutory undertakers, the tenancy shall have effect as if that shorter length of notice were specified in such an agreement as is mentioned in subsection (2) or (3) of section fifty-eight of this Act, as the case may be, and the agreement were embodied in the tenancy.

(2) The last foregoing sub-paragraph shall apply in relation to a tenancy where the landlord's interest belongs or is held as aforesaid and which, immediately before the commencement of this Act, was terminable by the landlord without notice as if the tenancy had then been terminable by one month's notice to quit given by the landlord.

8. Where at the commencement of this Act any proceedings are pending on an application made before the commencement of this Act to the tribunal under section five of the Landlord and Tenant Act, 1927, no further step shall be taken in the proceedings except for the purposes of an order as to costs; and where the tribunal has made an interim order in the proceedings under subsection (13) of section five of that Act authorising the tenant to remain in possession of the property comprised in his tenancy for any period, the tenancy shall be deemed not to have come to an end before the expiration of that period, and section twenty-four of this Act shall have effect in relation to it accordingly.

11. Notwithstanding the repeal of Part II of the Leasehold Property (Temporary Provisions) Act, 1951, where immediately before the commencement of this Act a tenancy was being continued by subsection (3) of section eleven of that Act it shall not come to an end at the commencement of this Act, and section twenty-four of this Act shall have effect in relation to it accordingly.

COSTS OF LEASES ACT 1958
(1958, c. 52)

An Act to make provision for the incidence of the costs of leases.   [23 July, 1958]

1. Costs of leases.
Notwithstanding any custom to the contrary, a party to a lease shall, unless the parties thereto agree otherwise in writing, be under no obligation to pay the whole or any part of any other party's solicitor's costs of the lease.

2. Interpretation.
In this Act—

(a) "lease" includes an underlease and an agreement for a lease or underlease or for a tenancy or sub-tenancy;

(b) "costs" includes fees, charges, disbursements (including stamp duty), expenses and remuneration.

PERPETUITIES AND ACCUMULATIONS ACT 1964
(1964, c. 55)

[16 July 1964]

9.   Options relating to land.

(1)   The rule against perpetuities shall not apply to a disposition consisting of the conferring of an option to acquire for valuable consideration an interest reversionary (whether directly or indirectly) on the term of a lease if—

(a)   the option is exercisable only by the lessee or his successors in title, and

(b)   it ceases to be exercisable at or before the expiration of one year following the determination of the lease.

This subsection shall apply in relation to an agreement for a lease as it applies in relation to a lease, and "lessee" shall be construed accordingly.

(2)   In the case of a disposition consisting of the conferring of an option to acquire for valuable consideraton any interest in land, the perpetuity period under the rule against perpetuities shall be twenty-one years, and section 1 of this Act shall not apply:

Provided that this subsection shall not apply to a right of pre-emption conferred on a public or local authority in respect of land used or to be used for religious purposes where the right becomes exercisable only if the land ceases to be used for such purposes.

10.   Avoidance of contractual and other rights in cases of remoteness.

Where a disposition inter vivos would fall to be treated as void for remoteness if the rights and duties thereunder were capable of transmission to persons other than the original parties and had been so transmitted, it shall be treated as void as between the person by whom it was made and the person to whom or in whose favour it was made or any successor of his, and no remedy shall lie in contract or otherwise for giving effect to it or making restitution for its lack of effect.

DEFECTIVE PREMISES ACT 1972
(1972, c. 35)

[29 June 1972]

4.   Landlord's duty of care in virtue of obligation or right to repair premises demised.

(1)   Where premises are let under a tenancy which puts on the landlord an obligation to the tenant for the maintenance or repair of the premises, the landlord owes to all persons who might reasonably be expected to be affected by defects in the state of the premises a duty to take such care as is reasonable in all the circumstances to see that they are reasonably safe from personal injury or from damage to their property caused by a relevant defect.

(2)   The said duty is owed if the landlord knows (whether as the result of being notified by the tenant or otherwise) or if he ought in all the circumstances to have known of the relevant defect.

(3)   In this section "relevant defect" means a defect in the state of the premises existing at or after the material time and arising from, or continuing because of, an act or omission by the landlord which constitutes or would if he had had notice of the defect, have constituted a failure by him to carry out his obligation to the tenant for the maintenance or repair of the premises; and for the purposes of the foregoing provision "the material time" means—

(a)   where the tenancy commenced before this Act, the commencement of this Act; and

(b)   in all other cases, the earliest of the following times, that is to say—

(i)   the time when the tenancy commences;

    (ii)   the time when the tenancy agreement is entered into;

    (iii)   the time when possession is taken of the premises in contemplation of the letting.

    (4)   Where premises are let under a tenancy which expressly or impliedly gives the landlord the right to enter the premises to carry out any description of maintenance or repair of the premises, then, as from the time when he first is, or by notice or otherwise can put himself, in a position to exercise the right and so long as he is or can put himself in that position, he shall be treated for the purposes of subsections (1) to (3) above (but for no other purpose) as if he were under an obligation to the tenant for that description of maintenance or repair of the premises; but the landlord shall not owe the tenant any duty by virtue of this subsection in respect of any defect in the state of the premises arising from, or continuing because of, a failure to carry out an obligation expressly imposed on the tenant by the tenancy.

    (5)   For the purposes of this section obligations imposed or rights given by any enactment in virtue of a tenancy shall be treated as imposed or given by the tenancy.

    (6)   This section applies to a right of occupation given by contract or any enactment and not amounting to a tenancy as if the right were a tenancy, and "tenancy" and cognate expressions shall be construed accordingly.

6. Supplemental.

    (1)   In this Act—

    "disposal", in relation to premises, includes a letting, and an assignment or surrender of a tenancy, of the premises and the creation by contract of any other right to occupy the premises, and "dispose" shall be construed accordingly;

    "personal injury" includes any disease and any impairment of a person's physical or mental condition;

    "tenancy" means—

    (a)   a tenancy created either immediately or derivatively out of the freehold, whether by a lease or underlease, by an agreement for a lease or underlease or by a tenancy agreement, but not including a mortgage term or any interest arising in favour of a mortgagor by his attorning tenant to his mortgagee; or

    (b)   a tenancy at will or a tenancy on sufferance; or

    (c)   a tenancy, whether or not constituting a tenancy at common law, created by or in pursuance of any enactment;

    and cognate expressions shall be construed accordingly.

    (2)   Any duty imposed by or enforceable by virtue of any provision of this Act is in addition to any duty a person may owe apart from that provision.

    (3)   Any term of an agreement which purports to exclude or restrict, or has the effect of excluding or restricting, the operation of any of the provisions of this Act, or any liability arising by virtue of any such provision, shall be void.

LAND CHARGES ACT 1972

(1972, c. 61)

[9 August 1972]

Registration in register of land charges

2. The register of land charges.

    (1)   If a charge on or obligation affecting land falls into one of the classes described in this section, it may be registered in the register of land charges as a land charge of that class.

    (2)   A Class A land charge is—

    (a)   a rent or annuity or principal money payable by instalments or otherwise, with or without interest, which is not a charge created by deed but is a charge upon land (other than a rate) created pursuant to the application of some person under the provisions of any Act of Parliament, for securing to any person either the money spent by him or the costs, charges and expenses incurred by him under such Act, or the money advanced by him for repaying the money spent or the costs, charges and expenses incurred by another person under the authority of an Act of Parliament; or

(b) a rent or annuity or principal money payable as mentioned in paragraph (a) above which is not a charge created by deed but is a charge upon land (other than a rate) created pursuant to the application of some person under any of the enactments mentioned in Schedule 2 to this Act.

(3) A Class B land charge is a charge on land (not being a local land charge) of any of the kinds described in paragraph (a) of subsection (2) above, created otherwise than pursuant to the application of any person.

(4) A Class C land charge is any of the following (not being a local land charge), namely—

(i) a puisne mortgage;

(ii) a limited owner's charge;

(iii) a general equitable charge;

(iv) an estate contract;

and for this purpose—

(i) a puisne mortgage is a legal mortgage which is not protected by a deposit of documents relating to the legal estate affected;

(ii) a limited owner's charge is an equitable charge acquired by a tenant for life or statutory owner under the Inheritance Tax Act 1984 or under any other statute by reason of the discharge by him of any capital transfer tax or other liabilities and to which special priority is given by the statute;

(iii) a general equitable charge is any equitable charge which—

(a) is not secured by a deposit of documents relating to the legal estate affected; and

(b) does not arise or affect an interest arising under a trust for sale or a settlement; and

(c) is not a charge given by way of indemnity against rents equitably apportioned or charged exclusively on land in exoneration of other land and against the breach or non-observance of covenants or conditions; and

(d) is not included in any other class of land charge;

(iv) an estate contract is a contract by an estate owner or by a person entitled at the date of the contract to have a legal estate conveyed to him to convey or create a legal estate, including a contract conferring either expressly or by statutory implication a valid option to purchase, a right of pre-emption or any other like right.

(5) A Class D land charge is any of the following (not being a local land charge), namely—

(i) an Inland Revenue charge;

(ii) a restrictive covenant;

(iii) an equitable easement;

and for this purpose—

(i) an Inland Revenue charge is a charge on land, being a charge acquired by the Board under the Inheritance Tax Act 1984;

(ii) a restrictive covenant is a covenant or agreement (other than a covenant or agreement between a lessor and a lessee) restrictive of the user of land and entered into on or after 1st January 1926;

(iii) an equitable easement is an easement, right or privilege over or affecting land created or arising on or after 1st January 1926, and being merely an equitable interest.

(6) A Class E land charge is an annuity created before 1st January 1926 and not registered in the register of annuities.

(7)   A Class F land charge is a charge affecting any land by virtue of the Matrimonial Homes Act 1983.

(8)   A charge or obligation created before 1st January 1926 can only be registered as a Class B land charge or a Class C land charge if it is acquired under a conveyance made on or after that date.

3.   Registration of land charges.

(1)   A land charge shall be registered in the name of the estate owner whose estate is intended to be affected.

4.   Effect of land charges and protection of purchasers.

(1)   A land charge of Class A (other than a land improvement charge registered after 31st December 1969) or of Class B shall, when registered, take effect as if it had been created by a deed of charge by way of legal mortgage, but without prejudice to the priority of the charge.

(2)   A land charge of Class A created after 31st December 1888 shall be void as against a purchaser of the land charged with it or of any interest in such land, unless the land charge is registered in the register of land charges before the completion of the purchase.

(3)   After the expiration of one year from the first conveyance occurring on or after 1st January 1889 of a land charge of Class A created before that date the person entitled to the land charge shall not be able to recover the land charge or any part of it as against a purchaser of the land charged with it or of any interest in the land, unless the land charge is registered in the register of land charges before the completion of the purchase.

(4)   If a land improvement charge was registered as a land charge of Class A before 1st January 1970, any body corporate which, but for the charge, would have power to advance money on the security of the estate or interest affected by it shall have that power notwithstanding the charge.

(5)   A land charge of Class B and a land charge of Class C (other than an estate contract) created or arising on or after 1st January 1926 shall be void as against a purchaser of the land charged with it, or of any interest in such land, unless the land charge is registered in the appropriate register before the completion of the purchase.

(6)   An estate contract and a land charge of Class D created or entered into on or after 1st January 1926 shall be void as against a purchaser for money or money's worth or, in the case of an Inland Revenue charge, a purchaser within the meaning of the Inheritance Tax Act 1984 of a legal estate in the land charged with it, unless the land charge is registered in the appropriate register before the completion of the purchase.

(7)   After the expiration of one year from the first conveyance occurring on or after 1st January 1926 of a land charge of Class B or Class C created before that date the person entitled to the land charge shall not be able to enforce or recover the land charge or any part of it as against a purchaser of the land charged with it, or of any interest in the land, unless the land charge is registered in the appropriate register before the completion of the purchase.

(8)   A land charge of Class F shall be void as against a purchaser of the land charged with it, or of any interest in such land, unless the land charge is registered in the appropriate register before the completion of the purchase.

17.   Interpretation.

(1)   In this Act, unless the context otherwise requires,—

"annuity" means a rentcharge or an annuity for a life or lives or for any term of years or greater estate determinable on a life or on lives and created after 25th April 1855 and before 1st January 1926, but does not include an annuity created by a marriage settlement or will;

"the Board" means the Commissioners of Inland Revenue;

"conveyance" includes a mortgage, charge, lease, assent, vesting declaration, vesting instrument, release and every other assurance of property, or of an interest in property, by any instrument except a will, and "convey" has a corresponding meaning;

"court" means the High Court, or the county court in a case where that court has jurisdiction;

"deed of arrangement" has the same meaning as in the Deeds of Arrangement Act 1914;

"estate owner", "legal estate", "equitable interest", "trust for sale", "charge by way of legal mortgage", and "will" have the same meanings as in the Law of Property Act 1925;

"judgment" includes any order or decree having the effect of a judgment;

"land" includes land of any tenure and mines and minerals, whether or not severed from the surface, buildings or parts of buildings (whether the division is horizontal, vertical or made in any other way) and other corporeal hereditaments, also a manor, an advowson and a rent and other incorporeal hereditaments, and an easement, right, privilege or benefit in, over or derived from land, but not an undivided share in land, and "hereditament" means real property which, on an intestacy occuring before 1st January 1926, might have devolved on an heir;

"land improvement charge" means any charge under the Improvement of Land Act 1864 or under any special improvement Act within the meaning of the Improvement of Land Act 1899;

"pending land action" means any action or proceeding pending in court relating to land or any interest in or charge on land;

"prescribed" means prescribed by rules made pursuant to this Act;

"purchaser" means any person (including a mortgagee or lessee) who, for valuable consideration, takes any interest in land or in a charge on land, and "purchase" has a corresponding meaning;

"registrar" means the Chief Land Registrar, "registry" means Her Majesty's Land Registry, and "registered land" has the same meaning as in the Land Registration Act 1925;

"tenant for life", "statutory owner", "vesting instrument" and "settlement" have the same meanings as in the Settled Land Act 1925.

(2)   For the purposes of any provision in this Act requiring or authorising anything to be done at or delivered or sent to the registry, any reference to the registry shall, if the registrar so directs, be read as a reference to such office of the registry (whether in London or elsewhere) as may be specified in the direction.

(3)   Any reference in this Act to any enactment is a reference to it as amended by or under any other enactment, including this Act.

RENT ACT 1977
(1977, c. 42)

An Act to consolidate the Rent Act 1968, Parts III, IV and VIII of the Housing Finance Act 1972, the Rent Act 1974, sections 7 to 10 of the Housing Rents and Subsidies Act 1975, and certain related enactments, with amendments to give effect to recommendations of the Law Commission.   [29 July 1977]

PART I
PRELIMINARY

Protected and statutory tenancies

1.   Protected tenants and tenancies.
Subject to this Part of this Act, a tenancy under which a dwelling-house (which may be

a house or part of a house) is let as a separate dwelling is a protected tenancy for the purposes of this Act.

Any reference in this Act to a protected tenant shall be construed accordingly.

2. Statutory tenants and tenancies.

(1) Subject to this Part of this Act—

(a) after the termination of a protected tenancy of a dwelling-house the person who, immediately before that termination, was the protected tenant of the dwelling-house shall, if and so long as he occupies the dwelling-house as his residence, be the statutory tenant of it; and

(b) Part I of Schedule 1 to this Act shall have effect for determining what person (if any) is the statutory tenant of a dwelling-house or, as the case may be, is entitled to an assured tenancy of a dwelling-house by succession at any time after the death of a person who, immediately before his death, was either a protected tenant of the dwelling-house or the statutory tenant of it by virtue of paragraph (a) above.

(2) In this Act a dwelling-house is referred to as subject to a statutory tenancy when there is a statutory tenant of it.

(3) In subsection (1)(a) above and in Part I of Schedule 1, the phrase "if and so long as he occupies the dwelling-house as his residence" shall be construed as it was immediately before the commencement of this Act (that is to say, in accordance with section 3(2) of the Rent Act 1968).

(4) A person who becomes a statutory tenant of a dwelling-house as mentioned in subsection (1)(a) above is, in this Act, referred to as a statutory tenant by virtue of his previous protected tenancy.

(5) A person who becomes a statutory tenant as mentioned in subsection 1(b) above is, in this Act, referred to as a statutory tenant by succession.

3. Terms and conditions of statutory tenancies.

(1) So long as he retains possession, a statutory tenant shall observe and be entitled to the benefit of all the terms and conditions of the original contract of tenancy, so far as they are consistent with the provisions of this Act.

(2) It shall be a condition of a statutory tenancy of a dwelling-house that the statutory tenant shall afford to the landlord access to the dwelling-house and all reasonable facilities for executing therein any repairs which the landlord is entitled to execute.

(3) Subject to section 5 of the Protection from Eviction Act 1977 (under which at least 4 weeks' notice to quit is required), a statutory tenant of a dwelling-house shall be entitled to give up possession of the dwelling-house if, and only if, he gives such notice as would have been required under the provisions of the original contract of tenancy, or, if no notice would have been so required, on giving not less than 3 months' notice.

(4) Notwithstanding anything in the contract of tenancy, a landlord who obtains an order for possession of a dwelling-house as against a statutory tenant shall not be required to give to the statutory tenant any notice to quit.

(5) Part II of Schedule 1 to this Act shall have effect in relation to the giving up of possession of statutory tenancies and the changing of statutory tenants by agreement.

Exceptions

4. Dwelling-houses above certain rateable values.

(1) A tenancy which is entered into before 1st April 1990 or (where the dwelling-house had a rateable value on 31st March 1990) is entered into on or after 1st April 1990 in pursuance of a contract made before that date is not a protected tenancy if the dwelling-house falls within one of the Classes set out in subsection (2) below.

(2) Where alternative rateable values are mentioned in this subsection, the higher applies if the dwelling-house is in Greater London and the lower applies if it is elsewhere.

Class A

The appropriate day in relation to the dwelling-house falls or fell on or after 1st April 1973 and the dwelling-house on the appropriate day has or had a rateable value exceeding £1,500 or £750.

Class B

The appropriate day in relation to the dwelling-house fell on or after 22nd March 1973, but before 1st April 1973, and the dwelling-house—
(a)   on the appropriate day had a rateable value exceeding £600 or £300, and
(b)   on 1st April 1973 had a rateable value exceeding £1,500 or £750.

Class C

The appropriate day in relation to the dwelling-house fell before 22nd March 1973 and the dwelling-house—
(a)   on the appropriate day had a rateable value exceeding £400 or £200, and
(b)   on 22nd March 1973 had a rateable value exceeding £600 or £300, and
(c)   on 1st April 1973 had a rateable value exceeding £1,500 or £750.

(3)   If any question arises in any proceedings whether a dwelling-house falls within a Class in subsection (2) above, by virtue of its rateable value at any time, it shall be deemed not to fall within that Class unless the contrary is shown.

(4)   A tenancy is not a protected tenancy if—
(a)   it is entered into on or after 1st April 1990 (otherwise than, where the dwelling-house had a rateable value on 31st March 1990, in pursuance of a contract made before 1st April 1990), and
(b)   under it the rent payable for the time being is payable at a rate exceeding £25,000 a year.

(5)   In subsection (4) above "rent" does not include any sum payable by the tenant as is expressed (in whatever terms) to be payable in respect of rates, services, repairs, maintenance or insurance, unless it could not have been regarded by the parties as a sum so payable.

(6)   If any question arises in any proceedings whether a tenancy is precluded from being a protected tenancy by subsection (4) above, the tenancy shall be deemed to be a protected tenancy unless the contrary is shown.

(7)   The Secretary of State may by order replace the amount referred to in subsection (4) above by an amount specified in the order; and such an order shall be made by statutory instrument which shall be subject to annulment in pursuance of a resolution of either House of Parliament.

5.   Tenancies at low rents.

(1)   A tenancy which was entered into before 1st April 1990 or (where the dwelling-house under the tenancy had a rateable value on 31st March 1990) is entered into on or after 1st April 1990 in pursuance of a contract made before that date is not a protected tenancy if under the tenancy either no rent is payable or, the rent payable is less than two-thirds of the rateable value which is or was the rateable value of the dwelling-house on the appropriate day.

(2)   Where—
(a)   the appropriate day in relation to a dwelling-house fell before 22nd March 1973, and
(b)   the dwelling-house had on the appropriate day a rateable value exceeding, if it is in Greater London, £400 or, if it is elsewhere, £200,
subsection (1) above shall apply in relation to the dwelling-house as if the reference to the appropriate day were a reference to 22nd March 1973.

(2A)   A tenancy is not a protected tenancy if—

(a)   it is entered into on or after the 1st April 1990 (otherwise than, where the dwelling-house under the tenancy had a rateable value on 31st March 1990, in pursuance of a contract made before 1st April 1990), and

(b)   under the tenancy for the time being either no rent is payable or the rent is payable at a rate of, if the dwelling-house is in Greater London, £1,000 or less a year, and, if the dwelling-house is elsewhere, £250 or less a year.

(2B)   Subsection (7) of section 4 above shall apply to any amount referred to in subsection (2A) above as it applies to the amount referred to in subsection (4) of that section.

(3)   In this Act a tenancy falling within subsection (1) above is referred to as a "tenancy at low rent".

(4)   In determining whether a long tenancy is a tenancy at a low rent, there shall be disregarded such part (if any) of the sums payable by the tenant as is expressed (in whatever terms) to be payable in respect of rates, services, repairs, maintenance, or insurance, unless it could not have been regarded by the parties as a part so payable.

(5)   In subsection (4) above "long tenancy" means a tenancy granted for a term certain exceeding 21 years, other than a tenancy which is, or may become, terminable before the end of that term by notice given to the tenant.

5A.   Certain shared ownership leases.

(1)   A tenancy is not a protected tenancy if it is a qualifying shared ownership lease, that is—

(a)   a lease granted in pursuance of the right to be granted a shared ownership lease under Part V of the Housing Act 1985, or

(b)   a lease granted by a housing association and which complies with the conditions set out in subsection (2) below.

(2)   The conditions referred to in subsection (1)(b) above are that the lease—

(a)   was granted for a term of 99 years or more and is not (and cannot become) terminable except in pursuance of a provision for re-entry or forfeiture;

(b)   was granted at a premium, calculated by reference to the value of the dwelling-house or the cost of providing it, of not less than 25 per cent, or such other percentage as may be prescribed, of the figure by reference to which it was calculated;

(c)   provides for the tenant to acquire additional shares in the dwelling-house on terms specified in the lease and complying with such requirements as may be prescribed;

(d)   does not restrict the tenant's powers to assign, mortgage or charge his interest in the dwelling-house;

(e)   if it enables the landlord to require payment for outstanding shares in the dwelling-house, does so only in such circumstances as may be prescribed;

(f)   provides, in the case of a house, for the tenant to acquire the landlord's interest on terms specified in the lease and complying with such requirements as may be prescribed; and

(g)   states the landlord's opinion that by virtue of this section the lease is excluded from the operation of this Act.

(3)   The Secretary of State may by regulations prescribe anything requiring to be prescribed for the purposes of subsection (2) above.

(4)   The regulations may—

(a)   make different provision for different cases or descriptions of case, including different provision for different areas, and

(b)   contain such incidental, supplementary or transitional provisions as the Secretary of State considers appropriate,

and shall be made by statutory instrument which shall be subject to annulment in pursuance of a resolution of either House of Parliament.

(5)   In any proceedings the court may, if of opinion that it is just and equitable to do so, treat a lease as a qualifying shared ownership lease notwithstanding that the condition specified in subsection (2)(g) above is not satisfied.

(6)   In this section—

"house" has the same meaing as in Part I of the Leasehold Reform Act 1967;

"housing association" has the same meaning as in the Housing Associations Act 1985; and

"lease" includes an agreement for a lease, and references to the grant of a lease shall be construed accordingly.

6.   Dwelling-houses let with other land.

Subject to section 26 of this Act, a tenancy is not a protected tenancy if the dwelling-house which is subject to the tenancy is let together with land other than the site of the dwelling-house.

7.   Payments for board or attendance.

(1)   A tenancy is not a protected tenancy if under the tenancy the dwelling-house is bona fide let at a rent which includes payments in respect of board or attendance.

(2)   For the purposes of subsection (1) above, a dwelling-house shall not be taken to be bona fide let at a rent which includes payments in respect of attendance unless the amount of rent which is fairly attributable to attendance, having regard to the value of the attendance to the tenant, forms a substantial part of the whole rent.

8.   Lettings to students.

(1)   A tenancy is not a protected tenancy if it is granted to a person who is pursuing, or intends to pursue, a course of study provided by a specified educational institution and is so granted either by that institution or by another specified institution or body of persons.

(2)   In subsection (1) above "specified" means specified, or of a class specified, for the purposes of this section by regulations made by the Secretary of State by statutory instrument.

(3)   A statutory instrument containing any such regulations shall be subject to annulment in pursuance of a resolution of either House of Parliament.

9.   Holiday lettings.

A tenancy is not a protected tenancy if the purpose of the tenancy is to confer on the tenant the right to occupy the dwelling-house for a holiday.

10.   Agricultural holdings.

A tenancy is not a protected tenancy if the dwelling-house is comprised in an agricultural holding (within the meaning of the Agricultural Holdings Act 1986) and is occupied by the person responsible for the control (whether as tenant or as servant or agent of the tenant) of the farming of the holding.

11.   Licensed premises.

A tenancy of a dwelling-house which consists of or comprises premises licensed for the sale of intoxicating liquors for consumption on the premises shall not be a protected tenancy, nor shall such a dwelling-house be the subject of a statutory tenancy.

12.   Resident landlords.

(1)   Subject to subsection (2) below, a tenancy of a dwelling-house granted on or after 14th August 1974 shall not be a protected tenancy at any time if—

(a)   the dwelling-house forms part only of a building and, except in a case where the dwelling-house also forms part of a flat, the building is not a purpose-built block of flats; and

(b)   the tenancy was granted by a person who, at the time when he granted it, occupied as his residence another dwelling-house which—

     (i)   in the case mentioned in paragraph (a) above, also forms part of the flat; or

     (ii)   in any other case, also forms part of the building; and

(c)   subject to paragraph 1 of Schedule 2 to this Act, at all times since the tenancy was granted the interest of the landlord under the tenancy has belonged to a person who, at the time he owned that interest, occupied as his residence another dwelling-house which—

     (i)   in the case mentioned in paragraph (a) above, also formed part of the flat; or

     (ii)   in any other case, also formed part of the building.

(2)   This section does not apply to a tenancy of a dwelling-house which forms part of a building if the tenancy is granted to a person who, immediately before it was granted, was a protected or statutory tenant of that dwelling-house or of any other dwelling-house in that building.

(4)   Schedule 2 to this Act shall have effect for the purpose of supplementing this section.

13. Landlord's interest belonging to Crown.

(1)   Except as provided by subsection (2) below—

(a)   a tenancy shall not be a protected tenancy at any time when the interest of the landlord under the tenancy belongs to Her Majesty in right of the Crown or to a government department or is held in trust for Her Majesty for the purposes of a government department; and

(b)   a person shall not at any time be a statutory tenant of a dwelling-house if the interest of his immediate landlord would at that time belong or be held as mentioned in paragraph (a) above.

(2)   An interest belonging to Her Majesty in right of the Crown shall not prevent a tenancy from being a protected tenancy or a person from being a statutory tenant if the interest is under the management of the Crown Estate Commissioners.

14. Landlord's interest belonging to local authority, etc.

A tenancy shall not be a protected tenancy at any time when the interest of the landlord under that tenancy belongs to—

(a)   the council of a county;

(b)   the council of a district or, in the application of this Act to the Isles of Scilly, the Council of the Isles of Scilly;

(bb)   the Broads Authority;

(c)   the council of a London borough or the Common Council of the City of London;

(cb)   a joint authority established by Part IV of the Local Government Act 1985;

(d)   the Commission for the New Towns;

(e)   a development corporation established by an order made, or having effect as if made, under the New Towns Act 1981; or

(f)   the Development Board for Rural Wales; or

(g)   an urban development corporation within the meaning of Part XVI of the Local Government, Planning and Land Act 1980;

(h)   a housing action trust established under Part III of the Housing Act 1988; nor shall a person at any time be a statutory tenant of a dwelling-house if the interest of his immediate landlord would belong at that time to any of those bodies.

15. Landlord's interest belonging to housing association, etc.

(1)   A tenancy shall not be a protected tenancy at any time when the interest of the landlord under that tenancy belongs to a housing association falling within subsection

(3) below; nor shall a person at any time be a statutory tenant of a dwelling-house if the interest of his immediate landlord would belong at that time to such a housing association.

(2)   A tenancy shall not be a protected tenancy at any time when the interest of the landlord under that tenancy belongs to—

(a)   the Housing Corporation;

(aa)   Housing for Wales; or

(b)   a housing trust which is a charity within the meaning of the Charities Act 1960;

nor shall a person at any time be a statutory tenant of a dwelling-house if the interest of his immediate landlord would belong at that time to any of those bodies.

(3)   A housing association falls within this subsection if—

(a)   it is registered under the Housing Associations Act 1985, or

(b)   it is a co-operative housing association within the meaning of that Act.

(5)   In subsection (2) above "housing trust" means a corporation or body of persons which—

(a)   is required by the terms of its constituent instrument to use the whole of its funds, including any surplus which may arise from its operations, for the purpose of providing housing accommodation; or

(b)   is required by the terms of its constituent instrument to devote the whole, or substantially the whole, of its funds to charitable purposes and in fact uses the whole, or substantially the whole, of its funds for the purpose of providing housing accommodation.

16.   Landlord's interest belonging to housing co-operative.

A tenancy shall not be a protected tenancy at any time when the interest of the landlord under that tenancy belongs to a housing co-operative within the meaning of section 27B of the Housing Act 1985 (agreements with housing co-operatives under certain superseded provisions) and the dwelling-house is comprised in a housing co-operative agreement within the meaning of that section.

18.   Regulated tenancies.

(1)   Subject to sections 24(3) and 143 of this Act, a "regulated tenancy" is, for the purposes of this Act, a protected or statutory tenancy.

(2)   Where a regulated tenancy is followed by a statutory tenancy of the same dwelling-house, the two shall be treated for the purposes of this Act as together constituting one regulated tenancy.

18A.   Modification of Act for controlled tenancies converted into regulated tenancies.

Schedule 17 to this Act applies for the purpose of modifying the provisions of this Act in relation to a tenancy which, by virtue of any of the following enactments, was converted from a controlled tenancy into a regulated tenancy, that is to say—

(a)   section 18(3) of this Act;

(b)   paragraph 5 of Schedule 2 to the Rent Act 1968 (which was superseded by section 18(3));

(c)   Part VIII of this Act;

(d)   Part III of the Housing Finance Act 1972 (which was superseded by Part VIII);

(e)   Part IV of the Act of 1972 (conversion by reference to rateable values);

(f)   section 64 of the Housing Act 1980 (conversion of remaining controlled tenancies into regulated tenancies).

Restricted contracts

19. Restricted contracts.

(1)   A contract to which this section applies is, in this Act, referred to as a "restricted contract".

(2)   Subject to section 144 of this Act, this section applies to a contract, whether entered into before or after the commencement of this Act, whereby one person grants to another person, in consideration of a rent which includes payment for the use of furniture or for services, the right to occupy a dwelling as a residence.

(3)   A contract is not a restricted contract if the dwelling falls within one of the Classes set out in subsection (4) below.

(4)   Where alternative rateable values are mentioned in this subsection, the higher applies if the dwelling is in Greater London and the lower applies if it is elsewhere.

Class D

The appropriate day in relation to the dwelling falls or fell on or after 1st April 1973 and the dwelling on the appropriate day has or had a rateable value exceeding £1,500 or £750.

Class E

The appropriate day in relation to the dwelling fell before 1st April 1973 and the dwelling—
(a)   on the appropriate day had a rateable value exceeding £400 or £200, and
(b)   on 1st April 1973 had a rateable value exceeding £1,500 or £750.

(5)   A contract is not a restricted contract if—
(a)   it creates a regulated tenancy; or
(aa)   under the contract the interest of the lessor belongs to a body mentioned in section 14 of this Act;
(b)   under the contract the interest of the lessor belongs to Her Majesty in right of the Crown ... or to a government department or is held in trust for Her Majesty for the purposes of a government department; or
(c)   it is a contract for the letting of any premises at a rent which includes payment in respect of board if the value of the board to the lessee forms a substantial proportion of the whole rent;
(cc)   it creates a qualifying shared ownership lease within the meaning of section 5A of this Act; or
(d)   it is a protected occupancy as defined in the Rent (Agriculture) Act 1976; or
(e)   it creates a tenancy to which Part VI of this Act applies except that an interest belonging to Her Majesty in right of the Crown does not prevent a contract from being a restricted contract if the interest is under the management of the Crown Estate Commissioners, or
(f)   it creates an assured tenancy within the meaning of section 56 of the Housing Act 1980.

(6)   Subject to subsections (3) to (5) above, and to paragraph 17 of Schedule 24 to this Act, a contract falling within subsection (2) above and relating to a dwelling which consists of only part of a house is a restricted contract whether or not the lessee is entitled, in addition to exclusive occupation of that part, to the use in common with any other person of other rooms or accommodation in the house.

(7)   No right to occupy a dwelling for a holiday shall be treated for the purposes of this section as a right to occupy it as a residence.

(8)   In this section—
"dwelling" means a house or part of a house;
"lessee" means the person to whom is granted, under a restricted contract, the right to occupy the dwelling in question as a residence and any person directly or indirectly deriving title from the grantee; and

"lessor" means the person who, under a restricted contract, grants to another the right to occupy the dwelling in question as a residence and any person directly or indirectly deriving title from the grantor; and

"services" includes attendance, the provision of heating or lighting, the supply of hot water and any other privilege or facility connected with the occupancy of a dwelling, other than a privilege or facility requisite for the purposes of access, cold water supply or sanitary accommodation.

20. Certain unfurnished tenancies to be treated as restricted contracts.

If and so long as a tenancy is, by virtue only of section 12 of this Act, precluded from being a protected tenancy it shall be treated as a restricted contract notwithstanding that the rent may not include payment for the use of furniture or for services.

Shared accommodation

21. Tenant sharing accommodation with landlord.

Where under any contract—

    (a)   a tenant has the exclusive occupation of any accomodation, and

    (b)   the terms on which he holds the accommodation include the use of other accommodation in common with his landlord or in common with his landlord and other persons, and

    (c)   by reason only of the circumstances mentioned in paragraph *(b)* above, or by reason of those circumstances and the operation of section 12 of this Act, the accommodation referred to in paragraph *(a)* above is not a dwelling-house let on a protected tenancy, the contract is a restricted contract notwithstanding that the rent does not include payment for the use of furniture or for services.

22. Tenant sharing accommodation with persons other than landlord.

  (1)   Where a tenant has the exclusive occupation of any accommodation ("the separate accommodation") and—

    (a)   the terms as between the tenant and his landlord on which he holds the separate accommodation include the use of other accommodation ("the shared accommodation") in common with another person or other persons, not being or including the landlord, and

    (b)   by reason only of the circumstances mentioned in paragraph (a) above, the separate accommodation would not, apart from this section, be a dwelling-house let on or subject to a protected or statutory tenancy, the separate accommodation shall be deemed to be a dwelling-house let on a protected tenancy or, as the case may be, subject to a statutory tenancy and the following provisions of this section shall have effect.

  (2)   For the avoidance of doubt it is hereby declared that where, for the purpose of determining the rateable value of the separate accommodation, it is necessary to make an apportionment under this Act, regard is to be had to the circumstances mentioned in subsection (1)(a) above.

  (3)   While the tenant is in possession of the separate accommodation (whether as a protected or statutory tenant), any term or condition of the contract of tenancy terminating or modifying, or providing for the termination or modification of, his right to the use of any of the shared accommodation which is living accommodation shall be of no effect.

  (4)   Where the terms and conditions of the contract of tenancy are such that at any time during the tenancy the persons in common with whom the tenant is entitled to the use of the shared accommodation could be varied, or their number could be increased, nothing in subsection (3) above shall prevent those terms and conditions from having effect so far as they relate to any such variation or increase.

  (5)   Without prejudice to the enforcement of any order made under subsection (6)

below, while the tenant is in possession of the separate accommodation, no order shall be made for possession of any of the shared accommodation, whether on the application of the immediate landlord of the tenant or on the application of any person under whom that landlord derives title, unless a like order has been made, or is made at the same time, in respect of the separate accommodation; and the provisions of section 98(1) of this Act shall apply accordingly.

(6) On the application of the landlord, the county court may make such order either—

(a) terminating the right of the tenant to use the whole or any part of the shared accommodation other than living accommodation.

(b) modifying his right to use the whole or any part of the shared accommodation, whether by varying the persons or increasing the number of persons entitled to the use of that accommodation, or otherwise,

as the court thinks just.

(7) No order shall be made under subsection (6) above so as to effect any termination or modification of the rights of the tenant which, apart from subsection (3) above, could not be effected by or under the terms of the contract of tenancy.

(8) In this section "living accommodation" means accommodation of such a nature that the fact that it constitutes or is included in the shared accommodation is (or, if the tenancy has ended, was) sufficient, apart from this section, to prevent the tenancy from constituting a protected tenancy of a dwelling-house.

Sublettings

23. Certain sublettings not to exclude any part of sub-lessor's premises from protection.

(1) Where the tenant of any premises, consisting of a house or part of a house, has sublet a part but not the whole of the premises, then, as against his landlord or any superior landlord, no part of the premises shall be treated as not being a dwelling-house let on or subject to a protected or statutory tenancy by reason only that—

(a) the terms on which any person claiming under the tenant holds any part of the premises include the use of accommodation in common with other persons; or

(b) part of the premises is let to any such person at a rent which includes payments in respect of board or attendance.

(2) Nothing in this section shall affect the rights against, and liabilities to, each other of the tenant and any person claiming under him, or of any 2 such persons.

Business premises

24. Premises with a business use.

(3) A tenancy shall not be a regulated tenancy if it is a tenancy to which Part II of the Landlord and Tenant Act 1954 applies (but this provision is without prejudice to the application of any other provision of this Act to a sub-tenancy of any part of the premises comprised in such a tenancy).

Miscellaneous

25. Rateable value and meaning of "appropriate day".

(1) Except where this Act otherwise provides, the rateable value on any day of a dwelling-house shall be ascertained for the purposes of this Act as follows:—

(a) if the dwelling-house is a hereditament for which a rateable value is then shown in the valuation list, it shall be that rateable value;

(b) if the dwelling-house forms part only of such a hereditament or consists of or forms part of more than one such hereditament, its rateable value shall be taken to be such value as is found by a proper apportionment or aggregation of the rateable value or values so shown.

(2)   Any question arising under this section as to the proper apportionment or aggregation of any value or values shall be determined by the county court, and the decision of the county court shall be final.

(3)   In this Act "the appropriate day"—

(a)   in relation to any dwelling-house which, on 23rd March 1965, was or formed part of a hereditament for which a rateable value was shown in the valuation list then in force, or consisted or formed part of more than one such hereditament, means that date, and

(b)   in relation to any other dwelling-house, means the date on which such a value is or was first shown in the valuation list.

(4)   Where, after the date which is the appropriate day in relation to any dwelling-house, the valuation list is altered so as to vary the rateable value of the hereditament of which the dwelling-house consists or forms part and the alteration has effect from a date not later than the appropriate day, the rateable value of the dwelling-house on the appropriate day shall be ascertained as if the value shown in the valuation list on the appropriate day had been the value shown in the list as altered.

(5)   This section applies in relation to any other land as it applies in relation to a dwelling-house.

26.   Land and premises let with dwelling-house.

(1)   For the purposes of this Act, any land or premises let together with a dwelling-house shall, unless it consists of agricultural land exceeding 2 acres in extent, be treated as part of the dwelling-house.

(2)   For the purposes of subsection (1) above "agricultural land" has the meaning set out in section 26(3)(a) of the General Rate Act 1967 (exclusion of agricultural land and premises from liability for rating).

PART III
RENTS UNDER REGULATED TENANCIES

Regulation of rent

44.   Limit of rent during contractual periods.

(1)   Where a rent for a dwelling-house is registered under Part IV of this Act, the rent recoverable for any contractual period of a regulated tenancy of the dwelling-house shall be limited to the rent so registered.

This subsection is subject to the following provisions of this Act: subsection (4) below, section 71(3), paragraph 1(3) of Schedule 7, and paragraph 3 of Schedule 20.

(2)   Where a limit is imposed by subsection (1) above on the rent recoverable in relation to any contractual period of a regulated tenancy, the amount by which the rent payable under the tenancy exceeds that limit shall, notwithstanding anything in any agreement, be irrecoverable from the tenant.

(3)   In this Part of this Act "contractual rent limit" means the limit specified in subsection (1) above.

(4)   Schedule 7 to this Act shall have effect for the purpose of providing a special rent limit in relation to certain tenancies which became regulated tenancies by virtue of section 14 of the Counter-Inflation Act 1973.

45.   Limit of rent during statutory periods.

(1)   Except as otherwise provided by this Part of this Act, where the rent payable for any statutory period of a regulated tenancy of a dwelling-house would exceed the rent recoverable for the last contractual period thereof, the amount of the excess shall, notwithstanding anything in any agreement, be recoverable from the tenant.

(2)   Where a rent for the dwelling-house is registered under Part IV of this Act, the following provisions shall apply with respect to the rent for any statutory period of a

regulated tenancy of the dwelling-house:—

(a) if the rent payable for any statutory period would exceed the rent so registered, the amount of the excess shall, notwithstanding anything in any agreement, be irrecoverable from the tenant; and

(b) if the rent payable for any statutory period would be less than the rent so registered, it may be increased up to the amount of that rent by a notice of increase served by the landlord on the tenant and specifying the date from which the increase is to take effect.

This subsection is subject to the following provisions of this Act: section 71(3), paragraph 1(3) of Schedule 7, and paragraph 3 of Schedule 20.

(3) The date specified in a notice of increase under subsection (2)(b) above shall not be earlier than the date from which the registration of the rent took effect nor earlier than 4 weeks before the service of the notice.

(4) Where no rent for the dwelling-house is registered under Part IV of this Act, sections 46 and 47 of this Act shall have effect with respect to the rent recoverable for any statutory period under a regulated tenancy of the dwelling-house.

46. Adjustment, with respect to rates, of recoverable rent for statutory periods before registration.

(1) Where—

(a) section 45(4) of this Act applies, and

(b) any rates in respect of the dwelling-house are, or were during the last contractual period, borne by the landlord or a superior landlord,

then, for any statutory period for which the amount of the rates (ascertained in accordance with Schedule 5 to this Act) differs from the amount, so ascertained, of the rates for the last contractual period, the recoverable rent shall be increased or decreased by the amount of the difference.

(2) Where the amount of the recoverable rent is increased by virtue of this section, the increase shall not take effect except in pursuance of a notice of increase served by the landlord on the tenant and specifying the increase and the date from which it is to take effect.

(3) The date specified in a notice of increase under subsection (2) above shall be not earlier than 6 weeks before the service of the notice, and if it is earlier than the service of the notice any rent unpaid shall become due on the day after the service of the notice.

47. Adjustment, with respect to services and furniture, of recoverable rent for statutory periods before registration.

(1) Where section 45(4) of this Act applies and for any statutory period there is with respect to—

(a) the provision of services for the tenant by the landlord or a superior landlord, or

(b) the use of furniture by the tenant,

or any circumstances relating thereto any difference, in comparison with the last contractual period, such as to affect the amount of the rent which it is reasonable to charge, the recoverable rent for the statutory period shall be increased or decreased by an appropriate amount.

(2) Any question whether, or by what amount, the recoverable rent for any period is increased or decreased by virtue of this section shall be determined by agreement in writing between the landlord and the tenant or by the county court; and any such determination—

(a) may be made so as to relate to past statutory periods; and

(b) shall have effect with respect to statutory periods subsequent to the periods to which it relates until revoked or varied by any such agreement as is referred to in this subsection or by the county court.

49.   Notices of increase.

(1)   Any reference in this section to a notice of increase is a reference to a notice of increase under section 45(2), or 46 of this Act.

(2)   A notice of increase must be in the prescribed form.

(3)   Notwithstanding that a notice of increase relates to statutory periods, it may be served during a contractual period.

(4)   Where a notice of increase is served during a contractual period and the protected tenancy could, by a notice to quit served by the landlord at the same time, be brought to an end before the date specified in the notice of increase, the notice of increase shall operate to convert the protected tenancy into a statutory tenancy as from that date.

(5)   If the county court is satisfied that any error or omission in a notice of increase is due to a bona fide mistake on the part of the landlord, the court may by order amend the notice by correcting any errors or supplying any omission therein which, if not corrected or supplied, would render the notice invalid and, if the court so directs, the notice as so amended shall have effect and be deemed to have had effect as a valid notice.

(6)   Any amendment of a notice of increase under subsection (5) above may be made on such terms and conditions with respect to arrears of rent or otherwise as appear to the court to be just and reasonable.

(7)   No increase of rent which becomes payable by reason of an amendment of a notice of increase under subsection (5) above shall be recoverable in respect of any statutory period which ended more than 6 months before the date of the order making the amendment.

Rent agreements with tenants having security of tenure

51.   Protection of tenants with security of tenure.

(1)   In this Part of this Act a "rent agreement with a tenant having security of tenure" means—

(a)   an agreement increasing the rent payable under a protected tenancy which is a regulated tenancy, or

(b)   the grant to the tenant under a regulated tenancy, or to any person who might succeed him as a statutory tenant, of another regulated tenancy of the dwelling-house at a rent exceeding the rent under the previous tenancy.

(2)   Where any rates in respect of the dwelling-house are borne by the landlord or a superior landlord, any increase of rent shall be disregarded for the purposes of the definition in subsection (1) above if the increase is no more than one corresponding to an increase in the rates borne by the landlord or a superior landlord in respect of the dwelling-house.

(3)   If—

(a)   a rent agreement with a tenant having security of tenure takes effect on or after the commencement of this Act, and was made at a time when no rent was registered for the dwelling-house under Part IV of this Act,

the requirements of subsection (4) below shall be observed as respects the agreement.

(4)   The requirements are that—

(a)   the agreement is in writing signed by the landlord and the tenant, and

(b)   the document containing the agreement contains a statement, in characters not less conspicuous than those used in any other part of the agreement—

(i)   that the tenant's security of tenure under this Act will not be affected if he refuses to enter into the agreement, and

(ii)   that entry into the agreement will not deprive the tenant or landlord of the right to apply at any time to the rent officer for the registration of a fair rent under Part IV of this Act,

or words to that effect, and

(c)   the statement mentioned in paragraph (b) above is set out at the head of the document containing the agreement.

52.   Protection: special provisions following conversion.

(1)   This section applies to an agreement with a tenant having security of tenure which is entered into after the commencement of section 68(2) of the Housing Act 1980 if the tenancy has become or, as the case may be, the previous tenancy became a regulated tenancy by conversion.

(2)   Any such agreement which purports to increase the rent payable under a protected tenancy shall, if entered into at a time when no rent is registered for the dwelling-house under Part IV of this Act, be void.

(3)   If any such agreement constitutes a grant of a regulated tenancy and is made at a time when no rent is so registered, any excess of the rent payable under the tenancy so granted (for any contractual or statutory period of the tenancy) over the rent limit applicable to the previous tenancy, shall be irrecoverable from the tenant; but this subsection ceases to apply if a rent is subsequently so registered.

(4)   For the purposes of this section a tenancy is a regulated tenancy by conversion if it has become a regulated tenancy by virtue of—

(a)   Part VIII of this Act, section 43 of the Housing Act 1969 or Part III or IV of the Housing Finance Act 1972 (conversion of controlled tenancies into regulated tenancies); or

(b)   section 18(3) of this Act or paragraph 5 of Schedule 2 to the Rent Act 1968 (conversion on death of first successor); or

(c)   section 64 of the Housing Act 1980 (conversion of all remaining controlled tenancies).

(5)   This section does not apply to any agreement where the tenant is neither the person who, at the time of the conversion, was the tenant nor a person who might succeed the tenant at that time as a statutory tenant.

(6)   Where a rent is registered for the dwelling-house and the registration is subsequently cancelled, this section shall not apply to the agreement submitted to the rent officer in connection with the cancellation nor to any agreement made so as to take effect after the cancellation.

54.   Failure to comply with provisions for protection of tenants.

(1)   If, in the case of a variation of the terms of a regulated tenancy, there is a failure to observe any of the requirements of section 51, of this Act, any excess of the rent payable under the terms as varied over the terms without the variation shall be irrecoverable from the tenant.

(2)   If, in the case of the grant of a tenancy, there is a failure to observe any of those requirements, any excess of the rent payable under the tenancy so granted (for any contractual or any statutory period of the tenancy) over the previous limit shall be irrecoverable from the tenant.

(3)   In subsection (2) above the "previous limit" shall be taken to be the amount which (taking account of any previous operation of this section or of section 46 of the Housing Finance Act 1972, which is superseded by this section) was recoverable by way of rent for the last rental period of the previous tenancy of the dwelling-house, or which would have been so recoverable if all notices of increase authorised by this Act, the Rent Act 1968 and section 37(3) of the Act of 1972 had been served.

Enforcement provisions

57.   Recovery from landlord of sums paid in excess of recoverable rent, etc.

(1)   Where a tenant has paid on account of rent any amount which, by virtue of this Part of this Act, is irrecoverable by the landlord, the tenant who paid it shall be entitled to recover that amount from the landlord who received it or his personal representatives.

(2)   Any amount which a tenant is entitled to recover under subsection (1) above may, without prejudice to any other method of recovery, be deducted by the tenant from any rent payable by him to the landlord.

(3)   No amount which a tenant is entitled to recover under subsection (1) above shall be recoverable at any time after the expiry of—

(a)   one year, in the case of an amount which is irrecoverable by virtue of section 54 of this Act; or

(b)   two years, in any other case.

(4)   Any person who, in any rent book or similar document, makes an entry showing or purporting to show any tenant as being in arrears in respect of any sum on account of rent which is irrecoverable by virtue of this Part of this Act shall be liable to a fine not exceeding level 3 on the standard scale unless he proves that, at the time of the making of the entry, the landlord had a bona fide claim that the sum was recoverable.

(5)   If, where any such entry has been made by or on behalf of any landlord, the landlord on being requested by or on behalf of the tenant to do so, refuses or neglects to cause the entry to be deleted within 7 days, the landlord shall be liable to a fine not exceeding level 3 on the standard scale unless he proves that, at the time of the neglect or refusal to cause the entry to be deleted, he had a bona fide claim that the sum was recoverable.

58.   Rectification of rent books in light of determination of recoverable rent.
Where, in any proceedings, the recoverable rent of a dwelling-house subject to a regulated tenancy is determined by a court, then, on the application of the tenant (whether in those or in any subsequent proceedings), the court may call for the production of the rent book or any similar document relating to the dwelling-house and may direct the registrar or clerk of the court to correct any entries showing, or purporting to show, the tenant as being in arrears in respect of any sum which the court has determined to be irrecoverable.

General provisions

59.   Adjustment for differences in lengths of rental periods.
In ascertaining for the purposes of this Part of this Act whether there is any difference with respect to rents or rates between one rental period and another (whether of the same tenancy or not) or the amount of any such difference, any necessary adjustment shall be made to take account of periods of different lengths; and for the purposes of such an adjustment a period of one month shall be treated as equivalent to one-twelfth of a year and a period of a week as equivalent to one-fifty-second of a year.

60.   Regulations.
(1)   The Secretary of State may make regulations—

(a)   prescribing the form of any notice or other document to be given or used in pursuance of this Part of this Act; and

(b)   prescribing anything required or authorised to be prescribed by this Part of this Act.

(2)   Any such regulations shall be made by statutory instrument which shall be subject to annulment in pursuance of a resolution of either House of Parliament.

61.   Interpretation of Part III.
(1)   In this Part of this Act, except where the context otherwise requires—

"contractual period" means a rental period of a regulated tenancy which is a period beginning before the expiry or termination of the protected tenancy;

"contractual rent limit" has the meaning assigned to it by section 44(3) of this Act;

"prescribed" means prescribed by regulations under section 60 of this Act and references to a prescribed form include references to a form substantially to the same effect as the prescribed form;

"recoverable rent" means rent which, under a regulated tenancy, is or was for the time being recoverable, having regard to the provisions of this Part of this Act;

"rent agreement with a tenant having security of tenure" has the meaning assigned to it by section 51 of this Act;

"statutory period" means any rental period of a regulated tenancy which is not a contractual period.

(2) References in this Part of this Act to rates, in respect of a dwelling-house, include references to such proportion of any rates in respect of a hereditament of which the dwelling-house forms part as may be agreed in writing between the landlord and the tenant or determined by the county court.

PART IV
REGISTRATION OF RENTS UNDER REGULATED TENANCIES

62. Registration areas.

(1) The registration areas for the purpose of this Part of this Act are—

    (a) counties,

    (b) London boroughs, and

    (c) the City of London.

(2) For the purposes of this Part of this Act—

    (a) the area of the City of London shall be deemed to include the Inner Temple and the Middle Temple, and

    (b) the Isles of Scilly shall be a registration area and the Council of the Isles of Scilly shall be the local authority for that registration area.

63. Schemes for appointment of rent officers.

(1) The Secretary of State shall for every registration area make, after consultation with the local authority, a scheme providing for the appointment by the proper officer of the local authority—

    (a) of such number of rent officers for the area as may be determined by or in accordance with the scheme.

(2) A scheme under this section—

    (a) shall provide for the payment by the local authority to rent officers of remuneration and allowances in accordance with scales approved by the Secretary of State with the consent of the Treasury;

    (b) shall prohibit the dismissal of a rent officer except by the proper officer of the local authority on the direction, or with the consent, of the Secretary of State;

    (c) shall require the local authority to provide for the rent officers office accommodation and clerical and other assistance;

    (d) shall allocate, or confer on the proper officer of the local authority the duty of allocating, work as between the rent officers and shall confer on the proper officer the duty of supervising the conduct of rent officers.

(2A) A scheme under this section may make all or any of the following provisions—

    (a) provision requiring the consent of the Secretary of State to the appointment of rent officers;

    (b) provision with respect to the appointment of rent officers for fixed periods;

    (c) provision for the proper officer of the local authority, in such circumstances and subject to such conditions (as to consent or otherwise) as may be specified in the scheme,—

        (i) to designate a person appointed or to be appointed a rent officer as chief rent officer and to designate one or more such persons as senior rent officers;

(ii)   to delegate to a person so designated as chief rent officer such functions as may be specified in the scheme; and

(iii)   to revoke a designation under sub-paragraph (i) above and to revoke or vary a delegation under sub-paragraph (ii) above;

(d)   provision with respect to the delegation of functions by a chief rent officer to other rent officers (whether designated as senior rent officers or not);

(e)   provision as to the circumstances in which and the terms on which a rent officer appointed by the scheme may undertake functions outside the area to which the scheme relates in accordance with paragraph (f) below;

(f)   provision under which a rent officer appointed for an area other than that to which the scheme relates may undertake functions in the area to which the scheme relates and for such a rent officer to be treated for such purposes as may be specified in the scheme (which may include the purposes of paragraphs (c) and (d) above and paragraphs (c) and (d) of subsection (2) above) as if he were a rent officer appointed under the scheme; and

(g)   provision conferring functions on the proper officer of a local authority with respect to the matters referred to in paragraphs (d) to (f) above.

(3)   For the purposes of any local Act scheme, within the meaning of section 8 of the Superannuation Act 1972, rent officers appointed in pursuance of a scheme under this section shall be deemed to be officers in the employment of the local authority for whose area the scheme is made; and for the purposes of—

(a)   Part III of the Social Security Pensions Act 1975, and

(b)   the Social Security Act 1975,

they shall be deemed to be in that employment under a contract of service.

(4)   References in this Part of this Act to the rent officer are references to any rent officer appointed for any area who is authorised to act in accordance with a scheme under this section.

(5)   A scheme under this section may be varied or revoked by a subsequent scheme made thereunder.

(6)   The Secretary of State shall, in respect of each financial year, make to any local authority incurring expenditure which is of a kind mentioned in subsection (7) below, a grant equal to that expenditure.

(7)   The expenditure mentioned in subsection (6) above is any expenditure—

(a)   attributable to this section or an order under section 121 of the Housing Act 1988, or

(b)   incurred in respect of pensions, allowances or gratuities payable to or in respect of rent officers (appointed in pursuance of a scheme under this section) by virtue of regulations under section 7 or section 24 of the Superannuation Act 1972 or

(c)   incurred in respect of increases of pensions payable to or in respect of rent officers (so appointed) by virtue of the Pensions (Increase) Act 1971.

(8)   Any expenditure incurred by the Secretary of State by virtue of subsection (6) above shall be paid out of money provided by Parliament.

(9)   In the case of a registration area which is a metropolitan county this section shall apply as if—

(a)   the first reference to the local authority in subsection (1) were a reference to the council of each district in the county; and

(b)   the second reference to the local authority in that subsection, the references to the local authority in subsection (2) and the reference to the local authority for whose area the scheme is made in subsection (3) were references to such one of the councils of the district in that county as has been designated by the scheme.

64.   Default powers of Secretary of State.

(1)   If the Secretary of State is of opinion that a local authority have failed to carry

out any function conferred on them by a scheme under section 63 of this Act he may, after such enquiry as he thinks fit, by order revoke the scheme and, without consulting the local authority, make another scheme under that section.

(2) A scheme made by virtue of subsection (1) above may confer functions otherwise exercisable by the local authority or the proper officer of the local authority on a person appointed by the Secretary of State and that person may, if another local authority consent, be that other local authority or, as the case may be, the proper officer of that other local authority.

(3) If the Secretary of State is of opinion that the proper officer of the local authority has failed to carry out any functions conferred on the proper officer by a scheme under section 63 he may (after consultation with the local authority) exercise his power under subsection (5) of that section by making a scheme providing for all or any of the functions otherwise exercisable by the proper officer to be exercised by some other person.

(4) A scheme made by virtue of this section may contain such incidental and transitional provisions as appear to the Secretary of State to be necessary or expedient.

64A. Amalgamation schemes.

(1) If the Secretary of State is of the opinion—

(a) that there is at any time insufficient work in two or more registration areas to justify the existence of a separate service of rent officers for each area, or

(b) that it would at any time be beneficial for the efficient administration of the service provided by rent officers in two or more registration areas,

he may, after consultation with the local authorities concerned, make a scheme under section 63 above designating as an amalgamated registration area the areas of those authorities and making provision accordingly for that amalgamated area.

(2) Any reference in the following provisions of this Chapter to a registation area includes a reference to an amalgamated registration area and, in relation to such an area, "the constituent authorities" means the local authorities whose areas make up the amalgamated area.

(3) A scheme under section 63 above made for an amalgamated registration area—

(a) shall confer on the proper officer of one of the constituent authorities all or any of the functions which, in accordance with section 63 above, fall to be exercisable by the proper officer of the local authority for the registration area;

(b) may provide that any rent officer previously appointed for the area of any one of the constituent authorities shall be treated for such purposes as may be specified in the scheme as a rent officer appointed for the amalgamated registration area; and

(c) shall make such provision as appears to the Secretary of State to be appropriate for the payment by one or more of the constituent authorities of the remunerations, allowances and other expenditure which under section 63 above is to be paid by the local authority for the area.

(4) A scheme under section 63 above made for an amalgamated registration area may contain such incidental, transitional and supplementary provisions as appear to the Secretary of State to be necessary or expedient.

64B. New basis for administration of rent officer service.

(1) If, with respect to registration areas generally or any particular registration area or areas, it appears to the Secretary of State that it is no longer appropriate for the appointment, remuneration and administration of rent officers to be a function of local authorities, he may by order—

(a) provide that no scheme under section 63 above shall be made for the area or areas specified in the order; and

(b) make, with respect to the area or areas so specified, such provision as appears to him to be appropriate with respect to the appointment, remuneration and administration of rent officers and the payment of pensions, allowances or gratuities to or in respect of them.

(2)   An order under this section shall make provision for any expenditure attributable to the provisions of the order to be met by the Secretary of State in such manner as may be specified in the order (whether by way of grant, reimbursement or otherwise); and any expenditure incurred by the Secretary of State by virtue of this subsection shall be paid out of money provided by Parliament.

(3)   An order under this section—

(a)   may contain such incidental, transitional and supplementary provisions as appear to the Secretary of State to be appropriate, including provisions amending this Part of this Act; and

(b)   shall be made by statutory instrument which shall be subject to annulment in pursuance of a resolution of either House of Parliament.

65.   Rent assessment committees.

Rent assessment committees shall be constituted in accordance with Schedule 10 to this Act.

66.   Register of rents.

(1)   The rent officer for any area shall prepare and keep up to date a register for the purposes of this Part of this Act and shall make the register available for inspection in such place or places and in such manner as may be provided by the scheme made for the area under section 63 of this Act.

(2)   The register shall contain, in addition to the rent payable under a regulated tenancy of a dwelling-house—

(a)   the prescribed particulars with regard to the tenancy; and

(b)   a specification of the dwelling-house.

(3)   A copy of an entry in the register certified under the hand of the rent officer or any person duly authorised by him shall be receivable in evidence in any court and in any proceedings.

(4)   A person requiring such a certified copy shall be entitled to obtain it on payment of the prescribed fee.

67.   Application for registration of rent.

(1)   An application for the registration of a rent for a dwelling-house may be made to the rent officer by the landlord or the tenant, or jointly by the landlord and the tenant, under a regulated tenancy of the dwelling-house.

(2)   Any such application must be in the prescribed form and must—

(a)   specify the rent which it is sought to register;

(b)   where the rent includes any sum payable by the tenant to the landlord for services and the application is made by the landlord, specify that sum and be accompanied by details of the expenditure incurred by the landlord in providing those services; and

(c)   contain such other particulars as may be prescribed.

(3)   Subject to subsection (4) below, where a rent for a dwelling-house has been registered under this Part of this Act, no application by the tenant alone or by the landlord alone for the registration of a different rent for that dwelling-house shall be entertained before the expiry of 2 years from the relevant date (as defined in subsection (5) below) except on the ground that, since that date, there has been such a change in—

(a)   the condition of the dwelling-house (including the making of any improvement therein),

(b)   the terms of the tenancy,

(c)   the quantity, quality or condition of any furniture provided for use under the tenancy (deterioration by fair wear and tear excluded), or

(d)   any other circumstances taken into consideration when the rent was registered or confirmed,

as to make the registered rent no longer a fair rent.

(4)   Notwithstanding anything in subsection (3) above, an application such as is mentioned in that subsection which is made by the landlord alone and is so made within the last 3 months of the period of 2 years referred to in that subsection may be entertained notwithstanding that that period has not expired.

(5)   In this section "relevant date", in relation to a rent which has been registered under this Part of this Act, means the date from which the registration took effect or, in the case of a registered rent which has been confirmed, the date from which the confirmation (or, where there have been two or more successive confirmations, the last of them) took effect.

(7)   The provisions of Part I of Schedule 11 to this Act as modified by the Regulated Tenancies (Procedure) Regulations 1980 shall have effect with respect to the procedure to be followed on applications for the registration of rents.

70.   Determination of fair rent.

(1)   In determining, for the purposes of this Part of this Act, what rent is or would be a fair rent under a regulated tenancy of a dwelling-house, regard shall be had to all the circumstances (other than personal circumstances) and in particular to—

(a)   the age, character, locality and state of repair of the dwelling-house, and

(b)   if any furniture is provided for use under the tenancy, the quantity, quality and condition of the furniture, and

(c)   any premium, or sum in the nature of a premium, which has been or may be lawfully required or received on the grant, renewal, continuance or assignment of the tenancy.

(2)   For the purposes of the determination it shall be assumed that the number of persons seeking to become tenants of similar dwelling-houses in the locality on the terms (other than those relating to rent) of the regulated tenancy is not substantially greater than the number of such dwelling-houses in the locality which are available for letting on such terms.

(3)   There shall be disregarded—

(a)   any disrepair or other defect attributable to a failure by the tenant under the regulated tenancy or any predecessor in title of his to comply with any terms thereof;

(b)   any improvement carried out, otherwise than in pursuance of the terms of the tenancy, by the tenant under the regulated tenancy or any predecessor in title of his;

(e)   if any furniture is provided for use under the regulated tenancy, any improvement to the furniture by the tenant under the regulated tenancy or any predecessor in title of his or, as the case may be, any deterioration in the condition of the furniture due to any ill-treatment by the tenant, any person residing or lodging with him, or any sub-tenant of his.

(4)   In this section "improvement" includes the replacement of any fixture or fitting.

(4A)   In this section "premium" has the same meaning as in Part IX of this Act, and "sum in the nature of a premium" means—

(a)   any such loan as is mentioned in section 119 or 120 of this Act,

(b)   any such excess over the reasonable price of furniture as is mentioned in section 123 of this Act, and

(c)   any such advance payment of rent as is mentioned in section 126 of this Act.

71.   Amount to be registered as rent.

(1)   The amount to be registered as the rent of any dwelling-house shall include any sums payable by the tenant to the landlord for the use of furniture or for services, whether or not those sums are separate from the sums payable for the occupation of the dwelling-house or are payable under separate agreements.

(2) Where any rates in respect of a dwelling-house are borne by the landlord or a superior landlord, the amount to be registered under this Part of this Act as the rent of the dwelling-house shall be the same as if the rates were not so borne; but the fact that they are so borne shall be noted on the register.

(3) Where subsection (2) above applies, the amount of the rates for any rental period, ascertained in accordance with Schedule 5 to this Act—

(a)   shall be added to the limit imposed by section 44(1) of this Act; and

(b)   if the rental period is a statutory period, as defined in section 61 of this Act, shall be recoverable, without service of any notice of increase, in addition to the sums recoverable from the tenant apart from this subsection.

(4) Where, under a regulated tenancy, the sums payable by the tenant to the landlord include any sums varying according to the cost from time to time of—

(a)   any services provided by the landlord or a superior landlord, or

(b)   any works of maintenance or repair carried out by the landlord or a superior landlord,

the amount to be registered under this Part of this Act as rent may, if the rent officer is satisfied or, as the case may be, the rent assessment committee are satisfied, that the terms as to the variation are reasonable, be entered as an amount variable in accordance with those terms.

72.   Effect of registration of rent.

(1)   The registration of a rent for a dwelling-house takes effect—

(a)   if the rent is determined by the rent officer, from the date when it is registered, and

(b)   if the rent is determined by a rent assessment committee, from the date when the committee make their decision.

(2)   If the rent for the time being registered is confirmed, the confirmation takes effect—

(a)   if it is made by the rent officer, from the date when it is noted in the register, and

(b)   if it is made by a rent assessment committee, from the date when the committee make their decision.

(3)   If (by virtue of section 67(4) of this Act) an application for registration of a rent is made before the expiry of the period mentioned in section 67(3) and the resulting registration of a rent for the dwelling-house, or confirmation of the rent for the time being registered, would, but for this subsection, take effect before the expiry of that period it shall take effect on the expiry of that period.

(4)   The date from which the registration or confirmation of a rent takes effect shall be entered in the register.

(5)   As from the date on which the registration of a rent takes effect any previous registration of a rent for the dwelling-house ceases to have effect.

(6)   Where a valid notice of increase under any provision of Part III of this Act has been served on a tenant and, in consequence of the registration of a rent, part but not the whole of the increase specified in the notice becomes irrecoverable from the tenant, the registration shall not invalidate the notice, but the notice shall, as from the date from which the registration takes effect, have effect as if it specified such part only of the increase as has not become irrecoverable.

73.   Cancellation of registration of rent.

(1)   An application may be made in accordance with this section for the cancellation of the registration of a rent for a dwelling-house where—

(a)   a rent agreement as respects the dwelling-house takes effect, or is to take effect, after the expiration of a period of 2 years beginning with the relevant date (as defined in section 67(5) of this Act), and (b)　the period for which the tenancy has effect cannot end, or be brought to an end by the landlord (except for non-payment of rent or a breach of the terms of the tenancy), earlier than 12 months after the date of the application, and

(c)　the application is made jointly by the landlord and the tenant under the agreement.

(1A)　Such an application may also be made where—

(a)　not less than two years have elapsed since the relevant date (as defined in section 67(5) of this Act); and

(b)　the dwelling-house is not for the time being subject to a regulated tenancy; and

(c)　the application is made by the person who would be the landlord if the dwelling-house were let on such a tenancy.

(2)　The rent agreement may be one providing that the agreement does not take effect unless the application for cancellation of registration is granted.

(3)　An application under this section must—

(a)　be in the form prescribed for the application concerned and contain the prescribed particulars; and

(b)　be accompanied, in the case of an application under subsection (1) above, by a copy of the rent agreement.

(4)　If the application is made under subsection (1) above and the rent officer is satisfied that the rent, or the highest rent, payable under the rent agreement does not exceed a fair rent for the dwelling-house, he shall cancel the registration and he shall also cancel the registration if the application is made under subsection (1A) above.

(5)　Where the application is made under subsection (1) above and under the terms of the rent agreement the sums payable by the tenant to the landlord include any sums varying according to the cost from time to time of any services provided by the landlord or a superior landlord, or of any works of maintenance or repair carried out by the landlord or a superior landlord, the rent officer shall not cancel the registration unless he is satisfied that those terms are reasonable.

(6)　A cancellation made in pursuance of an application under subsection (1) above shall not take effect until the date when the agreement takes effect; and if the cancellation is registered before that date, the date on which it is to take effect shall be noted on the register.

(7)　The cancellation of the registration shall be without prejudice to a further registration of a rent at any time after cancellation.

(8)　The rent officer shall notify the applicants of his decision to grant, or to refuse, any application under this section.

(9)　In this section "rent agreement" means—

(a)　an agreement increasing the rent payable under a protected tenancy which is a regulated tenancy, or

(b)　where a regulated tenancy is terminated, and a new regulated tenancy is granted at a rent exceeding the rent under the previous tenancy, the grant of the new tenancy.

74.　Regulations.

(1)　The Secretary of State may make regulations—

(a)　prescribing the form of any notice, application, register or other document to be given, made or used in pursuance of this Part of this Act;

(b)　regulating the procedure to be followed by rent officers and rent assessment committees whether under this Act or Part I of the Housing Act 1988 or Schedule 10 to the Local Government and Housing Act 1989; and

(c)　prescribing anything required or authorised to be prescribed by this Part of this Act.

(2)   Regulations under subsection (1)(b) above may contain provisions modifying the following provisions of this Act:—
    (a)   Section 67, or 72;
    (b)   Part I of Schedule 11;
but no regulations containing such provisions shall have effect unless approved by a resolution of each House of Parliament.

(3)   Regulations made under this section shall be made by statutory instrument which, except in a case falling within subsection (2) above, shall be subject to annulment in pursuance of a resolution of either House of Parliament.

75.   Interpretation of Part IV.

(1)   In this Part of this Act, except where the context otherwise requires—
"improvement" includes structural alteration, extension or addition and the provision of additional fixtures or fittings but does not include anything done by way of decoration or repair;
"prescribed" means prescribed by regulations under section 74 of this Act, and references to a prescribed form include references to a form substantially to the same effect as the prescribed form.

(2)   References in this Part of this Act to rates, in respect of a dwelling-house, include references to such proportion of any rates in respect of a hereditament of which the dwelling-house forms part as may be agreed in writing between the landlord and the tenant or determined by the county court.

PART V
RENTS UNDER RESTRICTED CONTRACTS

Control of rents

77.   Reference of contracts to rent tribunals and obtaining by them of information.

(1)   Either the lessor or the lessee under a restricted contract may refer the contract to the rent tribunal.

(2)   Where a restricted contract is referred to a rent tribunal under subsection (1) above they may, by notice in writing served on the lessor, require him to give them, within such period (not less than 7 days from the date of the service of the notice) as may be specified in the notice, such information as they may reasonably require regarding such of the prescribed particulars relating to the contract as are specified in the notice.

(3)   If, within the period specified in a notice under subsection (2) above, the lessor fails without reasonable cause to comply with the provisions of the notice he shall be liable to a fine not exceeding level 3 on the standard scale.

(4)   Proceedings for an offence under this section shall not be instituted otherwise than by the local authority.

78.   Powers of rent tribunals on reference of contracts.

(1)   Where a restricted contract is referred to a rent tribunal and the reference is not, before the tribunal have entered upon consideration of it, withdrawn by the party or authority who made it, the tribunal shall consider it.

(2)   After making such inquiry as they think fit and giving to—
    (a)   each party to the contract, and
    (b)   if the general management of the dwelling is vested in and exercisable by a housing authority, that authority,
an opportunity of being heard or, at his or their option, of submitting representations in writing, the tribunal, subject to subsections (3) and (4) below,—
    (i)   shall approve the rent payable under the contract, or

(ii) shall reduce or increase the rent to such sum as they may, in all the circumstances, think reasonable, or

(iii) may, if they think fit in all the circumstances, dismiss the reference, and shall notify the parties of their decision.

(3) On the reference of a restricted contract relating to a dwelling for which a rent is registered under Part IV of this Act, the rent tribunal may not reduce the rent payable under the contract below the amount which would be recoverable from the tenant under a regulated tenancy of the dwelling.

(4) An approval, reduction or increase under this section may be limited to rent payable in respect of a particular period.

(5) In subsection (2) above "housing authority" means a local housing authority within the meaning of the Housing Act 1985.

79. Register of rents under restricted contracts.

(1) The president of every rent assessment panel shall prepare and keep up to date a register for the purposes of this Part of this Act and shall make the register available for inspection in such place or places and in such manner as the Secretary of State may direct.

(2) The register shall be so prepared and kept up to date as to contain, with regard to any contract relating to a dwelling situated in the area of the rent assessment panel and under which a rent is payable which has been approved, reduced or increased under section 78 of this Act, entries of—

(a) the prescribed particulars with regard to the contract;

(b) a specification of the dwelling to which the contract relates; and

(c) the rent as approved, reduced or increased by the rent tribunal, and, in a case in which the approval, reduction or increase is limited to rent payable in respect of a particular period, a specification of that period.

(3) Where any rates in respect of a dwelling are borne by the lessor or any person having any title superior to that of the lessor, the amount to be entered in the register under this section as the rent payable for the dwelling shall be the same as if the rates were not so borne; but the fact that they are so borne shall be noted in the register.

(5) A copy of an entry in the register certified under the hand of an officer duly authorised in that behalf by the president of the rent assessment panel concerned shall be receivable in evidence in any court and in any proceedings.

(6) A person requiring such a certified copy shall be entitled to obtain it on payment of the prescribed fee.

(6A) Every local authority shall, before the expiry of the period of three months beginning with the commencement of paragraph 44 of Schedule 25 to the Housing Act 1980, send to the president of the appropriate rent assessment panel the register previously kept by the authority under this section.

80. Reconsideration of rent after registration.

(1) Where the rent payable for any dwelling has been entered in the register under section 79 of this Act the lessor or the lessee may refer the case to the rent tribunal for reconsideration of the rent so entered.

(2) Where the rent under a restricted contract has been registered under section 79 of this Act, a rent tribunal shall not be required to entertain a reference, made otherwise than by the lessor and the lessee jointly, for the registration of a different rent for the dwelling concerned before the expiry of the period of 2 years beginning on the date on which the rent was last considered by the tribunal, except on the ground that, since that date, there has been such a change in—

(a) the condition of the dwelling,

(b) the furniture or services provided,

(c) the terms of the contract, or

(d)   any other circumstances taken into consideration when the rent was last considered,
as to make the registered rent no longer a reasonable rent.

81.   Effect of registration of rent.

(1)   Where the rent payable for any dwelling is entered in the register under section 79 of this Act, it shall not be lawful to require or receive on account of rent for that dwelling under a restricted contract payment of any amount in excess of the rent so registered—

(a)   in respect of any period subsequent to the date of the entry, or

(b)   where a particular period is specified in the register, in respect of that period.

(2)   Where subsection (3) of section 79 applies, the amount entered in the register under that section shall be treated for the purposes of this section as increased for any rental period by the amount of the rates for that period, ascertained in accordance with Schedule 5 to this Act.

(3)   Where any payment has been made or received in contravention of this section, the amount of the excess shall be recoverable by the person by whom it was paid.

(4)   Any person who requires or receives any payment in contravention of this section shall be liable to a fine not exceeding level 3 on the standard scale or to imprisonment for a term not exceeding 6 months or both, and, without prejudice to any other method of recovery, the court by which a person is found guilty of an offence under this subsection may order the amount paid in excess to be repaid to the person by whom the payment was made.

(5)   Proceedings for an offence under this section shall not be instituted otherwise than by the local authority.

81A.   Cancellation of registration of rent.

(1)   Where the rent payable for any dwelling is entered in the register under section 79 of this Act, the rent tribunal shall cancel the entry, on an application made under this section, if—

(b)   the dwelling is not for the time being subject to a restricted contract; and

(c)   the application is made by the person who would be the lessor if the dwelling were subject to a restricted contract.

(2)   An application under this section must be in the prescribed form, and contain the prescribed particulars.

(3)   Cancellation of the registration shall be without prejudice to a further registration of a rent at any time after the cancellation.

(4)   The rent tribunal shall notify the applicant of their decision to grant, or to refuse, any application under this section.

Miscellaneous and general

82.   Jurisdiction of rent tribunals.

Where a restricted contract is referred to a rent tribunal under this Part, or Part VII, of this Act and—

(a)   the contract relates to a dwelling consisting of or comprising part only of a hereditament, and

(b)   no apportionment of the rateable value of the hereditament has been made under section 25 of this Act,

then, unless the lessor in the course of the proceedings requires that such an apportionment shall be made and, within 2 weeks of making the requirement, brings proceedings in the county court for the making of the apportionment, the rent tribunal shall have jurisdiction to deal with the reference if it appears to them that, had the apportionment been made, they would have had jurisdiction.

83. Local authorities for Part V.

(1)   For the purposes of this Part of this Act, the local authority shall be—

(a)   in a district or London borough, the council of the district or borough in question, and

(b)   in the City of London, the Common Council.

(2)   The local authority shall have power to publish information regarding the provisions of this Part, and sections 103 to 106, of this Act.

84. Regulations.

The Secretary of State may by statutory instrument make regulations—

(c)   for prescribing anything which is required by this Part of this Act to be prescribed; and

(d)   generally for carrying into effect the provisions of this Part, and sections 103 to 106, of this Act.

85. Interpretation of Part V.

(1)   In this Part of this Act, except where the context otherwise requires,—

"dwelling" means a house or part of a house;

"lessee" means the person to whom is granted, under a restricted contract, the right to occupy the dwelling in question as a residence and any person directly or indirectly deriving title from the grantee;

"lessor" means the person who, under a restricted contract, grants to another the right to occupy the dwelling in question as a residence and any person directly or indirectly deriving title from the grantor;

"register" means the register kept by the president of the rent assessment panel concerned in pursuance of section 79 of this Act;

"rent tribunal" shall be construed in accordance with section 72 of the Housing Act 1980;

"services" includes attendance, the provision of heating or lighting, the supply of hot water and any other privilege or facility connected with the occupancy of a dwelling, other than a privilege or facility requisite for the purposes of access, cold water supply or sanitary accommodation.

(2)   References in this Part of this Act to a party to a contract include references to any person directly or indirectly deriving title from such a party.

(3)   Where separate sums are payable by the lessee of any dwelling to the lessor for any two or more of the following:—

(a)   occupation of the dwelling,

(b)   use of furniture, and

(c)   services,

any reference in this Part of this Act to "rent" in relation to that dwelling is a reference to the aggregate of those sums and, where those sums are payable under separate contracts, those contracts shall be deemed to be one contract.

(4)   The references in sections 79(3) and 81(2) of this Act to rates, in respect of a dwelling, include references to such proportion of any rates in respect of a hereditament of which the dwelling forms part as may be agreed in writing between the lessor and the lessee or determined by the county court.

PART VI
RENT LIMIT FOR DWELLINGS LET BY HOUSING ASSOCIATIONS, HOUSING TRUSTS AND THE HOUSING CORPORATION

Registration of rents

86. Tenancies to which Part VI applies.

(1)   In this Part of this Act "housing association tenancy" means a tenancy to which this Part of this Act applies.

(2)   This Part of this Act applies to a tenancy (other than a co-ownership tenancy) where—

(a)   the interest of the landlord under that tenancy belongs to a housing association or housing trust, or to the Housing Corporation or Housing for Wales, and

(b)   the tenancy would be a protected tenancy but for section 15 or 16 of this Act, and is not a tenancy to which Part II of the Landlord and Tenant Act 1954 applies.

(3)   In this Part of this Act "housing association" has the same meaning as in the Housing Associations Act 1985.

(3A)   For the purposes of this section a tenancy is a "co-ownership tenancy" if—

(a)   it was granted by a housing association which is a co-operative housing association within the meaning of the Housing Associations Act 1985; and

(b)   the tenant (or his personal representatives) will, under the terms of the tenancy agreement or of the agreement under which he became a member of the association, be entitled, on his ceasing to be a member and subject to any conditions stated in either agreement, to a sum calculated by reference directly or indirectly to the value of the dwelling-house.

(4)   In this Part of this Act "housing trust" has the same meaning as in section 15 of this Act.

87.   Rents to be registrable.

(1)   There shall be a part of the register under Part IV of this Act in which rents may be registered for dwelling-houses which are let, or are, or are to be, available for letting, under a housing association tenancy.

(2)   In relation to that part of the register the following (and no other) provisions of this Act:—

(a)   sections 67, 70, and 72,

(b)   section 71, except subsection (3), and

(c)   Schedule 11

shall apply in relation to housing association tenancies, and in their application to such tenancies shall have effect as if for any reference in those provisions to a regulated tenancy there were substituted a reference to a housing association tenancy.

(6)   A rent registered in any part of the register for a dwelling-house which becomes, or ceases to be, one subject to a housing association tenancy, shall be as effective as if it were registered in any other part of the register.

Rent limit

88.   Rent limit.

(1)   Where the rent payable under a tenancy would exceed the rent limit determined in accordance with this Part of this Act, the amount of the excess shall be irrecoverable from the tenant.

(2)   Where a rent for the dwelling-house is registered, the rent limit is the rent so registered.

(3)   Where any rates in respect of the dwelling-house are borne by the landlord, or a superior landlord, the amount of those rates for any rental period, ascertained in accordance with Schedule 5 to this Act, shall be added to the limit imposed by subsection (2) above, and in this Part of this Act references to the amount of the registered rent include any amount to be added under this subsection.

(4)   Where no rent for the dwelling-house is registered, then, subject to subsection (5) below, the rent limit shall be determined as follows:—

(a)   if the lease or agreement creating the tenancy was made before 1st January 1973, the rent limit is the rent recoverable under the tenancy, as varied by any agreement made before that date (but not as varied by any later agreement);

(b)   if paragraph (a) above does not apply, and, not more than 3 years before the tenancy began, the dwelling-house was subject to another tenancy (whether before 1973 or later) the rent limit is the rent recoverable under that other tenancy (or, if there was more than one, the last of them) for the last rental period thereof;

(c) if paragraphs (a) and (b) above do not apply, the rent limit is the rent payable under the terms of the lease or agreement creating the tenancy (and not the rent so payable under those terms as varied by any subsequent agreement).

(5) The reference in subsection (4)(b) above to another tenancy includes, in addition to a housing association tenancy, a regulated tenancy—

(a) which subsisted at any time after 1st April 1975; and

(b) under which, immediately before it came to an end, the interest of the landlord belonged to a housing association.

(6) Where for any period there is a difference between the amount (if any) of the rates borne by the landlord or a superior landlord in respect of the dwelling-house and the amount (if any) so borne in the rental period on which the rent limit is based, the rent limit under this Part of this Act shall be increased or decreased by the amount of the difference.

(7) A tenancy commencing (whether before or after the coming into force of this Act) while there is in operation a condition imposed under any of the following enactments:—

(a) section 2 of the Housing (Financial Provisions) Act 1924;

(b) paragraph 2 of Part II of Schedule 16 to the Housing Act 1985, or any corresponding earlier enactment;

(c) section 23 of the Housing Act 1949; and

(d) section 33 of the Housing Act 1985, or any corresponding earlier enactment; (which imposes a rent limit in respect of the dwelling-house) shall be disregarded for the purposes of subsection (4)(b) above in determining the rent limit under any subsequent tenancy of the dwelling-house.

Conversion to regulated tenancies

92. Conversion of housing association tenancies into regulated tenancies.

(1) If at any time, by virtue of subsections (1) and (3) of section 15 of this Act, a tenancy ceases to be one to which this Part of this Act applies and becomes a protected tenancy, that tenancy shall be a regulated tenancy and the housing association which is the landlord under that tenancy shall give notice in writing to the tenant, informing him that his tenancy is no longer excluded from protection under this Act.

(2) If, without reasonable excuse, a housing association fails to give notice to a tenant under subsection (1) above within the period of 21 days beginning on the day on which his tenancy becomes a protected tenancy, the association shall be liable to a fine not exceeding level 3 on the standard scale.

(3) Where an offence under subsection (2) above committed by a body corporate is proved to have been committed with the consent or connivance of, or to be attributable to any neglect on the part of, any director, manager or secretary or other similar officer of the body corporate or any person who was purporting to act in any such capacity, he as well as the body corporate shall be guilty of that offence and shall be liable to be proceeded against and punished accordingly.

(4) Schedule 14 to this Act shall have effect for supplementing this section.

(5) In this section—

"housing association" has the same meaning as in the Housing Associations Act 1985.

Miscellaneous

93. Increase of rent without notice to quit.

(1) Subject to subsections (2) and (3) below, where a housing association tenancy is a weekly or other periodical tenancy, the rent payable to the housing association or, as

the case may be, the housing trust or the Housing Corporation or Housing for Wales (in this section called "the landlord") may, without the tenancy being terminated, be increased with effect from the beginning of any rental period by a written notice of increase specifying the date on which the increase is to take effect and given by the landlord to the tenant not later than four weeks before that date.

(2)   Where a notice of increase is given under subsection (1) above and the tenant, before the date specified in the notice of increase, gives a valid notice to quit, the notice of increase does not take effect unless the tenant, with the written agreement of the landlord, withdraws his notice to quit before that date.

(4)   This section shall apply to a tenancy notwithstanding that the letting took place before the coming into force of this Act.

(5)   Nothing in this section shall authorise any rent to be increased above the rent limit, and any reference in section 88 of this Act to the variation by agreement of the rent recoverable under a tenancy shall include a reference to variation under this section.

94.   Recovery from landlord of sums paid in excess of recoverable rent, etc.

(1)   Where a tenant has paid on account of rent any amount which, by virtue of this Part of this Act, is irrecoverable by the landlord, the tenant who paid it shall be entitled to recover that amount from the landlord who received it or his personal representatives.

(2)   Any amount which a tenant is entitled to recover under sbsection (1) above may, without prejudice to any other method of recovery, be deducted by the tenant from any rent payable by him to the landlord.

(3)   No amount which a tenant is entitled to recover under subsection (1) above shall be recoverable at any time after the expiry of 2 years from the date of payment.

(4)   Any person who, in any rent book or similar document, makes an entry showing or purporting to show any tenant as being in arrears in respect of any sum on account of rent which is irrecoverable by virtue of this Part of this Act shall be liable to a fine not exceeding level 3 on the standard scale, unless he proves that, at the time of the making of the entry, the landlord had a bona fide claim that the sum was recoverable.

(5)   If, where any such entry has been made by or on behalf of any landlord, the landlord on being requested by or on behalf of the tenant to do so, refuses or neglects to cause the entry to be deleted within 7 days, the landlord shall be liable to a fine not exceeding level 3 on the standard scale, unless he proves that, at the time of the neglect or refusal to cause the entry to be deleted, he had a bona fide claim that the sum was recoverable.

95.   Duty of landlord to supply statement of rent under previous tenancy.

(1)   Where the rent payable under a tenancy is subject to the rent limit specified in section 88(4)(b) of this Act, the landlord shall, on being so requested in writing by the tenant, supply him with a statement in writing of the rent which was payable for the last rental period of the other tenancy referred to in that subsection.

(2)   If, without reasonable excuse, a landlord who has received such a request—

(a)   fails to supply the statement referred to in subsection (1) above within 21 days of receiving the request, or

(b)   supplies a statement which is false in any material particular,

he shall be liable to a fine not exceeding level 3 on the standard scale.

(3)   Where an offence under this section committed by a body corporate is proved to have been committed with the consent or connivance of, or to be attributable to any neglect on the part of, any director, manager or secretary or other similar officer of the body corporate or any person who was purporting to act in any such capacity, he as well as the body corporate shall be guilty of that offence and shall be liable to be proceeded against and punished accordingly.

96. Supplemental.

(3) A county court shall have jurisdiction, either in the course of any proceedings relating to a dwelling-house or on an application made for the purpose by the landlord or the tenant, to determine any question as to the rent limit under this Part of this Act, or as to any matter which is or may become material for determining any such question.

(4) In ascertaining for the purposes of this Part of this Act whether there is any difference with respect to rents or rates between one rental period and another (whether of the same tenancy or not) or the amount of any such difference, any necessary adjustments shall be made to take account of periods of different lengths.

(5) For the purposes of such an adjustment a period of one month shall be treated as equivalent to one-twelfth of a year and a period of a week as equivalent to one-fifty-second of a year.

97. Interpretation of Part VI.

(1) In this Part of this Act, except where the context otherwise requires—
"housing association", "housing association tenancy" and "housing trust" have the meanings assigned to them by section 86 of this Act; and
"tenancy" means a housing association tenancy.

(2) In this Part of this Act references to registration are, subject to section 87(5) of this Act and unless the context otherwise requires, references to registration pursuant to section 87.

(3) It is hereby declared that any power of giving directions conferred on the Secretary of State by this Part of this Act includes power to vary or revoke directions so given.

PART VII
SECURITY OF TENURE

Limitations on recovery of possession of dwelling-houses let on protected tenancies or subject to statutory tenancies

98. Grounds for possession of certain dwelling-houses.

(1) Subject to this Part of this Act, a court shall not make an order for possession of a dwelling-house which is for the time being let on a protected tenancy or subject to a statutory tenancy unless the court considers it reasonable to make such an order and either—

(a) the court is satisfied that suitable alternative accommodation is available for the tenant or will be available for him when the order in question takes effect, or

(b) the circumstances are as specified in any of the Cases in Part I of Schedule 15 to this Act.

(2) If, apart from subsection (1) above, the landlord would be entitled to recover possession of a dwelling-house which is for the time being let on or subject to a regulated tenancy, the court shall make an order for possession if the circumstances of the case are as specified in any of the Cases in Part II of Schedule 15.

(3) Part III of Schedule 15 shall have effect in relation to Case 9 in that Schedule and for determining the relevant date for the purposes of the Cases in Part II of that Schedule.

(4) Part IV of Schedule 15 shall have effect for determining whether, for the purposes of subsection (1)(a) above, suitable alternative accommodation is or will be available for a tenant.

(5) Part V of Schedule 15 shall have effect for the purpose of setting out conditions which are relevant to Cases 11 and 12 of that Schedule.

99. Grounds for possession of certain dwelling-houses let to agricultural workers, etc.

(1)   This section applies to any protected or statutory tenancy which—

(a)   if it were a tenancy at a low rent, and

(b)   if (where relevant) any earlier tenancy granted to the tenant, or to a member of his family, had been a tenancy at a low rent,

would be a protected occupancy or statutory tenancy as defined in the Rent (Agriculture) Act 1976.

(2)   Notwithstanding anything in section 98 of this Act, the court shall not make an order for possession of a dwelling-house which is for the time being let on or subject to a tenancy to which this section applies unless the court considers it reasonable to make such an order and the circumstances are as specified in any of the Cases (except Case 8) in Part I of Schedule 15 to this Act or in either of the Cases in Schedule 16 to this Act.

(3)   If, apart from subsection (2) above, the landlord would be entitled to recover possession of a dwelling-house which is for the time being let on or subject to a tenancy to which this section applies, the court shall make an order for possession if the circumstances are as specified in any of the Cases (except Cases 16 to 18) in Part II of Schedule 15 to this Act.

100. Extended discretion of court in claims for possession of certain dwelling-houses.

(1)   Subject to subsection (5) below, a court may adjourn, for such period or periods as it thinks fit, proceedings for possession of a dwelling-house which is let on a protected tenancy or subject to a statutory tenancy.

(2)   On the making of an order for possession of such a dwelling-house, or at any time before the execution of such an order (whether made before or after the commencement of this Act), the court, subject to subsection (5) below, may—

(a)   stay or suspend execution of the order, or

(b)   postpone the date of possession,

for such period or periods as the court thinks fit.

(3)   On any such adjournment as is referred to in subsection (1) above or any such stay, suspension or postponement as is referred to in subsection (2) above, the court shall, unless it considers that to do so would cause exceptional hardship to the tenant or would otherwise be unreasonable, impose conditions with regard to payment by the tenant of arrears of rent (if any) and rent or payments in respect of occupation after termination of the tenancy (mesne profits) and may impose such other conditions as it thinks fit.

(4)   If any such conditions as are referred to in subsection (3) above are complied with, the court may, if it thinks fit, discharge or rescind any such order as is referred to in subsection (2) above.

(4A)   Subsection (4B) below applies in any case where—

(a)   proceedings are brought for possession of a dwelling-house which is let on a protected tenancy or subject to a statutory tenancy;

(b)   the tenant's spouse or former spouse, having rights of occupation under the Matrimonial Homes Act 1967, is then in occupation of the dwelling-house; and

(c)   the tenancy is terminated as a result of those proceedings.

(4B)   In any case to which this subsection applies, the spouse or former spouse shall, so long as he or she remains in occupation, have the same rights in relation to, or in connection with, any such adjournment as is referred to in subsection (1) above or any such stay, suspension or postponement as is referred to in subsection (2) above, as he or she would have if those rights of occupation were not affected by the termination of the tenancy.

(5)   This section shall not apply if the circumstances are as specified in any of the Cases in Part II of Schedule 15.

101. Overcrowded dwelling-houses.

At any time when a dwelling-house is overcrowded within the meaning of Part X of the Housing Act 1985 in such circumstances as to render the occupier guilty of an offence, nothing in this Part of this Act shall prevent the immediate landlord of the occupier from obtaining possession of the dwelling-house.

102. Compensation for misrepresentation or concealment in Cases 8 and 9.

Where, in such circumstances as are specified in Case 8 or Case 9 in Schedule 15 to this Act, a landlord obtains an order for possession of a dwelling-house let on a protected tenancy or subject to a statutory tenancy and it is subsequently made to appear to the court that the order was obtained by misrepresentation or concealment of material facts, the court may order the landlord to pay to the former tenant such sum as appears sufficient as compensation for damage or loss sustained by that tenant as a result of the order.

Restricted contracts

102A. Restricted application of sections 103 to 106.

Sections 103 to 106 of this Act apply only to restricted contracts entered into before the commencement of section 69 of the Housing Act 1980.

103. Notice to quit served after reference of contract to rent tribunal.

(1) If, after a restricted contract has been referred to a rent tribunal by the lessee under section 77 or 80 of this Act, a notice to quit the dwelling to which the contract relates is served by the lessor on the lessee at any time before the decision of the tribunal is given or within the period of 6 months thereafter, then, subject to sections 105 and 106 of this Act, the notice shall not take effect before the expiry of that period.

(2) In a case falling within subsection (1) above,—

(a) the rent tribunal may, if they think fit, direct that a shorter period shall be substituted for the period of 6 months specified in that subsection; and

(b) if the reference to the rent tribunal is withdrawn, the period during which the notice to quit is not to take effect shall end on the expiry of 7 days from the withdrawal of the reference.

104. Application to tribunal for security of tenure where notice to quit is served.

(1) Subject to sections 105 and 106(3) of this Act, where—

(a) a notice to quit a dwelling the subject of a restricted contract has been served, and

(b) the restricted contract has been referred to a rent tribunal under section 77 or 80 of this Act (whether before or after the service of the notice to quit) and the reference has not been withdrawn, and

(c) the period at the end of which the notice to quit takes effect (whether by virtue of the contract, of section 103 of this Act or of this section) has not expired,

the lessee may apply to the rent tribunal for the extension of that period.

(2) Where an application is made under this section, the notice to quit to which the application relates shall not have effect before the determination of the application unless the application is withdrawn.

(3) On an application under this section, the rent tribunal after making such inquiry as they think fit and giving to each party an opportunity of being heard or, at his option, of submitting representations in writing, may direct that the notice to quit shall not have effect until the end of such period, not exceeding 6 months from the date on which the notice to quit would have effect apart from the direction, as may be specified in the direction.

(4) If the rent tribunal refuse to give a direction under this section,—

(a)   the notice to quit shall not have effect before the expiry of 7 days from the determination of the application; and

(b)   no subsequent application under this section shall be made in relation to the same notice to quit.

(5)   On coming to a determination on an application under this section, the rent tribunal shall notify the parties of their determination.

105.   Notices to quit served by owner-occupiers.

Where a person who has occupied a dwelling as a residence (in this section referred to as "the owner-occupier") has, by virtue of a restricted contract, granted the right to occupy the dwelling to another person and—

(a)   at or before the time when the right was granted (or, if it was granted before 8th December 1965, not later than 7th June 1966) the owner-occupier has given notice in writing to that other person that he is the owner-occupier within the meaning of this section, and

(b)   if the dwelling is part of a house, the owner-occupier does not occupy any other part of the house as his residence,

neither section 103 nor 104 of this Act shall apply where a notice to quit the dwelling is served if, at the time the notice is to take effect, the dwelling is required as a residence for the owner-occupier or any member of his family who resided with him when he last occupied the dwelling as a residence.

106.   Reduction of period of notice on account of lessee's default.

(1)   Subsections (2) and (3) below apply where a restricted contract has been referred to a rent tribunal and the period at the end of which a notice to quit will take effect has been determined by virtue of section 103 of this Act or extended under section 104.

(2)   If, in a case where this subsection applies, it appears to the rent tribunal, on an application made by the lessor for a direction under this section,—

(a)   that the lessee has not complied with the terms of the contract, or

(b)   that the lessee or any person residing or lodging with him has been guilty of conduct which is a nuisance or annoyance to adjoining occupiers or has been convicted of using the dwelling, or allowing the dwelling to be used, for an immoral or illegal purpose, or

(c)   that the condition of the dwelling has deteriorated owing to any act or neglect of the lessee or any person residing or lodging with him, or

(d)   that the condition of any furniture provided for the use of the lessee under the contract has deteriorated owing to any ill-treatment by the lessee or any person residing or lodging with him,

the rent tribunal may direct that the period referred to in subsection (1) above shall be reduced so as to end at a date specified in the direction.

(3)   No application may be made under section 104 of this Act with respect to a notice to quit if a direction has been given under subsection (2) above reducing the period at the end of which the notice is to take effect.

(4)   In any case where—

(a)   a notice to quit a dwelling which is the subject of a restricted contract has been served, and

(b)   the period at the end of which the notice to quit takes effect is for the time being extended by virtue of section 103 or 104 of this Act, and

(c)   at some time during that period the lessor institutes proceedings in the county court for the recovery of possession of the dwelling, and

(d)   in those proceedings the county court is satisfied that any of paragraphs (a) to (d) of subsection (2) above applies,

the court may direct that the period referred to in paragraph (b) above shall be reduced so as to end at a date specified in the direction.

106A. Discretion of court in certain proceedings for possession.

(1) This section applies to any dwelling-house which is the subject of a restricted contract entered into after the commencement of section 69 of the Housing Act 1980.

(2) On the making of an order for possession of such a dwelling-house, or at any time before the execution of such an order, the court may—

(a) stay or suspend execution of the order, or

(b) postpone the date of possession,

for such period or periods as, subject to subsection (3) below, the court thinks fit.

(3) Where a court makes an order for possession of such a dwelling-house, the giving up of possession shall not be postponed (whether by the order or any variation, suspension or stay of execution) to a date later than 3 months after the making of the order.

(4) On any such stay, suspension or postponement as is referred to in subsection (2) above, the court shall, unless it considers that to do so would cause exceptional hardship to the lessee or would otherwise be unreasonable, impose conditions with regard to payment by the lessee of arrears of rent (if any) and rent or payments in respect of occupation after termination of the tenancy (mesne profits) and may impose such other conditions as it thinks fit.

(5) Subsection (6) below applies in any case where—

(a) proceedings are brought for possession of such a dwelling-house;

(b) the lessee's spouse or former spouse, having rights of occupation under the Matrimonial Homes Act 1967, is then in occupation of the dwelling-house; and

(c) the restricted contract is terminated as a result of those proceedings.

(6) In any case to which this subsection applies, the spouse or former spouse shall, so long as he or she remains in occupation, have the same rights in relation to, or in connection with, any such stay, suspension or postponement as is referred to in subsection (2) above, as he or she would have if those rights of occupation were not affected by the termination of the restricted contract.

Miscellaneous

107. Interpretation of Part VII.

(1) In this Part of this Act, except where the context otherwise requires—

"dwelling" means a house or part of a house;

"lessee" means the person to whom is granted, under a restricted contract, the right to occupy the dwelling in question as a residence and any person directly or indirectly deriving title from the grantee; and

"lessor" means the person who, under a restricted contract, grants to another the right to occupy the dwelling in question as a residence and any person directly or indirectly deriving title from the grantor.

(2) References in this Part of this Act to a party to a contract include references to any person directly or indirectly deriving title from such a party.

PART VIII
CONVERSION OF CONTROLLED TENANCIES INTO REGULATED TENANCIES

Miscellaneous

116. Consent of tenant.

(1) This section applies where a dwelling-house is subject to a statutory tenancy and the landlord wishes to carry out works which cannot be carried out without the consent of the tenant.

(2) If the tenant is unwilling to give his consent, then, if the condition specified in any of paragraphs (a) to (c) of subsection (3) below is satisfied, the county court may,

on the application of the landlord, make an order empowering him to enter and carry out the works.

(3)　The condition is—

(a)　that the works were specified in an application for an improvement grant, intermediate grant or common parts grant under Part XV of the Housing Act 1985 and the application has been approved, or

(b)　that the works are specified in a certificate issued by the local housing authority within the meaning of that Act and stating that if an application were to be made by the landlord for such a grant in respect of the works, the application would be likely to be approved, or

(c)　that the works were specified in an application for a renovation grant, a common parts grant, a disabled facilities grant or an HMO grant under Part VIII of the Local Government and Housing Act 1989 and the application has been approved.

(4)　An order under subsection (2) above may be made subject to such conditions as to the time at which the works are to be carried out and as to any provision to be made for the accommodation of the tenant and his household while they are carried out as the court may think fit.

(5)　Where such an order is made subject to any condition as to time, compliance with that condition shall be deemed to be also compliance with any condition imposed by the local housing authority under section 512(2) of the Housing Act 1985, or, as the case may be, with any condition under section 118(2) of the Local Government and Housing Act 1989.

(6)　In determining whether to make such an order and, if it is made, what (if any) conditions it should be subject to, the court shall have regard to all the circumstances and in particular to—

(a)　any disadvantage to the tenant that might be expected to result from the works, and

(b)　the accommodation that might be available for him whilst the works are carried out, and

(c)　the age and health of the tenant,

but the court shall not take into account the means or resources of the tenant.

PART IX

PREMIUMS, ETC.

119.　Prohibition of premiums and loans on grant of protected tenancies.

(1)　Any person who, as a condition of the grant, renewal or continuance of a protected tenancy, requires, in addition to the rent, the payment of any premium or the making of any loan (whether secured or unsecured) shall be guilty of an offence.

(2)　Any person who, in connection with the grant, renewal or continuance of a protected tenancy, receives any premium in addition to the rent shall be guilty of an offence.

(3)　A person guilty of an offence under this section shall be liable to a fine not exceeding level 3 on the standard scale.

(4)　The court by which a person is convicted of an offence under this section relating to requiring or receiving any premium may order the amount of the premium to be repaid to the person by whom it was paid.

120.　Prohibition of premiums and loans on assignment of protected tenancies.

(1)　Subject to section 121 of this Act, any person who, as a condition of the assignment of a protected tenancy, requires the payment of any premium or the making of any loan (whether secured or unsecured) shall be guilty of an offence.

(2) Subject to section 121 of this Act, any person who, in connection with the assignment of a protected tenancy, receives any premium shall be guilty of an offence.

(3) Notwithstanding anything in subsections (1) and (2) above, an assignor of a protected tenancy of a dwelling-house may, if apart from this section he would be entitled to do so, require the payment by the assignee or receive from the assignee a payment—

(a) of so much of any outgoings discharged by the assignor as is referable to any period after the assignment takes effect;

(b) of a sum not exceeding the amount of any expenditure reasonably incurred by the assignor in carrying out any structural alteration of the dwelling-house or in providing or improving fixtures therein, being fixtures which, as against the landlord, he is not entitled to remove;

(c) where the assignor became a tenant of the dwelling-house by virtue of an assignment of the protected tenancy, of a sum not exceeding any reasonable amount paid by him to his assignor in respect of expenditure incurred by that assignor, or by any previous assignor of the tenancy, in carrying out any such alteration or in providing or improving any such fixtures as are mentioned in paragraph (b) above; or

(d) where part of the dwelling-house is used as a shop or office, or for business, trade or professional purposes, of a reasonable amount in respect of any goodwill of the business, trade or profession, being goodwill transferred to the assignee in connection with the assignment or accruing to him in consequence thereof.

(4) Without prejudice to subsection (3) above, the assignor shall not be guilty of an offence under this section by reason only that—

(a) any payment of outgoings required or received by him on the assignment was a payment of outgoings referable to a period before the assignment took effect; or

(b) any expenditure which he incurred in carrying out structural alterations of the dwelling-house or in providing or improving fixtures therein and in respect of which he required or received the payment of any sum on the assignment was not reasonably incurred; or

(c) any amount paid by him as mentioned in subsection (3)(c) above was not a reasonable amount; or

(d) any amount which he required to be paid, or which he received, on the assignment in respect of goodwill was not a reasonable amount.

(5) Notwithstanding anything in subsections (1) and (2) above, Part I of Schedule 18 to this Act shall have effect in relation to the assignment of protected tenancies which are regulated tenancies in cases where a premium was lawfully required or received at the commencement of the tenancy.

(6) A person guilty of an offence under this section shall be liable to a fine not exceeding level 3 on the standard scale.

(7) The court by which a person is convicted of an offence under this section relating to requiring or receiving any premium may order the amount of the premium, or so much of it as cannot lawfully be required or received under this section (including any amount which, by virtue of subsection (4) above, does not give rise to an offence), to be repaid to the person by whom it was paid.

121. Tenancies which became regulated by virtue of Counter-Inflation Act 1973.

Part II of Schedule 18 to this Act shall have effect where a premium was lawfully required and paid on the grant, renewal or continuance of a regulated tenancy—

(a) which was granted before 8th March 1973, and

(b) which would not have been a regulated tenancy, but for section 14(1) of the Counter-Inflation Act 1973 (which brought certain tenancies of dwelling-houses with high rateable values within the protection of the Rent Act 1968).

122. Prohibition of premiums on grant or assignment of rights under restricted contracts.

(1)   This section applies in relation to any premises if—

(a)   under Part V of this Act, a rent is registered for those premises in the register kept in pursuance of section 79 of this Act; and

(b)   in a case where the approval, reduction or increase of the rent by the rent tribunal is limited to rent payable in respect of a particular period, that period has not expired.

(2)   Any person who, as a condition of the grant, renewal, continuance or assignment of rights under a restricted contract, requires the payment of any premium shall be guilty of an offence.

(3)   Nothing in subsection (2) above shall prevent a person from requiring—

(a)   that there shall be paid so much of any outgoings discharged by a grantor or assignor as is referable to any period after the grant or assignment takes effect; or

(b)   that there shall be paid a reasonable amount in respect of goodwill of a business, trade, or profession, where the goodwill is transferred to a grantee or assignee in connection with the grant or assignment or accrues to him in consequence thereof.

(4)   A person guilty of an offence under this section shall be liable to a fine not exceeding level 3 on the standard scale.

(5)   The court by which a person is convicted of an offence under this section may order the amount of the premium, or so much of it as cannot lawfully be required under this section, to be repaid to the person by whom it was paid.

123. Excessive price for furniture to be treated as premium.

Where the purchase of any furniture has been required as a condition of the grant, renewal, continuance or assignment—

(a)   of a protected tenancy, or

(b)   of rights under a restricted contract which relates to premises falling within section 122(1) of this Act,

then, if the price exceeds the reasonable price of the furniture, the excess shall be treated, for the purposes of this Part of this Act, as if it were a premium required to be paid as a condition of the grant, renewal, continuance or assignment of the protected tenancy or, as the case may be, the rights under the restricted contract.

124. Punishment of attempts to obtain from prospective tenants excessive prices for furniture.

(1)   Any person who, in connection with the proposed grant, renewal, continuance or assignment, on terms which require the purchase of furniture, of a protected tenancy—

(a)   offers the furniture at a price which he knows or ought to know is unreasonably high or otherwise seeks to obtain such a price for the furniture, or

(b)   fails to furnish, to any person seeking to obtain or retain accommodation whom he provides with particulars of the tenancy, a written inventory of the furniture, specifying the price sought for each item,

shall be liable to a fine not exceeding level 3 on the standard scale.

(2)   Where a local authority have reasonable grounds for suspecting that an offence under subsection (1)(a) above has been committed with respect to a protected tenancy or proposed protected tenancy of a dwelling-house, they may give notice to the person entitled to possession of the dwelling-house or his agent that, on such date as may be specified in the notice, which shall not be earlier than—

(a)   24 hours after the giving of the notice, or

(b)   if the dwelling-house is unoccupied, the expiry of such period after the giving of the notice as may be reasonable in the circumstances, facilities will be required for entry to the dwelling-house and inspection of the furniture therein.

(3)   A notice under this section may be given by post.

(4)   Where a notice is given under this section, any person authorised by the local authority may avail himself of any facilities for such entry and inspection as are referred to in subsection (2) above which are provided on the specified date but shall, if so required, produce some duly authenticated document showing that he is authorised by the local authority.

(5)   If it is shown to the satisfaction of a justice of the peace, on sworn information in writing, that a person required to give facilities under this section has failed to give them, the justice may, by warrant under his hand, empower the local authority, by any person authorised by them, to enter the dwelling-house in question, if need be by force, and inspect the furniture therein.

(6)   A person empowered by or under the preceding provisions of this section to enter a dwelling-house may take with him such other persons as may be necessary and, if the dwelling-house is unoccupied, shall leave it as effectively secured against trespassers as he found it.

(7)   Any person who wilfully obstructs a person acting in pursuance of a warrant issued under subsection (5) above shall be liable to a fine not exceeding level 3 on the standard scale.

(8)   In this section "local authority" means the council of a district or of a London borough or the Common Council of the City of London.

125.   Recovery of premiums and loans unlawfully required or received.

(1)   Where under any agreement (whether made before or after the commencement of this Act) any premium is paid after the commencement of this Act and the whole or any part of that premium could not lawfully be required or received under the preceding provisions of this Part of this Act, the amount of the premium or, as the case may be, so much of it as could not lawfully be required or received, shall be recoverable by the person by whom it was paid.

(2)   Nothing in section 119 or 120 of this Act shall invalidate any agreement for the making of a loan or any security issued in pursuance of such an agreement but, notwithstanding anything in the agreement for the loan, any sum lent in circumstances involving a contravention of either of those sections shall be repayable to the lender on demand.

126.   Avoidance of requirements for advance payment of rent in certain cases.

(1)   Where a protected tenancy which is a regulated tenancy is granted, continued or renewed, any requirement that rent shall be payable—

(a)   before the beginning of the rental period in respect of which it is payable, or

(b)   earlier than 6 months before the end of the rental period in respect of which it is payable (if that period is more than 6 months),

shall be void, whether the requirement is imposed as a condition of the grant, renewal or continuance of the tenancy or under the terms thereof.

(2)   Any requirement avoided by subsection (1) above is, in this section, referred to as a "prohibited requirement".

(3)   Rent for any rental period to which a prohibited requirement relates shall be irrecoverable from the tenant.

(4)   Any person who purports to impose any prohibited requirement shall be liable to a fine not exceeding level 3 on the standard scale, and the court by which he is convicted may order any amount of rent paid in compliance with the prohibited requirement to be repaid to the person by whom it was paid.

(5)   Where a tenant has paid on account of rent any amount which, by virtue of this section, is irrecoverable the tenant shall be entitled to recover that amount from the landlord who received it or his personal representatives.

(6)   Any amount which a tenant is entitled to recover under subsection (5) above may, without prejudice to any other method of recovery, be deducted by the tenant from any rent payable by him to the landlord.

(7)   No amount which a tenant is entitled to recover under subsection (5) above shall be recoverable at any time after the expiry of 2 years from the date of payment.

(8)   Any person who, in any rent book or similar document makes an entry showing or purporting to show any tenant as being in arrears in respect of any sum on account of rent which is irrecoverable by virtue of this section shall be liable to a fine not exceeding level 3 on the standard scale, unless he proves that, at the time of the making of the entry, the landlord had a bona fide claim that the sum was recoverable.

(9)   If, where any such entry has been made by or on behalf of any landlord, the landlord on being requested by or on behalf of the tenant to do so, refuses or neglects to cause the entry to be deleted within 7 days, the landlord shall be liable to a fine not exceeding level 3 on the standard scale, unless he proves that, at the time of the neglect or refusal to cause the entry to be deleted, he had a bona fide claim that the sum was recoverable.

127.   Allowable premiums in relation to certain long tenancies.

(1)   Where a tenancy is both a long tenancy within the meaning of Part I of the Landlord and Tenant Act 1954 and a protected tenancy, then—

(a)   if the conditions specified in subsection (2) below are satisfied with respect to it, nothing in this Part of this Act or in Part VII of the Rent Act 1968 (provisions superseded by this Part) or the enactments replaced by the said Part VII shall apply or be deemed ever to have applied to the tenancy;

(b)   if any of those conditions are not satisfied with respect to it, Part II of Schedule 18 to this Act shall apply and, if the tenancy was granted before the passing of this Act, be deemed always to have applied to it.

(2)   The conditions mentioned in subsection (1)(a) above are—

(a)   that the tenancy is not, and cannot become, terminable within 20 years of the date when it was granted by notice given to the tenant; and

(b)   that, unless the tenancy was granted before 25th July 1969 or was granted in pursuance of Part I of the Leasehold Reform Act 1967, the sums payable by the tenant otherwise than in respect of rates, services, repairs, maintenance or insurance are not, under the terms of the tenancy, varied or liable to be varied within 20 years of the date when it was granted nor, thereafter, more than once in any 21 years; and

(c)   that the terms of the tenancy do not inhibit both the assignment and the underletting of the whole of the premises comprised in the tenancy.

(3)   Where the condition specified in subsection (2)(b) above would be satisfied with respect to a sub-tenancy but for a term providing for one variation, within 20 years of the date when the sub-tenancy was granted, of the sums payable by the sub-tenant, that condition shall be deemed to be satisfied notwithstanding that term, if it is satisfied with respect to a superior tenancy of the premises comprised in the sub-tenancy (or of those and other premises).

(3A)   If the conditions in subsection (3B) below are satisfied in respect of a tenancy, this Part of this Act shall not apply to that tenancy and, together with Part VII of the Rent Act 1968 and the enactments replaced by Part VII, shall be deemed never to have applied to it.

(3B)   The conditions are that—

(a)   the tenancy was granted before 16th July 1980;

(b)   a premium was lawfully required and paid on the grant of the tenancy;

(c) the tenancy was, at the time when it was granted, a tenancy at a low rent; and

(d) the terms of the tenancy do not inhibit both the assignment and the underletting of the whole of the premises comprised in the tenancy.

(3C) If the conditions in subsection (3D) below are satisfied in respect of a tenancy, this section shall have effect, in relation to that tenancy, as if for the words "20 years" and "21 years", in subsections (2)(b) and (3) above there were substituted, respectively, the words "6 years" and "7 years".

(3D) The conditions are that—

(a) the tenancy is granted after 15th July 1980;

(b) at the time when it is granted it is a tenancy at a low rent; and

(c) the terms of the tenancy ensure that any variation of the sums payable by the tenant otherwise than in respect of rates, services, repairs or maintenance, cannot lead to those sums exceeding an annual rate of two-thirds of the rateable value of the dwelling-house at the date when the variation is made.

For the purposes of this subsection the rateable value of a dwelling-house shall be ascertained in accordance with section 25 of this Act (disregarding subsection (4)) by reference to the value shown in the valuation list at the date when the variation is made.

(4) Nothing in this section shall affect the recovery, in pursuance of any judgment given or order or agreement made before 20th May 1969, of any amount which it was not lawful to receive under the law in force at the time it was received.

(5) In this section "grant" includes continuance and renewal and for the purposes of subsections (2)(c) and (3B)(d) above the terms of a tenancy inhibit an assignment or underletting if they—

(a) preclude it; or

(b) permit it subject to a consent but exclude section 144 of the Law of Property Act 1925 (no payment in nature of fine); or

(c) permit it subject to a consent but require in connection with a request for consent the making of an offer to surrender the tenancy.

128. Interpretation of Part IX.

(1) In this Part of this Act, unless the context otherwise requires,—

"furniture" includes fittings and other articles; and

"premium" includes

(a) any fine or other like sum;

(b) any other pecuniary consideration in addition to rent; and

(c) any sum paid by way of deposit, other than one which does not exceed one-sixth of the annual rent and is reasonable in relation to the potential liability in respect of which it is paid.

(2) For the avoidance of doubt it is hereby declared that nothing in this Part of this Act shall render any amount recoverable more than once.

PART X
MORTGAGES

129. Mortgages to which Part X applies.

(1) This Part of this Act is concerned with mortgages which—

(a) were created before the relevant date, and

(b) are regulated mortgages, as defined in section 131 of this Act.

(2) For the purposes of this Part of this Act, "relevant date"—

(a) in a case where, on 28th November 1967, land consisting of or including a dwelling-house was subject to a long tenancy which became a regulated tenancy on that date by virtue of section 39 of the Leasehold Reform Act 1967, means, in relation to that land, 28th November 1967;

(b)   in a case where, on 22nd March 1973, land consisting of or including a dwelling-house was subject to a tenancy which became a regulated tenancy by virtue of section 14 of the Counter-Inflation Act 1973, means, in relation to that land, 22nd March 1973;

(c)   in the case of land consisting of or including a dwelling-house subject to a regulated furnished tenancy, means, in relation to that land, 14th August 1974; and

(d)   in any other case, means 8th December 1965.

131.   Regulated mortgages.

(1)   Subject to subsection (2) below, a mortgage which falls within section 129(1)(a) of this Act is a regulated mortgage if—

(a)   it is a legal mortgage of land consisting of or including a dwelling-house which is let on or subject to a regulated tenancy, and

(b)   the regulated tenancy is binding on the mortgagee.

(2)   Notwithstanding that a mortgage falls within subsection (1) above, it is not a regulated mortgage if—

(a)   the rateable value on the appropriate day of the dwelling-house which falls within subsection (1)(a) above or, if there is more than one such dwelling-house comprised in the mortgage, the aggregate of the rateable values of those dwelling-houses on the appropriate day is less than one-tenth of the rateable value on the appropriate day of the whole of the land comprised in the mortgage, or

(b)   the mortgagor is in breach of covenant, but for this purpose a breach of the covenant for the repayment of the principal money otherwise than by instalments shall be disregarded.

(3)   Subsection (2)(a) above shall have effect, in the case of land consisting of or including a dwelling-house which on 22nd March 1973 was subject to a tenancy which became a regulated tenancy by virtue of section 14 of the Counter-Inflation Act 1973, as if for the reference to the appropriate day there were substituted a reference to 7th March 1973.

(4)   In this section "legal mortgage" includes a charge by way of legal mortgage.

(5)   Any reference in this Part of this Act to a regulated mortgage shall be construed in accordance with this section.

132.   Powers of court to mitigate hardship to mortgagors under regulated mortgages.

(1)   The powers of the court under this section become exercisable, in relation to a regulated mortgage only on an application made by the mortgagor within 21 days, or such longer time as the court may allow, after the occurrence of one of the following events:—

(a)   the rate of interest payable in respect of the mortgage is increased; or

(b)   a rent for a dwelling-house comprised in the mortgage is registered under Part IV of this Act and the rent so registered is lower than the rent which was payable immediately before the registration; or

(c)   the mortgagee, not being a mortgagee who was in possession on the relevant date, demands payment of the principal money secured by the mortgage or takes any steps for exercising any right of foreclosure or sale or for otherwise enforcing his security.

Paragraph (b) above shall not apply to a case falling within section 129(2)(b) of this Act.

(2)   If the court is satisfied on any such application that, by reason of the event in question and of the operation of this Act, the mortgagor would suffer severe financial hardship unless relief were given under this section, the court may by order make such provision—

(a)   limiting the rate of interest,

(b)   extending the time for the repayment of the principal money, or

(c)   otherwise varying the terms of the mortgage or imposing any limitation or condition on the exercise of any right or remedy in respect thereof,

as it thinks appropriate.

(3)   Where the court makes an order under subsection (2) above in relation to a mortgage which comprises other land as well as a dwelling-house or dwelling-houses subject to a regulated tenancy the order may, if the mortgagee so requests, make provision for apportioning the money secured by the mortgage between that other land and the dwelling-house or dwelling-houses.

(4)   Where such an apportionment is made, the other provisions of the order made by the court shall not apply in relation to the other land referred to in that subsection and the money secured by the other land, and the mortgage shall have effect for all purposes as two separate mortgages of the apportioned parts.

(5)   Where the court has made an order under this section it may vary or revoke it by a subsequent order.

(6)   The court for the purposes of this section is a county court, except that where an application under subsection (1) above is made in pursuance of any step taken by the mortgagee in the High Court, it is the High Court.

136.   Interpretation of Part X.

In this Part of this Act, except where the context otherwise requires—

(a)   "mortgagee" and "mortgagor" include any person from time to time deriving title under the original mortgagee or mortgagor; and

(b)   "legal mortgage" in relation to regulated mortgages, includes any charge registered under the Land Registration Act 1925.

PART XI
GENERAL

Sublettings

137.   Effect on sub-tenancy of determination of superior tenancy.

(1)   If a court makes an order for possession of a dwelling-house from—

(a)   a protected or statutory tenant, or

(b)   a protected occupier or statutory tenant as defined in the Rent (Agriculture) Act 1976,

and the order is made by virtue of section 98(1) or 99(2) of this Act or, as the case may be, under Part I of Schedule 4 to that Act, nothing in the order shall affect the right of any sub-tenant to whom the dwelling-house or any part of it has been lawfully sublet before the commencement of the proceedings to retain possession by virtue of this Act, nor shall the order operate to give a right to possession against any such sub-tenant.

(2)   Where a statutorily protected tenancy of a dwelling-house is determined, either as a result of an order for possession or for any other reason, any sub-tenant to whom the dwelling-house or any part of it has been lawfully sublet shall, subject to this Act, be deemed to become the tenant of the landlord on the same terms as if the tenant's statutorily protected tenancy had continued.

(3)   Where a dwelling-house—

(a)   forms part of premises which have been let as a whole on a superior tenancy but do not constitute a dwelling-house let on a statutorily protected tenancy; and

(b)   is itself subject to a protected or statutory tenancy,

then, from the coming to an end of the superior tenancy, this Act shall apply in relation to the dwelling-house as if, in lieu of the superior tenancy, there had been separate tenancies of the dwelling-house and of the remainder of the premises, for the like purposes as under the superior tenancy, and at rents equal to the just proportion of the rent under the superior tenancy.

In this subsection "premises" includes, if the sub-tenancy in question is a protected or statutory tenancy to which section 99 of this Act applies, an agricultural holding within the meaning of the Agricultural Holdings Act 1986.

(4)   In subsections (2) and (3) above "statutorily protected tenancy" means—

(a)   a protected or statutory tenancy;

(b)   a protected occupancy or statutory tenancy as defined in the Rent (Agriculture) Act 1976; or

(c)   if the sub-tenancy in question is a protected or statutory tenancy to which section 99 of this Act applies, a tenancy of an agricultural holding within the meaning of the Agricultural Holdings Act 1986.

(5)   Subject to subsection (6) below, a long tenancy of a dwelling-house which is also a tenancy at a low rent but which, had it not been a tenancy at a low rent, would have been a protected tenancy or an assured tenancy, within the meaning of Part I of the Housing Act 1988, shall be treated for the purposes of subsection (2) above as a statutorily protected tenancy.

(6)   Notwithstanding anything in subsection (5) above, subsection (2) above shall not have effect where the sub-tenancy in question was created (whether immediately or derivatively) out of a long tenancy falling within subsection (5) above and, at the time of the creation of the sub-tenancy—

(a)   a notice to terminate the long tenancy had been given under section 4(1) of the Landlord and Tenant Act 1954 or, as the case may be, served under paragraph 4(1) of Schedule 10 to the Local Government and Housing Act 1989; or

(b)   the long tenancy was being continued by section 3(1) of the said Act of 1954 or, as the case may be, paragraph 3 of the said Schedule 10;

unless the sub-tenancy was created with the consent in writing of the person who at the time when it was created was the landlord, within the meaning of Part I of the said Act of 1954 or, as the case may be, the said Schedule 10.

(7)   This section shall apply equally where a protected occupier of a dwelling-house, or part of a dwelling-house, has a relevant licence as defined in the Rent (Agriculture) Act 1976, and in this section "tenancy" and all cognate expressions shall be construed accordingly.

138.   Effect on furnished sub-tenancy of determination of superior unfurnished tenancy.

(1)   If, in a case where section 137(2) of this Act applies, the conditions mentioned in subsection (2) below are fulfilled, the terms on which the sub-tenant is, by virtue of section 137(2), deemed to become the tenant of the landlord shall not include any terms as to the provision by the landlord of furniture or services.

(2)   The conditions are:—

(a)   that the statutorily protected tenancy which is determined as mentioned in section 137(2) was neither a protected furnished tenancy nor a statutory furnished tenancy; and

(b)   that, immediately before the determination of that statutorily protected tenancy, the sub-tenant referred to in section 137(2) was the tenant under a protected furnished tenancy or a statutory furnished tenancy; and

(c)   that the landlord, within the period of 6 weeks beginning with the day on which the statutorily protected tenancy referred to in section 137(2) is determined, serves notice on the sub-tenant that this section is to apply to his tenancy or statutory tenancy.

(3)   In this section "statutorily protected tenancy" has the same meaning as it has for the purposes of section 137(2) of this Act.

139. Obligation to notify sublettings of dwelling-houses let on or subject to protected or statutory tenancies.

(1) If the tenant of a dwelling-house let on or subject to a protected or statutory tenancy sublets any part of the dwelling-house on a protected tenancy, then, subject to subsection (2) below, he shall, within 14 days after the subletting, supply the landlord with a statement in writing of the subletting giving particulars of occupancy, including the rent charged.

(2) Subsection (1) above shall not require the supply of a statement in relation to a subletting of any part of a dwelling-house if the particulars which would be required to be included in the statement as to the rent and other conditions of the sub-tenancy would be the same as in the last statement supplied in accordance with that subsection with respect to a previous subletting of that part.

(3) A tenant who is required to supply a statement in accordance with subsection (1) above and who, without reasonable excuse—

(a) fails to supply a statement, or

(b) supplies a statement which is false in any material particular,

shall be liable to a fine not exceeding level 2 on the standard scale.

(4) In this section—

(a) "protected tenancy" includes a protected occupancy under the Rent (Agriculture) Act 1976;

(b) "statutory tenancy" includes a statutory tenancy under that Act.

Fire Precautions

140. Modification of Act in relation to fire precautions.

Schedule 20 to this Act shall have effect for the purpose of modifying this Act in connection with certain provisions of the Fire Precautions Act 1971.

Jurisdiction and procedure

141. County court jurisdiction.

(1) A county court shall have jurisdiction, either in the course of any proceedings relating to a dwelling or on an application made for the purpose by the landlord or the tenant, to determine any question—

(a) as to whether a tenancy is a protected tenancy or whether any person is a statutory tenant of a dwelling-house; or

(b) as to the rent limit; or

(d) as to the application of Part V and sections 103 to 106 of this Act to a contract; or

(e) as to whether a protected, statutory or regulated tenancy is a protected, statutory or regulated furnished tenancy;

or as to any matter which is or may become material for determining any such question.

(3) A county court shall have jurisdiction to deal with any claim or other proceedings arising out of any of the provisions of this Act specified in subsection (5) below, notwithstanding that by reason of the amount of the claim or otherwise the case would not, apart from this subsection, be within the jurisdiction of a county court.

(4) If, under any of the provisions of this Act specified in subsection (5) below, a person takes proceedings in the High Court which he could have taken in the county court, he shall not be entitled to recover any costs.

(5) The provisions referred to in subsections (3) and (4) above are—

(b) in Part III, section 57;

(c) Part VII, except sections 98(2) and 101;

(d) in Part IX, sections 125 and 126;

(e) in Part X, sections 133(1), 134 and 135; and

(f) in this Part of this Act, sections 145 and 147.

142. Rules as to procedure.

(1)   The Lord Chancellor may make such rules and give such directions as he thinks fit for the purpose of giving effect to the provisions of this Act and may, by those rules or directions, provide for the conduct so far as desirable in private of any proceedings for the purposes of those provisions and for the remission of any fees.

(2)   The power vested in the Lord Chancellor by subsection (1) above may, when the Great Seal is in commission, be exercised by any Lord Commissioner.

(3)   The power conferred by subsection (1) above shall not be exercisable in relation to the following provisions of this Act:—

(a)   Part IV, except section 75(2);

(b)   Part V;

(c)   Part VI;

(d)   sections 103 to 106, except subsection (4).

(4)   Any rules made under this section shall be contained in a statutory instrument.

Release from provisions of Act

143. Release from rent regulation.

(1)   Where the Secretary of State is satisfied with respect to every part of any area that the number of persons seeking to become tenants there—

(a)   of dwelling-houses exceeding a specified rateable value, or

(b)   of any class or description of dwelling-house or of dwelling-house exceeding a specified rateable value,

is not substantially greater than the number of such dwelling-houses in that part, he may by order provide that no such dwelling-house in the area shall be the subject of a regulated tenancy or the subject of a protected occupancy or statutory tenancy under the Rent (Agriculture) Act 1976.

(2)   An order under this section may contain such transitional provisions, including provisions to avoid or mitigate hardship, as appear to the Secretary of State to be desirable.

(3)   The power to make an order under this section shall be exercisable by statutory instrument and no such order shall have effect unless it is approved by a resolution of each House of Parliament.

144. Release from restricted contract provisions.

(1)   The Secretary of State may by order provide that, as from such date as may be specified in the order, section 19 of this Act shall not apply to a dwelling the rateable value of which on such day as may be specified in the order exceeds such amount as may be so specified.

(2)   An order under this section—

(a)   may be made so as to relate to the whole of England and Wales or to such area in England and Wales as may be specified in the order, and so as to apply generally or only to, or except to, such classes or descriptions of dwellings as may be specified in the order; and

(b)   may contain such transitional provisions as appear to the Secretary of State to be desirable.

(3)   The power to make an order under this section shall be exercisable by statutory instrument and no such order shall have effect unless it is approved by a resolution of each House of Parliament.

Miscellaneous

146. Long tenancies at a low rent.

(1)   In determining whether a long tenancy was, at any time,—

(a)   a tenancy at a low rent within the meaning of the Rent Act 1968; or

(b) a tenancy to which, by virtue of section 12(7) of the Act of 1920, the Rent Acts did not apply;

there shall be disregarded such part (if any) of the sums payable by the tenant as is expressed (in whatever terms) to be payable in respect of rates, services, repairs, maintenance, or insurance, unless it could not have been regarded by the parties as a part so payable.

(2) In subsection (1) above—

"long tenancy" means a tenancy granted for a term certain exceeding 21 years, other than a tenancy which is, or may become, terminable before the end of that term by notice given to the tenant;

"the Act of 1920" means the Increase of Rent and Mortgage Interest (Restrictions) Act 1920; and

"the Rent Acts" means the Rent and Mortgage Interest Restrictions Acts 1920 to 1939.

147. Restriction on levy of distress for rent.

(1) No distress for the rent of any dwelling-house let on a protected tenancy or subject to a statutory tenancy shall be levied except with the leave of the county court; and the court shall, with respect to any application for such leave, have the same or similar powers with respect to adjournment, stay, suspension, postponement and otherwise as are conferred by section 100 of this Act in relation to proceedings for possession of such a dwelling-house.

(2) Nothing in subsection (1) above shall apply to distress levied under section 102 of the County Courts Act 1984.

148. Implied term in all protected tenancies.

It shall be a condition of a protected tenancy of a dwelling-house that the tenant shall afford to the landlord access to the dwelling-house and all reasonable facilities for executing therein any repairs which the landlord is entitled to execute.

Supplemental

149. Powers of local authorities for the purposes of giving information.

(1) Any local authority to which this section applies shall have power—

(a) to publish information, for the assistance of landlords and tenants and others, as to their rights and duties under—

(i) sections 4 to 7 (provision of rent books) and sections 18 to 30 (service charges) of the Landlord and Tenant Act 1985,

(ii) the Protection from Eviction Act 1977,

(iii) Part II of the Housing Act 1980,

(iv) this Act,

(v) Chapters I to III of Part I of the Housing Act 1988

and as to the procedure for enforcing those rights or securing the performance of those duties, and

(b) to publish information, for the assistance of owners and occupiers of dwelling-houses and others, as to their rights and duties under the Rent (Agriculture) Act 1976 and as to the procedure for enforcing those rights or securing the performance of those duties, and

(c) to make any such information as is mentioned in paragraph (a) or (b) above available in any other way, and

(d) to furnish particulars as to the availability, extent and character of alternative accommodation.

(2) This section applies to the following local authorities:—

(a) councils of districts and of London boroughs;

(b) the Common Council of the City of London; and

(c)   the Council of the Isles of Scilly.

150. Prosecution of offences.

(1)   Offences under this Act are punishable summarily.

(2)   Proceedings for an offence under this Act may be instituted by any local authority to which section 149 of this Act applies.

151. Service of notices on landlord's agents.

(1)   Any document required or authorised by this Act to be served by the tenant of a dwelling-house on the landlord thereof shall be deemed to be duly served on him if it is served—

(a)   on any agent of the landlord named as such in the rent book or other similar document; or

(b)   on the person who receives the rent of the dwelling-house.

(2)   Where a dwelling-house is subject to a regulated tenancy, subsection (1) above shall apply also in relation to any document required or authorised by this Act to be served on the landlord by a person other than the tenant.

(3)   If for the purpose of any proceedings (whether civil or criminal) brought or intended to be brought under this Act, any person serves upon any such agent or other person as is referred to in paragraph (a) or paragraph (b) of subsection (1) above a notice in writing requiring the agent or other person to disclose to him the full name and place of abode or place of business of the landlord, that agent or other person shall forthwith comply with the notice.

(4)   If any such agent or other person as is referred to in subsection (3) above fails or refuses forthwith to comply with a notice served on him under that subsection, he shall be liable to a fine not exceeding level 4 on the standard scale, unless he shows to the satisfaction of the court that he did not know, and could not with reasonable diligence have ascertained, such of the facts required by the notice to be disclosed as were not disclosed by him.

(5)   So far as this section relates to Part V or IX or sections 103 to 107, of this Act, references to a landlord and to a tenant shall respectively include references to a lessor and to a lessee as defined by section 85 of this Act.

152. Interpretation.

(1)   In this Act, except where the context otherwise requires,—

"the appropriate day" has the meaning assigned to it by section 25(3) of this Act;

"landlord" includes any person from time to time deriving title under the original landlord and also includes, in relation to any dwelling-house, any person other than the tenant who is, or but for Part VII of this Act would be, entitled to possession of the dwelling-house;

"let" includes "sublet";

"long tenancy" means a tenancy granted for a term of years certain exceeding 21 years, whether or not subsequently extended by act of the parties or by any enactment;

"protected furnished tenancy", "regulated furnished tenancy" and "statutory furnished tenancy" mean a protected or, as the case may be, regulated or statutory tenancy—

(a)   under which the dwelling-house concerned is bona fide let at a rent which includes payments in respect of furniture, and

(b)   in respect of which the amount of rent which is fairly attributable to the use of furniture, having regard to the value of that use to the tenant, forms a substantial part of the whole rent;

"protected tenant" and "protected tenancy" shall be construed in accordance with section 1 of this Act;

"rates" includes water rates and charges but does not include an owner's drainage rate as defined in section 63(2)(a) of the Land Drainage Act 1976;

"rateable value" shall be construed in accordance with section 25 of this Act;

"regulated tenancy" shall be construed in accordance with section 18 of this Act;

"rent tribunal" has the meaning given by section 76(1) of this Act;

"rental period" means a period in respect of which a payment of rent falls to be made;

"restricted contract" shall be construed in accordance with section 19 of this Act;

"statutory tenant" and "statutory tenancy" shall be construed in accordance with section 2 of this Act;

"tenant" includes statutory tenant and also includes a sub-tenant and any person deriving title under the original tenant or sub-tenant;

"tenancy" includes "sub-tenancy";

"tenancy at a low rent" has the meaning assigned to it by section 5 of this Act.

(2)   Except in so far as the context otherwise requires, any reference in this Act to any other enactment shall be taken as referring to that enactment as amended by or under any other enactment, including this Act.

153.   Application to Isles of Scilly.

(1)   With the exception of Part V, and sections 102A to 106A, of this Act (which do not apply to the Isles of Scilly) this Act applies to the Isles subject to such exceptions, adaptations and modifications as the Secretary of State may by order direct.

(2)   The power to make an order under this section shall be exercisable by statutory instrument which shall be subject to annulment in pursuance of a resolution of either House of Parliament.

(3)   An order under this section may be varied or revoked by a subsequent order.

154.   Application to Crown property.

(1)   Subject to sections 13 and 19(5)(b) of this Act this Act shall apply in relation to premises in which there subsists, or at any material time subsisted, a Crown interest as it applies in relation to premises in which no such interest subsists or ever subsisted.

(2)   In this section "Crown interest" means an interest which belongs to Her Majesty in right of the Crown or of the Duchy of Lancaster or to the Duchy of Cornwall, or to a government department, or which is held in trust for Her Majesty for the purposes of a government department.

155.   Modifications, amendments, transitional provisions, repeals etc.

(2)   Subject to subsection (3) below, the enactments specified in Schedule 23 to this Act shall have effect subject to the amendments specified in that Schedule.

(3)   The savings and transitional provisions in Schedule 24 to this Act shall have effect.

(4)   The inclusion in this Act of any express saving, transitional provision or amendment shall not be taken as prejudicing the operation of section 38 of the Interpretation Act 1889 (which relates to the effect of repeals).

(5)   Subject to subsection (3) above, the enactments specified in Schedule 25 to this Act (which include enactments which were spent before the passing of this Act) are hereby repealed to the extent specified in the third column of that Schedule.

156.   Short title, commencement and extent.

(1)   This Act may be cited as the Rent Act 1977.

(2)   This Act shall come into force on the expiry of the period of one month beginning with the date on which it is passed.

(3)   This Act does not extend to Scotland or Northern Ireland.

SCHEDULES

Sections 2, 3.

SCHEDULE 1
STATUTORY TENANCIES

PART I
STATUTORY TENANTS BY SUCCESSION

1. Paragraph 2 or, as the case may be, paragraph 3 below shall have effect, subject to section 2(3) of this Act, for the purpose of determining who is the statutory tenant of a dwelling-house by succession after the death of the person (in this Part of this Schedule referred to as "the original tenant") who, immediately before his death, was a protected tenant of the dwelling-house or the statutory tenant of it by virtue of his previous protected tenancy.

2. The surviving spouse (if any) of the original tenant, if residing in the dwelling-house immediately before the death of the original tenant, shall after the death be the statutory tenant if and so long as he or she occupies the dwelling-house as his or her residence.

3. Where paragraph 2 above does not apply, but a person who was a member of the original tenant's family was residing with him at the time of and for the period of 6 months immediately before his death then, after his death, that person or if there is more than one such person such one of them as may be decided by agreement, or in default of agreement by the county court, shall be the statutory tenant if and so long as he occupies the dwelling-house as his residence.

4. A person who becomes the statutory tenant of a dwelling-house by virtue of paragraph 2 or 3 above is in this Part of this Schedule referred to as "the first successor".

5. If, immediately before his death, the first successor was still a statutory tenant, paragraph 6 or, as the case may be, paragraph 7 below shall have effect, subject to section 2(3) of this Act, for the purpose of determining who is the statutory tenant after the death of the first successor.

6. The surviving spouse (if any) of the first successor, if residing in the dwelling-house immediately before the death of the first successor, shall after the death be the statutory tenant if and so long as he or she occupies the dwelling-house as his or her residence.

7. Where paragraph 6 above does not apply but a person who was a member of the first successor's family was residing with him at the time of and for the period of 6 months immediately before his death then, after his death, that person or if there is more than one such person such one of them as may be decided by agreement, or in default of agreement by the county court, shall be the statutory tenant if and so long as he occupies the dwelling-house as his residence.

9. Paragraphs 5 to 8 above do not apply where the statutory tenancy of the original tenant arose by virtue of section 4 of the Requisitioned Houses and Housing (Amendment) Act 1955 or section 20 of the Rent Act 1965.

10.—(1) Where after a succession the successor becomes the tenant of the dwelling-house by the grant to him of another tenancy, "the original tenant" and "the first successor" in this Part of this Schedule shall, in relation to that other tenancy, mean the persons who were respectively the original tenant and the first successor at the time of the succession, and accordingly—

 (a) if the successor was the first successor, and, immediately before his death he was still the tenant (whether protected or statutory), paragraphs 6 and 7 above shall apply on his death,

 (b) if the successor was not the first successor, no person shall become a statutory tenant on his death by virtue of this Part of this Schedule.

 (2) Sub-paragraph (1) above applies—

(a) even if a successor enters into more than one other tenancy of the dwelling-house, and

(b) even if both the first successor and the successor on his death enter into other tenancies of the dwelling-house.

(3) In this paragraph "succession" means the occasion on which a person becomes the statutory tenant of a dwelling-house by virtue of this Part of this Schedule and "successor" shall be construed accordingly.

(4) This paragraph shall apply as respects a succession which took place before 27th August 1972 if, and only if, the tenancy granted after the succession, or the first of those tenancies, was granted on or after that date, and where it does not apply as respects a succession, no account should be taken of that succession in applying this paragraph as respects any later succession.

11.—(1) Paragraphs 5 to 8 above do not apply where—

(a) the tenancy of the original tenant was granted on or after the operative date within the meaning of the Rent (Agriculture) Act 1976, and

(b) both that tenancy and the statutory tenancy of the first successor were tenancies to which section 99 of this Act applies.

(2) If the tenants under both of the tenancies falling within sub-paragraph (1)(b) above were persons to whom paragraph 7 of Schedule 9 to the Rent (Agriculture) Act 1976 applies, the reference in sub-paragraph (1)(a) above to the operative date shall be taken as a reference to the date of operation for forestry workers within the meaning of that Act.

PART II
RELINQUISHING TENANCIES AND CHANGING TENANTS

Payments demanded by statutory tenants as a condition of giving up possession

12.—(1) A statutory tenant of a dwelling-house who, as a condition of giving up possession of the dwelling-house, asks for or receives the payment of any sum, or the giving of any other consideration, by any person other than the landlord, shall be guilty of an offence.

(2) Where a statutory tenant of a dwelling-house requires that furniture or other articles shall be purchased as a condition of his giving up possession of the dwelling-house, the price demanded shall, at the request of the person on whom the demand is made, be stated in writing, and if the price exceeds the reasonable price of the articles the excess shall be treated, for the purposes of sub-paragraph (1) above, as a sum asked to be paid as a condition of giving up possession.

(3) A person guilty of an offence under this paragraph shall be liable to a fine not exceeding level 3 on the standard scale.

(4) The court by which a person is convicted of an offence under this paragraph may order the payment—

(a) to the person who made any such payment, or gave any such consideration, as is referred to in sub-paragraph (1) above, of the amount of that payment or the value of that consideration, or

(b) to the person who paid any such price as is referred to in sub-paragraph (2) above, of the amount by which the price paid exceeds the reasonable price.

Change of statutory tenant by agreement

13.—(1) Where it is so agreed in writing between a statutory tenant ("the outgoing tenant") and a person proposing to occupy the dwelling ("the incoming tenant"), the incoming tenant shall be deemed to be the statutory tenant of the dwelling as from such date as may be specified in the agreement ("the transfer date").

(2)   Such an agreement shall not have effect unless the landlord is a party thereto, and, if the consent of any superior landlord would have been required to an assignment of the previous contractual tenancy, the agreement shall not have effect unless the superior landlord is a party thereto.

(3)   If the outgoing tenant is the statutory tenant by virtue of his previous protected tenancy, then, subject to sub-paragraph (6) below, this Act shall have effect, on and after the transfer date, as if the incoming tenant had been a protected tenant and had become the statutory tenant by virtue of his previous protected tenancy.

(4)   Subject to sub-paragraphs (5) and (6) below, if the outgoing tenant is a statutory tenant by succession, then, on and after the transfer date—

(a)   this Act shall have effect as if the incoming tenant were a statutory tenant by succession, and

(b)   the incoming tenant shall be deemed to have become a statutory tenant by virtue of that paragraph of Part I of this Schedule by virtue of which the outgoing tenant became (or is deemed to have become) a statutory tenant.

(5)   If the outgoing tenant is a statutory tenant by succession, the agreement may provide that, notwithstanding anything in sub-paragraph (4) above, on and after the transfer date, this Act shall have effect, subject to sub-paragraph (6) below, as if the incoming tenant had been a protected tenant and had become the statutory tenant by virtue of his previous protected tenancy.

(6)   Unless the incoming tenant is deemed, by virtue of sub-paragraph (4)(b) above, to have become a statutory tenant by virtue of paragraph 6 or 7 of Part I of this Schedule, paragraphs 5 to 7 of that Part shall not apply where a person has become a statutory tenant by virtue of this paragraph.

(7)   In this paragraph "the dwelling" means the aggregate of the premises comprised in the statutory tenancy of the outgoing tenant.

No pecuniary consideration to be required on change of tenant under paragraph 13

14.—(1)   Any person who requires the payment of any pecuniary consideration for entering into such an agreement as is referred to in paragraph 13(1) above shall be liable to a fine not exceeding level 3 on the standard scale.

(2)   The court by which a person is convicted of an offence under sub-paragraph (1) above may order the amount of the payment to be repaid by the person to whom it was paid.

(3)   Without prejudice to sub-paragraph (2) above, the amount of any such payment as is referred to in sub-paragraph (1) above shall be recoverable by the person by whom it was made either by proceedings for its recovery or, if it was made to the landlord by a person liable to pay rent to the landlord, by deduction from any rent so payable.

(4)   Notwithstanding anything in sub-paragraph (1) above, if apart from this paragraph he would be entitled to do so, the outgoing tenant may require the payment by the incoming tenant—

(a)   of so much of any outgoings discharged by the outgoing tenant as is referable to any period after the transfer date;

(b)   of a sum not exceeding the amount of any expenditure reasonably incurred by the outgoing tenant in carrying out any structural alteration of the dwelling or in providing or improving fixtures therein, being fixtures which, as against the landlord, the outgoing tenant is not entitled to remove;

(c)   where the outgoing tenant became a tenant of the dwelling by virtue of an assignment of the previous protected tenancy, of a sum not exceeding any reasonable amount paid by him to his assignor in respect of expenditure incurred by the assignor, or by any previous assignor of the tenancy, in carrying out any such alteration or in providing or improving any such fixtures as are mentioned in paragraph (b) above; or

(d)   where part of the dwelling is used as a shop or office, or for business, trade or professional purposes, of a reasonable amount in respect of any goodwill of the business, trade or profession, being goodwill transferred to the incoming tenant in connection with his becoming a statutory tenant of the dwelling or accruing to him in consequence thereof.

(5) In this paragraph "outgoing tenant", "incoming tenant", "the transfer date" and "the dwelling" have the same meanings as in paragraph 13 above.

Section 12(4).   SCHEDULE 2
                          RESIDENT LANDLORDS

PART I
PROVISIONS FOR DETERMINING APPLICATION OF SECTION 12

1.   In determining whether the condition in section 12(1)(c) of this Act is at any time fulfilled with respect to a tenancy, there shall be disregarded—

(a)   any period of not more than 28 days beginning with the date on which the interest of the landlord under the tenancy becomes vested at law and in equity in an individual who, during that period, does not occupy as his residence another dwelling-house which forms part of the building or, as the case may be, flat concerned;

(b)   if, within a period falling within paragraph (a) above, the individual concerned notifies the tenant in writing of his intention to occupy as his residence another dwelling-house in the building or, as the case may be, flat concerned, the period beginning with the date on which the interest of the landlord under the tenancy becomes vested in that individual as mentioned in that paragraph and ending—

(i)   at the expiry of the period of 6 months beginning on that date, or

(ii)   on the date on which that interest ceases to be so vested, or

(iii)   on the date on which the condition in section 12(1)(c) again applies, whichever is the earlier; and

(c)   any period of not more than 2 years beginning with the date on which the interest of the landlord under the tenancy becomes, and during which it remains, vested—

(ii)   in trustees as such; or

(iii)   by virtue of section 9 of the Administration of Estates Act 1925, in the Probate Judge, within the meaning of that Act.

(2)   During any period when—

(a)   the interest of the landlord under the tenancy referred to in section 12(1) is vested in trustees as such, and

(b)   that interest is or, if it is held on trust for sale, the proceeds of its sale are held on trust for any person who occupies as his residence a dwelling-house which forms part of the building or, as the case may be, flat referred to in section 12(1)(a), the condition in section 12(1)(c) shall be deemed to be fulfilled and, accordingly, no part of that period shall be disregarded by virtue of paragraph 1 above.

2A.—(1)   The tenancy referred to in section 12(1) falls within this paragraph if the interest of the landlord under the tenancy becomes vested in the personal representatives of a deceased person acting in that capacity.

(2)   If the tenancy falls within this paragraph, the condition in section 12(1)(c) shall be deemed to be fulfilled for any period, beginning with the date on which the interest becomes vested in the personal representatives and not exceeding two years, during which the interest of the landlord remains so vested.

3.   Throughout any period which, by virtue of paragraph 1 above, falls to be disregarded for the purpose of determining whether the condition in section 12(1)(c) is fulfilled with respect to a tenancy, no order shall be made for possession of the dwelling-house subject to that tenancy, other than an order which might be made if that tenancy were or, as the case may be, had been a regulated tenancy.

4.   For the purposes of section 12, a building is a purpose-built block of flats if as constructed it contained, and it contains, 2 or more flats; and for this purpose "flat" means a dwelling-house which—

(a)   forms part only of a building; and

(b)   is separated horizontally from another dwelling-house which forms part of the same building.

5.   For the purposes of section 12, a person shall be treated as occupying a dwelling-house as his residence if, so far as the nature of the case allows, he fulfils the same conditions as, by virtue of section 2(3) of this Act, are required to be fulfilled by a statutory tenant of a dwelling-house.

PART II
Tenancies ceasing to fall within section 12

6.—(1)   In any case where—

(a)   a tenancy which, by virtue only of section 12, was precluded from being a protected tenancy ceases to be so precluded and accordingly becomes a protected tenancy, and

(b)   before it became a protected tenancy a rent was registered for the dwelling concerned under Part V of this Act,

the amount which is so registered shall be deemed to be registered under Part IV of this Act as the rent for the dwelling-house which is let on that tenancy, and that registration shall be deemed to take effect on the day the tenancy becomes a protected tenancy.

(2)   Section 67(3) of this Act shall not apply to an application for the registration under Part IV of a rent different from that which is deemed to be registered as mentioned in sub-paragraph (1) above.

(4)   If, immediately before a tenancy became a protected tenancy as mentioned in sub-paragraph (1)(a) above, the rates in respect of the dwelling-house concerned were borne as mentioned in sub-section (3) of section 79 of this Act and the fact that they were so borne was noted as required by that subsection, then, in the application of Part IV in relation to the protected tenancy, section 71(2) of this Act shall be deemed to apply.

7.   If, in a case where a tenancy becomes a protected tenancy as mentioned in sub-paragraph (1)(a) above—

(a)   a notice to quit had been served in respect of the dwelling concerned before the date on which the tenancy became a protected tenancy, and

(b)   the period at the end of which that notice to quit takes effect had, before that date, been extended under Part VII of this Act, and

(c)   that period has not expired before that date,

the notice to quit shall take effect on the day following that date (whenever it would otherwise take effect) and, accordingly, on that day the protected tenancy shall become a statutory tenancy.

Section 27.   SCHEDULE 5

CALCULATION OF AMOUNT OF RATES

1.   For the purposes of this Act, the amount of rates for any rental period shall be taken, subject to this Schedule, to be an amount which bears to the total rates payable during the relevant rating period the same proportion as the length of the rental period bears to the length of the relevant rating period.

2.   In this Schedule "the relevant rating period", in relation to a rental period, means the rating period during which the rent for that rental period is payable.

3.   The amount of the rates for any rental period which precedes the making, by the authority levying the rates, of their first demand for, or for an instalment of, the rates

for the relevant rating period shall be calculated on the basis that the rates for that rating period will be the same as for the last preceding rating period.

4.—(1) On the making, by the authority levying the rates, of their first such demand, and on the making by them of any subsequent such demand, the amount of the rates for any rental period shall if necessary be recalculated on the basis that the rates for the relevant rating period will be such as appears from the information given in the demand and any previous demands.

(2) Any such recalculation shall not affect the ascertainment of the rates for any rental period beginning more than 6 weeks before the date of the service of the demand giving rise to the recalculation.

5. If, as a result of the settlement of a proposal, the rates payable for the relevant rating period are decreased, the amount of the rates for a rental period shall be recalculated so as to give effect to the decrease; but any such recalculation shall not affect the ascertainment of the rates for any rental period beginning more than 6 weeks before the date of the settlement of the proposal.

6. In computing the rates for any rental period for the purposes of this Schedule, any discount, and any allowance made under any of the enactments relating to allowances given where rates are paid by the owner instead of by the occupier, shall be left out of account, and accordingly those rates shall be computed as if no such discount or allowance had fallen to be, or had been, allowed or made.

Section 44(4).

SCHEDULE 7

RENT LIMIT FOR CERTAIN TENANCIES FIRST REGULATED BY VIRTUE OF THE COUNTER-INFLATION ACT 1973

Special rent limit

1.—(1) This paragraph applies to a regulated tenancy—

(a) which was granted before 8th March 1973, and

(b) which would not have been a regulated tenancy but for section 14(1) of the Counter-Inflation Act 1973 (which brought certain tenancies of dwelling-houses with high rateable values within the protection of the Rent Act 1968).

(2) Subject to this Schedule, the recoverable rent for any contractual period of a tenancy to which this paragraph applies shall not exceed the limit specified in paragraph 2 below, and the amount of any excess shall, notwithstanding anything in any agreement, be irrecoverable from the tenant.

(3) Where a rent for the dwelling-house is registered under Part IV of this Act which is less than the limit specified in paragraph 2 below, neither section 44(1) nor section 45(2) of this Act shall apply to a tenancy to which this paragraph applies.

(4) Sub-paragraphs (2) and (3) above shall cease to apply if the landlord and the tenant so provide by an agreement conforming with the requirements of section 51(4) of this Act.

(5) Sub-paragraph (2) above shall not apply where a rent for the dwelling-house is registered under Part IV of this Act which is not less than the limit specified in paragraph 2 below.

2.—(1) Where, at 22nd March 1973, Article 10 of the Counter-Inflation (Rents) (England and Wales) Order 1972 applied to the rent under the tenancy (to which paragraph 1 above applies) the said limit is the rent payable under the tenancy as limited by the said Article 10 immediately before that date.

(2) In any other case the said limit is the rent payable under the terms of the tenancy (to which paragraph 1 above applies) at 22nd March 1973.

Adjustment for repairs, services or rates

3.—(1) This paragraph applies to a contractual period the rent for which is subject to paragraph 1(2) above.

(2)   In this paragraph "the previous terms" means the terms of the tenancy (to which paragraph 1 above applies) as at 22nd March 1973, and "the limit" means the limit in paragraph 2 above.

(3)   Where under the terms of the tenancy there is with respect to—
    (a)   the responsibility for any repairs, or
    (b)   the provision of services by the landlord or any superior landlord, or
    (c)   the use of furniture by the tenant,
any difference compared with the previous terms, such as to affect the amount of the rent which it is reasonable to charge, the limit shall be increased or decreased by an appropriate amount.

(4)   Where for the contractual period there is a difference between the amount (if any) of the rates borne by the landlord or a superior landlord in respect of the dwelling-house and the amount (if any) so borne during the first rental period for which the previous terms were agreed, the limit shall be increased or decreased by the difference.

(5)   Where for the contractual period there is an increase in the cost of the provision of the services (if any) provided for the tenant by the landlord or a superior landlord compared with that cost at the time when the previous terms were agreed, such as to affect the amount of the rent which it is reasonable to charge, the limit shall be increased by an appropriate amount.

(6)   Where the previous terms provide for a variation of the rent in any of the circumstances mentioned in this paragraph, the limit shall not be further varied under this paragraph by reason of the same circumstances.

(7)   Any question whether, or by what amount, the limit is increased or decreased by sub-paragraph (3) or (5) above shall be determined by the county court, and any such determination—
    (a)   may be made so as to relate to past rental periods, and
    (b)   shall have effect with respect to rental periods subsequent to the periods to which it relates until revoked or varied by a subsequent determination.

Section 65.   SCHEDULE 10
                     RENT ASSESSMENT COMMITTEES

1.   The Secretary of State shall draw up and from time to time revise panels of persons to act as chairmen and other members of rent assessment committees for such areas, comprising together every registration area, as the Secretary of State may from time to time determine.

2.   Each panel shall consist of a number of persons appointed by the Lord Chancellor and a number of persons appointed by the Secretary of State.

3.   The Secretary of State shall nominate one of the persons appointed by the Lord Chancellor to act as president of the panel, and one or more such persons to act as vice-president or vice-presidents.

4.   Subject to this Schedule, the number of rent assessment committees to act for an area and the constitution of those committees shall be determined by the president of the panel formed for that area or, in the case of the president's absence or incapacity, by the vice-president or, as the case may be, one of the vice-presidents.

5.   Subject to paragraphs 6 and 6A below, each rent assessment committee shall consist of a chairman and one or two other members, and the chairman shall be either the president or vice-president (or, as the case may be, one of the vice-presidents) of the panel or one of the other members appointed by the Lord Chancellor.

6.   The president of the panel may, if he thinks fit, direct that when dealing with such cases or dealing with a case in such circumstances as may be specified in the direction, the chairman sitting alone may, with the consent of the parties, exercise the functions of a rent assessment committee.

6A. When dealing with an application under section 81A of this Act a rent assessment committee carrying out the functions of a rent tribunal shall consist of the chairman of the committee sitting alone.

7. There shall be paid to members of panels such remuneration and allowances as the Secretary of State, with the consent of the Minister for the Civil Service, may determine.

7A. The Secretary of State may, with the consent of the Minister for the Civil Service, provide for the payment of pensions, allowances or gratuities to or in respect of any person nominated to act as president or vice-president of a panel.

8. The President of the panel may appoint, with the approval of the Secretary of State as to numbers, such clerks and other officers and servants of rent assessment committees as he thinks fit, and there shall be paid to the clerks and other officers and servants such salaries and allowances as the Secretary of State, with the consent of the Minister for the Civil Service, may determine.

9. There shall be paid out of moneys provided by Parliament—

    (a) the remuneration and allowances of members of panels;

    (b) the salaries and allowances of clerks and other officers and servants appointed under this Schedule; and

    (c) such other expenses of a panel as the Minister for the Civil Service may determine.

Section 67.

SCHEDULE 11
APPLICATIONS FOR REGISTRATION OF RENT

PART I
APPLICATION UNSUPPORTED BY CERTIFICATE OF FAIR RENT

Procedure on application to rent officer

1. On receiving any application for the registration of a rent, the rent officer may, by notice in writing served on the landlord or on the tenant (whether or not the applicant or one of the applicants) require him to give to the rent officer, within such period of not less than 7 days from the service of the notice as may be specified in the notice, such information as he may reasonably require regarding such of the particulars contained in the application as may be specified in the notice.

2.—(1) Where the application is made jointly by the landlord and the tenant and it appears to the rent officer, after making such inquiry, if any, as he thinks fit and considering any information supplied to him in pursuance of paragraph 1 above, that the rent specified in the application is a fair rent, he may register that rent without further proceedings.

(2) Where the rent officer registers a rent under this paragraph he shall notify the landlord and tenant accordingly.

3.—(1) In the case of an application which does not fall within paragraph 2 above, the rent officer shall serve on the landlord and on the tenant a notice inviting the person on whom the notice is served to state in writing, within a period of not less than seven days after the service of the notice, whether he wishes the rent officer to consider, in consultation with the landlord and the tenant, what rent ought to be registered for the dwelling-house.

(2) A notice served under sub-paragraph (1) above on the person who did not make the application shall be accompanied—

    (a) by a copy of the application; and

    (b) where, in pursuance of section 67(2)(b), the application was accompanied by details of the landlord's expenditure in connection with the provisions of services, by a copy of those details.

3A.   If, after service of a notice by the rent officer under paragraph 3 above, no request in writing is made within the period specified in the notice for the rent to be considered as mentioned in that paragraph, the rent officer after considering what rent ought to be registered or, as the case may be, whether a different rent ought to be registered, may—

(a)   determine a fair rent and register it as the rent for the dwelling-house; or

(b)   confirm the rent for the time being registered and note the confirmation in the register; or

(c)   serve a notice under paragraph 4(2) below.

4.—(1)   Where, in response to a notice served by the rent officer under paragraph 3(1) above, the landlord or the tenant states in writing that he wishes the rent to be considered as mentioned in that paragraph, the rent officer shall serve a notice under this paragraph.

(2)   A notice under this paragraph shall be served on the landlord and on the tenant informing them that the rent officer proposes, at a time (which shall not be earlier than 7 days after the service of the notice, or 14 days in a case falling within paragraph 3(2)(b) above) and place specified in the notice, to consider in consultation with the landlord and the tenant, or such of them as may appear at that time and place, what rent ought to be registered for the dwelling-house or, as the case may be, whether a different rent ought to be so registered.

(3)   At any such consultation the landlord and the tenant may each be represented by a person authorised by him in that behalf, whether or not that person is of counsel or a solicitor.

(4)   The rent officer may, where he considers it appropriate, arrange for consultations in respect of one dwelling-house to be held together with consultations in respect of one or more other dwelling-houses.

5.   After considering, in accordance with paragraph 4 above, what rent ought to be registered or, as the case may be, whether a different rent ought to be registered, the rent officer shall, as the case may require,—

(a)   determine a fair rent and register it as the rent for the dwelling-house; or

(b)   confirm the rent for the time being registered and note the confirmation in the register.

5A.   Where a rent has been registered or confirmed by the rent officer under paragraph 3A or 5 above, he shall notify the landlord and the tenant accordingly by a notice stating that if, within 28 days of the service of the notice or such longer period as he or a rent assessment committee may allow, an objection in writing is received by the rent officer from the landlord or the tenant the matter will be referred to a rent assessment committee.

6.—(1)   If such an objection as is mentioned in paragraph 5A above is received then—

(a)   if it is received within the period of 28 days specified in that paragraph or a rent assessment committee so direct, the rent officer shall refer the matter to a rent assessment committee;

(b)   if it is received after the expiry of that period the rent officer may either refer the matter to a rent assessment committee or seek the directions of a rent assessment committee whether so to refer it.

(2)   The rent officer shall indicate in the register whether the matter has been referred to a rent assessment committee in pursuance of this paragraph.

Determination of fair rent by rent assessment committee

7.—(1)   The rent assessment committee to whom a matter is referred under paragraph 6 above—

(a)   may by notice in the prescribed form served on the landlord or the tenant require him to give to the committee, within such period of not less than 14 days from the service of the notice as may be specified in the notice, such further information, in addition to any given to the rent officer in pursuance of paragraph 1 above, as they may reasonably require; and

(b)   shall serve on the landlord and on the tenant a notice specifying a period of not less than 7 days from the service of the notice during which either representations in writing or a request to make oral representations may be made by him to the committee.

(2)   If any person fails without reasonable cause to comply with any notice served on him under sub-paragraph (1)(a) above, he shall be liable to a fine not exceeding level 3 on the standard scale.

(3)   Where an offence under sub-paragraph (2) above committed by a body corporate is proved to have been committed with the consent or connivance of, or to be attributable to any neglect on the part of, any director, manager or secretary or other similar officer of the body corporate or any person who was purporting to act in any such capacity, he as well as the body corporate shall be guilty of that offence and shall be liable to be proceeded against and punished accordingly.

8.   Where, within the period specified in paragraph 7(1)(b) above, or such further period as the committee may allow, the landlord or the tenant requests to make oral representations the committee shall give him an opportunity to be heard either in person or by a person authorised by him in that behalf, whether or not that person is of counsel or a solicitor.

9.—(1)   The committee shall make such inquiry, if any, as they think fit and consider any information supplied or representation made to them in pursuance of paragraph 7 or paragraph 8 above and—

(a)   if it appears to them that the rent registered or confirmed by the rent officer is a fair rent, they shall confirm that rent;

(b)   if it does not appear to them that that rent is a fair rent, they shall determine a fair rent for the dwelling-house.

(2)   Where the committee confirm or determine a rent under this paragraph they shall notify the landlord, the tenant and the rent officer of their decision and of the date on which it was made.

(3)   On receiving the notification, the rent officer shall, as the case may require, either indicate in the register that the rent has been confirmed or register the rent determined by the committee as the rent for the dwelling-house.

Section 92.   SCHEDULE 14
CONVERSION OF HOUSING ASSOCIATION TENANCIES INTO
REGULATED TENANCIES

1.—(1)   This paragraph applies in any case where—

(a)   a tenancy of a dwelling-house under which the interest of the landlord belonged to a housing association came to an end at a time before 1st April 1975, and

(b)   on the date when it came to an end, the tenancy was one to which Part VIII of the 1972 Act (which is superseded by Part VI of this Act) applied, and

(c)   if the tenancy had come to an end on 1st April 1975 it would, by virtue of section 18(1) of the 1974 Act have then been a protected tenancy for the purposes of the Rent Act 1968.

(2)   If on 1st April 1975 a person who was the tenant under the tenancy which came to an end duly retained possession of the dwelling-house, he shall be deemed to have done so as a statutory tenant under a regulated tenancy and as a person who became a statutory tenant on the termination of a protected tenancy under which he was the tenant.

(3)   If on 1st April 1975 a person duly retained possession of the dwelling-house as being a person who, in the circumstances described in sub-paragraph (5) below, would have been the first successor, within the meaning of Schedule 1 to the Rent Act 1968, he shall be deemed to have done so as the statutory tenant under a regulated tenancy and as a person who became a statutory tenant by virtue of paragraph 2 or 3 of Schedule 1 to this Act.

(4)   If on 1st April 1975 a person duly retained possession of the dwelling-house as being a person who, in the circumstances described in sub-paragraph (5) below, would have become the statutory tenant on the death of a first successor, he shall be deemed to have done so as a statutory tenant under a regulated tenancy and as a person who became a statutory tenant by virtue of paragraph 6 or 7 of Schedule 1 to this Act.

(5)   The circumstances mentioned in sub-paragraphs (3) and (4) above are that—

(a)   the tenant under the tenancy, or any person to whom the dwelling-house or any part thereof had been lawfully sublet has died; and

(b)   if the deceased had been the original tenant within the meaning of Schedule 1 to the Rent Act 1968, the person duly retaining possession of the dwelling-house would have been the first successor within the meaning of that Schedule or would have become the statutory tenant on the death of that first successor.

(6)   References in this paragraph to a person duly retaining possession of a dwelling-house are references to his retaining possession without any order for possession having been made or, where such an order has been made—

(a)   during any period while its operation is postponed or its execution is suspended; or

(b)   after it has been rescinded.

(7)   Subject to sub-paragraph (8) below, the tenancy referred to in sub-paragraph (1) above shall be treated as the original contract of tenancy for the purposes of section 3 of this Act in relation to a statutory tenancy imposed by any of sub-paragraphs (2) to (4) above.

(8)   The High Court or the county court may by order vary all or any of the terms of a statutory tenancy imposed by any of sub-paragraphs (2) to (4) above in any way appearing to the court to be just and equitable (and whether or not in a way authorised by sections 46 and 47 of this Act).

2.—(1)   If, in a case where either a tenancy has become a protected tenancy by virtue of section 18(1) of the 1974 Act or by virtue of subsections (1) and (3) of section 15 of this Act or a statutory tenancy has been imposed by virtue of paragraph 1 above—

(a)   a rent (the "previous registered rent") was registered for the dwelling-house at a time when Part VIII of the 1972 Act or Part VI of this Act applied to that tenancy or, as the case may be, to the tenancy referred to in paragraph 1(1) above; and

(b)   a rent has subsequently been registered for the dwelling-house under Part IV of this Act but the rent so registered is less than the previous registered rent, then subject to paragraph 4 below, until such time as a rent is registered under Part IV which is higher than the previous registered rent, the contractual rent limit or, as the case may be, the maximum rent recoverable during any statutory period of the regulated tenancy concerned shall be the previous registered rent.

(2)   If in a case falling within sub-paragraph (1) above, the Secretary of State has, in a direction under section 90 of this Act, specified a rent limit for the dwelling-house higher than the previous registered rent, then, during the period for which that direction has effect as mentioned in that section, sub-paragraph (1) above shall have effect with the substitution for any reference to the previous registered rent of a reference to the rent limit so specified.

(3)   Nothing in this paragraph shall affect the operation of section 73 of this Act and, accordingly, where the registration of a rent is cancelled in accordance with that section,

sub-paragraph (1) above shall cease to apply in relation to the rent of the dwelling-house concerned.

3.—(1)   This paragraph applies for the purposes of the application of Part III of this Act in relation to—

(a)   a tenancy which has become a protected tenancy by virtue of section 18(1) of the 1974 Act or by virtue of subsections (1) and (3) of section 15 of this Act,

(b)   a statutory tenancy arising on the termination of such a tenancy, and

(c)   a statutory tenancy imposed by virtue of paragraph 1 above,

in any case where at the time when Part VIII of the 1972 Act or Part VI of this Act applied to the tenancy referred to in paragraph (a) above or, as the case may require, paragraph 1(1) above, section 83(3) of the 1972 Act or section 88(4) of this Act, applied.

(2)   Where this paragraph applies, the rent limit applicable to the tenancy or statutory tenancy referred to in sub-paragraph (1) above shall be deemed to be (or, as the case may be, to have been) the contractual rent limit under the relevant tenancy, but without prejudice to the subsequent registration of a rent for the dwelling-house under Part IV of this Act or (during the currency of a protected tenancy) the making of an agreement under section 51 of this Act increasing the rent payable.

(3)   Sub-paragraph (2) above shall have effect notwithstanding the repeal by the 1972 Act of section 20(3) of the Rent Act 1968 (contractual rent limit before registration), but nothing in this paragraph shall be taken as applying any provisions of section 88 of this Act to a tenancy at a time when it is a protected tenancy.

(4)   In this paragraph "the relevant tenancy" means—

(a)   in the case of a tenancy falling within sub-paragraph (1)(a) above, that tenancy;

(b)   in the case of a statutory tenancy falling within sub-paragraph (1)(b) above, the tenancy referred to in sub-paragraph (1)(a) above; and

(c)   in the case of a statutory tenancy falling within sub-paragraph (1)(c) above, the protected tenancy referred to in sub-paragraph (2) of paragraph 1 above or, in a case where sub-paragraph (3) or (4) of that paragraph applies, a notional protected tenancy which, when taken with that regulated tenancy would, by virtue of section 18(2) of this Act, be treated for the purposes of this Act as constituting one regulated tenancy when taken together with the statutory tenancy.

5.—(1)   This paragraph has effect with respect to the application of Schedule 9 to this Act in relation to a regulated tenancy consisting of—

(a)   a tenancy which has become a protected tenancy by virtue of section 18(1) of the 1974 Act or by virtue of subsections (1) and (3) of section 15 of this Act, or

(b)   a statutory tenancy imposed by virtue of paragraph 1 above,

together with any subsequent statutory tenancy which, when taken with that regulated tenancy, is by virtue of section 18(2) of this Act treated for the purposes of this Act as constituting one regulated tenancy.

(2)   For the purposes of paragraph 1(1)(b) of Schedule 9, a tenancy falling within sub-paragraph (1)(a) above shall be deemed to have been a regulated tenancy throughout the period when Part VIII of the 1972 Act or Part VI of this Act applied to it.

(3)   In the case of a regulated tenancy falling within sub-paragraph (1)(b) above, paragraph 1(1)(b) of Schedule 9 shall have effect as if the reference to the completion of works during the existence of the regulated tenancy included a reference to their completion during the period beginning on the day on which Part VIII of the 1972 Act or Part VI of this Act first applied to the tenancy referred to in paragraph 1(1) above and ending on the day on which the regulated tenancy came into existence.

(4)   The reference in paragraph 3(1) of Schedule 9 to notices of increase authorised by this Act shall include a reference to notices of increase under section 87 of the 1972 Act.

7.   In the application of section 70 of this Act in relation to a tenancy which has become a protected tenancy by virtue of section 18(1) of the 1974 Act or by virtue of subsections (1) and (3) of section 15 of this Act or a statutory tenancy which is imposed by virtue of paragraph 1 above, the reference in subsection (3) to a failure to comply with any terms of a regulated tenancy or to carrying out an improvement includes a reference to a failure occurring or an improvement carried out before the tenancy became a regulated tenancy or, as the case may be, before the statutory tenancy was imposed.

8.   In this Schedule "the 1972 Act" means the Housing Finance Act 1972 and "the 1974 Act" means the Housing Act 1974.

Section 98.   SCHEDULE 15
      GROUNDS FOR POSSESSION OF DWELLING-HOUSES LET ON
        OR SUBJECT TO PROTECTED OR STATUTORY TENANCIES

PART I
CASES IN WHICH COURT MAY ORDER POSSESSION

Case 1

Where any rent lawfully due from the tenant has not been paid, or any obligation of the protected or statutory tenancy which arises under this Act, or—

(a)   in the case of a protected tenancy, any other obligation of the tenancy, in so far as is consistent with the provisions of Part VII of this Act, or

(b)   in the case of a statutory tenancy, any other obligation of the previous protected tenancy which is applicable to the statutory tenancy,

has been broken or not performed.

Case 2

Where the tenant or any person residing or lodging with him or any sub-tenant of his has been guilty of conduct which is a nuisance or annoyance to adjoining occupiers, or has been convicted of using the dwelling-house or allowing the dwelling-house to be used for immoral or illegal purposes.

Case 3

Where the condition of the dwelling-house has, in the opinion of the court, deteriorated owing to acts of waste by, or the neglect or default of, the tenant or any person residing or lodging with him or any sub-tenant of his and, in the case of any act of waste by, or the neglect or default of, a person lodging with the tenant or a sub-tenant of his, where the court is satisfied that the tenant has not, before the making of the order in question, taken such steps as he ought reasonably to have taken for the removal of the lodger or sub-tenant, as the case may be.

Case 4

Where the condition of any furniture provided for use under the tenancy has, in the opinion of the court, deteriorated owing to ill-treatment by the tenant or any person residing or lodging with him or any sub-tenant of his and, in the case of any ill-treatment by a person lodging with the tenant or a sub-tenant of his, where the court is satisfied that the tenant has not, before the making of the order in question, taken such steps as he ought reasonably to have taken for the removal of the lodger or sub-tenant, as the case may be.

Case 5

Where the tenant has given notice to quit and, in consequence of that notice, the landlord has contracted to sell or let the dwelling-house or has taken any other steps as the result of which he would, in the opinion of the court, be seriously prejudiced if he could not obtain possession.

Case 6

Where, without the consent of the landlord, the tenant has, at any time after—
    (b)   22nd March 1973, in the case of a tenancy which became a regulated tenancy by virtue of section 14 of the Counter-Inflation Act 1973;
    (bb)   the commencement of section 73 of the Housing Act 1980, in the case of a tenancy which became a regulated tenancy by virtue of that section;
    (c)   14th August 1974, in the case of a regulated furnished tenancy; or
    (d)   8th December 1965, in the case of any other tenancy,
assigned or sublet the whole of the dwelling-house or sublet part of the dwelling-house, the remainder being already sublet.

Case 8

Where the dwelling-house is reasonably required by the landlord for occupation as a residence for some person engaged in his whole-time employment, or in the whole-time employment of some tenant from him or with whom, conditional on housing being provided, a contract for such employment has been entered into, and the tenant was in the employment of the landlord or a former landlord, and the dwelling-house was let to him in consequence of that employment and he has ceased to be in that employment.

Case 9

Where the dwelling-house is reasonably required by the landlord for occupation as a residence for—
    (a)   himself, or
    (b)   any son or daughter of his over 18 years of age, or
    (c)   his father or mother, or
    (d)   if the dwelling-house is let on or subject to a regulated tenancy, the father or mother of his wife or husband,
and the landlord did not become landlord by purchasing the dwelling-house or any interest therein after—
    (i)   7th November 1956, in the case of a tenancy which was then a controlled tenancy;
    (ii)   8th March 1973, in the case of a tenancy which became a regulated tenancy by virtue of section 14 of the Counter-Inflation Act 1973;
    (iii)   24th May 1974, in the case of a regulated furnished tenancy; or
    (iv)   23rd March 1965, in the case of any other tenancy.

Case 10

Where the court is satisfied that the rent charged by the tenant—
    (a)   for any sublet part of the dwelling-house which is a dwelling-house let on a protected tenancy or subject to a statutory tenancy is or was in excess of the maximum rent for the time being recoverable for that part, having regard to Part III of this Act, or
    (b)   for any sublet part of the dwelling-house which is subject to a restricted contract is or was in excess of the maximum (if any) which it is lawful for the lessor, within the meaning of Part V of this Act to require or receive having regard to the provisions of that Part.

PART II
CASES IN WHICH COURT MUST ORDER POSSESSION WHERE
DWELLING-HOUSE SUBJECT TO REGULATED TENANCY

Case 11

Where a person (in this Case referred to as "the owner-occupier") who let the dwelling-house on a regulated tenancy had, at any time before the letting, occupied it as his residence and—

(a)   not later than the relevant date the landlord gave notice in writing to the tenant that possession might be recovered under this Case, and

(b)   the dwelling-house has not, since—

(i)   22nd March 1973, in the case of a tenancy which became a regulated tenancy by virtue of section 14 of the Counter-Inflation Act 1973;

(ii)   14th August 1974, in the case of a regulated furnished tenancy; or

(iii)   8th December 1965, in the case of any other tenancy,

been let by the owner-occupier on a protected tenancy with respect to which the condition mentioned in paragraph (a) above was not satisfied, and

(c)   the court is of the opinion that of the conditions set out in Part V of this Schedule one of those in paragraphs (a) and (c) to (f) is satisfied.

If the court is of the opinion that, notwithstanding that the condition in paragraph (a) or (b) above is not complied with, it is just and equitable to make an order for possession of the dwelling-house, the court may dispense with the requirements of either or both of those paragraphs, as the case may require.

The giving of a notice before 14th August 1974 under section 79 of the Rent Act 1968 shall be treated, in the case of a regulated furnished tenancy, as compliance with paragraph (a) of this Case.

Where the dwelling-house has been let by the owner-occupier on a protected tenancy (in this paragraph referred to as "the earlier tenancy") granted on or after 16th November 1984 but not later than the end of the period of two months beginning with the commencement of the Rent (Amendment) Act 1985 and either—

(i)   the earlier tenancy was granted for a term certain (whether or not to be followed by a further term or to continue thereafter from year to year or some other period) and was during that term a protected shorthold tenancy as defined in section 52 of the Housing Act 1980, or

(ii)   the conditions mentioned in paragraphs (a) to (c) of Case 20 were satisfied with respect to the dwelling-house and the earlier tenancy,

then for the purposes of paragraph (b) above the condition in paragraph (a) above is to be treated as having been satisfied with respect to the earlier tenancy.

Case 12

Where the landlord (in this Case referred to as "the owner") intends to occupy the dwelling-house as his residence at such time as he might retire from regular employment and has let it on a regulated tenancy before he has so retired and—

(a)   not later than the relevant date the landlord gave notice in writing to the tenant that possession might be recovered under this Case; and

(b)   the dwelling-house has not, since 14th August 1974, been let by the owner on a protected tenancy with respect to which the condition mentioned in paragraph (a) above was not satisfied; and

(c)   the court is of the opinion that of the conditions set out in Part V of this Schedule one of those in paragraphs (b) to (e) is satisfied.

If the court is of the opinion that, notwithstanding that the condition in paragraph (a) or (b) above is not complied with, it is just and equitable to make an order for possession of the dwelling-house, the court may dispense with the requirements of either or both of those paragraphs, as the case may require.

Case 13

Where the dwelling-house is let under a tenancy for a term of years certain not exceeding 8 months and—

    (a)   not later than the relevant date the landlord gave notice in writing to the tenant that possession might be recovered under this Case; and

    (b)   the dwelling-house was, at some time within the period of 12 months ending on the relevant date, occupied under a right to occupy it for a holiday.

For the purposes of this Case a tenancy shall be treated as being for a term of years certain notwithstanding that it is liable to determination by re-entry or on the happening of any event other than the giving of notice by the landlord to determine the term.

Case 14

Where the dwelling-house is let under a tenancy for a term of years certain not exceeding 12 months and—

    (a)   not later than the relevant date the landlord gave notice in writing to the tenant that possession might be recovered under this Case; and

    (b)   at some time within the period of 12 months ending on the relevant date, the dwelling-house was subject to such a tenancy as is referred to in Section 8(1) of this Act.

For the purposes of this Case a tenant shall be treated as being for a term of years certain notwithstanding that it is liable to determination by re-entry or on the happening of any event other than the giving of notice by the landlord to determine the term.

Case 15

Where the dwelling-house is held for the purpose of being available for occupation by a minister of religion as a residence from which to perform the duties of his office and—

    (a)   not later than the relevant date the tenant was given notice in writing that possession might be recovered under this Case, and

    (b)   the court is satisfied that the dwelling-house is required for occupation by a minister of religion as such a residence.

Case 16

Where the dwelling-house was at any time occupied by a person under the terms of his employment as a person employed in agriculture, and

    (a)   the tenant neither is nor at any time was so employed by the landlord and is not the widow of a person who was so employed, and

    (b)   not later than the relevant date, the tenant was given notice in writing that possession might be recovered under this Case, and

    (c)   the court is satisfied that the dwelling-house is required for occupation by a person employed, or to be employed, by the landlord in agriculture.

For the purposes of this Case "employed", "employment" and "agriculture" have the same meanings as in the Agricultural Wages Act 1948.

Case 17

Where proposals for amalgamation, approved for the purposes of a scheme under section 26 of the Agriculture Act 1967, have been carried out and, at the time when the proposals were submitted, the dwelling-house was occupied by a person responsible (whether as owner, tenant, or servant or agent of another) for the control of the farming of any part of the land comprised in the amalgamation and

(a) after the carrying out of the proposals, the dwelling-house was let on a regulated tenancy otherwise than to, or to the widow of, either a person ceasing to be so responsible as part of the amalgamation or a person who is, or at any time was, employed by the landlord in agriculture, and

(b) not later than the relevant date the tenant was given notice in writing that possession might be recovered under this Case, and

(c) the court is satisfied that the dwelling-house is required for occupation by a person employed, or to be employed, by the landlord in agriculture, and

(d) the proceedings for possession are commenced by the landlord at any time during the period of 5 years beginning with the date on which the proposals for the amalgamation were approved or, if occupation of the dwelling-house after the amalgamation continued in, or was first taken by, a person ceasing to be responsible as mentioned in paragraph (a) above or his widow, during a period expiring 3 years after the date on which the dwelling-house next became unoccupied.

For the purposes of this Case "employed" and "agriculture" have the same meanings as in the Agricultural Wages Act 1948 and "amalgamation" has the same meaning as in Part II of the Agriculture Act 1967.

Case 18

Where—

(a) the last occupier of the dwelling-house before the relevant date was a person, or the widow of a person, who was at some time during his occupation responsible (whether as owner, tenant, or servant or agent of another) for the control of the farming of land which formed, together with the dwelling-house, an agricultural unit within the meaning of the Agriculture Act 1947, and

(b) the tenant is neither—

(i) a person, or the widow of a person, who is or has at any time been responsible for the control of the farming of any part of the said land, nor

(ii) a person, or the widow of a person, who is or at any time was employed by the landlord in agriculture, and

(c) the creation of the tenancy was not preceded by the carrying out in connection with any of the said land of an amalgamation approved for the purposes of a scheme under section 26 of the Agriculture Act 1967, and

(d) not later than the relevant date the tenant was given notice in writing that possession might be recovered under this Case, and

(e) the court is satisfied that the dwelling-house is required for occupation either by a person responsible or to be responsible (whether as owner, tenant, or servant or agent of another) for the control of the farming of any part of the said land or by a person employed or to be employed by the landlord in agriculture, and

(f) in a case where the relevant date was before 9th August 1972, the proceedings for possession are commenced by the landlord before the expiry of 5 years from the date on which the occupier referred to in paragraph (a) above went out of occupation.

For the purposes of this Case "employed" and "agriculture" have the same meanings as in the Agricultural Wages Act 1948 and "amalgamation" has the same meaning as in Part II of the Agriculture Act 1967.

Case 19

Where the dwelling-house was let under a protected shorthold tenancy (or is treated under section 55 of the Housing Act 1980 as having been so let) and—

(a) there either has been no grant of a further tenancy of the dwelling-house since the end of the protected shorthold tenancy or, if there was such a grant, it was to a person who immediately before the grant was in possession of the dwelling-house as a protected or statutory tenant; and

(b)   the proceedings for possession were commenced after appropriate notice by the landlord to the tenant and not later than 3 months after the expiry of the notice.
A notice is appropriate for this Case if—

(i)   it is in writing and states that proceedings for possession under this Case may be brought after its expiry; and

(ii)   it expires not earlier than 3 months after it is served nor, if, when it is served, the tenancy is a periodic tenancy, before that periodic tenancy could be brought to an end by a notice to quit served by the landlord on the same day;

(iii)   it is served—

(a)   in the period of 3 months immediately preceding the date on which the protected shorthold tenancy comes to an end; or

(b)   if that date has passed, in the period of 3 months immediately preceding any anniversary of that date; and

(iv)   in a case where a previous notice has been served by the landlord on the tenant in respect of the dwelling-house, and that notice was an appropriate notice, it is served not earlier than 3 months after the expiry of the previous notice.

Case 20

Where the dwelling-house was let by a person (in this Case referred to as "the owner") at any time after the commencement of section 67 of the Housing Act 1980 and—

(a)   at the time when the owner acquired the dwelling-house he was a member of the regular armed forces of the Crown;

(b)   at the relevant date the owner was a member of the regular armed forces of the Crown;

(c)   not later than the relevant date the owner gave notice in writing to the tenant that possession might be recovered under this Case;

(d)   the dwelling-house has not, since the commencement of section 67 of the Act of 1980 been let by the owner on a protected tenancy with respect to which the condition mentioned in paragraph (c) above was not satisfied; and

(e)   the court is of the opinion that—

(i)   the dwelling-house is required as a residence for the owner; or

(ii)   of the conditions set out in Part V of this Schedule one of those in paragraphs (c) to (f) is satisfied.

If the court is of the opinion that, notwithstanding that the condition in paragraph (c) or (d) above is not complied with, it is just and equitable to make an order for possession of the dwelling-house, the court may dispense with the requirements of either or both of these paragraphs, as the case may require.

For the purposes of this Case "regular armed forces of the Crown" has the same meaning as in section 1 of the House of Commons Disqualification Act 1975.

PART III
PROVISIONS APPLICABLE TO CASE 9 AND PART II OF THIS SCHEDULE

Provision for Case 9

1.   A court shall not make an order for possession of a dwelling-house by reason only that the circumstances of the case fall within Case 9 in Part I of this Schedule if the court is satisfied that, having regard to all the circumstances of the case, including the question whether other accommodation is available for the landlord or the tenant, greater hardship would be caused by granting the order than by refusing to grant it.

Provision for Part II

2.   Any reference in Part II of this Schedule to the relevant date shall be construed as follows:—

(a)   except in a case falling within paragraph (b) or (c) below, if the protected tenancy, or, in the case of a statutory tenancy, the previous contractual tenancy, was created before 8th December 1965, the relevant date means 7th June 1966; and

(b)   except in a case falling within paragraph (c) below, if the tenancy became a regulated tenancy by virtue of section 14 of the Counter-Inflation Act 1973 and the tenancy or, in the case of a statutory tenancy, the previous contractual tenancy, was created before 22nd March 1973, the relevant date means 22nd September 1973; and

(c)   in the case of a regulated furnished tenancy, if the tenancy or, in the case of a statutory furnished tenancy, the previous contractual tenancy was created before 14th August 1974, the relevant date means 13th February 1975; and

(d)   in any other case, the relevant date means the date of the commencement of the regulated tenancy in question.

PART IV
SUITABLE ALTERNATIVE ACCOMMODATION

3.   For the purposes of section 98(1)(a) of this Act, a certificate of the local housing authority for the district in which the dwelling-house in question is situated, certifying that the authority will provide suitable alternative accommodation for the tenant by a date specified in the certificate, shall be conclusive evidence that suitable alternative accommodation will be available for him by that date.

4.—(1)   Where no such certificate as is mentioned in paragraph 3 above is produced to the court, accommodation shall be deemed to be suitable for the purposes of section 98(1)(a) of this Act if it consists of either—

(a)   premises which are to be let as a separate dwelling such that they will then be let on a protected tenancy (other than one under which the landlord might recover possession of the dwelling-house under one of the Cases in Part II of this Schedule), or

(b)   premises to be let as a separate dwelling on terms which will, in the opinion of the court, afford to the tenant security of tenure reasonably equivalent to the security afforded by Part VII of this Act in the case of a protected tenancy of a kind mentioned in paragraph (a) above,

and, in the opinion of the court, the accommodation fulfils the relevant conditions as defined in paragraph 5 below.

5.—(1)   For the purposes of paragraph 4 above, the relevant conditions are that the accommodation is reasonably suitable to the needs of the tenant and his family as regards proximity to place of work, and either—

(a)   similar as regards rental and extent to the accommodation afforded by dwelling-houses provided in the neighbourhood by any local housing authority for persons whose needs as regards extent are, in the opinion of the court, similar to those of the tenant and of his family; or

(b)   reasonably suitable to the means of the tenant and to the needs of the tenant and his family as regards extent and character; and

that if any furniture was provided for use under the protected or statutory tenancy in question, furniture is provided for use in the accommodation which is either similar to that so provided or is reasonably suitable to the needs of the tenant and his family.

(2)   For the purposes of sub-paragraph (1)(a) above, a certificate of a local housing authority stating—

(a)   the extent of the accommodation afforded by dwelling-houses provided by the authority to meet the needs of tenants with families of such number as may be specified in the certificate, and

(b)   the amount of the rent charged by the authority for dwelling-houses affording accommodation of that extent,
shall be conclusive evidence of the facts so stated.

6.   Accommodation shall not be deemed to be suitable to the needs of the tenant and his family if the result of their occupation of the accommodation would be that it would be an overcrowded dwelling-house for the purposes of Part X of the Housing Act 1985.

7.   Any document purporting to be a certificate of a local housing authority named therein issued for the purposes of this Schedule and to be signed by the proper officer of that authority shall be received in evidence and, unless the contrary is shown, shall be deemed to be such a certificate without further proof.

8.   In this Part "local housing authority" and "district" in relation to such an authority have the same meaning as in the Housing Act 1985.

PART V
Provisions applying to Cases 11, 12 and 20

1.   In this Part of this Schedule—
"mortgage" includes a charge and "mortgagee" shall be construed accordingly;
"owner" means, in relation to Case 11, the owner-occupier; and
"successor in title" means any person deriving title from the owner, other than a purchaser for value or a person deriving title from a purchaser for value.

2.   The conditions referred to in paragraph (c) in each of Cases 11 and 12 and in paragraph (e)(ii) of Case 20 are that—
(a)   the dwelling-house is required as a residence for the owner or any member of his family who resided with the owner when he last occupied the dwelling-house as a residence;
(b)   the owner has retired from regular employment and requires the dwelling-house as a residence;
(c)   the owner has died and the dwelling-house is required as a residence for a member of his family who was residing with him at the time of his death;
(d)   the owner has died and the dwelling-house is required by a successor in title as his residence or for the purpose of disposing of it with vacant possession;
(e)   the dwelling-house is subject to a mortgage, made by deed and granted before the tenancy, and the mortgagee—
(i)   is entitled to exercise a power of sale conferred on him by the mortgage or by section 101 of the Law of Property Act 1925; and
(ii)   requires the dwelling-house for the purpose of disposing of it with vacant possession in exercise of that power; and
(f)   the dwelling-house is not reasonably suitable to the needs of the owner, having regard to his place of work, and he requires it for the purpose of disposing of it with vacant possession and of using the proceeds of that disposal in acquiring, as his residence, a dwelling-house which is more suitable to those needs.

Section 99.   SCHEDULE 16

FURTHER GROUNDS FOR POSSESSION OF DWELLING-HOUSES LET ON OR SUBJECT TO TENANCIES TO WHICH SECTION 99 APPLIES

CASE I
Alternative accommodation not provided or arranged by housing authority

1.   The court is satisfied that suitable alternative accommodation is available for the tenant, or will be available for him when the order for possession takes effect.

2.   Accommodation shall be deemed suitable in this Case if it consists of—
   (a)   premises which are to be let as a separate dwelling such that they will then be let on a protected tenancy, or
   (b)   premises which are to be let as a separate dwelling on terms which will, in the opinion of the court, afford to the tenant security of tenure reasonably equivalent to the security afforded by Part VII of this Act in the case of a protected tenancy,
and, in the opinion of the court, the accommodation fulfils the conditions in paragraph 3 below.

3.—(1)   The accommodation must be reasonably suitable to the needs of the tenant and his family as regards proximity to place of work and either—
   (a)   similar as regards rental and extent to the accommodation afforded by dwelling-houses provided in the neighbourhood by the housing authority concerned for persons whose needs as regards extent are similar to those of the tenant and his family, or
   (b)   reasonably suitable to the means of the tenant, and to the needs of the tenant and his family as regards extent and character.
   (2)   For the purposes of sub-paragraph (1)(a) above, a certificate of the housing authority concerned stating—
   (a)   the extent of the accommodation afforded by dwelling-houses provided by the authority to meet the needs of tenants with families of such number as may be specified in the certificate, and
   (b)   the amount of the rent charged by the local housing authority concerned for dwelling-houses affording accommodation of that extent,
shall be conclusive evidence of the facts so stated.
   (3)   If any furniture was provided by the landlord for use under the tenancy, furniture must be provided for use in the alternative accommodation which is either similar, or is reasonably suitable to the needs of the tenant and his family.

4.   Accommodation shall not be deemed to be suitable to the needs of the tenant and his family if the result of their occupation of the accommodation would be that it would be an overcrowded dwelling-house for the purposes of Part X of the Housing Act 1985.

5.   Any document purporting to be a certificate of the local housing authority concerned issued for the purposes of this Case and to be signed by the proper officer of the authority shall be received in evidence and, unless the contrary is shown, shall be deemed to be such a certificate without further proof.

6.   In this Case no account shall be taken of accommodation as respects which an offer has been made, or notice has been given, as mentioned in paragraph 1 of Case II below.

7.   In this Case and in Case II below "the local housing authority" has the same meaning as in the Housing Act 1985.

CASE II
Alternative accommodation provided or arranged by housing authority

1.   The local housing authority concerned have made an offer in writing to the tenant of alternative accommodation which appears to them to be suitable, specifying the date when the accommodation will be available and the date (not being less than 14 days from the date of offer) by which the offer must be accepted.

OR

The local housing authority concerned have given notice in writing to the tenant that they have received from a person specified in the notice an offer in writing to rehouse the tenant in alternative accommodation which appears to the housing authority concerned to be suitable, and the notice specifies both the date when the accommodation will be available and the date (not being less than 14 days from the date when the notice was given to the tenant) by which the offer must be accepted.

2.   The landlord shows that the tenant accepted the offer (by the local housing authority or other person) within the time duly specified in the offer.

OR

The landlord shows that the tenant did not so accept the offer, and the tenant does not satisfy the court that he acted reasonably in failing to accept the offer.

3.—(1)   The accommodation offered must in the opinion of the court fulfil the conditions of this paragraph.

(2)   The accommodation must be reasonably suitable to the needs of the tenant and his family as regards proximity to place of work.

(3)   The accommodation must be reasonably suitable to the means of the tenant, and to the needs of the tenant and his family as regards extent.

(4)   If the accommodation offered is available for a limited period only, the local housing authority's offer or notice under paragraph 1 of this Case must contain an assurance that other accommodation—

   (a)   the availability of which is not so limited,

   (b)   which appears to them to be suitable, and

   (c)   which fulfils the conditions in paragraph 3 above,

will be offered to the tenant as soon as practicable.

Section 18A.   SCHEDULE 17

CONVERTED TENANCIES: MODIFICATION OF ACT

1.   In this Schedule—

"converted tenancy" means a tenancy which has become a regulated tenancy by virtue of any of the enactments mentioned in section 18A of this Act.

"the conversion" means the time when the tenancy became a regulated tenancy.

2.   In relation to any rental period beginning after the conversion, sections 45 to 47 of this Act shall have effect as if references therein to the last contractual period were references to the last rental period beginning before the conversion.

5.   Section 5(1) of this Act shall not apply to the converted tenancy after the conversion.

6.   Section 70 of this Act shall apply in relation to the converted tenancy as if the references in subsection (3) of that section to the tenant under the regulated tenancy included references to the tenant under the tenancy before the conversion.

7.   None of the enactments mentioned in section 18A of this Act shall be taken as affecting any court proceedings, instituted under this Act (or, as the case may be, the Rent Act 1968) before the conversion, which may affect the recoverable rent before the conversion, or the rent under the regulated tenancy after the conversion so far as that depends on the previous rent.

8.   Any court order in any proceedings to which paragraph 7 above applies which is made after the conversion may exclude from the effect of the order rent for any rental period beginning before the conversion, or for any later rental period beginning before the making of the order.

9.   Any right conferred on a tenant by section 38 of, or paragraph 6(4) of Schedule 6 to, this Act to recover any amount by deducting it from rent shall be exercisable by deducting it from rent for any rental period beginning after the conversion to the same extent as the right would have been exercisable if the conversion had not taken place.

Section 120(5), 121, 127(1).   SCHEDULE 18
ALLOWABLE PREMIUMS
PART I
PREMIUM ALLOWED ON ASSIGNMENT OF TENANCY WHERE PREMIUM LAWFULLY PAID ON GRANT

1.—(1) This Part of this Schedule applies where—

(a) a premium was lawfully required and paid, or lawfully received, in respect of the grant, renewal or continuance of a protected tenancy of a dwelling-house which is a regulated tenancy; and

(b) since that grant, renewal or continuance the landlord has not granted a tenancy of the dwelling-house under which, as against the landlord, a person became entitled to possession, other than the person who was so entitled to possession of the dwelling-house immediately before that tenancy began; and

(c) a rent for the dwelling-house is registered under Part IV of this Act and the rent so registered is higher than the rent payable under the tenancy.

(2) Any reference in this Part of this Schedule to a premium does not include a premium which consisted only of any such outgoings, sum or amount as fall within section 120(3) of this Act and, in the case of a premium which included any such outgoings, sum or amount, so much only of the premium as does not consist of those outgoings, sum or amount shall be treated as the premium for the purposes of this Part of this Schedule.

2. In a case where this Part of this Schedule applies, nothing in section 120 of this Act shall prevent any person from requiring or receiving, on an assignment of the protected tenancy referred to in paragraph 1(1)(a) above or any subsequent protected tenancy of the same dwelling-house, a premium which does not exceed an amount calculated (subject to paragraph 4 below) in accordance with the formula—

$$\frac{P \times A}{G}$$

where

P is the premium referred to in paragraph 1(1)(a) above;

A is the length of the period beginning on the date on which the assignment in question takes effect and ending on the relevant date; and

G is the length of the period beginning on the date of the grant, renewal or continuance in respect of which the premium was paid and ending on the relevant date.

3.—(1) If, although the registered rent is higher than the rent payable under the tenancy, the lump sum equivalent of the difference is less than the premium, paragraph 2 above shall have effect as if P were the lump sum equivalent.

(2) For the purposes of this Part of this Schedule, the lump sum equivalent of the difference between the two rents referred to in sub-paragraph (1) above shall be taken to be that difference multiplied by the number of complete rental periods falling within the period beginning with the grant, renewal or continuance in respect of which the premium was paid and ending on the relevant date.

4. Where any rates in respect of the dwelling-house are borne by the landlord or a superior landlord, the amount of the registered rent shall be taken, for the purposes of this Part of this Schedule, to be increased by the amount of the rates so borne in respect of the rental period comprising the date from which the registration took effect.

5.—(1) Any reference in this Part of this Schedule to the relevant date shall be construed in accordance with this paragraph.

(2) Where the tenancy referred to in paragraph 1(1)(a) above was granted, renewed or continued for a term of years certain exceeding 7 years and that term has not expired when the assignment takes effect, the relevant date is the date of the expiry of that term.

(3) In any other case, the relevant date is the date of the expiry of 7 years from the

commencement of the term, or, as the case may be, the renewal or continuance of the term in respect of which the premium was paid.

(4)   For the purposes of this paragraph—

(a)   a term of years shall be treated as certain notwithstanding that it is liable to determination by re-entry or on the happening of any event other than the giving of notice by the landlord to determine the term; and

(b)   a term of years determinable by the landlord giving notice to determine it shall be treated as a term of years certain expiring on the earliest date on which such a notice given after the date of the assignment would be capable of taking effect.

PART II
PREMIUM ALLOWED UNDER SECTIONS 121 AND 127

6.   Where this Part of this Schedule applies to any tenancy and a premium was lawfully required and paid on the grant or an assignment of the tenancy, nothing in section 120 of this Act shall prevent any person from requiring or receiving, on an assignment of the tenancy, the fraction of the premium specified below (without prejudice, however, to his requiring or receiving a greater sum in a case where he may lawfully do so under Part I of this Schedule).

(2)   If there was more than one premium, sub-paragraph (1) above shall apply to the last of them.

7.—(1)   The fraction is $\dfrac{X}{Y}$ where—

X is the residue of the term of the tenancy at the date of the assignment, and

Y is the term for which the tenancy was granted.

(2)   Sub-paragraph (1) above shall apply where a tenancy has been assigned as it applies where a tenancy has been granted and then Y in the fraction shall be the residue, at the date of that assignment, of the term for which the tenancy was granted.

8.   Where the tenancy was granted on the surrender of a previous tenancy, and a premium had been lawfully required and paid on the grant or an assignment of the previous tenancy, the surrender value of the previous tenancy shall be treated, for the purposes of this Part of this Schedule, as a premium, or as the case may be, as part of the premium, paid on the grant of the tenancy.

9.   For the purposes of paragraph 8 above, the surrender value of the previous tenancy shall be taken to be the amount which, had the previous tenancy been assigned instead of being surrendered and had this Part of this Schedule applied to it, would have been the amount that could have been required and received on the assignment in pursuance of this Part of this Schedule.

10.   In determining for the purposes of this Part of this Schedule the amount which may or could have been required and received on the assignment of a tenancy terminable, before the end of the term for which it was granted, by notice to the tenant, that term shall be taken to be a term expiring at the earliest date on which such a notice given after the date of the assignment would have been capable of taking effect.

11.   In this Part of this Schedule "grant" includes continuance and renewal.

Section 140.   SCHEDULE 20

MODIFICATION OF ACT IN RELATION TO FIRE PRECAUTIONS

Steps mentioned in certain notices under the Fire Precautions Act 1971 to count as improvements for certain purposes of this Act

1.—(1)   This paragraph applies where a dwelling which is the subject of a regulated tenancy consists of or is comprised in premises with respect to which there has been issued a fire certificate covering (in whatever terms) the use of the dwelling as a dwelling.

(2)   The amount of any expenditure incurred by the landlord in taking, in relation to the relevant building, a step mentioned in a fire precaution notice served in connection with the premises, shall for the purposes of this Act be treated (whether or not apart from this paragraph it would be so treated) as expenditure incurred by the landlord on an improvement effected in the dwelling.

(3)   If from the taking, in relation to the relevant building, of any such step as is referred to in sub-paragraph (2) above, there accrues benefit not only to the dwelling but also to other premises of the landlord comprised in the relevant building, the amount to be treated as mentioned in that sub-paragraph shall be so much only of the expenditure as may be determined, by agreement in writing between the landlord and the tenant or by the county court, to be properly apportionable to the dwelling, having regard to the benefit accruing, from the taking of the step, to the dwelling and the other premises.

(4)   Any apportionment made by the county court under sub-paragraph (3) above shall be final.

(5)   For the purposes of this paragraph, the amount of any expenditure shall be treated as diminished by the amount of any grant paid in respect of that expenditure under any enactment.

2.—(1)   This paragraph applies in relation to a dwelling-house consisting of or comprised in premises—

(a)   with respect to which there has been issued a fire certificate covering (in whatever terms) the use of the dwelling-house as a dwelling; or

(b)   which are the subject of an application for a fire certificate specifying as a use of the premises which it is desired to have covered by the certificate a use such that, if a certificate covering that use were issued, it would cover (in whatever terms) the use of the dwelling-house as a dwelling.

Cases where rent is increased by virtue of section 28(3)(b) of the Act of 1971

3.—(1)   This paragraph applies where, in the case of any premises consisting of a dwelling-house let on a protected tenancy which is a regulated tenancy, the rent payable in respect of the premises is increased by a section 28 order.

(2)   If the increase takes effect while a rent for the dwelling-house is registered under Part IV of this Act, and was so registered before the completion of the relevant alterations—

(a)   the contractual rent limit for any contractual period beginning while the registration of that rent continues to have effect shall be what it would be for that period under section 44(1) of this Act if the rent so registered had been simultaneously increased by the same amount (and the reference in section 71(3)(a) of this Act to the limit imposed by section 44(1) shall be construed accordingly); and

(b)   if the regulated tenancy of the dwelling-house becomes a statutory tenancy, section 45(2) of this Act shall have effect, in relation to any statutory period of that tenancy beginning while the registration of that rent continues to have effect, as if the rent so registered had been simultaneously increased by the same amount;

(3)   Where the rent payable under a tenancy to which Part VI of this Act applies is increased by a section 28 order, the rent limit for the dwelling-house under Part VI (including the rent limit specified in a direction of the Secretary of State) shall be increased by an amount equal to the increase effected by the order in the rent payable for the rental period in question.

(4)   If, at any time after the court order takes effect, a rent is registered for the dwelling-house (whether it is the first or any subsequent registration) sub-paragraph (2) above shall not apply to any rental period beginning after that time.

Interpretation

5.　In this Schedule—

"contractual period" means a rental period of a regulated tenancy which is a period beginning before the expiry or termination of the protected tenancy;

"contractual rent limit" has the meaning assigned to it by section 44(3) of this Act;

"fire certificate" has the meaning given in section 1(1) of the Fire Precautions Act 1971;

"fire precautions notice" means a notice served under section 5(4), 8(4) or (5) or 12(8)(b) of the Act of 1971;

"landlord" includes a superior landlord;

"relevant alterations" means the alterations or other things falling within section 28(3) of the Act of 1971 the expense of which was taken into account by the court in making a section 28 order;

"section 28 order" means an order made by a court by virtue of section 28(3)(b) of the Act of 1971; and

"statutory period" means any rental period of a regulated tenancy which is not a contractual period.

Section 155(3). SCHEDULE 24

SAVINGS AND TRANSITIONAL PROVISIONS

General transitional provisions

1.—(1)　In so far as anything done, or having effect as if done, under an enactment repealed by this Act could have been done under a corresponding provision in this Act, it shall not be invalidated by the repeal but shall have effect as if done under that provision.

(2)　Sub-paragraph (1) above applies, in particular, to any regulation, order, scheme, agreement, dissent, election, application, reference, representation, appointment or apportionment made, notice served, certificate issued, statement supplied, undertaking or direction given or rent registered.

(3)　Subject to this Schedule, any document made, served or issued before the passing of this Act or at any time thereafter (whether before or after the commencement of this Act) and containing a reference to an enactment repealed by this Act, or having effect as if containing such a reference, shall, except in so far as a contrary intention appears, be construed as referring, or as the context requires, as including a reference, to the corresponding provision of this Act.

(4)　Where a period of time specified in an enactment repealed by this Act is current at the commencement of this Act, this Act shall have effect as if the corresponding provision thereof had been in force when that period began to run.

(5)　Nothing in this Act shall affect the enactments repealed thereby in their operation in relation to offences committed before the commencement of this Act.

(6)　A conviction for an offence under an enactment repealed by this Act shall be treated for the purposes of this Act as a conviction of an offence under the corresponding provision of this Act.

(7)　Subject to the provisions of this Act, any reference in any document or enactment to a dwelling-house which is let on or subject to a protected or statutory tenancy (including any reference which, immediately before the commencement of this Act, was to be construed as such a reference by virtue of paragraph 5 of Schedule 16 to the Rent Act 1968) shall be construed, except in so far as the context otherwise requires, as a reference to a dwelling-house let on or subject to a protected or statutory tenancy within the meaning of this Act.

(8) Subject to the provisions of this Act, any reference in any document or enactment to a Part VI contract (within the meaning of Part VI of the Rent Act 1968) shall be construed, except in so far as the context otherwise requires, as a reference to a restricted contract.

Existing statutory tenants

2.—(1) If, immediately before the commencement of this Act, a person (the "existing statutory tenant") was a statutory tenant of a dwelling-house by virtue of any enactment repealed by this Act (a "repealed enactment") that person shall, on the commencement of this Act, be a statutory tenant of the dwelling-house for the purposes of this Act.

(2) If, immediately before the existing statutory tenant became a statutory tenant, he was a tenant of the dwelling-house under a tenancy then, for the purposes of this Act, he shall be the statutory tenant by virtue of his previous protected tenancy.

(3) If the existing statutory tenant became a statutory tenant on the death of a person who was himself a tenant or statutory tenant of the dwelling-house then, for the purposes of this Act, the existing statutory tenant shall be a statutory tenant by succession; and, unless he became a statutory tenant by virtue of section 13 of the Rent Act 1965, or paragraph 6 or 7 of Schedule 1 to the Rent Act 1968, he shall be deemed to be the first successor within the meaning of Schedule 1 to this Act.

(4) If the existing statutory tenant became a statutory tenant by virtue of an exchange under section 17 of the Rent Act 1957 or section 14 of the Rent Act 1968 then, for the purposes of this Act, he shall be deemed to be the statutory tenant by virtue of his previous protected tenancy or, as the case may be, a statutory tenant by succession, if immediately before the commencement of this Act he was so deemed for the purposes of the Rent Act 1968.

(5) If, by virtue of sub-paragraph (4) above, the existing statutory tenant is for the purposes of this Act a statutory tenant by succession, he shall be deemed to be the first successor, within the meaning of Schedule 1 to this Act if, and only if, the person who was a statutory tenant immediately before the date of exchange was not a statutory tenant by virtue of section 13 of the Rent Act 1965 or paragraph 6 or 7 of Schedule 1 to the Rent Act 1968.

(6) Without prejudice to the case where by virtue of sub-paragraph (4) or (5) above, the existing statutory tenant is deemed to be a statutory tenant by succession but is not deemed to be the first successor, within the meaning of Schedule 1 to this Act, paragraphs 5 to 7 of that Schedule shall not apply where the existing statutory tenant, or the person on whose death he became a statutory tenant, became a statutory tenant by virtue of an exchange under section 17 of the Rent Act 1957 or section 14 of the Rent Act 1968.

3.—(1) A person who, at any time before the commencement of this Act, became a statutory tenant of a dwelling-house by virtue of—

(a) section 12(10) of the Increase of Rent and Mortgage Interest (Restrictions) Act 1920 (under which workmen housed in certain dwelling-houses taken over by the Government during the 1914-18 war were to be treated as tenants of the landlords of those houses); and

(b) section 4 of the Requisitioned Houses and Housing (Amendment) Act 1955 (under which certain requisitioned dwelling-houses were returned to their owners on condition that the owners accepted the existing licensees as statutory tenants),

(and not by way of succession to a previous statutory tenancy) shall be treated for the purposes of this Act as having become the statutory tenant of that dwelling-house on the expiry of a protected tenancy thereof.

(2) A person who, on or after the commencement of the Rent Act 1965, retained possession of a dwelling-house by virtue of section 20 of that Act (which made

transitional provisions in relation to tenancies which expired before the commencement of that Act) shall be deemed to have done so under a statutory tenancy arising on the termination of a tenancy which was a regulated tenancy, and the terms as to rent and otherwise of that tenancy shall be deemed to have been the same, subject to any variation specified by the court, as those of the tenancy mentioned in subsection (1) of that section (that is to say, the tenancy which ended before the commencement of the Rent Act 1965 but which would have been a regulated tenancy if that Act had then been in force).

4.   A statutory tenancy subsisting at the commencement of this Act under section 4 of the Requisitioned Houses and Housing (Amendment) Act 1955 shall be treated, for the purposes of this Act—

(a)   as a regulated tenancy if, by virtue of section 10 of the Rent Act 1965, it fell to be treated as a regulated tenancy after 31st March 1966; and

(b)   in any other case, as a controlled tenancy.

Tenancies which ended before passing of Counter-Inflation Act 1973 (c. 9)

5.—(1)   This paragraph applies where the tenancy of a dwelling-house came to an end at a time before 22nd March 1973 and the tenancy would have been a regulated tenancy, for the purposes of the Rent Act 1968, if section 14 of the Counter-Inflation Act 1973 had been in force at that time.

(2)   If the tenant under the tenancy which came to an end duly retained possession of the dwelling-house after 22nd March 1973 without any order for possession having been made, or after the rescission of such an order, he shall be deemed to have done so under a statutory tenancy arising on the termination of the tenancy which came to an end and, subject to sub-paragraph (6) below the terms of that tenancy (including the rent) shall be deemed to have been the same as those of the tenancy which came to an end.

(3)   Any statutory tenancy arising by virtue of sub-paragraph (2) above, shall be treated as a statutory tenancy arising on the termination of a protected tenancy which was a regulated tenancy.

(4)   Where Article 10 of the Counter-Inflation (Rents) (England and Wales) Order 1972 applied to the rent under the tenancy, the rent under the tenancy imposed by sub-paragraph (2) above shall be the rent as limited by Article 10.

(5)   Schedule 7 to this Act shall not apply to a statutory tenancy arising under sub-paragraph (2) above.

(6)   The High Court or the county court may by order vary all or any of the terms of the tenancy imposed by sub-paragraph (2) above in any way appearing to the court to be just and equitable (and whether or not in a way authorised by the provisions of sections 46 and 47 of this Act).

(7)   If at 22nd March 1973 the dwelling-house was occupied by a person who would, if the tenancy had been a regulated tenancy, have been the "first successor" within the meaning of paragraph 4 of Schedule 1 to the Rent Act 1968 (which is re-enacted in Schedule 1 to this Act), sub-paragraphs (2), (4) and (5) above shall apply where that person retained possession as they apply where the tenant retained possession.

Protected furnished tenancies

6.—(1)   In any case where—

(a)   before 14th August 1974 a dwelling was subject to a tenancy which was a Part VI contract within the meaning of the Rent Act 1968, and

(b)   the dwelling forms part only of a building, and that building is not a purpose-built block of flats within the meaning of section 12 of this Act, and

(c)   on that date the interest of the lessor, within the meaning of Part VI of the Rent Act 1968, under the tenancy—

(i)   belonged to a person who occupied as his residence another dwelling which also formed part of that building, or

(ii)   was vested in trustees as such and was or, if it was held on trust for sale, the proceeds of its sale were held on trust for a person who occupied as his residence another dwelling which also formed part of that building, and

(d)   apart from paragraph 1 of Schedule 3 to the Rent Act 1974 the tenancy would, on that date, have become a protected furnished tenancy,

this Act shall apply, subject to sub-paragraph (2) below, as if the tenancy had been granted on that date and as if the condition in section 12(1)(b) of this Act were fulfilled in relation to the grant of the tenancy.

(2)   In the application of this Act to a tenancy by virtue of this paragraph—

(a)   subsection (2) of section 12 shall be omitted; and

(b)   in section 20 and Part II of Schedule 2 any reference to section 12 of this Act shall be construed as including a reference to this paragraph.

(3)   In any case where paragraphs (a), (b) and (d) of sub-paragraph (1) above apply but on 14th August 1974 the interest referred to in paragraph (c) of that sub-paragraph was vested—

(a)   in the personal representatives of a deceased person acting in that capacity, or

(b)   by virtue of section 9 of the Administration of Estates Act 1925, in the Probate Judge within the meaning of that Act, or

(c)   in trustees as such.

then, if the deceased immediately before his death or, as the case may be, the settlor immediately before the creation of the trust occupied as his residence another dwelling which also formed part of the building referred to in paragraph (b) of sub-paragraph (1) above, that sub-paragraph shall apply as if the condition in paragraph (c) thereof were fulfilled.

(4)   In the application of paragraph 1(c) of Schedule 2 to this Act in a case falling within sub-paragraph (3) above, any period before 14th August 1974 during which the interest of the landlord vested as mentioned in that subsection shall be disregarded in calculating the period of 12 months specified therein.

7.—(1)   This paragraph applies where the tenancy of a dwelling-house came to an end before 14th August 1974 and, if it had come to an end immediately after that date it would then have been a protected furnished tenancy within the meaning of the Rent Act 1974.

(2)   If the tenant under the tenancy which came to an end duly retained possession of the dwelling-house on 14th August 1974 without an order for possession having been made or after the rescission of such an order he shall be deemed to have done so as a statutory tenant under a regulated tenancy and, subject to sub-paragraph (5) below, as a person who became a statutory tenant on the termination of a protected tenancy under which he was the tenant; and, subject to sub-paragraphs (4) and (5) below, the tenancy referred to in sub-paragraph (1) above shall be treated, in relation to his statutory tenancy,—

(a)   as the original contractual tenancy for the purposes of section 3 of this Act, and

(b)   as the previous contractual tenancy for the purposes of paragraph 2 of Part III of Schedule 15 to this Act.

(3)   In any case where—

(a)   immediately before 14th August 1974 a rent was registered for a dwelling under Part VI of the Rent Act 1968, and

(b)   on that date a person became a statutory tenant of that dwelling by virtue of paragraph 3(4) of Schedule 3 to the Rent Act 1974,

the amount which was so registered under Part VI shall be deemed to be registered under Part IV of this Act as the rent for that dwelling and that registration shall be deemed to have taken effect on 14th August 1974.

(4)   The High Court or the county court may by order vary all or any of the terms of the statutory tenancy imposed by sub-paragraph (2) above in any way appearing to the court to be just and equitable (and whether or not in a way authorised by the provisions of sections 46 and 47 of this Act).

(5)   If on 14th August 1974 the dwelling-house was occupied by a person who would, if the tenancy had been a protected tenancy for the purposes of the Rent Act 1968, have been "the first successor" as defined in paragraph 4 of Schedule 1 to that Act, sub-paragraph (2) above shall apply where that person retained possession as it applies where the tenant retained possession, except that he shall be the first successor as so defined.

8.—(1)   Where, immediately before the commencement of this Act, a rent was deemed (by virtue of section 5 of the Rent Act 1974) to have been registered under Part IV of the Rent Act 1968 with effect from 14th August 1974, it shall for the purposes of this Act be deemed to be registered under Part IV of this Act with effect from that date.

(2)   Section 67(3) of this Act shall not apply to an application for the registration under Part IV of this Act of a rent different from that which is deemed to be registered as mentioned in sub-paragraph (1) above.

(4)   A statutory furnished tenancy which arose on 15th August 1974, by virtue of section 5(4) of the Rent Act 1974, shall be treated as a statutory furnished tenancy for the purposes of this Act and as having arisen on that date.

Regulated tenancies of formerly requisitioned houses

9.—(1)   This paragraph applies in relation to a regulated tenancy of a dwelling-house which is a statutory tenancy subsisting under section 4 of the Requisitioned Houses and Housing (Amendment) Act 1955 (under which licensees of previously requisitioned property became statutory tenants of the owners) and which, by virtue of section 10(1) of the Rent Act 1965, fell to be treated as a regulated tenancy after 31st March 1966.

(2)   In relation to any rental period of a regulated tenancy to which this paragraph applies, sections 45 to 48 of this Act shall have effect as if—

(a)   references therein to the last contractual period were references to the last rental period beginning before 31st March 1966, and

(b)   the rent recoverable for that last rental period has included any sum payable for that period by the local authority to the landlord under section 4(4) of the said Act of 1955 (which provided for payments to make up the difference between the rent actually paid and the amount which would normally have been recoverable).

Miscellaneous

10.   Any registration of a rent under Part IV of the Rent Act 1968 which, by virtue of paragraph 33(2) of Schedule 13 to the Housing Act 1974, fell to be treated as if it had been effected pursuant to an application under section 44 of the Rent Act 1968 shall continue to be so treated for the purposes of this Act.

11.   In the case of a registration of a rent before 1st January 1973 which, by virtue of subsection (3) of section 82 of the Housing Finance Act 1972 (provision corresponding to section 87(3) of this Act), was provisional only, the date of registration for the purposes of this Act shall be 1st January 1973.

12.   Where, by virtue of section 1(1)(b) of the Rent Act 1974, any reference in an enactment or instrument was, immediately before the coming into force of this Act, to be construed as having the same meaning as in the Rent Act 1968 as amended by section 1 of the Rent Act 1974, that reference shall be construed as having the same meaning as in this Act.

13.   If, immediately before the commencement of this Act, a person's statutory tenancy was a regulated tenancy (and not a controlled tenancy), for the purposes of the

Rent Act 1968, by virtue of paragraph 5 of Schedule 2 to that Act (second successors) it shall be a regulated tenancy for the purposes of this Act by virtue of that paragraph.

14. If, immediately before the commencement of this Act, a person's statutory tenancy was a regulated tenancy for the purposes of the Rent Act 1968, by virtue of paragraph 10 of Schedule 16 to that Act (statutory tenancies deemed to arise by virtue of section 20 of the Rent Act 1965) it shall be a regulated tenancy for the purposes of this Act.

15. In relation to any time before 1st January 1960, paragraph (a) of section 34(1) of this Act shall have effect as if it included a reference to section 150 of the Public Health Act 1875 and to the Private Street Works Act 1892.

16. Sections 44(1), 45(2), 57 and 72(7) of this Act shall have effect in relation to rent determined or confirmed in pursuance of Schedule 3 to the Housing Rents and Subsidies Act 1975.

17. If, immediately before the revocation of regulation 68CB of the Defence (General) Regulations 1939 accommodation was registered for the purposes of that regulation and was let in accordance with the terms and conditions so registered, any contract for the letting of the accommodation shall be treated, for the purposes of this Act, as not being a restricted contract, so long as any letting continues under which the accommodation was let in accordance with the terms and conditions on which it was let immediately before the revocation.

18. Section 54 of, and paragraph 5 of Schedule 9 to, this Act shall apply in relation to a failure to observe any of the requirements of section 43, 44(5) or 45 of the Housing Finance Act 1972 as they apply in relation to a failure to observe any of the corresponding requirements of section 51, 52(6) or 53 of this Act.

20. For the purposes of paragraph 3(3) of Schedule 9 to this Act a case where Schedule 2 to the Housing Rents and Subsidies Act 1975 had effect shall be treated as if it were a case where Schedule 8 to this Act had effect.

21. Subject to the provisions of this Act, any reference in any document or enactment to a Part VI letting (within the meaning of Part II of the Housing Finance Act 1972) shall be construed, except in so far as the context otherwise requires, as a reference to a restricted letting (within the meaning of Part II as amended by this Act).

Transitional provisions from Rent Act 1957

22. If the rent recoverable under a controlled tenancy for any rental period beginning immediately before the commencement of this Act was, by virtue of section 1(4) of the Rent Act 1957 and paragraph 15 of Schedule 16 to the Rent Act 1968, the same as the rent recoverable for the rental period comprising the commencement of the Act of 1957 then, after the commencement of this Act, that rent shall remain the rent recoverable under that tenancy for any rental period for which it is neither increased nor reduced under Part II of this Act (but without prejudice to paragraph 1 of this Schedule).

23. If, immediately before the commencement of this Act, an agreement or determination of a tribunal made or given for the purposes of paragraph (b) of section 24(3) of the Housing Repairs and Rents Act 1954 was deemed, by virtue of paragraph 1 of Schedule 7 to the Rent Act 1957 and paragraph 16 of Schedule 16 to the Rent Act 1968, to be an agreement or determination made under paragraph (c) of section 52(1) of the Act of 1968 then, after the commencement of this Act, that agreement or determination shall, until an agreement or determination is made as is mentioned in paragraph (c) of section 27(1) of this Act, be deemed to be an agreement or determination made as mentioned in paragraph (c) of section 27(1).

24.—(1) If, immediately before the commencement of this Act, the rent limit under a controlled tenancy of a dwelling was increased, by virtue of paragraph 2 of Schedule 7 to the Rent Act 1957 and paragraph 17 of Schedule 16 to the Rent Act 1968, on account of an improvement, or a notice of increase relating to an improvement, completed before the commencement of the Act of 1957, the like increase shall apply after the commencement of this Act to the rent limit under that controlled tenancy.

(2)   In sub-paragraph (1) above, "the rent limit", in relation to any time before the commencement of this Act, has the same meaning as in the Rent Act 1968, and in relation to any time after that commencement, has the same meaning as in Part II of this Act.

25.—(1)   If, immediately before the commencement of this Act, a certificate of a local authority under section 26(1) of the Housing Repairs and Rents Act 1954 or a certificate of a sanitary authority having effect as if it were a certificate under Part II of that Act had effect, by virtue of paragraph 3 of Schedule 7 to the Rent Act 1957 and paragraph 18 of Schedule 16 to the Rent Act 1968, as a certificate of disrepair under Schedule 9 to the Act of 1968, then, after the commencement of this Act, the certificate shall have effect, to the like extent as before that commencement, as if it were a certificate of disrepair under Schedule 6 to this Act.

(2)   where any such certificate ceases to have effect (whether by virtue of an order of the court or in consequence of being cancelled by the local authority) sections 27 and 28 of this Act shall have effect, in relation to any rental period beginning afer the date as from which the certificate ceases to have effect as if it had ceased to have effect immediately before the basic rental period (within the meaning of Part II of this Act).

26.   Where any increase in the rent recoverable under a controlled tenancy current on 6th July 1957 took effect before that date but after the beginning of the basic rental period (within the meaning of Part II of this Act), section 27 of this Act shall have effect as if for references to the rent recoverable for the basic rental period there were substituted references to the rent which would have been recoverable for that period if the increase had taken effect before the beginning thereof.

Savings

27.—(1)   Notwithstanding the repeal by this Act of the Rent Act 1968 and section 42 of the Housing Finance Act 1972—

(a)   sections 20(3) and 21 of the Rent Act 1968 (rent limit where no registered rent) shall continue to apply in relation to a regulated tenancy granted before 1st January 1973 if the rent under the tenancy, as varied by any agreement made before that date, exceeded the rent limit under section 20(3) (with any adjustment under section 21);

(b)   sections 30 (certain regulated tenancies to be disregarded in determining contractual rent limit) and 35 (duty of landlord to supply statement of rent under previous tenancy) of the Rent Act 1968 shall continue to apply in any case where section 20(3)(a) applies by virtue of this paragraph.

(2)   In any case to which section 21 of the Rent Act 1968 applies by virtue of sub-paragraph (1) above, the reference in subsection (5) of that section to the amount expended on the improvement shall be construed as a reference to that amount diminished by the amount of any grant or repayment of the kind mentioned in section 48(2)(a) or (b) of this Act.

(3)   This paragraph shall cease to apply if the landlord and the tenant enter into an agreement which is a rent agreement with a tenant having security of tenure (within the meaning of section 51 of this Act) which complies with the requirements of subsection (4) of that section, or if they provide that this paragraph is not to apply by an agreement conforming with those requirements.

28.—(1)   Section 47 of the Housing Act 1969 (first registration of a rent after issue of qualification certificate) shall continue to have effect as respects an application for the first registration of a rent where the tenancy became a regulated tenancy before the date of the repeal of Part III of that Act by the Housing Finance Act 1972, but with the substitution, for the references to Part IV of the Rent Act 1968 and Schedule 6 to that

Act, of references respectively to Part IV of, and Part II of Schedule 11 to, this Act.

(2)   Paragraph 3 of Schedule 17 to this Act shall apply to a conversion under the said Part III as it applies to a conversion under Part VIII of this Act.

(3)   Notwithstanding the said repeal, section 51(2)(a) of the Act of 1969 shall continue to have effect.

(4)   Sections 45 to 47 of this Act shall have effect in relation to a tenancy which has become a regulated tenancy by virtue of the said Part III as if references therein to the last contractual period were references to the last rental period beginning before the tenancy became a regulated tenancy.

29.   Subsections (2) and (5) of section 48 of this Act shall have effect, in relation to any grant paid under section 30 of the Housing (Financial Provisions) Act 1958 (improvement grants) or section 4 of the House Purchase and Housing Act 1959 (standard grants) in pursuance of an application made before 25th August 1969, as they have effect in relation to any of the grants mentioned in those subsections.

30.   Notwithstanding the repeal by this Act of the Rent Act 1968, the amendments made in other enactments ("the amended enactments") by that Act shall, to the extent that they had effect immediately before the coming into force of this Act, continue to have effect subject to any amendment of any of the amended enactments by this Act.

31.   Any registration of a rent made before the commencement of this Act—

(a)   in the part of the register provided for by section 82 of the Housing Finance Act 1972, and

(b)   in reliance on subsection (3A) of section 44 of the Rent Act 1968,

shall be as valid, and shall have effect, as if this Act had then been in force.

32.   Notwithstanding the repeal by this Act of paragraphs 20 to 26 of Schedule 16 to the Rent Act 1968 (miscellaneous savings) any enactment which, immediately before the commencement of this Act, had effect by virtue of any of those paragraphs shall continue to have effect; and this Act shall have effect in relation to cases falling within any of those paragraphs as the Act of 1968 had effect immediately before the commencement of this Act.

PROTECTION FROM EVICTION ACT 1977
(1977, c. 43)

An Act to consolidate section 16 of the Rent Act 1957 and Part III of the Rent Act 1965, and related enactments.   [29 July 1977]

PART I
UNLAWFUL EVICTION AND HARASSMENT

1.   Unlawful eviction and harassment of occupier.

(1)   In this section 'residential occupier', in relation to any premises, means a person occupying the premises as a residence, whether under a contract or by virtue of any enactment or rule of law giving him the right to remain in occupation or restricting the right of any other person to recover possession of the premises.

(2)   If any person unlawfully deprives the residential occupier of any premises of his occupation of the premises or any part thereof, or attempts to do so, he shall be guilty of an offence unless he proves that he believed, and had reasonable cause to believe, that the residential occupier had ceased to reside in the premises.

(3)   If any person with intent to cause the residential occupier of any premises—

(a)   to give up the occupation of the premises or any part thereof; or

(b)   to refrain from exercising any right or pursuing any remedy in respect of the premises or part thereof;

does acts likely to interfere with the peace or comfort of the residential occupier or members of his household, or persistently withdraws or withholds services reasonably required for the occupation of the premises as a residence he shall be guilty of an offence.

(3A)   Subject to subsection (3B) below, the landlord of a residential occupier or an agent of the landlord shall be guilty of an offence if—

(a)   he does acts likely to interfere with the peace or comfort of the residential occupier or members of his household, or

(b)   he persistently withdraws or withholds services reasonably required for the occupation of the premises in question as a residence,

and (in either case) he knows, or has reasonable cause to believe, that the conduct is likely to cause the residential occupier to give up the occupation of the whole or part of the premises or to refrain from exercising any right or pursuing any remedy in respect of the whole or part of the premises.

(3B)   A person shall not be guilty of an offence under subsection (3A) above if he proves that he had reasonable grounds for doing the acts or withdrawing or withholding the services in question.

(3C)   In subsection (3A) above 'landlord', in relation to a residential occupier of any premises, means the person who, but for—

(a)   the residential occupier's right to remain in occupation of the premises, or

(b)   a restriction on the person's right to recover possession of the premises,

would be entitled to occupation of the premises and any superior landlord under whom that person derives title.

(4)   A person guilty of an offence under this section shall be liable—

(a)   on summary conviction, to a fine not exceeding the prescribed sum or to imprisonment for a term not exceeding six months or to both;

(b)   on conviction on indictment, to a fine or to imprisonment for a term not exceeding two years or to both.

(5)   Nothing in this section shall be taken to prejudice any liability or remedy to which a person guilty of an offence thereunder may be subject in civil proceedings.

(6)   Where an offence under this section committed by a body corporate is proved to have been committed with the consent or connivance of, or to be attributable to any neglect on the part of, any director, manager or secretary or other similar officer of the body corporate or any person who was purporting to act in any such capacity, he as well as the body corporate shall be guilty of that offence and shall be liable to be proceeded against and punished accordingly.

2.   Restriction on re-entry without due process of law.

Where any premises are let as a dwelling on a lease which is subject to a right of re-entry or forfeiture it shall not be lawful to enforce that right otherwise than by proceedings in the court while any person is lawfully residing in the premises or part of them.

3.   Prohibition of eviction without due process of law.

(1)   Where any premises have been let as a dwelling under a tenancy which is neither a statutorily protected tenancy nor an excluded tenancy and—

(a)   the tenancy (in this section referred to as the former tenancy) has come to an end, but

(b)   the occupier continues to reside in the premises or part of them,

it shall not be lawful for the owner to enforce against the occupier, otherwise than by proceedings in the court, his right to recover possession of the premises.

(2)   In this section 'the occupier', in relation to any premises, means any person lawfully residing in the premises or part of them at the termination of the former tenancy.

(2A)   Subsections (1) and (2) above apply in relation to any restricted contract (within the meaning of the Rent Act 1977) which—

(a)   creates a licence; and

(b)   is entered into after the commencement of section 69 of the Housing Act 1980;

as they apply in relation to a restricted contract which creates a tenancy.

(2B)   Subsections (1) and (2) above apply in relation to any premises occupied as a dwelling under a licence, other than an excluded licence, as they apply in relation to premises let as a dwelling under a tenancy, and in those subsections the expressions 'let' and 'tenancy' shall be construed accordingly.

(2C)   References in the preceding provisions of this section and section 4(2A) below to an excluded tenancy do not apply to—

(a)   a tenancy entered into before the date on which the Housing Act 1988 came into force, or

(b)   a tenancy entered into on or after that date but pursuant to a contract made before that date,

but, subject to that, 'excluded tenancy' and 'excluded licence' shall be construed in accordance with section 3A below.

(3)   This section shall, with the necessary modifications, apply where the owner's right to recover possession arises on the death of the tenant under a statutory tenancy within the meaning of the Rent Act 1977 or the Rent (Agriculture) Act 1976.

3A.   Excluded tenancies and licences.

(1)   Any reference in this Act to an excluded tenancy or an excluded licence is a reference to a tenancy or licence which is excluded by virtue of any of the following provisions of this section.

(2)   A tenancy or licence is excluded if—

(a)   under its terms the occupier shares any accommodation with the landlord or licensor; and

(b)   immediately before the tenancy or licence was granted and also at the time it comes to an end, the landlord or licensor occupied as his only or principal home premises of which the whole or part of the shared accommodation formed part.

(3)   A tenancy or licence is also excluded if—

(a)   under its terms the occupier shares any accommodation with a member of the family of the landlord or licensor;

(b)   immediately before the tenancy or licence was granted and also at the time it comes to an end, the member of the family of the landlord or licensor occupied as his only or principal home premises of which the whole or part of the shared accommodation formed part; and

(c)   immediately before the tenancy or licence was granted and also at the time it comes to an end, the landlord or licensor occupied as his only or principal home premises in the same building as the shared accommodation and that building is not a purpose-built block of flats.

(4)   For the purposes of subsections (2) and (3) above, an occupier shares accommodation with another person if he has the use of it in common with that person (whether or not also in common with others) and any reference in those subsections to shared accommodation shall be construed accordingly, and if, in relation to any tenancy or licence, there is at any time more than one person who is the landlord or licensor, any reference in those subsections to the landlord or licensor shall be construed as a reference to any one of those persons.

(5)   In subsections (2) to (4) above—

(a)   'accommodation' includes neither an area used for storage nor a staircase, passage, corridor or other means of access;

(b)   'occupier' means, in relation to a tenancy, the tenant and, in relation to a licence, the licensee; and

(c)   'purpose-built block of flats' has the same meaning as in Part III of Schedule 1 to the Housing Act 1988;

and section 113 of the Housing Act 1985 shall apply to determine whether a person is for the purposes of subsection (3) above a member of another's family as it applies for the purposes of Part IV of that Act.

(6)   A tenancy or licence is excluded if it was granted as a temporary expedient to a person who entered the premises in question or any other premises as a trespasser (whether or not, before the beginning of that tenancy or licence, another tenancy or licence to occupy the premises or any other premises had been granted to him).

(7)   A tenancy or licence is excluded if—

(a)   it confers on the tenant or licensee the right to occupy the premises for a holiday only; or

(b)   it is granted otherwise than for money or money's worth.

(8)   A licence is excluded if it confers rights of occupation in a hostel, within the meaning of the Housing Act 1985, which is provided by—

(a)   the council of a county, district or London Borough, the Common Council of the City of London, the Council of the Isles of Scilly, the Inner London Education Authority, a joint authority within the meaning of the Local Government Act 1985 or a residuary body within the meaning of that Act;

(b)   a development corporation within the meaning of the New Towns Act 1981;

(c)   the Commission for the New Towns;

(d)   an urban development corporation established by an order under section 135 of the Local Government, Planning and Land Act 1980;

(e)   a housing action trust established under Part III of the Housing Act 1988;

(f)   the Development Board for Rural Wales;

(g)   the Housing Corporation or Housing for Wales;

(h)   a housing trust which is a charity or a registered housing association, within the meaning of the Housing Associations Act 1985; or

(i)   any other person who is, or who belongs to a class of person which is, specified in an order made by the Secretary of State.

(9)   The power to make an order under subsection (8)(i) above shall be exercisable by statutory instrument which shall be subject to annulment in pursuance of a resolution of either House of Parliament.

4.   Special provisions for agricultural employees.

(1)   This section shall apply where the tenant under the former tenancy (within the meaning of section 3 of this Act) occupied the premises under the terms of his employment as a person employed in agriculture, as defined in section 1 of the Rent (Agriculture) Act 1976, but is not a statutory tenant as defined in that Act.

(2)   In this section 'the occupier', in relation to any premises means—

(a)   the tenant under the former tenancy; or

(b)   the widow or widower of the tenant under the former tenancy residing with him at his death or, if the former tenant leaves no such widow or widower, any member of his family residing with him at his death.

(2A)   In accordance with section 3(2B) above, any reference in subsections (1) and (2) above to the tenant under the former tenancy includes a reference to the licensee under a licence (other than an excluded licence) which has come to an end (being a licence to occupy premises as a dwelling); and in the following provisions of this section the expressions 'tenancy' and 'rent' and any other expressions referable to a tenancy shall be construed accordingly.

(3)   Without prejudice to any power of the court apart from this section to postpone the operation or suspend the execution of an order for possession, if in proceedings by the owner against the occupier the court makes an order for the possession of the premises the court may suspend the execution of the order on such terms and conditions, including conditions as to the payment by the occupier of arrears of rent, mesne profits and otherwise as the court thinks reasonable.

(4)   Where the order for possession is made within the period of six months

beginning with the date when the former tenancy came to an end, then, without prejudice to any powers of the court under the preceding provisions of this section or apart from this section to postpone the operation or suspend the execution of the order for a longer period, the court shall suspend the execution of the order for the remainder of the said period of six months unless the court—

  (a) is satisfied either—

    (i) that other suitable accommodation is, or will within that period be made, available to the occupier; or

    (ii) that the efficient management of any agricultural land or the efficient carrying on of any agricultural operations would be seriously prejudiced unless the premises are available for occupation by a person employed or to be employed by the owner; or

    (iii) that greater hardship (being hardship in respect of matters other than the carrying on of such a business as aforesaid) would be caused by the suspension of the order until the end of that period than by its execution within that period; or

    (iv) that the occupier, or any person residing or lodging with the occupier, has been causing damage to the premises or has been guilty of conduct which is a nuisance or annoyance to persons occupying other premises; and

  (b) considers that it would be reasonable not to suspend the execution of the order for the remainder of that period.

  (5) Where the court suspends the execution of an order for possession under subsection (4) above it shall do so on such terms and conditions, including conditions as to the payment by the occupier of arrears of rent, mesne profits and otherwise as the court thinks reasonable.

  (6) A decision of the court not to suspend the execution of the order under subsection (4) above shall not prejudice any other power of the court to postpone the operation or suspend the execution of the order for the whole or part of the period of six months mentioned in that subsection.

  (7) Where the court has, under the preceding provisions of this section, suspended the execution of an order for possession, it may from time to time vary the period of suspension or terminate it and may vary any terms and conditions imposed by virtue of this section.

  (8) In considering whether or how to exercise powers under subsection (3) above, the court shall have regard to all the circumstances and, in particular, to—

  (a) whether other suitable accommodation is or can be made available to the occupier;

  (b) whether the efficient management of any agricultural land or the efficient carrying on of any agricultural operations would be seriously prejudiced unless the premises were available for occupation by a person employed or to be employed by the owner; and

  (c) whether greater hardship would be caused by the suspension of the execution of the order than by its execution without suspension or further suspension.

  (9) Where in proceedings for the recovery of possession of the premises the court makes an order for possession but suspends the execution of the order under this section, it shall make no order for costs, unless it appears to the court, having regard to the conduct of the owner or of the occupier, that there are special reasons for making such an order.

  (10) Where, in the case of an order for possession of the premises to which subsection (4) above applies, the execution of the order is not suspended under that subsection or, the execution of the order having been so suspended, the suspension is terminated, then, if it is subsequently made to appear to the court that the failure to suspend the execution of the order or, as the case may be, the termination of the suspension was—

(a)   attributable to the provisions of paragraph (a)(ii) of subsection (4), and

(b)   due to misrepresentation or concealment of material facts by the owner of the premises,

the court may order the owner to pay to the occupier such sum as appears sufficient as compensation for damage or loss sustained by the occupier as a result of that failure or termination.

PART II
NOTICE TO QUIT

5.   Validity of notices to quit.

(1)   Subject to subsection (1B) below no notice by a landlord or a tenant to quit any premises let (whether before or after the commencement of this Act) as a dwelling shall be valid unless—

(a)   it is in writing and contains such information as may be prescribed, and

(b)   it is given not less than four weeks before the date on which it is to take effect.

(1A)   Subject to subsection (1B) below, no notice by a licensor or a licensee to determine a periodic licence to occupy premises as a dwelling (whether the licence was granted before or after the passing of this Act) shall be valid unless—

(a)   it is in writing and contains such information as may be prescribed, and

(b)   it is given not less than four weeks before the date on which it is to take effect.

(1B)   Nothing in subsection (1) or subsection (1A) above applies to—

(a)   premises let on an excluded tenancy which is entered into on or after the date on which the Housing Act 1988 came into force unless it is entered into pursuant to a contract made before that date; or

(b)   premises occupied under an excluded licence.

(2)   In this section 'prescribed' means prescribed by regulations made by the Secretary of State by statutory instrument, and a statutory instrument containing any such regulations shall be subject to annulment in pursuance of a resolution of either House of Parliament.

(3)   Regulations under this section may make different provision in relation to different descriptions of lettings and different circumstances.

PART III
SUPPLEMENTAL PROVISIONS

6.   Prosecution of offences.

Proceedings for an offence under this Act may be instituted by any of the following authorities:—

(a)   councils of districts and London boroughs;

(b)   the Common Council of the City of London;

(c)   the Council of the Isles of Scilly.

7.   Service of notices.

(1)   If for the purpose of any proceedings (whether civil or criminal) brought or intended to be brought under this Act, any person serves upon—

(a)   any agent of the landlord named as such in the rent book or other similar document, or

(b)   the person who receives the rent of the dwelling,

a notice in writing requiring the agent or other person to disclose to him the full name and place of abode or place of business of the landlord, that agent or other person shall forthwith comply with the notice.

(2)   If any such agent or other person as is referred to in subsection (1) above fails or refuses forthwith to comply with a notice served on him under that subsection, he shall be liable on summary conviction to a fine not exceeding level 4 on the standard

scale unless he shows to the satisfaction of the court that he did not know, and could not with reasonable diligence have ascertained, such of the facts required by the notice to be disclosed as were not disclosed by him.

(3)   In this section 'landlord' includes—

(a)   any person from time to time deriving title under the original landlord,

(b)   in relation to any dwelling-house, any person other than the tenant who is or, but for Part VII of the Rent Act 1977 would be, entitled to possession of the dwelling-house, and

(c)   any person who grants to another the right to occupy the dwelling in question as a residence and any person directly or indirectly deriving title from the grantor.

8.   Interpretation.

(1)   In this Act 'statutorily protected tenancy' means—

(a)   a protected tenancy within the meaning of the Rent Act 1977 or a tenancy to which Part I of the Landlord and Tenant Act 1954 applies;

(b)   a protected occupancy or statutory tenancy as defined in the Rent (Agriculture) Act 1976;

(c)   a tenancy to which Part II of the Landlord and Tenant Act 1954 applies;

(d)   a tenancy of an agricultural holding within the meaning of the Agricultural Holdings Act 1986;

(e)   an assured tenancy or assured agricultural occupancy under Part 1 of the Housing Act 1988;

(f)   a tenancy to which Schedule 10 to the Local Government and Housing Act 1989 applies.

(2)   For the purposes of Part I of this Act a person who, under the terms of his employment, had exclusive possession of any premises other than as a tenant shall be deemed to have been a tenant and the expressions 'let' and 'tenancy' shall be construed accordingly.

(3)   In Part I of this Act 'the owner', in relation to any premises, means the person who, as against the occupier, is entitled to possession thereof.

(4)   In this Act 'excluded tenancy' and 'excluded licence' have the meaning assigned by section 3A of this Act.

(5)   If, on or after the date on which the Housing Act 1988 came into force, the terms of an excluded tenancy or excluded licence entered into before that date are varied, then—

(a)   ⁻if the variation affects the amount of the rent which is payable under the tenancy or licence, the tenancy or licence shall be treated for the purposes of sections 3(2C) and 5(1B) above as a new tenancy or licence entered into at the time of the variation; and

(b)   if the variation does not affect the amount of the rent which is so payable, nothing in this Act shall affect the determination of the question whether the variation is such as to give rise to a new tenancy or licence.

(6)   Any reference in subsection (5) above to a variation affecting the amount of the rent which is payable under a tenancy or licence does not include a reference to—

(a)   a reduction or increase effected under Part III or Part VI of the Rent Act 1977 (rents under regulated tenancies and housing association tenancies), section 78 of that Act (power of rent tribunal in relation to restricted contracts) or sections 11 to 14 of the Rent (Agriculture) Act 1976; or

(b)   a variation which is made by the parties and has the effect of making the rent expressed to be payable under the tenancy or licence the same as a rent for the dwelling which is entered in the register under Part IV or section 79 of the Rent Act 1977.

9.   The court for purposes of Part I.

(1)   The court for the purposes of Part I of this Act shall, subject to this section, be—

(a) the county court, in relation to premises with respect to which the county court has for the time being jurisdiction in actions for the recovery of land; and

(b) the High Court, in relation to other premises.

(2) Any powers of a county court in proceedings for the recovery of possession of any premises in the circumstances mentioned in section 3(1) of this Act may be exercised with the leave of the judge by any registrar of the court, except in so far as rules of court otherwise provide.

(3) Nothing in this Act shall affect the jurisdiction of the High Court in proceedings to enforce a lessor's right of re-entry or forfeiture or to enforce a mortgagee's right of possession in a case where the former tenancy was not binding on the mortgagee.

(4) Nothing in this Act shall affect the operation of—

(a) section 59 of the Pluralities Act 1838;

(b) section 19 of the Defence Act 1842;

(c) section 6 of the Lecturers and Parish Clerks Act 1844;

(d) paragraph 3 of Schedule 1 to the Sexual Offences Act 1956; or

(e) section 13 of the Compulsory Purchase Act 1965.

10. Application to Crown.

In so far as this Act requires the taking of proceedings in the court for the recovery of possession or confers any powers on the court it shall (except in the case of section 4(10)) be binding on the Crown.

11. Application to Isles of Scilly.

(1) In its application to the Isles of Scilly, this Act (except in the case of section 5) shall have effect subject to such exceptions, adaptations and modifications as the Secretary of State may by order direct.

(2) The power to make an order under this section shall be exercisable by statutory instrument which shall be subject to annulment, in pursuance of a resolution of either House of Parliament.

(3) An order under this section may be varied or revoked by a subsequent order.

12. Consequential amendments, etc.

(1) Schedule 1 to this Act contains amendments consequential on the provisions of this Act.

(2) Schedule 2 to this Act contains transitional provisions and savings.

(3) The enactments mentioned in Schedule 3 to this Act are hereby repealed to the extent specified in the third column of that Schedule.

(4) The inclusion in this Act of any express savings, transitional provisions or amendment shall not be taken to affect the operation in relation to this Act of section 38 of the Interpretation Act 1889 (which relates to the effect of repeals).

13. Short title, etc.

(1) This Act may be cited as the Protection from Eviction Act 1977.

(2) This Act shall come into force on the expiry of the period of one month beginning with the date on which it is passed.

(3) This Act does not extend to Scotland or Northern Ireland.

(4) References in this Act to any enactment are references to that enactment as amended, and include references thereto as applied by any other enactment including, except where the context otherwise requires, this Act.

SCHEDULE 2
TRANSITIONAL PROVISIONS AND SAVINGS

1.—(1) Insofar as anything done under an enactment repealed by this Act could have been done under a corresponding provision of this Act, it shall not be invalidated by the repeal but shall have effect as if done under that provision.

(2) Subparagraph (1) above applies, in particular, to any regulation, rule, notice or order.

2. The enactments mentioned in Schedule 6 to the Rent Act 1965 shall, notwithstanding the repeal of that Act by this Act, continue to have effect as they had effect immediately before the commencement of this Act.

CRIMINAL LAW ACT 1977
(1977, c. 45)

[29 July 1977]

PART II
OFFENCES RELATING TO ENTERING AND REMAINING ON PROPERTY

6. Violence for securing entry.
(1) Subject to the following provisions of this section, any person who, without lawful authority, uses or threatens violence for the purpose of securing entry into any premises for himself or for any other person is guilty of an offence, provided that—
(a) there is someone present on those premises at the time who is opposed to the entry which the violence is intended to secure; and
(b) the person using or threatening the violence knows that that is the case.
(2) The fact that a person has any interest in or right to possession or occupation of any premises shall not for the purposes of subsection (1) above constitute lawful authority for the use or threat of violence by him or anyone else for the purpose of securing his entry into those premises.
(3) In any proceedings for an offence under this section it shall be a defence for the accused to prove—
(a) that at the time of the alleged offence he or any other person on whose behalf he was acting was a displaced residential occupier of the premises in question; or
(b) that part of the premises in question constitutes premises of which he or any other person on whose behalf he was acting was a displaced residential occupier and that the part of the premises to which he was seeking to secure entry constitutes an access of which he or, as the case may be, that other person is also a displaced residential occupier.
(4) It is immaterial for the purposes of this section—
(a) whether the violence in question is directed against the person or against property; and
(b) ⁻whether the entry which the violence is intended to secure is for the purpose of acquiring possession of the premises in question or for any other purpose.
(5) A person guilty of an offence under this section shall be liable on summary conviction to imprisonment for a term not exceeding six months or to a fine not exceeding level 5 on the standard scale or to both.
(6) A constable in uniform may arrest without warrant anyone who is, or whom he, with reasonable cause, suspects to be, guilty of an offence under this section.
(7) Section 12 below contains provisions which apply for determining when any person is to be regarded for the purposes of this Part of this Act as a displaced residential occupier of any premises or of any access to any premises.

12. Supplementary provisions.
(1) In this Part of this Act—
(a) "premises" means any building, any part of a building under separate occupation, any land ancillary to a building, the site comprising any building or buildings together with any land ancillary thereto, and (for the purposes only of sections 10 and 11 above) any other place; and
(b) "access" means, in relation to any premises, any part of any site or building within which those premises are situated which contitutes an ordinary means of access

to those premises (whether or not that is its sole or primary use).

(2) References in this section to a building shall apply also to any structure other than a movable one, and to any movable structure, vehicle or vessel designed or adapted for use for residential purposes; and for the purposes of subsection (1) above—

(a) part of a building is under separate occupation if anyone is in occupation or entitled to occupation of that part as distinct from the whole; and

(b) land is ancillary to a building if it is adjacent to it and used (or intended for use) in connection with the occupation of that building or any part of it.

(3) Subject to subsection (4) below, any person who was occupying any premises as a residence immediately before being excluded from occupation by anyone who entered those premises, or any access to those premises, as a trespasser is a displaced residential occupier of the premises for the purposes of this Part of this Act so long as he continues to be excluded from occupation of the premises by the original trespasser or by any subsequent trespasser.

(4) A person who was himself occupying the premises in question as a trespasser immediately before being excluded from occupation shall not by virture of subsection (3) above be a displaced residential occupier of the premises for the purposes of this Part of this Act.

(5) A person who by virtue of subsection (3) above is a displaced residential occupier of any premises shall be regarded for the purposes of this Part of this Act as a displaced residential occupier also of any access to those premises.

(6) Anyone who enters or is on or in occupation of any premises by virtue of—

(a) any title derived from a trespasser; or

(b) any licence or consent given by a trespasser or by a person deriving title from a trespasser,

shall himself be treated as a trespasser for the purposes of this Part of this Act (without prejudice to whether or not he would be a trespasser apart from this provision); and references in this Part of this Act to a person's entering or being on or occupying any premises as a trespasser shall be construed accordingly.

(7) Anyone who is on any premises as a trespasser shall not cease to be a trespasser for the purposes of this Part of this Act by virtue of being allowed time to leave the premises, nor shall anyone cease to be a displaced residential occupier of any premises by virtue of any such allowance of time to a trespasser.

(8) No rule of law ousting the jurisdiction of magistrates' courts to try offences where a dispute of title to property is involved shall preclude magistrates' courts from trying offences under this Part of this Act.

HOUSING ACT 1980
(1980, c. 51)

[8 August 1980]

PART II
PRIVATE SECTOR TENANTS

Protected shorthold tenancies

51. Preliminary.

Sections 53 to 55 below modify the operation of the 1977 Act in relation to protected shorthold tenancies as defined in section 52 below.

52. Protected shorthold tenancies.

(1) A protected shorthold tenancy is a protected tenancy granted after the commencement of this section which is granted for a term certain of not less than one year nor more than five years and satisfies the following conditions, that is to say,—

(a)   it cannot be brought to an end by the landlord before the expiry of the term, except in pursuance of a provision for re-entry or forfeiture for non-payment of rent or breach of any other obligation of the tenancy; and

(b)   before the grant the landlord has given the tenant a valid notice stating that the tenancy is to be a protected shorthold tenancy.

(2)   A tenancy of a dwelling-house is not a protected shorthold tenancy if it is granted to a person who, immediately before it was granted, was a protected or statutory tenant of that dwelling-house.

(3)   A notice is not valid for the purposes of subsection (1)(b) above unless it complies with the requirements of regulations made by the Secretary of State.

(4)   The Secretary of State may by order direct that subsection (1) above shall have effect, either generally or in relation to any registration area specified in the order, as if paragraph (c) were omitted.

(5)   If a protected tenancy is granted after the commencement of this section—

(a)   for such a term certain as is mentioned in subsection (1) above, to be followed, at the option of the tenant, by a further term; or

(b)   for such a term certain and thereafter from year to year or some other period; and satisfies the conditions stated in that subsection, the tenancy is a protected shorthold tenancy until the end of the term certain.

53.   Right of tenant to terminate protected shorthold tenancy.

(1)   A protected shorthold tenancy may be brought to an end (by virtue of this section and notwithstanding anything in the terms of the tenancy) before the expiry of the term certain by notice in writing of the appropriate length given by the tenant to the landlord; and the appropriate length of the notice is—

(a)   one month if the term certain is two years or less; and

(b)   three months if it is more than two years.

(2)   Any agreement relating to a protected shorthold tenancy (whether or not contained in the instrument creating the tenancy) shall be void in so far as it purports to impose any penalty or disability on the tenant in the event of his giving a notice under this section.

54.   Subletting or assignment.

(1)   Where the whole or part of a dwelling-house let under a protected shorthold tenancy has been sublet at any time during the continuous period specified in subsection (3) below, and, during that period, the landlord becomes entitled, as against the tenant, to possession of the dwelling-house, he shall also be entitled to possession against the sub-tenant and section 137 of the 1977 Act shall not apply.

(2)   A protected shorthold tenancy of a dwelling-house and any protected tenancy of the same dwelling-house granted during the continuous period specified in subsection (3) below shall not be capable of being assigned, except in pursuance of an order under section 24 of the Matrimonial Causes Act 1973.

(3)   The continuous period mentioned in subsections (1) and (2) above is the period beginning with the grant of the protected shorthold tenancy and continuing until either—

(a)   no person is in possession of the dwelling-house as a protected or statutory tenant; or

(b)   a protected tenancy of the dwelling-house is granted to a person who is not, immediately before the grant, in possession of the dwelling-house as a protected or statutory tenant.

55.   Orders for possession.

(2)   If, in proceedings for possession under Case 19 set out above, the court is of opinion that, notwithstanding that the condition of paragraph (b) or (c) of section 52(1)

above is not satisfied, it is just and equitable to make an order for possession, it may treat the tenancy under which the dwelling-house was let as a protected shorthold tenancy.

PART III
TENANT'S REPAIRS AND IMPROVEMENTS

81. Tenant's improvements.

(1) The following provisions of this section have effect with respect to protected tenancies and statutory tenancies in place of section 19(2) of the Landlord and Tenant Act 1927.

(2) It is by virtue of this section a term of every such tenancy that the tenant will not make any improvement without the written consent of the landlord.

(3) The consent required by virtue of subsection (2) above is not to be unreasonably withheld and, if unreasonably withheld, shall be treated as given.

(4) Subsections (1) to (3) above do not apply in any case where the tenant has been given a notice—

(a) of a kind mentioned in one of Cases 11 to 18 and 20 in Schedule 15 to the 1977 Act (notice that possession might be recovered under that Case); or

(b) under section 52(1)(b) of this Act (notice that a tenancy is to be a protected shorthold tenancy);

unless the tenant proves that, at the time when the landlord gave the notice, it was unreasonable for the landlord to expect to be able in due course to recover possession of the dwelling-house under that Case or, as the case may be, Case 19 of Schedule 15 (added by section 55 of this Act).

(5) In Part I, and in this Part, of this Act "improvement" means any alteration in, or addition to, a dwelling-house and includes—

(a) any addition to, or alteration in, landlord's fixtures and fittings and any addition or alteration connected with the provision of any services to a dwelling-house;

(b) the erection of any wireless or television aerial; and

(c) the carrying out of external decoration;

but paragraph (c) above does not apply in relation to a protected or statutory tenancy if the landlord is under an obligation to carry out external decoration or to keep the exterior of the dwelling-house in repair.

82. Provisions as to consents required by section 81.

(1) If any question arises whether the withholding of a consent required by virtue of section 81 above was unreasonable it is for the landlord to show that it was not; and in determining that question the court shall, in particular, have regard to the extent to which the improvement would be likely—

(a) to make the dwelling-house, or any other premises, less safe for occupiers;

(b) to cause the landlord to incur expenditure which it would be unlikely to incur if the improvement were not made; or

(c) to reduce the price which the dwelling-house would fetch if sold on the open market or the rent which the landlord would be able to charge on letting the dwelling-house.

(2) A consent required by virtue of section 81 may be validly given notwithstanding that it follows, instead of preceding, the action requiring it and may be given subject to a condition.

(3) Where the tenant has applied in writing for a consent which is required by virtue of section 81 then—

(a) if the landlord refuses to give the consent it shall give to the tenant a written statement of the reasons why the consent was refused; and

(b) if the landlord neither gives nor refuses to give the consent within a reasonable time, the consent shall be taken to have been withheld, and if the landlord gives the consent but subject to an unreasonable condition, the consent shall be taken to have been unreasonably withheld.

(4)   If any question arises whether a condition attached to a consent was reasonable, it is for the landlord to show that it was.

83.   Conditional consent to tenant's improvements.

Any failure by a protected tenant or a statutory tenant to satisfy any reasonable condition imposed by his landlord in giving consent to an improvement which the tenant proposes to make, or has made, shall be treated for the purposes of Chapter II of Part I of this Act or, as the case may be, for the purposes of the 1977 Act as a breach by the tenant of an obligation of his tenancy or, as the case may be, of an obligation of the previous protected tenancy which is applicable to the statutory tenancy.

84.   Exclusion of certain housing associations from Part III.

This part of this Act does not apply in relation to a housing association which falls within paragraph (d) of section 15(3) of the 1977 Act (certain societies registered under the Industrial and Provident Societies Act 1965).

85.   Interpretation and application of Part III.

(1)   In this Part of this Act any expression used in the 1977 Act has the same meaning as in that Act.

(2)   This Part of this Act applies to tenancies granted before as well as tenancies granted after the commencement of this Part of this Act.

PART IV
JURISDICTION AND PROCEDURE

86.   Jurisdiction of county court and rules of procedure.

(1)   A county court has jurisdiction to determine any question arising under Part III of this Act (tenant's improvements) and to entertain any proceedings brought thereunder.

(2)   The jurisdiction conferred by this section includes jurisdiction to entertain proceedings on any question whether any consent required by section 81 was withheld or unreasonably withheld, notwithstanding that no other relief is sought than a declaration.

(3)   If a person takes proceedings in the High Court which, by virtue of this section, he could have taken in the county court he is not entitled to recover any costs.

(4)   The Lord Chancellor may make such rules and give such directions as he thinks fit for the purpose of giving effect to this Part of this Act.

(5)   The rules and directions may provide—

(a)   for the exercise by any registrar of a county court of any jurisdiction exercisable under this section; and

(b)   for the conduct of any proceedings in private.

(6)   The power to make rules under this section is exercisable by statutory instrument and any such instrument is subject to annulment in pursuance of a resolution of either House of Parliament.

88.   Discretion of court in certain proceedings for possession.

(1)   Where, under the terms of a rental purchase agreement, a person has been let into possession of a dwelling-house and, on the termination of the agreement or of his right to possession under it, proceedings are brought for the possession of the dwelling-house, the court may—

(a)   adjourn the proceedings; or

(b)   on making an order for the possession of the dwelling-house, stay or suspend execution of the order or postpone the date of possession;

for such period or periods as the court thinks fit.

(2) On any such adjournment, stay, suspension or postponement the court may impose such conditions with regard to payments by the person in possession in respect of his continued occupation of the dwelling-house and such other conditions as the court thinks fit.

(3) The court may revoke or from time to time vary any condition imposed by virtue of this section.

(4) In this section "rental purchase agreement" means an agreement for the purchase of a dwelling-house (whether freehold or leasehold property) under which the whole or part of the purchase price is to be paid in three or more instalments and the completion of the purchase is deferred until the whole or a specified part of the purchase price has been paid.

(5) This section extends to proceedings for the possession of a dwelling-house which were begun before the commencement of this section unless an order for the possession of the dwelling-house was made in the proceedings and executed before the commencement of this section.

89. Restriction on discretion of court in making orders for possession of land.

(1) Where a court makes an order for the possession of any land in a case not falling within the exceptions mentioned in subsection (2) below, the giving up of possession shall not be postponed (whether by the order or any variation, suspension or stay of execution) to a date later than fourteen days after the making of the order, unless it appears to the court that exceptional hardship would be caused by requiring possession to be given up by that date; and shall not in any event be postponed to a date later than six weeks after the making of the order.

(2) The restrictions in subsection (1) above do not apply if—

    (a) the order is made in an action by a mortgagee for possession; or

    (b) the order is made in an action for forfeiture of a lease; or

    (c) the court had power to make the order only if it considered it reasonable to make it; or

    (d) the order relates to a dwelling-house which is the subject of a restricted contract (within the meaning of section 19 of the 1977 Act); or

    (e) the order is made in proceedings brought as mentioned in section 88(1) above.

LIMITATION ACT 1980
(1980, c. 58)

[13 November 1980]

Actions to recover land and rent

15. Time limit for actions to recover land.

(1) No action shall be brought by any person to recover any land after the expiration of twelve years from the date on which the right of action accrued to him or, if it first accrued to some person through whom he claims, to that person.

(2) Subject to the following provisions of this section, where—

    (a) the estate or interest claimed was an estate or interest in reversion or remainder or any other future estate or interest and the right of action to recover the land accrued on the date on which the estate or interest fell into possession by the determination of the preceding estate or interest; and

    (b) the person entitled to the preceding estate or interest (not being a term of years absolute) was not in possession of the land on that date;

no action shall be brought by the person entitled to the succeeding estate or interest after the expiration of twelve years from the date on which the right of action accrued to the person entitled to the preceding estate or interest or six years from the date on which the right of action accrued to the person entitled to the succeeding estate or interest, whichever period last expires.

(3)   Subsection (2) above shall not apply to any estate or interest which falls into possession on the determination of an entailed interest and which might have been barred by the person entitled to the entailed interest.

(4)   No person shall bring an action to recover any estate or interest in land under an assurance taking effect after the right of action to recover the land had accrued to the person by whom the assurance was made or some person through whom he claimed or some person entitled to a preceding estate or interest, unless the action is brought within the period during which the person by whom the assurance was made could have brought such an action.

(5)   Where any person is entitled to any estate or interest in land in possession and, while so entitled, is also entitled to any future estate or interest in that land, and his right to recover the estate or interest in possession is barred under this Act, no action shall be brought by that person, or by any person claiming through him, in respect of the future estate or interest, unless in the meantime possession of the land has been recovered by a person entitled to an intermediate estate or interest.

(6)   Part I of Schedule 1 to this Act contains provisions for determining the date of accrual of rights of action to recover land in the cases there mentioned.

(7)   Part II of that Schedule contains provisions modifying the provisions of this section in their application to actions brought by, or by a person claiming through, the Crown or any spiritual or eleemosynary corporation sole.

19.   Time limit for actions to recover rent.
No action shall be brought, or distress made, to recover arrears of rent, or damages in respect of arrears of rent, after the expiration of six years from the date on which the arrears became due.

SCHEDULES

Section 15(6)(7).   SCHEDULE 1

PROVISIONS WITH RESPECT TO ACTIONS TO RECOVER LAND

PART I
ACCRUAL OF RIGHTS OF ACTION TO RECOVER LAND

Accrual of right of action in case of present interests in land

1.   Where the person bringing an action to recover land, or some person through whom he claims, has been in possession of the land, and has while entitled to the land been dispossessed or discontinued his possession, the right of action shall be treated as having accrued on the date of the dispossession or discontinuance.

2.   Where any person brings an action to recover any land of a deceased person (whether under a will or on intestacy) and the deceased person—

(a)   was on the date of his death in possession of the land or, in the case of a rentcharge created by will or taking effect upon his death, in possession of the land charged; and

(b)   was the last person entitled to the land to be in possession of it;
the right of action shall be treated as having accrued on the date of his death.

3.   Where any person brings an action to recover land, being an estate or interest in possession assured otherwise than by will to him, or to some person through whom he claims, and—

(a)   the person making the assurance was on the date when the assurance took effect in possession of the land or, in the case of a rentcharge created by the assurance, in possession of the land charged; and

(b)   no person has been in possession of the land by virtue of the assurance; the right of action shall be treated as having accrued on the date when the assurance took effect.

Accrual of right of action in case of future interests

4.   The right of action to recover any land shall, in a case where—

(a)   the estate or interest claimed was an estate or interest in reversion or remainder or any other future estate or interest; and

(b)   no person has taken possession of the land by virtue of the estate or interest claimed;

be treated as having accrued on the date on which the estate or interest fell into possession by the determination of the preceding estate or interest.

5.—(1)   Subject to sub-paragraph (2) below, a tenancy from year to year or other period, without a lease in writing, shall for the purposes of this Act be treated as being determined at the expiration of the first year or other period; and accordingly the right of action of the person entitled to the land subject to the tenancy shall be treated as having accrued at the date on which in accordance with this sub-paragraph the tenancy is determined.

(2)   Where any rent has subsequently been received in respect of the tenancy, the right of action shall be treated as having accrued on the date of the last receipt of rent.

6.—(1)   Where—

(a)   any person is in possession of land by virtue of a lease in writing by which a rent of not less than ten pounds a year is reserved; and

(b)   the rent is received by some person wrongfully claiming to be entitled to the land in reversion immediately expectant on the determination of the lease; and

(c)   no rent is subsequently received by the person rightfully so entitled; the right of action to recover the land of the person rightfully so entitled shall be treated as having accrued on the date when the rent was first received by the person wrongfully claiming to be so entitled and not on the date of the determination of the lease.

(2)   Sub-paragraph (1) above shall not apply to any lease granted by the Crown.

Accrual of right of action in case of forfeiture or breach of condition

7.—(1)   Subject to sub-paragraph (2) below, a right of action to recover land by virtue of a forfeiture or breach of condition shall be treated as having accrued on the date on which the forfeiture was incurred or the condition broken.

(2)   If any such right has accrued to a person entitled to an estate or interest in reversion or remainder and the land was not recovered by virtue of that right, the right of action to recover the land shall not be treated as having accrued to that person until his estate or interest fell into possesson, as if no such forfeiture or breach of condition had occurred.

Right of action not to accrue or continue unless there is adverse possession

8.—(1)   No right of action to recover land shall be treated as accruing unless the land is in the possession of some person in whose favour the period of limitation can run (referred to below in this paragraph as "adverse possession"); and where under the preceding provisions of this Schedule any such right of action is treated as accruing on a certain date and no person is in adverse possession on that date, the right of action shall not be treated as accruing unless and until adverse possession is taken of the land.

(2)   Where a right of action to recover land has accrued and after its accrual, before the right is barred, the land ceases to be in adverse possession, the right of action shall

no longer be treated as having accrued and no fresh right of action shall be treated as accruing unless and until the land is again taken into adverse possession.

(3)   For the purposes of this paragraph—

(a)   possession of any land subject to a rentcharge by a person (other than the person entitled to the rentcharge) who does not pay the rent shall be treated as adverse possession of the rentcharge; and

(b)   receipt of rent under a lease by a person wrongfully claiming to be entitled to the land in reversion immediately expectant on the determination of the lease shall be treated as adverse possession of the land.

(4)   For the purpose of determining whether a person occupying any land is in adverse possession of the land it shall not be assumed by implication of law that his occupation is by permission of the person entitled to the land merely by virtue of the fact that his occupation is not inconsistent with the latter's present or future enjoyment of the land.

This provision shall not be taken as prejudicing a finding to the effect that a person's occupation of any land is by implied permission of the person entitled to the land in any case where such a finding is justified on the actual facts of the case.

Possession of beneficiary not adverse to others interested in settled land or land held on trust for sale

9.   Where any settled land or any land held on trust for sale is in the possession of a person entitled to a beneficial interest in the land or in the proceeds of sale (not being a person solely or absolutely entitled to the land or the proceeds), no right of action to recover the land shall be treated for the purposes of this Act as accruing during that possession to any person in whom the land is vested as tenant for life, statutory owner or trustee, or to any other person entitled to a beneficial interest in the land or the proceeds of sale.

PART II
MODIFICATIONS OF SECTION 15 WHERE CROWN OR CERTAIN CORPORATIONS SOLE ARE INVOLVED

10.   Subject to paragraph 11 below, section 15(1) of this Act shall apply to the bringing of an action to recover any land by the Crown or by any spiritual or eleemosynary corporation sole with the substitution for the reference to twelve years of a reference to thirty years.

11.—(1)   An action to recover foreshore may be brought by the Crown at any time before the expiration of sixty years from the date mentioned in section 15(1) of this Act.

(2)   Where any right of action to recover land which has ceased to be foreshore but remains in the ownership of the Crown accrued when the land was foreshore, the action may be brought at any time before the expiraton of—

(a)   sixty years from the date of accrual of the right of action; or

(b)   thirty years from the date when the land ceased to be foreshore;

whichever period first expires.

(3)   In this paragraph "foreshore" means the shore and bed of the sea and of any tidal water, below the line of the medium high tide between the spring tides and the neap tides.

12.   Notwithstanding section 15(1) of this Act, where in the case of any action brought by a person other than the Crown or a spiritual or eleemosynary corporation sole the right of action first accrued to the Crown or any such corporation sole through whom the person in question claims, the action may be brought at any time before the expiration of—

(a)   the period during which the action could have been brought by the Crown or the corporation sole; or

(b)   twelve years from the date on which the right of action accrued to some person other than the Crown or the corporation sole;

whichever period first expires.

13.   Section 15(2) of this Act shall apply in any case where the Crown or a spiritual or eleemosynary corporation sole is entitled to the succeeding estate or interest with the substitution—

(a)   for the reference to twelve years of a reference to thirty years; and

(b)   for the reference to six years of a reference to twelve years.

SUPREME COURT ACT 1981
(1981, c. 54)

[28 July 1981]

PART II
JURISDICTION: THE HIGH COURT

Powers

37.   Powers of High Court with respect to injunctions and receivers.

(1)   The High Court may by order (whether interlocutory or final) grant an injunction or appoint a receiver in all cases in which it appears to the court to be just and convenient to do so.

(2)   Any such order may be made either unconditionally or on such terms and conditions as the court thinks just.

(3)   The power of the High Court under subsection (1) to grant an interlocutory injunction restraining a party to any proceedings from removing from the jurisdiction of the High Court, or otherwise dealing with, assets located within that jurisdiction shall be exercisable in cases where that party is, as well as in cases where he is not, domiciled, resident or present within that jurisdiction.

(4)   The power of the High Court to appoint a receiver by way of equitable execution shall operate in relation to all legal estates and interests in land; and that power—

(a)   may be exercised in relation to an estate or interest in land whether or not a charge has been imposed on that land under section 1 of the Charging Orders Act 1979 for the purpose of enforcing the judgment, order or award in question; and

(b)   shall be in addition to, and not in derogation of, any power of any court to appoint a receiver in proceedings for enforcing such a charge.

(5)   Where an order under the said section 1 imposing a charge for the purpose of enforcing a judgment, order or award has been, or has effect as if, registered under section 6 of the Land Charges Act 1972, subsection (4) of the said section 6 (effect of non-registration of writs and orders registrable under that section) shall not apply to an order appointing a receiver made either—

(a)   in proceedings for enforcing the charge; or

(b)   by way of equitable execution of the judgment, order or award or, as the case may be, of so much of it as requires payment of moneys secured by the charge.

38.   Relief against forfeiture for non-payment of rent.

(1)   In any action in the High Court for the forfeiture of a lease for non-payment of rent, the court shall have power to grant relief against forfeiture in a summary manner, and may do so subject to the same terms and conditions as to the payment of rent, costs or otherwise as could have been imposed by it in such an action immediately before the commencement of this Act.

(2)   Where the lessee or a person deriving title under him is granted relief under this section, he shall hold the demised premises in accordance with the terms of the lease without the necessity for a new lease.

MATRIMONIAL HOMES ACT 1983
(1983, c. 19)

An Act to consolidate certain enactments relating to the rights of a husband or wife to occupy a dwelling house that has been a matrimonial home.   [9 May 1983]

1. Rights concerning matrimonial home where one spouse has no estate, etc.

(1)   Where one spouse is entitled to occupy a dwelling house by virtue of a beneficial estate or interest or contract or by virtue of any enactment giving him or her the right to remain in occupation, and the other spouse is not so entitled, then, subject to the provisions of this Act, the spouse not so entitled shall have the following rights (in this Act referred to as "rights of occupation")—

(a)   if in occupation, a right not to be evicted or excluded from the dwelling house or any part thereof by the other spouse except with the leave of the court given by an order under this section;

(b)   if not in occupation, a right with the leave of the court so given to enter into and occupy the dwelling house.

(2)   So long as one spouse has rights of occupation, either of the spouses may apply to the court for an order—

(a)   declaring, enforcing, restricting or terminating those rights, or

(b)   prohibiting, suspending or restricting the exercise by either spouse of the right to occupy the dwelling house, or

(c)   requiring either spouse to permit the exercise by the other of that right.

(3)   On an application for an order under this section, the court may make such order as it thinks just and reasonable having regard to the conduct of the spouses in relation to each other and otherwise, to their respective needs and financial resources, to the needs of any children and to all the circumstances of the case, and, without prejudice to the generality of the foregoing provision—

(a)   may except part of the dwelling house from a spouse's rights of occupation (and in particular a part used wholly or mainly for or in connection with the trade, business or profession of the other spouse),

(b)   may order a spouse occupying the dwelling house or any part thereof by virtue of this section to make periodical payments to the other in respect of the occupation,

(c)   may impose on either spouse obligations as to the repair and maintenance of the dwelling house or the discharge of any liabilities in respect of the dwelling house.

(4)   Orders under this section may, in so far as they have a continuing effect, be limited so as to have effect for a period specified in the order or until further order.

(5)   Where a spouse is entitled under this section to occupy a dwelling house or any part thereof, any payment or tender made or other thing done by that spouse in or towards satisfaction of any liability of the other spouse in respect of rent, rates, mortgage payments or other outgoings affecting the dwelling house shall, whether or not it is made or done in pursuance of an order under this section, be as good as if made or done by the other spouse.

(6)   A spouse's occupation by virtue of this section shall, for the purposes of the Rent (Agriculture) Act 1976, and of the Rent Act 1977 (other than Part V and sections 103 to 106), be treated as possession by the other spouse and for purposes of Part IV of the Housing Act 1985 (secure tenancies) and Part I of the Housing Act 1988 be treated as occupation by the other spouse.

(7)   Where a spouse is entitled under this section to occupy a dwelling house or any part thereof and makes any payment in or towards satisfaction of any liability of the other spouse in respect of mortgage payments affecting the dwelling house, the person to whom the payment is made may treat it as having been made by that other spouse, but the fact that that person has treated any such payment as having been so made shall

not affect any claim of the first-mentioned spouse against the other to an interest in the dwelling house by virtue of the payment.

(8)   Where a spouse is entitled under this section to occupy a dwelling house or part thereof by reason of an interest of the other spouse under a trust, all the provisions of subsections (5) to (7) above shall apply in relation to the trustees as they apply in relation to the other spouse.

(9)   The jurisdiction conferred on the court by this section shall be exercisable by the High Court or by a county court, and shall be exercisable by a county court notwithstanding that by reason of the amount of the net annual value for rating of the dwelling house or otherwise the jurisdiction would not but for this subsection be exercisable by a county court.

(10)   This Act shall not apply to a dwelling house which has at no time been a matrimonial home of the spouses in question; and a spouse's rights of occupation shall continue only so long as the marriage subsists and the other spouse is entitled as mentioned in subsection (1) above to occupy the dwelling house, except where provision is made by section 2 of this Act for those rights to be a charge on an estate or interest in the dwelling house.

(11)   It is hereby declared that a spouse who has an equitable interest in a dwelling house or in the proceeds of sale thereof, not being a spouse in whom is vested (whether solely or as a joint tenant) a legal estate in fee simple or a legal term of years absolute in the dwelling house, is to be treated for the purpose only of determining whether he or she has rights of occupation under this section as not being entitled to occupy the dwelling house by virtue of that interest.

SCHEDULES

Section 7.   SCHEDULE 1

TRANSFER OF CERTAIN TENANCIES ON DIVORCE, ETC.

PART I
General

1.—(1)   Where one spouse is entitled, either in his or her own right or jointly with the other spouse, to occupy a dwelling house by virtue of—

(a)   a protected tenancy or statutory tenancy within the meaning of the Rent Act 1977, or

(b)   a statutory tenancy within the meaning of the Rent (Agriculture) Act 1976, or

(c)   a secure tenancy within the meaning of section 79 of the Housing Act 1985, or

(d)   an assured tenancy or assured agricultural occupancy, within the meaning of Part I of the Housing Act 1988,

then, on granting a decree of divorce, a decree of nullity of marriage or a decree of judicial separation, or at any time thereafter (whether, in the case of a decree of divorce or nullity of marriage, before or after the decree is made absolute), the court by which the decree is granted may make an order under Part II below.

(2)   References in this Schedule to a spouse being entitled to occupy a dwelling house by virtue of a protected, statutory or secure tenancy or an assured tenancy or assured agricultural occupancy, apply whether that entitlement is in his or her own right, or jointly with the other spouse.

PART II
Protected or secure tenancy

2.—(1)   Where a spouse is entitled to occupy the dwelling house by virtue of a protected tenancy within the meaning of the Rent Act 1977, or a secure tenancy within the meaning of the Housing Act 1985 or an assured tenancy or assured agricultural occupancy within the meaning of Part I of the Housing Act 1988, the court may by order direct that, as from such date as may be specified in the order, there shall, by virtue of the order and without further assurance, be transferred to, and vested in, the other spouse—

(a)   the estate or interest which the spouse so entitled had in the dwelling house immediately before that date by virtue of the lease or agreement creating the tenancy and any assignment of that lease or agreement, with all rights, privileges and appurtenances attaching to that estate or interest but subject to all covenants, obligations, liabilities and incumbrances to which it is subject; and

(b)   where the spouse so entitled is an assignee of such lease or agreement, the liability of that spouse under any covenant of indemnity by the assignee expressed or implied in the assignment of the lease or agreement to that spouse.

(2)   Where an order is made under this paragraph, any liability or obligation to which the spouse so entitled is subject under any covenant having reference to the dwelling house in the lease or agreement, being a liability or obligation falling due to be discharged or performed on or after the date so specified, shall not be enforceable against that spouse.

(3)   Where the spouse so entitled is a successor within the meaning of Part IV of the Housing Act 1985, his or her former spouse (or, in the case of judicial separation, his or her spouse) shall be deemed also to be a successor within the meaning of that Chapter.

(4)   Where the spouse so entitled is for the purposes of section 17 of the Housing Act 1988 a successor in relation to the tenancy or occupancy, his or her former spouse (or, in the case of judicial separation, his or her spouse) shall be deemed to be a successor in relation to the tenancy or occupancy for the purposes of that section.

(5)   If the transfer under sub-paragraph (1) above is of an assured agricultural occupancy, then, for the purposes of Chapter III of Part I of the Housing Act 1988,—

(a)   the agricultural worker condition shall be fulfilled with respect to the dwelling-house while the spouse to whom the assured agricultural occupancy is transferred continues to be the occupier under that occupancy; and

(b)   that condition shall be treated as so fulfilled by virtue of the same paragraph of Schedule 3 to the Housing Act 1988 as was applicable before the transfer.

Statutory tenancy within the meaning of the Rent Act 1977

3.—(1)   Where the spouse is entitled to occupy the dwelling house by virtue of a statutory tenancy within the meaning of the Rent Act 1977, the court may by order direct that, as from such date as may be specified in the order, that spouse shall cease to be entitled to occupy the dwelling house and that the other spouse shall be deemed to be the tenant or, as the case may be, the sole tenant under that statutory tenancy.

(2)   The question whether the provisions of paragraphs 1 to 3 or, as the case may be, paragraphs 5 to 7 of Schedule 1 to the Rent Act 1977 as to the succession by the surviving spouse of a deceased tenant, or by a member of the deceased tenant's family, to the right to retain possession are capable of having effect in the event of the death of the person deemed by an order under this paragraph to be the tenant or sole tenant under the statutory tenancy shall be determined according as those provisions have or have not already had effect in relation to the statutory tenancy.

Statutory tenancy within the meaning of the Rent (Agriculture) Act 1976

4.   Where the spouse is entitled to occupy the dwelling house by virtue of a statutory tenancy within the meaning of the Rent (Agriculture) Act 1976, the court may by order direct that, as from such date as may be specified in the order, that spouse shall cease to be entitled to occupy the dwelling house and that the other spouse shall be deemed to

be the tenant or, as the case may be, the sole tenant under that statutory tenancy; and a spouse who is deemed as aforesaid to be the tenant under a statutory tenancy in his own right, or a statutory tenant by succession, according as the other spouse was a statutory tenant in his own right or a statutory tenant by succession.

PART III

Ancillary jurisdiction

5. Where the court makes an order under Part II of this Schedule, it may by the order direct that both spouses shall be jointly and severally liable to discharge or perform any or all of the liabilities and obligations in respect of the dwelling house (whether arising under the tenancy or otherwise) which have at the date of the order fallen due to be discharged or performed by one only of the spouses or which, but for the direction, would before the date specified as the date on which the order is to take effect fall due to be discharged or performed by one only of them; and where the court gives such a direction it may further direct that either spouse shall be liable to indemnify the other in whole or in part against any payment made or expenses incurred by the other in discharging or performing any such liability or obligation.

Date when order is to take effect

6. In the case of a decree of divorce or nullity of marriage, the date specified in an order under Part II of this Schedule as the date on which the order is to take effect shall not be earlier than the date on which the decree is made absolute.

Remarriage of either spouse

7. If after the grant of a decree dissolving or annulling a marriage either spouse remarries, that spouse shall not be entitled to apply, by reference to the grant of that decree, for an order under Part II of this Schedule.

Rules of court

8.—(1) Rules of court shall be made requiring the court before it makes an order under this Schedule to give the landlord of the dwelling house to which the order will relate an opportunity of being heard.

(2) Rules of court may provide that an application for an order under this Schedule shall not, without the leave of the court by which the decree of divorce, nullity of marriage or judicial separation was granted, be made after the expiration of such period from the grant of the decree as may be prescribed by the rules.

Saving for sections 1 and 2 of this Act

9. Where a spouse is entitled to occupy a dwelling house by virtue of a tenancy, this Schedule shall not affect the operation of sections 1 and 2 of this Act in relation to the other spouse's rights of occupation, and the court's power to make orders under this Schedule shall be in addition to the powers conferred by those sections.

Interpretation

10.—(1) In this Schedule—
"landlord" includes any person from time to time deriving title under the original landlord and also includes, in relation to any dwelling house, any person other than the tenant who is, or but for Part VII of the Rent Act 1977 or Part II of the Rent (Agriculture) Act 1976 would be, entitled to possession of the dwelling house;
"tenancy" includes sub-tenancy.

(2) For the avoidance of doubt it is hereby declared that the reference in paragraph 7 above to remarriage includes a reference to a marriage which is by law void or voidable.

COUNTY COURTS ACT 1984
(1984, c. 28)

[26 June 1984]

PART IX
MISCELLANEOUS AND GENERAL

Forfeiture for non-payment of rent

138.   Provisions as to forfeiture for non-payment of rent.

(1)   This section has effect where a lessor is proceeding by action in a county court (being an action in which the county court has jurisdiction) to enforce against a lessee a right of re-entry or forfeiture in respect of any land for non-payment of rent.

(2)   If the lessee pays into court not less than 5 clear days before the return day all the rent in arrear and the costs of the action, the action shall cease, and the lessee shall hold the land according to the lease without any new lease.

(3)   If—

(a)   the action does not cease under subsection (2); and

(b)   the court at the trial is satisfied that the lessor is entitled to enforce the right of re-entry or forfeiture,

the court shall order possession of the land to be given to the lessor at the expiration of such period, not being less than 4 weeks from the date of the order, as the court thinks fit, unless within that period the lessee pays into court all the rent in arrear and the costs of the action.

(4)   The court may extend the period specified under subsection (3) at any time before possession of the land is recovered in pursuance of the order under that subsection.

(5)   If—

(a)   within the period specified in the order; or

(b)   within that period as extended under subsection (4),

the lessee pays into court—

(i)   all the rent in arrear; and

(ii)   the costs of the action,

he shall hold the land according to the lease without any new lease.

(6)   Subsection (2) shall not apply where the lessor is proceeding in the same action to enforce a right of re-entry of forfeiture on any other ground as well as for non-payment of rent, or to enforce any other claim as well as the right of re-entry or forfeiture and the claim for arrears of rent.

(7)   If the lessee does not—

(a)   within the period specified in the order; or

(b)   within that period as extended under subsection (4),

pay into court—

(i)   all the rent in arrear; and

(ii)   the costs of the action,

the order shall be enforceable in the prescribed manner and so long as the order remains unreversed the lessee shall, subject to subsections (8) and (9A), be barred from all relief.

(8)   The extension under subsection (4) of a period fixed by a court shall not be treated as relief from which the lessee is barred by subsection (7) if he fails to pay into court all the rent in arrears and the costs of the action within that period.

(9)   Where the court extends a period under subsection (4) at a time when—

(a)   that period has expired; and

(b)   a warrant has been issued for the possession of the land,

the court shall suspend the warrant for the extended period; and, if, before the expiration of the extended period, the lessee pays into court all the rent in arrear and all the costs of the action, the court shall cancel the warrant.

(9A)   Where the lessor recovers possession of the land at any time after the making of the order under subsection (3) (whether as a result of the enforcement of the order or otherwise) the lessee may, at any time within six months from the date on which the lessor recovers possession, apply to the court for relief; and on any such application the court may, if it thinks fit, grant to the lessee such relief, subject to such terms and conditions, as it thinks fit.

(9B)   Where the lessee is granted relief on an application under subsection (9A) he shall hold the land according to the lease without any new lease.

(9C)   An application under subsection (9A) may be made by a person with an interest under a lease of the land derived (whether immediately or otherwise) from the lessee's interest therein in like manner as if he were the lessee; and on any such application the court may make an order which (subject to such terms and conditions as the court thinks fit) vests the land in such a person, as lessee of the lessor, for the remainder of the term of the lease under which he has any such interest as aforesaid, or for any lesser term.

In this subsection any reference to the land includes a reference to a part of the land.

(10)   Nothing in this section or section 139 shall be taken to affect—

(a)   the power of the court to make any order which it would otherwise have power to make as respects a right of re-entry or forfeiture on any ground other than non-payment of rent; or

(b)   section 146(4) of the Law of Property Act 1925 (relief against forfeiture).

139.   Service of summons and re-entry.

(1)   In a case where section 138 has effect, if—

(a)   one-half-year's rent is in arrear at the time of the commencement of the action; and

(b)   the lessor has a right to re-enter for non-payment of that rent; and

(c)   no sufficient distress is to be found on the premises countervailing the arrears then due,

the service of the summons in the action in the prescribed manner shall stand in lieu of a demand and re-entry.

(2)   Where a lessor has enforced against a lessee, by re-entry without action, a right of re-entry or forfeiture as respects any land for non-payment of rent, the lessee may, if the net annual value for rating of the land does not exceed the county court limit, at any time within six months from the date on which the lessor re-entered apply to the county court for relief, and on any such application the court may, if it thinks fit, grant to the lessee such relief as the High Court could have granted.

(3)   Subsections (9B) and (9C) of section 138 shall have effect in relation to an application under subsection (2) of this section as they have effect in relation to an application under subsection (9A) of that section.

140.   Interpretation of sections 138 and 139.

For the purposes of sections 138 and 139—

"lease" includes—

(a)   an original or derivative under-lease;

(b)   an agreement for a lease where the lessee has become entitled to have his lease granted; and

(c)   a grant at a fee farm rent, or under a grant securing a rent by condition;

"lessee" includes—

(a)   an original or derivative under-lessee;

(b)   the persons deriving title under a lessee;

(c)   a grantee under a grant at a fee farm rent, or under a grant securing a rent by condition; and

(d)   the persons deriving title under such a grantee;
"lessor" includes—
(a)   an original or derivative under-lessor;
(b)   the persons deriving title under a lessor;
(c)   a person making a grant at a fee farm rent, or a grant securing a rent by condition; and
(d)   the persons deriving title under such a grantor;
"under-lease" includes an agreement for an under-lease where the under-lessee has become entitled to have his under-lease granted; and
"under-lessee" includes any person deriving title under an under-lessee.

HOUSING ACT 1985
(1985, c. 68)

[30 October 1985]

PART IV
SECURE TENANCIES AND RIGHTS OF SECURE TENANTS

Security of tenure

79.   Secure tenancies.

(1)   A tenancy under which a dwelling-house is let as a separate dwelling is a secure tenancy at any time when the conditions described in sections 80 and 81 as the landlord condition and the tenant condition are satisfied.

(2)   Subsection (1) has effect subject to—
(a)   the exceptions in Schedule 1 (tenancies which are not secure tenancies),
(b)   sections 89(3) and (4) and 90(3) and (4) (tenancies ceasing to be secure after death of tenant), and
(c)   sections 91(2) and 93(2) (tenancies ceasing to be secure in consequence of assignment or subletting).

(3)   The provisions of this Part apply in relation to a licence to occupy a dwelling-house (whether or not granted for a consideration) as they apply in relation to a tenancy.

(4)   Subsection (3) does not apply to a licence granted as a temporary expedient to a person who entered the dwelling-house or any other land as a trespasser (whether or not, before the grant of that licence, another licence to occupy that or another dwelling-house had been granted to him).

80.   The landlord condition.

(1)   The landlord condition is that the interest of the landlord belongs to one of the following authorities or bodies—
a local authority,
a new town corporation,
a housing action trust,
an urban development corporation,
the Development Board for Rural Wales,
a housing co-operative to which this section applies.

(3)   If a co-operative housing association ceases to be registered, it shall, within the period of 21 days beginning with the date on which it ceases to be registered, notify each of its tenants who thereby becomes a secure tenant, in writing, that he has become a secure tenant.

(4)   This section applies to a housing co-operative within the meaning of section 27B (agreements under certain superseded provisions) where the dwelling-house is comprised in a housing co-operative agreement within the meaning of that section.

81. The tenant condition.

The tenant condition is that the tenant is an individual and occupies the dwelling-house as his only or principal home; or, where the tenancy is a joint tenancy, that each of the joint tenants is an individual and at least one of them occupies the dwelling-house as his only or principal home.

82. Security of tenure.

(1) A secure tenancy which is either—

    (a) a weekly or other periodic tenancy, or

    (b) a tenancy for a term certain but subject to termination by the landlord,

cannot be brought to an end by the landlord except by obtaining an order of the court for the possession of the dwelling-house or an order under subsection (3).

(2) Where the landlord obtains an order for the possession of the dwelling-house, the tenancy ends on the date on which the tenant is to give up possession in pursuance of the order.

(3) Where a secure tenancy is a tenancy for a term certain but with a provision for re-entry or forfeiture, the court shall not order possession of the dwelling-house in pursuance of that provision, but in a case where the court would have made such an order it shall instead make an order terminating the tenancy on a date specified in the order and section 86 (periodic tenancy arising on termination of fixed term) shall apply.

(4) Section 146 of the Law of Property Act 1925 (restriction on and relief against forfeiture), except subsection (4) (vesting in under-lessee), and any other enactment or rule of law relating to forfeiture, shall apply in relation to proceedings for an order under subsection (3) of this section as if they were proceedings to enforce a right of re-entry or forfeiture.

83. Notice of proceedings for possession or termination.

(1) The court shall not entertain—

    (a) proceedings for the possession of a dwelling-house let under a secure tenancy, or

    (b) proceedings for the termination of a secure tenancy,

unless the landlord has served on the tenant a notice complying with the provisions of this section.

(2) The notice shall—

    (a) be in a form prescribed by regulations made by the Secretary of State,

    (b) specify the ground on which the court will be asked to make an order for the possession of the dwelling-house or for the termination of the tenancy, and

    (c) give particulars of that ground.

(3) Where the tenancy is a periodic tenancy the notice—

    (a) shall also specify a date after which proceedings for the possession of the dwelling-house may be begun, and

    (b) ceases to be in force twelve months after the date so specified;

and the date so specified must not be earlier than the date on which the tenancy could, apart from this Part, be brought to an end by notice to quit given by the landlord on the same date as the notice under this section.

(4) Where the tenancy is a periodic tenancy, the court shall not entertain any such proceedings unless they are begun after the date specified in the notice and at a time when the notice is still in force.

(5) Where a notice under this section is served with respect to a secure tenancy for a term certain, it has effect also with respect to any periodic tenancy arising on the termination of that tenancy by virtue of section 86; and subsections (3) and (4) of this section do not apply to the notice.

(6) Regulations under this section shall be made by statutory instrument and may make different provision with respect to different cases or descriptions of case, including different provision for different areas.

84. Grounds and orders for possession.

(1) The court shall not make an order for the possession of a dwelling-house let under a secure tenancy except on one or more of the grounds set out in Schedule 2.

(2) The court shall not make an order for possession—

(a) on the grounds set out in Part I of that Schedule (grounds 1 to 8), unless it considers it reasonable to make the order,

(b) on the grounds set out in Part II of that Schedule (grounds 9 to 11), unless it is satisfied that suitable accommodation will be available for the tenant when the order takes effect,

(c) on the grounds set out in Part III of that Schedule (grounds 12 to 16), unless it both considers it reasonable to make the order and is satisfied that suitable accommodation will be available for the tenant when the order takes effect;

and Part IV of the Schedule has effect for determining whether suitable accommodation will be available for a tenant.

(3) The court shall not make such an order on any of those grounds unless the ground is specified in the notice in pursuance of which proceedings for possession are begun; but the grounds so specified may be altered or added to with the leave of the court.

85. Extended discretion of court in certain proceedings for possession.

(1) Where proceedings are brought for possession of a dwelling-house let under a secure tenancy on any of the grounds set out in Part I or Part III of Schedule 2 (grounds 1 to 8 and 12 to 16: cases in which the court must be satisfied that it is reasonable to make a possession order), the court may adjourn the proceedings for such period or periods as it thinks fit.

(2) On the making of an order for possession of such a dwelling-house on any of those grounds, or at any time before the execution of the order, the court may—

(a) stay or suspend the execution of the order, or

(b) postpone the date of possession,

for such period or periods as the court thinks fit.

(3) On such an adjournment, stay, suspension or postponement the court—

(a) shall impose conditions with respect to the payment by the tenant of arrears of rent (if any) and rent or payments in respect of occupation after the termination of the tenancy (mesne profits), unless it considers that to do so would cause exceptional hardship to the tenant or would otherwise be unreasonable, and

(b) may impose such other conditions as it thinks fit.

(4) If the conditions are complied with, the court may, if it thinks fit, discharge or rescind the order for possession.

(5) Where proceedings are brought for possession of a dwelling-house which is let under a secure tenancy and—

(a) the tenant's spouse or former spouse, having rights of occupation under the Matrimonial Homes Act 1983, is then in occupation of the dwelling-house, and

(b) the tenancy is terminated as a result of those proceedings,

the spouse or former spouse shall, so long as he or she remains in occupation, have the same rights in relation to, or in connection with, any adjournment, stay, suspension or postponement in pursuance of this section as he or she would have if those rights of occupation were not affected by the termination of the tenancy.

86. Periodic tenancy arising on termination of fixed term.

(1) Where a secure tenancy ("the first tenancy") is a tenancy for a term certain and comes to an end—

(a) by effluxion of time, or

(b) by an order of the court under section 82(3) (termination in pursuance of provision for re-entry or forfeiture), a periodic tenancy of the same dwelling-house arises by virtue of this section, unless the tenant is granted another secure tenancy of the same dwelling-house (whether a tenancy for a term certain or a periodic tenancy) to begin on the coming to an end of the first tenancy.

(2) Where a periodic tenancy arises by virtue of this section—

(a) the periods of the tenancy are the same as those for which rent was last payable under the first tenancy, and

(b) the parties and the terms of the tenancy are the same as those of the first tenancy at the end of it;

except that the terms are confined to those which are compatible with a periodic tenancy and do not include any provision for re-entry or forfeiture.

Succession on death of tenant

87. Persons qualified to succeed tenant.

A person is qualified to succeed the tenant under a secure tenancy if he occupies the dwelling-house as his only or principal home at the time of the tenant's death and either—

(a) he is the tenant's spouse, or

(b) he is another member of the tenant's family and has resided with the tenant throughout the period of twelve months ending with the tenant's death;

unless, in either case, the tenant was himself a successor, as defined in section 88.

88. Cases where the tenant is a successor.

(1) The tenant is himself a successor if—

(a) the tenancy vested in him by virtue of section 89 (succession to a periodic tenancy), or

(b) he was a joint tenant and has become the sole tenant, or

(c) the tenancy arose by virtue of section 86 (periodic tenancy arising on ending of term certain) and the first tenancy there mentioned was granted to another person or jointly to him and another person, or

(d) he became the tenant on the tenancy being assigned to him (but subject to subsections (2) and (3)), or

(e) he became the tenant on the tenancy being vested in him on the death of the previous tenant.

(2) A tenant to whom the tenancy was assigned in pursuance of an order under section 24 of the Matrimonial Causes Act 1973 (property adjustment orders in connection with matrimonial proceedings) is a successor only if the other party to the marriage was a successor.

(3) A tenant to whom the tenancy was assigned by virtue of section 92 (assignments by way of exchange) is a successor only if he was a successor in relation to the tenancy which he himself assigned by virtue of that section.

(4) Where within six months of the coming to an end of a secure tenancy which is a periodic tenancy ("the former tenancy") the tenant becomes a tenant under another secure tenancy which is a periodic tenancy, and—

(a) the tenant was a successor in relation to the former tenancy, and

(b) under the other tenancy either the dwelling-house or the landlord, or both, are the same as under the former tenancy,

the tenant is also a successor in relation to the other tenancy unless the agreement creating that tenancy otherwise provides.

89. Succession to periodic tenancy.

(1) This section applies where a secure tenant dies and the tenancy is a periodic tenancy.

(2)   Where there is a person qualified to succeed the tenant, the tenancy vests by virtue of this section in that person, or if there is more than one such person in the one to be preferred in accordance with the following rules—

(a)   the tenant's spouse is to be preferred to another member of the tenant's family;

(b)   of two or more other members of the tenant's family such of them is to be preferred as may be agreed between them or as may, where there is no such agreement, be selected by the landlord.

(3)   Where there is no person qualified to succeed the tenant and the tenancy is vested or otherwise disposed of in the course of the administration of the tenant's estate, the tenancy ceases to be a secure tenancy unless the vesting or other disposal is in pursuance of an order made under section 24 of the Matrimonial Causes Act 1973 (property adjustment orders in connection with matrimonial proceedings).

(4)   A tenancy which ceases to be a secure tenancy by virtue of this section cannot subsequently become a secure tenancy.

90.   Devolution of term certain.

(1)   This section applies where a secure tenant dies and the tenancy is a tenancy for a term certain.

(2)   The tenancy remains a secure tenancy until—

(a)   it is vested or otherwise disposed of in the course of the administration of the tenant's estate, as mentioned in subsection (3), or

(b)   it is known that when it is so vested or disposed of it will not be a secure tenancy.

(3)   The tenancy ceases to be a secure tenancy on being vested or otherwise disposed of in the course of administration of the tenant's estate, unless—

(a)   the vesting or other disposal is in pursuance of an order made under section 24 of the Matrimonial Causes Act 1973 (property adjustment orders in connection with matrimonial proceedings), or

(b)   the vesting or other disposal is to a person qualified to succeed the tenant.

(4)   A tenancy which ceases to be a secure tenancy by virtue of this section cannot subsequently become a secure tenancy.

Assignment, lodgers and subletting

91.   Assignment in general prohibited.

(1)   A secure tenancy which is—

(a)   a periodic tenancy, or

(b)   a tenancy for a term certain granted on or after 5th November 1982,

is not capable of being assigned except in the cases mentioned in subsection (3).

(2)   If a secure tenancy for a term certain granted before 5th November 1982 is assigned, then, except in the cases mentioned in subsection (3), it ceases to be a secure tenancy and cannot subsequently become a secure tenancy.

(3)   The exceptions are—

(a)   an assignment in accordance with section 92 (assignment by way of exchange);

(b)   an assignment in pursuance of an order made under section 24 of the Matrimonial Causes Act 1973 (property adjustment orders in connection with matrimonial proceedings);

(c)   an assignment to a person who would be qualified to succeed the tenant if the tenant died immediately before the assignment.

92.   Assignments by way of exchange.

(1)   It is a term of every secure tenancy that the tenant may, with the written consent of the landlord, assign the tenancy to another secure tenant who satisfies the condition in subsection (2) or to an assured tenant who satisfies the conditions in subsection (2A).

(2)   The condition is that the other secure tenant has the written consent of his landlord to an assignment of his tenancy either to the first-mentioned tenant or to another secure tenant who satisfies the condition in this subsection.

(2A)   The conditions to be satisfied with respect to an assured tenant are—

(a)   that the landlord under his assured tenancy is either the Housing Corporation, Housing for Wales, a registered housing association or a housing trust which is a charity; and

(b)   that he intends to confirm his assured tenancy to the secure tenant referred to in subsection (1) or to another secure tenant who satisfies the condition in subsection (2).

(3)   The consent required by virtue of this section shall not be withheld except on one or more of the grounds set out in Schedule 3, and if withheld otherwise than on one of those grounds shall be treated as given.

(4)   The landlord may not rely on any of the grounds set out in Schedule 3 unless he has, within 42 days of the tenant's application for the consent, served on the tenant a notice specifying the ground and giving particulars of it.

(5)   Where rent lawfully due from the tenant has not been paid or an obligation of the tenancy has been broken or not performed, the consent required by virtue of this section may be given subject to a condition requiring the tenant to pay the outstanding rent, remedy the breach or perform the obligation.

(6)   Except as provided by subsection (5), a consent required by virtue of this section cannot be given subject to a condition, and a condition imposed otherwise than as so provided shall be disregarded.

93.   Lodgers and subletting.

(1)   It is a term of every secure tenancy that the tenant—

(a)   may allow any persons to reside as lodgers in the dwelling-house, but

(b)   will not, without the written consent of the landlord, sublet or part with possession of part of the dwelling-house.

(2)   If the tenant under a secure tenancy parts with the possession of the dwelling-house or sublets the whole of it (or sublets first part of it and then the remainder), the tenancy ceases to be a secure tenancy and cannot subsequently become a secure tenancy.

94.   Consent to subletting.

(1)   This section applies to the consent required by virtue of section 93(1)(b) (landlord's consent to subletting of part of dwelling-house).

(2)   Consent shall not be unreasonably withheld (and if unreasonably withheld shall be treated as given), and if a question arises whether the withholding of consent was unreasonable it is for the landlord to show that it was not.

(3)   In determining that question the following matters, if shown by the landlord, are among those to be taken into account—

(a)   that the consent would lead to overcrowding of the dwelling-house within the meaning of Part X (overcrowding);

(b)   that the landlord proposes to carry out works on the dwelling-house, or on the building of which it forms part, and that the proposed works will affect the accommodation likely to be used by the sub-tenant who would reside in the dwelling-house as a result of the consent.

(4)   Consent may be validly given notwithstanding that it follows, instead of preceding, the action requiring it.

(5)   Consent cannot be given subject to a condition (and if purporting to be given subject to a condition shall be treated as given unconditionally).

(6)   Where the tenant has applied in writing for consent, then—

(a)   if the landlord refuses to give consent, it shall give the tenant a written statement of the reasons why consent was refused, and

(b)   if the landlord neither gives nor refuses to give consent within a reasonable time, consent shall be taken to have been withheld.

95.   Assignment or subletting where tenant condition not satisfied.

(1)   This section applies to a tenancy which is not a secure tenancy but would be if the tenant condition referred to in section 81 (occupation by the tenant) were satisfied.

(2)   Sections 91 and 93(2) (restrictions on assignment or subletting of whole dwelling-house) apply to such a tenancy as they apply to a secure tenancy, except that—

(a)   section 91(3)(b) and (c) (assignments excepted from restrictions) do not apply to such a tenancy for a term certain granted before 5th November 1982, and

(b)   references to the tenancy ceasing to be secure shall be disregarded, without prejudice to the application of the remainder of the provisions in which those references occur.

Repairs and improvements

96.   Right to carry out repairs.

(1)   The Secretary of State may by regulations make a scheme for entitling secure tenants, subject to and in accordance with the provisions of the scheme—

(a)   to carry out to the dwelling-houses of which they are secure tenants repairs which their landlords are obliged by repairing covenants to carry out, and

(b)   after carrying out the repairs, to recover from their landlords such sums as may be determined by or under the scheme.

(2)   The regulations may make such procedural, incidental, supplementary and transitional provision as may appear to the Secretary of State to be necessary or expedient, and may in particular—

(a)   provide for questions arising under the scheme to be referred to and determined by the county court;

(b)   provide that where a secure tenant makes application under the scheme his landlord's obligation under the repairing covenants shall cease to apply for such period and to such extent as may be determined by or under the scheme.

(3)   The regulations may make different provision with respect to different cases or descriptions of case, including different provision for different areas.

(4)   Regulations under this section shall be made by statutory instrument which shall be subject to annulment in pursuance of a resolution of either House of Parliament.

(5)   In this section "repairing covenant", in relation to a dwelling-house, means a covenant, whether express or implied, obliging the landlord to keep in repair the dwelling-house or any part of the dwelling-house.

97.   Tenant's improvements require consent.

(1)   It is a term of every secure tenancy that the tenant will not make any improvement without the written consent of the landlord.

(2)   In this Part "improvement" means any alteration in, or addition to, a dwelling-house, and includes—

(a)   any addition to or alteration in landlord's fixtures and fittings,

(b)   any addition or alteration connected with the provision of services to the dwelling-house,

(c)   the erection of a wireless or television aerial, and

(d)   the carrying out of external decoration.

(3)   The consent required by virtue of subsection (1) shall not be unreasonably withheld, and if unreasonably withheld shall be treated as given.

(4)   The provisions of this section have effect, in relation to secure tenancies, in place of section 19(2) of the Landlord and Tenant Act 1927 (general provisions as to covenants, &c. not to make improvements without consent).

98.   Provisions as to consents required by s. 97.

(1)   If a question arises whether the withholding of a consent required by virtue of

section 97 (landlord's consent to improvements) was unreasonable, it is for the landlord to show that it was not.

(2) In determining that question the court shall, in particular, have regard to the extent to which the improvement would be likely—

(a) to make the dwelling-house, or any other premises, less safe for occupiers,

(b) to cause the landlord to incur expenditure which it would be unlikely to incur if the improvement were not made, or

(c) to reduce the price which the dwelling-house would fetch if sold on the open market or the rent which the landlord would be able to charge on letting the dwelling-house.

(3) A consent required by virtue of section 97 may be validly given notwithstanding that it follows, instead of preceding, the action requiring it.

(4) Where a tenant has applied in writing for a consent which is required by virtue of section 97—

(a) the landlord shall if it refuses consent give the tenant a written statement of the reason why consent was refused, and

(b) if the landlord neither gives nor refuses to give consent within a reasonable time, consent shall be taken to have been withheld.

99. Conditional consent to improvements.

(1) Consent required by virtue of section 97 (landlord's consent to improvements) may be given subject to conditions.

(2) If the tenant has applied in writing for consent and the landlord gives consent subject to an unreasonable condition, consent shall be taken to have been unreasonably withheld.

(3) If a question arises whether a condition was reasonable, it is for the landlord to show that it was.

(4) A failure by a secure tenant to satisfy a reasonable condition imposed by his landlord in giving consent to an improvement which the tenant proposes to make, or has made, shall be treated for the purposes of this Part as a breach by the tenant of an obligation of his tenancy.

100. Power to reimburse cost of tenant's improvements.

(1) Where a secure tenant has made an improvement and—

(a) the work on the improvement was begun on or after 3rd October 1980,

(b) the landlord, or a predecessor in title of the landlord, has given its written consent to the improvement or is treated as having given its consent, and

(c) the improvement has materially added to the price which the dwelling-house may be expected to fetch if sold on the open market, or the rent which the landlord may be expected to be able to charge on letting the dwelling-house,

the landlord may, at or after the end of the tenancy, make to the tenant (or his personal representatives) such payment in respect of the improvement as the landlord considers to be appropriate.

(2) The amount which a landlord may pay under this section in respect of an improvement shall not exceed the cost, or likely cost, of the improvement after deducting the amount of any improvement grant, intermediate grant, special grant, repairs grant or common parts grant under Part XV in respect of the improvement.

(3) The power conferred by this section to make such payments as are mentioned in subsection (1) is in addition to any other power of the landlord to make such payments.

101. Rent not to be increased on account of tenant's improvements.

(1) This section applies where a person (the "improving tenant") who is or was the secure tenant of a dwelling-house has lawfully made an improvement and has borne the

whole or part of its cost; and for the purposes of this section a person shall be treated as having borne any cost which he would have borne but for an improvement grant, intermediate grant, special grant, repairs grant or common parts grant under Part XV.

(1A)   In subsection (1)—

(a)   the reference to an improvement grant under Part XV includes a reference to a renovation grant, disabled facilities grant or HMO grant under Part VIII of the Local Government and Housing Act 1989; and

(b)   the reference to a common parts grant under Part XV includes a reference to a common parts grant under the said Part VIII.

(2)   In determining, at any time whilst the improving tenant or his qualifying successor is a secure tenant of the dwelling-house, whether or to what extent to increase the rent, the landlord shall treat the improvement as justifying only such part of an increase which would otherwise be attributable to the improvement as corresponds to the part of the cost which was not borne by the tenant (and accordingly as not justifying an increase if he bore the whole cost).

(3)   The following are qualifying successors of an improving tenant—

(a)   a person in whom the tenancy vested under section 89 (succession to periodic tenancy) on the death of the tenant;

(b)   a person to whom the tenancy was assigned by the tenant and who would have been qualified to succeed him if he had died immediately before the assignment;

(c)   a person to whom the tenancy was assigned by the tenant in pursuance of an order made under section 24 of the Matrimonial Causes Act 1973 (property adjustment orders in connection with matrimonial proceedings);

(d)   a spouse or former spouse of the tenant to whom the tenancy has been transferred by an order under paragraph 2 of Schedule 1 to the Matrimonial Homes Act 1983.

(4)   This section does not apply to an increase of rent attributable to rates.

Variation of terms of tenancy

102.   Variation of terms of secure tenancy.

(1)   The terms of a secure tenancy may be varied in the following ways, and not otherwise—

(a)   by agreement between the landlord and the tenant;

(b)   to the extent that the variation relates to rent or to payments in respect of rates or services, by the landlord or the tenant in accordance with a provision in the lease or agreement creating the tenancy, or in an agreement varying it;

(c)   in accordance with section 103 (notice of variation of periodic tenancy).

(2)   References in this section and section 103 to variation include addition and deletion; and for the purposes of this section the conversion of a monthly tenancy into a weekly tenancy, or a weekly tenancy into a monthly tenancy, is a variation of a term of the tenancy, but a variation of the premises let under a tenancy is not.

(3)   This section and section 103 do not apply to a term of a tenancy which—

(a)   is implied by an enactment, or

(b)   may be varied under section 93 of the Rent Act 1977 (housing association and other tenancies: increase of rent without notice to quit).

(4)   This section and section 103 apply in relation to the terms of a periodic tenancy arising by virtue of section 86 (periodic tenancy arising on termination of a fixed term) as they would have applied to the terms of the first tenancy mentioned in that section had that tenancy been a periodic tenancy.

103.   Notice of variation of periodic tenancy.

(1)   The terms of a secure tenancy which is a periodic tenancy may be varied by the landlord by a notice of variation served on the tenant.

(2)   Before serving a notice of variation on the tenant the landlord shall serve on him a preliminary notice—

    (a) informing the tenant of the landlord's intention to serve a notice of variation,

    (b) specifying the proposed variation and its effect, and

    (c) inviting the tenant to comment on the proposed variation within such time, specified in the notice, as the landlord considers reasonable;

and the landlord shall consider any comments made by the tenant within the specified time.

(3)   Subsection (2) does not apply to a variation of the rent, or of payments in respect of services or facilities provided by the landlord or of payments in respect of rates.

(4)   The notice of variation shall specify—

    (a) the variation effected by it, and

    (b) the date on which it takes effect;

and the period between the date on which it is served and the date on which it takes effect must be at least four weeks or the rental period, whichever is the longer.

(5)   The notice of variation, when served, shall be accompanied by such information as the landlord considers necessary to inform the tenant of the nature and effect of the variation.

(6)   If after the service of a notice of variation the tenant, before the date on which the variation is to take effect, gives a valid notice to quit, the notice of variation shall not take effect unless the tenant, with the written agreement of the landlord, withdraws his notice to quit before that date.

Provision of information and consultation

104.   Provision of information about tenancies.

(1)   Every body which lets dwelling-houses under secure tenancies shall from time to time publish information about its secure tenancies in such form as it considers best suited to explain in simple terms, and so far as it considers it appropriate, the effect of—

    (a) the express terms of its secure tenancies,

    (b) the provisions of this Part and Part V (the right to buy), and

    (c) the provisions of sections 11 to 16 of the Landlord and Tenant Act 1985 (landlord's repairing obligations),

and shall ensure that so far as is reasonably practicable the information so published is kept up to date.

(2)   The landlord under a secure tenancy shall supply the tenant with—

    (a) a copy of the information for secure tenants published by it under subsection (1), and

    (b) a written statement of the terms of the tenancy, so far as they are neither expressed in the lease or written tenancy agreement (if any) nor implied by law;

and the statement required by paragraph (b) shall be supplied on the grant of the tenancy or as soon as practicable afterwards.

105.   Consultation on matters of housing management.

(1)   A landlord authority shall maintain such arrangements as it considers appropriate to enable those of its secure tenants who are likely to be substantially affected by a matter of housing management to which this section applies—

    (a) to be informed of the authority's proposals in respect of the matter, and

    (b) to make their views known to the authority within a specified period;

and the authority shall, before making any decision on the matter, consider any representations made to it in accordance with those arrangements.

(2)   For the purposes of this section, a matter is one of housing management if, in the opinion of the landlord authority, it relates to—

    (a) the management, maintenance, improvement or demolition of dwelling-houses let by the authority under secure tenancies, or

(b)   the provision of services or amenities in connection with such dwelling-houses;

but not so far as it relates to the rent payable under a secure tenancy or to charges for services or facilities provided by the authority.

(3)   This section applies to matters of housing management which, in the opinion of the landlord authority, represent—

(a)   a new programme of maintenance, improvement or demolition, or

(b)   a change in the practice or policy of the authority,

and are likely substantially to affect either its secure tenants as a whole or a group of them who form a distinct social group or occupy dwelling-houses which constitute a distinct class (whether by reference to the kind of dwelling-house, or the housing estate or other larger area in which they are situated).

(4)   In the case of a landlord authority which is a local housing authority, the reference in subsection (2) to the provision of services or amenities is a reference only to the provision of services or amenities by the authority acting in its capacity as landlord of the dwelling-houses concerned.

(5)   A landlord authority shall publish details of the arrangements which it makes under this section, and a copy of the documents published under this subsection shall—

(a)   be made available at the authority's principal office for inspection at all reasonable hours, without charge, by members of the public, and

(b)   be given, on payment of a reasonable fee, to any member of the public who asks for one.

(6)   A landlord authority which is a registered housing association shall, instead of complying with paragraph (a) of subsection (5), send a copy of any document published under that subsection—

(a)   to the Corporation, and

(b)   to the council of any district or London borough in which there are dwelling-houses let by the association under secure tenancies;

and a council to whom a copy is sent under this subsection shall make it available at its principal office for inspection at all reasonable hours, without charge, by members of the public.

106.   Information about housing allocation.

(1)   A landlord authority shall publish a summary of its rules—

(a)   for determining priority as between applicants in the allocation of its housing accommodation, and

(b)   governing cases where secure tenants wish to move (whether or not by way of exchange of dwelling-houses) to other dwelling-houses let under secure tenancies by that authority or another body.

(2)   A landlord authority shall—

(a)   maintain a set of the rules referred to in subsection (1) and of the rules which it has laid down governing the procedure to be followed in allocating its housing accommodation, and

(b)   make them available at its principal office for inspection at all reasonable hours, without charge, by members of the public.

(3)   A landlord authority which is a registered housing association shall, instead of complying with paragraph (b) of subsection (2), send a set of the rules referred to in paragraph (a) of that subsection—

(a)   to the Corporation, and

(b)   to the council of any district or London borough in which there are dwelling-houses let or to be let by the association under secure tenancies;

and a council to whom a set of rules is sent under this subsection shall make it available at its principal office for inspection at all reasonable hours, without charge, by members of the public.

(4)   A copy of the summary published under subsection (1) shall be given without charge, and a copy of the set of rules maintained under subsection (2) shall be given on payment of a reasonable fee, to any member of the public who asks for one.

(5)   At the request of a person who has applied to it for housing accommodation, a landlord authority shall make available to him, at all reasonable times and without charge, details of the particulars which he has given to the authority about himself and his family and which the authority has recorded as being relevant to his application for accommodation.

106A.   Consultation before disposal to private sector landlord.

(1)   The provisions of Schedule 3A have effect with respect to the duties of—

(a)   a local authority proposing to dispose of dwelling-houses subject to secure tenancies, and

(b)   the Secretary of State in considering whether to give his consent to such a disposal,

to have regard to the views of tenants liable as a result of the disposal to cease to be secure tenants.

(2)   In relation to a disposal to which that Schedule applies, the provisions of that Schedule apply in place of the provisions of section 105 (consultation on matters of housing management).

Miscellaneous

108.   Heating charges.

(1)   This section applies to secure tenants of dwelling-houses to which a heating authority supply heat produced at a heating installation.

(2)   The Secretary of State may by regulations require heating authorities to adopt such methods for determining heating charges payable by such tenants as will secure that the proportion of heating costs borne by each of those tenants is no greater than is reasonable.

(3)   The Secretary of State may by regulations make provision for entitling such tenants, subject to and in accordance with the regulations, to require the heating authority—

(a)   to give them, in such form as may be prescribed by the regulations, such information as to heating charges and heating costs as may be so prescribed, and

(b)   where such informatoon has been given, to afford them reasonable facilities for inspecting the accounts, receipts and other documents supporting the information and for taking copies or extracts from them.

(4)   Regulations under this section—

(a)   may make different provision with respect to different cases or descriptions of case, including different provision for different areas;

(b)   may make such procedural, incidental, supplementary and transitional provision as appears to the Secretary of State to be necessary or expedient, and may in particular provide for any question arising under the regulations to be referred to and determined by the county court; and

(c)   shall be made by statutory instrument which shall be subject to annulment in pursuance of a resolution of either House of Parliament.

(5)   In this section—

(a)   "heating authority" means a housing authority or housing action trust who operate a heating installation and supply to premises heat produced at the installation;

(b)   "heating installation" means a generating station or other installation for producing heat;

(c)   references to heat produced at an installation include steam produced from, and air and water heated by, heat so produced;

(d)   "heating charge" means an amount payable to a heating authority in respect of heat produced at a heating installation and supplied to premises, including in the case of heat supplied to premises let by the authority such an amount payable as part of the rent;

(e)   "heating costs" means expenses incurred by a heating authority in operating a heating installation.

109. Provisions not applying to tenancies of co-operative housing associations.

Sections 91 to 108 (assignment and subletting, repairs and improvements, variation of terms, provision of information and consultation, contributions to costs of transfers and heating charges) do not apply to a tenancy when the interest of the landlord belongs to a co-operative housing association.

Supplementary provisions

109A.   Acquisition of dwelling-house subject to statutory tenancy.

Where an authority or body within section 80 (the landlord condition for secure tenancies) becomes the landlord of a dwelling-house subject to a statutory tenancy, the tenancy shall be treated for all purposes as if it were a contractual tenancy on the same terms, and the provisions of this Part apply accordingly.

110.   Jurisdiction of county court.

(1)   A county court has jurisdiction to determine questions arising under this Part and to entertain proceedings brought under this Part and claims, for whatever amount, in connection with a secure tenancy.

(2)   That jurisdiction includes jurisdiction to entertain proceedings on the following questions—

(a)   whether a consent required by section 92 (assignment by way of exchange) was withheld otherwise than on one or more of the grounds set out in Schedule 3,

(b)   whether a consent required by section 93(1)(b) or 97(1) (landlord's consent to subletting of part of dwelling-house or to carrying out of improvements) was withheld or unreasonably withheld, or

(c)   whether a statement supplied in pursuance of section 104(2)(b) (written statement of certain terms of tenancy) is accurate,

notwithstanding that no other relief is sought than a declaration.

(3)   If a person takes proceedings in the High Court which, by virtue of this section, he could have taken in the county court, he is not entitled to recover any costs.

111.   County court rules and directions.

(1)   The Lord Chancellor may make such rules and give such directions as he thinks fit for the purpose of giving effect to—

(a)   section 85 (extended discretion of court in certain proceedings for possession), and

(b)   section 110 (jurisdiction of county court to determine questions arising under this Part).

(2)   The rules and directions may provide—

(a)   for the exercise by a registrar of a county court of any jurisdiction exercisable under the provisions mentioned in subsection (1), and

(b)   for the conduct of proceedings in private.

(3)   The power to make rules is exercisable by statutory instrument which shall be subject to annulment in pursuance of a resolution of either House of Parliament.

112. Meaning of "dwelling-house".

(1) For the purposes of this Part a dwelling-house may be a house or a part of a house.

(2) Land let together with a dwelling-house shall be treated for the purposes of this Part as part of the dwelling-house unless the land is agricultural land (as defined in section 26(3)(a) of the General Rate Act 1967) exceeding two acres.

113. Members of a person's family.

(1) A person is a member of another's family within the meaning of this Part if—

(a) he is the spouse of that person, or he and that person live together as husband and wife, or

(b) he is that person's parent, grandparent, child, grandchild, brother, sister, uncle, aunt, nephew or niece.

(2) For the purpose of subsection (1)(b)—

(a) a relationship by marriage shall be treated as a relationship by blood,

(b) a relationship of the half-blood shall be treated as a relationship of the whole blood,

(c) the stepchild of a person shall be treated as his child, and

(d) an illegitimate child shall be treated as the legitimate child of his mother and reputed father.

114. Meaning of "landlord authority".

(1) In this Part "landlord authority" means—

a local housing authority,

a registered housing association other than a co-operative housing association,

a housing trust which is a charity,

a development corporation,

a housing action trust,

an urban development corporation, or

the Development Board for Rural Wales,

other than an authority in respect of which an exemption certificate has been issued.

(2) The Secretary of State may, on an application duly made by the authority concerned, issue an exemption certificate to—

a development corporation,

a housing action trust,

an urban development corporation, or

the Development Board for Rural Wales,

if he is satisfied that it has transferred, or otherwise disposed of, at least three-quarters of the dwellings which have at any time before the making of the application been vested in it.

(3) The application shall be in such form and shall be accompanied by such information as the Secretary of State may, either generally or in relation to a particular case, direct.

115. Meaning of "long tenancy".

In this part—

(1) The following are long tenancies for the purposes of this Part, subject to subsection (2)—

(a) a tenancy granted for a term certain exceeding 21 years, whether or not it is (or may become) terminable before the end of that term by notice given by the tenant or by re-entry or forfeiture;

(b) a tenancy for a term fixed by law under a grant with a covenant or obligation for perpetual renewal, other than a tenancy by sub-demise from one which is not a long tenancy;

(c)   any tenancy granted in pursuance of Part V (the right to buy).

(2)   A tenancy granted so as to become terminable by notice after a death is not a long tenancy for the purposes of this Part, unless—

(a)   it is granted by a housing association which at the time of the grant is registered,

(b)   it is granted at a premium calculated by reference to a percentage of the value of the dwelling-house or of the cost of providing it, and

(c)   at the time it is granted it complies with the requirements of the regulations then in force under section 140(4)(b) of the Housing Act 1980 or paragraph 4(2)(b) of Schedule 4A to the Leasehold Reform Act 1967 (conditions for exclusion of shared ownership leases from Part I of the Leasehold Reform Act 1967) or, in the case of a tenancy granted before any such regulations were brought into force, with the first such regulations to be in force.

116.   Minor definitions.

"common parts", in relation to a dwelling-house let under a tenancy, means any part of a building comprising the dwelling-house and any other premises which the tenant is entitled under the terms of the tenancy to use in common with the occupiers of other dwelling-houses let by the landlord;

"housing purposes" means the purposes for which dwelling-houses are held by local housing authorities under Part II (provision of housing) or purposes corresponding to those purposes;

"rental period" means a period in respect of which a payment of rent falls to be made;

"term", in relation to a secure tenancy, includes a condition of the tenancy.

117.   Index of defined expressions: Part IV.

The following Table shows provisions defining or otherwise explaining expressions used in this Part (other than provisions defining or explaining an expression in the same section or paragraph):—

assured tenancy	section 622
cemetery	section 622
charity	section 622
common parts (in relation to a dwelling-house let under a tenancy)	section 116
consent (in Schedule 3A)	paragraph 2(3) of that Schedule
co-operative housing association	section 5(2)
the corporation	section 6A
development corporation	section 4(c)
dwelling-house	section 112
family (member of)	section 113
housing association	section 5(1)
housing authority	section 4(a)
housing purposes	section 116
housing trust	section 6
improvement	section 97(2)
landlord (in Part V of Schedule 2)	paragraph 7 of that Part
landlord authority	section 114
local authority	section 4(e)
local housing authority	section 1, 2(2)
long tenancy	section 115
management agreement and manager	sections 27(2) and 27B(4)
new town corporation	section 4(b)
qualified to succeed (on the death of a secure tenant)	section 87

LANDLORD AND TENANT ACT 1985
(1985, c. 70)

An Act to consolidate certain provisions of the law of landlord and tenant formerly found in the Housing Acts, together with the Landlord and Tenant Act 1962, with amendments to give effect to recommendations of the Law Commission.   **[30 October 1985]**

Information to be given to tenant

1. Disclosure of landord's identity.

(1) If the tenant of premises occupied as a dwelling makes a written request for the landlord's name and address to—

(a) any person who demands, or the last person who received, rent payable under the tenancy, or

(b) any other person for the time being acting as agent for the landlord, in relation to the tenancy,

that person shall supply the tenant with a written statement of the landlord's name and address within the period of 21 days beginning with the day on which he receives the request.

(2) A person who, without reasonable excuse, fails to comply with subsection (1) commits a summary offence and is liable on conviction to a fine not exceeding level 4 on the standard scale.

(3) In this section and section 2—

(a) "tenant" includes a statutory tenant; and

(b) "landlord" means the immediate landlord.

2. Disclosure of directors, &c. of corporate landlord.

(1) Where a tenant is supplied under section 1 with the name and address of his landlord and the landlord is a body corporate, he may make a further written request to the landlord for the name and address of every director and of the secretary of the landlord.

(2) The landlord shall supply the tenant with a written statement of the information requested within the period of 21 days beginning with the day on which he receives the request.

(3) A request under this section is duly made to the landlord if it is made to—

(a) an agent of the landlord, or

(b) a person who demands the rent of the premises concerned;

and any such agent or person to whom such a request is made shall forward it to the landlord as soon as may be.

(4) A landlord who, without reasonable excuse, fails to comply with a request under this section, and a person who, without reasonable excuse, fails to comply with a requirement imposed on him by subsection (3), commits a summary offence and is liable on conviction to a fine not exceeding level 4 on the standard scale.

3. Duty to inform tenant of assignment of landlord's interest.

(1) If the interest of the landlord under a tenancy of premises which consist of or include a dwelling is assigned, the new landlord shall give notice in writing of the

assignment, and of his name and address, to the tenant not later than the next day on which rent is payable under the tenancy or, if that is within two months of the assignment, the end of that period of two months.

(2)   If trustees constitute the new landlord, a collective description of the trustees as the trustees of the trust in question may be given as the name of the landlord, and where such a collective description is given—

(a)   the address of the new landlord may be given as the address from which the affairs of the trust are conducted, and

(b)   a change in the persons who are for the time being the trustees of the trust shall not be treated as an assignment of the interest of the landlord.

(3)   A person who is the new landlord under a tenancy falling within subsection (1) and who fails, without reasonable excuse, to give the notice required by that subsection, commits a summary offence and is liable on conviction to a fine not exceeding level 4 on the standard scale.

(3A)   The person who was the landlord under the tenancy immediately before the assignment ("the old landlord") shall be liable to the tenant in respect of any breach of any covenant, condition or agreement under the tenancy occurring before the end of the relevant period in like manner as if the interest assigned were still vested in him; and where the new landlord is also liable to the tenant in respect of any such breach occurring within that period, he and the old landlord shall be jointly and severally liable in respect of it.

(3B)   In subsection (3A) "the relevant period" means the period beginning with the date of the assignment and ending with the date when—

(a)   notice in writing of the assignment, and of the new landlord's name and address, is given to the tenant by the new landlord (whether in accordance with subection (1) or not), or

(b)   notice in writing of the assignment, and of the new landlord's name and last-known address, is given to the tenant by the old landlord,
whichever happens first.

(4)   In this section

(a)   "tenancy" includes a statutory tenancy, and

(b)   references to the assignment of the landlord's interest include any conveyance other than a mortgage or charge.

Provision of rent books

4.   Provision of rent books.

(1)   Where a tenant has a right to occupy premises as a residence in consideration of a rent payable weekly, the landlord shall provide a rent book or other similar document for use in respect of the premises.

(2)   Subsection (1) does not apply to premises if the rent includes a payment in respect of board and the value of that board to the tenant forms a substantial proportion of the whole rent.

(3)   In this section and sections 5 to 7—

(a)   "tenant" includes a statutory tenant and a person having a contractual right to occupy the premises; and

(b)   "landlord", in relation to a person having such a contractual right, means the person who granted the right or any successor in title of his, as the case may require.

5.   Information to be contained in rent books.

(1)   A rent book or other similar document provided in pursuance of section 4 shall contain notice of the name and address of the landlord of the premises and—

(a)   if the premises are occupied by virtue of a restricted contract, particulars of the rent and of the other terms and conditions of the contract and notice of such other matters as may be prescribed;

(b) if the premises are let on or subject to a protected or statutory tenancy or let on an assured tenancy within the meaning of Part I of the Housing Act 1988, notice of such matters as may be prescribed.

(2) If the premises are occupied by virtue of a restricted contract or let on or subject to a protected or statutory tenancy or let on an assured tenancy within the meaning of Part I of the Housing Act 1988, the notice and particulars required by this section shall be in the prescribed form.

(3) In this section "prescribed" means prescribed by regulations made by the Secretary of State, which—

(a) may make different provision for different cases, and

(b) shall be made by statutory instrument which shall be subject to annulment in pursuance of a resolution of either House of Parliament.

6. Information to be supplied by companies.

(1) Where the landlord of premises to which section 4(1) applies (premises occupied as a residence at a weekly rent) is a company, and the tenant serves on the landlord a request in writing to that effect, the landlord shall give the tenant in writing particulars of the name and address of every director and of the secretary of the company.

(2) A request under this section is duly served on the landlord if it is served—

(a) on an agent of the landlord named as such in the rent book or other similar document, or

(b) on the person who receives the rent of the premises;

and a person on whom a request is so served shall forward it to the landlord as soon as may be.

7. Offences.

(1) If the landlord of premises to which section 4(1) applies (premises occupied as a residence at a weekly rent) fails to comply with any relevant requirement of—

section 4 (provision of rent book), or

section 5 (information to be contained in rent book), or

section 6 (information to be supplied by companies),

he commits a summary offence and is liable on conviction to a fine not exceeding level 4 on the standard scale.

(2) If a person demands or receives rent on behalf of the landlord of such premises while any relevant requirement of—

section 4 (provision of rent book), or

section 5 (information to be contained in rent book),

is not complied with, then, unless he shows that he neither knew nor had reasonable cause to suspect that any such requirement had not been complied with, he commits a summary offence and is liable to a fine not exceeding level 4 on the standard scale.

(3) If a person fails to comply with a requirement imposed on him by section 6(2) (duty to forward request to landlord), he commits a summary offence and is liable on conviction to a fine not exceeding level 4 on the standard scale.

(4) If a default in respect of which—

(a) a landlord is convicted of an offence under subsection (1), or

(b) another person is convicted of an offence under subsection (3),

continues for more than 14 days after the conviction, the landlord or other person commits a further offence under that subsection in respect of the default.

Implied terms as to fitness for human habitation

8. Implied terms as to fitness for human habitation.

(1) In a contract to which this section applies for the letting of a house for human habitation there is implied, notwithstanding any stipulation to the contrary—

(a)   a condition that the house is fit for human habitation at the commencement of the tenancy, and

(b)   an undertaking that the house will be kept by the landlord fit for human habitation during the tenancy.

(2)   The landlord, or a person authorised by him in writing, may at reasonable times of the day, on giving 24 hours' notice in writing to the tenant or occupier, enter premises to which this section applies for the purpose of viewing their state and condition.

(3)   This section applies to a contract if—

(a)   the rent does not exceed the figure applicable in accordance with subsection (4), and

(b)   the letting is not on such terms as to the tenant's responsibility as are mentioned in subsection (5).

(4)   The rent limit for the application of this section is shown by the following Table, by reference to the date of making of the contract and the situation of the premises:

TABLE

Date of making of contract	Rent limit
Before 31st July 1923.	In London: £40. Elsewhere: £26 or £16 (see Note 1).
On or after 31st July 1923 and before 6th July 1957.	In London: £40. Elsewhere: £26.
On or after 6th July 1957.	In London: £80. Elsewhere: £52.

NOTES

1.   The applicable figure for contracts made before 31st July 1923 is £26 in the case of premises situated in a borough or urban district which at the date of the contract had according to the last published census a population of 50,000 or more. In the case of a house situated elsewhere, the figure is £16.

2.   The references to "London" are, in relation to contracts made before 1st April 1965, to the administrative county of London and, in relation to contracts made on or after that date, to Greater London exclusive of the outer London boroughs.

(5)   This section does not apply where a house is let for a term of three years or more (the lease not being determinable at the option of either party before the expiration of three years) upon terms that the tenant puts the premises into a condition reasonably fit for human habitation.

(6)   In this section "house" includes—

(a)   a part of a house, and

(b)   any yard, garden, outhouses and appurtenances belonging to the house or usually enjoyed with it.

9.   Application of s. 8 to certain houses occupied by agricultural workers.

(1)   Where under the contract of employment of a worker employed in agriculture the provision of a house for his occupation forms part of his remuneration and the provisions of section 8 (implied terms as to fitness for human habitation) are inapplicable by reason only of the house not being let to him—

(a)   there are implied as part of the contract of employment, notwithstanding any stipulation to the contrary, the like condition and undertaking as would be implied under that section if the house were so let, and

(b)   the provisions of that section apply accordingly, with the substitution of "employer" for "landlord" and such other modifications as may be necessary.

(2)   This section does not affect any obligation of a person other than the employer to repair a house to which this section applies, or any remedy for enforcing such an obligation.

(3) In this section "house" includes—

    (a) a part of a house, and

    (b) any yard, garden, outhouses and appurtenances belonging to the house or usually enjoyed with it.

10. Fitness for human habitation.

In determining for the purposes of this Act whether a house is unfit for human habitation, regard shall be had to its condition in respect of the following matters—

    repair,

    stability,

    freedom from damp,

    internal arrangement,

    natural lighting,

    ventilation,

    water supply,

    drainage and sanitary conveniences,

    facilities for preparation and cooking of food and for the disposal of waste water;

and the house shall be regarded as unfit for human habitation if, and only if, it is so far defective in one or more of those matters that it is not reasonably suitable for occupation in that condition.

Repairing obligations

11. Repairing obligations in short leases.

(1) In a lease to which this section applies (as to which, see sections 13 and 14) there is implied a covenant by the lessor—

    (a) to keep in repair the structure and exterior of the dwelling-house (including drains, gutters and external pipes),

    (b) to keep in repair and proper working order the installations in the dwelling-house for the supply of water, gas and electricity and for sanitation (including basins, sinks, baths and sanitary conveniences, but not other fixtures, fittings and appliances for making use of the supply of water, gas or electricity), and

    (c) to keep in repair and proper working order the installations in the dwelling-house for space heating and heating water.

(2) The covenant implied by subsection (1) ("the lessor's repairing covenant") shall not be construed as requiring the lessor—

    (a) to carry out works or repairs for which the lessee is liable by virtue of his duty to use the premises in a tenant-like manner, or would be so liable but for an express covenant on his part,

    (b) to rebuild or reinstate the premises in the case of destruction or damage by fire, or by tempest, flood or other inevitable accident, or

    (c) to keep in repair or maintain anything which the lessee is entitled to remove from the dwelling-house.

(3) In determining the standard of repair required by the lessor's repairing covenant, regard shall be had to the age, character and prospective life of the dwelling-house and the locality in which it is situated.

(4) A covenant by the lessee for the repair of the premises is of no effect so far as it relates to the matters mentioned in subsection (1)(a) to (c), except so far as it imposes on the lessor any of the requirements mentioned in subsection (2)(a) or (c).

(5) The reference in subsection (4) to a covenant by the lessee for the repair of the premises includes a covenant—

    (a) to put in repair or deliver up in repair,

    (b) to paint, point or render,

    (c) to pay money in lieu of repairs by the lessee, or

(d)   to pay money on account of repairs by the lessor.

(6)   In a lease in which the lessor's repairing covenant is implied there is also implied a covenant by the lessee that the lessor, or any person authorised by him in writing, may at reasonable times of the day and on giving 24 hours' notice in writing to the occupier, enter the premises comprised in the lease for the purpose of viewing their condition and state of repair.

12.   Restriction on contracting out of s. 11.

(1)   A covenant or agreement, whether contained in a lease to which section 11 applies or in an agreement collateral to such a lease, is void in so far as it purports—

(a)   to exclude or limit the obligations of the lessor or the immunities of the lessee under that section, or

(b)   to authorise any forfeiture or impose on the lessee any penalty, disability or obligation in the event of his enforcing or relying upon those obligations or immunities, unless the inclusion of the provision was authorised by the county court.

(2)   The county court may, by order made with the consent of the parties, authorise the inclusion in a lease, or in an agreement collateral to a lease, of provisions excluding or modifying in relation to the lease, the provisions of section 11 with respect to the repairing obligations of the parties if it appears to the court that it is reasonable to do so, having regard to all the circumstances of the case, including the other terms and conditions of the lease.

13.   Leases to which s. 11 applies: general rule.

(1)   Section 11 (repairing obligations) applies to a lease of a dwelling-house granted on or after 24th October 1961 for a term of less than seven years.

(2)   In determining whether a lease is one to which section 11 applies—

(a)   any part of the term which falls before the grant shall be left out of account and the lease shall be treated as a lease for a term commencing with the grant,

(b)   a lease which is determinable at the option of the lessor before the expiration of seven years from the commencement of the term shall be treated as a lease for a term of less than seven years, and

(c)   a lease (other than a lease to which paragraph (b) applies) shall not be treated as a lease for a term of less than seven years if it confers on the lessee an option for renewal for a term which, together with the original term, amounts to seven years or more.

(3)   This section has effect subject to—

section 14 (leases to which section 11 applies: exceptions), and

section 32(2) (provisions not applying to tenancies within Part II of the Landlord and Tenant Act 1954).

14.   Leases to which s. 11 applies: exceptions.

(1)   Section 11 (repairing obligations) does not apply to a new lease granted to an existing tenant, or to a former tenant still in possession, if the previous lease was not a lease to which section 11 applied (and, in the case of a lease granted before 24th October 1961, would not have been if it had been granted on or after that date).

(2)   In subsection (1)—

"existing tenant" means a person who is when, or immediately before, the new lease is granted, the lessee under another lease of the dwelling-house;

"former tenant still in possession" means a person who—

(a)   was the lessee under another lease of the dwelling-house which terminated at some time before the new lease was granted, and

(b)   between the termination of that other lease and the grant of the new lease was continuously in possession of the dwelling-house or of the rents and profits of the dwelling-house; and

"the previous lease" means the other lease referred to in the above definitions.

(3)   Section 11 does not apply to a lease of a dwelling-house which is a tenancy of an agricultural holding within the meaning of the Agricultural Holdings Act 1986.

(4)   Section 11 does not apply to a lease granted on or after 3rd October 1980 to—
a local authority,
a new town corporation,
an urban development corporation,
the Development Board for Rural Wales,
a registered housing association,
a co-operative housing association, or
an educational institution or other body specified, or of a class specified, by regulations under section 8 of the Rent Act 1977 or paragraph 8 of Schedule 1 to the Housing Act 1988 (bodies making student lettings),
a housing action trust established under Part III of the Housing Act 1988.

(5)   Section 11 does not apply to a lease granted on or after 3rd October 1980 to—
(a)   Her Majesty in right of the Crown (unless the lease is under the management of the Crown Estate Commissioners), or
(b)   a government department or a person holding in trust for Her Majesty for the purposes of a government department.

15.   Jurisdiction of county court.
The county court has jurisdiction to make a declaration that section 11 (repairing obligations) applies, or does not apply, to a lease—
(a)   whatever the net annual value of the property in question, and
(b)   notwithstanding that no other relief is sought than a declaration.

16.   Meaning of "lease" and related expressions.
In sections 11 to 15 (repairing obligations in short leases)—
(a)   "lease" does not include a mortgage term;
(b)   "lease of a dwelling-house" means a lease by which a building or part of a building is let wholly or mainly as a private residence, and "dwelling-house" means that building or part of a building;
(c)   "lessee" and "lessor" mean, respectively, the person for the time being entitled to the term of a lease and to the reversion expectant on it.

17.   Specific preformance of landlord's repairing obligations.
(1)   In proceedings in which a tenant of a dwelling alleges a breach on the part of his landlord of a repairing covenant relating to any part of the premises in which the dwelling is comprised, the court may order specific performance of the covenant whether or not the breach relates to a part of the premises let to the tenant and notwithstanding any equitable rule restricting the scope of the remedy, whether on the basis of a lack of mutuality or otherwise.

(2)   In this section—
(a)   "tenant" includes a statutory tenant,
(b)   in relation to a statutory tenant the reference to the premises let to him is to the premises of which he is a statutory tenant,
(c)   "landlord", in relation to a tenant, includes any person against whom the tenant has a right to enforce a repairing covenant, and
(d)   "repairing covenant" means a covenant to repair, maintain, renew, construct or replace any property.

Service charges

18.   Meaning of "service charge" and "relevant costs".
(1)   In the following provisions of this Act "service charge" means an amount payable by a tenant of a dwelling as part of or in addition to the rent—

(a)   which is payable, directly or indirectly, for services, repairs, maintenance or insurance or the landlord's costs of management, and

(b)   the whole or part of which varies or may vary according to the relevant costs.

(2)   The relevant costs are the costs or estimated costs incurred or to be incurred by or on behalf of the landlord, or a superior landlord, in connection with the matters for which the service charge is payable.

(3)   For this purpose—

(a)   "costs" includes overheads, and

(b)   costs are relevant costs in relation to a service charge whether they are incurred, or to be incurred, in the period for which the service charge is payable or in an earlier or later period.

19.   Limitation of service charges: reasonableness.

(1)   Relevant costs shall be taken into account in determining the amount of a service charge payable for a period—

(a)   only to the extent that they are reasonably incurred, and

(b)   where they are incurred on the provision of services or the carrying out of works, only if the services or works are of a reasonable standard;

and the amount payable shall be limited accordingly.

(2)   Where a service charge is payable before the relevant costs are incurred, no greater amount than is reasonable is so payable, and after the relevant costs have been incurred any necessary adjustment shall be made by repayment, reduction or subsequent charges or otherwise.

(3)   An agreement by the tenant of a dwelling (other than an arbitration agreement within the meaning of section 32 of the Arbitration Act 1950) is void in so far as it purports to provide for a determination in a particular manner, or on particular evidence, of any question—

(a)   whether costs incurred for services, repairs, maintenance, insurance or management were reasonably incurred,

(b)   whether services or works for which costs were incurred are of a reasonable standard, or

(c)   whether an amount payable before costs are incurred is reasonable.

(4)   A county court may make a declaration—

(a)   that any such costs were or were not reasonably incurred,

(b)   that any such services or works are or are not of a reasonable standard, or

(c)   that any such amount is or is not reasonable,

notwithstanding that no other relief is sought in the proceedings.

(5)   If a person takes any proceedings in the High Court in pursuance of any of the provisions of this Act relating to service charges and he could have taken these proceedings in the county court, he shall not be entitled to recover any costs.

20.   Limitation of service charges: estimates and consultation.

(1)   Where relevant costs incurred on the carrying out of any qualifying works exceed the limit specified in subsection (3), the excess shall not be taken into account in determining the amount of a service charge unless the relevant requirements have been either—

(a)   complied with, or

(b)   dispensed with by the court in accordance with subsection (9);

and the amount payable shall be limited accordingly.

(2)   In subsection (1) "qualifying works", in relation to a service charge, means works (whether on a building or on any other premises) to the costs of which the tenant by whom the service charge is payable may be required under the terms of his lease to contribute by the payment of such a charge.

(3)   The limit is whichever is the greater of—

(a)   £25, or such other amount as may be prescribed by order of the Secretary of State, multiplied by the number of dwellings let to the tenants concerned, or

(b)   £500, or such other amount as may be so prescribed.

(4)   The relevant requirements in relation to such of the tenants concerned as are not represented by a recognised tenants' association are—

(a)   At least two estimates for the works shall be obtained, one of them from a person wholly unconnected with the landlord.

(b)   A notice accompanied by a copy of the estimates shall be given to each of those tenants concerned or shall be displayed in one or more places where it is likely to come to the notice of all those tenants.

(c)   The notice shall describe the works to be carried out and invite observations on them and on the estimates and shall state the name and the address in the United Kingdom of the person to whom the observations may be sent and the date by which they are to be received.

(d)   The date stated in the notice shall not be earlier than one month after the date on which the notice is given or displayed as required by paragraph (b).

(e)   The landlord shall have regard to any observations received in pursuance of the notice; and unless the works are urgently required they shall not be begun earlier than the date specified in the notice.

(5)   The relevant requirements in relation to such of the tenants concerned as are represented by a recognised tenants' association are—

(a)   The landlord shall give to the secretary of the association a notice containing a detailed specification of the works in question and specifying a reasonable period within which the association may propose to the landlord the names of one or more persons from whom estimates for the works should in its view be obtained by the landlord.

(b)   At least two estimates for the works shall be obtained, one of them from a person wholly unconnected with the landlord.

(c)   A copy of each of the estimates shall be given to the secretary of the association.

(d)   A notice shall be given to each of the tenants concerned represented by the association, which shall—

(i)   describe briefly the works to be carried out,

(ii)   summarise the estimates,

(iii)   inform the tenant that he has a right to inspect and take copies of a detailed specification of the works to be carried out and of the estimates,

(iv)   invite observations on those works and on the estimates, and

(v)   specify the name and the address in the United Kingdom of the person to whom the observations may be sent and the date by which they are to be received.

(e)   The date stated in the notice shall not be earlier than one month after the date on which the notice is given as required by paragraph (d).

(f)   If any tenant to whom the notice if given so requests, the landlord shall afford him reasonable facilities for inspecting a detailed specification of the works to be carried out and the estimates, free of charge, and for taking copies of them on payment of such reasonable charge as the landlord may determine.

(g)   The landlord shall have regard to any observations received in pursuance of the notice and, unless the works are urgently required, they shall not be begun earlier than the date specified in the notice.

(6)   Paragraphs (d)(ii) and (iii) and (f) of subsection 5 shall not apply to any estimate of which a copy is enclosed with the notice given in pursuance of paragraph (d).

(7)   The requirement imposed on the landlord by subsection (5)(f) to make any facilities available to a person free of charge shall not be construed as precluding the landlord from treating as part of his costs of management any costs incurred by him in

connection with making those facilities so available.

(8)   In this section "the tenants concerned" means all the landlord's tenants who may be required under the terms of their leases to contribute to the cost of the works in question by the payment of service charges.

(9)   In proceedings relating to a service charge the court may, if satisfied that the landlord acted reasonably, dispense with all or any of the relevant requirements.

(10)   An order under this section—

(a)   may make different provision with respect to different cases or descriptions of case, including different provision for different areas, and

(b)   shall be made by statutory instrument which shall be subject to annulment in pursuance of a resolution of either House of Parliament.

20A.   Limitation of service charges: grant-aided works.

(1)   Where relevant costs are incurred or to be incurred on the carrying out of works in respect of which a grant has been or is to be paid under Part XV of the Housing Act 1985 or Part VIII of the Local Government and Housing Act 1989 (grants for works of improvement, repair or conversion), the amount of the grant shall be deducted from the costs and the amount of the service charge payable shall be reduced accordingly.

(2)   In any case where—

(a)   relevant costs are incurred or to be incurred on the carrying out of works which are included in the external works specified in a group repair scheme, within the meaning of Part VIII of the Local Government and Housing Act 1989, and

(b)   the landlord participated or is participating in that scheme as an assisted participant,

the amount which, in relation to the landlord, is the outstanding balance determined in accordance with subsections (3) and (4) of section 130 of that Act shall be deducted from the costs, and the amount of the service charge payable shall be reduced accordingly.

20B.   Limitation of service charges: time limit on making demands.

(1)   If any of the relevant costs taken into account in determining the amount of any service charge were incurred more than 18 months before a demand for payment of the service charge is served on the tenant, then (subject to subsection (2)), the tenant shall not be liable to pay so much of the service charge as reflects the costs so incurred.

(2)   Subsection (1) shall not apply if, within the period of 18 months beginning with the date when the relevant costs in question were incurred, the tenant was notified in writing that those costs had been incurred and that he would subsequently be required under the terms of his lease to contribute to them by the payment of a service charge.

20C.   Limitation of service charges: costs of court proceedings.

(1)   A tenant may make an application to the appropriate court for an order that all or any of the costs incurred, or to be incurred, by the landlord in connection with any proceedings are not to be regarded as relevant costs to be taken into account in determining the amount of any service charge payable by the tenant or any other person or persons specified in the application; and the court may make such order on the application as it considers just and equitable in the circumstances.

(2)   In subsection (1) "the appropriate court" means—

(a)   if the application is made in the course of the proceedings in question, the court before which the proceedings are taking place; and

(b)   if the application is made after those proceedings are concluded, a county court.

21.   Request for summary of relevant costs.

(1)   A tenant may require the landlord in writing to supply him with a written summary of the costs incurred—

(a)   if the relevant accounts are made up for periods of twelve months, in the last such period ending not later than the date of the request, or

(b) if the accounts are not so made up, in the period of twelve months ending with the date of the request,
and which are relevant costs in relation to the service charges payable or demanded as payable in that or any other period.

(2) If the tenant is represented by a recognised tenants' association and he consents, the request may be made by the secretary of the association instead of by the tenant and may then be for the supply of the summary to the secretary.

(3) A request is duly served on the landlord if it is served on—
(a) an agent of the landlord named as such in the rent book or similar document, or
(b) the person who receives the rent on behalf of the landlord;
and a person on whom a request is so served shall forward it as soon as may be to the landlord.

(4) The landlord shall comply with the request within one month of the request or within six months of the end of the period referred to in subsection (1)(a) or (b) whichever is the later.

(5) The summary shall state whether any of the costs relate to works in respect of which a grant has been or is to be paid under Part XV of the Housing Act 1985 or Part VIII of the Local Government and Housing Act 1989 (grants for works of improvement, repair or conversion) and set out the costs in a way showing how they have been or will be reflected in demands for service charges and, in addition, shall summarise each of the following items, namely—
(a) any of the costs in respect of which no demand for payment was received by the landlord within the period referred to in subsection (1)(a) or (b),
(b) any of the costs in respect of which—
(i) a demand for payment was so received, but
(ii) no payment was made by the landlord within that period, and
(c) any of the costs in respect of which—
(i) a demand for payment was so received, and
(ii) payment was made by the landlord within that period,
and specify the aggregate of any amounts received by the landlord down to the end of that period on account of service charges in respect of relevant dwellings and still standing to the credit of the tenants of those dwellings at the end of that period.

(5A) In subsection (5) "relevant dwelling" means a dwelling whose tenant is either—
(a) the person by or with the consent of whom the request was made, or
(b) a person whose obligations under the terms of his lease as regards contributing to relevant costs relate to the same costs as the corresponding obligations of the person mentioned in paragraph (a) above relate to.

(5B) The summary shall state whether any of the costs relate to works which are included in the external works specified in a group repair scheme, within the meaning of Part VIII of the Local Government and Housing Act 1989, in which the landlord participated or is participating as an assisted participant.

(6) If the service charges in relation to which the costs are relevant costs as mentioned in subsection (1) are payable by the tenants of more than four dwellings, the summary shall be certified by a qualified accountant as—
(a) in this opinion a fair summary complying with the requirements of subsection (5), and
(b) being sufficiently supported by accounts, receipts and other documents which have been produced to him.

22. Request to inspect supporting accounts, etc.

(1) This section applies where a tenant, or the secretary of a recognised tenant's association, has obtained such a summary as is referred to in section 21(1) (summary of

relevant costs), whether in pursuance of that section or otherwise.

(2)　The tenant, or the secretary with the consent of the tenant, may within six months of obtaining the summary require the landlord in writing to afford him reasonable facilities—

　　(a)　for inspecting the accounts, receipts and other documents supporting the summary, and

　　(b)　for taking copies or extracts from them.

(3)　A request under this section is duly served on the landlord if it is served on—

　　(a)　an agent of the landlord named as such in the rent book or similar document, or

　　(b)　the person who receives the rent on behalf of the landlord;

and a person on whom a request is so served shall forward it as soon as may be to the landlord.

(4)　The landlord shall make such facilities available to the tenant or secretary for a period of two months beginning not later than one month after the request is made.

(5)　The landlord shall—

　　(a)　where such facilities are for the inspection of any documents, make them so available free of charge;

　　(b)　where such facilities are for the taking of copies or extracts, be entitled to make them so available on payment of such reasonable charge as he may determine.

(6)　The requirement imposed on the landlord by subsection (5)(a) to make any facilities available to a person free of charge shall not be construed as precluding the landlord from treating as part of his costs of management any costs incurred by him in connection with making those facilities so available.

23.　Request relating to information held by superior landlord.

(1)　If a request under section 21 (request for summary of relevant costs) relates in whole or in part to relevant costs incurred by or on behalf of a superior landlord, and the landlord to whom the request is made is not in possession of the relevant information—

　　(a)　he shall in turn make a written request for the relevant information to the person who is his landlord (and so on, if that person is not himself the superior landlord),

　　(b)　the superior landlord shall comply with that request within a reasonable time, and

　　(c)　the immediate landlord shall then comply with the tenant's or secretary's request, or that part of it which relates to the relevant costs incurred by or on behalf of the superior landlord, within the time allowed by section 21 or such further time, if any, as is reasonable in the circumstances.

(2)　If a request under section 22 (request for facilities to inspect supporting accounts, &c.) relates to a summary of costs incurred by or on behalf of a superior landlord—

　　(a)　the landlord to whom the request is made shall forthwith inform the tenant or secretary of that fact and of the name and address of the superior landlord, and

　　(b)　section 22 shall then apply to the superior landlord as it applies to the immediate landlord.

24.　Effect of assignment on request.

The assignment of a tenancy does not affect the validity of a request made under section 21, 22 or 23 before the assignment; but a person is not obliged to provide a summary or make facilities available more than once for the same dwelling and for the same period.

25.　Failure to comply with ss. 21, 22, or 23 an offence.

(1)　It is a summary offence for a person to fail, without reasonable excuse, to perform a duty imposed on him by section 21, 22 or 23.

(2)   A person committing such an offence is liable on conviction to a fine not exceeding level 4 on the standard scale.

26.   Exception: tenants of certain public authorities.

(1)   Sections 18 to 25 (limitation on service charges and requests for information about costs) do not apply to a service charge payable by a tenant of—

a local authority,

a new town corporation, or

the Development Board for Rural Wales,

unless the tenancy is a long tenancy, in which case sections 18 to 24 apply but section 25 (offence of failure to comply) does not.

(2)   The following are long tenancies for the purposes of subsection (1), subject to subsection (3)—

(a)   a tenancy granted for a term certain exceeding 21 years, whether or not it is (or may become) terminable before the end of that term by notice given by the tenant or by re-entry or forfeiture;

(b)   a tenancy for a term fixed by law under a grant with a covenant or obligation for perpetual renewal, other than a tenancy by sub-demise from one which is not a long tenancy;

(c)   any tenancy granted in pursuance of Part V of the Housing Act 1985 (the right to buy).

(3)   A tenancy granted so as to become terminable by notice after a death is not a long tenancy for the purposes of subsection (1), unless—

(a)   it is granted by a housing association which at the time of the grant is registered,

(b)   it is granted at a premium calculated by reference to a percentage of the value of the dwelling-house or the cost of providing it, and

(c)   at the time it is granted it complies with the requirements of the regulations then in force under section 140(4)(b) of the Housing Act 1980 or paragraph 4(2)(b) of Schedule 4A to the Leasehold Reform Act 1967 (conditions for exclusion of shared ownership leases from Part I of Leasehold Reform Act 1967) or, in the case of a tenancy granted before any such regulations were brought into force, with the first such regulations to be in force.

27.   Exception: rent registered and not entered as variable.

Sections 18 to 25 (limitation on service charges and requests for information about costs) do not apply to a service charge payable by the tenant of a dwelling the rent of which is registered under Part IV of the Rent Act 1977, unless the amount registered is, in pursuance of section 71(4) of that Act, entered as a variable amount.

28.   Meaning of "qualified accountant".

(1)   The reference to a "qualified accountant" in section 21(6) (certification of summary of information about relevant costs) is to a person who, in accordance with the following provisions, has the necessary qualification and is not disqualified from acting.

(2)   A person has the necessary qualification if he is a member of one of the following bodies—

the Institute of Chartered Accountants in England and Wales,

the Institute of Chartered Accountants in Scotland,

the Association of Certified Accountants,

the Institute of Chartered Accountants in Ireland, or

any other body of accountants established in the United Kingdom and recognised by the Secretary of State for the purposes of section 389(1)(a) of the Companies Act 1985, or if he is a person who is for the time being authorised by the Secretary of State under section 389(1)(b) of that Act (or the corresponding provision of the Companies Act 1948) as being a person with similar qualifications obtained outside the United Kingdom.

(3)   A Scottish firm has the necessary qualification if each of the partners in it has the necessary qualification.

(4)   The following are disqualified from acting—

(a)   a body corporate, except a Scottish firm;

(b)   an officer, employee or partner of the landlord or, where the landlord is a company, of an associated company;

(c)   a person who is a partner or employee of any such officer or employee;

(d)   an agent of the landlord who is a managing agent for any premises to which any of the costs covered by the summary in question relate;

(e)   an employee or partner of any such agent.

(5)   For the purposes of subsection (4)(b) a company is associated with a landlord company if it is (within the meaning of section 736 of the Companies Act 1985) the landlord's holding company, a subsidiary of the landlord or another subsidiary of the landlord's holding company.

(5A)   For the purposes of subsection (4)(d) a person is a managing agent for any premises to which any costs relate if he has been appointed to discharge any of the landlord's obligations relating to the management by him of the premises and owed to the tenants who may be required under the terms of their leases to contribute to those costs by the payment of service charges.

(6)   Where the landlord is a local authority, a new town corporation or the Development Board for Rural Wales—

(a)   the persons who have the necessary qualification include members of the Chartered Institute of Public Finance and Accountancy, and

(b)   subsection (4)(b) (disqualification of officers and employees of landlord) does not apply.

29.   Meaning of "recognised tenants' association".

(1)   A recognised tenants' association is an association of qualifying tenants (whether with or without other tenants) which is recognised for the purposes of the provisions of this Act relating to service charges either—

(a)   by notice in writing given by the landlord to the secretary of the association, or

(b)   by a certificate of a member of the local rent assessment committee panel.

(2)   A notice given under subsection (1)(a) may be withdrawn by the landlord by notice in writing given to the secretary of the association not less than six months before the date on which it is to be withdrawn.

(3)   A certificate given under subsection (1)(b) may be cancelled by any member of the local rent assessment committee panel.

(4)   In this section the "local rent assessment committee panel" means the persons appointed by the Lord Chancellor under the Rent Act 1977 to the panel of persons to act as members of a rent assessment committee for the registration area in which the dwellings let to the qualifying tenants are situated, and for the purposes of this section a number of tenants are qualifying tenants if each of them may be required under the terms of his lease to contribute to the same costs by the payment of a service charge.

(5)   The Secretary of State may by regulations specify—

(a)   the procedure which is to be followed in connection with an application for, or for the cancellation of, a certificate under subsection (1)(b);

(b)   the matters to which regard is to be had in giving or cancelling such a certificate;

(c)   the duration of such a certificate; and

(d)   any circumstances in which a certificate is not to be given under subsection (1)(b).

(6)   Regulations under subsection (5)—

(a)   may make different provisions with respect to different cases or descriptions of case, including different provision for different areas, and

(b)   shall be made by statutory instrument which shall be subject to annulment in pursuance of a resolution of either House of Parliament.

30.   Meaning of "flat", "landlord" and "tenant".

In the provisions of this Act relating to service charges—

"landlord" includes any person who has a right to enforce payment of a service charge;

"tenant" includes

(a)   a statutory tenant, and

(b)   where the dwelling or part of it is sub-let, the sub-tenant.

Insurance

30A.   Rights of tenants with respect to insurance.

The Schedule to this Act (which confers on tenants certain rights with respect to the insurance of their dwellings) shall have effect.

Managing agents

30B.   Recognised tenants' associations to be consulted about managing agents.

(1)   A recognised tenants' association may at any time serve a notice on the landlord requesting him to consult the association in accordance with this section on matters relating to the appointment or employment by him of a managing agent for any relevant premises.

(2)   Where, at the time when any such notice is served by a recognised tenants' association, the landlord does not employ any managing agent for any relevant premises, the landlord shall, before appointing such a managing agent, serve on the association a notice specifying—

(a)   the name of the proposed managing agent;

(b)   the landlord's obligations to the tenants represented by the association which it is proposed that the managing agent should be required to discharge on his behalf; and

(c)   a period of not less than one month beginning with the date of service of the notice within which the association may make observations on the proposed appointment.

(3)   Where, at the time when a notice is served under subsection (1) by a recognised tenants' association, the landlord employs a managing agent for any relevant premises, the landlord shall, within the period of one month beginning with the date of service of that notice, serve on the association a notice specifying—

(a)   the landlord's obligations to the tenants represented by the association which the managing agent is required to discharge on his behalf; and

(b)   a reasonable period within which the association may make observations on the manner in which the managing agent has been discharging those obligations, and on the desirability of his continuing to discharge them.

(4)   Subject to subsection (5), a landlord who has been served with a notice by an association under subsection (1) shall, so long as he employs a managing agent for any relevant premises—

(a)   serve on that association at least once in every five years a notice specifying—

(i)   any change occurring since the date of the last notice served by him on the association under this section in the obligations which the managing agent has been required to discharge on his behalf; and

    (ii)   a reasonable period within which the association may make observations on the manner in which the managing agent has discharged those obligations since that date, and on the desirability of his continuing to discharge them;

  (b)   serve on that association, whenever he proposes to appoint any new managing agent for any relevant premises, a notice specifying the matters mentioned in paragraphs (a) to (c) of subsection (2).

(5) A landlord shall not, by virtue of a notice served by an association under subsection (1), be required to serve on the association a notice under subsection (4)(a) or (b) if the association subsequently serves on the landlord a notice withdrawing its request under subsection (1) to be consulted by him.

(6) Where—

  (a)   a recognised tenants' association has served a notice under subsection (1) with respect to any relevant premises, and

  (b)   the interest of the landlord in those premises becomes vested in a new landlord,

that notice shall cease to have effect with respect to those premises (without prejudice to the service by the association on the new landlord of a fresh notice under that subsection with respect to those premises).

(7) Any notice served by a landlord under this section shall specify the name and the address in the United Kingdom of the person to whom any observations made in pursuance of the notice are to be sent; and the landlord shall have regard to any such observations that are received by that person within the period specified in the notice.

(8) In this section—

    "landlord", in relation to a recognised tenants' association, means the immediate landlord of the tenants represented by the association or a person who has a right to enforce payment of service charges payable by any of those tenants;

    "managing agent", in relation to any relevant premises, means an agent of the landlord appointed to discharge any of the landlord's obligations to the tenants represented by the recognised tenants' association in question which relate to the management by him of those premises; and

    "tenant" includes a statutory tenant;

and for the purposes of this section any premises (whether a building or not) are relevant premises in relation to a recognised tenants' association if any of the tenants represented by the association may be required under the terms of their leases to contribute by the payment of service charges to costs relating to those premises.

Miscellaneous

31. Reserve power to limit rents.

(1) The Secretary of State may by order provide for—

  (a)   restricting or preventing increases of rent for dwellings which would otherwise take place, or

  (b)   restricting the amount of rent which would otherwise be payable on new lettings of dwellings;

and may so provide either generally or in relation to any specified description of dwelling.

(2) An order may contain supplementary or incidental provisions, including provisions excluding, adapting or modifying any provision made by or under an enactment (whenever passed) relating to rent or the recovery of overpaid rent.

(3) In this section—

    "new letting" includes any grant of a tenancy, whether or not the premises were previously let, and any grant of a licence;

    "rent" includes a sum payable under a licence, but does not include a sum

attributable to rates or, in the case of dwellings of local authorities or new town corporations, to the use of furniture, or the provision of services;
and for the purposes of this section an increase in rent takes place at the beginning of the rental period for which the increased rent is payable.

(4) An order under this section shall be made by statutory instrument which shall be subject to annulment in pursuance of a resolution of either House of Parliament.

Supplementary provisions

32. Provisions not applying to tenancies within Part II of the Landlord and Tenant Act 1954.

(1) The following provisions do not apply to a tenancy to which Part II of the Landlord and Tenant Act 1954 (business tenancies) applies—
sections 1 to 3 (information to be given to tenant),
section 17 (specific performance of landlord's repairing obligations).

(2) Section 11 (repairing obligations) does not apply to a new lease granted to an existing tenant, or to a former tenant still in possession, if the new lease is a tenancy to which Part II of the Landlord and Tenant Act 1954 applies and the previous lease either is such a tenancy or would be but for section 28 of that Act (tenancy not within Part II if renewal agreed between the parties).

In this subsection "existing tenant", "former tenant still in possession" and "previous lease" have the same meaning as in section 14(2).

(3) Section 31 (reserve power to limit rents) does not apply to a dwelling forming part of a property subject to a tenancy to which Part II of the Landlord and Tenant Act 1954 applies; but without prejudice to the application of that section in relation to a sub-tenancy of a part of the premises comprised in such a tenancy.

33. Liability of directors, &c. for offences by body corporate.

(1) Where an offence under this Act which has been committed by a body corporate is proved—
(a) to have been committed with the consent or connivance of a director, manager, secretary or other similar officer of the body corporate, or a person purporting to act in any such capacity, or
(b) to be attributable to any neglect on the part of such an officer or person,
he, as well as the body corporate, is guilty of an offence and liable to be proceeded against and punished accordingly.

(2) Where the affairs of a body corporate are managed by its members, subsection (1) applies in relation to the acts and defaults of a member in connection with his functions of management as if he were a director of the body corporate.

34. Power of local housing authority to prosecute.

Proceedings for an offence under any provision of this Act may be brought by a local housing authority.

35. Application to Isles of Scilly.

(1) This Act applies to the Isles of Scilly subject to such exceptions, adaptations and modifications as the Secretary of State may by order direct.

(2) An order shall be made by statutory instrument which shall be subject to annulment in pursuance of a resolution of either House of Parliament.

36. Meaning of "lease" and "tenancy" and related expressions.

(1) In this Act "lease" and "tenancy" have the same meaning.
(2) Both expressions include—
(a) a sub-lease or sub-tenancy, and
(b) an agreement for a lease or tenancy (or sub-lease or sub-tenancy).
(3) The expressions "lessor" and "lessee" and "landlord" and "tenant", and

references to letting, to the grant of a lease or to covenants or terms, shall be construed accordingly.

37. Meaning of "statutory tenant" and related expressions.

In this Act—

(a) "statutory tenancy" and "statutory tenant" mean a statutory tenancy or statutory tenant within the meaning of the Rent Act 1977 or the Rent (Agriculture) Act 1976; and

(b) "landlord", in relation to a statutory tenant, means the person who, apart from the statutory tenancy, would be entitled to possession of the premises.

38. Minor definitions.

In this Act—

"address" means a person's place of abode or place of business or, in the case of a company, its registered office;

"co-operative housing association" has the same meaning as in the Housing Associations Act 1985;

"dwelling" means a building or part of a building occupied or intended to be occupied as a separate dwelling, together with any yard, garden, outhouses and appurtenances belonging to it or usually enjoyed with it;

"housing association" has the same meaning as in the Housing Associations Act 1985;

"local authority" means a district, county or London borough council, the Common Council of the City of London or the Council of the Isles of Scilly and in sections 14(4), 26(1) and 28(6) includes the Broads Authority and a joint authority established by Part IV of the Local Government Act 1985;

"local housing authority" has the meaning given by section 1 of the Housing Act 1985;

"new town corporation" means—

(a) a development corporation established by an order made, or treated as made, under the New Towns Act 1981, or

(b) the Commission for the New Towns;

"protected tenancy" has the same meaning as in the Rent Act 1977;

"registered", in relation to a housing association, means registered under the Housing Associations Act 1985;

"restricted contract" has the same meaning as in the Rent Act 1977;

"urban development corporation" has the same meaning as in Part XVI of the Local Government, Planning and Land Act 1980.

39. Index of defined expressions.

The following Table shows provisions defining or otherwise explaining expressions used in this Act (other than provisions defining or explaining an expression in the same section):

address	section 38
co-operative housing association	section 38
dwelling	section 38
dwelling-house (in the provisions relating to repairing obligations)	section 16
fit for human habitation	section 10
flat (in the provisions relating to service charges)	section 30
housing association	section 38
landlord—	
(generally)	section 36(3)

Final provisions

40.   Short title, commencement and extent.

(1)   This Act may be cited as the Landlord and Tenant Act 1985.

(2)   This Act comes into force on 1st April 1986.

(3)   This Act extends to England and Wales.

Section 30A.   SCHEDULE

RIGHTS OF TENANTS WITH RESPECT TO INSURANCE

Construction

1.   In this Schedule—

"landlord", in relation to a tenant by whom a service charge is payable which includes an amount payable directly or indirectly for insurance includes any person who has a right to enforce payment of that service charge;

"relevant policy", in relation to a dwelling, means any policy of insurance under which the dwelling is insured (being, in the case of a flat, a policy covering the building containing it); and

"tenant" includes a statutory tenant.

Request for summary of insurance cover

2.—(1)   Where a service charge is payable by the tenant of a dwelling which consists of or includes an amount payable directly or indirectly for insurance, the tenant may require the landlord in writing to supply him with a written summary of the insurance for the time being effected in relation to the dwelling.

(2)   If the tenant is represented by a recognised tenants' association and he consents, the request may be made by the secretary of the association instead of by the tenant and may then be for the supply of the summary to the secretary.

(3)   A request is duly served on the landlord if it is served on—

(a)   an agent of the landlord named as such in the rent book or similar document, or

(b)   the person who receives the rent on behalf of the landlord;

and a person on whom a request is so served shall forward it as soon as may be to the landlord.

(4)   The landlord shall, within one month of the request, comply with it by supplying to the tenant or the secretary of the recognised tenants' association (as the case may require) such a summary as is mentioned in sub-paragraph (1), which shall include—

(a)   the insured amount or amounts under any relevant policy, and

(b)   the name of the insurer under any such policy, and

(c)   the risks in respect of which the dwelling or (as the case may be) the building containing it is insured under any such policy.

(5)   In sub-paragraph (4)(a) "the insured amount or amounts", in relation to a relevant policy, means—

(a)   in the case of a dwelling other than a flat, the amount for which the dwelling is insured under the policy; and

(b)   in the case of a flat, the amount for which the building containing it is insured under the policy and, if specified in the policy, the amount for which the flat is insured under it.

(6)   The landlord shall be taken to have complied with the request if, within the period mentioned in sub-paragraph (4), he instead supplies to the tenant or the secretary (as the case may require) a copy of every relevant policy.

(7)   In a case where two or more buildings are insured under any relevant policy, the summary or copy supplied under sub-paragraph (4) or (6) so far as relating to that policy need only be of such parts of the policy as relate—

(a)   to the dwelling, and

(b)   if the dwelling is a flat, to the building containing it.

Request to inspect insurance policy etc.

3.—(1)   This paragraph applies where a tenant, or the secretary of a recognised tenants' association, has obtained either—

(a)   such a summary as is referred to in paragraph 2(1), or

(b)   a copy of any relevant policy or of any such parts of any relevant policy as relate to the premises referred to in paragraph 2(7)(a) or (b),

whether in pursuance of paragraph 2 or otherwise.

(2)   The tenant, or the secretary with the consent of the tenant, may within six months of obtaining any such summary or copy as is mentioned in subparagraph (1)(a) or (b) require the landlord in writing to afford him reasonable facilities—

(a)   for inspecting any relevant policy,

(b)   for inspecting any accounts, receipts or other documents which provide evidence of payment of any premiums due under any such policy in respect of the period of insurance which is current when the request is made and the period of insurance immediately preceding that period, and

(c)   for taking copies of or extracts from any of the documents referred to in paragraphs (a) and (b).

(3)   Any reference in this paragraph to a relevant policy includes a reference to a policy of insurance under which the dwelling in question was insured for the period of

insurance immediately preceding that current when the request is made under this paragraph (being, in the case of a flat, a policy covering the building containing it).

(4)   Subsections (3) to (6) of section 22 shall have effect in relation to a request made under this paragraph as they have effect in relation to a request made under that section.

Request relating to insurance effected by superior landlord

4.—(1)   If a request is made under paragraph 2 in a case where a superior landlord has effected, in whole or in part, the insurance of the dwelling in question and the landlord to whom the request is made is not in possession of the relevant information—

(a)   he shall in turn make a written request for the relevant information to the person who is his landlord (and so on, if that person is not himself the superior landlord),

(b)   the superior landlord shall comply with that request within a reasonable time, and

(c)   the immediate landlord shall then comply with the tenants' or secretary's request in the manner provided by sub-paragraphs (4) to (7) of paragraph 2 within the time allowed by that paragraph or such further time, if any, as is reasonable in the circumstances.

(2)   If, in a case where a superior landlord has effected, in whole or in part, the insurance of the dwelling in question, a request under paragraph 3 relates to any policy of insurance effected by the superior landlord—

(a)   the landlord to whom the request is made shall forthwith inform the tenant or secretary of that fact and of the name and address of the superior landlord, and

(b)   that paragraph shall then apply to the superior landlord in relation to that policy as it applies to the immediate landlord.

Effect of assignment on request

5.   The assignment of a tenancy does not affect the validity of a request made under paragraph 2, 3 or 4 before the assignment; but a person is not obliged to provide a summary or make facilities available more than once for the same dwelling and for the same period.

Failure to comply with paragraph 2, 3 or 4 an offence

6.—(1)   It is a summary offence for a person to fail, without reasonable excuse, to perform a duty imposed on him by or by virtue of paragraph 2, 3 or 4.

(2)   A person committing such an offence is liable on conviction to a fine not exceeding level 4 on the standard scale.

Tenants' right to notify insurers of possible claim

7.—(1)   This paragraph applies to any dwelling in respect of which the tenant pays to the landlord a service charge consisting of or including an amount payable directly or indirectly for insurance.

(2)   Where—

(a)   it appears to the tenant of any such dwelling that damage has been caused—

(i)   to the dwelling, or

(ii)   if the dwelling is a flat, to the dwelling or to any other part of the building containing it,

in respect of which a claim could be made under the terms of a policy of insurance, and

(b)   it is a term of that policy that the person insured under the policy should give notice of any claim under it to the insurer within a specified period,

the tenant may, within that specified period, serve on the insurer a notice in writing stating that it appears to him that damage has been caused as mentioned in paragraph (a) and describing briefly the nature of the damage.

(3) Where—

(a) any such notice is served on an insurer by a tenant in relation to any such damage, and

(b) the specified period referred to in sub-paragraph (2)(b) would expire earlier than the period of six months beginning with the date on which the notice is served, the policy in question shall have effect as regards any claim subsequently made in respect of that damage by the person insured under the policy as if for the specified period there were substituted that period of six months.

(4) Where the tenancy of a dwelling to which this paragraph applies is held by joint tenants, a single notice under this paragraph may be given by any one or more of those tenants.

(5) The Secretary of State may by regulations prescribe the form of notices under this paragraph and the particulars which such notices must contain.

(6) Any such regulations—

(a) may make different provision with respect to different cases or descriptions of case, including different provision for different areas, and

(b) shall be made by statutory instrument.

Right to challenge landlord's choice of insurers

8.—(1) This paragraph applies to a tenant of a dwelling which requires the tenant to insure the dwelling with an insurer nominated by the landlord.

(2) Where, on an application made by the tenant under any such tenancy, the court is satisfied—

(a) that the insurance which is available from the nominated insurer for insuring the tenant's dwelling is unsatisfactory in any respect, or

(b) that the premiums payable in respect of any such insurance are excessive, the court may make either an order requiring the landlord to nominate such other insurer as is specified in the order or an order requiring him to nominate another insurer who satisfies such requirements in relation to the insurance of the dwelling as are specified in the order.

(3) A county court shall have jurisdiction to hear and determine any application under this paragraph.

Exception for tenants of certain public authorities

9.—(1) Paragraphs 2 to 8 do not apply to a tenant of—

a local authority,

a new town corporation, or

the Development Board for Rural Wales,

unless the tenancy is a long tenancy, in which case paragraphs 2 to 5 and 7 and 8 apply but paragraph 6 does not.

(2) Subsections (2) and (3) of section 26 shall apply for the purposes of subparagraph (1) as they apply for the purposes of subsection (1) of that section.

LANDLORD AND TENANT ACT 1987
(1987, c. 31)

An Act to confer on tenants of flats rights with respect to the acquisition by them of their landlord's reversion; to make provision for the appointment of a manager at the instance of such tenants and for the variation of long leases held by such tenants; to make further provision with respect to service charges payable by tenants of flats and other dwellings; to make other provision with respect to such tenants; to make further provision with respect to the permissible purposes and objects of registered housing associations as regards the management of leasehold property; and for connected purposes. [15 May 1987]

PART I

TENANTS' RIGHTS OF FIRST REFUSAL

Preliminary

1. Qualifying tenants to have rights of first refusal on disposals by landlord.

(1)   A landlord shall not make a relevant disposal affecting any premises to which at the time of the disposal this Part applies unless—

(a)   he has in accordance with section 5 previously served a notice under that section with respect to the disposal on the qualifying tenants of the flats contained in those premises (being a notice by virtue of which rights of first refusal are conferred on those tenants); and

(b)   the disposal is made in accordance with the requirements of sections 6 to 10.

(2)   Subject to subsections (3) and (4), this Part applies to premises if—

(a)   they consist of the whole or part of a building; and

(b)   they contain two or more flats held by qualifying tenants; and

(c)   the number of flats held by such tenants exceeds 50 per cent. of the total number of flats contained in the premises.

(3)   This Part does not apply to premises falling within subsection (2) if—

(a)   any part or parts of the premises is or are occupied or intended to be occupied otherwise than for residential purposes; and

(b)   the internal floor area of that part or those parts (taken together) exceeds 50 per cent. of the internal floor area of the premises (taken as a whole);

and for the purposes of this subsection the internal floor area of any common parts shall be disregarded.

(4)   This Part also does not apply to any such premises at a time when the interest of the landlord in the premises is held by an exempt landlord or a resident landlord.

(5)   The Secretary of State may by order substitute for the percentage for the time being specified in subsection (3)(b) such other percentage as is specified in the order.

2. Landlords for the purposes of Part I.

(1)   Subject to subsection (2) and section 4(1A), a person is for the purposes of this Part the landlord in relation to any premises consisting of the whole or part of a building if he is—

(a)   the immediate landlord of the qualifying tenants of the flats contained in those premises, or

(b)   where any of those tenants is a statutory tenant, the person who, apart from the statutory tenancy, would be entitled to possession of the flat in question.

(2)   Where the person who is, in accordance with subsection (1), the landlord in relation to any such premises for the purposes of this Part ("the immediate landlord") is himself a tenant of those premises under a tenancy which is either—

(a)   a tenancy for a term of less than seven years, or

(b)   a tenancy for a longer term but terminable within the first seven years at the option of the person who is the landlord under that tenancy ("the superior landlord"),

the superior landlord shall also be regarded as the landlord in relation to those premises for the purposes of this Part and, if the superior landlord is himself a tenant of those premises under a tenancy falling within paragraph (a) or (b) above, the person who is the landlord under that tenancy shall also be so regarded (and so on).

3. Qualifying tenants.

(1)   Subject to the following provisions of this section, a person is for the purposes of this Part a qualifying tenant of a flat if he is the tenant of the flat under a tenancy other than—

(a)   a protected shorthold tenancy as defined in section 52 of the Housing Act 1980;

(b)   a tenancy to which Part II of the Landlord and Tenant Act 1954 (business tenancies) applies;

(c)   a tenancy terminable on the cessation of his employment; or

(d)   an assured tenancy or assured agricultural occupancy within the meaning of Part I of the Housing Act 1988.

(2)   A person is not to be regarded as being a qualifying tenant of any flat contained in any particular premises consisting of the whole or part of a building if by virtue of one or more tenancies none of which falls within paragraphs (a) to (d) of subsection (1), he is the tenant not only of the flat in question but also of at least two other flats contained in those premises.

(3)   For the purposes of subsection (2) any tenant of a flat contained in the premises in question who is a body corporate shall be treated as the tenant of any other flat so contained and let to an associated company.

(4)   A tenant of a flat whose landlord is a qualifying tenant of that flat is not to be regarded as being a qualifying tenant of that flat.

4.   Relevant disposals.

(1)   In this Part references to a relevant disposal affecting any premises to which this Part applies are references to the disposal by the landlord of any estate or interest (whether legal or equitable) in any such premises, including the disposal of any such estate or interest in any common parts of any such premises but excluding—

(a)   the grant of any tenancy under which the demised premises consist of a single flat (whether with or without any appurtenant premises); and

(b)   any of the disposals falling within subsection (2).

(1A)   Where an estate or interest of the landlord has been mortgaged, the reference in subsection (1) above to the disposal of an estate or interest by the landlord includes a reference to its disposal by the mortgagee in exercise of a power of sale or leasing, whether or not the disposal is made in the name of the landlord; and, in relation to such a proposed disposal by the mortgagee, any reference in the following provisions of this Part to the landlord shall be construed as a reference to the mortgagee.

(2)   The disposals referred to in subsection (1)(b) are—

(a)   a disposal of—

(i)   any interest of a beneficiary in settled land within the meaning of the Settled Land Act 1925, or

(iii)   any incorporeal hereditament;

(aa)   a disposal consisting of the creation of an estate or interest by way of security for a loan;

(b)   a disposal to a trustee in bankruptcy or to the liquidator of a company;

(c)   a disposal in pursuance of an order made under section 24 or 24A of the Matrimonial Causes Act 1973 or section 2 of the Inheritance (Provision for Family and Dependants) Act 1975;

(d)   a disposal in pursuance of a compulsory purchase order or in pursuance of an agreement entered into in circumstances where, but for the agreement, such an order would have been made or (as the case may be) carried into effect;

(e)   a disposal by way of gift to a member of the landlord's family or to a charity;

(f)   a disposal by one charity to another of an estate or interest in land which prior to the disposal is functional land of the first-mentioned charity and which is intended to be functional land of the other charity once the disposal is made;

(g)   a disposal consisting of the transfer of an estate or interest held on trust for any person where the disposal is made in connection with the appointment of a new trustee or in connection with the discharge of any trustee;

(h)   a disposal consisting of a transfer by two or more persons who are members of the same family either—

(i)   to fewer of their number, or

(ii)   to a different combination of members of the family (but one that includes at least one of the transferors);

(i)   a disposal in pursuance of—

(i)   any option or right of pre-emption binding on the landlord (whether granted before or after the commencement of this section), or

(ii)   any other obligation binding on him and created before that commencement;

(j)   a disposal consisting of the surrender of a tenancy in pursuance of any covenant, condition or agreement contained in it;

(k)   a disposal to the Crown; and

(l)   where the landlord is a body corporate, a disposal to an associated company.

(3)   In this Part "disposal" means a disposal whether by the creation or the transfer of an estate or interest and—

(a)   includes the surrender of a tenancy and the grant of an option or right of pre-emption, but

(b)   excludes a disposal under the terms of a will or under the law relating to intestacy;

and references in this Part to the transferee in connection with a disposal shall be construed accordingly.

(4)   In this section "appurtenant premises", in relation to any flat, means any yard, garden, outhouse or appurtenance (not being a common part of the building containing the flat) which belongs to, or is usually enjoyed with, the flat.

(5)   A person is a member of another's family for the purposes of this section if—

(a)   that person is the spouse of that other person, or the two of them live together as husband and wife, or

(b)   that person is that other person's parent, grandparent, child, grandchild, brother, sister, uncle, aunt, nephew or niece.

(6)   For the purposes of subsection (5)(b)—

(a)   a relationship by marriage shall be treated as a relationship by blood,

(b)   a relationship of the half-blood shall be treated as a relationship of the whole blood,

(c)   the stepchild of a person shall be treated as his child, and

(d)   an illegitimate child shall be treated as the legitimate child of his mother and reputed father.

Notices conferring rights of first refusal

5.   Requirement to serve notice conferring rights of first refusal.

(1)   Where, in the case of any premises to which this Part applies, the landlord proposes to make a relevant disposal affecting the premises, he shall serve a notice under this section on the qualifying tenants of the flats contained in the premises.

(2)   A notice under this section must—

(a)   contain particulars of the principal terms of the disposal proposed by the landlord, including in particular—

(i)   the property to which it relates and the estate or interest in that property proposed to be disposed of, and

(ii)   the consideration required by the landlord for making the disposal;

(b)   state that the notice constitutes an offer by the landlord to dispose of the property on those terms which may be accepted by the requisite majority of qualifying tenants of the constituent flats;

(c)   specify a period within which that offer may be so accepted, being a period of not less than two months which is to begin with the date of service of the notice; and

(d)   specify a further period within which a person or persons may be nominated for the purposes of section 6, being a period of not less than two months which is to begin with the end of the period specified under paragraph (c).

(3)   Where, as the result of a notice under this section being served on different tenants on different dates, the period specified in the notice under subsection (2)(c) would, apart from this subsection, end on different dates—

(a)   the notice shall have effect in relation to all the qualifying tenants on whom it is served as if it provided for that period to end with the latest of those dates, and for the period specified in the notice under subsection (2)(d) to begin with the end of that period; and

(b)   references in this Part to the period specified in the notice under subsection (2)(c) or (as the case may be) subsection (2)(d) shall be construed accordingly.

(4)   Where a landlord has not served a notice under this section on all of the qualifying tenants on whom it was required to be served by virtue of subsection (1), he shall nevertheless be treated as having complied with that subsection if—

(a)   he has served such a notice on not less than 90 per cent. of the qualifying tenants on whom it was so required to be served, or

(b)   where the qualifying tenants on whom it was so required to be served number less than ten, he has served such a notice on all but one of them.

(5)   Where a landlord proposes to effect a transaction that would involve both—

(a)   a disposal of an estate or interest in the whole or part of a building constituting a relevant disposal affecting any premises to which this Part applies, and

(b)   a disposal of an estate or interest in the whole or part of another building (whether or not constituting a relevant disposal affecting any premises to which this Part applies) or more than one such disposal,

the landlord shall, for the purpose of complying with this section in relation to any relevant disposal falling within paragraph (a) or (b) above, sever the transaction in such a way as to secure that, in the notice served by him under this section with respect to that disposal, the terms specified in pursuance of subsection (2)(a) are the terms on which he is willing to make that disposal.

(6)   References in this Part to the requisite majority of qualifying tenants of the constituent flats are references to qualifying tenants of those flats with more than 50 per cent. of the available votes; and for the purposes of this subsection—

(a)   the total number of available votes shall be determined as follows, namely—

(i)   in a case where a notice has been served under this section, that number shall correspond to the total number of constituent flats let to qualifying tenants on the date when the period specified in that notice under subsection (2)(c) expires,

(ii)   in a case where a notice is served under section 11 without a notice having been previously served under this section, that number shall correspond to the total number of constituent flats let to qualifying tenants on the date of service of the notice under section 11, and

(iii)   in a case where a notice is served under section 12 or 15 without a notice having been previously served under this section or under section 11, that number shall correspond to the total number of constituent flats let to qualifying tenants on the date of service of the notice under section 12 or 15; and

(b)   there shall be one available vote in respect of each of the flats so let on the date referred to in the relevant provision of paragraph (a) which shall be attributed to the qualifying tenant to whom it is let.

(7)   Nothing in this Part shall be construed as requiring the persons constituting the requisite majority of qualifying tenants in any one context to be the same as the persons constituting any such majority in any other context.

(8)   For the purposes of—
    (a)   subsection (2) above and sections 6 to 10, and
    (b)   subsection (6) above so far as it has effect for the purposes of those provisions,
a flat is a constituent flat if it is contained in the premises affected by the relevant disposal
with respect to which the notice was served under this section; and for the purposes of
sections 11 to 17, and subsection (6) above so far as it has effect for the purposes of those
sections, a flat is a constituent flat if it is contained in the premises affected by the
relevant disposal referred to in section 11(1)(a).

6.   Acceptance of landlord's offer.

(1)   Where—
    (a)   the landlord has, in accordance with the provisions of section 5, served an offer
notice on the qualifying tenants of the constituent flats, and
    (b)   within the period specified in that notice under section 5(2)(c), a notice is served
on him by the requisite majority of qualifying tenants of the constituent flats informing
him that the persons by whom it is served accept the offer contained in his notice,
the landlord shall not during the relevant period dispose of the protected interest except
to a person or persons nominated for the purposes of this section by the requisite
majority of qualifying tenants of the constituent flats.

(2)   In subsection (1) "the relevant period" means—
    (a)   in every case, the period beginning with the date of service of the acceptance
notice and ending with the end of the period specified in the offer notice under section
5(2)(d), and
    (b)   if any person is nominated for the purposes of this section within that period,
an additional period of three months beginning with the end of the period so specified.

(3)   If no person has been nominated for the purposes of this section during the
period so specified, the landlord may, during the period of 12 months beginning with
the end of that period, dispose of the protected interest to such person as he thinks fit,
but subject to the following restrictions, namely—
    (a)   that the consideration required by him for the disposal must not be less than
that specified in the offer notice, and
    (b)   that the other terms on which the disposal is made must, so far as relating to
any matters covered by the terms specified in the offer notice, correspond to those terms.

(4)   It is hereby declared that the entitlement of a landlord, by virtue of subsection
(3) or any other corresponding provision of this Part, to dispose of a particular estate or
interest in any property during a specified period of 12 months extends only to a disposal
of that estate or interest in the property, and accordingly the requirements of section
1(1) must be satisfied with respect to any other disposal by him affecting that property
and made during that period of 12 months (unless the disposal is not a relevant disposal
affecting any premises to which at the time of the disposal this Part applies).

(5)   A person nominated for the purposes of this section by the requisite majority of
qualifying tenants of the constituent flats may only be replaced by another person so
nominated if he has (for any reason) ceased to be able to act as a person so nominated.

(6)   Where two or more persons have been so nominated and any of them ceases to
act as such a person without being replaced in accordance with subsection (5), any
remaining person or persons so nominated shall be entitled to continue to act in his or
their capacity as such.

(7)   Where subsection (1) above applies to the landlord, and he is precluded by virtue
of any covenant, condition or other obligation from disposing of the protected interest
to the nominated person unless the consent of some other person is obtained, then,
subject to subsection (8)—
    (a)   he shall use his best endeavours to secure that the consent of that person to
that disposal is given, and

(b)   if it appears to him that that person is obliged not to withhold his consent unreasonably but has nevertheless so withheld it, he shall institute proceedings for a declaration to that effect.

(8)   Subsection (7) shall not apply once a notice is served by or on the landlord in accordance with any provision of section 9 or 10.

(9)   In this Part—

"acceptance notice" means a notice served on the landlord in pursuance of subsection (1)(b);

"offer notice" means a notice served under section 5; and

"the protected interest" means (subject to section 9(9)) any such estate or interest in any property as is specified in an offer notice in pursuance of section 5(2)(a).

7.   Rejection of landlord's offer: counter-offer by tenants.

(1)   Where—

(a)   a landlord has, in accordance with section 5, served an offer notice on the qualifying tenants of the constituent flats, and

(b)   an acceptance notice is not served on the landlord by the requisite majority of qualifying tenants of the constituent flats within the period specified in the offer notice under section 5(2)(c), and

(c)   paragraph (b) of subsection (2) below does not apply,

the landlord may, during the period of 12 months beginning with the end of that period, dispose of the protected interest to such person as he thinks fit, but subject to the restrictions mentioned in section 6(3)(a) and (b).

(2)   Where—

(a)   a landlord has served an offer notice as mentioned in subsection (1)(a), and

(b)   within the period specified in the offer notice under section 5(2)(c), a notice is served on the landlord by the requisite majority of qualifying tenants of the constituent flats stating that the persons by whom it is served are making him a counter-offer for the acquisition by them of such estate or interest in the property specified in the offer notice under section 5(2)(a) as is specified in their notice,

the landlord shall serve on such person as is specified in that notice in pursuance of subsection (3)(b) a notice which either accepts the counter-offer or rejects it.

(3)   Any notice making a counter-offer in accordance with subsection (2)(b) must specify—

(a)   the terms (including those relating to the consideration payable) on which the counter-offer is made; and

(b)   the name and address of a person on whom any notice by the landlord under subsection (2) is to be served.

(4)   If the landlord serves a notice under subsection (2) above accepting the counter-offer, section 6(1) and the other provisions of section 6 shall apply to him as if an acceptance notice had been served on him as mentioned in section 6(1)(b), except that—

(a)   any reference to the protected interest shall be read as a reference to any such estate or interest as is specified in the notice making the counter-offer in accordance with subsection (2)(b) above;

(b)   any reference in section 6(3) to the offer notice shall be read as a reference to the notice making the counter-offer; and

(c)   where the landlord's notice is served under subsection (2) above after the end of the period specified under section 5(2)(c), section 6(2) and (3) shall have effect as if the period specified under section 5(2)(d) began with the date of service of the landlord's notice.

(5)   If the landlord serves a notice under subsection (2) above rejecting the counter-offer, then, unless it is a notice falling within section 8(1), subsection (1) above shall apply to him as if no such notice as is mentioned in subsection (2)(b) above had

been served on him (except that where he serves his notice under subsection (2) above after the end of the period specified under section 5(2)(c), subsection (1) above shall have effect as if the period of 12 months there mentioned began with the date of service of that notice).

8. Fresh offer by landlord: further negotiations between parties.

(1) This section applies where the landlord serves a notice under subsection (2) of section 7 rejecting a counter-offer but the notice—

(a) states that it constitutes a fresh offer by the landlord to dispose of an estate or interest in the property specified in the offer notice under section 5(2)(a) which may be accepted by the requisite majority of qualifying tenants of the constituent flats;

(b) contains particulars of the estate or interest in that property which he proposes to dispose of, the consideration required by him for the disposal and the other principal terms of the disposal; and

(c) specifies a period within which the offer may be accepted as mentioned in paragraph (a) above.

(2) If, within the period specified in the landlord's notice under subsection (1)(c) above, a notice is served on the landlord by the requisite majority of qualifying tenants of the constituent flats informing him that the persons by whom it is served accept the offer contained in the landlord's notice, section 6(1) and the other provisions of section 6 shall apply to the landlord as if an acceptance notice had been served on him as mentioned in section 6(1)(b), except that—

(a) any reference to the protected interest shall be read as a reference to any such estate or interest as is specified in the landlord's notice in pursuance of subsection (1)(b) above; and

(b) any reference in section 6(3) to the offer notice shall be read as a reference to the landlord's notice under subsection (1) above; and

(c) where the notice served on the landlord in pursuance of this subsection is served after the end of the period specified under section 5(2)(c), section 6(2) and (3) shall have effect as if the period specified under section 5(2)(d) began with the date of service of that notice.

(3) If, within the period specified in the landlord's notice under subsection (1)(c) above, no notice is served on the landlord as mentioned in subsection (2) above and subsection (4) below does not apply, the landlord may, during the period of 12 months beginning with the end of that period dispose of any such estate or interest as is specified in the landlord's notice under subsection (1)(b) above to such person as he thinks fit, but subject to the following restrictions, namely—

(a) that the consideration required by him for the disposal must not be less than that specified in his notice under subsection (1), and

(b) that the other terms on which the disposal is made must, so far as relating to any matters covered by the terms specified in that notice, correspond to those terms.

(4) If, within the period so specified in the landlord's notice, a notice is served on him by the requisite majority of qualifying tenants of the constituent flats stating that the persons by whom it is served are making him a further counter-offer for the acquisition by them of such estate or interest in the property specified in the offer notice under section 5(2)(a) as is specified in their notice, the provisions of subsections (2) to (5) of section 7 and the provisions of this section (including this subsection) shall apply, with any necessary modifications, in relation to any such notice as they apply in relation to a notice served as mentioned in subsection (2)(b) of section 7.

9. Withdrawal of either party from transaction.

(1) Where—

(a) section 6(1) applies to a landlord by virtue of any provision of sections 6 to 8, and

(b)   any person has been nominated for the purposes of section 6 by the requisite majority of qualifying tenants of the constituent flats within the period specified by the landlord in his offer notice under section 5(2)(d) (taking into account any postponement of the commencement of that period effected by any of the preceding provisions of this Part), and

(c)   the nominated person serves a notice on the landlord indicating an intention no longer to proceed with the acquisition of the protected interest,

the landlord may, during the period of 12 months beginning with the date of service of the nominated person's notice, dispose of the protected interest to such person as he thinks fit, but subject to the restrictions mentioned in subsection (2).

(2)   The restrictions referred to in subsection (1) are—

(a)   that the consideration required by him for the disposal must not be less than the amount which has been agreed to by the parties (subject to contract) for the disposal of the protected interest, and

(b)   that the other terms on which the disposal is made must correspond to those so agreed to by the parties in relation to the disposal.

(3)   If at any time the nominated person becomes aware that the number of the qualifying tenants of the constituent flats desiring to proceed with the acquisition of the protected interest is less than the requisite majority of qualifying tenants of those flats, he shall forthwith serve on the landlord such a notice as is mentioned in subsection (1)(c).

(4)   Where—

(a)   paragraphs (a) and (b) of subsection (1) apply, and

(b)   the landlord serves a notice on the nominated person indicating an intention no longer to proceed with the disposal of the protected interest,

the landlord shall not be entitled to dispose of that interest in accordance with that subsection but the notice shall have the consequences set out in subsection (5) or (6) (as the case may be).

(5)   If any notice served in pursuance of subsection (1), (3) or (4) above is served not later than the end of the first four weeks of the period referred to in subsection (1)(b) above, the party serving it shall not be liable for any costs incurred by the other party in connection with the disposal.

(6)   If any such notice is served after the end of those four weeks, the party on whom it is served may recover from the other party any costs reasonably incurred by the first-mentioned party in connection with the disposal between the end of those four weeks and the time when that notice is served on him.

(7)   For the purposes of this section the parties are—

(a)   the landlord, and

(b)   the qualifying tenants who served the acceptance notice or other notice accepting an offer by the landlord, or (as the case may be) the notice making the counter-offer which was accepted by the landlord, together with the nominated person,

and any liability of those tenants and the nominated person which arises under this section shall be a joint and several liability.

(8)   Nothing in this section applies where a binding contract for the disposal of the protected interest has been entered into by the landlord and the nominated person.

(9)   In this section and section 10—

"the nominated person" means the person or persons for the time being nominated for the purposes of section 6 by the requisite majority of qualifying tenants of the constituent flats; and

"the protected interest" means—

(a)   except where section 6(1) applies to the landlord by virtue of section 7(4) or 8(2), the protected interest as defined by section 6(9); and

(b)   where section 6(1) applies to the landlord by virtue of section 7(4) or 8(2), any such estate or interest as is mentioned in section 7(4)(a) or (as the case may be) in section 8(2)(a).

10.   Lapse of landlord's offer.

(1)   If, at any time after a landlord has served an offer notice with respect to any relevant disposal affecting any premises to which this Part applies, those premises cease to be premises to which this Part applies, the landlord may serve a notice on the qualifying tenants of the constituent flats stating—

(a)   that the premises have ceased to be premises to which this Part applies, and

(b)   that the offer notice, and anything done in pursuance of it, is to be treated as not having been served or done;

and, on the service of any such notice, the provisions of this Part shall cease to have effect in relation to that disposal.

(2)   Subsection (4) of section 5 shall apply to a notice under subsection (1) above as it applies to a notice under that section, but as if the references to the qualifying tenants on whom such a notice is required to be served by virtue of subsection (1) of that section were references to the qualifying tenants mentioned in subsection (1) above.

(3)   In a case where a landlord is entitled to serve a notice under subsection (1) above but does not do so, this Part shall continue to have effect in relation to the disposal in question as if the premises in question were still premises to which this Part applies.

(4)   Where—

(a)   in the case of a landlord to whom section 6(7) applies—

(i)   the landlord has discharged any duty imposed on him by that provision, and

(ii)   any such consent as is there mentioned has been withheld, and

(iii)   no such declaration as is there mentioned has been made, or

(b)   the period specified in section 6(2)(b) has expired without any binding contract having been entered into between the landlord and the nominated person,

and the landlord serves a notice on the nominated person stating that paragraph (a) or (b) above applies, the landlord may, during the period of 12 months beginning with the end of the period specified in section 6(2)(b), dispose of the protected interest to such person as he thinks fit, but subject to the restrictions mentioned in section 9(2). References in this subsection to section 6(2)(b) include references to that provision as it has effect by virtue of section 7(4)(c) or 8(2)(c).

(5)   Where any such notice is served in a case to which paragraph (b) of subsection (4) applies, the landlord may recover from the other party any costs reasonably incurred by him in connection with the disposal to the nominated person between the end of the first four weeks of the period referred to in section 9(1)(b) and the time when that notice is served by him; and section 9(7) shall apply for the purposes of this section as it applies for the purposes of section 9.

(6)   Where any binding contract with respect to the disposal of the protected interest has been entered into between the landlord and the nominated person but it has been lawfully rescinded by the landlord, the landlord may, during the period of 12 months beginning with the date of the rescission of the contract, dispose of that interest to such person (and on such terms) as he thinks fit.

(7)   Section 9(9) applies for the purposes of this section.

Enforcement by tenants of rights against new landlords

11.   Duty of new landlord to furnish particulars of disposal made in contravention of Part I.

(1)   Where—

(a)   a landlord has made a relevant disposal affecting any premises to which at the time of the disposal this Part applied ("the original disposal"), and

(b)   either no notice was served by the landlord under section 5 with respect to that disposal or it was made in contravention of any provision of sections 6 to 10, and

(c)   those premises are still premises to which this Part applies,

the requisite majority of qualifying tenants of the constituent flats may, before the end of the period specified in subsection (2) below, serve a notice on the transferee under the original disposal requiring him to furnish a person (whose name and address are specified for the purpose in the notice) with particulars of the terms on which the original disposal was made (including those relating to the consideration payable) and the date on which it was made; and in the following provisions of this Part the transferee under that disposal is referred to as "the new landlord".

(2)   The period referred to in subsection (1) is the period of two months beginning with the date by which—

(a)   notices under section 3 of the Landlord and Tenant Act 1985 (in this Act referred to as "the 1985 Act") relating to the original disposal, or

(b)   documents of any other description indicating that the original disposal has taken place,

have been served on the requisite majority of qualifying tenants of the constituent flats.

(3)   Any person served with a notice in accordance with subsection (1) shall comply with the notice within the period of one month beginning with the date on which it is served on him.

12.   Right of qualifying tenants to compel sale etc. by new landlord.

(1)   Where—

(a)   paragraphs (a) and (b) of section 11(1) apply to a relevant disposal affecting any premises to which at the time of the disposal this Part applied (other than a disposal consisting of such a surrender as is mentioned in section 15(1)(b)), and

(b)   those premises are still premises to which this Part applies,

the requisite majority of qualifying tenants of the constituent flats may, before the end of the period specified in subsection (2), serve a notice ("a purchase notice") on the new landlord requiring him (except as provided by the following provisions of this Part) to dispose of the estate or interest that was the subject-matter of the original disposal, on the terms on which it was made (including those relating to the consideration payable), to a person or persons nominated for the purposes of this section by any such majority of qualifying tenants of those flats.

(2)   The period referred to in subsection (1) is—

(a)   in a case where a notice has been served on the new landlord under section 11(1), the period of three months beginning with the date on which a notice is served by him under section 11(3); and

(b)   in any other case, the period of three months beginning with the date mentioned in section 11(2).

(3)   A purchase notice—

(a)   shall, where the estate or interest that was the subject-matter of the original disposal related to any property in addition to the premises to which this Part applied at the time of the disposal—

(i)   require the new landlord to dispose of that estate or interest only so far as relating to those premises, and

(ii)   require him to do so on the terms referred to in subsection (1) subject to such modifications as are necessary or expedient in the circumstances;

(b)   may, instead of specifying the estate or interest to be disposed of or any particular terms on which the disposal is to be made by the new landlord (whether doing so expressly or by reference to the original disposal), provide for that estate or interest, or (as the case may be) for any such terms, to be determined by a rent assessment committee in accordance with section 13.

(4) Where the property which the new landlord is required to dispose of in pursuance of the purchase notice has at any time since the original disposal become subject to any charge or other incumbrance, then, unless the court by order directs otherwise—

(a) in the case of a charge to secure the payment of money or the performance of any other obligation by the new landlord or any other person, the instrument by virtue of which the property is disposed of by the new landlord to the person or persons nominated for the purposes of this section shall (subject to the provisions of Part I of Schedule 1) operate to discharge the property from that charge; and

(b) in the case of any other incumbrance, the property shall be so disposed of subject to the incumbrance but with a reduction in the consideration payable to the new landlord corresponding to the amount by which the existence of the incumbrance reduces the value of the property.

(5) Subsection (4)(a) and Part I of Schedule 1 shall apply, with any necessary modifications, to mortgages and liens as they apply to charges; but nothing in those provisions shall apply to a rentcharge.

(6) Where the property referred to in subsection (4) has at any time since the original disposal increased in monetary value owing to any change in circumstances (other than a change in the value of money), the amount of the consideration payable to the new landlord for the disposal by him of the property in pursuance of the purchase notice shall be the amount that might reasonably have been obtained on a corresponding disposal made on the open market at the time of the original disposal if the change in circumstances had already taken place.

(7) The person or persons initially nominated for the purposes of this section shall be so nominated in the purchase notice; and any such person may only be replaced by another person so nominated by the requisite majority of qualifying tenants of the constituent flats if he has (for any reason) ceased to be able to act as person so nominated.

(8) Where two or more persons have been so nominated and any of them ceases to act as such a person without being replaced in accordance with subsection (7), any remaining person or persons so nominated shall be entitled to continue to act in his or their capacity as such.

(9) Where, in the exercise of its power to award costs, the court or the Lands Tribunal makes, in connection with any proceedings arising under or by virtue of this Part, an award of costs against the person or persons so nominated, the liability for those costs shall be the joint and several liability of that person or those persons together with the qualifying tenants by whom the relevant purchase notice was served.

13. Determination by rent assessment committees of questions relating to purchase notices.

(1) A rent assessment committee shall have jurisdiction to hear and determine—

(a) any question arising in relation to any matters specified in a purchase notice (whether relating to the nature of the estate or interest, or the identity of the property, to be disposed of or relating to any other terms on which the disposal by the new landlord is to be made); and

(b) any question arising for determination in consequence of a provision in a purchase notice such as is mentioned in section 12(3)(b).

(2) An application to a rent assessment committee under this section must be in such form, and contain such particulars, as the Secretary of State may by regulations prescribe.

(3) On any application under this section the interests of the persons by whom a purchase notice has been served shall be represented by the nominated person, and accordingly the parties to any such application shall not include those persons.

(4) Any costs incurred by a party to an application under this section in connection

with the application shall be borne by that party.

(5) A rent assessment committee shall, when constituted for the purpose of hearing and determining any question falling within subsection (1) above, be known as a leasehold valuation tribunal, and paragraphs 1 to 3 and 7 of Schedule 22 to the Housing Act 1980 (provisions relating to leasehold valuation tribunals) shall accordingly apply to any such committee when so constituted.

(6) In this section and sections 14, 16 and 17 "the nominated person" means (subject to section 15(5)) the person or persons for the time being nominated for the purposes of section 12 by the requisite majority of qualifying tenants of the constituent flats.

14. Withdrawal of nominated person from transaction.

(1) Where, at any time before a binding contract is entered into in pursuance of a purchase notice, the nominated person serves a notice on the new landlord indicating an intention no longer to proceed with the disposal required by the purchase notice, the new landlord may recover from that person any costs reasonably incurred by him in connection with that disposal down to the time when the notice is served on him under this subsection.

(2) If, at any such time as is mentioned in subsection (1) above, the nominated person becomes aware that the number of qualifying tenants of the constituent flats desiring to proceed with the disposal required by the purchase notice is less than the requisite majority of those tenants, he shall forthwith serve on the new landlord a notice indicating such an intention as is mentioned in subsection (1), and that subsection shall apply accordingly.

(3) If a notice is served under this section at a time when any proceedings arising under or by virtue of this Part are pending before the court or the Lands Tribunal, the liability of the nominated person for any costs incurred by the new landlord as mentioned in subsection (1) above shall be such as may be determined by the court or (as the case may be) by the Tribunal.

(4) By virtue of section 13(4) the costs that may be recovered by the new landlord under the preceding provisions of this section do not include any costs incurred by him in connection with an application to a rent assessment committee.

(5) Any liability for costs to which a nominated person becomes subject by virtue of this section shall be such a joint and several liability as is mentioned in section 12(9).

(6) Section 13(6) applies for the purposes of this section.

15. Right of qualifying tenants to compel grant of new tenancy by superior landlord.

(1) Where—

(a) paragraphs (a) and (b) of section 11(1) apply to a relevant disposal affecting any premises to which at the time of the disposal this Part applied, and

(b) the disposal consisted of the surrender by the landlord of a tenancy held by him ("the relevant tenancy"), and

(c) those premises are still premises to which this Part applies,

the requisite majority of qualifying tenants of the constituent flats may, before the end of the period specified in section 12(2), serve a notice on the new landlord requiring him (except as provided by the following provisions of this Part) to grant a new tenancy of the premises subject to the relevant tenancy, on the terms referred to in subsection (2) below and expiring on the date on which that tenancy would have expired, to a person or persons nominated for the purposes of this section by any such majority of qualifying tenants of those flats.

(2) Those terms are—

(a) the terms of the relevant tenancy; and

(b) if the new landlord paid any amount to the landlord as consideration for the surrender by him of that tenancy, that any such amount is paid to the new landlord by the person or persons so nominated.

(3)   A notice under this section—

(a)   shall, where the premises subject to the relevant tenancy included premises other than those to which this Part applied at the time of the original disposal—

(i)   require the new landlord to grant a new tenancy only of the premises to which this Part so applied, and

(ii)   require him to do so on the terms referred to in subsection (2) subject to such modifications as are necessary or expedient in the circumstances;

(b)   may, instead of specifying the premises to be demised under the new tenancy or any particular terms on which that tenancy is to be granted by the new landlord (whether doing so expressly or by reference to the relevant tenancy), provide for those premises, or (as the case may be) for any such terms, to be determined by a rent assessment committee in accordance with section 13 (as applied by subsection (4) below).

(4)   The following provisions, namely—

section 12(7) to (9),

sections 13 and 14, and

sections 16 and 17,

shall apply in relation to a notice under this section as they apply in relation to a purchase notice (whether referred to as such or as a notice served under section 12(1)) but subject to the modifications specified in subsection (5) below.

(5)   Those modifications are as follows—

(a)   any reference to the purposes of section 12 shall be read as a reference to the purposes of this section;

(b)   the reference in section 13(1)(b) to section 12(3)(b) shall be read as a reference to subsection (3)(b) above;

(c)   the references in section 16 to the estate or interest that was the subject-matter of the original disposal shall be read as a reference to the estate or interest which, prior to the surrender of the relevant tenancy, constituted the reversion immediately expectant on it; and

(d)   the references in sections 16 and 17 to sections 12 to 14 shall be read as references to sections 12(7) to (9), 13 and 14 (as applied by subsection (4) above) and this section.

Enforcement by tenants of rights against subsequent purchasers

16.   Right of qualifying tenants to compel sale etc. by subsequent purchaser.

(1)   Where, at the time when a notice is served under section 11(1) or 12(1) on the new landlord, he no longer holds the estate or interest that was the subject-matter of the original disposal, then—

(a)   in the case of a notice served under section 11(1), the new landlord shall, within the period specified in section 11(3)—

(i)   furnish such person as is specified in the notice with the information that he is required to furnish by virtue of it, and

(ii)   serve on that person a notice informing him of the name and address of the person to whom the new landlord disposed of that estate or interest ("the subsequent purchaser"), and

(iii)   serve on the subsequent purchaser a copy of the notice under section 11(1) and of the information furnished by him under sub-paragraph (i) above;

(b)   in the case of a notice served under section 12(1), the new landlord shall forthwith—

(i)   forward the notice to the subsequent purchaser, and

(ii)   serve on the nominated person such a notice as is mentioned in paragraph (a)(ii) above.

(2)   If the new landlord serves a notice in accordance with subsection (1)(a)(ii) or (b)(ii) above, sections 12 to 14 shall, instead of applying to the new landlord, apply to the subsequent purchaser as if he were the transferee under the original disposal.

(3)   Subsections (1) and (2) above shall have effect, with any necessary modifications, in a case where, instead of disposing of the whole of the estate or interest referred to in subsection (1) to another person, the new landlord has disposed of it in part or in parts to one or more other persons and accordingly sections 12 to 14 shall—

(a)   in relation to any part of that estate or interest retained by the new landlord, apply to the new landlord, and

(b)   in relation to any part of that estate or interest disposed of to any other person, apply to that other person instead as if he were (as respects that part) the transferee under the original disposal.

(4)   Subsection (1) shall not apply in a case where the premises affected by the original disposal have ceased to be premises to which this Part applies.

(5)   Section 13(6) applies for the purposes of this section.

Termination of rights against new landlords etc.

17.   Termination of rights against new landlord or subsequent purchaser.

(1)   If, at any time after a notice has been served under section 11(1) or 12(1), the premises affected by the original disposal cease to be premises to which this Part applies, the new landlord may serve a notice on the qualifying tenants of the constituent flats stating—

(a)   that the premises have ceased to be premises to which this Part applies, and

(b)   that any notice served on him under section 11(1) or 12(1), and anything done in pursuance of it, is to be treated as not having been served or done.

(2)   Subsection (4) of section 5 shall apply to a notice under subsection (1) above as it applies to a notice under that section, but as if the references to the qualifying tenants on whom such a notice is required to be served by virtue of subsection (1) of that section were references to the qualifying tenants mentioned in subsection (1) above.

(3)   Where a period of three months beginning with the date of service of a purchase notice on the new landlord has expired—

(a)   without any binding contract having been entered into between the new landlord and the nominated person, and

(b)   without there having been made any application in connection with the purchase notice to the court or to a rent assessment committee under section 13, the new landlord may serve on the nominated person a notice containing such a statement as is mentioned in subsection (1)(b) above.

(4)   Where—

(a)   any such application as is mentioned in paragraph (b) of subsection (3) was made within the period of three months referred to in that subsection, but

(b)   a period of two months beginning with the date of the determination of that application has expired, and

(c)   no binding contract has been entered into between the new landlord and the nominated person, and

(d)   no other such application as is mentioned in subsection (3)(b) is pending, the new landlord may serve on the nominated person a notice containing such a statement as is mentioned in subsection (1)(b).

(5)   Where the new landlord serves a notice in accordance with subsection (1), (3) or (4), this Part shall cease to have effect in relation to him in connection with the original disposal.

(6)   In a case where a new landlord is entitled to serve a notice under subsection (1) above but does not do so, this Part shall continue to have effect in relation to him in connection with the original disposal as if the premises in question were still premises to which this Part applies.

(7)   References in this section to the new landlord shall be read as including references to any other person to whom sections 12 to 14 apply by virtue of section 16(2) or (3).

(8)   Section 13(6) applies for the purposes of this section.

Notices served by prospective purchasers

18.   Notices served by prospective purchasers to ensure that rights of first refusal do not arise.

(1)   Where—

(a)   any disposal of an estate or interest in any premises consisting of the whole or part of a building is proposed to be made by a landlord, and

(b)   it appears to the person who would be the transferee under that disposal ("the purchaser") that any such disposal would, or might, be a relevant disposal affecting premises to which this Part applies,

the purchaser may serve notices under this subsection on the tenants of the flats contained in the premises referred to in paragraph (a) ("the flats affected").

(2)   Any notice under subsection (1) shall—

(a)   inform the person on whom it is served of the general nature of the principal terms of the proposed disposal, including in particular—

(i)   the property to which it would relate and the estate or interest in that property proposed to be disposed of by the landlord, and

(ii)   the consideration required by him for making the disposal;

(b)   invite that person to serve a notice on the purchaser stating—

(i)   whether the landlord has served on him, or on any predecessor in title of his, a notice under section 5 with respect to the disposal, and

(ii)   if the landlord has not so served any such notice, whether he is aware of any reason why he is not entitled to be served with any such notice by the landlord, and

(iii)   if he is not so aware, whether he would wish to avail himself of the right of first refusal conferred by any such notice if it were served; and

(c)   inform that person of the effect of the following provisions of this section.

(3)   Where the purchaser has served notices under subsection (1) on at least 80 per cent. of the tenants of the flats affected and—

(a)   not more than 50 per cent. of the tenants on whom those notices have been served by the purchaser have served notices on him in pursuance of subsection (2)(b) by the end of the period of 28 days beginning with the date on which the last of them was served by him with a notice under this section, or

(b)   more than 50 per cent. of the tenants on whom those notices have been served by the purchaser have served notices on him in pursuance of subsection (2)(b) but the notices in each case indicate that the tenant serving it either—

(i)   does not regard himself as being entitled to be served by the landlord with a notice under section 5 with respect to the disposal, or

(ii)   would not wish to avail himself of the right of first refusal conferred by such a notice if it were served,

the premises affected by the disposal shall, in relation to the disposal, be treated for the purposes of this Part as premises to which this Part does not apply.

(4)   For the purposes of subsection (3) each of the flats affected shall be regarded as having one tenant, who shall count towards any of the percentages specified in that subsection whether he is a qualifying tenant of the flat or not.

Supplementary

19.   Enforcement of obligations under Part I.

(1)   The court may, on the application of any person interested, make an order requiring any person who has made default in complying with any duty imposed on him

by any provision of this Part to make good the default within such time as is specified in the order.

(2)   An application shall not be made under subsection (1) unless—

(a)   a notice has been previously served on the person in question requiring him to make good the default, and

(b)   more than 14 days have elapsed since the date of service of that notice without his having done so.

(3)   The restriction imposed by section 1(1) may be enforced by an injunction granted by the court.

20.   Construction of Part I and power of Secretary of State to prescribe modifications. 1985 c. 6.

(1)   In this Part—

"acceptance notice" means a notice served on a landlord in pursuance of section 6(1)(b);

"associated company", in relation to a body corporate, means another body corporate which is (within the meaning of section 736 of the Companies Act 1985) that body's holding company, a subsidiary of that body or another subsidiary of that body's holding company;

"constituent flat" shall be construed in accordance with section 5(8);

"disposal" has the meaning given by section 4(3), and references to the acquisition of an estate or interest shall be construed accordingly;

"landlord", in relation to any premises, shall be construed in accordance with section 2;

"the new landlord" means any such transferee under a relevant disposal as is mentioned in section 11(1);

"offer notice" means a notice served by a landlord under section 5;

"the original disposal" means the relevant disposal referred to in section 11(1);

"the protected interest" means (subject to section 9(9)) any such estate or interest in any property as is specified in an offer notice in pursuance of section 5(2)(a);

"purchase notice" means a notice served on a new landlord in pursuance of section 12(1);

"qualifying tenant", in relation to a flat, shall be construed in accordance with section 3;

"relevant disposal" shall be construed in accordance with section 4;

"the requisite majority", in relation to qualifying tenants, shall be construed in accordance with section 5(6) and (7);

"transferee", in relation to a disposal, shall be construed in accordance with section 4(3).

(2)   In this Part—

(a)   any reference to an offer or counter-offer is a reference to an offer or counter-offer made subject to contract, and

(b)   any reference to the acceptance of an offer or counter-offer is a reference to its acceptance subject to contract.

(3)   Any reference in this Part to a tenant of a particular description shall be construed, in relation to any time when the interest under his tenancy has ceased to be vested in him, as a reference to the person who is for the time being the successor in title to that interest.

(4)   The Secretary of State may by regulations make such modifications of any of the provisions of sections 5 to 18 as he considers appropriate, and any such regulations may contain such incidental, supplemental or transitional provisions as he considers appropriate in connection with the regulations.

(5)   In subsection (4) "modifications" includes additions, omissions and alterations.

PART II

APPOINTMENT OF MANAGERS BY THE COURT

21. Tenant's right to apply to court for appointment of manager.

(1)   The tenant of a flat contained in any premises to which this Part applies may, subject to the following provisions of this Part, apply to the court for an order under section 24 appointing a manager to act in relation to those premises.

(2)   Subject to subsection (3), this Part applies to premises consisting of the whole or part of a building if the building or part contains two or more flats.

(3)   This Part does not apply to any such premises at a time when—

(a)   the interest of the landlord in the premises is held by an exempt landlord or a resident landlord, or

(b)   the premises are included within the functional land of any charity.

(4)   An application for an order under section 24 may be made—

(a)   jointly by tenants of two or more flats if they are each entitled to make such an application by virtue of this section, and

(b)   in respect of two or more premises in which this Part applies;

and, in relation to any such joint application as is mentioned in paragraph (a), references in this Part to a single tenant shall be construed accordingly.

(5)   Where the tenancy of a flat contained in any such premises is held by joint tenants, an application for an order under section 24 in respect of those premises may be made by any one or more of those tenants.

(6)   An application to the court for it to exercise in relation to any premises any jurisdiction existing apart from this Act to appoint a receiver or manager shall not be made by a tenant (in his capacity as such) in any circumstances in which an application could be made by him for an order under section 24 appointing a manager to act in relation to those premises.

(7)   References in this Part to a tenant do not include references to a tenant under a tenancy to which Part II of the Landlord and Tenant Act 1954 applies.

22. Preliminary notice by tenant.

(1)   Before an application for an order under section 24 is made in respect of any premises to which this Part applies by a tenant of a flat contained in those premises, a notice under this section must (subject to subsection (3)) be served on the landlord by the tenant.

(2)   A notice under this section must—

(a)   specify the tenant's name, the address of his flat and an address in England and Wales (which may be the address of his flat) at which the landlord may serve notices, including notices in proceedings, on him in connection with this Part;

(b)   state that the tenant intends to make an application for an order under section 24 to be made by the court in respect of such premises to which this Part applies as are specified in the notice, but (if paragraph (d) is applicable) that he will not do so if the landlord complies with the requirement specified in pursuance of that paragraph;

(c)   specify the grounds on which the court would be asked to make such an order and the matters that would be relied on by the tenant for the purpose of establishing those grounds;

(d)   where those matters are capable of being remedied by the landlord, require the landlord, within such reasonable period as is specified in the notice, to take such steps for the purpose of remedying them as are so specified; and

(e)   contain such information (if any) as the Secretary of State may by regulations prescribe.

(3)   The court may (whether on the hearing of an application for an order under section 24 or not) by order dispense with the requirement to serve a notice under this

section in a case where it is satisfied that it would not be reasonably practicable to serve such a notice on the landlord, but the court may, when doing so, direct that such other notices are served, or such other steps are taken, as it thinks fit.

(4)   In a case where—

(a)   a notice under this section has been served on the landlord, and

(b)   his interest in the premises specified in pursuance of subsection (2)(b) is subject to a mortgage,

the landlord shall, as soon as is reasonably practicable after receiving the notice, serve on the mortgagee a copy of the notice.

23.   Application to court for appointment of manager.

(1)   No application for an order under section 24 shall be made to the court unless—

(a)   in a case where a notice has been served under section 22, either—

(i)   the period specified in pursuance of paragraph (d) of subsection (2) of that section has expired without the landlord having taken the steps that he was required to take in pursuance of that provision, or

(ii)   that paragraph was not applicable in the circumstances of the case; or

(b)   in a case where the requirement to serve such a notice has been dispensed with by an order under subsection (3) of that section, either—

(i)   any notices required to be served, and any other steps required to be taken, by virtue of the order have been served or (as the case may be) taken, or

(ii)   no direction was given by the court when making the order.

(2)   Rules of court shall make provision—

(a)   for requiring notice of an application for an order under section 24 in respect of any premises to be served on such descriptions of persons as may be specified in the rules; and

(b)   for enabling persons served with any such notice to be joined as parties to the proceedings.

24.   Appointment of manager by the court.

(1)   The court may, on an application for an order under this section, by order (whether interlocutory or final) appoint a manager to carry out in relation to any premises to which this Part applies—

(a)   such functions in connection with the management of the premises, or

(b)   such functions of a receiver,

or both, as the court thinks fit.

(2)   The court may only make an order under this section in the following circumstances, namely—

(a)   where the court is satisfied—

(i)   that the landlord either is in breach of any obligation owed by him to the tenant under his tenancy and relating to the management of the premises in question or any part of them or (in the case of an obligation dependent on notice) would be in breach of any such obligation but for the fact that it has not been reasonably practicable for the tenant to give him the appropriate notice, and

(ii)   that the circumstances by virtue of which he is (or would be) in breach of any such obligation are likely to continue, and

(iii)   that it is just and convenient to make the order in all the circumstances of the case; or

(b)   where the court is satisfied that other circumstances exist which make it just and convenient for the order to be made.

(3)   The premises in respect of which an order is made under this section may, if the court thinks fit, be either more or less extensive than the premises specified in the application on which the order is made.

(4)   An order under this section may make provision with respect to—

(a)   such matters relating to the exercise by the manager of his functions under the order, and

(b)   such incidental or ancillary matters,

as the court thinks fit; and, on any subsequent application made for the purpose by the manager, the court may give him directions with respect to any such matters.

(5)   Without prejudice to the generality of subsection (4), an order under this section may provide—

(a)   for rights and liabilities arising under contracts to which the manager is not a party to become rights and liabilities of the manager;

(b)   for the manager to be entitled to prosecute claims in respect of causes of action (whether contractual or tortious) accruing before or after the date of his appointment;

(c)   for remuneration to be paid to the manager by the landlord, or by the tenants of the premises in respect of which the order is made or by all or any of those persons;

(d)   for the manager's functions to be exercisable by him (subject to subsection (9)) either during a specified period or without limit of time.

(6)   Any such order may be granted subject to such conditions as the court thinks fit, and in particular its operation may be suspended on terms fixed by the court.

(7)   In a case where an application for an order under this section was preceded by the service of a notice under section 22, the court may, if it thinks fit, make such an order notwithstanding—

(a)   that any period specified in the notice in pursuance of subsection (2)(d) of that section was not a reasonable period, or

(b)   that the notice failed in any other respect to comply with any requirement contained in subsection (2) of that section or in any regulations applying to the notice under section 54(3).

(8)   The Land Charges Act 1972 and the Land Registration Act 1925 shall apply in relation to an order made under this section as they apply in relation to an order appointing a receiver or sequestrator of land.

(9)   The court may, on the application of any person interested, vary or discharge (whether conditionally or unconditionally) an order made under this section; and if the order has been protected by an entry registered under the Land Charges Act 1972 or the Land Registration Act 1925, the court may by order direct that the entry shall be cancelled.

(10)   An order made under this section shall not be discharged by the court by reason only that, by virtue of section 21(3), the premises in respect of which the order was made have ceased to be premises to which this Part applies.

(11)   References in this section to the management of any premises include references to the repair, maintenance or insurance of those premises.

PART III
COMPULSORY ACQUISITION BY TENANTS OF THEIR LANDLORD'S INTEREST

25.   Compulsory acquisition of landlord's interest by qualifying tenants.

(1)   This Part has effect for the purpose of enabling qualifying tenants of flats contained in any premises to which this Part applies to make an application to the court for an order providing for a person nominated by them to acquire their landlord's interest in the premises without his consent; and any such order is referred to in this Part as "an acquisition order".

(2)   Subject to subsections (4) and (5), this Part applies to premises if—

(a)   they consist of the whole or part of a building; and

(b)   they contain two or more flats held by tenants of the landlord who are qualifying tenants; and

(c) the appropriate requirement specified in subsection (3) is satisfied with respect to them.

(3) For the purposes of subsection (2)(c) the appropriate requirement is—

(a) where the premises contain less than four flats, that all of the flats are let by the landlord on long leases;

(b) where the premises contain more than three but less than ten flats, that all, or all but one, of the flats are so let; and

(c) where the premises contain ten or more flats, that at least 90 per cent. of the flats are so let.

(4) This Part does not apply to premises falling within subsection (2) if—

(a) any part or parts of the premises is or are occupied or intended to be occupied otherwise than for residential purposes; and

(b) the internal floor area of that part or those parts (taken together) exceeds 50 per cent. of the internal floor area of the premises (taken as a whole); and for the purposes of this subsection the internal floor area of any common parts shall be disregarded.

(5) This Part also does not apply to any such premises at a time when—

(a) the interest of the landlord in the premises is held by an exempt landlord or a resident landlord, or

(b) the premises are included within the functional land of any charity.

(6) The Secretary of State may by order substitute for the percentage for the time being specified in subsection (4)(b) such other percentage as is specified in the order.

26. Qualifying tenants.

(1) Subject to subsections (2) and (3), a person is a qualifying tenant of a flat for the purposes of this Part if he is the tenant of the flat under a long lease other than one constituting a tenancy to which Part II of the Landlord and Tenant Act 1954 applies.

(2) A person is not to be regarded as being a qualifying tenant of a flat contained in any particular premises consisting of the whole or part of a building if by virtue of one or more long leases none of which constitutes a tenancy to which Part II of the Landlord and Tenant Act 1954 applies, he is the tenant not only of the flat in question but also of at least two other flats contained in those premises.

(3) A tenant of a flat under a long lease whose landlord is a qualifying tenant of that flat is not to be regarded as being a qualifying tenant of that flat.

(4) For the purposes of subsection (2) any tenant of a flat contained in the premises in question who is a body corporate shall be treated as the tenant of any other flat so contained and let to an associated company, as defined in section 20(1).

27. Preliminary notice by tenants.

(1) Before an application for an acquisition order is made in respect of any premises to which this Part applies, a notice under this section must (subject to subsection (3)) be served on the landlord by qualifying tenants of the flats contained in the premises who, at the date when it is served, constitute the requisite majority of such tenants.

(2) A notice under this section must—

(a) specify the names of the qualifying tenants by whom it is served, the addresses of their flats and the name and the address in England and Wales of a person on whom the landlord may serve notices (including notices in proceedings) in connection with this Part instead of serving them on those tenants;

(b) state that those tenants intend to make an application for an acquisition order to be made by the court in respect of such premises to which this Part applies as are specified in the notice, but (if paragraph (d) is applicable) that they will not do so if the landlord complies with the requirement specified in pursuance of that paragraph;

(c) specify the grounds on which the court would be asked to make such an order and the matters that would be relied on by the tenants for the purpose of establishing those grounds;

(d)   where those matters are capable of being remedied by the landlord, require the landlord, within such reasonable period as is specified in the notice, to take such steps for the purpose of remedying them as are so specified; and

(e)   contain such information (if any) as the Secretary of State may by regulations prescribe.

(3)   The court may by order dispense with the requirement to serve a notice under this section in a case where it is satisfied that it would not be reasonably practicable to serve such a notice on the landlord, but the court may, when doing so, direct that such other notices are served, or such other steps are taken, as it thinks fit.

(4)   Any reference in this Part to the requisite majority of qualifying tenants of the flats contained in any premises is a reference to qualifying tenants of the flats so contained with more than 50 per cent. of the available votes; and for the purposes of this subsection—

(a)   the total number of available votes shall correspond to the total number of those flats for the time being let to qualifying tenants; and

(b)   there shall be one available vote in respect of each of the flats so let which shall be attributed to the qualifying tenant to whom it is let.

(5)   Nothing in this Part shall be construed as requiring the persons constituting any such majority in any one context to be the same as the persons constituting any such majority in any other context.

28.   Applications for acquisition orders.

(1)   An application for an acquisition order in respect of any premises to which this Part applies must be made by qualifying tenants of the flats contained in the premises who, at the date when it is made, constitute the requisite majority of such tenants.

(2)   No such application shall be made to the court unless—

(a)   in a case where a notice has been served under section 27, either—

(i)   the period specified in pursuance of paragraph (d) of subsection (2) of that section has expired without the landlord having taken the steps that he was required to take in pursuance of that provision, or

(ii)   that paragraph was not applicable in the circumstances of the case; or

(b)   in a case where the requirement to serve such a notice has been dispensed with by an order under subsection (3) of that section, either—

(i)   any notices required to be served, and any other steps required to be taken, by virtue of the order have been served or (as the case may be) taken, or

(ii)   no direction was given by the court when making the order.

(3)   An application for an acquisition order may, subject to the preceding provisions of this Part, be made in respect of two or more premises to which this Part applies.

(4)   Rules of court shall make provision—

(a)   for requiring notice of an application for an acquisition order in respect of any premises to be served on such descriptions of persons as may be specified in the rules; and

(b)   for enabling persons served with any such notice to be joined as parties to the proceedings.

(5)   The Land Charges Act 1972 and the Land Registration Act 1925 shall apply in relation to an application for an acquisition order as they apply in relation to other pending land actions.

(6)   The persons applying for an acquisition order in respect of any premises to which this Part applies shall be treated for the purposes of section 57 of the Land Registration Act 1925 (inhibitions) as persons interested in relation to any registered land containing the whole or part of those premises.

29. Conditions for making acquisition orders.

(1)   The court may, on an application for an acquisition order, make such an order in respect of any premises if—

(a)   the court is satisfied—

(i)   that those premises were, at the date of service on the landlord of the notice (if any) under section 27 and on the date when the application was made, premises to which this Part applies, and

(ii)   that they have not ceased to be such premises since the date when the application was made, and

(b)   either of the conditions specified in subsections (2) and (3) is fulfilled with respect to those premises, and

(c)   the court considers it appropriate to make the order in the circumstances of the case.

(2)   The first of the conditions referred to in subsection (1)(b) is that the court is satisfied—

(a)   that the landlord either is in breach of any obligation owed by him to the applicants under their leases and relating to the repair, maintenance, insurance or management of the premises in question, or any part of them, or (in the case of an obligation dependent on notice) would be in breach of any such obligation but for the fact that it has not been reasonably practicable for the tenant to give him the appropriate notice, and

(b)   that the circumstances by virtue of which he is (or would be) in breach of any such obligation are likely to continue, and

(c)   that the appointment of a manager under Part II to act in relation to those premises would not be an adequate remedy.

(3)   The second of those conditions is that, both at the date when the application was made and throughout the period of three years immediately preceding that date, there was in force an appointment under Part II of a person to act as manager in relation to the premises in question.

(4)   An acquisition order may, if the court thinks fit—

(a)   include any yard, garden, outhouse or appurtenance belonging to, or usually enjoyed with, the premises specified in the application on which the order is made;

(b)   exclude any part of the premises so specified.

(5)   Where—

(a)   the premises in respect of which an application for an acquisition order is made consist of part only of more extensive premises in which the landlord has an interest, and

(b)   it appears to the court that the landlord's interest in the latter premises is not reasonably capable of being severed, either in the manner contemplated by the application or in any manner authorised by virtue of subsection (4)(b),

then, notwithstanding that paragraphs (a) and (b) of subsection (1) apply, the court shall not make an acquisition order on the application.

(6)   In a case where an application for an acquisition order was preceded by the service of a notice under section 27, the court may, if it thinks fit, make such an order notwithstanding—

(a)   that any period specified in the notice in pursuance of subsection (2)(d) of that section was not a reasonable period, or

(b)   that the notice failed in any other respect to comply with any requirement contained in subsection (2) of that section or in any regulations applying to the notice under section 54(3).

(7)   Where any premises are premises to which this Part applies at the time when an application for an acquisition order is made in respect of them, then, for the purposes of this section and the following provisions of this Part, they shall not cease to be such

premises by reason only that—

    (a)   the interest of the landlord in them subsequently becomes held by an exempt landlord or a resident landlord, or

    (b)   they subsequently become included within the functional land of any charity.

30. Content of acquisition orders.

(1)   Where an acquisition order is made by the court, the order shall (except in a case falling within section 33(1)) provide for the nominated person to be entitled to acquire the landlord's interest in the premises specified in the order on such terms as may be determined—

    (a)   by agreement between the landlord and the qualifying tenants in whose favour the order is made, or

    (b)   in default of agreement, by a rent assessment committee under section 31.

(2)   An acquisition order may be granted subject to such conditions as the court thinks fit, and in particular its operation may be suspended on terms fixed by the court.

(3)   References in this Part, in relation to an acquisition order, to the nominated person are references to such person or persons as may be nominated for the purposes of this Part by the persons applying for the order.

(4)   Those persons must secure that the nominated person is joined as a party to the application, and no further nomination of a person for the purposes of this Part shall be made by them after the order is made (whether in addition to, or in substitution for, the existing nominated person) except with the approval of the court.

(5)   Where the landlord is, by virtue of any covenant, condition or other obligation, precluded from disposing of his interest in the premises in respect of which an acquisition order has been made unless the consent of some other person is obtained—

    (a)   he shall use his best endeavours to secure that the consent of that person to that disposal is obtained and, if it appears to him that that person is obliged not to withhold his consent unreasonably but has nevertheless so withheld it, shall institute proceedings for a declaration to that effect; but

    (b)   if—

        (i)   the landlord has discharged any duty imposed on him by paragraph (a), and

        (ii)   the consent of that person has been withheld, and

        (iii)   no such declaration has been made,

the order shall cease to have effect.

(6)   The Land Charges Act 1972 and the Land Registration Act 1925 shall apply in relation to an acquisition order as they apply in relation to an order affecting land made by the court for the purpose of enforcing a judgment or recognisance.

31. Determination of terms by rent assessment committees.

(1)   A rent assessment committee shall have jurisdiction to determine the terms on which the landlord's interest in the premises specified in an acquisition order may be acquired by the nominated person to the extent that those terms have not been determined by agreement between the landlord and either—

    (a)   the qualifying tenants in whose favour the order was made, or

    (b)   the nominated person;

and (subject to subsection (2)) such a committee shall determine any such terms on the basis of what appears to them to be fair and reasonable.

(2)   Where an application is made under this section for such a committee to determine the consideration payable for the acquisition of a landlord's interest in any premises, the committee shall do so by determining an amount equal to the amount which, in their opinion, that interest might be expected to realise if sold on the open market by a willing seller on the appropriate terms and on the assumption that none of the tenants of the landlord of any premises comprised in those premises was buying or seeking to buy that interest.

(3) In subsection (2) "the appropriate terms" means all of the terms to which the acquisition of the landlord's interest in pursuance of the order is to be subject (whether determined by agreement as mentioned in subsection (1) or on an application under this section) apart from those relating to the consideration payable.

(4) On any application under this section the interests of the qualifying tenants in whose favour the acquisition order was made shall be represented by the nominated person, and accordingly the parties to any such application shall not include those tenants.

(5) Subsections (2), (4) and (5) of section 13 shall apply for the purposes of this section as they apply for the purposes of that section, but as if the reference in subsection (5) to subsection (1) of that section were a reference to subsection (1) of this section.

(6) Nothing in this section shall be construed as authorising a rent assessment committee to determine any terms dealing with matters in relation to which provision is made by section 32 or 33.

32. Discharge of existing mortgages.

(1) Where the landlord's interest in any premises is acquired in pursuance of an acquisition order, the instrument by virtue of which it is so acquired shall (subject to subsection (2) and Part II of Schedule 1) operate to discharge the premises from any charge on that interest to secure the payment of money or the performance of any other obligation by the landlord or any other person.

(2) Subsection (1) does not apply to any such charge if—

(a) it has been agreed between the landlord and either—

(i) the qualifying tenants in whose favour the order was made, or

(ii) the nominated person,

that the landlord's interest should be acquired subject to the charge, or

(b) the court is satisfied, whether on the application for the order or on an application made by the person entitled to the benefit of the charge, that in the exceptional circumstances of the case it would be fair and reasonable that the landlord's interest should be so acquired, and orders accordingly.

(3) This section and Part II of Schedule 1 shall apply, with any necessary modifications, to mortgages and liens as they apply to charges; but nothing in those provisions shall apply to a rentcharge.

33. Acquisition order where landlord cannot be found.

(1) Where an acquisition order is made by the court in a case where the landlord cannot be found, or his identity cannot be ascertained, the order shall provide for the landlord's interest in the premises specified in the order to vest in the nominated person on the following terms, namely—

(a) such terms as to payment as are specified in subsection (2), and

(b) such other terms as the court thinks fit, being terms which, in the opinion of the court, correspond so far as possible to those on which the interest might be expected to be transferred if it were being transferred by the landlord.

(2) The terms as to payment referred to in subsection (1)(a) are terms requiring the payment into court of—

(a) such amount as a surveyor selected by the President of the Lands Tribunal may certify to be in his opinion the amount which the landlord's interest might be expected to realise if sold as mentioned in section 31(2); and

(b) any amounts or estimated amounts remaining due to the landlord from any tenants of his of any premises comprised in the premises in respect of which the order is made, being amounts or estimated amounts determined by the court as being due from those persons under the terms of their leases.

(3) Where any amount or amounts required by virtue of subsection (2) to be paid into court are so paid, the landlord's interest shall, by virtue of this section, vest in the nominated person in accordance with the order.

34. Discharge of acquisition order and withdrawal by tenants.

(1) If, on an application by a landlord in respect of whose interest an acquisition order has been made, the court is satisfied—

(a) that the nominated person has had a reasonable time within which to effect the acquisition of that interest in pursuance of the order but has not done so, or

(b) that the number of qualifying tenants of flats contained in the premises in question who desire to proceed with the acquisition of the landlord's interest is less than the requisite majority of qualifying tenants of the flats contained in those premises, or

(c) that the premises in question have ceased to be premises to which this Part applies,

the court may discharge the order.

(2) Where—

(a) a notice is served on the landlord by the qualifying tenants by whom a notice has been served under section 27 or (as the case may be) by whom an application has been made for an acquisition order, or by the person nominated for the purposes of this Part by any such tenants, and

(b) the notice indicates an intention no longer to proceed with the acquisition of the landlord's interest in the premises in question,

the landlord may (except in a case where subsection (4) applies) recover under this subsection any costs reasonably incurred by him in connection with the disposal by him of that interest down to the time when the notice is served; and, if the notice is served after the making of an acquisition order, that order shall cease to have effect.

(3) If (whether before or after the making of an acquisition order) the nominated person becomes aware—

(a) that the number of qualifying tenants of flats contained in the premises in question who desire to proceed with the acquisition of the landlord's interest is less than the requisite majority of qualifying tenants of the flats contained in those premises, or

(b) that those premises have ceased to be premises to which this Part applies,

he shall forthwith serve on the landlord a notice indicating an intention no longer to proceed with the acquisition of that interest, and subsection (2) shall apply accordingly.

(4) If, at any time when any proceedings taken under or by virtue of this Part are pending before the court or the Lands Tribunal—

(a) such a notice as is mentioned in subsection (2) or (3) is served on the landlord, or

(b) the nominated person indicates that he is no longer willing to act in the matter and nobody is nominated for the purposes of this Part in his place, or

(c) the number of qualifying tenants of flats contained in the premises in question who desire to proceed with the acquisition of the landlord's interest falls below the requisite majority of qualifying tenants of the flats contained in those premises, or

(d) those premises cease to be premises to which this Part applies,

or if the court discharges an acquisition order under subsection (1), the landlord may recover such costs incurred by him in connection with the disposal by him of his interest in those premises as the court or (as the case may be) the Tribunal may determine.

(5) The costs that may be recovered by the landlord under subsection (2) or (4) include costs incurred by him in connection with any proceedings under this Part (other than proceedings before a rent assessment committee).

(6) Any liability for costs arising under this section shall be the joint and several liability of the following persons, namely—

(a) where the liability arises before the making of an application for an acquisition order, the tenants by whom a notice was served under section 27, or

(b) where the liability arises after the making of such an application, the tenants by whom the application was made,

together with (in either case) any person nominated by those tenants for the purposes of this Part.

(7)   In relation to any time when a tenant falling within paragraph (a) or (b) of subsection (6) has ceased to have vested in him the interest under his lease, that paragraph shall be construed as applying instead to the person who is for the time being the successor in title to that interest.

(8)   Nothing in this section shall be construed as authorising the court to discharge an acquisition order where the landlord's interest has already been acquired in pursuance of the order.

(9)   If—

(a)   an acquisition order is discharged, or ceases to have effect, by virtue of any provision of this Part, and

(b)   the order has been protected by an entry registered under the Land Charges Act 1972 or the Land Registration Act 1925,

the court may by order direct that that entry shall be cancelled.

PART IV
VARIATION OF LEASES

Applications relating to flats

35.   Application by party to lease for variation of lease.

(1)   Any party to a long lease of a flat may make an application to the court for an order varying the lease in such manner as is specified in the application.

(2)   The grounds on which any such application may be made are that the lease fails to make satisfactory provision with respect to one or more of the following matters, namely—

(a)   the repair or maintenance of—

(i)   the flat in question, or

(ii)   the building containing the flat, or

(iii)   any land or building which is let to the tenant

under the lease or in respect of which rights are conferred on him under it;

(b)   the insurance of the flat or of any such building or land as is mentioned in paragraph (a)(ii) or (iii);

(c)   the repair or maintenance of any installations (whether they are in the same building as the flat or not) which are reasonably necessary to ensure that occupiers of the flat enjoy a reasonable standard of accommodation;

(d)   the provision or maintenance of any services which are reasonably necessary to ensure that occupiers of the flat enjoy a reasonable standard of accommodation (whether they are services connected with any such installations or not, and whether they are services provided for the benefit of those occupiers or services provided for the benefit of the occupiers of a number of flats including that flat);

(e)   the recovery by one party to the lease from another party to it of expenditure incurred or to be incurred by him, or on his behalf, for the benefit of that other party or of a number of persons who include that other party;

(f)   the computation of a service charge payable under the lease.

(3)   For the purposes of subsection (2)(c) and (d) the factors for determining, in relation to the occupiers of a flat, what is a reasonable standard of accommodation may include—

(a)   factors relating to the safety and security of the flat and its occupiers and of any common parts of the building containing the flat; and

(b)   other factors relating to the condition of any such common parts.

(4)   For the purposes of subsection (2)(f) a lease fails to make satisfactory provision with respect to the computation of a service charge payable under it if—

(a)   it provides for any such charge to be a proportion of expenditure incurred, or to be incurred, by or on behalf of the landlord or a superior landlord; and

(b)   other tenants of the landlord are also liable under their leases to pay by way of service charges proportions of any such expenditure; and

(c)   the aggregate of the amounts that would, in any particular case, be payable by reference to the proportions referred to in paragraphs (a) and (b) would exceed the whole of any such expenditure.

(5)   Rules of court shall make provision—

(a)   for requiring notice of any application under this Part to be served by the person making the application, and by any respondent to the application, on any person who the applicant, or (as the case may be) the respondent, knows or has reason to believe is likely to be affected by any variation specified in the application, and

(b)   for enabling persons served with any such notice to be joined as parties to the proceedings.

(6)   For the purposes of this Part a long lease shall not be regarded as a long lease of a flat if—

(a)   the demised premises consist of or include three or more flats contained in the same building; or

(b)   the lease constitutes a tenancy to which Part II of the Landlord and Tenant Act 1954 applies.

(8)   In this section "service charge" has the meaning given by section 18(1) of the 1985 Act.

36.   Application by respondent for variation of other leases.

(1)   Where an application ("the original application") is made under section 35 by any party to a lease, any other party to the lease may make an application to the court asking it, in the event of its deciding to make an order effecting any variation of the lease in pursuance of the original application, to make an order which effects a corresponding variation of each of such one or more other leases as are specified in the application.

(2)   Any lease so specified—

(a)   must be a long lease of a flat under which the landlord is the same person as the landlord under the lease specified in the original application; but

(b)   need not be a lease of a flat which is in the same building as the flat let under that lease, nor a lease drafted in terms identical to those of that lease.

(3)   The grounds on which an application may be made under this section are—

(a)   that each of the leases specified in the application fails to make satisfactory provision with respect to the matter or matters specified in the original application; and

(b)   that, if any variation is effected in pursuance of the original application, it would be in the interests of the person making the application under this section, or in the interests of the other persons who are parties to the leases specified in that application, to have all of the leases in question (that is to say, the ones specified in that application together with the one specified in the original application) varied to the same effect.

37.   Application by majority of parties for variation of leases.

(1)   Subject to the following provisions of this section, an application may be made to the court in respect of two or more leases for an order varying each of those leases in such manner as is specified in the application.

(2)   Those leases must be long leases of flats under which the landlord is the same person, but they need not be leases of flats which are in the same building, nor leases which are drafted in identical terms.

(3)   The grounds on which an application may be made under this section are that the object to be achieved by the variation cannot be satisfactorily achieved unless all the leases are varied to the same effect.

(4)   An application under this section in respect of any leases may be made by the landlord or any of the tenants under the leases.

(5) Any such application shall only be made if—

(a) in a case where the application is in respect of less than nine leases, all, or all but one, of the parties concerned consent to it; or

(b) in a case where the application is in respect of more than eight leases, it is not opposed for any reason by more than 10 per cent. of the total number of the parties concerned and at least 75 per cent. of that number consent to it.

(6) For the purposes of subsection (5)—

(a) in the case of each lease in respect of which the application is made, the tenant under the lease shall constitute one of the parties concerned (so that in determining the total number of the parties concerned a person who is the tenant under a number of such leases shall be regarded as constituting a corresponding number of the parties concerned); and

(b) the landlord shall also constitute one of the parties concerned.

Orders varying leases

38. Orders by the court varying leases.

(1) If, on an application under section 35, the grounds on which the application was made are established to the satisfaction of the court, the court may (subject to subsections (6) and (7)) make an order varying the lease specified in the application in such manner as is specified in the order.

(2) If—

(a) an application under section 36 was made in connection with that application, and

(b) the grounds set out in subsection (3) of that section are established to the satisfaction of the court with respect to the leases specified in the application under section 36,

the court may (subject to subsections (6) and (7)) also make an order varying each of those leases in such manner as is specified in the order.

(3) If, on an application under section 37, the grounds set out in subsection (3) of that section are established to the satisfaction of the court with respect to the leases specified in the application, the court may (subject to subsections (6) and (7)) make an order varying each of those leases in such manner as is specified in the order.

(4) The variation specified in an order under subsection (1) or (2) may be either the variation specified in the relevant application under section 35 or 36 or such other variation as the court thinks fit.

(5) If the grounds referred to in subsection (2) or (3) (as the case may be) are established to the satisfaction of the court with respect to some but not all of the leases specified in the application, the power to make an order under that subsection shall extend to those leases only.

(6) The court shall not make an order under this section effecting any variation of a lease if it appears to the court—

(a) that the variation would be likely substantially to prejudice—

(i) any respondent to the application, or

(ii) any person who is not a party to the application,

and that an award under subsection (10) would not afford him adequate compensation, or

(b) that for any other reason it would not be reasonable in the circumstances for the variation to be effected.

(7) The court shall not, on an application relating to the provision to be made by a lease with respect to insurance, make an order under this section effecting any variation of the lease—

(a) which terminates any existing right of the landlord under its terms to nominate an insurer for insurance purposes; or

(b)   which requires the landlord to nominate a number of insurers from which the tenant would be entitled to select an insurer for those purposes; or

(c)   which, in a case where the lease requires the tenant to effect insurance with a specified insurer, requires the tenant to effect insurance otherwise than with another specified insurer.

(8)   The court may, instead of making an order varying a lease in such manner as is specified in the order, make an order directing the parties to the lease to vary it in such manner as is so specified; and accordingly any reference in this Part (however expressed) to an order which effects any variation of a lease or to any variation effected by an order shall include a reference to an order which directs the parties to a lease to effect a variation of it or (as the case may be) a reference to any variation effected in pursuance of such an order.

(9)   The court may by order direct that a memorandum of any variation of a lease effected by an order under this section shall be endorsed on such documents as are specified in the order.

(10)   Where the court makes an order under this section varying a lease the court may, if it thinks fit, make an order providing for any party to the lease to pay, to any other party to the lease or to any other person, compensation in respect of any loss or disadvantage that the court considers he is likely to suffer as a result of the variation.

39.   Effect of orders varying leases: applications by third parties.

(1)   Any variation effected by an order under section 38 shall be binding not only on the parties to the lease for the time being but also on other persons (including any predecessors in title of those parties), whether or not they were parties to the proceedings in which the order was made or were served with a notice by virtue of section 35(5).

(2)   Without prejudice to the generality of subsection (1), any variation effected by any such order shall be binding on any surety who has guaranteed the performance of any obligation varied by the order; and the surety shall accordingly be taken to have guaranteed the performance of that obligation as so varied.

(3)   Where any such order has been made and a person was, by virtue of section 35(5), required to be served with a notice relating to the proceedings in which it was made, but he was not so served, he may—

(a)   bring an action for damages for breach of statutory duty against the person by whom any such notice was so required to be served in respect of that person's failure to serve it;

(b)   apply to the court for the cancellation or modification of the variation in question.

(4)   The court may, on an application under subsection (3)(b) with respect to any variation of a lease—

(a)   by order cancel that variation or modify it in such manner as is specified in the order, or

(b)   make such an order as is mentioned in section 38(10) in favour of the person making the application,

as it thinks fit.

(5)   Where a variation is cancelled or modified under paragraph (a) of subsection (4)—

(a)   the cancellation or modification shall take effect as from the date of the making of the order under that paragraph or as from such later date as may be specified in the order, and

(b)   the court may by order direct that a memorandum of the cancellation or modification shall be endorsed on such documents as are specified in the order;

and, in a case where a variation is so modified, subsections (1) and (2) above shall, as from the date when the modification takes effect, apply to the variation as modified.

Applications relating to dwellings other than flats

40. Application for variation of insurance provisions of lease of dwelling other than a flat.

(1)   Any party to a long lease of a dwelling may make an application to the court for an order varying the lease, in such manner as is specified in the application, on the grounds that the lease fails to make satisfactory provision with respect to any matter relating to the insurance of the dwelling, including the recovery of the costs of such insurance.

(2)   Sections 36 and 38 shall apply to an application under subsection (1) subject to the modifications specified in subsection (3).

(3)   Those modifications are as follows—

    (a)   in section 36—

      (i)   in subsection (1), the reference to section 35 shall be read as a reference to subsection (1) above, and

      (ii)   in subsection (2), any reference to a flat shall be read as a reference to a dwelling; and

    (b)   in section 38—

      (i)   any reference to an application under section 35 shall be read as a reference to an application under subsection (1) above, and

      (ii)   any reference to an application under section 36 shall be read as a reference to an application under section 36 as applied by subsection (2) above.

(4)   For the purpose of this section, a long lease shall not be regarded as a long lease of a dwelling if—

    (a)   the demised premises consist of three or more dwellings; or

    (b)   the lease constitutes a tenancy to which Part II of the Landlord and Tenant Act 1954 applies.

(4A)   Without prejudice to subsection (4), an application under subsection (1) may not be made by a person who is a tenant under a long lease of a dwelling if, by virtue of that lease and one or more other long leases of dwellings, he is also a tenant from the same landlord of at least two other dwellings.

(4B)   For the purposes of subsection (4A), any tenant of a dwelling who is a body corporate shall be treated as a tenant of any other dwelling held from the same landlord which is let under a long lease to an associated company, as defined in section 20(1).

(5)   In this section "dwelling" means a dwelling other than a flat.

PART V
MANAGEMENT OF LEASEHOLD PROPERTY

Service charges

42. Service charge contributions to be held in trust.

(1)   This section applies where the tenants of two or more dwellings may be required under the terms of their leases to contribute to the same costs by the payment of service charges; and in this section—

    "the contributing tenants" means those tenants;

    "the payee" means the landlord or other person to whom any such charges are payable by those tenants under the terms of their leases;

    "relevant service charges" means any such charges;

    "service charge" has the meaning given by section 18(1) of the 1985 Act, except that it does not include a service charge payable by the tenant of a dwelling the rent of which is registered under Part IV of the Rent Act 1977, unless the amount registered is, in pursuance of section 71(4) of that Act, entered as a variable amount;

    "tenant" does not include a tenant of an exempt landlord; and "trust fund" means the fund, or (as the case may be) any of the funds, mentioned in subsection (2) below.

(2) Any sums paid to the payee by the contributing tenants by way of relevant service charges, and any investments representing those sums, shall (together with any income accruing thereon) be held by the payee either as a single fund or, if he thinks fit, in two or more separate funds.

(3) The payee shall hold any trust fund—

(a) on trust to defray costs incurred in connection with the matters for which the relevant service charges were payable (whether incurred by himself or by any other person), and

(b) subject to that, on trust for the persons who are the contributing tenants for the time being.

(4) Subject to subsections (6) to (8), the contributing tenants shall be treated as entitled by virtue of subsection (3)(b) to such shares in the residue of any such fund as are proportionate to their respective liabilities to pay relevant service charges.

(5) If the Secretary of State by order so provides, any sums standing to the credit of any trust fund may, instead of being invested in any other manner authorised by law, be invested in such manner as may be specified in the order; and any such order may contain such incidental, supplemental or transitional provisions as the Secretary of State considers appropriate in connection with the order.

(6) On the termination of the lease of a contributing tenant the tenant shall not be entitled to any part of any trust fund, and (except where subsection (7) applies) any part of any such fund which is attributable to relevant service charges paid under the lease shall accordingly continue to be held on the trusts referred to in subsection (3).

(7) If after the termination of any such lease there are no longer any contributing tenants, any trust fund shall be dissolved as at the date of the termination of the lease, and any assets comprised in the fund immediately before its dissolution shall—

(a) if the payee is the landlord, be retained by him for his own use and benefit, and

(b) in any other case, be transferred to the landlord by the payee.

(8) Subsections (4), (6) and (7) shall have effect in relation to a contributing tenant subject to any express terms of his lease which relate to the distribution, either before or (as the case may be) at the termination of the lease, of amounts attributable to relevant service charges paid under its terms (whether the lease was granted before or after the commencement of this section).

(9) Subject to subsection (8), the provisions of this section shall prevail over the terms of any express or implied trust created by a lease so far as inconsistent with those provisions, other than an express trust so created before the commencement of this section.

PART VI
INFORMATION TO BE FURNISHED TO TENANTS

46. Application of Part VI, etc.

(1) This Part applies to premises which consist of or include a dwelling and are not held under a tenancy to which Part II of the Landlord and Tenant Act 1954 applies.

(2) In this Part "service charge" has the meaning given by section 18(1) of the 1985 Act.

47. Landlord's name and address to be contained in demands for rent etc.

(1) Where any written demand is given to a tenant of premises to which this Part applies, the demand must contain the following information, namely—

(a) the name and address of the landlord, and

(b) if that address is not in England and Wales, an address in England and Wales at which notices (including notices in proceedings) may be served on the landlord by the tenant.

(2) Where—
    (a) a tenant of any such premises is given such a demand, but
    (b) it does not contain any information required to be contained in it by virtue of
subsection (1),
then (subject to subsection (3)) any part of the amount demanded which consists of a
service charge ("the relevant amount") shall be treated for all purposes as not being due
from the tenant to the landlord at any time before that information is furnished by the
landlord by notice given to the tenant.

    (3) The relevant amount shall not be so treated in relation to any time when, by
virtue of an order of any court, there is in force an appointment of a receiver or manager
whose functions include the receiving of service charges from the tenant.

    (4) In this section "demand" means a demand for rent or other sums payable to the
landlord under the terms of the tenancy.

48. Notification by landlord of address for service of notices.

    (1) A landlord of premises to which this Part applies shall by notice furnish the
tenant with an address in England and Wales at which notices (including notices in
proceedings) may be served on him by the tenant.

    (2) Where a landlord of any such premises fails to comply with subsection (1), any
rent or service charge otherwise due from the tenant to the landlord shall (subject to
subsection (3)) be treated for all purposes as not being due from the tenant to the
landlord at any time before the landlord does comply with that subsection.

    (3) Any such rent or service charge shall not be so treated in relation to any time
when, by virtue of an order of any court, there is in force an appointment of a receiver
or manager whose functions include the receiving of rent or (as the case may be) service
charges from the tenant.

49. Extension of circumstances in which notices are sufficiently served.

In section 196 of the Law of Property Act 1925 (regulations respecting notices), any
reference in subsection (3) or (4) to the last-known place of abode or business of the
person to be served shall have effect, in its application to a notice to be served by a tenant
on a landlord of premises to which this Part applies, as if that reference included a
reference to—
    (a) the address last furnished to the tenant by the landlord in accordance with
section 48, or
    (b) if no address has been so furnished in accordance with section 48, the address
last furnished to the tenant by the landlord in accordance with section 47.

PART VII

GENERAL

52. Jurisdiction of county courts.

    (1) A county court shall have jurisdiction to hear and determine any question arising
under any provision to which this section applies (other than a question falling within
the jurisdiction of a rent assessment committee by virtue of section 13(1) or 31(1)).

    (2) This section applies to—
    (a) any provision of Parts I to IV;
    (b) any provision of section 42; and
    (c) any provision of sections 46 to 48.

    (3) Where any proceedings under any provision to which this section applies are
being taken in a county court, the county court shall have jurisdiction to hear and
determine any other proceedings joined with those proceedings, notwithstanding that
the other proceedings would, apart from this subsection, be outside the court's
jurisdiction.

    (4) If a person takes any proceedings under any such provision in the High Court

he shall not be entitled to recover any more costs of those proceedings than those to which he would have been entitled if the proceedings had been taken in a county court; and in any such case the taxing master shall have the same power of directing on what county court scale costs are to be allowed, and of allowing any item of costs, as the judge would have had if the proceedings had been taken in a county court.

(5)   Subsection (4) shall not apply where the purpose of taking the proceedings in the High Court was to enable them to be joined with any proceedings already pending before that court (not being proceedings taken under any provision to which this section applies).

53.   Regulations and orders.

(1)   Any power of the Secretary of State to make an order or regulations under this Act shall be exercisable by statutory instrument and may be exercised so as to make different provision for different cases, including different provision for different areas.

(2)   A statutory instrument containing—

(a)   an order made under section 1(5), 25(6), 42(5) or 55, or

(b)   any regulations made under section 13(2) (including any made under that provision as it applies for the purposes of section 31) or under section 20(4),

shall be subject to annulment in pursuance of a resolution of either House of Parliament.

54.   Notices.

(1)   Any notice required or authorised to be served under this Act—

(a)   shall be in writing; and

(b)   may be sent by post.

(2)   Any notice purporting to be a notice served under any provision of Part I or III by the requisite majority of any qualifying tenants (as defined for the purposes of that provision) shall specify the names of all of the persons by whom it is served and the addresses of the flats of which they are qualifying tenants.

(3)   The Secretary of State may by regulations prescribe—

(a)   the form of any notices required or authorised to be served under or in pursuance of any provision of Parts I to III, and

(b)   the particulars which any such notices must contain (whether in addition to, or in substitution for, any particulars required by virtue of the provision in question).

(4)   Subsection (3)(b) shall not be construed as authorising the Secretary of State to make regulations under subsection (3) varying either of the periods specified in section 5(2) (which accordingly can only be varied by regulations under section 20(4)).

55.   Application to Isles of Scilly.

This Act shall apply to the Isles of Scilly subject to such exceptions, adaptations and modifications as the Secretary of State may by order direct.

56.   Crown land.

(1)   This Act shall apply to a tenancy from the Crown if there has ceased to be a Crown interest in the land subject to it.

(2)   A variation of any such tenancy effected by or in pursuance of an order under section 38 shall not, however, be treated as binding on the Crown, as a predecessor in title under the tenancy, by virtue of section 39(1).

(3)   Where there exists a Crown interest in any land subject to a tenancy from the Crown and the person holding that tenancy is himself the landlord under any other tenancy whose subject-matter comprises the whole or part of that land, this Act shall apply to that other tenancy, and to any derivative sub-tenancy, notwithstanding the existence of that interest.

(4)   For the purposes of this section "tenancy from the Crown" means a tenancy of land in which there is, or has during the subsistence of the tenancy been, a Crown interest superior to the tenancy, and "Crown interest" means—

(a)   an interest comprised in the Crown Estate;
(b)   an interest belonging to Her Majesty in right of the Duchy of Lancaster;
(c)   an interest belonging to the Duchy of Cornwall;
(d)   any other interest belonging to a government department or held on behalf of
Her Majesty for the purposes of a government department.

57. Financial provision.
There shall be paid out of money provided by Parliament any increase attributable to
this Act in the sums payable out of money so provided under any other Act.

58. Exempt landlords and resident landlords.
(1)   In this Act "exempt landlord" means a landlord who is one of the following
bodies, namely—
(a)   a district, county or London borough council, the Common Council of the
City of London, the Council of the Isles of Scilly, or a joint authority established by
Part IV of the Local Government Act 1985;
(b)   the Commission for the New Towns or a development corporation established
by an order made (or having effect as if made) under the New Towns Act 1981;
(c)   an urban development corporation within the meaning of Part XVI of the
Local Government, Planning and Land Act 1980;
(ca)   a housing action trust established under Part III of The Housing Act 1988;
(d)   the Development Board for Rural Wales;
(dd)   the Broads Authority;
(e)   the Housing Corporation;
(ea)   Housing for Wales;
(f)   a housing trust (as defined in section 6 of the Housing Act 1985) which is a
charity;
(g)   a registered housing association, or an unregistered housing association which
is a fully mutual housing association, within the meaning of the Housing Associations
Act 1985; or
(h)   an authority established under section 10 of the Local Government Act 1985
(joint arrangements for waste disposal functions).
(2)   For the purposes of this Act the landlord of any premises consisting of the whole
or part of a building is a resident landlord of those premises at any time if—
(a)   the premises are not, and do not form part of, a purpose-built block of flats;
and
(b)   at that time the landlord occupies a flat contained in the premises as his only
or principal residence; and
(c)   he has so occupied such a flat throughout a period of not less than 12 months
ending with that time.
(3)   In subsection (2) "purpose-built block of flats" means a building which
contained as constructed, and contains, two or more flats.

59. Meaning of "lease", "long lease" and related expressions.
(1)   In this Act "lease" and "tenancy" have the same meaning; and both expressions
include—
(a)   a sub-lease or sub-tenancy, and
(b)   an agreement for a lease or tenancy (or for a sub-lease or sub-tenancy).
(2)   The expressions "landlord" and "tenant", and references to letting, to the grant
of a lease or to covenants or the terms of a lease shall be construed accordingly.
(3)   In this Act "long lease" means—
(a)   a lease granted for a term certain exceeding 21 years, whether or not it is (or
may become) terminable before the end of that term by notice given by the tenant or by
re-entry or forfeiture;

(b)   a lease for a term fixed by law under a grant with a covenant or obligation for perpetual renewal, other than a lease by sub-demise from one which is not a long lease; or

(c)   a lease granted in pursuance of Part V of the Housing Act 1985 (the right to buy).

60.   General interpretation.

(1)   In this Act—

"the 1985 Act" means the Landlord and Tenant Act 1985;

"charity" means a charity within the meaning of the Charities Act 1960, and "charitable purposes", in relation to a charity, means charitable purposes whether of that charity or of that charity and other charities;

"common parts", in relation to any building or part of a building, includes the structure and exterior of that building or part and any common facilities within it;

"the court" means the High Court or a county court;

"dwelling" means a building or part of a building occupied or intended to be occupied as a separate dwelling, together with any yard, garden, outhouses and appurtenances belonging to it or usually enjoyed with it;

"exempt landlord" has the meaning given by section 58(1);

"flat" means a separate set of premises, whether or not on the same floor, which—

(a)   forms part of a building, and

(b)   is divided horizontally from some other part of that building, and

(c)   is constructed or adapted for use for the purposes of a dwelling;

"functional land", in relation to a charity, means land occupied by the charity, or by trustees for it, and wholly or mainly used for charitable purposes;

"landlord" (except for the purposes of Part I) means the immediate landlord or, in relation to a statutory tenant, the person who, apart from the statutory tenancy, would be entitled to possession of the premises subject to the tenancy;

"lease" and related expressions shall be construed in accordance with section 59(1) and (2);

"long lease" has the meaning given by section 59(3);

"mortgage" includes any charge or lien, and references to a mortgagee shall be construed accordingly;

"notices in proceedings" means notices or other documents served in, or in connection with, any legal proceedings;

"rent assessment committee" means a rent assessment committee constituted under Schedule 10 to the Rent Act 1977;

"resident landlord" shall be construed in accordance with section 58(2);

"statutory tenancy" and "statutory tenant" mean a statutory tenancy or statutory tenant within the meaning of the Rent Act 1977 or the Rent (Agriculture) Act 1976;

"tenancy" includes a statutory tenancy.

61.   Consequential amendments and repeals.

(1)   The enactments mentioned in Schedule 4 shall have effect subject to the amendments there specified (being amendments consequential on the preceding provisions of this Act).

(2)   The enactments mentioned in Schedule 5 are hereby repealed to the extent specified in the third column of that Schedule.

62.   Short title, commencement and extent.

(1)   This Act may be cited as the Landlord and Tenant Act 1987.

(2)   This Act shall come into force on such day as the Secretary of State may by order appoint.

(3)   An order under subsection (2)—

(a)   may appoint different days for different provisions or for different purposes; and

(b)   may make such transitional, incidental, supplemental or consequential provision or saving as the Secretary of State considers necessary or expedient in connection with the coming into force of any provision of this Act or the operation of any enactment which is repealed or amended by a provision of this Act during any period when the repeal or amendment is not wholly in force.

(4)   This Act extends to England and Wales only.

SCHEDULES

Sections 12 and 32.   SCHEDULE 1

DISCHARGE OF MORTGAGES ETC.: SUPPLEMENTARY PROVISIONS

PART I
DISCHARGE IN PURSUANCE OF PURCHASE NOTICES

Construction

1.   In this Part of this Schedule—
"the consideration payable" means the consideration payable to the new landlord for the disposal by him of the property referred to in section 12(4);
"the new landlord" has the same meaning as in section 12, and accordingly includes any person to whom that section applies by virtue of section 16(2) or (3); and
"the nominated person" means the person or persons nominated as mentioned in section 12(1).

Duty of nominated person to redeem mortgages

2.—(1)   Where in accordance with section 12(4)(a) an instrument will operate to discharge any property from a charge to secure the payment of money, it shall be the duty of the nominated person to apply the consideration payable, in the first instance, in or towards the redemption of any such charge (and, if there are more than one, then according to their priorities).

(2)   Where sub-paragraph (1) applies to any charge or charges, then if (and only if) the consideration payable is applied by the nominated person in accordance with that sub-paragraph or paid into court by him in accordance with paragraph 4, the instrument in question shall operate as mentioned in sub-paragraph (1) notwithstanding that the consideration payable is insufficient to enable the charge or charges to be redeemed in its or their entirety.

(3)   Subject to sub-paragraph (4), sub-paragraph (1) shall not apply to a charge which is a debenture holders' charge, that is to say, a charge (whether a floating charge or not) in favour of the holders of a series of debentures issued by a company or other body of persons, or in favour of trustees for such debenture holders; and any such charge shall be disregarded in determining priorities for the purposes of sub-paragraph (1).

(4)   Sub-paragraph (3) above shall not have effect in relation to a charge in favour of trustees for debenture holders which at the date of the instrument by virtue of which the property is disposed of by the new landlord is (as regards that property) a specific and not a floating charge.

Determination of amounts due in respect of mortgages

3.—(1)   For the purpose of determining the amount payable in respect of any charge under paragraph 2(1), a person entitled to the benefit of a charge to which that provision applies shall not be permitted to exercise any right to consolidate that charge with a separate charge on other property.

(2) For the purpose of discharging any property from a charge to which paragraph 2(1) applies, a person may be required to accept three months or any longer notice of the intention to pay the whole or part of the principal secured by the charge, together with interest to the date of payment, notwithstanding that the terms of the security make other provision or no provision as to the time and manner of payment; but he shall be entitled, if he so requires, to receive such additional payment as is reasonable in the circumstances in respect of the costs of re-investment or other incidental costs and expenses and in respect of any reduction in the rate of interest obtainable on re-investment.

Payments into court

4.—(1) Where under section 12(4)(a) any property is to be discharged from a charge and, in accordance with paragraph 2(1), a person is or may be entitled in respect of the charge to receive the whole or part of the consideration payable, then if—

(a) for any reason difficulty arises in ascertaining how much is payable in respect of the charge, or

(b) for any reason mentioned in sub-paragraph (2) below difficulty arises in making a payment in respect of the charge,

the nominated person may pay into court on account of the consideration payable the amount, if known, of the payment to be made in respect of the charge or, if that amount is not known, the whole of that consideration or such lesser amount as the nominated person thinks right in order to provide for that payment.

(2) Payment may be made into court in accordance with sub-paragraph (1)(b) where the difficulty arises for any of the following reasons, namely—

(a) because a person who is or may be entitled to receive payment cannot be found or ascertained;

(b) because any such person refuses or fails to make out a title, or to accept payment and give a proper discharge, or to take any steps reasonably required of him to enable the sum payable to be ascertained and paid; or

(c) because a tender of the sum payable cannot, by reason of complications in the title to it or the want of two or more trustees or for other reasons, be effected, or not without incurring or involving unreasonable cost or delay.

(3) Without prejudice to sub-paragraph (2)(a), the whole or part of the consideration payable shall be paid into court by the nominated person if, before execution of the instrument referred to in paragraph 2(1), notice is given to him—

(a) that the new landlord or a person entitled to the benefit of a charge on the property in question requires him to do so for the purpose of protecting the rights of persons so entitled, or for reasons related to the bankruptcy or winding up of the new landlord, or

(b) that steps have been taken to enforce any charge on the new landlord's interest in that property by the bringing of proceedings in any court, or by the appointment of a receiver or otherwise;

and where payment into court is to be made by reason only of a notice under this sub-paragraph, and the notice is given with reference to proceedings in a court specified in the notice other than a county court, payment shall be made into the court so specified.

Savings

5.—(1) Where any property is discharged by section 12(4)(a) from a charge (without the obligations secured by the charge being satisfied by the receipt of the whole or part of the consideration payable), the discharge of that property from the charge shall not prejudice any right or remedy for the enforcement of those obligations against other property comprised in the same or any other security, nor prejudice any personal liability as principal or otherwise of the new landlord or any other person.

(2)   Nothing in this Schedule shall be construed as preventing a person from joining in the instrument referred to in paragraph 2(1) for the purpose of discharging the property in question from any charge without payment or for a lesser payment than that to which he would otherwise be entitled; and, if he does so, the persons to whom the consideration payable ought to be paid shall be determined accordingly.

PART II
DISCHARGE IN PURSUANCE OF ACQUISITION ORDERS

Construction

6.   In this Part of this Schedule—
"the consideration payable" means the consideration payable for the acquisition of the landlord's interest referred to in section 32(1); and
"the nominated person" means the person or persons nominated for the purposes of Part III by the persons who applied for the acquisition order in question.

Duty of nominated person to redeem mortgages

7.—(1)   Where in accordance with section 32(1) an instrument will operate to discharge any premises from a charge to secure the payment of money, it shall be the duty of the nominated person to apply the consideration payable, in the first instance, in or towards the redemption of any such charge (and, if there are more than one, then according to their priorities).

(2)   Where sub-paragraph (1) applies to any charge or charges, then if (and only if) the consideration payable is applied by the nominated person in accordance with that sub-paragraph or paid into court by him in accordance with paragraph 9, the instrument in question shall operate as mentioned in sub-paragraph (1) notwithstanding that the consideration payable is insufficient to enable the charge or charges to be redeemed in its or their entirety.

(3)   Subject to sub-paragraph (4), sub-paragraph (1) shall not apply to a charge which is a debenture holders' charge within the meaning of paragraph 2(3) in Part I of this Schedule; and any such charge shall be disregarded in determining priorities for the purposes of sub-paragraph (1).

(4)   Sub-paragraph (3) above shall not have effect in relation to a charge in favour of trustees for debenture holders which at the date of the instrument by virtue of which the landlord's interest in the premises in question is acquired is (as regards those premises) a specific and not a floating charge.

Determination of amounts due in respect of mortgages

8.—(1)   For the purpose of determining the amount payable in respect of any charge under paragraph 7(1), a person entitled to the benefit of a charge to which that provision applies shall not be permitted to exercise any right to consolidate that charge with a separate charge on other property.

(2)   For the purpose of discharging any premises from a charge to which paragraph 7(1) applies, a person may be required to accept three months or any longer notice of the intention to pay the whole or part of the principal secured by the charge, together with interest to the date of payment, notwithstanding that the terms of the security make other provision or no provision as to the time and manner of payment; but he shall be entitled, if he so requires, to receive such additional payment as is reasonable in the

circumstances in respect of the costs of re-investment or other incidental costs and expenses and in respect of any reduction in the rate of interest obtainable on re-investment.

Payments into court

9.—(1) Where under section 32 any premises are to be discharged from a charge and, in accordance with paragraph 7(1), a person is or may be entitled in respect of the charge to receive the whole or part of the consideration payable, then if—

(a) for any reason difficulty arises in ascertaining how much is payable in respect of the charge, or

(b) for any reason mentioned in sub-paragraph (2) below difficulty arises in making a payment in respect of the charge,

the nominated person may pay into court on account of the consideration payable the amount, if known, of the payment to be made in respect of the charge or, if that amount is not known, the whole of that consideration or such lesser amount as the nominated person thinks right in order to provide for that payment.

(2) Payment may be made into court in accordance with sub-paragraph (1)(b) where the difficulty arises for any of the following reasons, namely—

(a) because a person who is or may be entitled to receive payment cannot be found or ascertained;

(b) because any such person refuses or fails to make out a title, or to accept payment and give a proper discharge, or to take any steps reasonably required of him to enable the sum payable to be ascertained and paid; or

(c) because a tender of the sum payable cannot, by reason of complications in the title to it or the want of two or more trustees or for other reasons be effected, or not without incurring or involving unreasonable cost or delay.

(3) Without prejudice to sub-paragraph (1)(a), the whole or part of the consideration payable shall be paid into court by the nominated person if, before execution of the instrument referred to in paragraph 7(1), notice is given to him—

(a) that the landlord or a person entitled to the benefit of a charge on the premises in question requires him to do so for the purpose of protecting the rights of persons so entitled, or for reasons related to the bankruptcy or winding up of the landlord, or

(b) that steps have been taken to enforce any charge on the landlord's interest in those premises by the bringing of proceedings in any court, or by the appointment of a receiver or otherwise;

and where payment into court is to be made by reason only of a notice under this sub-paragraph, and the notice is given with reference to proceedings in a court specified in the notice other than a county court, payment shall be made into the court so specified.

Savings

10.—(1) Where any premises are discharged by section 32 from a charge (without the obligations secured by the charge being satisfied by the receipt of the whole or part of the consideration payable), the discharge of those premises from the charge shall not prejudice any right or remedy for the enforcement of those obligations against other property comprised in the same or any other security, nor prejudice any personal liability as principal or otherwise of the landlord or any other person.

(2) Nothing in this Schedule shall be construed as preventing a person from joining in the instrument referred to in paragraph 7(1) for the purpose of discharging the premises in question from any charge without payment or for a lesser payment than that to which he would otherwise be entitled; and, if he does so, the persons to whom the consideration payable ought to be paid shall be determined accordingly.

LANDLORD AND TENANT ACT 1988
(1988, c. 26)

An Act to make new provision for imposing statutory duties in connection with covenants in tenancies against assigning, underletting, charging or parting with the possession of premises without consent. [29 July 1988]

1. Qualified duty to consent to assigning, underletting etc. of premises.

(1)   This section applies in any case where—

(a)   a tenancy includes a covenant on the part of the tenant not to enter into one or more of the following transactions, that is—

(i)   assigning,

(ii)   underletting,

(iii)   charging, or

(iv)   parting with the possession of,

the premises comprised in the tenancy or any part of the premises without the consent of the landlord or some other person, but

(b)   the covenant is subject to the qualification that the consent is not to be unreasonably withheld (whether or not it is also subject to any other qualification).

(2)   In this section and section 2 of this Act—

(a)   references to a proposed transaction are to any assignment, underletting, charging or parting with possession to which the covenant relates, and

(b)   references to the person who may consent to such a transaction are to the person who under the covenant may consent to the tenant entering into the proposed transaction.

(3)   Where there is served on the person who may consent to a proposed transaction a written application by the tenant for consent to the transaction, he owes a duty to the tenant within a reasonable time—

(a)   to give consent, except in a case where it is reasonable not to give consent,

(b)   to serve on the tenant written notice of his decision whether or not to give consent specifying in addition—

(i)   if the consent is given subject to conditions, the conditions,

(ii)   if the consent is withheld, the reasons for withholding it.

(4)   Giving consent subject to any condition that is not a reasonable condition does not satisfy the duty under subsection (3)(a) above.

(5)   For the purposes of this Act it is reasonable for a person not to give consent to a proposed transaction only in a case where, if he withheld consent and the tenant completed the transaction, the tenant would be in breach of a covenant.

(6)   It is for the person who owed any duty under subsection (3) above—

(a)   if he gave consent and the question arises whether he gave it within a reasonable time, to show that he did,

(b)   if he gave consent subject to any condition and the question arises whether the condition was a reasonable condition, to show that it was,

(c)   if he did not give consent and the question arises whether it was reasonable for him not to do so, to show that it was reasonable,

and, if the question arises whether he served notice under that subsection within a reasonable time, to show that he did.

2. Duty to pass on applications.

(1)   If, in a case where section 1 of this Act applies, any person receives a written application by the tenant for consent to a proposed transaction and that person—

(a)   is a person who may consent to the transaction or (though not such a person) is the landlord, and

(b) believes that another person, other than a person who he believes has received the application or a copy of it, is a person who may consent to the transaction, he owes a duty to the tenant (whether or not he owes him any duty under section 1 of this Act) to take such steps as are reasonable to secure the receipt within a reasonable time by the other person of a copy of the application.

(2) The reference in section 1(3) of this Act to the service of an application on a person who may consent to a proposed transaction includes a reference to the receipt by him of an application or a copy of an application (whether it is for his consent or that of another).

3. Qualified duty to approve consent by another.

(1) This section applies in any case where—

(a) a tenancy includes a covenant on the part of the tenant not without the approval of the landlord to consent to the sub-tenant—

(i) assigning,

(ii) underletting,

(iii) charging, or

(iv) parting with the possession of,

the premises comprised in the sub-tenancy or any part of the premises, but

(b) the covenant is subject to the qualification that the approval is not to be unreasonably withheld (whether or not it is also subject to any other qualification).

(2) Where there is served on the landlord a written application by the tenant for approval or a copy of a written application to the tenant by the sub-tenant for consent to a transaction to which the covenant relates the landlord owes a duty to the sub-tenant within a reasonable time—

(a) to give approval, except in a case where it is reasonable not to give approval,

(b) to serve on the tenant and the sub-tenant written notice of his decision whether or not to give approval specifying in addition—

(i) if approval is given subject to conditions, the conditions,

(ii) if approval is withheld, the reasons for withholding it.

(3) Giving approval subject to any condition that is not a reasonable condition does not satisfy the duty under subsection (2)(a) above.

(4) For the purposes of this section it is reasonable for the landlord not to give approval only in a case where, if he withheld approval and the tenant gave his consent, the tenant would be in breach of covenant.

(5) It is for a landlord who owed any duty under subsection (2) above—

(a) if he gave approval and the question arises whether he gave it within a reasonable time, to show that he did,

(b) if he gave approval subject to any condition and the question arises whether the condition was a reasonable condition, to show that it was,

(c) if he did not give approval and the question arises whether it was reasonable for him not to do so, to show that it was reasonable,

and, if the question arises whether he served notice under that subsection within a reasonable time, to show that he did.

4. Breach of duty.

A claim that a person has broken any duty under this Act may be made the subject of civil proceedings in like manner as any other claim in tort for breach of statutory duty.

5. Interpretation.

(1) In this Act—

"covenant" includes condition and agreement,

"consent" includes licence,

"landlord" includes any superior landlord from whom the tenant's immediate landlord directly or indirectly holds,

"tenancy", subject to subsection (3) below, means any lease or other tenancy (whether made before or after the coming into force of this Act) and includes—
  (a)   a sub-tenancy, and
  (b)   an agreement for a tenancy
and references in this Act to the landlord and to the tenant are to be interpreted accordingly, and
"tenant", where the tenancy is affected by a mortgage (within the meaning of the Law of Property Act 1925) and the mortgagee proposes to exercise his statutory or express power of sale, includes the mortgagee.
  (2)   An application or notice is to be treated as served for the purposes of this Act if—
  (a)   served in any manner provided in the tenancy, and
  (b)   in respect of any matter for which the tenancy makes no provision, served in any manner provided by section 23 of the Landlord and Tenant Act 1927.
  (3)   This Act does not apply to a secure tenancy (defined in section 79 of the Housing Act 1985).
  (4)   This Act applies only to applications for consent or approval served after its coming into force.

6. Application to Crown.

This Act binds the Crown; but as regards the Crown's liability in tort shall not bind the Crown further than the Crown is made liable in tort by the Crown Proceedings Act 1947.

7. Short title, commencement and extent.

  (1)   This Act may be cited as the Landlord and Tenant Act 1988.
  (2)   This Act shall come into force at the end of the period of two months beginning with the day on which it is passed.
  (3)   This Act extends to England and Wales only.

HOUSING ACT 1988
(1988, c. 50)

An Act to make further provision with respect to dwelling-houses let on tenancies or occupied under licences; to amend the Rent Act 1977 and the Rent (Agriculture) Act 1976; to establish a body, Housing for Wales, having functions relating to housing associations; to amend the Housing Associations Act 1985 and to repeal and re-enact with amendments certain provisions of Part II of that Act; to make provision for the establishment of housing action trusts for areas designated by the Secretary of State; to confer on persons approved for the purpose the right to acquire from public sector landlords certain dwelling-houses occupied by secure tenants; to make further provision about rent officers, the administration of housing benefit and rent allowance subsidy, the right to buy, repair notices and certain disposals of land and the application of capital money arising thereon; to make provision consequential upon the Housing (Scotland) Act 1988; and for connected purposes.

[15 November 1988]

PART I
RENTED ACCOMMODATION
CHAPTER I
ASSURED TENANCIES

Meaning of assured tenancy etc.

1. Assured tenancies.

  (1)   A tenancy under which a dwelling-house is let as a separate dwelling is for the purposes of this Act an assured tenancy if and so long as—

(a)   the tenant or, as the case may be, each of the joint tenants is an individual; and

(b)   the tenant or, as the case may be, at least one of the joint tenants occupies the dwelling-house as his only or principal home; and

(c)   the tenancy is not one which, by virtue of subsection (2) or subsection (6) below, cannot be an assured tenancy.

(2)   Subject to subsection (3) below, if and so long as a tenancy falls within any paragraph in Part I of Schedule 1 to this Act, it cannot be an assured tenancy; and in that Schedule—

(a)   "tenancy" means a tenancy under which a dwelling-house is let as a separate dwelling;

(b)   Part II has effect for determining the rateable value of a dwelling-house for the purposes of Part I; and

(c)   Part III has effect for supplementing paragraph 10 in Part I.

(2A)   The Secretary of State may by order replace any amount referred to in paragraphs 2 and 3A of Schedule 1 to this Act by such amount as is specified in the order; and such an order shall be made by statutory instrument which shall be subject to annulment in pursuance of a resolution of either House of Parliament.

(3)   Except as provided in Chapter V below, at the commencement of this Act, a tenancy—

(a)   under which a dwelling-house was then let as a separate dwelling, and

(b)   which immediately before that commencement was an assured tenancy for the purposes of sections 56 to 58 of the Housing Act 1980 (tenancies granted by approved bodies),

shall become an assured tenancy for the purposes of this Act.

(4)   In relation to an assured tenancy falling within subsection (3) above—

(a)   Part I of Schedule 1 to this Act shall have effect, subject to subsection (5) below, as if it consisted only of paragraphs 11 and 12; and

(b)   sections 56 to 58 of the Housing Act 1980 (and Schedule 5 to that Act) shall not apply after the commencement of this Act.

(5)   In any case where—

(a)   immediately before the commencement of this Act the landlord under a tenancy is a fully mutual housing association, and

(b)   at the commencement of this Act the tenancy becomes an assured tenancy by virtue of subsection (3) above,

then, so long as that association remains the landlord under that tenancy (and under any statutory periodic tenancy which arises on the coming to an end of that tenancy), paragraph 12 of Schedule 1 to this Act shall have effect in relation to that tenancy with the omission of subparagraph (1)(h).

(6)   If, in pursuance of its duty under—

(a)   section 63 of the Housing Act 1985 (duty to house pending inquiries in case of apparent priority need),

(b)   section 65(3) of that Act (duty to house temporarily person found to have priority need but to have become homeless intentionally), or

(c)   section 68(1) of that Act (duty to house pending determination whether conditions for referral of application are satisfied),

a local housing authority have made arrangements with another person to provide accommodation, a tenancy granted by that other person in pursuance of the arrangements to a person specified by the authority cannot be an assured tenancy before the expiry of the period of twelve months beginning with the date specified in subsection (7) below unless, before the expiry of that period, the tenant is notified by the landlord (or, in the case of joint landlords, at least one of them) that the tenancy is to be regarded as an assured tenancy.

(7)   The date referred to in subsection (6) above is the date on which the tenant

received the notification required by section 64(1) of the Housing Act 1985 (notification of decision on question of homelessness or threatened homelessness) or, if he received a notification under section 68(3) of that Act (notification of which authority has duty to house), the date on which he received that notification.

2. Letting of a dwelling-house together with other land.

(1) If, under a tenancy, a dwelling-house is let together with other land, then, for the purposes of this Part of this Act,—

(a) if and so long as the main purpose of the letting is the provision of a home for the tenant or, where there are joint tenants, at least one of them, the other land shall be treated as part of the dwelling-house; and

(b) if and so long as the main purpose of the letting is not as mentioned in paragraph (a) above, the tenancy shall be treated as not being one under which a dwelling-house is let as a separate dwelling.

(2) Nothing in subsection (1) above affects any question whether a tenancy is precluded from being an assured tenancy by virtue of any provision of Schedule 1 to this Act.

3. Tenant sharing accommodation with persons other than landlord.

(1) Where a tenant has the exclusive occupation of any accommodation (in this section referred to as "the separate accommodation") and—

(a) the terms as between the tenant and his landlord on which he holds the separate accommodation include the use of other accommodation (in this section referred to as "the shared accommodation") in common with another person or other persons, not being or including the landlord, and

(b) by reason only of the circumstances mentioned in paragraph (a) above, the separate accommodation would not, apart from this section, be a dwelling-house let on an assured tenancy,

the separate accommodation shall be deemed to be a dwelling-house let on an assured tenancy and the following provisions of this section shall have effect.

(2) For the avoidance of doubt it is hereby declared that where, for the purpose of determining the rateable value of the separate accommodation, it is necessary to make an apportionment under Part II of Schedule 1 to this Act, regard is to be had to the circumstances mentioned in subsection (1)(a) above.

(3) While the tenant is in possession of the separate accommodation, any term of the tenancy terminating or modifying, or providing for the termination or modification of, his right to the use of any of the shared accommodation which is living accommodation shall be of no effect.

(4) Where the terms of the tenancy are such that, at any time during the tenancy, the persons in common with whom the tenant is entitled to the use of the shared accommodation could be varied or their number could be increased, nothing in subsection (3) above shall prevent those terms from having effect so far as they relate to any such variation or increase.

(5) In this section "living accommodation" means accommodation of such a nature that the fact that it constitutes or is included in the shared accommodation is sufficient, apart from this section, to prevent the tenancy from constituting an assured tenancy of a dwelling-house.

4. Certain sublettings not to exclude any part of sublessor's premises from assured tenancy.

(1) Where the tenant of a dwelling-house has sublet a part but not the whole of the dwelling-house, then, as against his landlord or any superior landlord, no part of the dwelling-house shall be treated as excluded from being a dwelling-house let on an assured tenancy by reason only that the terms on which any person claiming under the

tenant holds any part of the dwelling-house include the use of accommodation in common with other persons.

(2)   Nothing in this section affects the rights against, and liabilities to, each other of the tenant and any person claiming under him, or of any two such persons.

Security of tenure

5. Security of tenure.

(1)   An assured tenancy cannot be brought to an end by the landlord except by obtaining an order of the court in accordance with the following provisions of this Chapter or Chapter II below or, in the case of a fixed term tenancy which contains power for the landlord to determine the tenancy in certain circumstances, by the exercise of that power and, accordingly, the service by the landlord of a notice to quit shall be of no effect in relation to a periodic assured tenancy.

(2)   If an assured tenancy which is a fixed term tenancy comes to an end otherwise than by virtue of—

(a)   an order of the court, or

(b)   a surrender or other action on the part of the tenant,

then, subject to section 7 and Chapter II below, the tenant shall be entitled to remain in possession of the dwelling-house let under that tenancy and, subject to subsection (4) below, his right to possession shall depend upon a periodic tenancy arising by virtue of this section.

(3)   The periodic tenancy referred to in subsection (2) above is one—

(a)   taking effect in possession immediately on the coming to an end of the fixed term tenancy;

(b)   deemed to have been granted by the person who was the landlord under the fixed term tenancy immediately before it came to an end to the person who was then the tenant under that tenancy;

(c)   under which the premises which are let are the same dwelling-house as was let under the fixed term tenancy;

(d)   under which the periods of the tenancy are the same as those for which rent was last payable under the fixed term tenancy; and

(e)   under which, subject to the following provisions of this Part of this Act, the other terms are the same as those of the fixed term tenancy immediately before it came to an end, except that any term which makes provision for determination by the landlord or the tenant shall not have effect while the tenancy remains an assured tenancy.

(4)   The periodic tenancy referred to in subsection (2) above shall not arise if, on the coming to an end of the fixed term tenancy, the tenant is entitled, by virtue of the grant of another tenancy, to possession of the same or substantially the same dwelling-house as was let to him under the fixed term tenancy.

(5)   If, on or before the date on which a tenancy is entered into or is deemed to have been granted as mentioned in subsection (3)(b) above, the person who is to be the tenant under that tenancy—

(a)   enters into an obligation to do any act which (apart from this subsection) will cause the tenancy to come to an end at a time when it is an assured tenancy, or

(b)   executes, signs or gives any surrender, notice to quit or other document which (apart from this subsection) has the effect of bringing the tenancy to an end at a time when it is an assured tenancy,

the obligation referred to in paragraph (a) above shall not be enforceable or, as the case may be, the surrender, notice to quit or other document referred to in paragraph (b) above shall be of no effect.

(6)   If, by virtue of any provision of this Part of this Act, Part I of Schedule 1 to this Act has effect in relation to a fixed term tenancy as if it consisted only of paragraphs 11 and 12, that Part shall have the like effect in relation to any periodic tenancy which arises

by virtue of this section on the coming to an end of the fixed term tenancy.

(7)   Any reference in this Part of this Act to a statutory periodic tenancy is a reference to a periodic tenancy arising by virtue of this section.

6.   Fixing of terms of statutory periodic tenancy.

(1)   In this section, in relation to a statutory periodic tenancy,—

(a)   "the former tenancy" means the fixed term tenancy on the coming to an end of which the statutory periodic tenancy arises; and

(b)   "the implied terms" means the terms of the tenancy which have effect by virtue of section 5(3)(e) above, other than terms as to the amount of the rent;
but nothing in the following provisions of this section applies to a statutory periodic tenancy at a time when, by virtue of paragraph 11 or paragraph 12 in Part 1 of Schedule 1 to this Act, it cannot be an assured tenancy.

(2)   Not later than the first anniversary of the day on which the former tenancy came to an end, the landlord may serve on the tenant, or the tenant may serve on the landlord, a notice in the prescribed form proposing terms of the statutory periodic tenancy different from the implied terms and, if the landlord or the tenant considers it appropriate, proposing an adjustment of the amount of the rent to take account of the proposed terms.

(3)   Where a notice has been served under subsection (2) above,—

(a)   within the period of three months beginning on the date on which the notice was served on him, the landlord or the tenant, as the case may be, may, by an application in the prescribed form, refer the notice to a rent assessment committee under subsection (4) below; and

(b)   if the notice is not so referred, then, with effect from such date, not falling within the period referred to in paragraph (a) above, as may be specified in the notice, the terms proposed in the notice shall become terms of the tenancy in substitution for any of the implied terms dealing with the same subject matter and the amount of the rent shall be varied in accordance with any adjustment so proposed.

(4)   Where a notice under subsection (2) above is referred to a rent assessment committee, the committee shall consider the terms proposed in the notice and shall determine whether those terms, or some other terms (dealing with the same subject matter as the proposed terms), are such as, in the committee's opinion, might reasonably be expected to be found in an assured periodic tenancy of the dwelling-house concerned, being a tenancy—

(a)   which begins on the coming to an end of the former tenancy; and

(b)   which is granted by a willing landlord on terms which, except in so far as they relate to the subject matter of the proposed terms, are those of the statutory periodic tenancy at the time of the committee's consideration.

(5)   Whether or not a notice under subsection (2) above proposes an adjustment of the amount of the rent under the statutory periodic tenancy, where a rent assessment committee determine any terms under subsection (4) above, they shall, if they consider it appropriate, specify such an adjustment to take account of the terms so determined.

(6)   In making a determination under subsection (4) above, or specifying an adjustment of an amount of rent under subsection (5) above, there shall be disregarded any effect on the terms or the amount of the rent attributable to the granting of a tenancy to a sitting tenant.

(7)   Where a notice under subsection (2) above is referred to a rent assessment committee, then, unless the landlord and the tenant otherwise agree, with effect from such date as the committee may direct—

(a)   the terms determined by the committee shall become terms of the statutory periodic tenancy in substitution for any of the implied terms dealing with the same subject matter; and

(b)   the amount of the rent under the statutory periodic tenancy shall be altered to accord with any adjustment specified by the committee;

but for the purposes of paragraph (b) above the committee shall not direct a date earlier than the date specified, in accordance with subsection (3)(b) above, in the notice referred to them.

(8)   Nothing in this section requires a rent assessment committee to continue with a determination under subsection (4) above if the landlord and tenant give notice in writing that they no longer require such a determination or if the tenancy has come to an end.

7.   Orders for possession.

(1)   The court shall not make an order for possession of a dwelling-house let on an assured tenancy except on one or more of the grounds set out in Schedule 2 to this Act; but nothing in this Part of this Act relates to proceedings for possession of such a dwelling-house which are brought by a mortgagee, within the meaning of the Law of Property Act 1925, who has lent money on the security of the assured tenancy.

(2)   The following provisions of this section have effect, subject to section 8 below, in relation to proceedings for the recovery of possession of a dwelling-house let on an assured tenancy.

(3)   If the court is satisfied that any of the grounds in Part I of Schedule 2 to this Act is established then, subject to subsections (5A) and (6) below, the court shall make an order for possession.

(4)   If the court is satisfied that any of the grounds in Part II of Schedule 2 to this Act is established, then, subject to subsections (5A) and (6) below, the court may make an order for possession if it considers it reasonable to do so.

(5)   Part III of Schedule 2 to this Act shall have effect for supplementing Ground 9 in that Schedule and Part IV of that Schedule shall have effect in relation to notices given as mentioned in Grounds 1 to 5 of that Schedule.

(5A)   The court shall not make an order for possession of a dwelling-house let on an assured periodic tenancy arising under Schedule 10 to the Local Government and Housing Act 1989 on any of the following grounds, that is to say,—

(a)   Grounds 1, 2 and 5 in Part I of Schedule 2 to this Act;

(b)   Ground 16 in Part II of that Schedule; and

(c)   if the assured periodic tenancy arose on the termination of a former 1954 Act tenancy, within the meaning of the said Schedule 10, Ground 6 in Part I of Schedule 2 to this Act.

(6)   The court shall not make an order for possession of a dwelling-house to take effect at a time when it is let on an assured fixed term tenancy unless—

(a)   the ground for possession is Ground 2 or Ground 8 in Part I of Schedule 2 to this Act or any of the grounds in Part II of that Schedule, other than Ground 9 or Ground 16; and

(b)   the terms of the tenancy make provision for it to be brought to an end on the ground in question (whether that provision takes the form of a provision for re-entry, for forfeiture, for determination by notice or otherwise).

(7)   Subject to the preceding provisions of this section, the court may make an order for possession of a dwelling-house on grounds relating to a fixed term tenancy which has come to an end; and where an order is made in such circumstances, any statutory periodic tenancy which has arisen on the ending of the fixed term tenancy shall end (without any notice and regardless of the period) on the day on which the order takes effect.

8.   Notice of proceedings for possession.

(1)   The court shall not entertain proceedings for possession of a dwelling-house let on an assured tenancy unless—

(a)   the landlord or, in the case of joint landlords, at least one of them has served on the tenant a notice in accordance with this section and the proceedings are begun within the time-limits stated in the notice in accordance with subsections (3) and (4) below; or

(b)   the court considers it just and equitable to dispense with the requirement of such a notice.

(2)   The court shall not make an order for possession on any of the grounds in Schedule 2 to this Act unless that ground and particulars of it are specified in the notice under this section; but the grounds specified in such a notice may be altered or added to with the leave of the court.

(3)   A notice under this section is one in the prescribed form informing the tenant that—

(a)   the landlord intends to begin proceedings for possession of the dwelling-house on one or more of the grounds specified in the notice; and

(b)   those proceedings will not begin earlier than a date specified in the notice which, without prejudice to any additional limitation under subsection (4) below, shall not be earlier than the expiry of the period of two weeks from the date of service of the notice; and

(c)   those proceedings will not begin later than 12 months from the date of service of the notice.

(4)   If a notice under this section specifies, in accordance with subsection (3)(a) above, any of Grounds 1, 2, 5 to 7, 9 and 16 in Schedule 2 to this Act (whether with or without other grounds), the date specified in the notice as mentioned in subsection (3)(b) above shall not be earlier than—

(a)   two months from the date of service of the notice; and

(b)   if the tenancy is a periodic tenancy, the earliest date on which, apart from section 5(1) above, the tenancy could be brought to an end by a notice to quit given by the landlord on the same date as the date of service of the notice under this section.

(5)   The court may not exercise the power conferred by subsection (1)(b) above if the landlord seeks to recover possession on Ground 8 in Schedule 2 to this Act.

(6)   Where a notice under this section—

(a)   is served at a time when the dwelling-house is let on a fixed term tenancy, or

(b)   is served after a fixed term tenancy has come to an end but relates (in whole or in part) to events occurring during that tenancy,

the notice shall have effect notwithstanding that the tenant becomes or has become tenant under a statutory periodic tenancy arising on the coming to an end of the fixed term tenancy.

9.   Extended discretion of court in possession claims.

(1)   Subject to subsection (6) below, the court may adjourn for such period or periods as it thinks fit proceedings for possession of a dwelling-house let on an assured tenancy.

(2)   On the making of an order for possession of a dwelling-house let on an assured tenancy or at any time before the execution of such an order, the court, subject to subsection (6) below, may—

(a)   stay or suspend execution of the order, or

(b)   postpone the date of possession,

for such period or periods as the court thinks just.

(3)   On any such adjournment as is referred to in subsection (1) above or on any such stay, suspension or postponement as is referred to in subsection (2) above, the court, unless it considers that to do so would cause exceptional hardship to the tenant or would otherwise be unreasonable, shall impose conditions with regard to payment by the tenant of arrears of rent (if any) and rent or payments in respect of occupation after the

termination of the tenancy (mesne profits) and may impose such other conditions as it thinks fit.

(4)   If any such conditions as are referred to in subsection (3) above are complied with, the court may, if it thinks fit, discharge or rescind any such order as is referred to in subsection (2) above.

(5)   In any case where—

(a)   at a time when proceedings are brought for possession of a dwelling-house let on an assured tenancy, the tenant's spouse or former spouse, having rights of occupation under the Matrimonial Homes Act 1983, is in occupation of the dwelling-house, and

(b)   the assured tenancy is terminated as a result of those proceedings,

the spouse or former spouse, so long as he or she remains in occupation, shall have the same rights in relation to, or in connection with, any such adjournment as is referred to in subsection (1) above or any such stay, suspension or postponement as is referred to in subsection (2) above, as he or she would have if those rights of occupation were not affected by the termination of the tenancy.

(6)   This section does not apply if the court is satisfied that the landlord is entitled to possession of the dwelling-house—

(a)   on any of the grounds in Part I of Schedule 2 to this Act; or

(b)   by virtue of subsection (1) or subsection (4) of section 21 below.

10.   Special provisions applicable to shared accommodation.

(1)   This section applies in a case falling within subsection (1) of section 3 above and expressions used in this section have the same meaning as in that section.

(2)   Without prejudice to the enforcement of any order made under subsection (3) below, while the tenant is in possession of the separate accommodation, no order shall be made for possession of any of the shared accommodation, whether on the application of the immediate landlord of the tenant or on the application of any person under whom that landlord derives title, unless a like order has been made, or is made at the same time, in respect of the separate accommodation; and the provisions of section 6 above shall have effect accordingly.

(3)   On the application of the landlord, the court may make such order as it thinks just either—

(a)   terminating the right of the tenant to use the whole or any part of the shared accommodation other than living accommodation; or

(b)   modifying his right to use the whole or any part of the shared accommodation, whether by varying the persons or increasing the number of persons entitled to the use of that accommodation or otherwise.

(4)   No order shall be made under subsection (3) above so as to effect any termination or modification of the rights of the tenant which, apart from section 3(3) above, could not be effected by or under the terms of the tenancy.

11.   Payment of removal expenses in certain cases.

(1)   Where a court makes an order for possession of a dwelling-house let on an assured tenancy on Ground 6 or Ground 9 in Schedule 2 to this Act (but not on any other ground), the landlord shall pay to the tenant a sum equal to the reasonable expenses likely to be incurred by the tenant in removing from the dwelling-house.

(2)   Any question as to the amount of the sum referred to in subsection (1) above shall be determined by agreement between the landlord and the tenant or, in default of agreement, by the court.

(3)   Any sum payable to a tenant by virtue of this section shall be recoverable as a civil debt due from the landlord.

12. Compensation for misrepresentation or concealment.

Where a landlord obtains an order for possession of a dwelling-house let on an assured tenancy on one or more of the grounds in Schedule 2 to this Act and it is subsequently made to appear to the court that the order was obtained by misrepresentation or concealment of material facts, the court may order the landlord to pay to the former tenant such sum as appears sufficient as compensation for damage or loss sustained by that tenant as a result of the order.

Rent and other terms

13. Increases of rent under assured periodic tenancies.

(1) This section applies to—

(a) a statutory periodic tenancy other than one which, by virtue of paragraph 11 or paragraph 12 in Part I of Schedule 1 to this Act, cannot for the time being be an assured tenancy; and

(b) any other periodic tenancy which is an assured tenancy, other than one in relation to which there is a provision, for the time being binding on the tenant, under which the rent for a particular period of the tenancy will or may be greater than the rent for an earlier period.

(2) For the purpose of securing an increase in the rent under a tenancy to which this section applies, the landlord may serve on the tenant a notice in the prescribed form proposing a new rent to take effect at the beginning of a new period of the tenancy specified in the notice, being a period beginning not earlier than—

(a) the minimum period after the date of the service of the notice; and

(b) except in the case of a statutory periodic tenancy, the first anniversary of the date on which the first period of the tenancy began; and

(c) if the rent under the tenancy has previously been increased by virtue of a notice under this subsection or a determination under section 14 below, the first anniversary of the date on which the increased rent took effect.

(3) The minimum period referred to in subsection (2) above is—

(a) in the case of a yearly tenancy, six months;

(b) in the case of a tenancy where the period is less than a month, one month; and

(c) in any other case, a period equal to the period of the tenancy.

(4) Where a notice is served under subsection (2) above, a new rent specified in the notice shall take effect as mentioned in the notice unless, before the beginning of the new period specified in the notice,—

(a) the tenant by an application in the prescribed form refers the notice to a rent assessment committee; or

(b) the landlord and the tenant agree on a variation of the rent which is different from that proposed in the notice or agree that the rent should not be varied.

(5) Nothing in this section (or in section 14 below) affects the right of the landlord and the tenant under an assured tenancy to vary by agreement any term of the tenancy (including a term relating to rent).

14. Determination of rent by rent assessment committee.

(1) Where, under subsection (4)(a) of section 13 above, a tenant refers to a rent assessment committee a notice under subsection (2) of that section, the committee shall determine the rent at which, subject to subsections (2) and (4) below, the committee consider that the dwelling-house concerned might reasonably be expected to be let in the open market by a willing landlord under an assured tenancy—

(a) which is a periodic tenancy having the same periods as those of the tenancy to which the notice relates;

(b) which begins at the beginning of the new period specified in the notice;

(c) the terms of which (other than relating to the amount of the rent) are the same as those of the tenancy to which the notice relates; and

(d)   in respect of which the same notices, if any, have been given under any of Grounds 1 to 5 of Schedule 2 to this Act, as have been given (or have effect as if given) in relation to the tenancy to which the notice relates.

(2)   In making a determination under this section, there shall be disregarded—

(a)   any effect on the rent attributable to the granting of a tenancy to a sitting tenant;

(b)   any increase in the value of the dwelling-house attributable to a relevant improvement carried out by a person who at the time it was carried out was the tenant, if the improvement—

(i)   was carried out otherwise than in pursuance of an obligation to his immediate landlord, or

(ii)   was carried out pursuant to an obligation to his immediate landlord being an obligation which did not relate to the specific improvement concerned but arose by reference to consent given to the carrying out of that improvement; and

(c)   any reduction in the value of the dwelling-house attributable to a failure by the tenant to comply with any terms of the tenancy.

(3)   For the purposes of subsection (2)(b) above, in relation to a notice which is referred by a tenant as mentioned in subsection (1) above, an improvement is a relevant improvement if either it was carried out during the tenancy to which the notice relates or the following conditions are satisfied, namely—

(a)   that it was carried out not more than 21 years before the date of service of the notice; and

(b)   that, at all times during the period beginning when the improvement was carried out and ending on the date of service of the notice, the dwelling-house has been let under an assured tenancy; and

(c)   that, on the coming to an end of an assured tenancy at any time during that period, the tenant (or, in the case of joint tenants, at least one of them) did not quit.

(4)   In this section "rent" does not include any service charge, within the meaning of section 18 of the Landlord and Tenant Act 1985, but, subject to that, includes any sums payable by the tenant to the landlord on account of the use of furniture or for any of the matters referred to in subsection (1)(a) of that section, whether or not those sums are separate from the sums payable for the occupation of the dwelling-house concerned or are payable under separate agreements.

(5)   Where any rates in respect of the dwelling-house concerned are borne by the landlord or a superior landlord, the rent assessment committee shall make their determination under this section as if the rates were not so borne.

(6)   In any case where—

(a)   a rent assessment committee have before them at the same time the reference of a notice under section 6(2) above relating to a tenancy (in this subsection referred to as "the section 6 reference") and the reference of a notice under section 13(2) above relating to the same tenancy (in this subsection referred to as "the section 13 reference"), and

(b)   the date specified in the notice under section 6(2) above is not later than the first day of the new period specified in the notice under section 13(2) above, and

(c)   the committee propose to hear the two references together,

the committee shall make a determination in relation to the section 6 reference before making their determination in relation to the section 13 reference and, accordingly, in such a case the reference in subsection (1)(c) above to the terms of the tenancy to which the notice relates shall be construed as a reference to those terms as varied by virtue of the determination made in relation to the section 6 reference.

(7)   Where a notice under section 13(2) above has been referred to a rent assessment committee, then, unless the landlord and the tenant otherwise agree, the rent determined by the committee (subject, in a case where subsection (5) above applies, to

the addition of the appropriate amount in respect of rates) shall be the rent under the tenancy with effect from the beginning of the new period specified in the notice or, if it appears to the rent assessment committee that that would cause undue hardship to the tenant, with effect from such later date (not being later than the date the rent is determined) as the committee may direct.

(8)   Nothing in this section requires a rent assessment committee to continue with their determination of a rent for a dwelling-house if the landlord and tenant give notice in writing that they no longer require such a determination or if the tenancy has come to an end.

15.   Limited prohibition on assignment etc. without consent.

(1)   Subject to subsection (3) below, it shall be an implied term of every assured tenancy which is a periodic tenancy that, except with the consent of the landlord, the tenant shall not—

(a)   assign the tenancy (in whole or in part); or

(b)   sublet or part with possession of the whole or any part of the dwelling-house let on the tenancy.

(2)   Section 19 of the Landlord and Tenant Act 1927 (consents to assign not to be unreasonably withheld etc.) shall not apply to a term which is implied into an assured tenancy by subsection (1) above.

(3)   In the case of a periodic tenancy which is not a statutory periodic tenancy or an assured periodic tenancy arising under Schedule 10 to the Local Government and Housing Act 1989 subsection (1) above does not apply if—

(a)   there is a provision (whether contained in the tenancy or not) under which the tenant is prohibited (whether absolutely or conditionally) from assigning or subletting or parting with possession or is permitted (whether absolutely or conditionally) to assign, sublet or part with possession; or

(b)   a premium is required to be paid on the grant or renewal of the tenancy.

(4)   In subsection (3)(b) above "premium" includes—

(a)   any fine or other like sum;

(b)   any other pecuniary consideration in addition to rent; and

(c)   any sum paid by way of deposit, other than one which does not exceed one-sixth of the annual rent payable under the tenancy immediately after the grant or renewal in question.

16.   Access for repairs.

It shall be an implied term of every assured tenancy that the tenant shall afford to the landlord access to the dwelling-house let on the tenancy and all reasonable facilities for executing therein any repairs which the landlord is entitled to execute.

Miscellaneous

17.   Succession to assured periodic tenancy by spouse.

(1)   In any case where—

(a)   the sole tenant under an assured periodic tenancy dies, and

(b)   immediately before the death, the tenant's spouse was occupying the dwelling-house as his or her only or principal home, and

(c)   the tenant was not himself a successor, as defined in subsection (2) or subsection (3) below,

then, on the death, the tenancy vests by virtue of this section in the spouse (and, accordingly, does not devolve under the tenant's will or intestacy).

(2)   For the purposes of this section, a tenant is a successor in relation to a tenancy if—

(a)   the tenancy became vested in him either by virtue of this section or under the will or intestacy of a previous tenant; or

(b)   at some time before the tenant's death the tenancy was a joint tenancy held by himself and one or more other persons and, prior to his death, he became the sole tenant by survivorship; or

(c)   he became entitled to the tenancy as mentioned in section 39(5) below.

(3)   For the purposes of this section, a tenant is also a successor in relation to a tenancy (in this subsection referred to as "the new tenancy") which was granted to him (alone or jointly with others) if—

(a)   at some time before the grant of the new tenancy, he was, by virtue of subsection (2) above, a successor in relation to an earlier tenancy of the same or substantially the same dwelling-house as is let under the new tenancy; and

(b)   at all times since he became such a successor he has been a tenant (alone or jointly with others) of the dwelling-house which is let under the new tenancy or of a dwelling-house which is substantially the same as that dwelling-house.

(4)   For the purposes of this section, a person who was living with the tenant as his or her wife or husband shall be treated as the tenant's spouse.

(5)   If, on the death of the tenant, there is, by virtue of subsection (4) above, more than one person who fulfils the condition in subsection (1)(b) above, such one of them as may be decided by agreement or, in default of agreement, by the county court shall be treated as the tenant's spouse for the purposes of this section.

18.   Provisions as to reversions on assured tenancies.

(1)   If at any time—

(a)   a dwelling-house is for the time being lawfully let on an assured tenancy, and

(b)   the landlord under the assured tenancy is himself a tenant under a superior tenancy; and

(c)   the superior tenancy comes to an end,

then, subject to subsection (2) below, the assured tenancy shall continue in existence as a tenancy held of the person whose interest would, apart from the continuance of the assured tenancy, entitle him to actual possession of the dwelling-house at that time.

(2)   Subsection (1) above does not apply to an assured tenancy if the interest which, by virtue of that subsection, would become that of the landlord, is such that, by virtue of Schedule 1 to this Act, the tenancy could not be an assured tenancy.

(3)   Where, by virtue of any provision of this Part of this Act, an assured tenancy which is a periodic tenancy (including a statutory periodic tenancy) continues beyond the beginning of a reversionary tenancy which was granted (whether before, on or after the commencement of this Act) so as to begin on or after—

(a)   the date on which the previous contractual assured tenancy came to an end, or

(b)   a date on which, apart from any provision of this Part, the periodic tenancy could have been brought to an end by the landlord by notice to quit,

the reversionary tenancy shall have effect as if it had been granted subject to the periodic tenancy.

(4)   The reference in subsection (3) above to the previous contractual assured tenancy applies only where the periodic tenancy referred to in that subsection is a statutory periodic tenancy and is a reference to the fixed term tenancy which immediately preceded the statutory periodic tenancy.

19.   Restriction on levy of distress for rent.

(1)   Subject to subsection (2) below, no distress for the rent of any dwelling-house let on an assured tenancy shall be levied except with the leave of the county court; and, with respect to any application for such leave, the court shall have the same powers with respect to adjournment, stay, suspension, postponement and otherwise as are conferred by section 9 above in relation to proceedings for possession of such a dwelling-house.

(2)   Nothing in subsection (1) above applies to distress levied under section 102 of the County Courts Act 1984.

CHAPTER II

ASSURED SHORTHOLD TENANCIES

20. Assured shorthold tenancies.

(1) Subject to subsection (3) below, an assured shorthold tenancy is an assured tenancy—

(a) which is a fixed term tenancy granted for a term certain of not less than six months; and

(b) in respect of which there is no power for the landlord to determine the tenancy at any time earlier than six months from the beginning of the tenancy; and

(c) in respect of which a notice is served as mentioned in subsection (2) below.

(2) The notice referred to in subsection (1)(c) above is one which—

(a) is in such form as may be prescribed;

(b) is served before the assured tenancy is entered into;

(c) is served by the person who is to be the landlord under the assured tenancy on the person who is to be the tenant under that tenancy; and

(d) states that the assured tenancy to which it relates is to be a shorthold tenancy.

(3) Notwithstanding anything in subsection (1) above, where—

(a) immediately before a tenancy (in this subsection referred to as "the new tenancy") is granted, the person to whom it is granted or, as the case may be, at least one of the persons to whom it is granted was a tenant under an assured tenancy which was not a shorthold tenancy, and

(b) the new tenancy is granted by the person who, immediately before the beginning of the tenancy, was the landlord under the assured tenancy referred to in paragraph (a) above,

the new tenancy cannot be an assured shorthold tenancy.

(4) Subject to subsection (5) below, if, on the coming to an end of an assured shorthold tenancy (including a tenancy which was an assured shorthold but ceased to be assured before it came to an end), a new tenancy of the same or substantially the same premises comes into being under which the landlord and the tenant are the same as at the coming to an end of the earlier tenancy, then, if and so long as the new tenancy is an assured tenancy, it shall be an assured shorthold tenancy, whether or not it fulfils the conditions in paragraphs (a) to (c) of subsection (1) above.

(5) Subsection (4) above does not apply if, before the new tenancy is entered into (or, in the case of a statutory periodic tenancy, takes effect in possession), the landlord serves notice on the tenant that the new tenancy is not to be a shorthold tenancy.

(6) In the case of joint landlords—

(a) the reference in subsection (2)(c) above to the person who is to be the landlord is a reference to at least one of the persons who are to be joint landlords; and

(b) the reference in subsection (5) above to the landlord is a reference to at least one of the joint landlords.

(7) Section 14 above shall apply in relation to an assured shorthold tenancy as if in subsection (1) of that section the reference to an assured tenancy were a reference to an assured shorthold tenancy.

21. Recovery of possession on expiry or termination of assured shorthold tenancy.

(1) Without prejudice to any right of the landlord under an assured shorthold tenancy to recover possession of the dwelling-house let on the tenancy in accordance with Chapter I above, on or after the coming to an end of an assured shorthold tenancy which was a fixed term tenancy, a court shall make an order for possession of the dwelling-house if it is satisfied—

(a) that the assured shorthold tenancy has come to an end and no further assured tenancy (whether shorthold or not) is for the time being in existence, other than an assured shorthold periodic tenancy (whether statutory or not); and

(b)   the landlord or, in the case of joint landlords, at least one of them has given to the tenant not less than two months' notice stating that he requires possession of the dwelling-house.

(2)   A notice under paragraph (b) of subsection (1) above may be given before or on the day on which the tenancy comes to an end; and that subsection shall have effect notwithstanding that on the coming to an end of the fixed term tenancy a statutory periodic tenancy arises.

(3)   Where a court makes an order for possession of a dwelling-house by virtue of subsection (1) above, any statutory periodic tenancy which has arisen on the coming to an end of the assured shorthold tenancy shall end (without further notice and regardless of the period) on the day on which the order takes effect.

(4)   Without prejudice to any such right as is referred to in subsection (1) above, a court shall make an order for possession of a dwelling-house let on an assured shorthold tenancy which is a periodic tenancy if the court is satisfied—

(a)   that the landlord or, in the case of joint landlords, at least one of them has given to the tenant a notice stating that, after a date specified in the notice, being the last day of a period of the tenancy and not earlier than two months after the date the notice was given, possession of the dwelling-house is required by virtue of this section; and

(b)   that the date specified in the notice under paragraph (a) above is not earlier than the earliest day on which, apart from section 5(1) above, the tenancy could be brought to an end by a notice to quit given by the landlord on the same date as the notice under paragraph (a) above.

22.   Reference of excessive rents to rent assessment committee.

(1)   Subject to section 23 and subsection (2) below, the tenant under an assured shorthold tenancy in respect of which a notice was served as mentioned in section 20(2) above may make an application in the prescribed form to a rent assessment committee for a determination of the rent which, in the committee's opinion, the landlord might reasonably be expected to obtain under the assured shorthold tenancy.

(2)   No application may be made under this section if—

(a)   the rent payable under the tenancy is a rent previously determined under this section; or

(b)   the tenancy is an assured shorthold tenancy falling within subsection (4) of section 20 above (and, accordingly, is one in respect of which notice need not have been served as mentioned in subsection (2) of that section).

(3)   Where an application is made to a rent assessment committee under subsection (1) above with respect to the rent under an assured shorthold tenancy, the committee shall not make such a determination as is referred to in that subsection unless they consider—

(a)   that there is a sufficient number of similar dwelling-houses in the locality let on assured tenancies (whether shorthold or not); and

(b)   that the rent payable under the assured shorthold tenancy in question is significantly higher than the rent which the landlord might reasonably be expected to be able to obtain under the tenancy, having regard to the level of rents payable under the tenancies referred to in paragraph (a) above.

(4)   Where, on an application under this section, a rent assessment committee make a determination of a rent for an assured shorthold tenancy—

(a)   the determination shall have effect from such date as the committee may direct, not being earlier than the date of the application;

(b)   if, at any time on or after the determination takes effect, the rent which, apart from this paragraph, would be payable under the tenancy exceeds the rent so determined, the excess shall be irrecoverable from the tenant; and

(c)   no notice may be served under section 13(2) above with respect to a tenancy of the dwelling-house in question until after the first anniversary of the date on which the determination takes effect.

(5)   Subsections (4), (5) and (8) of section 14 above apply in relation to a determination of rent under this section as they apply in relation to a determination under that section and, accordingly, where subsection (5) of that section applies, any reference in subsection (4)(b) above to rent is a reference to rent exclusive of the amount attributable to rates.

23.   Termination of rent assessment committee's functions.

(1)   If the Secretary of State by order made by statutory instrument so provides, section 22 above shall not apply in such cases or to tenancies of dwelling-houses in such areas or in such other circumstances as may be specified in the order.

(2)   An order under this section may contain such transitional, incidental and supplementary provisions as appear to the Secretary of State to be desirable.

(3)   No order shall be made under this section unless a draft of the order has been laid before, and approved by a resolution of, each House of Parliament.

CHAPTER III

ASSURED AGRICULTURAL OCCUPANCIES

24.   Assured agricultural occupancies.

(1)   A tenancy or licence of a dwelling-house is for the purposes of this Part of this Act an "assured agricultural occupancy" if—

(a)   it is of a description specified in subsection (2) below; and

(b)   by virtue of any provision of Schedule 3 to this Act the agricultural worker condition is for the time being fulfilled with respect to the dwelling-house subject to the tenancy or licence.

(2)   The following are the tenancies and licences referred to in subsection (1)(a) above—

(a)   an assured tenancy which is not an assured shorthold tenancy;

(b)   a tenancy which does not fall within paragraph (a) above by reason only of paragraph 3, 3A, 3B or paragraph 7 of Schedule 1 to this Act (or of more than one of those paragraphs); and

(c)   a licence under which a person has the exclusive occupation of a dwelling-house as a separate dwelling and which, if it conferred a sufficient interest in land to be a tenancy, would be a tenancy falling within paragraph (a) or paragraph (b) above.

(3)   For the purposes of Chapter I above and the following provisions of this Chapter, every assured agricultural occupancy which is not an assured tenancy shall be treated as if it were such a tenancy and any reference to a tenant, a landlord or any other expression appropriate to a tenancy shall be construed accordingly; but the provisions of Chapter I above shall have effect in relation to every assured agricultural occupancy subject to the provisions of this Chapter.

(4)   Section 14 above shall apply in relation to an assured agricultural occupancy as if in subsection (1) of that section the reference to an assured tenancy were a reference to an assured agricultural occupancy.

25.   Security of tenure.

(1)   If a statutory periodic tenancy arises on the coming to an end of an assured agricultural occupancy—

(a)   it shall be an assured agricultural occupancy as long as, by virtue of any provision of Schedule 3 to this Act, the agricultural worker condition is for the time being fulfilled with respect to the dwelling-house in question; and

(b) if no rent was payable under the assured agricultural occupancy which constitutes the fixed term tenancy referred to in subsection (2) of section 5 above, subsection (3)(d) of that section shall apply as if for the words "the same as those for which rent was last payable under" there were substituted "monthly beginning on the day following the coming to an end of".

(2) In its application to an assured agricultural occupancy, Part II of Schedule 2 to this Act shall have effect with the omission of Ground 16.

(3) In its application to an assured agricultural occupancy, Part III of Schedule 2 to this Act shall have effect as if any reference in paragraph 2 to an assured tenancy included a reference to an assured agricultural occupancy.

(4) If the tenant under an assured agricultural occupancy gives notice to terminate his employment then, notwithstanding anything in any agreement or otherwise, that notice shall not constitute a notice to quit as respects the assured agricultural occupancy.

(5) Nothing in subsection (4) above affects the operation of an actual notice to quit given in respect of an assured agricultural occupancy.

CHAPTER IV

PROTECTION FROM EVICTION

27. Damages for unlawful eviction.

(1) This section applies if, at any time after 9th June 1988, a landlord (in this section referred to as "the landlord in default") or any person acting on behalf of the landlord in default unlawfully deprives the residential occupier of any premises of his occupation of the whole or part of the premises.

(2) This section also applies if, at any time after 9th June 1988, a landlord (in this section referred to as "the landlord in default") or any person acting on behalf of the landlord in default—

(a) attempts unlawfully to deprive the residential occupier of any premises of his occupation of the whole or part of the premises, or

(b) knowing or having reasonable cause to believe that the conduct is likely to cause the residential occupier of any premises—

(i) to give up his occupation of the premises or any part thereof, or

(ii) to refrain from exercising any right or pursuing any remedy in respect of the premises or any part thereof,

does acts likely to interfere with the peace or comfort of the residential occupier or members of his household, or persistently withdraws or withholds services reasonably required for the occupation of the premises as a residence,

and, as a result, the residential occupier gives up his occupation of the premises as a residence.

(3) Subject to the following provisions of this section, where this section applies, the landlord in default shall, by virtue of this section, be liable to pay to the former residential occupier, in respect of his loss of the right to occupy the premises in question as his residence, damages assessed on the basis set out in section 28 below.

(4) Any liability arising by virtue of subsection (3) above—

(a) shall be in the nature of a liability in tort; and

(b) subject to subsection (5) below, shall be in addition to any liability arising apart from this section (whether in tort, contract or otherwise).

(5) Nothing in this section affects the right of a residential occupier to enforce any liability which arises apart from this section in respect of his loss of the right to occupy premises as his residence; but damages shall not be awarded both in respect of such a liability and in respect of a liability arising by virtue of this section on account of the same loss.

(6) No liability shall arise by virtue of subsection (3) above if—

(a) before the date on which proceedings to enforce the liability are finally disposed of, the former residential occupier is reinstated in the premises in question in such circumstances that he becomes again the residential occupier of them; or

(b) at the request of the former residential occupier, a court makes an order (whether in the nature of an injunction or otherwise) as a result of which he is reinstated as mentioned in paragraph (a) above;

and, for the purposes of paragraph (a) above, proceedings to enforce a liability are finally disposed of on the earliest date by which the proceedings (including any proceedings on or in consequence of an appeal) have been determined and any time for appealing or further appealing has expired, except that if any appeal is abandoned, the proceedings shall be taken to be disposed of on the date of the abandonment.

(7) If, in proceedings to enforce a liability arising by virtue of subsection (3) above, it appears to the court—

(a) that, prior to the event which gave rise to the liability, the conduct of the former residential occupier or any person living with him in the premises concerned was such that it is reasonable to mitigate the damages for which the landlord in default would otherwise be liable, or

(b) that, before the proceedings were begun, the landlord in default offered to reinstate the former residential occupier in the premises in question and either it was unreasonable of the former residential occupier to refuse that offer or, if he had obtained alternative accommodation before the offer was made, it would have been unreasonable of him to refuse that offer if he had not obtained that accommodation,

the court may reduce the amount of damages which would otherwise be payable to such amount as it thinks appropriate.

(8) In proceedings to enforce a liability arising by virtue of subsection (3) above, it shall be a defence for the defendant to prove that he believed, and had reasonable cause to believe—

(a) that the residential occupier had ceased to reside in the premises in question at the time when he was deprived of occupation as mentioned in subsection (1) above or, as the case may be, when the attempt was made or the acts were done as a result of which he gave up his occupation of those premises; or

(b) that, where the liability would otherwise arise by virtue only of the doing of acts or the withdrawal or withholding of services, he had reasonable grounds for doing the acts or withdrawing or withholding the services in question.

(9) In this section—

(a) "residential occupier", in relation to any premises, has the same meaning as in section 1 of the 1977 Act;

(b) "the right to occupy", in relation to a residential occupier, includes any restriction on the right of another person to recover possession of the premises in question;

(c) "landlord", in relation to a residential occupier, means the person who, but for the occupier's right to occupy, would be entitled to occupation of the premises and any superior landlord under whom that person derives title;

(d) "former residential occupier", in relation to any premises, means the person who was the residential occupier until he was deprived of or gave up his occupation as mentioned in subsection (1) or subsection (2) above (and, in relation to a former residential occupier, "the right to occupy" and "landlord" shall be construed accordingly).

28. The measure of damages.

(1) The basis for the assessment of damages referred to in section 27(3) above is the difference in value, determined as at the time immediately before the residential occupier ceased to occupy the premises in question as his residence, between—

(a)   the value of the interest of the landlord in default determined on the assumption that the residential occupier continues to have the same right to occupy the premises as before that time; and

(b)   the value of that interest determined on the assumption that the residential occupier has ceased to have that right.

(2)   In relation to any premises, any reference in this section to the interest of the landlord in default is a reference to his interest in the building in which the premises in question are comprised (whether or not that building contains any other premises) together with its curtilage.

(3)   For the purposes of the valuations referred to in subsection (1) above, it shall be assumed—

(a)   that the landlord in default is selling his interest on the open market to a willing buyer;

(b)   that neither the residential occupier nor any member of his family wishes to buy; and

(c)   that it is unlawful to carry out any substantial development of any of the land in which the landlord's interest subsists or to demolish the whole or part of any building on that land.

(4)   In this section "the landlord in default" has the same meaning as in section 27 above and subsection (9) of that section applies in relation to this section as it applies in relation to that.

(5)   Section 113 of the Housing Act 1985 (meaning of "members of a person's family") applies for the purposes of subsection (3)(b) above.

(6)   The reference in subsection (3)(c) above to substantial development of any of the land in which the landlord's interest subsists is a reference to any development other than—

(a)   development for which planning permission is granted by a general development order for the time being in force and which is carried out so as to comply with any condition or limitation subject to which planning permission is so granted; or

(b)   a change of use resulting in the building referred to in subsection (2) above or any part of it being used as, or as part of, one or more dwelling-houses;
and in this subsection "general development order" has the meaning given in section 56(6) of the Town and Country Planning Act 1990 and other expressions have the same meaning as in that Act.

33.   Interpretation of Chapter IV and the 1977 Act.

(1)   In this Chapter "the 1977 Act" means the Protection from Eviction Act 1977.

CHAPTER V

PHASING OUT OF RENT ACTS AND OTHER TRANSITIONAL PROVISIONS

34.   New protected tenancies and agricultural occupancies restricted to special cases.

(1)   A tenancy which is entered into on or after the commencement of this Act cannot be a protected tenancy, unless—

(a)   it is entered into in pursuance of a contract made before the commencement of this Act; or

(b)   it is granted to a person (alone or jointly with others) who, immediately before the tenancy was granted, was a protected or statutory tenant and is so granted by the person who at that time was the landlord (or one of the joint landlords) under the protected or statutory tenancy; or

(c) it is granted to a person (alone or jointly with others) in the following circumstances—

(i) prior to the grant of the tenancy, an order for possession of a dwelling-house was made against him (alone or jointly with others) on the court being satisfied as mentioned in section 98(1)(a) of, or Case 1 in Schedule 16 to, the Rent Act 1977 or Case 1 in Schedule 4 to the Rent (Agriculture) Act 1976 (suitable alternative accommodation available); and

(ii) the tenancy is of the premises which constitute the suitable alternative accommodation as to which the court was so satisfied; and

(iii) in the proceedings for possession the court considered that, in the circumstances, the grant of an assured tenancy would not afford the required security and, accordingly, directed that the tenancy would be a protected tenancy; or

(d) it is a tenancy under which the interest of the landlord was at the time the tenancy was granted held by a new town corporation, within the meaning of section 80 of the Housing Act 1985, and, before the date which has effect by virtue of paragraph (a) or paragraph (b) of subsection (4) of section 38 below, ceased to be so held by virtue of a disposal by the Commission for the New Towns made pursuant to a direction under section 37 of the New Towns Act 1981.

(2) In subsection (1)(b) above "protected tenant" and "statutory tenant" do not include—

(a) a tenant under a protected shorthold tenancy;

(b) a protected or statutory tenant of a dwelling-house which was let under a protected shorthold tenancy which ended before the commencement of this Act and in respect of which at that commencement either there has been no grant of a further tenancy or any grant of a further tenancy has been to the person who, immediately before the grant, was in possession of the dwelling-house as a protected or statutory tenant;

and in this subsection "protected shorthold tenancy" includes a tenancy which, in proceedings for possession under Case 19 in Schedule 15 to the Rent Act 1977, is treated as a protected shorthold tenancy.

(3) In any case where—

(a) by virtue of subsections (1) and (2) above, a tenancy entered into on or after the commencement of this Act is an assured tenancy, but

(b) apart from subsection (2) above, the effect of subsection (1)(b) above would be that the tenancy would be a protected tenancy, and

(c) the landlord and the tenant under the tenancy are the same as at the coming to an end of the protected or statutory tenancy which, apart from subsection (2) above, would fall within subsection (1)(b) above,

the tenancy shall be an assured shorthold tenancy (whether or not it fulfils the conditions in section 20(1) above) unless, before the tenancy is entered into, the landlord serves notice on the tenant that it is not to be a shorthold tenancy.

(4) A licence or tenancy which is entered into on or after the commencement of this Act cannot be a relevant licence or relevant tenancy for the purposes of the Rent (Agriculture) Act 1976 (in this subsection referred to as "the 1976 Act") unless—

(a) it is entered into in pursuance of a contract made before the commencement of this Act; or

(b) it is granted to a person (alone or jointly with others) who, immediately before the licence or tenancy was granted, was a protected occupier or statutory tenant, within the meaning of the 1976 Act, and is so granted by the person who at that time was the landlord or licensor (or one of the joint landlords or licensors) under the protected occupancy or statutory tenancy in question.

(5) Except as provided in subsection (4) above, expressions used in this section have the same meaning as in the Rent Act 1977.

35. Removal of special regimes for tenancies of housing associations etc.

(1) In this section "housing association tenancy" has the same meaning as in Part VI of the Rent Act 1977.

(2) A tenancy which is entered into on or after the commencement of this Act cannot be a housing association tenancy unless—

(a) it is entered into in pursuance of a contract made before the commencement of this Act; or

(b) it is granted to a person (alone or jointly with others) who, immediately before the tenancy was granted, was a tenant under a housing association tenancy and is so granted by the person who at that time was the landlord under that housing association tenancy; or

(c) it is granted to a person (alone or jointly with others) in the following circumstances—

(i) prior to the grant of the tenancy, an order for possession of a dwelling-house was made against him (alone or jointly with others) on the court being satisfied as mentioned in paragraph (b) or paragraph (c) of subsection (2) of section 84 of the Housing Act 1985; and

(ii) the tenancy is of the premises which constitute the suitable accommodation as to which the court was so satisfied; and

(iii) in the proceedings for possession the court directed that the tenancy would be a housing association tenancy; or

(d) it is a tenancy under which the interest of the landlord was at the time the tenancy was granted held by a new town corporation, within the meaning of section 80 of the Housing Act 1985, and, before the date which has effect by virtue of paragraph (a) or paragraph (b) of subsection (4) of section 38 below, ceased to be so held by virtue of a disposal by the Commission for the New Towns made pursuant to a direction under section 37 of the New Towns Act 1981.

(3) Where, on or after the commencement of this Act, a registered housing association, within the meaning of the Housing Associations Act 1985, grants a secure tenancy pursuant to an obligation under section 554(2A) of the Housing Act 1985 (as set out in Schedule 17 to this Act) then, in determining whether that tenancy is a housing association tenancy, it shall be assumed for the purposes only of section 86(2)(b) of the Rent Act 1977 (tenancy would be a protected tenancy but for section 15 or 16 of that Act) that the tenancy was granted before the commencement of this Act.

(4) Subject to section 38(4A) below a tenancy or licence which is entered into on or after the commencement of this Act cannot be a secure tenancy unless—

(a) the interest of the landlord belongs to a local authority, a new town corporation or an urban development corporation, all within the meaning of section 80 of the Housing Act 1985, a housing action trust established under Part III of this Act or the Development Board for Rural Wales; or

(b) the interest of the landlord belongs to a housing cooperative within the meaning of section 27B of the Housing Act 1985 (agreements between local housing authorities and housing cooperatives) and the tenancy or licence is of a dwelling-house comprised in a housing cooperative agreement falling within that section; or

(c) it is entered into in pursuance of a contract made before the commencement of this Act; or

(d) it is granted to a person (alone or jointly with others) who, immediately before it was entered into, was a secure tenant and is so granted by the body which at that time was the landlord or licensor under the secure tenancy; or

(e) it is granted to a person (alone or jointly with others) in the following circumstances—

(i) prior to the grant of the tenancy or licence, an order for possession of a dwelling-house was made against him (alone or jointly with others) on the court being satisfied as mentioned in paragraph (b) or paragraph (c) of subsection (2) of section 84 of the Housing Act 1985; and

(ii)   the tenancy or licence is of the premises which constitute the suitable accommodation as to which the court was so satisfied; and

(iii)   in the proceedings for possession the court considered that, in the circumstances, the grant of an assured tenancy would not afford the required security and, accordingly, directed that the tenancy or licence would be a secure tenancy; or

(f)   it is granted pursuant to an obligation under section 554(2A) of the Housing Act 1985 (as set out in Schedule 17 to this Act).

(5)   If, on or after the commencement of this Act, the interest of the landlord under a protected or statutory tenancy becomes held by a housing association, a housing trust, the Housing Corporation or Housing for Wales, nothing in the preceding provisions of this section shall prevent the tenancy from being a housing association tenancy or a secure tenancy and, accordingly, in such a case section 80 of the Housing Act 1985 (and any enactment which refers to that section) shall have effect without regard to the repeal of provisions of that section effected by this Act.

(6)   In subsection (5) above "housing association" and "housing trust" have the same meaning as in the Housing Act 1985.

36.   New restricted contracts limited to transitional cases.

(1)   A tenancy or other contract entered into after the commencement of this Act cannot be a restricted contract for the purposes of the Rent Act 1977 unless it is entered into in pursuance of a contract made before the commencement of this Act.

(2)   If the terms of a restricted contract are varied after this Act comes into force then, subject to subsection (3) below,—

(a)   if the variation affects the amount of the rent which, under the contract, is payable for the dwelling in question, the contract shall be treated as a new contract entered into at the time of the variation (and subsection (1) above shall have effect accordingly); and

(b)   if the variation does not affect the amount of the rent which, under the contract, is so payable, nothing in this section shall affect the determination of the question whether the variation is such as to give rise to a new contract.

(3)   Any reference in subsection (2) above to a variation affecting the amount of the rent which, under a contract, is payable for a dwelling does not include a reference to—

(a)   a reduction or increase effected under section 78 of the Rent Act 1977 (power of rent tribunal); or

(b)   a variation which is made by the parties and has the effect of making the rent expressed to be payable under the contract the same as the rent for the dwelling which is entered in the register under section 79 of the Rent Act 1977.

(4)   In subsection (1) of section 81A of the Rent Act 1977 (cancellation of registration of rent relating to a restricted contract) paragraph (a) (no cancellation until two years have elapsed since the date of the entry) shall cease to have effect.

(5)   In this section "rent" has the same meaning as in Part V of the Rent Act 1977.

37.   No further assured tenancies under Housing Act 1980.

(1)   A tenancy which is entered into on or after the commencement of this Act cannot be an assured tenancy for the purposes of sections 56 to 58 of the Housing Act 1980 (in this section referred to as a "1980 Act tenancy").

(2)   In any case where—

(a)   before the commencement of this Act, a tenant under a 1980 Act tenancy made an application to the court under section 24 of the Landlord and Tenant Act 1954 (for the grant of a new tenancy), and

(b)   at the commencement of this Act the 1980 Act tenancy is continuing by virtue of that section or of any provision of Part IV of the said Act of 1954, section 1(3) of this Act shall not apply to the 1980 Act tenancy.

(3)   If, in a case falling within subsection (2) above, the court makes an order for the grant of a new tenancy under section 29 of the Landlord and Tenant Act 1954, that tenancy shall be an assured tenancy for the purposes of this Act.

(4)   In any case where—

(a)   before the commencement of this Act a contract was entered into for the grant of a 1980 Act tenancy, but

(b)   at the commencement of this Act the tenancy had not been granted,

the contract shall have effect as a contract for the grant of an assured tenancy (within the meaning of this Act).

(5)   In relation to an assured tenancy falling within subsection (3) above or granted pursuant to a contract falling within subsection (4) above, Part I of Schedule 1 to this Act shall have effect as if it consisted only of paragraphs 11 and 12; and, if the landlord granting the tenancy is a fully mutual housing association, then, so long as that association remains the landlord under that tenancy (and under any statutory periodic tenancy which arises on the coming to an end of that tenancy), the said paragraph 12 shall have effect in relation to that tenancy with the omission of sub-paragraph (1)(h).

(6)   Any reference in this section to a provision of the Landlord and Tenant Act 1954 is a reference only to that provision as applied by section 58 of the Housing Act 1980.

38.   Transfer of existing tenancies from public to private sector.

(1)   The provisions of subsection (3) below apply in relation to a tenancy which was entered into before, or pursuant to a contract made before, the commencement of this Act if,—

(a)   at that commencement or, if it is later, at the time it is entered into, the interest of the landlord is held by a public body (within the meaning of subsection (5) below); and

(b)   at some time after that commencement, the interest of the landlord ceases to be so held.

(2)   The provisions of subsection (3) below also apply in relation to a tenancy which was entered into before, or pursuant to a contract made before, the commencement of this Act if,—

(a)   at the commencement of this Act or, if it is later, at the time it is entered into, it is a housing association tenancy; and

(b)   at some time after that commencement, it ceases to be such a tenancy.

(3)   Subject to subsections (4) and (4A) below on and after the time referred to in subsection (1)(b) or, as the case may be, subsection (2)(b) above—

(a)   the tenancy shall not be capable of being a protected tenancy, a protected occupancy or a housing association tenancy;

(b)   the tenancy shall not be capable of being a secure tenancy unless (and only at a time when) the interest of the landlord under the tenancy is (or is again) held by a public body; and

(c)   paragraph 1 of Schedule 1 to this Act shall not apply in relation to it, and the question whether at any time thereafter it becomes (or remains) an assured tenancy shall be determined accordingly.

(4)   In relation to a tenancy under which, at the commencement of this Act or, if it is later, at the time the tenancy is entered into, the interest of the landlord is held by a new town corporation, within the meaning of section 80 of the Housing Act 1985 and which subsequently ceases to be so held by virtue of a disposal by the Commission for the New Towns made pursuant to a direction under section 37 of the New Towns Act 1981, subsections (1) and (3) above shall have effect as if any reference in subsection (1) above to the commencement of this Act were a reference to—

(a)   the date on which expires the period of two years beginning on the day this Act is passed; or

(b)   if the Secretary of State by order made by statutory instrument within that period so provides, such other date (whether earlier or later) as may be specified by the order for the purposes of this subsection.

(4A)   Where, by virtue of a disposal falling within subsection (4) above and made before the date which has effect by virtue of paragraph (a) or paragraph (b) of that subsection, the interest of the landlord under a tenancy passes to a registered housing association, then, notwithstanding anything in subsection (3) above, so long as the tenancy continues to be held by a body which would have been specified in subsection (1) of section 80 of the Housing Act 1985 if the repeal of provisions of that section effected by this Act had not been made, the tenancy shall continue to be a secure tenancy and to be capable of being a housing association tenancy.

(5)   For the purposes of this section, the interest of a landlord under a tenancy is held by a public body at a time when—

(a)   it belongs to a local authority, a new town corporation or an urban development corporation, all within the meaning of section 80 of the Housing Act 1985; or

(b)   it belongs to a housing action trust established under Part III of this Act; or

(c)   it belongs to the Development Board for Rural Wales; or

(d)   it belongs to Her Majesty in right of the Crown or to a government department or is held in trust for Her Majesty for the purposes of a government department.

(6)   In this section—

(a)   "housing association tenancy" means a tenancy to which Part VI of the Rent Act 1977 applies;

(b)   "protected tenancy" has the same meaning as in that Act; and

(c)   "protected occupancy" has the same meaning as in the Rent (Agriculture) Act 1976.

39.   Statutory tenants: succession.

(2)   Where the person who is the original tenant, within the meaning of Part I of Schedule 1 to the Rent Act 1977, dies after the commencement of this Act, that Part shall have effect subject to the amendments in Part I of Schedule 4 to this Act.

(3)   Where subsection (2) above does not apply but the person who is the first successor, within the meaning of Part I of Schedule 1 to the Rent Act 1977, dies after the commencement of this Act, that Part shall have effect subject to the amendments in paragraphs 5 to 9 of Part I of Schedule 4 to this Act.

(4)   In any case where the original occupier, within the meaning of section 4 of the Rent (Agriculture) Act 1976 (statutory tenants and tenancies) dies after the commencement of this Act, that section shall have effect subject to the amendments in Part II of Schedule 4 to this Act.

(5)   In any case where, by virtue of any provision of—

(a)   Part I of Schedule 1 to the Rent Act 1977, as amended in accordance with subsection (2) or subsection (3) above, or

(b)   section 4 of the Rent (Agriculture) Act 1976, as amended in accordance with subsection (4) above,

a person (in the following provisions of this section referred to as "the successor") becomes entitled to an assured tenancy of a dwelling-house by succession, that tenancy shall be a periodic tenancy arising by virtue of this section.

(6)   Where, by virtue of subsection (5) above, the successor becomes entitled to an assured periodic tenancy, that tenancy is one—

(a)   taking effect in possession immediately after the death of the protected or statutory tenant or protected occupier (in the following provisions of this section referred to as "the predecessor") on whose death the successor became so entitled;

(b)   deemed to have been granted to the successor by the person who, immediately before the death of the predecessor, was the landlord of the predecessor under his tenancy;

(c)   under which the premises which are let are the same dwelling-house as, immediately before his death, the predecessor occupied under his tenancy;

(d)   under which the periods of the tenancy are the same as those for which rent was last payable by the predecessor under his tenancy;

(e)   under which, subject to sections 13 to 15 above, the other terms are the same as those on which, under his tenancy, the predecessor occupied the dwelling-house immediately before his death; and

(f)   which, for the purposes of section 13(2) above, is treated as a statutory periodic tenancy;

and in paragraphs (b) to (e) above "under his tenancy", in relation to the predecessor, means under his protected tenancy or protected occupancy or in his capacity as a statutory tenant.

(7)   If, immediately before the death of the predecessor, the landlord might have recovered possession of the dwelling-house under Case 19 in Schedule 15 to the Rent Act 1977, the assured periodic tenancy to which the successor becomes entitled shall be an assured shorthold tenancy (whether or not it fulfils the conditions in section 20(1) above).

(8)   If, immediately before his death, the predecessor was a protected occupier or statutory tenant within the meaning of the Rent (Agriculture) Act 1976, the assured periodic tenancy to which the successor becomes entitled shall be an assured agricultural occupancy (whether or not it fulfils the conditions in section 24(1) above).

(9)   Where, immediately before his death, the predecessor was a tenant under a fixed term tenancy, section 6 above shall apply in relation to the assured periodic tenancy to which the successor becomes entitled on the predecessor's death subject to the following modifications—

(a)   for any reference to a statutory period tenancy there shall be substituted a reference to the assured periodic tenancy to which the successor becomes so entitled;

(b)   in subsection (1) of that section, paragraph (a) shall be omitted and the reference in paragraph (b) to section 5(3) (e) above shall be construed as a reference to subsection (6)(e) above; and

(c)   for any reference to the coming to an end of the former tenancy there shall be substituted a reference to the date of the predecessor's death.

(10)   If and so long as a dwelling-house is subject to an assured tenancy to which the successor has become entitled by succession, section 7 above and Schedule 2 to this Act shall have effect subject to the modifications in Part III of Schedule 4 to this Act; and in that Part "the predecessor" and "the successor" have the same meaning as in this section.

CHAPTER VI

GENERAL PROVISIONS

40.   Jurisdiction of county courts.

(1)   A county court shall have jurisdiction to hear and determine any question arising under any provision of—

(a)   Chapters I to III and V above, or

(b)   sections 27 and 28 above,

other than a question falling within the jurisdiction of a rent assessment committee by virtue of any such provision.

(2)   Subsection (1) above has effect notwithstanding that the damages claimed in any proceedings may exceed the amount which, for the time being, is the county court limit for the purposes of the County Courts Act 1984.

(3)   Where any proceedings under any provision mentioned in subsection (1) above are being taken in a county court, the court shall have jurisdiction to hear and determine any other proceedings joined with those proceedings, notwithstanding that, apart from this subsection, those other proceedings would be outside the court's jurisdiction.

(4)   If any person takes any proceedings under any provision mentioned in subsection (1) above in the High Court, he shall not be entitled to recover any more costs of those proceedings than those to which he would have been entitled if the proceedings had been taken in a county court: and in such a case the taxing master shall have the same power of directing on what county court scale costs are to be allowed, and of allowing any item of costs, as the judge would have had if the proceedings had been taken in a county court.

(5)   Subsection (4) above shall not apply where the purpose of taking the proceedings in the High Court was to enable them to be joined with any proceedings already pending before that court (not being proceedings taken under any provision mentioned in subsection (1) above).

41.   Rent assessment committees: procedure and information powers.

(2)   The rent assessment committee to whom a matter is referred under Chapter I or Chapter II above may by notice in the prescribed form served on the landlord or the tenant require him to give to the committee, within such period of not less than fourteen days from the service of the notice as may be specified in the notice, such information as they may reasonably require for the purposes of their functions.

(3)   If any person fails without reasonable excuse to comply with a notice served on him under subsection (2) above, he shall be liable on summary conviction to a fine not exceeding level 3 on the standard scale.

(4)   Where an offence under subsection (3) above committed by a body corporate is proved to have been committed with the consent or connivance of, or to be attributable to any neglect on the part of, any director, manager or secretary or other similar officer of the body corporate or any person who was purporting to act in any such capacity, he as well as the body corporate shall be guilty of that offence and shall be liable to be proceeded against and punished accordingly.

42.   Information as to determinations of rents.

(1)   The President of every rent assessment panel shall keep and make publicly available, in such manner as is specified in an order made by the Secretary of State, such information as may be so specified with respect to rents under assured tenancies and assured agricultural occupancies which have been the subject of references or applications to, or determinations by, rent assessment committees.

(2)   A copy of any information certified under the hand of an officer duly authorised by the President of the rent assessment panel concerned shall be receivable in evidence in any court and in any proceedings.

(3)   An order under subsection (1) above—

(a)   may prescribe the fees to be charged for the supply of a copy, including a certified copy, of any of the information kept by virtue of that subsection; and

(b)   may make different provision with respect to different cases or descriptions of case, including different provision for different areas.

(4)   The power to make an order under subsection (1) above shall be exercisable by statutory instrument which shall be subject to annulment in pursuance of a resolution of either House of Parliament.

44.   Application to Crown Property.

(1)   Subject to paragraph 11 of Schedule 1 to this Act and subsection (2) below, Chapters I to IV above apply in relation to premises in which there subsists, or at any

material time subsisted, a Crown interest as they apply in relation to premises in relation to which no such interest subsists or ever subsisted.

(2) In Chapter IV above—

(a) sections 27 and 28 do not bind the Crown; and

(b) the remainder binds the Crown to the extent provided for in section 10 of the Protection from Eviction Act 1977.

(3) In this section "Crown interest" means an interest which belongs to Her Majesty in right of the Crown or of the Duchy of Lancaster or to the Duchy of Cornwall, or to a government department, or which is held in trust for Her Majesty for the purposes of a government department.

(4) Where an interest belongs to Her Majesty in right of the Duchy of Lancaster, then, for the purposes of Chapters I to IV above, the Chancellor of the Duchy of Lancaster shall be deemed to be the owner of the interest.

45. Interpretation of Part I.

(1) In this Part of this Act, except where the context otherwise requires,—

"dwelling-house" may be a house or part of a house;

"fixed term tenancy" means any tenancy other than a periodic tenancy;

"fully mutual housing association" has the same meaning as in Part I of the Housing Associations Act 1985;

"landlord" includes any person from time to time deriving title under the original landlord and also includes, in relation to a dwelling-house, any person other than a tenant who is, or but for the existence of an assured tenancy would be, entitled to possession of the dwelling-house;

"let" includes "sub-let";

"prescribed" means prescribed by regulations made by the Secretary of State by statutory instrument;

"rates" includes water rates and charges but does not include an owner's drainage rate, as defined in section 63(2)(a) of the Land Drainage Act 1976;

"secure tenancy" has the meaning assigned by section 79 of the Housing Act 1985;

"statutory periodic tenancy" has the meaning assigned by section 5(7) above;

"tenancy" includes a sub-tenancy and an agreement for a tenancy or sub-tenancy; and

"tenant" includes a sub-tenant and any person deriving title under the original tenant or sub-tenant.

(2) Subject to paragraph 11 of Schedule 2 to this Act, any reference in this Part of this Act to the beginning of a tenancy is a reference to the day on which the tenancy is entered into or, if it is later, the day on which, under the terms of any lease, agreement or other document, the tenant is entitled to possession under the tenancy.

(3) Where two or more persons jointly constitute either the landlord or the tenant in relation to a tenancy, then, except where this Part of this Act otherwise provides, any reference to the landlord or to the tenant is a reference to all the persons who jointly constitute the landlord or the tenant, as the case may require.

(4) For the avoidance of doubt, it is hereby declared that any reference in this Part of this Act (however expressed) to a power for a landlord to determine a tenancy does not include a reference to a power of re-entry or forfeiture for breach of any term or condition of the tenancy.

(5) Regulations under subsection (1) above may make different provision with respect to different cases or descriptions of case, including different provision for different areas.

PART V

MISCELLANEOUS AND GENERAL

Leases

115. Premiums on long leases.

(1) With respect to—
    (a) any premium received or required to be paid after the commencement of this Act, or
    (b) any loan required to be made after that commencement,
section 127 of the Rent Act 1977 (allowable premiums in relation to certain long tenancies) shall have effect subject to the amendments in subsections (2) and (3) below.

(2) For subsections (2) and (3) there shall be substituted the following subsections—

    "(2) The conditions mentioned in subsection (1)(a) above are—
      (a) that the landlord has no power to determine the tenancy at any time within twenty years beginning on the date when it was granted; and
      (b) that the terms of the tenancy do not inhibit both the assignment and the underletting of the whole of the premises comprised in the tenancy;
but for the purpose of paragraph (b) above there shall be disregarded any term of the tenancy which inhibits assignment and underletting only during a period which is or falls within the final seven years of the term for which the tenancy was granted.

    (3) The reference in subsection (2) above to a power of the landlord to determine a tenancy does not include a reference to a power of re-entry or forfeiture for breach of any term or condition of the tenancy."

(3) Subsections (3C) and (3D) shall be omitted and in subsection (5) for "(2)(c)" there shall be substituted "(2)(b)".

(4) Expressions used in subsection (1) above have the same meaning as in Part IX of the Rent Act 1977.

116. Repairing obligations in short leases. 1985 c. 70.

(1) In section 11 of the Landlord and Tenant Act 1985 (repairing obligations in short leases) after subsection (1) there shall be inserted the following subsections—

    "(1A) If a lease to which this section applies is a lease of a dwelling-house which forms part only of a building, then, subject to subsection (1B), the covenant implied by subsection (1) shall have effect as if—
      (a) the reference in paragraph (a) of that subsection to the dwelling-house included a reference to any part of the building in which the lessor has an estate or interest; and
      (b) any reference in paragraphs (b) and (c) of that subsection to an installation in the dwelling-house included a reference to an installation which, directly or indirectly, serves the dwelling-house and which either—
        (i) forms part of any part of a building in which the lessor has an estate or interest; or
        (ii) is owned by the lessor or under his control.

    (1B) Nothing in subsection (1A) shall be construed as requiring the lessor to carry out any works or repairs unless the disrepair (or failure to maintain in working order) is such as to affect the lessee's enjoyment of the dwelling-house or of any common parts, as defined in section 60(1) of the Landlord and Tenant Act 1987, which the lessee, as such, is entitled to use."

(2) After subsection (3) of that section there shall be inserted the following subsection—
    "(3A) In any case where—

(a)   the lessor's repairing covenant has effect as mentioned in subsection (1A), and

(b)   in order to comply with the covenant the lessor needs to carry out works or repairs otherwise than in, or to an installation in, the dwelling-house, and

(c)   the lessor does not have a sufficient right in the part of the building or the installation concerned to enable him to carry out the required works or repairs, then, in any proceedings relating to a failure to comply with the lessor's repairing covenant, so far as it requires the lessor to carry out the works or repairs in question, it shall be a defence for the lessor to prove that he used all reasonable endeavours to obtain, but was unable to obtain, such rights as would be adequate to enable him to carry out the works or repairs."

(3)   At the end of section 14(4) of the said Act of 1985 (which excludes from section 11 certain leases granted to various bodies) there shall be added—

"a housing action trust established under Part III of the Housing Act 1988".

(4)   The amendments made by this section do not have effect with respect to—

(a)   a lease entered into before the commencement of this Act; or

(b)   a lease entered into pursuant to a contract made before the commencement of this Act.

121.   Rent officers: additional functions relating to housing benefit etc.

(1)   The Secretary of State may by order require rent officers to carry out such functions as may be specified in the order in connection with housing benefit and rent allowance subsidy.

(2)   An order under this section—

(a)   shall be made by statutory instrument which, except in the case of the first order to be made, shall be subject to annulment in pursuance of a resolution of either House of Parliament;

(b)   may make different provision for different cases or classes of case and for different areas; and

(c)   may contain such transitional, incidental and supplementary provisions as appear to the Secretary of State to be desirable;

and the first order under this section shall not be made unless a draft of it has been laid before, and approved by a resolution of, each House of Parliament.

Supplementary

138.   Financial provisions.

(1)   There shall be paid out of money provided by Parliament—

(a)   any sums required for the payment by the Secretary of State of grants under this Act;

(b)   any sums required to enable the Secretary of State to make payments to housing action trusts established under Part III of this Act;

(c)   any other expenses of the Secretary of State under this Act; and

(d)   any increase attributable to this Act in the sums so payable under any other enactment.

(2)   Any sums received by the Secretary of State under this Act, other than those required to be paid into the National Loans Fund, shall be paid into the Consolidated Fund.

139.   Application to Isles of Scilly.

(1)   This Act applies to the Isles of Scilly subject to such exceptions, adaptations and modifications as the Secretary of State may by order direct.

(2)   The power to make an order under this section shall be exercisable by statutory instrument which shall be subject to annulment in pursuance of a resolution or either House of Parliament.

141. Short title, commencement and extent.

(1)   This Act may be cited as the Housing Act 1988.

(2)   The provisions of Parts II and IV of this Act and sections 119, 122, 124, 128, 129, 135 and 140 above shall come into force on such day as the Secretary of State may by order made by statutory instrument appoint, and different days may be so appointed for different provisions or for different purposes.

(3)   Part I and this Part of this Act, other than sections 119, 122, 124, 128, 129, 132, 133, 134, 135 and 138 onwards, shall come into force at the expiry of the period of two months beginning on the day it is passed; and any reference in those provisions to the commencement of this Act shall be construed accordingly.

(4)   An order under subsection (2) above may make such transitional provisions as appear to the Secretary of State necessary or expedient in connection with the provisions brought into force by the order.

(5)   Parts I, III and IV of this Act and this Part, except sections 118, 128, 132, 134, 135 and 137 onwards, extend to England and Wales only.

(6)   This Act does not extend to Northern Ireland.

SCHEDULES

Section 1   SCHEDULE 1

TENANCIES WHICH CANNOT BE ASSURED TENANCIES

PART I
THE TENANCIES

Tenancies entered into before commencement

1.   A tenancy which is entered into before, or pursuant to a contract made before the commencement of this Act.

Tenancies of dwelling-houses with high rateable values

2.—(1)   A tenancy—

(a)   which is entered into on or after 1st April 1990 (otherwise than, where the dwelling-house had a rateable value on 31st March 1990, in pursuance of a contract made before 1st April 1990), and

(b)   under which the rent payable for the time being is payable at a rate exceeding £25,000 a year.

(2)   In sub-paragraph (1) "rent" does not include any sum payable by the tenant as is expressed (in whatever terms) to be payable in respect of rates, services, management, repairs, maintenance or insurance, unless it could not have been regarded by the parties to the tenancy as a sum so payable.

2A.   A tenancy—

(a)   which was entered into before the 1st April 1990, or on or after that date in pursuance of a contract made before that date, and

(b)   under which the dwelling-house had a rateable value on the 31st March 1990 which, if it is in Greater London, exceeded £1,500 and, if it is elsewhere, exceeded £750.

Tenancies at a low rent

3.   A tenancy under which for the time being no rent is payable.

3A.   A tenancy—

(a)   which is entered into on or after 1st April 1990 (otherwise than, where the dwelling-house had a rateable value on 31st March 1990, in pursuance of a contract made before 1st April 1990), and

(b)   under which the rent payable for the time being is payable at a rate of, if the dwelling-house is in Greater London, £1,000 or less a year and, if it is elsewhere, £250 or less a year.

3B.   A tenancy—

(a)   which was entered into before 1st April 1990 or, where the dwelling-house had a rateable value on the 31st March 1990, on or after 1st April 1990 in pursuance of a contract made before that date, and

(b)   under which the rent for the time being payable is less than two-thirds of the rateable value of the dwelling-house on 31st March 1990.

3C.   Paragraph 2(2) above applies for the purposes of paragraphs 3, 3A and 3B as it applies for the purposes of paragraph 2(1).

Business tenancies

4.   A tenancy to which Part II of the Landlord and Tenant Act 1954 applies (business tenancies).

Licensed premises

5.   A tenancy under which the dwelling-house consists of or comprises premises licensed for the sale of intoxicating liquors for consumption on the premises.

Tenancies of agricultural land

6.—(1)   A tenancy under which agricultural land, exceeding two acres, is let together with the dwelling-house.

(2)   In this paragraph "agricultural land" has the meaning set out in section 26(3)(a) of the General Rate Act 1967 (exclusion of agricultural land and premises from liability for rating).

Tenancies of agricultural holdings

7.   A tenancy under which the dwelling-house—

(a)   is comprised in an agricultural holding (within the meaning of the Agricultural Holdings Act 1986); and

(b)   is occupied by the person responsible for the control (whether as tenant or as servant or agent of the tenant) of the farming of the holding.

Lettings to students

8.—(1)   A tenancy which is granted to a person who is pursuing, or intends to pursue, a course of study provided by a specified educational institution and is so granted either by that institution or by another specified institution or body of persons.

(2)   In sub-paragraph (1) above "specified" means specified, or of a class specified, for the purposes of this paragraph by regulations made by the Secretary of State by statutory instrument.

(3)   A statutory instrument made in the exercise of the power conferred by sub-paragraph (2) above shall be subject to annulment in pursuance of a resolution of either House of Parliament.

Holiday lettings

9.   A tenancy the purpose of which is to confer on the tenant the right to occupy the dwelling-house for a holiday.

Resident landlords

10.—(1)   A tenancy in respect of which the following conditions are fulfilled—

(a)   that the dwelling-house forms part only of a building and, except in a case where the dwelling-house also forms part of a flat, the building is not a purpose-built block of flats; and

(b)   that, subject to Part III of this Schedule, the tenancy was granted by an individual who, at the time when the tenancy was granted, occupied as his only or principal home another dwelling-house which,—

(i)   in the case mentioned in paragraph (a) above, also forms part of the flat; or

(ii)   in any other case, also forms part of the building; and

(c)   that, subject to Part III of this Schedule, at all times since the tenancy was granted the interest to the landlord under the tenancy has belonged to an individual who, at the time he owned that interest, occupied as his only or principal home another dwelling-house which,—

(i)   in the case mentioned in paragraph (a) above, also formed part of the flat; or

(ii)   in any other case, also formed part of the building; and

(d)   that the tenancy is not one which is excluded from this sub-paragraph by sub-paragraph (3) below.

(2)   If a tenancy was granted by two or more persons jointly, the reference in sub-paragraph (1)(b) above to an individual is a reference to any one of those persons and if the interest of the landlord is for the time being held by two or more persons jointly, the reference in sub-paragraph (1)(c) above to an individual is a reference to any one of those persons.

(3)   A tenancy (in this sub-paragraph referred to as "the new tenancy") is excluded from sub-paragraph (1) above if—

(a)   it is granted to a person (alone, or jointly with others) who, immediately before it was granted, was a tenant under an assured tenancy (in this sub-paragraph referred to as "the former tenancy") of the same dwelling-house or of another dwelling-house which forms part of the building in question; and

(b)   the landlord under the new tenancy and under the former tenancy is the same person or, if either of those tenancies is or was granted by two or more persons jointly, the same person is the landlord or one of the landlords under each tenancy.

Crown tenancies

11.—(1)   A tenancy under which the interest of the landlord belongs to Her Majesty in right of the Crown or to a government department or is held in trust for Her Majesty for the purposes of a government department.

(2)   The reference in sub-paragraph (1) above to the case where the interest of the landlord belongs to Her Majesty in right of the Crown does not include the case where that interest is under the management of the Crown Estate Commissioners.

Local authority tenancies etc.

12.—(1)   A tenancy under which the interest of the landlord belongs to—

(a)   a local authority, as defined in sub-paragraph (2) below;

(b)   the Commission for the New Towns;

(c)   the Development Board for Rural Wales;

(d)   an urban development corporation established by an order under section 135 of the Local Government, Planning and Land Act 1980;

(e)   a development corporation, within the meaning of the New Towns Act 1981;

(f)   an authority established under section 10 of the Local Government Act 1985 (waste disposal authorities);

(g)   a residuary body, within the meaning of the Local Government Act 1985;

(h)   a fully mutual housing association; or

(i)   a housing action trust established under Part III of this Act.

(2)   The following are local authorities for the purposes of sub-paragraph (1)(a) above—

(a)   the council of a county, district or London borough;

(b)   the Common Council of the City of London;

(c) the Council of the Isles of Scilly;
(d) the Broads Authority;
(e) the Inner London Education Authority; and
(f) a joint authority, within the meaning of the Local Government Act 1985.

Transitional cases

13.—(1) A protected tenancy, within the meaning of the Rent Act 1977.

(2) A housing association tenancy, within the meaning of Part VI of that Act.

(3) A secure tenancy.

(4) Where a person is a protected occupier of a dwelling-house, within the meaning of the Rent (Agriculture) Act 1976, the relevant tenancy, within the meaning of that Act, by virtue of which he occupies the dwelling-house.

PART II
RATEABLE VALUES

14.—(1) The rateable value of a dwelling-house at any time shall be ascertained for the purposes of Part I of this Schedule as follows—

(a) if the dwelling-house is a hereditament for which a rateable value is then shown in the valuation list, it shall be that rateable value;

(b) if the dwelling-house forms part only of such a hereditament or consists of or forms part of more than one such hereditament, its rateable value shall be taken to be such value as is found by a proper apportionment or aggregation of the rateable value or values so shown.

(2) Any question arising under this Part of this Schedule as to the proper apportionment or aggregation of any value or values shall be determined by the county court and the decision of that court shall be final.

15. Where, after the time at which the rateable value of a dwelling-house is material for the purposes of any provision of Part I of this Schedule, the valuation list is altered so as to vary the rateable value of the hereditament of which the dwelling-house consists (in whole or in part) or forms part and the alteration has effect from that time or from an earlier time, the rateable value of the dwelling-house at the material time shall be ascertained as if the value shown in the valuation list at the material time had been the value shown in the list as altered.

16. Paragraphs 14 and 15 above apply in relation to any other land which, under section 2 of this Act, is treated as part of a dwelling-house as they apply in relation to the dwelling-house itself.

PART III
PROVISIONS FOR DETERMINING APPLICATION OF PARAGRAPH 10 (RESIDENT LANDLORDS)

17.—(1) In determining whether the condition in paragraph 10(1)(c) above is at any time fulfilled with respect to a tenancy, there shall be disregarded—

(a) any period of not more than twenty-eight days, beginning with the date on which the interest of the landlord under the tenancy becomes vested at law and in equity in an individual who, during that period, does not occupy as his only or principal home another dwelling-house which forms part of the building or, as the case may be, flat concerned;

(b) if, within a period falling within paragraph (a) above, the individual concerned notifies the tenant in writing of his intention to occupy as his only or principal home another dwelling-house in the building or, as the case may be, flat concerned, the period beginning with the date on which the interest of the landlord under the tenancy becomes vested in that individual as mentioned in that paragraph and ending—

(i) at the expiry of the period of six months beginning on that date, or

    (ii)   on the date on which that interest ceases to be so vested, or

    (iii)   on the date on which that interest becomes again vested in such an individual as is mentioned in paragraph 10(1)(c) or the condition in that paragraph becomes deemed to be fulfilled by virtue of paragraph 18(1) or paragraph 20 below. whichever is the earlier; and

    (c)   any period of not more than two years beginning with the date on which the interest of the landlord under the tenancy becomes, and during which it remains, vested—

    (i)   in trustees as such; or

    (ii)   by virtue of section 9 of the Administration of Estates Act 1925, in the Probate Judge, within the meaning of that Act.

    (2)   Where the interest of the landlord under a tenancy becomes vested at law and in equity in two or more persons jointly, of whom at least one was an individual, sub-paragraph (1) above shall have effect subject to the following modifications—

    (a)   in paragraph (a) for the words from "an individual" to "occupy" there shall be substituted "the joint landlords if, during that period none of them occupies"; and

    (b)   in paragraph (b) for the words "the individual concerned" there shall be substituted "any of the joint landlords who is an individual" and for the words "that individual" there shall be substituted "the joint landlords".

    18.—(1)   During any period when—

    (a)   the interest of the landlord under the tenancy referred to in paragraph 10 above is vested in trustees as such, and

    (b)   that interest is or, if it is held on trust for sale, the proceeds of its sale are held on trust for any person who or for two or more persons of whom at least one occupies as his only or principal home a dwelling-house which forms part of the building or, as the case may be, flat referred to in paragraph 10(1)(a), the condition in paragraph 10(1)(c) shall be deemed to be fulfilled and accordingly, no part of that period shall be disregarded by virtue of paragraph 17 above.

    (2)   If a period during which the condition in paragraph 10(1)(c) is deemed to be fulfilled by virtue of sub-paragraph (1) above comes to an end on the death of a person who was in occupation of a dwelling-house as mentioned in paragraph (b) of that sub-paragraph, then, in determining whether that condition is at any time thereafter fulfilled, there shall be disregarded any period—

    (a)   which begins on the date of the death;

    (b)   during which the interest of the landlord remains vested as mentioned in sub-paragraph (1)(a) above; and

    (c)   which ends at the expiry of the period of two years beginning on the date of the death or on any earlier date on which the condition in paragraph 10(1)(c) becomes again deemed to be fulfilled by virtue of sub-paragraph (1) above.

    19.   In any case where—

    (a)   immediately before a tenancy comes to an end the condition in paragraph 10(1)(c) is deemed to be fulfilled by virtue of paragraph 18(1) above, and

    (b)   on the coming to an end of that tenancy the trustees in whom the interest of the landlord is vested grant a new tenancy of the same or substantially the same dwelling-house to a person (alone or jointly with others) who was the tenant or one of the tenants under the previous tenancy, the condition in paragraph 10(1)(b) above shall be deemed to be fulfilled with respect to the new tenancy.

    20.—(1)   The tenancy referred to in paragraph 10 above falls within this paragraph if the interest of the landlord under the tenancy becomes vested in the personal representatives of a deceased person acting in that capacity.

    (2)   If the tenancy falls within this paragraph, the condition in paragraph 10(1)(c) shall be deemed to be fulfilled for any period, beginning with the date on which the

interest becomes vested in the personal representatives and not exceeding two years, during which the interest of the landlord remains so vested.

21.   Throughout any period which, by virtue of paragraph 17 or paragraph 18(2) above, falls to be disregarded for the purpose of determining whether the condition in paragraph 10(1)(c) is fulfilled with respect to a tenancy, no order shall be made for possession of the dwelling-house subject to that tenancy, other than an order which might be made if that tenancy were or, as the case may be, had been an assured tenancy.

22.   For the purposes of paragraph 10 above, a building is a purpose-built block of flats if as constructed it contained, and it contains, two or more flats; and for this purpose "flat" means a dwelling-house which—

  (a)   forms part only of a building; and

  (b)   is separated horizontally from another dwelling-house which forms part of the same building.

Section 7.

SCHEDULE 2

GROUNDS FOR POSSESSION OF DWELLING-HOUSES LET ON ASSURED TENANCIES

PART I
GROUNDS ON WHICH COURT MUST ORDER POSSESSION

Ground 1

Not later than the beginning of the tenancy the landlord gave notice in writing to the tenant that possession might be recovered on this ground or the court is of the opinion that it is just and equitable to dispense with the requirement of notice and (in either case)—

  (a)   at some time before the beginning of the tenancy, the landlord who is seeking possession or, in the case of joint landlords seeking possession, at least one of them occupied the dwelling-house as his only or principal home; or

  (b)   the landlord who is seeking possession or, in the case of joint landlords seeking possession, at least one of them requires the dwelling-house as his or his spouse's only or principal home and neither the landlord (or, in the case of joint landlords, any one of them) nor any other person who, as landlord, derived title under the landlord who gave the notice mentioned above acquired the reversion on the tenancy for money or money's worth.

Ground 2

The dwelling-house is subject to a mortgage granted before the beginning of the tenancy and—

  (a)   the mortgagee is entitled to exercise a power of sale conferred on him by the mortgage or by section 101 of the Law of Property Act 1925; and

  (b)   the mortgagee requires possession of the dwelling-house for the purpose of disposing of it with vacant possession in exercise of that power; and

  (c)   either notice was given as mentioned in Ground 1 above or the court is satisfied that it is just and equitable to dispense with the requirement of notice;

and for the purposes of this ground "mortgage" includes a charge and "mortgagee" shall be construed accordingly.

Ground 3

The tenancy is a fixed term tenancy for a term not exceeding eight months and—

  (a)   not later than the beginning of the tenancy the landlord gave notice in writing to the tenant that possession might be recovered on this ground; and

(b)   at some time within the period of twelve months ending with the beginning of the tenancy, the dwelling-house was occupied under a right to occupy it for a holiday.

Ground 4

The tenancy is a fixed term tenancy for a term not exceeding twelve months and—

(a)   not later than the beginning of the tenancy the landlord gave notice in writing to the tenant that possession might be recovered on this ground; and

(b)   at some time within the period of twelve months ending with the beginning of the tenancy, the dwelling-house was let on a tenancy falling within paragraph 8 of Schedule 1 to this Act.

Ground 5

The dwelling-house is held for the purpose of being available for occupation by a minister of religion as a residence from which to perform the duties of his office and—

(a)   not later than the beginning of the tenancy the landlord gave notice in writing to the tenant that possession might be recovered on this ground; and

(b)   the court is satisfied that the dwelling-house is required for occupation by a minister of religion as such a residence.

Ground 6

The landlord who is seeking possession or, if that landlord is a registered housing association or charitable housing trust, a superior landlord intends to demolish or reconstruct the whole or a substantial part of the dwelling-house or to carry out substantial works on the dwelling-house or any part thereof or any building of which it forms part and the following conditions are fulfilled—

(a)   the intended work cannot reasonably be carried out without the tenant giving up possession of the dwelling-house because—

(i)   the tenant is not willing to agree to such a variation of the terms of the tenancy as would give such access and other facilities as would permit the intended work to be carried out, or

(ii)   the nature of the intended work is such that no such variation is practicable, or

(iii)   the tenant is not willing to accept an assured tenancy of such part only of the dwelling-house (in this sub-paragraph referred to as "the reduced part") as would leave in the possession of his landlord so much of the dwelling-house as would be reasonable to enable the intended work to be carried out and, where appropriate, as would give such access and other facilities over the reduced part as would permit the intended work to be carried out, or

(iv)   the nature of the intended work is such that such a tenancy is not practicable; and

(b)   either the landlord seeking possession acquired his interest in the dwelling-house before the grant of the tenancy or that interest was in existence at the time of that grant and neither that landlord (or, in the case of joint landlords, any of them) nor any other person who, alone or jointly with others, has acquired that interest since that time acquired it for money or money's worth; and

(c)   the assured tenancy on which the dwelling-house is let did not come into being by virtue of any provision of Schedule 1 to the Rent Act 1977, as amended by Part I of Schedule 4 to this Act or, as the case may be, section 4 of the Rent (Agriculture) Act 1976, as amended by Part II of that Schedule.

For the purposes of this ground, if, immediately before the grant of the tenancy, the tenant to whom it was granted or, if it was granted to joint tenants, any of them was the tenant or one of the joint tenants of the dwelling-house concerned under an earlier assured tenancy or, as the case may be, under a tenancy to which Schedule 10 to the

Local Government and Housing Act 1989 applied, any reference in paragraph (b) above to the grant of the tenancy is a reference to the grant of that earlier assured tenancy or, as the case may be, to the grant of the tenancy to which the said Schedule 10 applied.

For the purposes of this ground "registered housing association" has the same meaning as in the Housing Associations Act 1985 and "charitable housing trust" means a housing trust, within the meaning of that Act, which is a charity, within the meaning of the Charities Act 1960.

For the purposes of this ground, every acquisition under Part IV of this Act shall be taken to be an acquisition for money or money's worth; and in any case where—

(i)   the tenancy (in this paragraph referred to as "the current tenancy") was granted to a person (alone or jointly with others) who, immediately before it was granted, was a tenant under a tenancy of a different dwelling-house (in this paragraph referred to as "the earlier tenancy"), and

(ii)   the landlord under the current tenancy is the person who, immediately before that tenancy was granted, was the landlord under the earlier tenancy, and

(iii)   the condition in paragraph (b) above could not have been fulfilled with respect to the earlier tenancy by virtue of an acquisition under Part IV of this Act (including one taken to be such an acquisition by virtue of the previous operation of this paragraph),

the acquisition of the landlord's interest under the current tenancy shall be taken to have been under that Part and the landlord shall be taken to have acquired that interest after the grant of the current tenancy.

Ground 7

The tenancy is a periodic tenancy (including a statutory periodic tenancy) which has devolved under the will or intestacy of the former tenant and the proceedings for the recovery of possession are begun not later than twelve months after the death of the former tenant or, if the court so directs, after the date on which, in the opinion of the court, the landlord or, in the case of joint landlords, any one of them became aware of the former tenant's death.

For the purposes of this ground, the acceptance by the landlord of rent from a new tenant after the death of the former tenant shall not be regarded as creating a new periodic tenancy, unless the landlord agrees in writing to a change (as compared with the tenancy before the death) in the amount of the rent, the period of the tenancy, the premises which are let or any other term of the tenancy.

Ground 8

Both at the date of the service of the notice under section 8 of this Act relating to the proceedings for possession and at the date of the hearing—

(a)   if rent is payable weekly or fortnightly, at least thirteen weeks' rent is unpaid;

(b)   if rent is payable monthly, at least three months' rent is unpaid;

(c)   if rent is payable quarterly, at least one quarter's rent is more than three months in arrears; and

(d)   if rent is payable yearly, at least three months' rent is more than three months in arrears;

and for the purpose of this ground "rent" means rent lawfully due from the tenant.

PART II
GROUNDS ON WHICH COURT MAY ORDER POSSESSION
Ground 9

Suitable alternative accommodation is available for the tenant or will be available for him when the order for possession takes effect.

Ground 10

Some rent lawfully due from the tenant—
  (a)   is unpaid on the date on which the proceedings for possession are begun; and
  (b)   except where subsection (1)(b) of section 8 of this Act applies, was in arrears
at the date of the service of the notice under that section relating to those proceedings.

Ground 11

Whether or not any rent is in arrears on the date on which proceedings for possession are
begun, the tenant has persistently delayed paying rent which has become lawfully due.

Ground 12

Any obligation of the tenancy (other than one related to the payment of rent) has been
broken or not performed.

Ground 13

The condition of the dwelling-house or any of the common parts has deteriorated owing
to acts of waste by, or the neglect or default of, the tenant or any other person residing
in the dwelling-house and, in the case of an act of waste by, or the neglect or default of,
a person lodging with the tenant or a sub-tenant of his, the tenant has not taken such
steps as he ought reasonably to have taken for the removal of the lodger or sub-tenant.
  For the purposes of this ground, "common parts" means any part of a building
comprising the dwelling-house and any other premises which the tenant is entitled
under the terms of the tenancy to use in common with the occupiers of other
dwelling-houses in which the landlord has an estate or interest.

Ground 14

The tenant or any other person residing in the dwelling-house has been guilty of
conduct which is a nuisance or annoyance to adjoining occupiers, or has been convicted
of using the dwelling-house or allowing the dwelling-house to be used for immoral or
illegal purposes.

Ground 15

The condition of any furniture provided for use under the tenancy has, in the opinion
of the court, deteriorated owing to ill-treatment by the tenant or any other person
residing in the dwelling-house and, in the case of ill-treatment by a person lodging with
the tenant or by a sub-tenant of his, the tenant has not taken such steps as he ought
reasonably to have taken for the removal of the lodger or sub-tenant.

Ground 16

The dwelling-house was let to the tenant in consequence of his employment by the
landlord seeking possession or a previous landlord under the tenancy and the tenant has
ceased to be in that employment.
  For the purposes of this ground, at a time when the landlord is or was the Secretary
of State, employment by a health services body, as defined in section 60(7) of the
National Health Service and Community Care Act 1990, shall be regarded as
employment by the Secretary of State.

PART III
SUITABLE ALTERNATIVE ACCOMMODATION

  1.   For the purposes of Ground 9 above, a certificate of the local housing authority
for the district in which the dwelling-house in question is situated, certifying that the
authority will provide suitable alternative accommodation for the tenant by a date

specified in the certificate, shall be conclusive evidence that suitable alternative accommodation will be available for him by that date.

2. Where no such certificate as is mentioned in paragraph 1 above is produced to the court, accommodation shall be deemed to be suitable for the purposes of Ground 9 above if it consists of either—

(a) premises which are to be let as a separate dwelling such that they will then be let on an assured tenancy, other than—

(i) a tenancy in respect of which notice is given not later than the beginning of the tenancy that possession might be recovered on any of Grounds 1 to 5 above, or

(ii) an assured shorthold tenancy, within the meaning of Chapter II of Part I of this Act, or

(b) premises to be let as a separate dwelling on terms which will, in the opinion of the court, afford to the tenant security of tenure reasonably equivalent to the security afforded by Chapter I of Part I of this Act in the case of an assured tenancy of a kind mentioned in sub-paragraph (a) above,

and, in the opinion of the court, the accommodation fulfils the relevant conditions as defined in paragraph 3 below.

3.—(1) For the purposes of paragraph 2 above, the relevant conditions are that the accommodation is reasonably suitable to the needs of the tenant and his family as regards proximity to place of work, and either—

(a) similar as regards rental and extent to the accommodation afforded by dwelling-houses provided in the neighbourhood by any local housing authority for persons whose needs as regards extent are, in the opinion of the court, similar to those of the tenant and of his family; or

(b) reasonably suitable to the means of the tenant and to the needs of the tenant and his family as regards extent and character; and

that if any furniture was provided for use under the assured tenancy in question, furniture is provided for use in the accommodation which is either similar to that so provided or is reasonably suitable to the needs of the tenant and his family.

(2) For the purposes of sub-paragraph (1)(a) above, a certificate of a local housing authority stating—

(a) the extent of the accommodation afforded by dwelling-houses provided by the authority to meet the needs of tenants with families of such number as may be specified in the certificate, and

(b) the amount of the rent charged by the authority for dwelling-houses affording accommodation of that extent,

shall be conclusive evidence of the facts so stated.

4. Accommodation shall not be deemed to be suitable to the needs of the tenant and his family if the result of their occupation of the accommodation would be that it would be an overcrowded dwelling-house for the purposes of Part X of the Housing Act 1985.

5. Any document purporting to be a certificate of a local housing authority named therein issued for the purposes of this Part of this Schedule and to be signed by the proper officer of that authority shall be received in evidence and, unless the contrary is shown, shall be deemed to be such a certificate without further proof.

6. In this Part of this Schedule "local housing authority" and "district", in relation to such an authority, have the same meaning as in the Housing Act 1985.

PART IV
NOTICES RELATING TO RECOVERY OF POSSESSION

7. Any reference in Grounds 1 to 5 in Part I of this Schedule or in the following provisions of this Part to the landlord giving a notice in writing to the tenant is, in the case of joint landlords, a reference to at least one of the joint landlords giving such a notice.

8.—(1)　If, not later than the beginning of a tenancy (in this paragraph referred to as "the earlier tenancy"), the landlord gives such a notice in writing to the tenant as is mentioned in any of grounds 1 to 5 in Part I of this Schedule, then, for the purposes of the ground in question and any further application of this paragraph, that notice shall also have effect as if it had been given immediately before the beginning of any later tenancy falling within sub-paragraph (2) below.

(2)　Subject to sub-paragraph (3) below, sub-paragraph (1) above applies to a later tenancy—

(a)　which takes effect immediately on the coming to an end of the earlier tenancy; and

(b)　which is granted (or deemed to be granted) to the person who was the tenant under the earlier tenancy immediately before it came to an end; and

(c)　which is of substantially the same dwelling-house as the earlier tenancy.

(3)　Sub-paragraph (1) above does not apply in relation to a later tenancy if, not later than the beginning of the tenancy, the landlord gave notice in writing to the tenant that the tenancy is not one in respect of which possession can be recovered on the ground in question.

9.　Where paragraph 8(1) above has effect in relation to a notice given as mentioned in Ground 1 in Part I of this Schedule, the reference in paragraph (b) of that ground to the reversion on the tenancy is a reference to the reversion on the earlier tenancy and on any later tenancy falling within paragraph 8(2) above.

10.　Where paragraph 8(1) above has effect in relation to a notice given as mentioned in Ground 3 or Ground 4 in Part I of this Schedule, any second or subsequent tenancy in relation to which the notice has effect shall be treated for the purpose of that ground as beginning at the beginning of the tenancy in respect of which the notice was actually given.

11.　Any reference in Grounds 1 to 5 in Part I of this Schedule to a notice being given not later than the beginning of the tenancy is a reference to its being given not later than the day on which the tenancy is entered into and, accordingly, section 45(2) of this Act shall not apply to any such reference.

Section 24.　　　　　　　　　　　　　　SCHEDULE 3

AGRICULTURAL WORKER CONDITIONS

Interpretation

1.—(1)　In this Schedule—

"the 1976 Act" means the Rent (Agriculture) Act 1976;

"agriculture" has the same meaning as in the 1976 Act; and

"relevant tenancy or licence" means a tenancy or licence of a description specified in section 24(2) of this Act.

(2)　In relation to a relevant tenancy or licence—

(a)　"the occupier" means the tenant or licensee; and

(b)　"the dwelling-house" means the dwelling-house which is let under the tenancy or, as the case may be, is occupied under the licence.

(3)　Schedule 3 to the 1976 Act applies for the purposes of this Schedule as it applies for the purposes of that Act and, accordingly, shall have effect to determine—

(a)　whether a person is a qualifying worker;

(b)　whether a person is incapable of whole-time work in agriculture, or work in agriculture as a permit worker, in consequence of a qualifying injury or disease; and

(c)　whether a dwelling-house is in qualifying ownership.

The conditions

2.   The agricultural worker condition is fulfilled with respect to a dwelling-house subject to a relevant tenancy or licence if—

(a)   the dwelling-house is or has been in qualifying ownership at any time during the subsistence of the tenancy or licence (whether or not it was at that time a relevant tenancy or licence); and

(b)   the occupier or, where there are joint occupiers, at least one of them—

(i)   is a qualifying worker or has been a qualifying worker at any time during the subsistence of the tenancy or licence (whether or not it was at that time a relevant tenancy or licence); or

(ii)   is incapable of whole-time work in agriculture or work in agriculture as a permit worker in consequence of a qualifying injury or disease.

3.—(1)   The agricultural worker condition is also fulfilled with respect to a dwelling-house subject to a relevant tenancy or licence if—

(a)   that condition was previously fulfilled with respect to the dwelling-house but the person who was then the occupier or, as the case may be, a person who was one of the joint occupiers (whether or not under the same relevant tenancy or licence) has died; and

(b)   that condition ceased to be fulfilled on the death of the occupier referred to in paragraph (a) above (hereinafter referred to as "the previous qualifying occupier"); and

(c)   the occupier is either—

(i)   the qualifying widow or widower of the previous qualifying occupier; or

(ii)   the qualifying member of the previous qualifying occupier's family.

(2)   For the purposes of sub-paragraph (1)(c)(i) above and sub-paragraph (3) below a widow or widower of the previous qualifying occupier of the dwelling-house is a qualifying widow or widower if she or he was residing in the dwelling-house immediately before the previous qualifying occupier's death.

(3)   Subject to sub-paragraph (4) below, for the purposes of sub-paragraph (1)(c)(ii) above, a member of the family of the previous qualifying occupier of the dwelling-house is the qualifying member of the family if—

(a)   on the death of the previous qualifying occupier there was no qualifying widow or widower; and

(b)   the member of the family was residing in the dwelling-house with the previous qualifying occupier at the time of, and for the period of two years before, his death.

(4)   Not more than one member of the previous qualifying occupier's family may be taken into account in determining whether the agricultural worker condition is fulfilled by virtue of this paragraph and, accordingly, if there is more than one member of the family—

(a)   who is the occupier in relation to the relevant tenancy or licence, and

(b)   who, apart from this sub-paragraph, would be the qualifying member of the family by virtue of sub-paragraph (3) above,

only that one of those members of the family who may be decided by agreement or, in default of agreement by the county court, shall be the qualifying member.

(5)   For the purposes of the preceding provisions of this paragraph a person who, immediately before the previous qualifying occupier's death, was living with the previous occupier as his or her wife or husband shall be treated as the widow or widower of the previous occupier.

(6)   If, immediately before the death of the previous qualifying occupier, there is, by virtue of sub-paragraph (5) above, more than one person who falls within sub-paragraph (1)(c)(i) above, such one of them as may be decided by agreement or, in default of agreement, by the county court shall be treated as the qualifying widow or widower for the purposes of this paragraph.

4.   The agricultural worker condition is also fulfilled with respect to a dwelling-house subject to a relevant tenancy or licence if—

(a)   the tenancy or licence was granted to the occupier or, where there are joint occupiers, at least one of them in consideration of his giving up possession of another dwelling-house of which he was then occupier (or one of joint occupiers) under another relevant tenancy or licence; and

(b)   immediately before he gave up possession of that dwelling-house, as a result of his occupation the agricultural worker condition was fulfilled with respect to it (whether by virtue of paragraph 2 or paragraph 3 above or this paragraph);

and the reference in paragraph (a) above to a tenancy or licence granted to the occupier or at least one of joint occupiers includes a reference to the case where the grant is to him together with one or more other persons.

5.—(1)   This paragraph applies where—

(a)   by virtue of any of paragraphs 2 to 4 above, the agricultural worker condition is fulfilled with respect to a dwelling-house subject to a relevant tenancy or licence (in this paragraph referred to as "the earlier tenancy or licence"); and

(b)   another relevant tenancy or licence of the same dwelling-house (in this paragraph referred to as "the later tenancy or licence") is granted to the person who, immediately before the grant, was the occupier or one of the joint occupiers under the earlier tenancy or licence and as a result of whose occupation the agricultural worker condition was fulfilled as mentioned in paragraph (a) above;

and the reference in paragraph (b) above to the grant of the later tenancy or licence to the person mentioned in that paragraph includes a reference to the case where the grant is to that person together with one or more other persons.

(2)   So long as a person as a result of whose occupation of the dwelling-house the agricultural worker condition was fulfilled with respect to the earlier tenancy or licence continues to be the occupier, or one of the joint occupiers, under the later tenancy or licence, the agricultural worker condition shall be fulfilled with respect to the dwelling-house.

(3)   For the purposes of paragraphs 3 and 4 above and any further application of this paragraph, where sub-paragraph (2) above has effect, the agricultural worker condition shall be treated as fulfilled so far as concerns the later tenancy or licence by virtue of the same paragraph of this Schedule as was applicable (or, as the case may be, last applicable) in the case of the earlier tenancy or licence.

Section 39.   SCHEDULE 4

STATUTORY TENANTS: SUCCESSION

PART I
AMENDMENTS OF SCHEDULE 1 TO RENT ACT 1977

1.   In paragraph 1 the words "or, as the case may be, paragraph 3" shall be omitted.

2.   At the end of paragraph 2 there shall be inserted the following sub-paragraphs—

"(2)   For the purposes of this paragraph, a person who was living with the original tenant as his or her wife or husband shall be treated as the spouse of the original tenant.

(3)   If, immediately after the death of the original tenant, there is, by virtue of sub-paragraph (2) above, more than one person who fulfils the conditions in sub-paragraph (1) above, such one of them as may be decided by agreement or, in default of agreement, by the county court shall be treated as the surviving spouse for the purposes of this paragraph."

3.   In paragraph 3—

(a) after the words "residing with him" there shall be inserted "in the dwelling-house";

(b) for the words "period of 6 months" there shall be substituted "period of 2 years";

(c) for the words from "the statutory tenant" onwards there shall be substituted "entitled to an assured tenancy of the dwelling-house by succession"; and

(d) at the end there shall be added the following sub-paragraph—

"(2) If the original tenant died within the period of 18 months beginning on the operative date, then, for the purposes of this paragraph, a person who was residing in the dwelling-house with the original tenant at the time of his death and for the period which began 6 months before the operative date and ended at the time of his death shall be taken to have been residing with the original tenant for the period of 2 years immediately before his death."

4. In paragraph 4 the words "or 3" shall be omitted.

5. In paragraph 5—

(a) for the words from "or, as the case may be" to "of this Act" there shall be substituted "below shall have effect"; and

(b) for the words "the statutory tenant" there shall be substituted "entitled to an assured tenancy of the dwelling-house by succession".

6. For paragraph 6 there shall be substituted the following paragraph—

"6.—(1) Where a person who—

(a) was a member of the original tenant's family immediately before that tenant's death, and

(b) was a member of the first successor's family immediately before the first successor's death,

was residing in the dwelling-house with the first successor at the time of, and for the period of 2 years immediately before, the first successor's death, that person or, if there is more than one such person, such one of them as may be decided by agreement or, in default of agreement, by the county court shall be entitled to an assured tenancy of the dwelling-house by succession.

(2) If the first successor died within the period of 18 months beginning on the operative date, then, for the purposes of this paragraph, a person who was residing in the dwelling-house with the first successor at the time of his death and for the period which began 6 months before the operative date and ended at the time of his death shall be taken to have been residing with the first successor for the period of 2 years immediately before his death."

7. Paragraph 7 shall be omitted.

8. In paragraph 10(1)(a) for the words "paragraphs 6 or 7" there shall be substituted "paragraph 6".

9. At the end of paragraph 11 there shall be inserted the following paragraph—

"11A. In this Part of this Schedule "the operative date" means the date on which Part I of the Housing Act 1988 came into force."

PART II
AMENDMENTS OF SECTION 4 OF RENT (AGRICULTURE) ACT 1976

10. In subsection (2) the words "or, as the case may be, subsection (4)" shall be omitted.

11. In subsection (4)—

(a) in paragraph (b) after the words "residing with him" there shall be inserted "in the dwelling-house" and for the words "period of six months" there shall be substituted "period of 2 years"; and

(b) for the words from "the statutory tenant" onwards there shall be substituted "entitled to an assured tenancy of the dwelling-house by succession".

12. In subsection (5) for the words "subsections (1), (3) and (4)" there shall be substituted "subsections (1) and (3)" and after that subsection there shall be inserted the following subsections—

"(5A) For the purposes of subsection (3) above, a person who was living with the original occupier as his or her wife or husband shall be treated as the spouse of the original occupier and, subject to subsection (5B) below, the references in subsection (3) above to a widow and in subsection (4) above to a surviving spouse shall be construed accordingly.

(5B) If, immediately after the death of the original occupier, there is, by virtue of subsection (5A) above, more than one person who fulfils the conditions in subsection (3) above, such one of them as may be decided by agreement or, in default of agreement by the county court, shall be the statutory tenant by virtue of that subsection.

(5C) If the original occupier dies within the period of 18 months beginning on the operative date, then, for the purposes of subsection (3) above, a person who was residing in the dwelling-house with the original occupier at the time of his death and for the period which began 6 months before the operative date and ended at the time of his death shall be taken to have been residing with the original occupier for the period of 2 years immediately before his death; and in this subsection "the operative date" means the date on which Part I of the Housing Act 1988 came into force."

PART III
MODIFICATIONS OF SECTION 7 AND SCHEDULE 2

13.—(1) Subject to sub-paragraph (2) below, in relation to the assured tenancy to which the successor becomes entitled by succession, section 7 of this Act shall have effect as if in subsection (3) after the word "established" there were inserted the words "or that the circumstances are as specified in any of Cases 11, 12, 16, 17, 18 and 20 in Schedule 15 to the Rent Act 1977".

(2) Sub-paragraph (1) above does not apply if, by virtue of section 39(8) of this Act, the assured tenancy to which the successor becomes entitled is an assured agricultural occupancy.

14. If by virtue of section 39(8) of this Act, the assured tenancy to which the successor becomes entitled is an assured agricultural occupancy, section 7 of this Act shall have effect in relation to that tenancy as if in subsection (3) after the word "established" there were inserted the words "or that the circumstances are as specified in Case XI or Case XII of the Rent (Agriculture) Act 1976".

15.—(1) In relation to the assured tenancy to which the successor becomes entitled by succession, any notice given to the predecessor for the purposes of Case 13, Case 14 or Case 15 in Schedule 15 to the Rent Act 1977 shall be treated as having been given for the purposes of whichever of Grounds 3 to 5 in Schedule 2 to this Act corresponds to the Case in question.

(2) Where sub-paragraph (1) above applies, the regulated tenancy of the predecessor shall be treated, in relation to the assured tenancy of the successor, as "the earlier tenancy" for the purposes of Part IV of Schedule 2 to this Act.

Section 140. SCHEDULE 18

ENACTMENTS REPEALED

1. The repeal of sections 19 to 21 of the Rent Act 1977 does not apply with respect to any tenancy or contract entered into before the coming into force of Part I of this Act

nor to any other tenancy or contract which, having regard to section 36 of be a restricted contract.

2. The repeal of section 52 of the Housing Act 1980 (protected shorthold does not apply with respect to any tenancy entered into before the coming in Part I of this Act nor to any other tenancy which, having regard to section Act, can be a protected shorthold tenancy.

3. The repeal of sections 56 to 58 of the Housing Act 1980 does not have effect in relation to any tenancy to which, by virtue of section 37(2) of this Act, section 1(3) of this Act does not apply.

4. The repeals in section 80 of the Housing Act 1985—

(a) have effect (subject to section 35(5) of this Act) in relation to any tenancy or licence entered into before the coming into force of Part I of this Act unless, immediately before that time, the landlord or, as the case may be, the licensor is a body which, in accordance with the repeals, would cease to be within the said section 80; and

(b) do not have effect in relation to a tenancy or licence entered into on or after the coming into force of Part I of this Act if the tenancy or licence falls within any of paragraphs (c) to (f) of subsection (4) of section 35 of this Act; and

(c) do not have effect in relation to a tenancy while it is a housing association tenancy.

LAW OF PROPERTY (MISCELLANEOUS PROVISIONS) ACT 1989
(1989, c. 34)

[27 July 1989]

2. Contracts for sale etc. of land to be made by signed writing.

(1) A contract for the sale or other disposition of an interest in land can only be made in writing and only by incorporating all the terms which the parties have expressly agreed in one document or, where contracts are exchanged, in each.

(2) The terms may be incorporated in a document either by being set out in it or by reference to some other document.

(3) The document incorporating the terms or, where contracts are exchanged, one of the documents incorporating them (but not necessarily the same one) must be signed by or on behalf of each party to the contract.

(4) Where a contract for the sale or other disposition of an interest in land satisfies the conditions of this section by reason only of the rectification of one or more documents in pursuance of an order of a court, the contract shall come into being, or be deemed to have come into being, at such time as may be specified in the order.

(5) This section does not apply in relation to—

(a) a contract to grant such a lease as is mentioned in section 54(2) of the Law of Property Act 1925 (short leases);

(b) a contract made in the course of a public auction; or

(c) a contract regulated under the Financial Services Act 1986;

and nothing in this section affects the creation or operation of resulting, implied or constructive trusts.

(6) In this section—

"disposition" has the same meaning as in the Law of Property Act 1925;

"interest in land" means any estate, interest or charge in or over land or in or over the proceeds of sale of land.

(7) Nothing in this section shall apply in relation to contracts made before this section comes into force.

(8) Section 40 of the Law of Property Act 1925 (which is superseded by this section) shall cease to have effect.

LOCAL GOVERNMENT AND HOUSING ACT 1989
(1989, c. 42)

[16 November 1989]

149. Statutory references to rating.

(6) Without prejudice to the generality of the powers conferred by this section, section 37 of the Landlord and Tenant Act 1954 (which provides for compensation by reference to rateable values) shall be amended in accordance with Schedule 7 to this Act.

186. Security of tenure on ending of long residential tenancies.

(1) Schedule 10 to this Act shall have effect (in place of Part I of the Landlord and Tenant Act 1954) to confer security of tenure on certain tenants under long tenancies and, in particular, to establish assured periodic tenancies when such long tenancies come to an end.

(2) Schedule 10 to this Act applies, and section 1 of the Landlord and Tenant Act 1954 does not apply, to a tenancy of a dwelling-house—

    (a) which is a long tenancy at a low rent, as defined in Schedule 10 to this Act; and

    (b) which is entered into on or after the day appointed for the coming into force of this section, otherwise than in pursuance of a contract made before that day.

(3) If a tenancy—

    (a) is in existence on 15th January 1999, and

    (b) does not fall within subsection (2) above, and

    (c) immediately before that date was, or was deemed to be, a long tenancy at a low rent for the purposes of Part I of the Landlord and Tenant Act 1954,

then, on and after that date (and so far as concerns any notice specifying a date of termination on or after that date and any steps taken in consequence thereof), section 1 of that Act shall cease to apply to it and Schedule 10 to this Act shall apply to it unless, before that date, the landlord has served a notice under section 4 of that Act specifying a date of termination which is earlier than that date.

(4) The provisions of Schedule 10 to this Act have effect notwithstanding any agreement to the contrary, but nothing in this subsection or that Schedule shall be construed as preventing the surrender of a tenancy.

(5) Section 18 of the Landlord and Tenant Act 1954 (duty of tenants of residential property to give information to landlords or superior landlords) shall apply in relation to property comprised in a long tenancy at a low rent, within the meaning of Schedule 10 to this Act, as it applies to property comprised in a long tenancy at a low rent within the meaning of Part I of that Act, except that the reference in that section to subsection (1) of section 3 of that Act shall be construed as a reference to sub-paragraph (1) of paragraph 3 of Schedule 10 to this Act.

(6) Where, by virtue of subsection (3) above, Schedule 10 to this Act applies to a tenancy which is not a long tenancy at a low rent as defined in that Schedule, it shall be deemed to be such a tenancy for the purposes of that Schedule.

Section 149.   **SCHEDULE 7**

COMPENSATION PROVISIONS OF LANDLORD AND TENANT ACT 1954, PART II

1. Any reference in this Schedule to a section which is not otherwise identified is a reference to that section of the Landlord and Tenant Act 1954, Part II of which relates to security of tenure for business, professional and other tenants.

2.—(1) Subject to the following provisions of this Schedule, section 37 (compensation where order for new tenancy precluded on certain grounds) shall have effect with the amendments set out below.

(2)   At the beginning of subsection (2) there shall be inserted the words "Subject to subsections (5A) to (5D) of this section".

(3)   After subsection (5) there shall be inserted the following subsections—

"(5A)   If part of the holding is domestic property, as defined in section 66 of the Local Government Finance Act 1988,—

(a)   the domestic property shall be disregarded in determining the rateable value of the holding under subsection (5) of this section; and

(b)   if, on the date specified in subsection (5)(a) of this section, the tenant occupied the whole or any part of the domestic property, the amount of compensation to which he is entitled under subsection (1) of this section shall be increased by the addition of a sum equal to his reasonable expenses in removing from the domestic property.

(5B)   Any question as to the amount of the sum referred to in paragraph (b) of subsection (5A) of this section shall be determined by agreement between the landlord and the tenant or, in default of agreement, by the court.

(5C)   If the whole of the holding is domestic property, as defined in section 66 of the Local Government Finance Act 1988, for the purposes of subsection (2) of this section the rateable value of the holding shall be taken to be an amount equal to the rent at which it is estimated the holding might reasonably be expected to let from year to year if the tenant undertook to pay all usual tenant's rates and taxes and to bear the cost of the repairs and insurance and the other expenses (if any) necessary to maintain the holding in a state to command that rent.

(5D)   The following provisions shall have effect as regards a determination of an amount mentioned in subsection (5C) of this section—

(a)   the date by reference to which such a determination is to be made is the date on which the landlord's notice under section 25 or, as the case may be, subsection (6) of section 26 of this Act is given;

(b)   any dispute arising, whether in proceedings before the court or otherwise, as to such a determination shall be referred to the Commissioners of Inland Revenue for decision by a valuation officer;

(c)   an appeal shall lie to the Lands Tribunal from such a decision, but subject to that, such a decision shall be final."

(4)   At the end of subsection (8) (definition of "the appropriate multiplier") there shall be added the words "and different multipliers may be so prescribed in relation to different cases".

3.   The amendments made by paragraph 2 above do not have effect unless the date which, apart from paragraph 4 below, is relevant for determining the rateable value of the holding under subsection (5) of section 37 is on or after 1st April 1990.

4.—(1)   Subject to paragraph 3 above and paragraph 5 below, in any case where—

(a)   the tenancy concerned was entered into before 1st April 1990 or was entered into on or after that date in pursuance of a contract made before that date, and

(b)   the landlord's notice under section 25 or, as the case may be, section 26(6) is given before 1st April 2000, and

(c)   within the period referred to in section 29(3) for the making of an application under section 24(1), the tenant gives notice to the landlord that he wants the special basis of compensation provided for by this paragraph,

the amendments made by paragraph 2 above shall not have effect and section 37 shall, instead, have effect with the modification specified in sub-paragraph (2) below.

(2)   The modification referred to in sub-paragraph (1) above is that the date which is relevant for the purposes of determining the rateable value of the holding under subsection (5) of section 37 shall be 31st March 1990 instead of the date on which the landlord's notice is given.

5.   In any case where—

(a)   paragraph 4(1)(a) above applies, and

(b)   on 31 March 1990, the rateable value of the holding could be determined only in accordance with paragraph (c) of subsection (5) of section 37, no notice may be given under paragraph 4(1)(b) above.

Section 186.   SCHEDULE 10

SECURITY OF TENURE ON ENDING OF LONG RESIDENTIAL TENANCIES

Preliminary

1.—(1)   This Schedule applies to a long tenancy of a dwelling-house at a low rent as respects which for the time being the following condition (in this Schedule referred to as "the qualifying condition") is fulfilled, that is to say, that the circumstances (as respects the property let under the tenancy, the use of that property and all other relevant matters) are such that, if the tenancy were not at a low rent, it would at that time be an assured tenancy within the meaning of Part I of the Housing Act 1988.

(2)   For the purpose only of determining whether the qualifying condition is fulfilled with respect to a tenancy, Schedule 1 to the Housing Act 1988 (tenancies which cannot be assured tenancies) shall have effect with the omission of paragraph 1 (which excludes tenancies entered into before, or pursuant to contracts made before, the coming into force of Part I of that Act).

(2A)   For the purpose only of determining whether the qualifying condition is fulfilled with respect to a tenancy which is entered into on or after 1st April 1990 (otherwise than, where the dwelling-house has a rateable value on 31st March 1990, in pursuance of a contract made before 1st April 1990), for paragraph 2(1)(b) and (2) of Schedule 1 to the Housing Act 1988 there shall be substituted—

"(b)   where (on the date the contract for the grant of the tenancy was made or, if there was no such contract, on the date the tenancy was entered into) R exceeded £25,000 under the formula—

$$R = \frac{P \times I}{1 - (1 + I)^{-T}}$$

where—

P is the premium payable as a condition of the grant of the tenancy (and includes a payment of money's worth) or, where no premium is so payable, zero,

I is 0.06,

T is the term, expressed in years, granted by the tenancy (disregarding any right to terminate the tenancy before the end of the term or to extend the tenancy)."

(3)   At any time within the period of twelve months ending on the day preceding the term date, application may be made to the court as respects any long tenancy of a dwelling-house at a low rent, not being at the time of the application a tenancy as respects which the qualifying condition is fulfilled, for an order declaring that the tenancy is not to be treated as a tenancy to which this Schedule applies.

(4)   Where an application is made under sub-paragraph (3) above—

(a)   the court, if satisfied that the tenancy is not likely immediately before the term date to be a tenancy to which this Schedule applies but not otherwise, shall make the order; and

(b)   if the court makes the order, then, notwithstanding anything in sub-paragraph (1) above the tenancy shall not thereafter be treated as a tenancy to which this Schedule applies.

(5)   A tenancy to which this Schedule applies is hereinafter referred to as a long residential tenancy.

(6) Anything authorised or required to be done under the following provisions of this Schedule in relation to a long residential tenancy shall, if done before the term date in relation to a long tenancy of a dwelling-house at a low rent, not be treated as invalid by reason only that at the time at which it was done the qualifying condition was not fulfilled as respects the tenancy.

(7) In determining for the purposes of any provision of this Schedule whether the property let under a tenancy was let as a separate dwelling, the nature of the property at the time of the creation of the tenancy shall be deemed to have been the same as its nature at the time in relation to which the question arises, and the purpose for which it was let under the tenancy shall be deemed to have been the same as the purpose for which it is or was used at the last-mentioned time.

(8) The Secretary of State may by order replace the number in the definition of "I" in sub-paragraph (2A) above and any amount referred to in that sub-paragraph and paragraph 2(4)(b) below by such number or amount as is specified in the order; and such an order shall be made by statutory instrument which shall be subject to annulment in pursuance of a resolution of either House of Parliament.

2.—(1) This paragraph has effect for the interpretation of certain expressions used in this Schedule.

(2) Except where the context otherwise requires, expressions to which a meaning is assigned for the purposes of the 1988 Act or Part I of that Act have the same meaning in this Schedule.

(3) "Long tenancy" means a tenancy granted for a term of years certain exceeding 21 years, whether or not subsequently extended by act of the parties or by any enactment, but excluding any tenancy which is, or may become, terminable before the end of the term by notice given to the tenant.

(4) A tenancy is "at a low rent" if under the tenancy—
  (a) no rent is payable,
  (b) where the tenancy is entered into on or after 1st April 1990 (otherwise than, where the dwelling-house had a rateable value on 31st March 1990, in pursuance of a contract made before 1st April 1990), the maximum rent payable at any time is payable at a rate of—
    (i) £1,000 or less a year if the dwelling-house is in Greater London and,
    (ii) £250 or less a year if the dwelling-house is elsewhere, or,
  (c) where the tenancy was entered into before 1st April 1990 or (where the dwelling-house had a rateable value on 31st March 1990) is entered into on or after 1st April 1990 in pursuance of a contract made before that date, and the maximum rent payable at any time under the tenancy is less than two-thirds of the rateable value of the dwelling-house on 31st March 1990.

(5) Paragraph 2(2) of Schedule 1 to the 1988 Act applies to determine whether the rent under a tenancy falls within sub-paragraph (4) above and Part II of that Schedule applies to determine the rateable value of a dwelling-house for the purposes of that sub-paragraph.

(6) "Long residential tenancy" and "qualifying condition" have the meaning assigned by paragraph 1 above and the following expressions shall be construed as follows—
  "the 1954 Act" means the Landlord and Tenant Act 1954;
  "the 1988 Act" means the Housing Act 1988;
  "assured periodic tenancy" shall be construed in accordance with paragraph 9(4) below;
  "the date of termination" has the meaning assigned by paragraph 4(4) below;
  "disputed terms" shall be construed in accordance with paragraph 11(1)(a) below;
  "election by the tenant to retain possession" shall be construed in accordance with paragraph 4(7) below;

"former 1954 Act tenancy" means a tenancy to which, by virtue of section 186(3) of this Act, this Schedule applies on and after 15th January 1999;

"the implied terms" shall be construed in accordance with paragraph 4(5)(a) below;

"landlord" shall be construed in accordance with paragraph 19(1) below;

"landlord's notice" means a notice under sub-paragraph (1) of paragraph 4 below and such a notice is—

(a)   a "landlord's notice proposing an assured tenancy" if it contains such proposals as are mentioned in sub-paragraph (5)(a) of that paragraph; and

(b)   a "landlord's notice to resume possession" if it contains such proposals as are referred to in sub-paragraph (5)(b) of that paragraph;

"specified date of termination", in relation to a tenancy in respect of which a landlord's notice is served, means the date specified in the notice as mentioned in paragraph 4(1)(a) below;

"tenant's notice" shall be construed in accordance with paragraph 10(1)(a) below;

"term date", in relation to a tenancy granted for a term of years certain, means the date of expiry of that term; and

"the terms of the tenancy specified in the landlord's notice" shall be construed in accordance with paragraph 4(6) below; and

"undisputed terms" shall be construed in accordance with paragraph 11(2) below.

Continuation of long residential tenancies

3.—(1)   A tenancy which, immediately before the term date, is a long residential tenancy shall not come to an end on that date except by being terminated under the provisions of this Schedule, and, if not then so terminated, shall subject to those provisions continue until so terminated and, while continuing by virtue of this paragraph, shall be deemed to be a long residential tenancy (notwithstanding any change in circumstances).

(2)   Sub-paragraph (1) above does not apply in the case of a former 1954 Act tenancy the term date of which falls before 15th January 1999 but if, in the case of such a tenancy,—

(a)   the tenancy is continuing immediately before that date by virtue of section 3 of the 1954 Act, and

(b)   on that date the qualifying condition (as defined in paragraph 1(1) above) is fulfilled, then, subject to the provisions of this Schedule, the tenancy shall continue until terminated under those provisions and, while continuing by virtue of this paragraph, shall be deemed to be a long residential tenancy (notwithstanding any change in circumstances).

(3)   Where by virtue of this paragraph a tenancy continues after the term date, the tenancy shall continue at the same rent and in other respects on the same terms as before the term date.

Termination of tenancy by the landlord

4.—(1)   Subject to sub-paragraph (2) below and the provisions of this Schedule as to the annulment of notices in certain cases, the landlord may terminate a long residential tenancy by a notice in the prescribed form served on the tenant—

(a)   specifying the date at which the tenancy is to come to an end, being either the term date or a later date; and

(b)   so served not more than twelve nor less than six months before the date so specified.

(2)   In any case where—

(a)   a landlord's notice has been served, and

(b)   an application has been made to the court or a rent assessment committee under the following provisions of this Schedule other than paragraph 6, and

    (c)   apart from this paragraph, the effect of the notice would be to terminate the tenancy before the expiry of the period of three months beginning with the date on which the application is finally disposed of,

the effect of the notice shall be to terminate the tenancy at the expiry of the said period of three months and not at any other time.

    (3)   The reference in sub-paragraph (2)(c) above to the date on which the application is finally disposed of shall be construed as a reference to the earliest date by which the proceedings on the application (including any proceedings on or in consequence of an appeal) have been determined and any time for appealing or further appealing has expired, except that if the application is withdrawn or any appeal is abandoned the reference shall be construed as a reference to the date of withdrawal or abandonment.

    (4)   In this Schedule "the date of termination", in relation to a tenancy in respect of which a landlord's notice is served, means,—

    (a)   where the tenancy is continued as mentioned in sub-paragraph (2) above, the last day of the period of three months referred to in that sub-paragraph; and

    (b)   in any other case, the specified date of termination.

    (5)   A landlord's notice shall not have effect unless—

    (a)   it proposes an assured monthly periodic tenancy of the dwelling-house and a rent for that tenancy (such that it would not be a tenancy at a low rent) and, subject to sub-paragraph (6) below, states that the other terms of the tenancy shall be the same as those of the long residential tenancy immediately before it is terminated (in this Schedule referred to as "the implied terms"); or

    (b)   it gives notice that, if the tenant is not willing to give up possession at the date of termination of the property let under the tenancy, the landlord proposes to apply to the court, on one or more of the grounds specified in paragraph 5(1) below, for the possession of the property let under the tenancy and states the ground or grounds on which he proposes to apply.

    (6)   In the landlord's notice proposing an assured tenancy the landlord may propose terms of the tenancy referred to in sub-paragraph (5)(a) above different from the implied terms; and any reference in the following provisions of this Schedule to the terms of the tenancy specified in the landlord's notice is a reference to the implied terms or, if the implied terms are varied by virtue of this sub-paragraph, to the implied terms as so varied.

    (7)   A landlord's notice shall invite the tenant, within the period of two months beginning on the date on which the notice was served, to notify the landlord in writing whether,—

    (a)   in the case of a landlord's notice proposing an assured tenancy, the tenant wishes to remain in possession; and

    (b)   in the case of a landlord's notice to resume possession, the tenant is willing to give up possession as mentioned in sub-paragraph (5)(b) above;

and references in this Schedule to an election by the tenant to retain possession are references to his notifying the landlord under this sub-paragraph that he wishes to remain in possession or, as the case may be, that he is not willing to give up possession.

    5.—(1)   Subject to the following provisions of this paragraph, the grounds mentioned in paragraph 4(5)(b) above are—

    (a)   Ground 6 in, and those in Part II of, Schedule 2 to the 1988 Act, other than Ground 16;

    (b)   the ground that, for the purposes of redevelopment after the termination of the tenancy, the landlord proposes to demolish or reconstruct the whole or a substantial part of the premises; and

    (c)   the ground that the premises or part of them are reasonably required by the landlord for occupation as a residence for himself or any son or daughter of his over eighteen years of age or his or his spouse's father or mother and, if the landlord is not the immediate landlord, that he will be at the specified date of termination.

(2) Ground 6 in Schedule 2 to the 1988 Act may not be specified in a landlord's notice to resume possession if the tenancy is a former 1954 Act tenancy; and in the application of that Ground in accordance with sub-paragraph (1) above in any other case, paragraph (c) shall be omitted.

(3) In its application in accordance with sub-paragraph (1) above, Ground 10 in Schedule 2 to the 1988 Act shall have effect as if, in paragraph (b)—

(a) the words "except where subsection (1)(b) of section 8 of this Act applies" were omitted; and

(b) for the words "notice under that section relating to those proceedings" there were substituted "landlord's notice to resume possession (within the meaning of Schedule 10 to the Local Government and Housing Act 1989)".

(4) The ground mentioned in sub-paragraph (1)(b) above may not be specified in a landlord's notice to resume possession unless the landlord is a body to which section 28 of the Leasehold Reform Act 1967 applies and the premises are required for relevant development within the meaning of that section; and on any application by such a body under paragraph 13 below for possession on that ground, a certificate given by a Minister of the Crown as provided by subsection (1) of that section shall be conclusive evidence that the premises are so required.

(5) The ground mentioned in sub-paragraph (1)(c) above may not be specified in a landlord's notice to resume possession if the interest of the landlord, or an interest which is merged in that interest and but for the merger would be the interest of the landlord, was purchased or created after 18th February 1966.

Interim rent

6.—(1) On the date of service of a landlord's notice proposing an assured tenancy, or at any time between that date and the date of termination, the landlord may serve a notice on the tenant in the prescribed form proposing an interim monthly rent to take effect from a date specified in the notice, being not earlier than the specified date of termination, and to continue while the tenancy is continued by virtue of the preceding provisions of this Schedule.

(2) Where a notice has been served under sub-paragraph (1) above,—

(a) within the period of two months beginning on the date of service, the tenant may refer the interim monthly rent proposed in the notice to a rent assessment committee; and

(b) if the notice is not so referred, then, with effect from the date specified in the notice or, if it is later, the expiry of the period mentioned in paragraph (a) above, the interim monthly rent proposed in the notice shall be the rent under the tenancy.

(3) Where, under sub-paragraph (2) above, the rent specified in a landlord's notice is referred to a rent assessment committee, the committee shall determine the monthly rent at which, subject to sub-paragraph (4) below, the committee consider that the premises let under the tenancy might reasonably be expected to be let on the open market by a willing landlord under a monthly periodic tenancy—

(a) which begins on the day following the specified date of termination;

(b) under which the other terms are the same as those of the existing tenancy at the date on which was given the landlord's notice proposing an assured tenancy; and

(c) which affords the tenant security of tenure equivalent to that afforded by Chapter I of Part I of the 1988 Act in the case of an assured tenancy (other than an assured shorthold tenancy) in respect of which possession may not be recovered under any of Grounds 1 to 5 in Part I of Schedule 2 to that Act.

(4) Subsections (2), (4) and (5) of section 14 of the 1988 Act shall apply in relation to a determination of rent under sub-paragraph (3) above as they apply in relation to a

determination under that section subject to the modifications in sub-paragraph (5) below; and in this paragraph "rent" shall be construed in accordance with subsection (4) of that section.

(5)   The modifications of section 14 of the 1988 Act referred to in sub-paragraph (4) above are that in subsection (2), the reference in paragraph (b) to a relevant improvement being carried out shall be construed as a reference to an improvement being carried out during the long residential tenancy and the reference in paragraph (c) to a failure to comply with any term of the tenancy shall be construed as a reference to a failure to comply with any term of the long residential tenancy.

(6)   Where a reference has been made to a rent assessment committee under sub-paragraph (2) above, then, the rent determined by the committee (subject, in a case where section 14(5) of the 1988 Act applies, to the addition of the appropriate amount in respect of rates) shall be the rent under the tenancy with effect from the date specified in the notice served under sub-paragraph (1) above or, if it is later, the expiry of the period mentioned in paragraph (a) of sub-paragraph (2) above.

7.—(1)   Nothing in paragraph 6 above affects the right of the landlord and the tenant to agree the interim monthly rent which is to have effect while the tenancy is continued by virtue of the preceding provisions of this Schedule and the date from which that rent is to take effect; and, in such a case,—

(a)   notwithstanding the provisions of paragraph 6 above, that rent shall be the rent under the tenancy with effect from that date; and

(b)   no steps or, as the case may be, no further steps may be taken by the landlord or the tenant under the provisions of that paragraph.

(2)   Nothing in paragraph 6 above requires a rent assessment committee to continue with a determination under sub-paragraph (3) of that paragraph—

(a)   if the tenant gives notice in writing that he no longer requires such a determination; or

(b)   if the long residential tenancy has come to an end on or before the specified date of termination.

(3)   Notwithstanding that a tenancy in respect of which an interim monthly rent has effect in accordance with paragraph 6 above or this paragraph is no longer at a low rent, it shall continue to be regarded as a tenancy at a low rent and, accordingly, shall continue to be a long residential tenancy.

Termination of tenancy by the tenant

8.—(1)   A long residential tenancy may be brought to an end at the term date by not less than one month's notice in writing given by the tenant to his immediate landlord.

(2)   A tenancy which is continuing after the term date by virtue of paragraph 3 above may be brought to an end at any time by not less than one month's notice in writing given by the tenant to his immediate landlord, whether the notice is given before or after the term date of the tenancy.

(3)   The fact that the landlord has served a landlord's notice or that there has been an election by the tenant to retain possession shall not prevent the tenant from giving notice under this paragraph terminating the tenancy at a date earlier than the specified date of termination.

The assured periodic tenancy

9.—(1)   Where a long residential tenancy (in this paragraph referred to as "the former tenancy") is terminated by a landlord's notice proposing an assured tenancy, then, subject to sub-paragraph (3) below, the tenant shall be entitled to remain in possession of the dwelling-house and his right to possession shall depend upon an assured periodic tenancy arising by virtue of this paragraph.

(2)   The assured periodic tenancy referred to in sub-paragraph (1) above is one—

(a) taking effect in possession on the day following the date of termination;

(b) deemed to have been granted by the person who was the landlord under the former tenancy on the date of termination to the person who was then the tenant under that tenancy;

(c) under which the premises let are the dwelling-house;

(d) under which the periods of the tenancy, and the intervals at which rent is to be paid, are monthly beginning on the day following the date of termination;

(e) under which the rent is determined in accordance with paragraphs 10 to 12 below; and

(f) under which the other terms are determined in accordance with paragraphs 10 to 12 below.

(3) If, at the end of the period of two months beginning on the date of service of the landlord's notice, the qualifying condition was not fulfilled as respects the tenancy, the tenant shall not be entitled to remain in possession as mentioned in sub-paragraph (1) above unless there has been an election by the tenant to retain possession; and if, at the specified date of termination, the qualifying condition is not fulfilled as respects the tenancy, then, notwithstanding that there has been such an election, the tenant shall not be entitled to remain in possession as mentioned in that sub-paragraph.

(4) Any reference in the following provisions of this Schedule to an assured periodic tenancy is a reference to an assured periodic tenancy arising by virtue of this paragraph.

Initial rent under and terms of assured periodic tenancy

10.—(1) Where a landlord's notice proposing an assured tenancy has been served on the tenant,—

(a) within the period of two months beginning on the date of service of the notice, the tenant may serve on the landlord a notice in the prescribed form proposing either or both of the following, that is to say,—

(i) a rent for the assured periodic tenancy different from that proposed in the landlord's notice; and

(ii) terms of the tenancy different from those specified in the landlord's notice, and such a notice is in this Schedule referred to as a "tenant's notice"; and

(b) if a tenant's notice is not so served, then, with effect from the date on which the assured periodic tenancy takes effect in possession,—

(i) the rent proposed in the landlord's notice shall be the rent under the tenancy; and

(ii) the terms of the tenancy specified in the landlord's notice shall be terms of the tenancy.

(2) Where a tenant's notice has been served on the landlord under sub-paragraph (1) above—

(a) within the period of two months beginning on the date of service of the notice, the landlord may by an application in the prescribed form refer the notice to a rent assessment committee; and

(b) if the notice is not so referred, then, with effect from the date on which the assured periodic tenancy takes effect in possession,—

(i) the rent (if any) proposed in the tenant's notice, or, if no rent is so proposed, the rent proposed in the landlord's notice, shall be the rent under the tenancy; and

(ii) the other terms of the tenancy (if any) proposed in the tenant's notice and, in so far as they do not conflict with the terms so proposed, the terms specified in the landlord's notice shall be terms of the tenancy.

11.—(1) Where, under sub-paragraph (2) of paragraph 10 above, a tenant's notice is referred to a rent assessment committee, the committee, having regard only to the contents of the landlord's notice and the tenant's notice, shall decide—

(a) whether there is any dispute as to the terms (other than those relating to the amount of the rent) of the assured periodic tenancy (in this Schedule referred to as "disputed terms") and, if so, what the disputed terms are; and

(b)   whether there is any dispute as to rent under the tenancy;

and where the committee decide that there are disputed terms and that there is a dispute as to the rent under the tenancy, they shall make a determination under sub-paragraph (3) below before they make a determination under sub-paragraph (5) below.

(2)   Where, under paragraph 10(2) above, a tenant's notice is referred to a rent assessment committee, any reference in this Schedule to the undisputed terms is a reference to those terms (if any) which—

(a)   are proposed in the landlord's notice or the tenant's notice; and

(b)   do not relate to the amount of the rent; and

(c)   are not disputed terms.

(3)   If the rent assessment committee decide that there are disputed terms, they shall determine whether the terms in the landlord's notice, the terms in the tenant's notice, or some other terms, dealing with the same subject matter as the disputed terms are such as, in the committee's opinion, might reasonably be expected to be found in an assured monthly periodic tenancy of the dwelling-house (not being an assured shorthold tenancy)—

(a)   which begins on the day following the date of termination;

(b)   which is granted by a willing landlord on terms which, except so far as they relate to the subject matter of the disputed terms, are the undisputed terms; and

(c)   in respect of which possession may not be recovered under any of Grounds 1 to 5 in Part I of Schedule 2 to the 1988 Act;

and the committee shall, if they consider it appropriate, specify an adjustment of the undisputed terms to take account of the terms so determined and shall, if they consider it appropriate, specify an adjustment of the rent to take account of the terms so determined and, if applicable, so adjusted.

(4)   In making a determination under sub-paragraph (3) above, or specifying an adjustment of the rent or undisputed terms under that sub-paragraph, there shall be disregarded any effect on the terms or the amount of rent attributable to the granting of a tenancy to a sitting tenant.

(5)   If the rent assessment committee decide that there is a dispute as to the rent under the assured periodic tenancy, the committee shall determine the monthly rent at which, subject to sub-paragraph (6) below, the committee consider that the dwelling-house might reasonably be expected to be let in the open market by a willing landlord under an assured tenancy (not being an assured shorthold tenancy)—

(a)   which is a monthly periodic tenancy;

(b)   which begins on the day following the date of termination;

(c)   in respect of which possession may not be recovered under any of Grounds 1 to 5 in Part I of Schedule 2 to the 1988 Act; and

(d)   the terms of which (other than those relating to the amount of the rent) are the same as—

(i)   the undisputed terms; or

(ii)   if there has been a determination under sub-paragraph (3) above, the terms determined by the committee under that sub-paragraph and the undisputed terms (as adjusted, if at all, under that sub-paragraph).

(6)   Subsections (2), (4) and (5) of section 14 of the 1988 Act shall apply in relation to a determination of rent under sub-paragraph (5) above as they apply in relation to a determination under that section subject to the modifications in sub-paragraph (7) below; and in this paragraph "rent" shall be construed in accordance with subsection (4) of that section.

(7)   The modifications of section 14 of the 1988 Act referred to in sub-paragraph (6) above are that in subsection (2), the reference in paragraph (b) to a relevant

improvement being carried out shall be construed as a reference to an improvement being carried out during the long residential tenancy and the reference in paragraph (c) to a failure to comply with any term of the tenancy shall be construed as a reference to a failure to comply with any term of the long residential tenancy.

(8) Where a reference has been made to a rent assessment committee under sub-paragraph (2) of paragraph 10 above, then,—

(a) if the committee decide that there are no disputed terms and that there is no dispute as to the rent, paragraph 10(2)(b) above shall apply as if the notice had not been so referred,

(b) where paragraph (a) above does not apply then, so far as concerns the amount of the rent under the tenancy, if there is a dispute as to the rent, the rent determined by the committee (subject, in a case where section 14(5) of the 1988 Act applies, to the addition of the appropriate amount in respect of rates) and, if there is no dispute as to the rent, the rent specified in the landlord's notice or, as the case may be, the tenant's notice (subject to any adjustment under sub-paragraph (3) above) shall be the rent under the tenancy, and

(c) where paragraph (a) above does not apply and there are disputed terms, then, so far as concerns the subject matter of those terms, the terms determined by the committee under sub-paragraph (3) above shall be terms of the tenancy and, so far as concerns any undisputed terms, those terms (subject to any adjustment under sub-paragraph (3) above) shall also be terms of the tenancy,

with effect from the date on which the assured periodic tenancy takes effect in possession.

(9) Nothing in this Schedule affects the right of the landlord and the tenant under the assured periodic tenancy to vary by agreement any term of the tenancy (including a term relating to rent).

12.—(1) Subsections (2) to (4) of section 41 of the 1988 Act (rent assessment committees: information powers) shall apply where there is a reference to a rent assessment committee under the preceding provisions of this Schedule as they apply where a matter is referred to such a committee under Chapter I or Chapter II of Part I of the 1988 Act.

(2) Nothing in paragraph 10 or paragraph 11 above affects the right of the landlord and the tenant to agree any terms of the assured periodic tenancy (including a term relating to the rent) before the tenancy takes effect in possession (in this sub-paragraph referred to as "the expressly agreed terms"); and, in such case,—

(a) the expressly agreed terms shall be terms of the tenancy in substitution for any terms dealing with the same subject matter which would otherwise, by virtue of paragraph 10 or paragraph 11 above, be terms of the tenancy; and

(b) where a reference has already been made to a rent assessment committee under sub-paragraph (2) of paragraph 10 above but there has been no determination by the committee under paragraph 11 above,—

(i) the committee shall have regard to the expressly agreed terms, as notified to them by the landlord and the tenant, in deciding, for the purposes of paragraph 11 above, what the disputed terms are and whether there is any dispute as to the rent; and

(ii) in making any determination under paragraph 11 above the committee shall not make any adjustment of the expressly agreed terms, as so notified.

(3) Nothing in paragraph 11 above requires a rent assessment committee to continue with a determination under that paragraph—

(a) if the long residential tenancy has come to an end; or

(b) if the landlord serves notice in writing on the committee that he no longer requires such a determination;

and, where the landlord serves notice as mentioned in paragraph (b) above, then, for the purposes of sub-paragraph (2) of paragraph 10 above, the landlord shall be treated as not having made a reference under paragraph (a) of that sub-paragraph and, accordingly, paragraph (b) of that sub-paragraph shall, subject to sub-paragraph (2) above, have effect for determining rent and other terms of the assured periodic tenancy.

Landlord's application for possession

13.—(1) Where a landlord's notice to resume possession has been served on the tenant and either—

(a) there is an election by the tenant to retain possession, or

(b) at the end of the period of two months beginning on the date of service of the notice, the qualifying condition is fulfilled as respects the tenancy, the landlord may apply to the court for an order under this paragraph on such of the grounds mentioned in paragraph 5(1) above as may be specified in the notice.

(2) The court shall not entertain an application under sub-paragraph (1) above unless the application is made—

(a) within the period of two months beginning on the date of the election by the tenant to retain possession; or

(b) if there is no election by the tenant to retain possession, within the period of four months beginning on the date of service of the landlord's notice.

(3) Where the ground or one of the grounds for claiming possession specified in the landlord's notice is Ground 6 in Part I of Schedule 2 to the 1988 Act, then, if on an application made under sub-paragraph (1) above the court is satisfied that the landlord has established that ground, the court shall order that the tenant shall, on the date of termination, give up possession of the property then let under the tenancy.

(4) Subject to sub-paragraph (6) below, where the ground or one of the grounds for claiming possession specified in the landlord's notice is any of Grounds 9 to 15 in Part II of Schedule 2 to the 1988 Act or the ground mentioned in paragraph 5(1)(c) above, then, if on an application made under sub-paragraph (1) above the court is satisfied that the landlord has established that ground and that it is reasonable that the landlord should be granted possession, the court shall order that the tenant shall, on the date of termination, give up possession of the property then let under the tenancy.

(5) Part III of Schedule 2 to the 1988 Act shall have effect for supplementing Ground 9 in that Schedule (as that ground applies in relation to this Schedule) as it has effect for supplementing that ground for the purposes of that Act, subject to the modification that in paragraph 3(1), in the words following paragraph (b) the reference to the assured tenancy in question shall be construed as a reference to the long residential tenancy in question.

(6) Where the ground or one of the grounds for claiming possession specified in the landlord's notice is that mentioned in paragraph 5(1)(c) above, the court shall not make the order mentioned in sub-paragraph (4) above on that ground if it is satisfied that, having regard to all the circumstances of the case, including the question whether other accommodation is available for the landlord or the tenant, greater hardship would be caused by making the order than by refusing to make it.

(7) Where the ground or one of the grounds for claiming possession specified in the landlord's notice is that mentioned in paragraph 5(1)(b) above, then, if on an application made under sub-paragraph (1) above the court is satisfied that the landlord has established that ground and is further satisfied—

(a) that on that ground possession of those premises will be required by the landlord on the date of termination, and

(b) that the landlord has made such preparations (including the obtaining or, if that is not reasonably practicable in the circumstances, preparations relating to the obtaining of any requisite permission or consent, whether from any authority whose permission or consent is required under any enactment or from the owner of any interest

in any property) for proceeding with the redevelopment as are reasonable in the circumstances.
the court shall order that the tenant shall, on the date of termination, give up possession of the property then let under the tenancy.

14.—(1) Where, in a case falling within sub-paragraph (7) of paragraph 13 above, the court is not satisfied as mentioned in that sub-paragraph but would be satisfied if the date of termination of the tenancy had been such date (in this paragraph referred to as "the postponed date") as the court may determine, being a date later, but not more than one year later, than the specified date of termination, the court shall, if the landlord so requires, make an order as mentioned in sub-paragraph (2) below.

(2) The order referred to in sub-paragraph (1) above is one by which the court specifies the postponed date and orders—

(a) that the tenancy shall not come to an end on the date of termination but shall continue thereafter, as respects the whole of the property let under the tenancy, at the same rent and in other respects on the same terms as before that date; and

(b) that, unless the tenancy comes to an end before the postponed date, the tenant shall on that date give up possession of the property then let under the tenancy.

(3) Notwithstanding the provisions of paragraph 13 above and the preceeding provisions of this paragraph and notwithstanding that there has been an election by the tenant to retain possession, if the court is satisfied, at the date of the hearing, that the qualifying condition is not fulfilled as respects the tenancy, the court shall order that the tenant shall, on the date of termination, give up possession of the property then let under the tenancy.

(4) Nothing in paragraph 13 above or the preceding provisions of this paragraph shall prejudice any power of the tenant under paragraph 8 above to terminate the tenancy; and sub-paragraph (2) of that paragraph shall apply where the tenancy is continued by an order under sub-paragraph (2) above as it applies where the tenancy is continued by virtue of paragraph 3 above.

Provisions where tenant not ordered to give up possession

15.—(1) The provisions of this paragraph shall have effect where the landlord is entitled to make an application under sub-paragraph (1) of paragraph 13 above but does not obtain an order under that paragraph or paragraph 14 above.

(2) If at the expiration of the period within which an application under paragraph 13(1) above may be made the landlord has not made such an application, the landlord's notice to resume possession, and anything done in pursuance thereof, shall cease to have effect.

(3) If before the expiration of the period mentioned in sub-paragraph (2) above the landlord has made an application under paragraph 13(1) above but the result of the application, at the time when it is finally disposed of, is that no order is made, the landlord's notice to resume possession shall cease to have effect.

(4) In any case where sub-paragraph (3) above applies, then, if within the period of one month beginning on the date that the application to the court is finally disposed of the landlord serves on the tenant a landlord's notice proposing an assured tenancy, the earliest date which may be specified in the notice as the date of termination shall, notwithstanding any thing in paragraph 4(1)(b) above, be the day following the last day of the period of four months beginning on the date of service of the subsequent notice.

(5) The reference in sub-paragraphs (3) and (4) above to the time at which an application is finally disposed of shall be construed as a reference to the earliest time at which the proceedings on the application (including any proceedings on or in consequence of an appeal) have been determined and any time for appealing or further appealing has expired, except that if the application is withdrawn or any appeal is

abandoned the reference shall be construed as a reference to the time of withdrawal or abandonment.

(6) A landlord's notice to resume possession may be withdrawn at any time by notice in writing served on the tenant (without prejudice, however, to the power of the court to make an order as to costs if the notice is withdrawn after the landlord has made an application under paragraph 13(1) above).

(7) In any case where sub-paragraph (6) above applies, then, if within the period of one month beginning on the date of withdrawal of the landlord's notice to resume possession the landlord serves on the tenant a landlord's notice proposing an assured tenancy, the earliest date which may be specified in the notice as the date of termination shall, notwithstanding anything in paragraph 4(1)(b) above, be the day following the last day of the period of four months beginning on the date of service of the subsequent notice or the day following the last day of the period of six months beginning on the date of service of the withdrawn notice, whichever is the later.

Tenancies granted in continuation of long tenancies

16.—(1) Where on the coming to the end of a tenancy at a low rent the person who was the tenant immediately before the coming to an end thereof becomes (whether by grant or by implication of the law) the tenant under another tenancy at a low rent of a dwelling-house which consists of the whole or any part of the property let under the previous tenancy, then, if the previous tenancy was a long tenancy or is deemed by virtue of this paragraph to have been a long tenancy, the new tenancy shall be deemed for the purposes of this Schedule to be a long tenancy, irrespective of its terms.

(2) In relation to a tenancy from year to year or other tenancy not granted for a term of years certain, being a tenancy which by virtue of sub-paragraph (1) above is deemed for the purposes of this Schedule to be a long tenancy, the preceding provisions of this Schedule shall have effect subject to the modifications set out below.

(3) In sub-paragraph (6) of paragraph 2 above for the expression beginning "term date" there shall be substituted—

"'term date', in relation to any such tenancy as is mentioned in paragraph 16(2) below, means the first date after the coming into force of this Schedule on which, apart from this Schedule, the tenancy could have been brought to an end by notice to quit given by the landlord".

(4) Notwithstanding anything in sub-paragraph (3) of paragraph 3 above, where by virtue of that paragraph the tenancy is continued after the term date, the provisions of this Schedule as to the termination of a tenancy by notice shall have effect, subject to sub-paragraph (5) below, in substitution for and not in addition to any such provisions included in the terms on which the tenancy had effect before the term date.

(5) The minimum period of notice referred to in paragraph 8(1) above shall be one month or such longer period as the tenant would have been required to give to bring the tenancy to an end at the term date.

(6) Where the tenancy is not terminated under paragraph 4 or paragraph 8 above at the term date, then, whether or not it would have continued after that date apart from the provisions of this Schedule, it shall be treated for the purposes of those provisions as being continued by virtue of paragraph 3 above.

Agreements as to the grant of new tenancies

17. In any case where, prior to the date of termination of a long residential tenancy, the landlord and the tenant agree for the grant to the tenant of a future tenancy of the whole or part of the property let under the tenancy at a rent other than a low rent and on terms and from a date specified in the agreement, the tenancy shall continue until that date but no longer; and, in such a case, the provisions of this Schedule shall cease to apply in relation to the tenancy with effect from the date of the agreement.

Assumptions on which to determine future questions

18.   Where under this Schedule any question falls to be determined by the court or a rent assessment committee by reference to circumstances at a future date, the court or committee shall have regard to all rights, interests and obligations under or relating to the tenancy as they subsist at the time of the determination and to all relevant circumstances as those then subsist and shall assume, except in so far as the contrary is shown, that those rights, interests, obligations and circumstances will continue to subsist unchanged until that future date.

Landlords and mortgagees in possession

19.—(1)   Section 21 of the 1954 Act (meaning of "the landlord" and provisions as to mesne landlords) shall apply in relation to this Schedule as it applies in relation to Part I of that Act but subject to the following modifications—

(a)   any reference to Part I of that Act shall be construed as a reference to this Schedule; and

(b)   subsection (4) (which relates to statutory tenancies arising under that Part) shall be omitted.

(2)   Section 67 of the 1954 Act (mortgagees in possession) applies for the purposes of this Schedule except that for the reference to that Act there shall be substituted a reference to this Schedule.

(3)   In accordance with sub-paragraph (1) above, Schedule 5 to the 1954 Act shall also apply for the purpose of this Schedule but subject to the following modifications—

(a)   any reference to Part I of the 1954 Act shall be construed as a reference to the provisions of this Schedule (other than this sub-paragraph);

(b)   any reference to section 21 of the 1954 Act shall be construed as a reference to that section as it applies in relation to this Schedule;

(c)   any reference to subsection (1) of section 4 of that Act shall be construed as a reference to sub-paragraph (1) of paragraph 4 above;

(d)   any reference to the court includes a reference to a rent assessment committee;

(e)   paragraphs 6 to 8 and 11 shall be omitted;

(f)   any reference to a particular subsection of section 16 of the 1954 Act shall be construed as a reference to that subsection as it applies in relation to this Schedule;

(g)   any reference to a tenancy to which section 1 of the 1954 Act applies shall be construed as a reference to a long residential tenancy; and

(h)   expressions to which a meaning is assigned by any provision of this Schedule (other than this sub-paragraph) shall be given that meaning.

Application of other provisions of the 1954 Act

20.—(1)   Section 16 of the 1954 Act (relief for tenant where landlord proceeding to enforce covenants) shall apply in relation to this Schedule as it applies in relation to Part I of that Act but subject to the following modifications—

(a)   in subsection (1) the reference to a tenancy to which section 1 of the 1954 Act applies shall be construed as a reference to a long residential tenancy;

(b)   in subsection (2) the reference to Part I of that Act shall be construed as a reference to this Schedule;

(c)   subsection (3) shall have effect as if the words "(without prejudice to section ten of this Act)" were omitted; and

(d)   in subsection (7) the reference to subsection (3) of section 2 of the 1954 Act shall be construed as a reference to paragraph 1(6) above.

(2)   Section 55 of the 1954 Act (compensation for possession obtained by misrepresentation) shall apply in relation to this Schedule as it applies in relation to Part I of that Act.

(3)   Section 63 of the 1954 Act (jurisdiction of court for purposes of Parts I and II of the 1954 Act and of Part I of the Landlord and Tenant Act 1927) shall apply in relation to this Schedule and section 186 of this Act as it applies in relation to Part I of that Act.

(4)   Section 65 of the 1954 Act (provisions as to reversions) applies for the purposes of this Schedule except that for any reference to that Act there shall be substituted a reference to this Schedule.

(5)   Subsection (4) of section 66 of the 1954 Act (services of notices) shall apply in relation to this Schedule as it applies in relation to that Act.

21.—(1)   Where this Schedule has effect in relation to a former 1954 Act tenancy the term date of which falls before 15th January 1999, any reference (however expressed) in the preceding provisions of this Schedule to the dwelling-house (or the property) let under the tenancy shall have effect as a reference to the premises qualifying for protection, within the meaning of the 1954 Act.

(2)   Notwithstanding that at any time section 1 of the 1954 Act does not, and this Schedule does, apply to a former 1954 Act tenancy, any question of what are the premises qualifying for protection or (in that context) what is the tenancy shall be determined for the purposes of this Schedule in accordance with Part I of that Act.

Crown application

22.—(1)   This Schedule shall apply where—
  (a)   there is an interest belonging to Her Majesty in right of the Crown and that interest is under the management of the Crown Estate Commissioners, or
  (b)   there is an interest belonging to Her Majesty in right of the Duchy of Lancaster or belonging to the Duchy of Cornwall,
as if it were an interest not so belonging.

(2)   Where an interest belongs to Her Majesty in right of the Duchy of Lancaster, then, for the purposes of this Schedule, the Chancellor of the Duchy of Lancaster shall be deemed to be the owner of the interest.

(3)   Where an interest belongs to the Duchy of Cornwall, then, for the purposes of this Schedule, such person as the Duke of Cornwall, or other possessor for the time being of the Duchy of Cornwall, appoints shall be deemed to be the owner of the interest.

LANDLORD AND TENANT (LICENSED PREMISES) ACT 1990
(1990, c. 39)

An Act to repeal section 43(1)(d) of the Landlord and Tenant Act 1954; and for connected purposes.   [1 November 1990]

1. Licensed premises: application of Landlord and Tenant Act 1954, Part II.
1954 c. 56

(1)   In the Landlord and Tenant Act 1954 (in this section referred to as "the 1954 Act"), in section 43 (tenancies excluded from Part II), paragraph (d) of subsection (1) (which excludes tenancies of premises licensed for the sale of intoxicating liquor for consumption on the premises) shall cease to have effect in relation to any tenancy entered into on or after 11th July 1989, otherwise than in pursuance of a contract made before that date.

(2)   If a tenancy—
  (a)   is of a description mentioned in paragraph (d) of subsection (1) of section 43 of the 1954 Act, and
  (b)   is in existence on 11th July 1992, and
  (c)   does not fall within subsection (1) above,

that paragraph shall cease to have effect in relation to the tenancy on and after 11th July 1992; and section 24(3)(b) of the 1954 Act (which, in certain cases, preserves the effect of a notice to quit given in respect of a tenancy which becomes one to which Part II of the 1954 Act applies) shall not have effect in the case of a tenancy which becomes one to which that Part applies by virtue of this subsection.

(3)   In relation to a tenancy falling within subsection (2) above, before 11th July 1992 the following notices may be given and any steps may be taken in consequence thereof as if section 43(1)(d) of the 1954 Act had already ceased to have effect—

(a)   a notice under section 25 of the 1954 Act (termination of tenancy by landlord) specifying as the date of termination 11th July 1992 or any later date;

(b)   a notice under section 26 of the 1954 Act (tenant's request for a new tenancy) requesting a new tenancy beginning not earlier than that date; and

(c)   a notice under section 27(1) of the 1954 Act (termination by tenant of tenancy for fixed term) stating that the tenant does not desire his tenancy to be continued.

(4)   In this section "tenancy" has the same meaning as in Part II of the 1954 Act.

2.   Short title, repeal, commencement and extent.

(1)   This Act may be cited as the Landlord and Tenant (Licensed Premises) Act 1990.

(2)   Subject to subsections (1) and (2) of section 1 of this Act,—

(a)   section 43(1)(d) of the Landlord and Tenant Act 1954, and

(b)   paragraph 5 of Schedule 2 to the Finance Act 1959 (which amended section 43 by substituting the present subsection (1)(d)),

are hereby repealed.

(3)   This Act shall come into force at the end of the period of two months beginning with the day on which it is passed.

(4)   This Act does not extend to Scotland or Northern Ireland.

INDEX